Morocco,
Algeria & Tunisia
a travel survival kit

Geoff Crowther
Hugh Finlay

Morocco, Algeria & Tunisia – a travel survival kit
  1st edition

Published by
  Lonely Planet Publications
  Head Office: PO Box 617, Hawthorn, Victoria 3122, Australia
  US Office: PO Box 2001A, Berkeley, CA 94702, USA

Printed by
  Singapore National Printers Ltd, Singapore

Photographs by
  Geoff Crowther (GC)
  Hugh Finlay (HF)
  Front cover: Sand Dunes at In Salah, Algeria (HF)
  Back cover: Souvenir shops in Medenine, Tunisia (HF)

Published
  July 1989

National Library of Australia Cataloguing in Publication Data

Crowther, Geoff 1944–
  Morocco, Algeria & Tunisia: a travel survival kit.

  1st ed.
  Includes index.
  ISBN 0 86442 034 X.

  1. Morocco – Description and travel – 1981– – Guide-books.
  2. Algeria – Description and travel – Guide-books. 3 Tunisia
  – Description and travel – Guide-books. I. Finlay, Hugh. II.
  Title.

  916. 4'045

© Copyright Hugh Finlay, Geoff Crowther, 1989

Geoff Crowther

Born in Yorkshire, England, Geoff took to his heels early on in the search for the miraculous. The lure of the unknown took him to Kabul, Kathmandu and Lamu in the days before the overland bus companies began digging up the dirt along the tracks of Africa. His experiences led him to join the the now legendary but sadly defunct alternative information centre BIT in the late '60s.

In 1977, he wrote his first guide for Lonely Planet – *Africa on the Cheap*, which is now *Africa on a shoestring*. He has also written *South America on a shoestring* as well as travel survival kits for *Korea* and *East Africa*. Geoff has also co-authored travel survival kits for *India* and *Malaysia, Singapore & Brunei*.

After travelling extensively, Geoff and Hyung Pun have recently discovered the joys of family life with baby Ashley. They expect to move out of a banana shed and into the house that Geoff (et al) built somewhere in the wilds of northern New South Wales. He continues to pursue noxious weeds and brew mango wine.

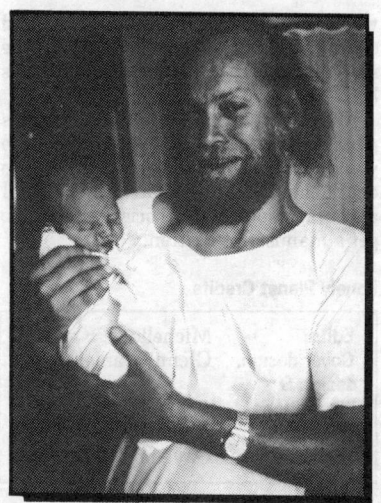

Hugh Finlay

After deciding there must be more to life than a career in civil engineering, Hugh first took off around Australia in the mid '70s, working at everything from parking cars to prospecting for diamonds in the back blocks of South Australia, before heading further afield. He spent three years travelling and working in three continents, including a stint on an irrigation project in Saudi Arabia, before joining Lonely Planet in 1985.

Hugh has also written the Lonely Planet guide *Jordan & Syria – a travel survival kit* and has contributed to others including *Africa on a shoestring* and *India – a travel survival kit*.

Hugh and Linda are now finding life considerably enlivened by their daughter, Ella. When not travelling and writing, Hugh spends a good deal of time striving for the perfect home-brew beer.

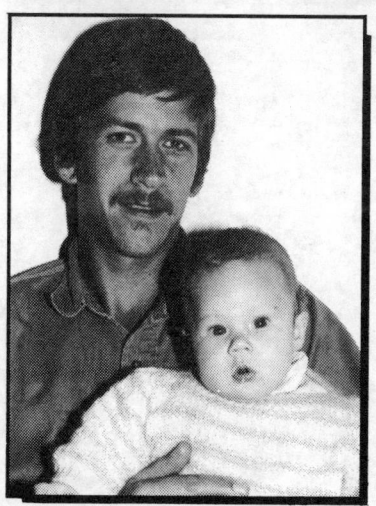

From the Authors

As with *East Africa – a travel survival kit*, this book is partly a response to feedback from travellers using *Africa on a shoestring* who felt a need for a lot more detail and a lot less weight!

Thanks must go to all those travellers

who have written in with ideas and comments, and to those we met on the road during the course of researching this book.

Many thanks also to Linda, Hugh's partner and travelling companion, who was not only a valuable extra pair of eyes out on the road, but also gave him the vital encouragement and criticism needed to get a manuscript written.

Lonely Planet Credits

Editor	Michelle de Kretser
Cover design, design & illustrations	Glenn Beanland
Typesetting	Ann Jeffree
	Gaylene Miller

Thanks also to Sharon Wertheim for compiling the index and to Susan Mitra for help with proofing.

A Warning & a Request
Things change – prices go up, schedules change, good places go bad and bad places go bankrupt – nothing stays the same. So if you find things better or worse, recently opened or long since closed, please write and tell us and help make the next edition better!

Your letters will be used to help update future editions and, where possible, important changes will also be included as a Stop Press section in reprints.

All information is greatly appreciated and the best letters will receive a free copy of the next edition, or any other Lonely Planet book of your choice.

Contents

Introduction

For most people, a trip to this region is one of two things: seeing the splendours of the imperial Moroccan cities, or crossing the greatest desert of them all – the Sahara. Without doubt, these are the two principal attractions of the area, but there is also much much more for the traveller, especially if your interest extends to Roman history and Islamic architecture.

Morocco is, of course, the star attraction, far overshadowing its Arab neighbours to the east. It's a fascinating mix of African, Islamic, Arab, Berber and even European influences and this, combined with its accessibility from Europe, makes it a popular and memorable place to visit. As well as the four imperial cities – Fès, Meknès, Marrakesh and Rabat – there are the natural attractions of the Atlantic beaches and the remote villages of the High Atlas and Rif mountains. The contrasts are great – poverty and opulence, hospitality and aggression. Despite the stories, it is far from being a dangerous country to travel in and, love it or hate it, you are hardly likely to quickly forget a trip to Morocco.

Algeria is the lumbering socialist giant of the Maghreb. While most people set out to conquer the Sahara, in itself a once-in-a-lifetime experience, few people take the time to explore the rich diversity of the north of the country. As a result, sites of great historical importance and areas of superb natural beauty are both unspoilt and uncrowded. The people of the country, too, go out of their way to make the visitor welcome – an invitation to have a meal or spend the night in a local home is not at all uncommon. Really it's a country

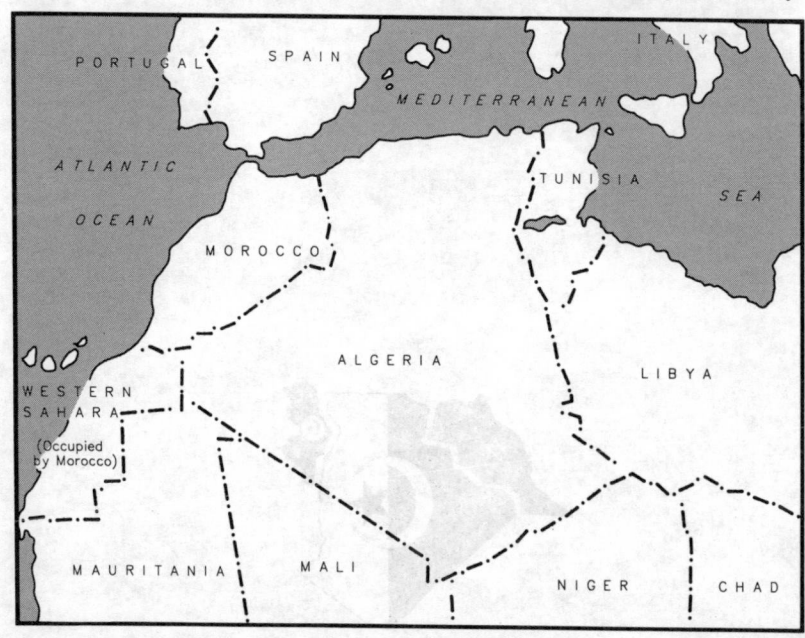

which more than amply rewards the traveller who wants to get off the beaten track.

Tunisia is very much the 'little brother' of the three countries as far as size goes. Because it has embraced the west so openly it has a well-developed tourist industry, helped in no small measure by the fact that the country has some of the best beaches in the Mediterranean. For most foreign visitors Tunisia comes as a neat package, which means that for the enterprising traveller who wants to get away from the resorts, there is plenty of scope for exploration in an unspoilt environment. Distances are small, transport is fast and efficient, and the variety of things worth seeing would do justice to a country many times bigger – ruined Roman towns, holy Islamic cities, Berber strongholds, underground villages, desert oases and sand seas, and of course the beaches. What are you waiting for!

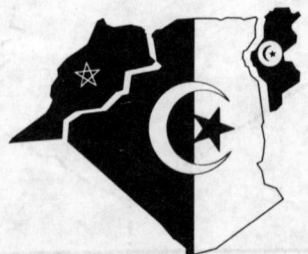

Facts about the Region

HISTORY
Prehistory

Although archaeological finds in the region date back to well over 200,000 years ago, it was not until around 3000 BC that human settlement became well established throughout the Maghreb (the Arab term for 'west' and now taken to include Morocco, Algeria and Tunisia). Prior to this, various groups of hunter-gatherers had existed in patches throughout the area, leaving behind traces such as the remarkable rock paintings in the Hoggar and Tassili ranges in the southern Sahara. These date from around 6000 BC and show mainly animals, many now extinct or found only much further to the south of the continent.

Around the 10th century BC a race of light-skinned invaders arrived from western Asia and by the 2nd century BC they had spread right across the north of the continent. This race is known as Capsian Man, after finds made at ancient Capsa (present-day Gafsa) in Tunisia. The finds are mainly of stone axes and other implements which were more sophisticated than anything else in the area at the time. It is from these people that the Berbers as a race are believed to be descended.

Carthaginian Dominance

The Phoenicians first came cruising the North African coast around 1000 BC. They were looking for staging posts for their trade vessels making the journey from the eastern Mediterranean shores to the Atlantic coast of Spain, a major source of raw metals. On the whole these ports remained largely undeveloped and little was done to exploit the interior of the continent. By about the 7th century BC settlements had been established at Utica, Carthage, Hadrumetum (Sousse) and Hippo Diarrhytus (Bizerte) in Tunisia; Hippo Regius (Annaba), Saldae (Bejaia) and Iol (Cherchell) in Algeria; and Tamuda (Tetouan), Lixus, Mogador (Essaouira) and Tingi (Tangier) in Morocco.

The foundation of Carthage is traditionally given as 814 BC and, in the traditional manner, it remained totally dependent on the mother culture in Tyre (modern-day Lebanon). Although the emergence of Carthage as an independent power came about partly as the power of Tyre was weakened by the Babylonians from the east, closer to the scene it was the Greeks in southern Italy who forced the Carthaginians to defend their outposts there as well as their trade routes in the Mediterranean.

By the 4th century BC, when Tyre had long been taken over by the Persians and had ceased to be actively involved in the Mediterranean, Carthage had become a major regional power controlling the coast all the way to the Atlantic in Morocco. The Carthaginians had developed the hinterland, particularly the fertile Cap Bon Peninsula, and did their utmost to guard the trade routes. This led to a clash with the Greeks in Sicily in 396 in which the Carthaginians were defeated. In 310 successful Greek raiders led by Agathocles, the ruler of Syracuse, landed in North Africa and left a trail of destruction for some three years before finally being defeated by Carthaginian mercenaries. It was also in Sicily that Carthaginian and Roman interests clashed, which led to the famous Punic Wars and, ultimately, the downfall of Carthage itself.

The first of the Punic Wars was a long-drawn-out affair lasting some 22 years from 263 to 241 BC. It saw the Carthaginians defeated in numerous naval battles, although they did defeat and capture the Roman general Regulus. Having lost their navy in a final skirmish, and being close to broke, they finally

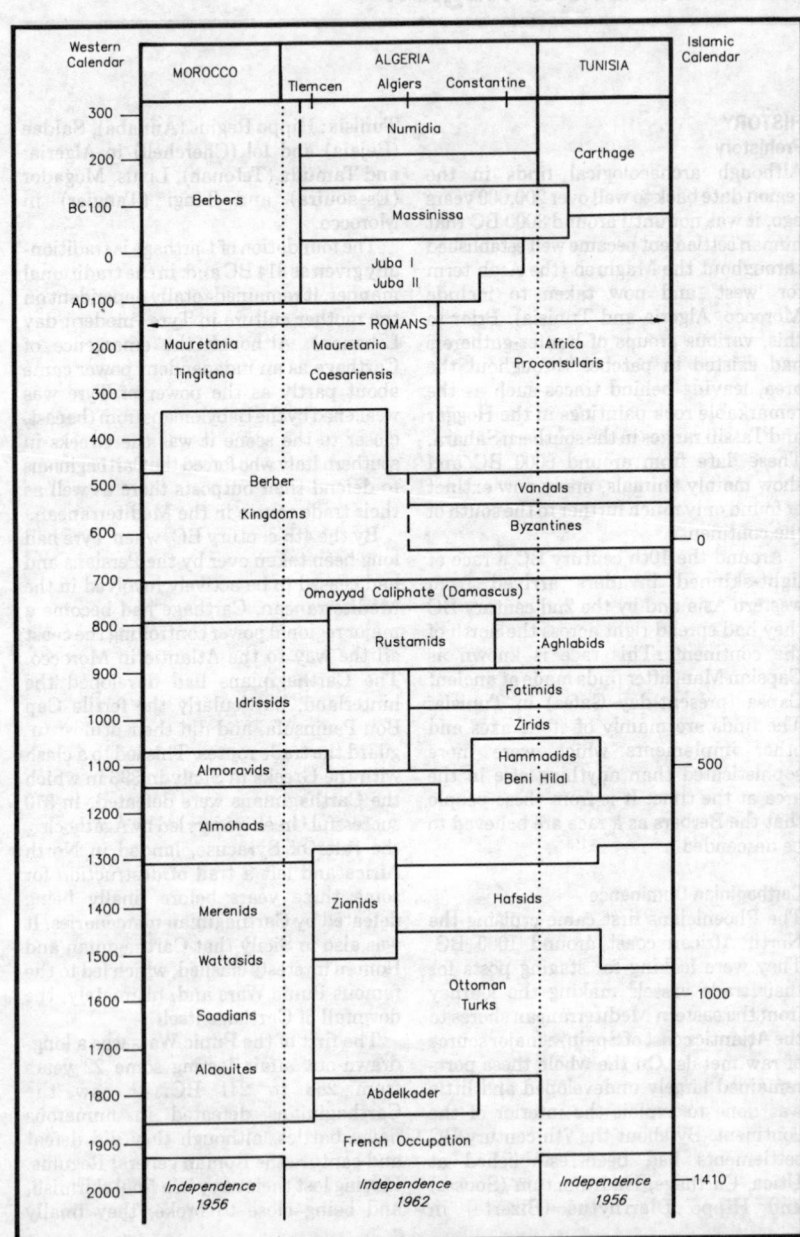

accepted Roman terms and gave up their hold in Sicily, followed soon by Sardinia and Corsica. They were soon to face troubles at home, however: there was no money in the coffers to pay the mercenaries, who promptly revolted and were only starved into submission after a prolonged period of brutality and a final stand-off. This came to be known as the Truceless War; it later inspired Gustave Flaubert's memorably bad novel *Salammbô*.

After the First Punic War, Carthage set about consolidating its position in Africa and establishing itself in Spain under the leadership of Hamilcar. His son, Hannibal, ignored Roman threats aimed at discouraging any Carthaginian expansion. At the age of 29 he led the now famous trek with elephants across the Alps, invading Italy in 218 and inflicting crushing defeats at Lake Trasimene (217) and Cannae (216). Rome seemed to be powerless. Only after Hannibal had been stranded in southern Italy for some seven years waiting for support were the Romans able to forget about the threat of being overrun by him and his 300-odd elephants.

The Roman emperor Scipio retook Spain and landed in Africa at Utica in 204. Carthage was teetering; Hannibal was recalled from Italy in 203 in an attempt to halt the Romans but was resoundingly beaten at Zama (near Le Kef) in 202. Carthage capitulated and paid an enormous price, giving up its fleet and overseas territories. Hannibal fled to Asia minor where he eventually committed suicide to avoid capture in 182.

For the next 50 or so years Carthage managed to hang on in North Africa despite incessant threats from the Numidian king Massinissa, who was based at Cirta (Constantine in Algeria) and had previously allied himself with the invading Scipio. Although Carthage was no longer a major power, many Romans felt that as long as it existed, it was a potential threat. Among these people was Cato the Elder, an eminent statesman and writer who became well known for his

vehement opposition to Carthage. So, in the Third Punic War, the Roman army once again landed in Utica, this time in 149; for the next three years the Romans laid siege to Carthage, and it finally fell in 146. Such was the Roman thoroughness that the city was utterly destroyed and the site symbolically sprinkled with salt and damned forever.

Overall, the Carthaginians were great traders and merchants. However, they were never particularly adept at getting the right people on side or fostering any sort of loyalty, even at home among the Berbers who, although not reduced to outright slavery, were forced to pay them heavy tribute and supply them with troops. The armies of Carthage consisted for the most part of paid mercenaries.

The Carthaginians greatly influenced the area by introducing advanced agricultural techniques; this was to lead to the Berbers changing from a semi-nomadic life style to a much more settled one.

The Romans

Roman settlement in Africa was brought about not through a desire to expand but just as a matter of survival when waging war with Carthage. Once Carthage had fallen, the area was ruled by a governor for over a century. Then the emperor Augustus refounded Carthage in 44 BC and installed a proconsul there to govern the new colony, which indicates the increasing importance of the area.

The areas to the west were still controlled by the Numidian rulers. It was Massinissa's grandson, Jugurtha, who got them into hot water by massacring some Italian opponents who were helping a Roman ally, Adherbal, defend the town of Cirta. Alarm bells rang in Rome, but Jugurtha managed to resist a couple of attempts to uproot him; however, he was finally betrayed by Bocchus I, a Mauretanian king, in 105. The boundaries of the Roman colony were extended and some settlers (mostly veterans) were given land in the area.

For a period of 50 or so years there was just a trickle of Roman settlers moving in of their own accord. Then state expansion went ahead in a big way, when the last of the formidable Numidian kings, Juba I, backed the wrong side in the Roman civil war and was defeated by Julius Caesar in 46 BC at Thapsus (near Mahdia). The new province of Africa Nova was amalgamated with the old and renamed Africa Proconsularis.

When the Mauretanian king Bocchus II died in 33 BC, Augustus installed Juba II, a renowned scholar married to Cleopatra Selene (the daughter of Mark Antony and Cleopatra), as king. After the murder of Juba II's son and successor Ptolemy, the western kingdom was split into the two provinces of Mauretania Caesariensis, which extended roughly from what is now Sétif to the Moroccan border, and Mauretania Tingitana from there to the Atlantic coast.

From here on until the decline of the Roman Empire in the 4th century AD, Roman North Africa proved to be a stable and integral part of the empire. Agriculture was all important, and by the 1st century AD Africa was supplying more than 60% of the empire's grain requirements. Animal husbandry and fishing were also widely practised; from Africa too came the majority of the wild animals used in amphitheatre shows.

The period of Roman rule saw a great spread in urbanisation throughout Tunisia and the North African coast. Colonies of veterans and civilians were established all the way along the coast. Many indigenous communities prospered and their members were granted Roman citizenship; many upper-class Roman citizens were actually of African origin. Several went on to hold high office and in fact in the 3rd century they made up the majority of Roman senators. The African colonies also provided a line of African emperors, the most notable being Septimus Serverus. It was these wealthy citizens who donated the monumental public buildings which graced the Roman cities of the region.

Even in the 3rd century there were signs that all was not well in North Africa. Landowners rebelled against increasingly harsh economic policies and there were tribal uprisings in Mauretania. Christianity spread rapidly, especially with the conversion of the emperor Constantine in 313 AD. It was hoped that this might give the empire's flagging fortunes a boost, but the Donatist controversy emerged in Carthage to spoil any such hopes. This controversy centred around a schism named after Donatus, a priest of Carthage, who split from the orthodox church. The movement gained popularity and, despite some banning and persecution, it is estimated that in the 4th century Donatists made up about 50% of all Christians. Following vigorous support for orthodoxy by St Augustine of Hippo Regius (Annaba, Algeria), a conference in Carthage formulated laws regarding religious unity which the Donatists were forced to obey, and the schism was healed.

The Vandals & the Byzantines

With Rome in a state of weakness, the Germanic Arian Vandals invaded from the north. They took Spain and wasted no time in crossing to Africa in 429 under the leadership of Gaiseric; by the end of the following year they were sitting pretty in Carthage. They confiscated large amounts of property and their exploitative policies only served to accelerate the general economic decline of the area. The Berbers became increasingly rebellious and, as the borders of the Vandal Empire receded, independent kingdoms became established, particularly in Mauretania and the west.

The Byzantine emperor Justinian, who was based in Istanbul, had revived the eastern empire and had similar plans for the lost western territories. His general Belisarius defeated the Vandals in 533; there followed a century of fairly ineffective Byzantine rule, which saw increasing Berber uprisings and the loss of territory under Byzantine control.

The Arabs

Following successes in Asia the Arabs looked westward for more areas to conquer, arriving in Tunisia in the middle of the 7th century. After numerous forays, Kairouan was founded by Aqbar ibn Nafi in 670; by 711 Islam had spread to the Atlantic coast despite some stubborn Berber resistance. One of the most famous instances was the defiant stand of the princess Kahina who, according to tradition, made her last stand in the amphitheatre at El Jem in Tunisia.

It seems that even once Islam became well established the Berbers, although accepting the religion, were not to be pacified. A mass rebellion inspired by the Muslim heresy of Kharijism set out from Morocco in 740 and conquered the Omayyad armies west of Kairouan.

With the shift of the caliphate from the Omayyads in Damascus to the Abbasids in Baghdad, the Muslim west (North Africa and Spain) split from the east. Although there was a great deal of unrest, there finally emerged three major Islamic kingdoms: the Idrissids in Fès, the Rustamids in Tahart and the Aghlabids in Kairouan.

Idriss was a *sherif* (a descendant of the Prophet) who, due to persecution from the Abbasids, fled to northern Morocco; here, on receiving support from the Berbers, he established the Idrissid kingdom. He and his son, Idriss II, founded the Islamic city of Fès (present-day Fès el-Bali) – a place of diverse influences from both Andalusia and Kairouan.

Arab knight

In 800 the Aghlabids were appointed by the caliph of Baghdad to promote religious orthodoxy in the Maghreb. This they did with some success, and the dynasty founded by Ibrahim ben Aghlab lasted until 909. This period saw the construction of the Great Mosque in Kairouan (their capital) and of the *ribats* (monastic forts) at Sousse and Mahdia.

The only people to embrace the Shia sect of Islam to any great extent were the Berbers of the Kabylie region of northern Algeria. Led by Obeid Allah, who declared himself *Mahdi* (Chosen One) they defeated the Aghlabids and installed themselves in Kairouan. The Fatimids, as they were called, built their new capital, Mahdia, on a small, easily defended headland on the coast. Obeid Allah's great ambition however, was to be the caliph of Islam; if he was ever to achieve this he needed a stronger base, so he set his sights on Egypt. After several unsuccessful attempts a new Fatimid leader, Emir al-Mu'izz, defeated the Egyptians and founded Cairo in 972.

Before leaving for Egypt, however, the Fatimids entrusted their North African territory (by now known as Ifriqiya) to the rule of the Berber Zirids. They and their neighbours to the west, the Hammadids, were unable to resist pressure for religious orthodoxy from within and officially returned to Sunnism in open defiance of the Fatimids in Cairo. The reply from Cairo was devastating: the Beni Hilal and Beni Sulaim tribes of upper Egypt were ordered to invade the Maghreb, and North Africa was reduced to ruins. The Zirids managed to hang on to a few coastal cities until 1148, while the Hammadids retreated to the coastal town of Bejaia.

These invading tribes were the first major influx of Arabs into the Maghreb; until that time the vast majority of people had been of Berber descent.

Berber Empires
In the south of Morocco, the Sanhaja confederation of Berber Touareg tribes comprised the Lemtunas, the Gudalah and the Massufah. It was a Lemtuna chief, Yahia ibn Ibrahim, who made the pilgrimage to Mecca and brought back with him a Moroccan scholar, Ibn Yasin, to reform the rather slack Islam of the desert tribe. This was the start of the Almoravid dynasty. Under the leadership of Ibn Tachfin the Almovarids had overrun the region as far east as Algeria by 1069 and had founded their new capital city, Marrakesh. By the end of the 11th century the Almoravids had conquered the Christians in Spain in response to pleas for assistance by the Spanish Muslims.

They were rulers who won support by making popular decisions such as abolishing taxes not sanctioned by the Koran and by presenting themselves as liberators from corrupt rule. They didn't win everyone over, however. In fact in the High Atlas a young Berber, Mohammed ibn-Tumart, feeling that the Almoravids were corrupting the oneness of God, went to study in Tunisia and there developed his doctrine of the divine unity. On his return to Morocco his followers adopted the name

al Muwahadin ('those who affirm the unity of God', ie the unitarians).

He retreated to the High Atlas and there preached and rallied support against the Almoravids. Although he died in 1130, by 1147 his successor, Abd el Moumen, had conquered the whole Maghreb and all Andalusia in the name of the Almohads. This marked the high point of Berber Islam and was the first and last time that the whole of the Maghreb would be a single Berber kingdom.

For over a century the Almohads were able to rule successfully. However, with increasing pressure from both the Christians in Spain and the Bedouin in the east, the caliph Mohammed an-Nasr was forced to split his government in two and appointed a member of the Hafsid family to govern in Tunisia. This was the beginning of the end for the Almohads. Before long, anarchy reigned; at the end of the 13th century the empire split into three kingdoms under the Hafsids in Tunisia and eastern Algeria, the weak Abd el Wadids based in Tlemcen in the centre and the powerful Merenids in Morocco.

The Hafsids managed to hang on until the middle of the 15th century, when Tunisia became the scene for rivalry between the Spanish and the Turks. In Morocco the Merenids prospered for a full century and a half before falling under the sway of the Wattasid dynasty of viziers in 1459. It was under the Merenids that Morocco really went through a golden age, which saw the establishment of Fès el-Jedid (Fès the New) and the building of fine medressas and mosques, many of which still stand today. The Abd el Wadids formed an alliance with Granada in an effort to survive, but fell to the greater power of the Merenids in 1352 and then to the Turks in 1555.

The Wattasids' biggest mistake was to allow Portuguese traders and raiders to settle at various points along the coast. It was ostensibly in opposition to the Portuguese that the Saadians rose from the Drâa oases in a holy war. In fact, they used the opportunity to conquer Morocco and set themselves up in Marrakesh.

The Saadian sultan Ahmed al-Mansour made only one major raid – against the Muslims of the southern Sahara in 1591 – in the course of which he captured Timbuktu, from where he obtained slaves and massive wealth in gold. Marrakesh became a rich and decadent city and so was ripe for overthrow.

Enter the Alawi *sherifs*, who took Fès in 1666 under the leadership of Moulay Rashid. He was assassinated in 1672 and, after a struggle for power between his sons, Moulay Ismail emerged on the top of the pile and was the last of the imperial rulers of any import. Although he built a splendid new capital at Meknès, he is probably best remembered for being extremely unpredictable and cruel; such was the state of the country, however, that ruthlessness was necessary to the survival of the dynasty.

Ibn Khaldoun

Ibn Khaldoun is, without any doubt, the greatest Arab historian who has ever lived. He developed the first philosophy of history which wasn't based on religion. Called the *Muqaddimah* (Introduction to History), it is regarded as a classic. The 20th-century historian Toynbee has called it 'a philosophy of history which is undoubtedly the greatest work of its kind that has ever yet been created by any mind in any time or place.' Ibn Khaldoun also wrote a definitive history of Muslim North Africa.

He was born in Tunisia in 1332 and spent the early years of his life there, but by the age of 23 had become a secretary to the Sultan of Fès. After being imprisoned for two years on suspicion of being involved in a palace rebellion, Ibn Khaldoun moved to Granada, then Bejaia, Tlemcen, Biskra and Fès before ending up back in Granada.

In 1375 he gave up the world of business and politics and retired to the village of Frenda in Algeria where, under the protection of the local emir, he spent the next four years writing the *Muqaddimah*.

He spent the later years of his life as a professor at the great Islamic university, Al Ahzar, in Cairo, and was appointed chief judge by the Mamluk ruler, Sultan Barquq.

When the Mongol emperor Tamerlane invaded Syria in 1400, Ibn Khaldoun found himself in besieged Damascus with the new Egyptian sultan, Faraj. Tamerlane asked to meet Ibn Khaldoun who, after filling Tamerlane in on North Africa, was able to secure permission to return to Egypt, where he died in 1406.

The Ottoman Turks

In the early 16th century, the pirate Barbarossa (or Khair ed Din) and his brother Aruj, sons of a Turk from the Greek island of Lesbos, were permitted to settle in Jerba (Tunisia). Aruj captured Algiers from the Spanish, but they retook the city and killed Aruj in 1518. Thereupon Khair ed Din decided to ally himself with the Turks in order to protect his Barbary (from Barbarossa) possessions. The Ottomans jumped at the chance, conferred on him the title of *beylerbey* (governor) and sent him 6000 artillery men. In 1529 he managed to boot the Spaniards out of Algiers once again and five years later was in control of Tunis as well. However, the following year saw Spain's Charles V take that city and the Hafsid ruler Moulay Hassan installed as a Spanish vassal.

There was a flurry of activity for a while as Spaniards and Turks fought for supremacy in North Africa. A Turkish pirate and associate of Barbarossa settled in Jerba and controlled Kairouan; Tunis was taken for the Turks in 1569 but it fell to Don John of Austria the next year. The Turks rallied and retook Tunis in 1574 and Tunisia, like Algeria, became an Ottoman province.

In both places piracy played a particularly important role, and the Barbary pirates were the scourge of Europe.

The two provinces had a complex system of government whereby the head man, the *pasha*, was assisted by a *dey*, who was the administrative chief, and a *bey*, who was in charge of the military. Power in fact resided more in the dey in Algeria and the bey in Tunisia and the pashas were little more than figureheads.

Deylical power declined in Algeria with the assassination of the last dey elected directly from Turkey in 1671.

In Tunisia, the beylical line carried on strongly until the beginning of the 19th century. Husein bin Ali, a Greek soldier from Crete, founded the last of the Tunisian dynasties, the Huseinids, when he had himself elected bey by the Turkish janissaries (the Ottoman army elite) in 1705.

Meanwhile, Back in Morocco...

After being enthroned, Moulay Ismail's first move was to raise an army of black slaves and Arab troops to assert his authority at home and to repel the Christian invaders who had set themselves up at various places on the coast. In both pursuits he was only partially successful: the mountain tribes refused to be pacified, and he only managed to drive out the European Christians from Tangier, Larache and Mahdia while reducing the Spanish presence to the small enclaves of Melilla and Ceuta. The unrest at home was due in no small measure to the high rates of taxation which he levied on the people in order to finance his lavish palaces and military undertakings.

After a 30-year period of decline following the death of Moulay Ismail in 1712, Morocco's fortunes revived somewhat under his grandson Sidi Mohammed. The latter kicked the Portuguese out of El Jadida and started trading with Europe. Again chaos followed, but order of a kind was restored by Moulay Sliman who ruled from 1792 to 1822. However, by this stage there was little left to govern and the British, French and Spanish were all looking to grab a bit of the action in North Africa.

The French

The French overran Algeria in 1830. Tunisia and Morocco were made protectorates in 1881 and 1912 respectively. The three countries' struggles for independence followed different paths, with Morocco

getting it first in 1956, followed by Tunisia later the same year and Algeria (after a bitter and bloody six-year war) in 1962. The 19th-century colonial era, independence and modern history to the present day are dealt with in the individual country chapters.

RELIGION

Islam is the predominant religion in the Maghreb. Muslims are called to prayer five times a day and, no matter where you might be, there always seems to be a mosque within earshot.

In the early 7th century in Mecca, Mohammed received the word of Allah (God) and called on the people to turn away from pagan worship and submit to the one true God. His teachings appealed to the poorer levels of society and angered the wealthy merchant class. By 622 life had become sufficiently unpleasant to force Mohammed and his followers to migrate to Medina, an oasis town some 300 km to the north. This migration – the Hejira – marks the beginning of the Islamic Calendar, year 1 AH or 622 AD. By 630 Mohammed had gained a sufficient following to return and take Mecca.

With seemingly unlimited zeal the followers of Mohammed spread the word, using force where necessary, and by 644 the Islamic state covered Syria, Persia, Mesopotamia, Egypt and North Africa; in following decades its influence would extend from the Atlantic to the Indian Ocean.

Islam is the Arabic word for submission, and the duty of every Muslim is to submit themselves to Allah. This profession of faith (the *Shahada*) is the first of the Five Pillars of Islam, the five tenets in the Koran which guide Muslims in their daily life:

Shahada 'There is no God but Allah and Mohammed is his prophet' – this profession of faith is the fundamental tenet of Islam. It is to Islam what The Lord's Prayer is to Christianity, and it is often quoted (eg to greet the newborn and farewell the dead).

Salah is the call to prayer. Five times a day – at dawn, midday, mid-afternoon, sunset and nightfall – Muslims must face Mecca and recite the prescribed prayer.

Zakat was originally the act of giving alms to the poor and needy and was originally fixed at 5% of one's income. It has been developed by some modern states into an obligatory land tax which goes to help the poor.

Ramadan is the ninth month of the Muslim calendar. During it Muslims must abstain from eating, drinking, smoking and sex from dawn to dusk. It commemorates the month when Mohammed had the Koran revealed to him; the purpose of the physical deprivation is to strengthen the will and forfeit the body to the spirit.

Hajj is the pilgrimage to Mecca, the holiest place in Islam. It is the duty of every Muslim who is fit and can afford it to make the pilgrimage at least once in their life. On the pilgrimage, the pilgrim (*hajji*) wears two plain white sheets and walks around the *kabbah*, the black stone in the centre of the mosque, seven times. Other ceremonies such as sacrificing an animal and shaving the pilgrim's head also take place.

According to Muslim belief, Allah is the

same as the God worshipped by Christians and Jews. Adam, Abraham, Noah, Moses, David, Jacob, Joseph, Job and Jesus are all recognised as prophets by Islam. Jesus is not, however, recognised as the son of God. According to Islam, all these prophets partly received the word of God but only Mohammed received the complete revelation.

In its early days Islam suffered a major schism that divided the faith into two streams: the Sunnis (or Sunnites) and the Shi'ites. The prophet's son-in-law, Ali, became the fourth caliph following the murder of Mohammed's third successor, and he in turn was assassinated in 661 by the governor of Syria, who set himself up as caliph. The Sunnis, who comprise the majority of Muslims today, are followers of the succession from this caliph, while the Shi'ites follow the descendants of Ali.

Islam & the West

Unfortunately, Islam has been much maligned and misunderstood in the west in recent years. Any mention of it usually brings to mind one of two images: the 'barbarity' of some aspects of Islamic law such as flogging, stoning or the amputation of hands; or the so-called fanatics out to terrorise the west.

For most Muslims, however, Islam provides stability in a very unstable world. They are not aware that they are seen as a threat to the west; in fact they see the inroads that western culture is making into their society as a threat to them.

While the west is offended by the anti-western rhetoric of the radical minority, the Muslims see the west, especially its support of Israel, as a direct challenge to their struggle for Islamic rights and political independence.

The western media condemn the political violence of 'fanatics' in Lebanon, while similar violence in Afghanistan was applauded because it was directed at the Soviet Union. Similarly, it is emphasised that political terrorism in the Middle East is motivated by religion, while in the coverage of similar events in Northern Ireland, for instance, the religious element barely rates a mention.

Just as the west receives a distorted and exaggerated view of Muslim society, so too are western values distorted in Islamic societies. The glamour of the west has lured those able to embrace it (usually the young, the rich and the well-educated); for others, the west is the bastion of moral decline and it is easier for them to reassert their faith in Islam than to seek what they cannot attain. Often what is being accepted or rejected by Muslims is a mish-mash of western values which may bear little relation to life in the west.

As long as these misunderstandings exist, the fact that Islam offers many people a code of religious and political behaviour that they can apply to their daily lives, making an often difficult life tolerable, will be overlooked. Instead, it'll be thought that the majority of Muslims, rather than an very small minority, are extremists, or radicals bent on revolution.

Islamic Customs

When a baby is born, the first words uttered to it are the call to prayer. A week later this is followed by a ceremony in which the baby's head is shaved and an animal is sacrificed.

The major event of a boy's childhood is

circumcision, which normally takes place sometime between the ages of seven and 12.

Marriage ceremonies are colourful and noisy affairs which usually take place in summer. One of the customs is for all the males to get in their cars and drive around the streets in a convoy making as much noise as possible. The ceremony usually takes place in either the mosque or the home of the bride or groom. The partying goes on until the early hours of the morning, often until sunrise.

The death ceremony is simple: a burial service is held at the mosque and the body is then buried with the feet facing Mecca.

When Muslims pray, they must follow certain rituals. First they must wash their hands, arms, feet, head and neck in running water before praying; all mosques have a small area set aside for this purpose. If they are not in a mosque and there is no water available, clean sand suffices; and where there is no sand, they must just go through the motions of washing.

Then they must face Mecca (all mosques are oriented so that the *mihrab* (prayer niche) faces the right direction) and follow a set pattern of gestures and genuflections – photos of rows of Muslims kneeling in the direction of Mecca with their heads touching the ground are legion. You regularly see Muslims praying by the side of the road or in the street as well as in mosques.

In everyday life, Muslims are prohibited from drinking alcohol and eating pork (as the animal is considered unclean), and must refrain from fraud, usury, slander and gambling.

ISLAMIC HOLIDAYS

As the Hejira (Islamic) calendar is 11 days shorter than the Gregorian (western) calendar, Islamic holidays fall 11 days earlier each year. July 24 1990 is the first day of Moharram 1410 (Islamic years are numbered from the Hejira – the flight of Mohammed to Medina in 622 AD.) The actual dates may vary, as they depend upon the sighting of the moon.

Ras al Sana
New Year's Day, celebrated on 1 Moharram (2 August 1989, 21 September 1990).
Mulid al Nabi
The Prophet Mohammed's birthday, celebrated on 12 Rabi al-Awal (13 to 14 October 1989, 2 to 12 October, 1990).
Ramadan
The ninth month of the Muslim calendar and the second pillar of Islam. During Ramadan pious Muslims who have reached puberty abstain from eating, drinking, smoking and sex during daylight hours for the whole month (28 March to 26 April 1990). There are no public holidays, but it is difficult to deal with officialdom because of unusual opening hours.

These prohibitions don't apply to travellers, but it would be insensitive to openly flaunt them and you might very well generate anger if you do. If you must do any of these things during Ramadan then be discreet. Better still, do what the locals do, because travelling at this time of year isn't really the feat of endurance which the above might suggest.

While it's true that most Muslims become a little frazzled by the end of the month, each evening when the sun goes down people pour onto the streets to eat, drink and promenade up and down. There's a feeling of relief and festivity in the air, and the cafés and restaurants stay open until very late. It's better to enter into the spirit of it than attempt to fight it. Why are you visiting the area if not to experience fully what it is like to live there?

Eid al Fitr
The end of the Ramadan fast celebrated on 1 Shawwal (25 April 1990). This is one of the major celebrations in Islam and is marked by feasting and attendance at the mosque. It is also a time of animal sacrifice, and in the days leading up to the festival many doorways have a sheep tied up outside; the bleating of the hapless animals can be heard all over the place.

Eid al Adhah
The time when Muslims fulfil the fifth pillar of Islam – the pilgrimage to Mecca. This period lasts from 10 to 13 Zuul Hijja (14 July 1989, 3 July 1990). The day is also celebrated by those who are not fortunate enough to be in Mecca.

LANGUAGE
Arabic is the official language of all three Maghreb countries, though most travellers make little effort to learn any. Unfortunately North African Arabic is difficult to learn, as it differs from the more common and accessible Classical (or Levantine) Arabic (which comes from the Middle East).

Obviously, French is the most commonly used European language and a basic knowledge of it is extremely helpful if you are going to be in Tunisia and, particularly, Algeria. Most people you come across will be bilingual in Arabic and French. Very few people speak more than a couple of words of English at most, so learn a bit of Arabic or French before you arrive if possible. At the very least you should learn the French words relevant to filling out visa applications and other forms, as these are nearly always in French (and Arabic) *only*.

In Morocco the situation is a little bit different: not only do the touts and guides speak French, Arabic and Berber, many of them are proficient in English, German and Spanish as well.

There are several Berber languages spoken in the Maghreb. Tamahaq is the language of the Touareg, Kabyle comes from the Kabylie region of northern Algeria, while Rif and Tamazight are spoken in Morocco.

Arabic Basics
Numbers Arabic numerals are simple

enough to learn and, unlike the written language, run from left to right.

0	•	sifr
1	١	wahid
2	٢	ithneen or zoosh
3	٣	thalatha
4	٤	arba'a
5	٥	khamsa
6	٦	sitta
7	٧	sabah
8	٨	tamanya
9	٩	tissa
10	١٠	ashera
11		wahidash
12		ithna'ash
13		tamantahsh
14		arba'atahsh
15		khamstahsh
16		sit'tahsh
17		sabahtahsh
18		thamantahsh
19		tissa'atahsh
20		ashreen
21		wahid wa ashreen
22		ithneen wa ashreen
30		talateen
40		arba'een
50		khamseen
60		sit'teen
70		saba'een
80		tamaneen
90		tissa'een
100		mia
101		mia wa wahid
125		mia wa khamsa wa ashreen
200		miatayn
300		talata mia
400		arba'a mia
1000		alf
2000		alftayn
3000		talat talaf
4000		arba'a talaf

Days of the Week

Monday	al-ithneen
Tuesday	at-talata
Wednesday	al-arbiya
Thursday	al-khamees
Friday	al-jumah
Saturday	al-assabt
Sunday	al-ahad

Months The Islamic year has 12 lunar months and is 11 days shorter than the western calendar, so important Muslim dates will fall 11 days earlier each (western) year.

When the western calendar is being used, which is usually the case, the French names are used. The Hejira months, however, have their own names:

1st	Moharram
2nd	Safar
3rd	Rabi al-Awal
4th	Rabi al-Akhir
5th	Jumada al-Awal
6th	Jumada al-Akhir
7th	Rajab
8th	Shaaban
9th	Ramadan
10th	Shawwal
11th	Zuul Qaada
12th	Zuul Hijja

French Basics

hello	bonjour
How are you?	comment ça va?
goodbye	au revoir
yes/no	oui/non
please	s'il vous plaît
thank you	merci
I/you	je/vous
he/she	il/elle
surname	nom
given names	prénoms
date of birth	date de naissance
place of birth	lieu de naissance
date of issue	date de délivrance
date of expiry	date d'expiration
visa	visa
passport	passeport

left/right	*gauche/droite*	room	*chambre, salle*
here/there	*ici/là*	bed	*lit*
next to	*à côté de*	shower	*douche*
opposite	*en face*	washbasin	*lavabo*
behind	*derrière*	key	*clé*
where?	*où?*	roof	*terrasse*
when?	*quand?*	full	*complet*
now	*maintenant*	blanket	*couverture*
at what time?	*à quelle heure?*	sheet	*drap*
what is the time?	*quelle heure est-il?*	hot water	*eau chaude*
today	*aujourd'hui*		
tomorrow	*demain*	**Numbers**	
yesterday	*hier*	1	*un*
after	*après*	2	*deux*
morning	*matin*	3	*trois*
afternoon	*après-midi*	4	*quatre*
evening	*soir*	5	*cinq*
day/night	*jour/nuit*	6	*six*
week/year	*semaine/an*	7	*sept*
quickly	*vite*	8	*huit*
slowly	*lentement*	9	*neuf*
		10	*dix*
How much?	*combien?*		
more/less	*plus/moins*	11	*onze*
too much	*trop*	12	*douze*
which	*quel*	13	*treize*
why	*pourquoi*	14	*quatorze*
big/small	*grand/petit*	15	*quinze*
Is/are there . . .?	*il y a . . .?*	16	*seize*
		17	*dix-sept*
bus	*car, autobus*	18	*dix-huit*
railway	*chemin de fer*	19	*dix-neuf*
train	*train*	20	*vingt*
boat	*bâteau*		
ferry	*bac*	21	*vingt et un*
station	*gare*	22	*vingt-deux*
bus station	*gare routière*	23	*vingt-trois*
ticket	*billet*		
rucksack	*sac*	30	*trente*
left-luggage office	*consigne*	40	*quarante*
		50	*cinquante*
money	*argent*	60	*soixante*
bank	*banque*	70	*soixante-dix*
post office	*poste*	80	*quatre-vingt*
stamps	*timbres*	90	*quatre-vingt dix*
parcel post office	*colis posteaux*	100	*cent*
open/closed	*ouvert/fermé*	101	*cent et un*
		125	*cent vingt-cinq*
hotel	*hôtel*		
youth hostel	*auberge de jeunesse*	200	*deux cents*

300	*trois cents*	1000	*mille*
400	*quatre cents*	2000	*deux mille*
500	*cinq cents*	3000	*trois mille*
600	*six cents*	4000	*quatre mille*

Facts for the Visitor

HEALTH

The medical services in all three countries are well developed in the larger towns and cities, and many of the doctors have been trained overseas and speak French. Your embassy or an expensive hotel will usually be able to recommend a reliable doctor or hospital if the need arises.

For minor complaints, pharmacies can usually supply what you need, although you will probably have to use sign language in out-of-the-way places. Drugs normally sold only on prescription in the west are often available over the counter.

Any special medication that you take regularly should be brought with you, as it may not be available locally.

Vaccinations

There are no inoculations needed for entry to any of the Maghreb countries unless you're coming from a disease-affected area, but it's a good idea to have preventive shots for tetanus, typhoid and cholera. Some border officials may not be aware of which countries are disease affected, so you could save yourself some hassle if you have an up-to-date, duly stamped International Health Card. Having a compulsory jab on a border with the same needle which has been stuck into a dozen other people because some vaccination is not on your card is worth avoiding at any cost. Keeping your jabs up to date is the best protection. If you are heading further south to sub-Saharan Africa, you will need to be vaccinated against yellow fever. It's a straightforward shot in the arm which is valid for 10 years.

Your local doctor can arrange to give you the necessary jabs, or you can go to any of the vaccinations centres in Europe. They are listed in the phone book but the bigger ones are:

Belgium
  Ministère de la Santé Publique et de la Famille, Cité Administrative de l'Etat, Quartier de l'Esplanade, 1000 Brussels
  Centre Médical du Ministere des Affaires Etrangères, 9 Rue Brederode, 1000 Brussels
France
  Direction Départementale d'Action Sanitaire et Sociale, 57 Boulevard de Sebastopol, 75001 Paris
Holland
  Any GGD office or the Academic Medical Centre, Amsterdam
Switzerland
  L'Institut d'Hygiène, 2 Quai du Cheval Blanc, 1200 Geneva (tel (022) 43 8075)
United Kingdom
  Hospital for Tropical Diseases, 4 St Pancras Way, London, NW1 (tel (01) 387 4411); injections here are free but they are often booked up about a month ahead.
  West London Designated Vaccination Centre, 53 Great Cumberland Place, London W1 (tel (01) 262 6546); no appointment is necessary and the fees vary depending on the vaccine.

Travel Insurance

Don't leave home without it! Hopefully you will never need it, but if you do, you'll be glad you've got it. There are literally dozens of policies around and any good travel agent will be able to put you on the right track. Most travel insurance packages include baggage and life insurance. Read the fine print, and find one that suits your needs and covers the countries you will be visiting.

Another thing to check is that the policy covers any money you might lose by forfeiting a booked flight, and that it will cover the cost of flying a travelling companion back home with you.

Medical Kit

It would be an unwise traveller who doesn't carry at least a basic medical kit. Items worth carrying include: Band-Aids, sterile gauze bandage, antiseptic cream or liquid, cotton wool, thermometer, tweezers, scissors, antibiotic cream, a course of a broad-spectrum antibiotic (check with your doctor), insect repellent, anti-malarial tablets and multi-vitamins.

Some medication for diarrhoea can be handy in emergencies – Lomotil is a popular one. Don't forget some paracetamol or codeine for aches and fevers.

Food & Water
Tap water in the major towns is safe to drink, but if your stomach is a bit delicate bottled water is available in most places. In Algeria there are shortages of it all the time but the tap water is OK, although at times unpalatable.

If you can't find bottled water you will probably have to settle for tea or soft drinks, both of which are safe.

When it comes to food, there are a few common-sense precautions to take. Never eat unwashed fruit or vegetables and steer clear of stalls where the food doesn't look fresh or the owner looks grubby.

Meat is always all right to eat, but make sure it is cooked thoroughly.

Contaminated food and water can give you all sorts of weird and not-so-wonderful diseases such as hepatitis A, typhoid, cholera, dysentery, giardia and polio. You can minimise the risk of catching any of them by being selective about where and what you eat and by exercising meticulous care with your personal hygiene. Always wash your hands before eating (restaurants always have a washbasin for this purpose) and, needless to say, after using the toilet.

Diarrhoea
It's inevitable that at some stage you'll be struck down with diarrhoea, maybe just as a result of a change of food or water, but more often because of a bug of some sort.

Don't go pumping yourself full of antibiotics at the first sign of trouble. This is not a good way to treat your stomach and you can often do more harm than good by destroying all the useful intestinal flora in your gut as well as the nasties that are giving you problems.

The best course of action is to starve the little bastards out. Rest, eat nothing and drink only unsweetened tea, citrus juice and clean water. Make sure you drink plenty of fluids, as diarrhoea can dehydrate you very quickly. It is also important to take salt to help your body retain water. If you must eat, stick to simple foods such as boiled vegetables, plain bread or toast, and yoghurt. Keep away from dairy products (other than yoghurt), anything sweet and non-citrus fruits.

If you have to be moving on and it's not practical to stick to this regimen, you may have to take something to block you up for a while. Lomotil is effective and handy because the pills are so tiny – take two tablets three times daily. Codeine phosphate tablets or a prescribed tincture of opium are other alternatives. If at the end of all this you are still suffering, you may have dysentery and should see a doctor.

Dysentery
It's not all that difficult to catch dysentery. The first sign that something is seriously wrong is blood and mucus in stools – indications that the bowel wall has started to break down. There are two types: bacillary dysentery, the most common variety, is short, sharp and nasty, but is rarely persistent and responds well to antibiotics; amoebic dysentery, which is caused by amoebic parasites rather than bacteria, is harder to treat, is often persistent and can do permanent damage to your intestines if left untreated. The recommended treatments for amoebic dysentery include Bactrim and Flagyl.

Hepatitis
This is a liver disease caused by a virus and again there are two types. Infectious hepatitis (type A) is the one you are most

likely to catch. It is highly contagious and you pick it up from drinking water, eating food or using utensils contaminated by an infected person. Serum hepatitis (type B) can only be contracted by having sex with a type B carrier or using a needle previously injected into a carrier.

Symptoms start to appear three to five weeks after infection and consist of fever, loss of appetite, nausea, depression, lethargy and pains around the base of your rib cage (ie the liver). The usual tell-tale signs are that the whites of your eyes start turning yellow and your urine turns a deep orange or brown.

The only cure for hepatitis is complete rest, good food and giving your liver a sporting chance by laying off the alcohol. You should be over the worst in about 10 days but it can last for months, so if you still feel really crook it might be time to cash in that medical insurance which you took out (you didn't?) and fly home.

If you are going to be away for less than six months consider getting a gamma globulin shot, which will give you some protection from type A for six months; however, its effectiveness is still being debated.

Cholera
Cholera usually occurs in epidemics and can be extremely dangerous. Symptoms are bad diarrhoea, vomiting, shallow breathing, wrinkled skin, stomach cramps, dehydration and a fast, faint heartbeat. If you think you have it see a doctor immediately, as you cannot treat it yourself.

Cholera vaccinations are valid for six months, and although they are only about 50% effective any protection is better than none at all. You should have no problem if you are sensible about what you eat and drink.

Typhoid
This is a dangerous infection that starts in the stomach and spreads throughout the body. The main symptom is a high fever. Typhoid can be caught from contaminated food and water. Vaccination is recommended.

Malaria
Malaria in the desert? Surprising as it may seem, there is a (very small) risk of catching malaria, particularly if you're going to be in the south of Morocco. Unless you are going to be in the area for months on end, it is unnecessary to take anti-malarials.

The disease is spread by mosquitoes which are fortunately few in number and, unlike in many places, the strains of malaria found in this region are not resistant to chloroquine. The period of highest risk is from May to October.

Yellow Fever
Although North Africa is not a yellow fever area, you will need to have this vaccination if you are travelling further south into West Africa. It is a simple shot which gives protection for 10 years.

Bilharzia
Bilharzia occurs in certain parts of Africa but it's rare this far north. If you want to be sure, keep out of rivers and pools edged or surrounded by reedy vegetation. The freshwater snail which carries the parasite lives in such environments. Boil or sterilise any water drawn from such sources. Bilharzia does not occur in salt water.

Other Diseases
You should also make sure you are vaccinated against polio and tetanus. You'll probably have been vaccinated as a child, so should only need boosters. Check with your doctor.

Coping with the Heat
It gets stinking hot during the summer and without adequate protection you'll be a sitting duck for heat exhaustion – headaches, nausea, dizziness and other fun things.

Your best insurance against this happening is wearing a hat and drinking plenty of fluids other than alcohol and coffee. Cotton clothes which cover as much skin as possible are cooler than brief clothes, because with cotton moisture is trapped against your skin.

Excessive fluid loss through perspiration (or diarrhoea) results in salt deficiency and you need to keep up your intake. The food in this area is usually cooked with enough salt to maintain a good balance in your body and you shouldn't have to take extra.

When it's practical, keep out of the sun altogether during the real heat of the day.

Toilets

Toilets are almost always the hole-in-the-floor variety and are in fact far more hygienic than sit-on toilets, as only your footwear comes into contact with anything.

It takes a little while to master the squatting technique without losing everything from your pockets. Always carry your own toilet paper or adopt the local habit of using your left hand and water. There is always a tap at a convenient height for this purpose – whether any water actually comes out of it is something else again!

Books

A useful book to browse through before leaving, but not worth carrying, is *The Traveller's Health Guide* Dr A C Turner (Lascelles, London, 1979).

Don't Panic!

This section may read like a Who's Who of exotic diseases. It is not designed to put you off, just to make you aware of what's out there, how to take reasonable steps to avoid catching it and what to do about it if you get ill.

Most travellers have no problems beyond the occasional mild doses of diarrhoea and often leave in better physical shape than when they arrived.

SAFETY

Anyone with any amount of common sense is going to have no trouble travelling in the Maghreb. Sure, you do hear of people getting ripped off, drugged and ripped off, or worse, and these things *do* happen; but they also happen in London, Melbourne and New York, and probably a lot more frequently. The trouble is that when relating their experiences in a country, people always tell you first about the *worst* things that happen. The fact that they were invited into someone's house to have a meal or were helped when lost is completely overshadowed by the fact that they got overcharged $10 by a wily carpet dealer who's had years of practice at squeezing the absolute maximum out of a deal.

Morocco has the worst reputation for this. Although the touts and hustlers are definitely out for a buck, their best weapon is the gullibility of the tourist rather than downright dishonesty on their own part. Yes, you *will* get taken for a ride if you are at all hesitant, but as long as you are firm, polite and up-front you'll have no serious problems. Don't think that the hustlers are going to leave you alone altogether; however, eventually they'll get the message that you are not a likely prospect and won't waste any more time on you.

In Algeria and Tunisia you face no such problems. It has to be said that the people here, particularly in Algeria where they see so few tourists, are some of the most hospitable you'll find anywhere. Getting invited into a house for a meal is not uncommon and people will invariably go out of their way to help.

Theft

Despite popular misconceptions, even in Morocco the general level of honesty is very high. This doesn't mean that your stuff won't get knocked off if you are careless with it, but if you are reasonably careful you stand little chance of losing anything. The time you need to be most vigilant is when you are in a jostling crowd, where wandering hands can find their way into your bag or pocket undetected. The place to carry your valuables, such as documents and money, is in a pouch against your skin, around either your waist or your neck. Neither method is foolproof, but both give a good measure of security and make it much harder to lose things. Leather pouches are far more comfortable to have against your skin than nylon and the moisture from perspiration is far less of a problem.

Items left in hotel rooms are generally safe, even in the smaller places, but your passport and camera should stay with you at all times. Many cheap hotels have an old cupboard which is often lockable, so you can leave some things in there; but cameras are best carried with you, even if it's only for peace of mind. (This is also a good habit to develop if you are heading for Black Africa, where theft is much more of a problem.) Even the cheap hotels prefer to keep your room key, and while I had no problem with this anywhere in North Africa, the staff are usually not too fussed if you insist on keeping it with you. It's cold comfort really because it's highly probable that they have a spare anyway.

The Evil Weed
Morocco is famous (or infamous – depending on your experiences) for its cannabis; Ketama became a household word among dope freaks in the 1970s. Dope is, however, illegal in Morocco although, judging from the number of people who smoke it, you wouldn't know that. Since alcohol is prohibited for Muslims, cannabis is the most widely used recreational drug and is available just about everywhere.

As a tourist, however, you need to be very discreet about using it. Blatant public use is going to land you in a heap of trouble involving possible jail. If you're a user, don't jump at the first offer. Take your time. Be especially careful in the north around Tetouan and Ketama.

There's plenty of money to be made selling you cannabis and then shopping you to the police. Many travellers have learnt this to their cost.

The quality of dope in Morocco is generally good and the cost very modest in comparison with Europe.

Ever since the northern European dealers descended upon Ketama in the early 1970s, the Rif has acquired a reputation for hassles. If you don't want those hassles, then avoid the area like the plague. Chechaouen is still sweet but Tetouan and Ketama can be very bad news. We get letters all the time from travellers who have been relentlessly pursued by hustlers wanting to sell them kilos of the stuff.

In Tunisia and Algeria there is not the tradition of smoking that there is in Morocco. Penalties are much stiffer and the law is enforced with much less flexibility. If you bring any dope with you from Morocco and get caught, the consequences could be disastrous. Algerian officials at the Moroccan border are looking specifically for two things – drugs and dinar. If they find the latter, it will be confiscated, if they find the former, you are in deep shit.

Women Alone
Women travellers in the Maghreb face an additional problem – sexual harassment. It *is* extremely constant, particularly in Algeria, the most conservative of the three countries. The harassment we're talking about may be limited to being stared at in ways that leave little to the imagination, or it may take other forms such as being followed or touched. Such harassment is uncomfortable and annoying, but it probably won't go any further than this.

If you're a woman travelling solo, in Morocco you'll find that you have local men as constant companions, in Algeria you'll get stared at and in Tunisia they won't exactly ignore you, but things are much more relaxed.

Even women travelling with a male

companion are not immune: it's quite possible that an Arab man will ask the male in a western couple if he can take liberties with his partner! It's pretty bizarre and indeed unfortunate that Arab men (especially Muslims) have this stereotyped idea that western women are promiscuous and ready to jump into bed at the drop of a hat. Western TV soapies only help to reinforce these ideas.

Despite all this, women are travelling, both alone and in pairs, throughout the Maghreb and are still having a great time. There are certain things you can do to minimise the friction. Modest dress is the first and most obvious thing. By tradition, Muslims are modest people when it comes to dress and westerners who travel in a Muslim country with no regard for the local customs are asking for trouble.

Women should wear tops that keep at least the shoulders covered, and dresses or pants which come at least to the knee. A scarf is not necessary but adds greatly to your respectability. A wedding ring too will increase your respectability in North African eyes. Dress modestly at all times but particularly in smaller towns, which are likely to be more conservative than the cities.

Also, you should avoid eye contact with a man you don't know, and ignore any rude remarks and act as if you didn't hear them. Women travelling alone or in pairs should experience few problems if they follow these tips.

The best way for female travellers to meet and talk to local women is to go to a *hammam* (bathhouse). Every town has one, and if there is not one that is exclusively for women there are times set aside each day for women and men.

FOOD

The Maghreb is not a place of gastronomic delights; still, it is possible to eat well and cheaply, although the lack of variety becomes tedious after a while. The places where you get the biggest variety and the best quality food are the places with the most tourists, so in parts of Tunisia and Morocco the choices are good.

The most basic local eateries barely warrant being called restaurants. These places will usually have just one or two dishes, and have often run out by early evening. As might be expected, the further south you go, the more basic the restaurants become and the less variety they have. Vegetables become rarer and the emphasis is on meat and starch, so soups and salads disappear and basically what you get is meat and *couscous*, spaghetti or bread.

In the larger towns there are restaurants which have a set menu, which will get you a soup, salad, main course and dessert. These places are usually out of the range of the budget traveller.

If you get totally pissed off with eating in basic restaurants, the fancy hotels always have a restaurant with fancy prices, although the food is often no better (and sometimes a good deal worse) than elsewhere.

The French influence is still very noticeable; 'French sticks' are virtually the only bread eaten, and every town has at least one *patisserie* which sells all manner of sticky cakes and often has a coffee bar at the back. Menus, where they are supplied, are always in French and/or Arabic. Croissants are available everywhere and, with a cup of coffee, make a reasonable breakfast.

The food is fairly uniform throughout the Maghreb, but there are a few specialities which are served in one country only.

Snacks

Tunisia The great invention here is the *casse-croûte*. It consists of a large hunk of French bread which is stuffed with any or all of the following: olives, tuna, egg, sausage, chips, oil; it always includes a generous slathering of *harissa*, a spicy chilli sauce which varies in strength but is often hot enough to bring tears to your eyes and have you reaching for a drink.

Many patisseries, particularly in Tunis, serve individual pizzas and savoury pastries. These are very rich and filling and can be a meal in themselves.

Soups & Starters

Soups (chorba, or harira in Morocco) are usually tasty and filling. Based on a meat stock, they have macaroni and vegetables as the other main ingredients. Any flavours these might impart are often cunningly concealed by a hefty dose of pepper or chilli. Moroccan soups are far and away the best and, with a chunk of bread, make a pretty good meal.

Salad is a great catch-all that can include anything from a limp piece of lettuce and a scabby tomato right through to a tasty mix of chopped vegetables, olives, tuna and spicy dressing. Unfortunately it's the former that you are most likely to encounter. It is generally unwise to eat salads if you have just arrived from Europe, as the ingredients are unlikely to have been washed thoroughly, if at all. After a while, when your stomach has had a chance to acclimatise, you should be able to handle them without any problem.

Tunisia One speciality (peculiarity?) here is the brik à l'oeuf. This is a strange creature: it consists of a thin crisp pastry which is fried like a pancake, has an egg is dropped in the middle and is folded in half. The result varies from a horrible greasy mess to a tasty snack. It should be tried at least once, and if the first one you get doesn't impress you try one more at a later date; a good one is really excellent.

Whether you've got a good or bad brik they are awkward things to eat, as the egg invariably oozes everywhere, the pastry cracks into dozens of pieces and you get oil over everything.

Another delight in Tunisia (and to a certain extent Algeria) is shakshuka. This is rather like a thick vegetable stew and consists of onions, peppers, tomatoes and egg all fried up in a spicy tomato sauce; it's usually excellent.

Main Courses

Most of the dishes are starch based, which usually means couscous, spaghetti or rice.

Couscous is the staple food of the region and is an enormous bowl of steamed semolina topped with a meat and vegetable sauce. It is available virtually everywhere and varies tremendously. It's actually the sauce which varies and can make the difference between a good meal and a plate of dry couscous not unlike sawdust. Fortunately there is enough variety most of the time for you not to have to live off it.

If you want to cut costs and aren't too bothered about not eating meat, ask how much the dishes are without meat (sans viande), as you still get the rest of the sauce and the price drops significantly.

Chicken has taken off in a big way right across North Africa and is often the only meat available. It is usually roasted and served with chips, which, unless you ask specifically, are always cold. There's something about cold chips which really make you feel as though you've hit rock bottom.

Brochettes are one of the most basic meals and are just pieces of meat on a skewer barbecued over hot coals.

Morocco The big dish here is tajine. This is basically a meat and vegetable stew cooked very slowly in an earthenware dish over hot coals. The meat used is usually lamb or chicken, but you can also find beef or rabbit.

The vegetables usually cooked with the meat are potatoes, onions and squash, but it's not unusual for fruits such as prunes, apricots and raisins to be included.

The other dish worth trying, although not widely available, is pastilla (b'stila in Arabic). It is a delicious and incredibly rich pigeon pie, which is made in layered ouarka pastry (like filo pastry) with nuts and spices and is then coated with sugar and baked. It is common in Fès, where you just get a chunk from a stall, but it is also served in some restaurants in other cities.

Tunisia This is the only country where any amount of fish is eaten. In the better restaurants in Tunis a tray of fresh fish is brought to your table and you select what you want. Elsewhere you take your chances, but it is rare to get one that doesn't taste fine.

Desserts

Desserts and sweets are more often available from patisseries than in restaurants, but things such as *crème caramel*, cakes and fruit are often served in the better restaurants.

Fruit

In season there is really a great variety of fruit available, particularly in the north of Tunisia. This includes apples, pears, peaches, grapes, melons, watermelons, figs, dates, cactus fruit and pomegranate.

Soup

| soup | *chorba* | potage |
| spicy bean | *harira* | |

Salads & Vegetables

mixed salad		salade variée
tomatoes	*tamatin*	tomates
chips		frites
peas	*baseela*	petits pois
green beans	*fasooliya*	haricots verts
haricot beans		haricots blancs
carrots	*gazar*	carottes
cucumber	*khiyaar*	concombre
lettuce	*kahss*	laitue
lentils	*'aads*	lentilles
onions	*bassal*	oignons
potatoes	*batatas*	pommes de terre
olives	*zitoun*	olives

Meat

meat	*al-luhum*	viande
lamb	*lahma danee*	agneau
camel	*lahma gamil*	chameau
chicken	*farooj*	poulet
liver		foie
kidneys	*kelawwi*	rognons

Fruit

fruit	*fawaka*	fruits
apricot	*meesh-meesh*	abricot
apple	*toofa*	pomme
orange	*burtuaan*	orange
banana	*mohz*	banane
dates	*tamr*	dattes
grapes	*einab*	raisins
figs	*tiin*	figues
pomegranate	*ruman*	grenade
watermelon	*bateeq*	pastèque

Miscellaneous

salt	*mehal*	sel
pepper	*filfil*	poivre
bread	*khobz*	pain
eggs	*bayd*	oeufs
cheese	*gibna*	fromage
sugar	*sukur*	sucre
yoghurt	*labanee*	yaourt
butter	*zibna*	beurre
oil	*zit*	huile

DRINKS
Tea & Coffee

Tea and coffee are the national obsessions in all three countries and are drunk in copious quantities. They are also extremely strong and, when your body is not used to them, drinking either in the evening is usually a recipe for a sleepless night.

The main pastime for men is sipping tea or coffee in a café while chatting or playing cards or backgammon. Every town has at least one café; they are the social centres and are a good place to meet the local men. Local women don't frequent these places but western women can enter. Often the tables and chairs are set out on the footpath, and are a good spot to sit and watch the world go by.

Tea is served in large glasses and is heavily sweetened. In Morocco it is also strongly mint flavoured, which is fine if you like mint.

Coffee is always strong and is served the French way: small black and large white.

Soft Drinks

Morocco and Tunisia both have the biggies such as Coca Cola and Pepsi. Algeria makes its own and, for the most part, these are quite OK, although it does depend on the quality of the water used. In places like In Salah, where the ground water is very salty, the drinks are quite unpalatable.

Alcohol

Despite the fact that Islam prohibits the use of alcohol, it is widely drunk and readily available.

In Algeria and Tunisia there are no bars and the only place to drink is in the hotels, usually the more expensive places. Tunis does have a few bars but they are hard-drinking places with a sleazy, smoky atmosphere.

Beer All three countries brew their own beer. In Tunisia, Celtia is a very weak and watery drop which really isn't that flash, no matter how many times you drink it.

Algerian beer comes in an anonymous bottle and is similar to what you get in Tunisia.

Morocco too brews its own beer. The favoured variety is Flag Special, a very palatable drop.

WINE

Wine North African wines definitely don't rank with western wines but are certainly drinkable, especially with a meal. Again, it is mainly in the better restaurants that wine is served.

WHAT TO BRING

Bring the minimum. When you have gathered all the stuff you think you're going to need, chuck half of it away and you'll probably be close to a sensible amount. There is nothing worse than having to lug kilos of excess stuff around, but once you've brought something it is much harder to throw it away and the longer you carry it the less inclined you are to chuck it out. Unless it's absolutely essential, *leave it at home*!

A rucksack is far more practical than an overnight bag and is much more likely to stand up to the rigours of African travel. It is worth paying for a good quality one, as a cheap one just becomes a nuisance: buckles and straps start falling off and before long all you have is a worthless bit of junk.

What type of pack you take is largely a matter of personal preference. I find that the internal-frame types are much less hassle than those with an external frame, the ends of which constantly get snagged on things. Berghaus, Lowe and Karrimor are three recommended brands. One of the best stockists in London is the YHA Adventure Centre, 14 Southampton St, London WC2.

A sleeping bag and closed-cell foam mat are essential for sleeping out in the Sahara, but if your route is confined to the north they are unnecessary. A youth-hostel-type sleeping sheet can be handy to keep the mosquitoes off when it is too hot to use a sleeping bag. In southern Algeria the climate is such that sleeping out is a viable option for much of the year, so a sleeping bag is invaluable. It also comes in handy to pad hard seats on long bus or truck journeys. If you are doing any sleeping out, a waterproof groundsheet is also well worth carrying.

Depending on your itinerary and the season, you are going to need clothes for all climates. Although this is desert and the desert is supposed to be hot, many people underestimate the severity of the colder months right across the north of the Maghreb. Snow is common, and bitterly cold winds can make life unbearable if you don't have a decent sweater to keep out the cold. A windproof and waterproof knee-length jacket also comes in handy, even if only to keep your pack dry.

Clothes must not only be practical but should also take local sensibilities into account. This is Muslim territory and large areas of exposed flesh are certainly frowned on. Women especially need to be careful about what they wear (particularly when you take a look at the women in central Algeria, who have everything covered except for one eye peering through a gap in the cloth). Tops should cover at least the shoulders, and skirts or pants should reach at least to the knee. Lightweight fabrics are often see-through, so be aware of that also. For men, long pants are preferable; if you really want to wear shorts this won't really be a problem, even though some of the locals will think that you are so dense that you have forgotten to put your pants on and are wandering around in your undies!

Some people take a stove and tent. If you are heading further south this is worth considering, but for just the Maghreb the extra weight and inconvenience aren't justifiable.

Overlooked by many people, but absolutely indispensable, is a good pair of sunglasses. The glare in the desert is not only uncomfortable but can damage your eyes. A hat which shades your face and neck is also worth considering but then you have the inconvenience of trying to pack it when you are not using it. Straw hats are as good as any. For my money, a water bottle is worth its weight in gold, despite the inconvenience of having an extra piece of luggage. It needs to be unbreakable, have a good seal, a carry-strap and, preferably, be insulated. Anything which holds less than a litre is not worth bothering with.

Most important are the little things which take up little room but make life just that little bit more comfortable: a Swiss Army knife, a small sewing kit (including a few metres of fishing line and a big needle for emergency rucksack surgery), contraceptives, tampons, a few metres of nylon cord, and half a tennis ball (which makes a good fits-all washbasin plug).

Most toiletries – soap, shampoo, toothpaste, toilet paper – are available all over Tunisia and Morocco. In Algeria, toilet paper is not hard to find, but the others can be difficult to obtain and even then the quality may not be all that fantastic. You need to carry at least some spare supplies.

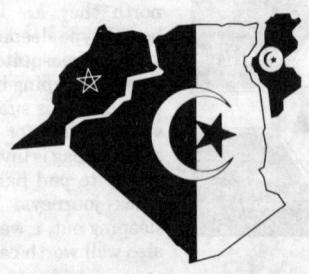

Getting There

The Maghreb is a popular place for a holiday, mainly because it is so easily accessible from Europe. Not only are there regular air connections with Europe from over a dozen North African cities, there is also a choice of at least as many ferry routes from Spain, France and Italy.

Since many travellers visit the Maghreb as part of a longer journey through Africa, often with a vehicle, these ferries are popular (especially with the overland route through Sudan being closed) and, obviously, are cheaper than flying.

AIR
To/From Europe
With the ferry connections being so good there is little need to fly from Europe to North Africa, but if you are short on time it may be the way to go.

There is little discounting to destinations north of the Sahara, so you will probably end up paying close to the full fare. The so-called bucket shops are the place to look for the best deal. These are travel agencies which sell discounted tickets, often at real bargain rates.

If you can't find a discounted fare, another option before paying full fare is an APEX (advance purchase excursion) ticket, which is usually discounted by up to 40%. The discount is offered because there are restrictions, such as buying the ticket at least 21 days before departure, staying away for a minimum period and returning within a certain time (usually six months). Another disadvantage is that there are often penalties to pay if you want to change the dates. Check carefully that the restrictions on an APEX ticket are not going to disadvantage you.

Another possibility is getting a seat on a charter flight. There are many operating in the summer to Tunisia and Morocco; although the seats are mostly reserved for people on package deals, they can be incredibly cheap if you can get on. Often an operator will sell tickets cheaply at the last minute to fill empty places. Good travel agents should be able to point you in the right direction.

To/From North America
The best way to find cheap travel deals is by checking the Sunday travel supplements in major newspapers such as the *Los Angeles Times* or the *San Francisco Examiner-Chronicle* in the west and the *New York Times* in the east.

It is unlikely that you will find any real bargains to North Africa from the USA. It will probably work out cheaper to take a cheap flight to Europe with a company like Virgin Atlantic (for around US$250 one-way and US$560 return) and then either fly or head overland from there.

To/From Australasia
There are no direct connections between North Africa and Australia. Again, the most convenient way is probably to go to London and then hunt around there for a cheap flight; else go overland through Europe.

If you do specifically want to go direct to North Africa, the cheapest deal costs around US$1200 return to Tunis or Casablanca from the Australian east coast. This fare uses British Airways between Australia and Singapore, and Royal Jordanian between Singapore and North Africa. The flights go via Amman and you may have to stop over there for a day or two, as the connections aren't that great; there is only one flight a week between Jordan and Tunisia and Morocco.

OVERLAND
To/From West Africa
If you are coming north from West Africa, the only way to enter North Africa is to go

from either Mali or Niger to Algeria. The crossing points are at In Guezzam on the route from Niger, and at Borj Mokhtar if coming from Mali.

The western routes down through Morocco and western Algeria to or from Mauritania are out of the question as long as the war in Western Sahara between the Polisario guerrillas and Morocco continues, and there is no end in sight at the moment.

See the Algeria Getting There chapter for details of the routes.

Taking Your Own Vehicle
Carnet A *carnet* (short for *carnet de passage en douane* and sometimes known as a *triptique*) is not required for Morocco, Algeria or Tunisia, but if you are heading through to West Africa and beyond they are mandatory. You also don't need to pre-arrange them for most West African countries (Nigeria is an exception); documentation can be arranged at the Niger or Mali borders. At the Niger border they'll charge you CFA 5500 per month and the documents will cover you for all CFA countries.

The purpose of a carnet is to allow you to take a vehicle into a country without paying the duties which would normally apply. It's a document which guarantees that if a vehicle is taken into a country but not exported, then the organisation which issued it will accept responsibility for payment of import duties. Carnets can only be issued by one of the national motoring organisations (in the UK, this is the AA or RAC; in Australia, the AAA). Consult one of these organisations if you plan on taking a vehicle into any other African country.

Full details regarding carnets and so on can be found in the Lonely Planet guides to the relevant areas such as *Africa on a shoestring*.

It is important to note the following: though you don't need a carnet to take a foreign-registered vehicle into Algeria, if you have to abandon it in the desert, you'll be up for import duties which are twice the new value of the car. And they won't let you out of the country until you pay. You might think this is unfair, since you haven't sold the car – you've simply been forced to abandon it. Tough luck! As far as customs is concerned, you've sold it and they are not prepared to go out into the desert to confirm that it had to be abandoned. Your only option for getting around paying the import duties is either to get the vehicle going again or have it towed in. The latter would cost a fortune.

The amount of import duty can vary considerably but, generally speaking, it's between one and 1½ times the new value of the vehicle. There are exceptions to this where duty can be as high as three times the new value.

The road between Tamanrasset and the Algeria-Niger border is littered with abandoned cars, so you won't be the first. The moral of the story is simple: make sure your vehicle is in top mechanical condition before you set off, carry sufficient spare parts and be able to fix it if anything goes wrong.

Insurance If you're going to be driving in Morocco, make sure you have a green card proving that you have third-party insurance. The police there can fine you 35 dirhams (over US$6) if you can't produce one.

Legislation about compulsory third-party insurance varies considerably from one country to another. It is compulsory in all three Maghreb countries and you must buy it at the border.

The liability limits on these policies is often absurdly low by western standards and if you have any bad accidents you could be in deep water. Also, you can only guess whether or not the premium is simply pocketed by the person collecting it or is actually passed on to the company, although this is more of a problem further south than in the Maghreb.

If you want more comprehensive and

reliable cover then you will have to arrange this before you leave. If you're starting from the UK, the company that everyone recommends for insurance policies and for detailed information on carnets is: Campbell Irvine Ltd (tel (01) 937 9407), 48 Earls Court Rd, London, W8 6EJ. The people who work here are very friendly, will give you personal attention, and, since they've been handling these kinds of enquiries for years, they know the business inside out. Most of the overland tour companies use them too. Write to them for a copy of their Overland Insurance leaflet or call round there and discuss it with them.

Books Taking a vehicle to Africa requires thorough preparation, and the detailed information and advice you need is really outside the scope of this book. An excellent guide which discusses all aspects of this is the *Sahara Handbook* by Simon & Jan Glen (Lascelles, London, 1987).

Another book, which has been recently updated and doesn't confine itself to the Sahara, is *Overland & Beyond* by Jon &

Theresa Hewatt (Lascelles, London). If you understand German a very good book is *Dürch Afrika* by K & E Darr (Touring Club Suisse, Zürich, 1977).

Selling Cars in West Africa For years now large numbers of French, German and Swiss travellers and small entrepreneurs have been buying second-hand cars in northern Europe, driving them across the Sahara Desert and selling them in West Africa. For most travellers this is a one-off affair, the object of which is to reduce the costs of an Africa trip, but there are quite a few people who do it full-time for a living by taking several cars at once on the back of a truck. It's still possible to make a reasonable profit on the transaction, but don't expect too much by the time you've deducted expenses and the wear and tear which a car inevitably goes through when it's driven through the desert. You'll certainly still cover your costs (including the purchase price of the car).

For the full details, see the Lonely Planet guide *Africa on a shoestring*.

Fuel Costs (per litre)

	regular	super	diesel
Algeria	AD 2.70	AD 3.20	AD 0.80
Morocco	Dr 5.94	Dr 6.05	Dr 3.56
Tunisia	TD 0.450	TD 0.470	TD 0.240

BOAT

Which ferry you want to take depends largely on where you want to travel and how much you want to pay. Obviously the shorter the route, the cheaper the fare, which makes the Spain/Morocco ferries the cheapest at around US$21 per person, US$90 for a large car or 4WD vehicle and around US$20 for a motorcycle.

Next on the fare scale are those from southern Italy to Tunis, the cheapest being from Trapani in Sicily which costs US$55 per person and around US$95 for a vehicle. A more convenient route may be the one from Genoa to Tunis (which costs US$105 per person and US$160 for a vehicle), as you don't have to drive right down through Italy.

There are also direct ferries from France to Algeria, but these are not that cheap at US$140 per person and US$300 for a vehicle from Marseilles to Algiers.

Whichever route you want to take, *all* are heavily subscribed in the summer months. If you plan to take a vehicle across it is imperative that you book well in advance, especially for the Tunisian and Algerian crossings. The situation is not quite as bad for Morocco, as there are many more crossings.

For full details of routes, schedules, operators and their addresses, check the Getting There chapters for each country.

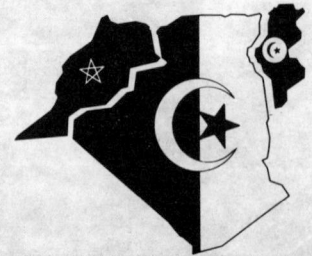

◼ ⁂ MOROCCO

Facts about the Country

HISTORY SINCE 1830

Unlike its neighbours to the east Morocco was able to retain its independence right through the 19th century, although this was due mainly to rivalry between the European nations rather than to Moroccan effort.

The British secured trade privileges in 1856. In 1894, the new sultan, Abd el Aziz, came to power at the age of ten and set about surrounding himself with expensive toys and European advisors, whose life style and customs he adopted. Naturally this disgusted the populace, particularly the religious leaders, and his rule became tenuous at best.

The European powers saw this period of uncertainty and weakness as an opportunity to further their own interests in Africa and bartered for whole regions. In 1904, Britain gave France a free rein in Morocco in exchange for an assurance that the French wouldn't interfere in Egypt; France pacified the Spanish by giving them north Morocco and the Italians were kept happy with Libya.

The end came for Abd el Aziz when his brother, Abd al-Hafid, led a rebellion against him in 1907, claiming that he (Abd el Aziz) had betrayed his Muslim origins. Abd al-Hafid installed himself in Fès but soon found himself besieged by hostile tribesmen and was forced to turn to the French for assistance. After the French had bailed him out, he had little choice but to accede to French terms. These were ratified by the 1912 Treaty of Fès, which saw Morocco become a French protectorate with provision for Spanish control of the north and the desert province of Tafaya in the south. Tangier became an international zone in 1923.

The terms of the protectorate recognised the Sultan of Morocco, but in practice his power was minimal. However, unlike the experience in Algeria where local culture was systematically wiped out, the first French resident general, Marshal Lyautey, had a deep-seated respect for the Arabs. Consequently, he didn't destroy the existing Moroccan towns but built French ones alongside them. A new capital was built on the Atlantic coast and the port of Casablanca was developed.

Marshal Lyautey's successor was a good deal less sympathetic. Local interests became less and less important in the administration of the protectorate, and French settlement went ahead at a great pace. One of the few problems faced by the French was an uprising in the Rif Mountains led by the Berber scholar Abd el-Krim. This revolt led to the declaration of the Republic of the Rif. The Rif was finally overrun by a combined Spanish-French force of over 250,000 in 1926, and Abd el-Krim surrendered to the French.

By 1934 the last of the mountain tribes had been 'pacified', and from here on nationalist feeling was channelled away from violence into moves towards gaining political concessions.

In 1943 the nationalist movement had become the Istiqlal ('independence') party and had put forward proposals demanding independence. Not only were the proposals ignored, the French reacted by detaining the party leaders.

After serving with distinction with the French in WW II, the Moroccans hoped (in vain, as it turned out) that their demands for independence might be treated more favourably. Violence by nationalist guerrilla groups increased and was met with violence by some of the 300,000 French settlers.

In a climate of increasing tension it became clear to the French that their governing days were numbered unless they could stem the growing nationalist feeling. Their last hope was to try and scare the nationalists with the threat of getting the mountain tribes to invade. To this end they co-operated with a Berber called Thami el-Glaoui who ruled briefly in 1953 when the French exiled the Alaouite sultan Sidi Mohammed (Mohammed V). The sultan immediately became a national hero and was allowed back in 1955.

Full independence was granted in 1956 by France, and Mohammed V formed a government. The Spanish withdrew as well, but held on to Ifni in the south, and Ceuta and Melilla in the north. Ifni was handed back to Morocco in 1970, but Ceuta and Melilla continue to this day as Spanish enclaves.

Independent Morocco

With the French gone, Mohammed V was free to resume his autocratic rule. Moulay Hassan (Hassan II) succeeded Mohammed V after the latter's sudden death in 1961.

Parliamentary elections were held in 1963, but Hassan II had to resume personal control when, after only one year, the opposition Istiqlal and the FDIC (the party supporting the king) came to a deadlock.

Attempts to introduce a new constitution in 1970 and 1972 both met with attempted coups against the monarchy. The leader of this second attempt, General Mohammed Oufkir, had been implicated in the kidnapping and assassination in 1963 of Mehdi Ben Barka; Barka, the former leader of the Istiqlal party, had been exiled after being implicated in a plot to overthrow Hassan II. Oufkir committed suicide after his coup failed.

In 1981 and 1984 there were riots across the country, but these were not so much a sign of united political opposition as popular protests at the increase in basic commodity prices.

Hassan's popularity soared in 1975 following the 'Green March' into Spanish Western Sahara. This was purely an exercise in gaining popularity and winning over the disaffected youth at home.

Another reason for Hassan's exceptional popularity is that he is a direct descendant of the Prophet and is therefore also the people's spiritual leader. Among his titles is Commander of the Faithful and Allah's Deputy on Earth.

While the king's grip on power certainly appears to be more secure than ever, with the army fully occupied with the war in Western Sahara and the trade unions and press restricted, it remains to be seen how long he can continue to outmanoeuvre the dissident factions in Moroccan society. These groups have so far failed to attract mass support but, as the economic climate gets worse, their influence is growing, especially in the shanty towns around the large cities and in the backward Rif Mountains.

It is estimated that half the population lives below the poverty line, and unemployment levels are unacceptably high. Resentment is inexorably growing against the privileges and standard of living of the elite who inhabit the Casablanca-Rabat region, particularly in view of the effects of the austerity measures demanded by the IMF which have made life much harder for many millions of Moroccans. There have already been riots in the main cities (during 1984) following price rises of staple foods. And that's not all. With a birth growth rate of 3% per year which will double the population by the early years of the 21st century, there clearly are major problems ahead.

On the other hand, it's probably true to say that Morocco is a relatively conservative society. It is in no hurry to jettison its centuries-old traditions and embrace radical political philosophies.

Western Sahara

With the discovery of enormous phosphate reserves in Western Sahara by the Spanish in the 1960s, Spain started to develop the infrastructure with an eye to exploiting the reserves. However, it soon

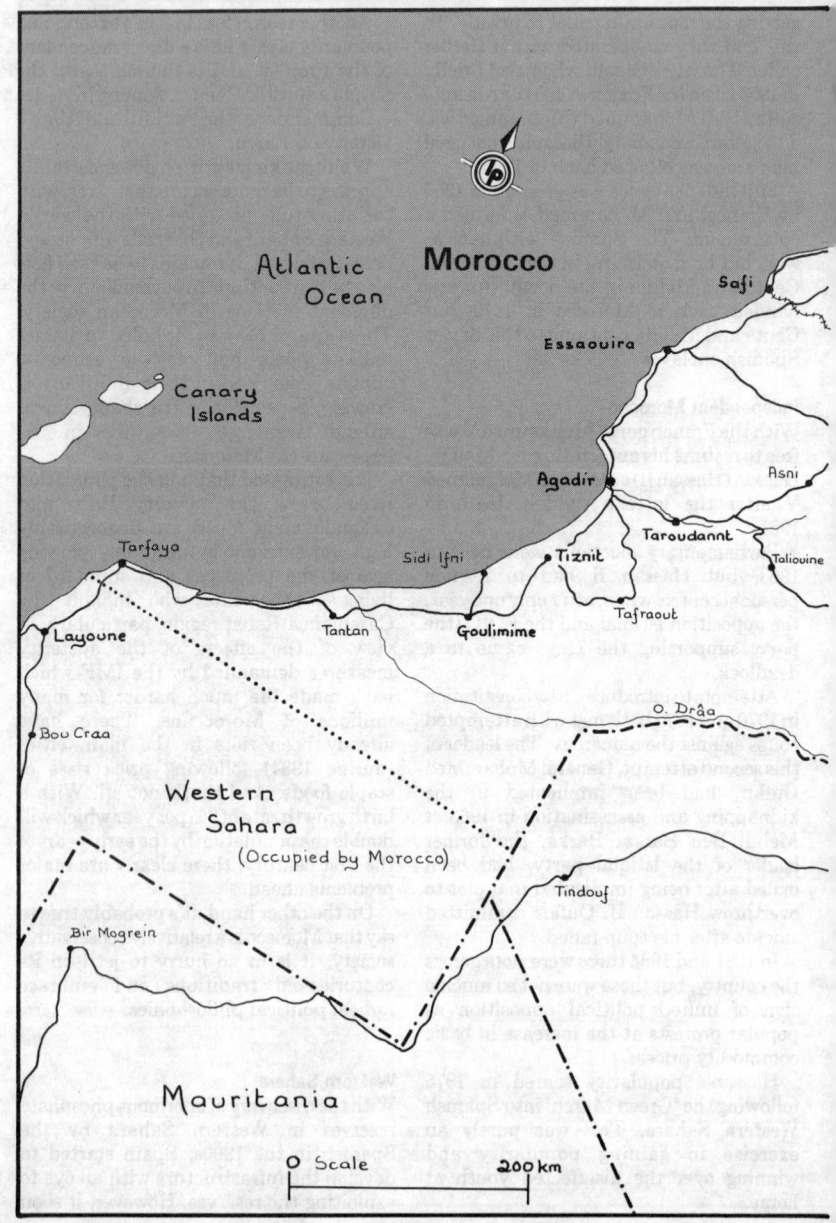

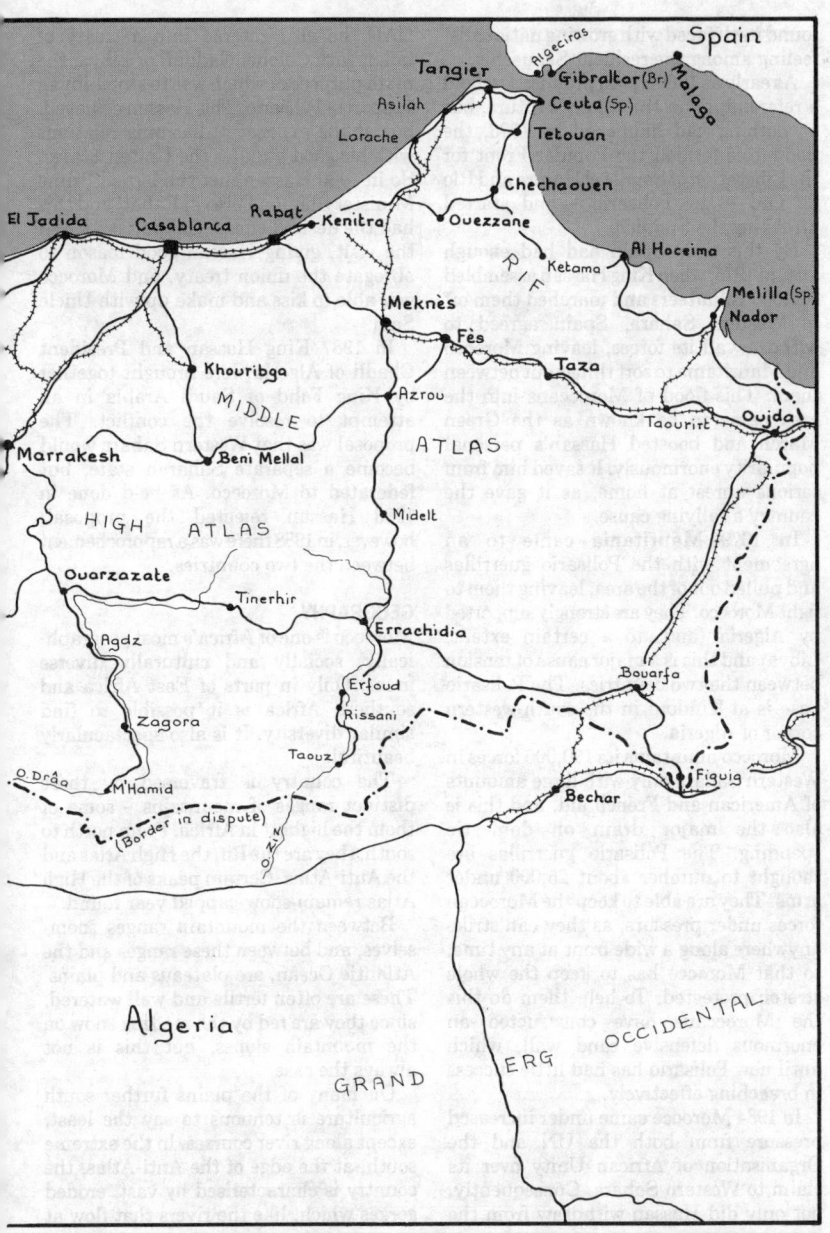

found itself faced with growing nationalist feeling among the resident Saouarhis.

As early as 1966 Spain promised to hold a referendum on the colony's future, but as nothing had happened by 1973, the Saouarhis formed the Popular Front for the Liberation of Saguia el Hamra and Río de Oro – the Polisario – and started attacking the Spanish.

By this time Spain had had enough and, in 1975, when King Hassan assembled 350,000 volunteers and marched them off to Western Sahara, Spain agreed to withdraw all its forces, leaving Morocco and Mauritania to sort things out between them. This flood of Moroccans into the area came to be known as the Green March and boosted Hassan's personal popularity enormously. It saved him from serious unrest at home, as it gave the country a rallying cause.

In 1979 Mauritania came to an agreement with the Polisario guerrillas and pulled out of the area, leaving them to fight Morocco. They are strongly supported by Algeria (and, to a certain extent, Libya) and this is a major cause of tension between the two countries. The Polisario base is at Tindouf in the south-western corner of Algeria.

Morocco maintains its 100,000 forces in Western Sahara only with large amounts of American and French aid, and this is also the major drain on domestic spending. The Polisario guerrillas are thought to number about 25,000 under arms. They are able to keep the Moroccan forces under pressure, as they can strike anywhere along a wide front at any time, so that Morocco has to keep the whole stretch protected. To help them do this the Moroccans have constructed an enormous defensive sand wall, which until now Polisario has had little success in breaching effectively.

In 1984 Morocco came under increased pressure from both the UN and the Organisation of African Unity over its claim to Western Sahara. Consequently, not only did Hassan withdraw from the OAU, he also entered into a treaty of union with Colonel Gaddafi of Libya, the main purpose of which was to stop Libyan support of Polisario. This Hassan achieved, but at the expense of harming relations with his good buddies the United States. So in 1986 Hassan met the Israeli Prime Minister Shimon Peres in Rabat, and this had the desired effect: Gaddafi criticised the visit, giving Hassan good reason to abrogate the union treaty, and Morocco was able to kiss and make up with Uncle Sam.

In 1987 King Hassan and President Chadli of Algeria were brought together by King Fahd of Saudi Arabia in an attempt to resolve the conflict. The proposal was that Western Sahara would become a separate Saharan state, but federated to Morocco. As he'd done in 1983 Hassan rejected the proposal; however, in 1988 there was a rapprochement between the two countries.

GEOGRAPHY

Morocco is one of Africa's most geographically, socially and culturally diverse areas. Only in parts of East Africa and southern Africa is it possible to find similar diversity. It is also spectacularly beautiful.

The country is traversed by three distinct ranges of mountains – some of them the highest in Africa. From north to south, they are the Rif, the High Atlas and the Anti-Atlas. Certain peaks of the High Atlas remain snow-capped year round.

Between the mountain ranges themselves, and between these ranges and the Atlantic Ocean, are plateaus and plains. These are often fertile and well watered, since they are fed by the melting snow on the mountain slopes, but this is not always the case.

On many of the plains further south agriculture is tenuous to say the least, except along river courses. In the extreme south, at the edge of the Anti-Atlas, the country is characterised by vast, eroded gorges which, like the rivers that flow at their bases, gradually peter out into the endless sand and gravel wastes of the Sahara Desert.

CLIMATE

The climatic variations in a country like this are endless. However, it's generally true to say that in winter the lowlands are pleasantly warm to hot (30°C) during the day and cool to cold (15°C) at night. In summer, it's very hot during the day (45°C) and uncomfortably warm at night (23°C).

Winter in the higher regions demands clothing suitable for Arctic conditions; this is true of anywhere in the vicinity of the High Atlas, since bitterly cold winds sweep down from the peaks at this time of year. In summer, it's hot during the day and cool at night.

Passes over the High Atlas can be blocked with snow during winter. Snowploughs usually clear them by the following day, but this can mean that you spend a bitterly cold night stuck in a bus in the snow without heating.

The main rainy season is between November and April but it brings only occasional light rain, which falls mainly on the coastal regions and on the high peaks. Rain rarely falls on the eastern parts of the country. Given the low rainfall, humidity is generally low.

The most pleasant seasons to explore Morocco are spring (April to May) and autumn (September to October). Midsummer can be very pleasant on the coast but viciously hot in the interior. Likewise, winter can be idyllic in Marrakesh and further south as far as the Algerian border during the day but you can be chilled to the bone at night.

GOVERNMENT

Morocco has been ruled by sultans ever since the Arab conquest and, until very recently, the power of the sultan was absolute – at least in theory. Just how far any sultan's writ extended, however, varied greatly from one reign to another and was dependent on the degree of control which he exercised over the always rebellious local chieftains.

Although King Hassan II, the present ruler, acts as the undisputed head of state and spiritual leader of the nation, the country remains a patchwork of ethnic and tribal groups. So far, the king has displayed considerable political acumen in maintaining at least a semblance of unity by playing off one region against another, the towns against the countryside and one political party against another. The war in Western Sahara has also been used to enhance his position by inspiring a sense of Moroccan nationalism and diverting attention from more pressing domestic problems.

It has not all been plain sailing, however. The monarchy has been forced to come to terms with the political developments of the 20th century and the aspirations of its subjects for a voice in government. The present constitution (the country's second since independence from France), which was adopted by referendum in 1972, provides for a 'constitutional and presidential monarchy' together with a multi-party national assembly.

There are five main political parties in Morocco. The oldest is Istiqlal, a nationalist conservative party founded in 1944, which draws its support from the middle classes. It previously had a much broader appeal but was weakened when many of its left-wing members split off to form the Union Nationale des Forces Populaires (UNFP) under the leadership of Ben Barka in 1959. Istiqlal came out badly in the 1984 general elections, losing half of the seats it had previously held.

Another party which enjoys a great deal of support – this time from the Berbers and other rural dwellers – is the pro-monarchist Mouvement Populaire (MP). Also close to the monarchy is the Mouvement Populaire Constitutionnel et Démocratique (MPCD), a splinter group of the Mouvement Populaire. Other parties with representatives in the national assembly include the Union Socialiste des Forces Populaires (USFP), which draws its main support from the working classes, students and intellectuals, and the Communist MPP (formerly the Parti du Progrès et du Socialisme) which was banned until 1983.

Until 1985, the ruling coalition was made up of the MP, MPCD, USFP, the Rassemblement National des Indépendents (RNI), the Union Constitutionelle (UC) and the Parti des Indépendents Démocrates (PID). The last three are all right-wing, pro-royalist parties and, together with the MP, they control 206 seats in the national assembly.

As a result of the war in Western Sahara, in 1985 the king demanded that the prime minister form a Government of National Unity. Both Istiqlal and the USFP refused to join, so parliament is currently controlled by a centre-right coalition comprising the UC, RNI and PID.

There are 306 members of parliament, two-thirds of whom are elected by universal suffrage. The remainder are nominated by an electoral college consisting of municipal councillors, representatives of the Chambers of Commerce and Agriculture, artisans' guilds and labour unions.

On a provincial and local level, Morocco is divided into 40 provinces each headed by a governor. Provinces are subdivided into *préfectures* headed by *chefs de cercle*. In turn, each préfecture is divided into *caidates* under the direction of *caids*. Caids have much the same powers as pashas, who are responsible for the administration of urban municipalities.

Despite Morocco's flirtation with democracy and the monarchy's apparently constitutional status, it is the king and a small circle of trusted advisors who make all the real decisions. The king retains the right to appoint or dismiss the prime minister and his cabinet and to dissolve the national assembly.

There have been serious confrontations in the past (centred on the universities) and two attempted coups (involving the armed forces). There are also occasional disturbances involving left-wing and Islamic fundamentalist groups but they have been suppressed, though Hassan only narrowly escaped death in the attempted coup of 1972.

ECONOMY

Morocco's economy has been going through hard times in recent years. The country has been forced to adopt austerity measures prescribed by the IMF in order to have its external debts rescheduled and to secure bridging loans. The total foreign debt in 1988 stands at around US$16 billion. The austerity programme has had serious social and political repercussions including rising unemployment and riots, the latter brought on by the reduction of subsidies on staple foods.

The main reasons for the downturn in the economy are droughts which have plagued the agricultural sector, a collapse of the world phosphate market, sluggish industrial growth and heavy dependence on imported oil, which accounts for some 80% of national energy requirements.

The war in Western Sahara is also a serious drain on the economy: it is estimated to be costing around US$2 million per day. Much of the debt with which Morocco is now saddled was run up in the 1970s, when the country was able to borrow heavily to fund an ambitious development programme on the strength of a boom in phosphate prices.

The mainstays of the economy are mining, agriculture, tourism, industry and remittances from Moroccans working overseas.

Morocco is the world's third largest producer of phosphates (15% of world production); it the largest exporter of phosphates, with estimated reserves of around 60 billion tonnes. Exports of phosphates and their derivatives (mainly fertilisers and phosphoric acid) account for up to 60% of foreign earnings. Since

conquerors were militarily too weak to oppose such syncretism.

It's also an historical fact that Islam co-existed with Christianity in the Iberian peninsula as well as in Sicily and southern Italy, until the advent of the Crusades. This sort of liberal interaction must have had profound effects on both religions.

None of this is to suggest that Islam in Morocco is in any way profoundly heretical. It isn't, but it has been tempered by regional sensibilities. Nevertheless, whenever it has been perceived as diverging too far from its basic tenets, there has been a fundamentalist reaction. This is as true of the present as it is of the past. Iran and Egypt are not the only Islamic nations which are either ruled by or have to deal with Islamic fundamentalism. Such forces exist in Morocco too and are perceived as a serious political issue. As a traveller you should be aware of this. It's conceivable that the growth of hard-line fundamentalism is directly related to the disrespect shown by many tourists to Islamic customs and strictures.

Certain local cults in Morocco extended their influence so far that they acquired national significance; their saints were endowed with real or imaginary lineages going back to the Prophet. The descendants of such saints acquired the title of *sherif* and many of them enjoyed a high political profile. The foremost of these was Moulay Idriss, whose tomb stands in the town of the same name outside Meknès. In the 8th century he founded the first Moroccan dynasty, which held sway until the advent of the Almoravids. He is held in such high esteem that, even today, non-Muslims are prohibited from staying overnight in the town and are only barely tolerated near his tomb.

Such cults later developed into brotherhoods not unlike those of the Sufis in the Middle East and, like them, they shared a mystical interpretation of Islam. Their magical powers and the trance-like states which they induced through dancing became legendary. Though active until fairly recently, these brotherhoods are now officially frowned on and their more extreme rituals outlawed. Nevertheless, loyalty to a particular saint's family remains an important part of Moroccan society.

Apart from the regionalism described above, almost everyone in Morocco is Muslim, and Sunni Muslim at that. While it is true that the Berber tribes took advantage of the great schism in Islam in the 7th century to re-assert their independence, they quickly rejoined the Sunni mainstream.

Until the establishment of Israel, Morocco was the home of many Jews. Traditionally, they lived in the *mellahs* of the main cities and were an important economic force in the life of the nation. Very few now remain, most of them having emigrated to Israel.

One last important facet of Islam which travellers should be aware of is that it is incumbent upon Muslims to help the poor. It's not that you are going to encounter many beggars in Morocco (they are few and far between). However, unemployment is high, so well-heeled tourists (ie virtually all foreigners) are regarded as employment opportunities. Hence the hassles at the entrance to most large city medinas. In your dealings with these people, remember that they have no access to welfare payouts. Such things do not exist in Morocco. If you refuse to help out by 'employing' them for the day then don't be too surprised if you get treated with contempt – but see the section on Bargaining in the Facts for the Visitor chapter in this section, because all is not as simple as that bald statement might imply.

HOLIDAYS & FESTIVALS

The main public holidays are:

New Year's Day
  1 January
Feast of the Throne
  3 March

Labour Day
1 May
Green March
6 November
Independence Day
18 November

These holidays are tied to the western calendar and, therefore, are accurately predictable in advance. On these days all banks and post offices are closed, as are most shops.

In addition to secular holidays there are many national and local religious holidays and festivals (known as *moussems* or *amouggars*). Some of these are national affairs celebrated country-wide but others are less elaborate local events. They are all tied to the lunar calendar; their approximate dates can be worked out if you know the phases of the moon but their exact dates cannot be predicted, since that decision rests with the religious authorities in Fès. The dates for local festivals are generally set by local caids, who take the weather into account, so they are even less predictable.

Probably the most important religious festival is that of Eid al Fitr which comes at the end of the Ramadan month-long fast. Ramadan takes place during the ninth month of the Muslim calendar and is a sort of parallel to the Christian Lent, with the difference that it is strictly observed by Muslims.

Another very important national festival is that of Aid el Kebir, which coincides with the beginning of the Islamic year. It commemorates Abraham's submission to God through his offer of his son Isaac for sacrifice. It takes the form of a traditional family gathering and those who can afford it slaughter a sheep for the occasion.

The third main religious festival, known as Mouloud, celebrates the Prophet Mohammed's birthday.

Local festivals are usually held in honour of marabouts (Muslim saints). They are often no more elaborate than an unusually lively and more extensive market day, though quite a few have

taken on regional and sometimes national importance. These sorts of festivals are common amongst the Berbers and are usually held during the summer months. It's worth making enquiries to determine when they are due to take place. The most important, in chronological order, are:

March
   Moussem of Moulay Aissa ben Driss in Beni Mellal.
May
   Fête des Roses (rose festival) at Kelaâ des M'Gouna in the Dadès Valley. Held late in the month.
   Moussem of Sidi Bou Selham south of Larache. This festival sometimes takes place in June.
June
   National Folklore Festival in Marrakesh (10 days). Held early in the month.
   Fête des Cerises (cherry festival) in Sefrou.
July
   Moussem at Mdiq, north-east of Tetouan. Takes place early in the month.
August
   Moussem of Moulay Idriss in Zerhoun, north of Meknès.
   Moussem of Moulay Abdallah south of El Jadida. Takes place late in the month.
   Moussem of Setti Fatma in the Ourika Valley, south of Marrakesh.
September
   Fête des Fiancés in Imilchil. Takes place late in the month.
   Moussem of Sidi Moussa Ou Quarquour near El Kelas du Straghna, north of Marrakesh.
October
   Moussem of Moulay Idriss in Fès.
   Fête du Cheval (horse festival) in Tissa, north-east of Fès. These two festivals take place in early October.
   Fête des Dattes (date festival) in Erfoud. This takes place in late October.

The Folklore Festival at Marrakesh is essentially a tourist event these days (even though it also attracts large numbers of Moroccans). Nevertheless, it's very colourful and well worth attending, since groups of dancers, musicians and other entertainers are invited in from all over the country.

LANGUAGE

Arabic, Berber, French and Spanish are the main languages. English is also spoken in many places. Spanish is more common in the north and French in the south. The country's official languages are Arabic and French, and both are taught in every school – even in the smallest villages.

Moroccans must be among the world's most accomplished linguists. There is probably no other country in the world where you will come across so many people – even children – who can speak so many different languages passably. The motivation – unemployment amid hordes of well-heeled tourists – might be obvious but their skill can only be admired. Even dish-washers at food stalls can manage one or two sentences of passable Japanese, not to mention any European language you can think of. Most of the people in this category are, naturally, involved in the tourist trade. Don't expect much beyond Moorish Arabic and French outside the main cities and popular tourist spots.

Although Arabic may be one of the official languages, its spoken form – Maghrebi Arabic – is considerably different from that which you hear in the Middle East. It's basically a regional dialect and is not radically different from the Arabic which you hear in Algeria and Tunisia. The written language, however, remains uniform.

Berber is widely spoken in the countryside and particularly in the mountains. Though related to Arabic, it's a language whose roots go back to pre-historic times. Prior to the Arab conquest of North Africa, it was spoken over much of the area between the Moroccan Atlantic coast and the Egyptian border. The original script of the language has disappeared but was probably not too dissimilar to that used today by the Touareg in the Sahara Desert. Berber is now rendered in Arabic script.

Berber has many dialects – some of them almost different languages – and this is especially true in Morocco. The country is, after all, one of the extremities of the Arab world, so it's not surprising that regional languages and dialects should have survived in the way they have done on the western extremities of Europe.

Moroccan Berber falls into three main colloquial groups – Rifian, Braber and Chleub. The first and the last are almost mutually unintelligible but Braber contains elements of both.

Rifian, as the name implies, refers to the dialect spoken by the inhabitants of the Rif Mountains. It is also spoken in the Middle Atlas and as far south as the oases around Figuig on the Algerian border.

Braber is the dialect spoken by the transient pastoralists of the Middle Atlas, the eastern High Atlas and the valleys which connect the High Atlas to the Sahara – the Ziz, Todra and Dadès.

Chleub is the dialect spoken by the settled tribes of the High Atlas, the Anti-Atlas, the Sous Valley and the south-western oases; it can also be found in the Ziz, Todra and Dadès valleys.

Unlike Basque, Breton and Welsh, however, the dialects which these people speak do not mark them off as belonging to any particular race or tribe. Most Berbers are bilingual (Berber and Arabic) and many are trilingual (Berber, Arabic and French).

Facts for the Visitor

VISAS

Visas are not required by the following: nationals of West European countries (with three exceptions – Belgium, the Netherlands and Portugal), Australia, Brazil, Canada, Chile, Japan, Mexico, New Zealand, Peru, the Philippines, the USA, Venezuela and most Arab countries. All other visitors must have a visa.

Nationals of Israel and South Africa are not admitted. What is more, if you do need a visa it's advisable not to have an Israeli stamp in your passport; else you may be refused a visa. Visas are not available at land borders or ports of entry.

Visas cost US$3 or the equivalent and are valid for a stay of up to 90 days.

Moroccan immigration officials not only do not believe that 'hippies' are an endangered species, they still subscribe to the enduring myth that hippies are the offal of western society. They represent a moral pollutant which must be turned back before it corrupts the fibre of Moroccan society. A 'hippie' is any male with long hair (and preferably an untidy beard) or untidy/outlandish clothes. Women face no such discrimination. And if a male fits the above description, the rules are applied with a frustrating capriciousness: some people get through; others are refused.

The ferry from Algeciras to Tangier is notorious for arbitrary refusals. The one from Algeciras to Ceuta doesn't have this problem, since Ceuta is Spanish territory and its border with Morocco is usually controlled in an easy-going fashion.

The Melilla border (Spain's other Moroccan enclave), on the other hand, is often staffed by officials whose main qualification for the job appears to be obnoxiousness. If you are planning on entering Morocco here, make sure you have on your Sunday best and that your razor was sharp that morning.

Visa Extensions

Visa extensions are free of charge but you may need a letter of recommendation from your own embassy. In theory, extensions are obtainable from the *gendarmerie* (police) headquarters in any regional capital but, in practice, you'll be told you have to go back to Rabat to get them. In Rabat you have to go to the Sûreté Nationale, Rue Soekarno. You can collect your extension the same day (at 6 pm) if you get there early.

If you intend to stay more than three months, you must apply for permission to do this within 15 days of arrival. Nationals of France and Spain are allowed unlimited stay so long as they report to the police within three months of arrival.

Travel Restrictions

It is prohibited to travel south of Tantan into Western Sahara without a special permit from the military authorities. Depending on the state of the war in that disputed part of Morocco, you may be able to get such a permit. If you do, it will usually allow you to travel south as far as Layoune (previously el-Aaiun) and even Dakhla (the regional capital). The war usually affects only the border area with Algeria, so it's safe to travel if you get the military permit. Recent travellers to this part of the country have been finding these permits much easier to obtain – at least as far as Layoune.

In late 1988 Morocco and Algeria announced they were to re-establish full diplomatic relations, so it may now be possible once again to travel on foot across the Oujda-Tlemcen border.

Other African Visas

Most of the developed nations of the world maintain embassies in the capital, Rabat. Where African countries are concerned, there are embassies for CAR, Egypt,

Equatorial Guinea, Gabon, Guinea, Ivory Coast, Libya, Mauritania, Nigeria, Senegal, Sudan, Tunisia and Zaire.

Algeria There are Algerian consulates in: Rabat (tel 242 15, 242 87) 8 Rue d'Azrou, just off Ave du Fas; Oujda (tel 37 40/41) Blvd Bir Anzarane; and Casablanca, 159 Blvd Moulay Idriss. The consulate in Rabat shares a building with the United Arab Emirates embassy and is open Monday to Friday from 8.30 am to 12 noon. Visas cost Dr 50, require four photos and can be issued the same day if your application does not have to be referred to Algiers.

If you have a West German passport *do not* apply for your visa in Morocco. You will be refused. I even met a West German man married to an Algerian woman who was refused a visa in Rabat. You must get your visa in Bonn before leaving. Much the same applies to Dutch nationals, who also should get their visas in Europe. Europe.

The consulate in Oujda has the nasty

habit of refusing to issue visas, so get them elsewhere or be prepared to backtrack to Rabat.

Egypt Visas cost Dr 170, require two photos and are issued in 24 hours. There's no fuss or money-showing. The embassy is at 31 Ave al Jazair (formerly called Ave d'Alger) on Place Abraham Lincoln, Rabat.

Mauritania Visas cost Dr 50 and are issued while you wait. The embassy is at 6 Rue Thami Lam Souissi, Rabat.

Niger There is no Niger Embassy in Rabat and the French Consulate in Rabat cannot issue visas. The nearest Niger diplomatic missions are in Algiers or Tamanrasset (Algeria).

MONEY

US$1	=	Dr 7.97
UK£1	=	Dr 14.05
DM 1	=	Dr 3.78
FFr 1	=	Dr 1.24

The unit of currency is the dirham. A dirham is made up of 100 centimes. The import or export of local currency is officially prohibited. There's no black market as such, though you will occasionally be made an offer. Even if you are, it will only be a few cents above the bank rate, so it's hardly worth the effort unless you're desperate to change.

Banks do not usually charge commission on travellers' cheques, though the Banque Populaire may take Dr 5 in some places (eg Azrou, Errachidia). Banking services are usually quick and efficient.

Credit cards are widely accepted in the main cities but not in the smaller places or in the countryside. American Express is represented by the travel agency Voyages Schwarz, which can be found in Agadir, Casablanca, Marrakesh, Rabat and Tangier. The Banque Crédit du Maroc represents the interests of the Visa and Access systems.

If you are going on to Algeria it is well worth considering buying Algerian dinars in Ceuta, Melilla or Oujda before you do. In Oujda the going rate is US$1 = AD 23, which is better than you'll get on the black market inside Algeria. Even dirhams hold their value remarkably well – you should be able to get one Algerian dinar for two dirham. However, it is illegal to import Algerian dinars into Algeria and the searches at the borders can be thorough, so you'll need to hide them well. There are plenty of money changers doing the rounds in Oujda and Melilla.

COSTS

Whether you are coming from Europe, America or Australasia, you'll find Moroccan prices refreshingly reasonable. A basic (ie unclassified) hotel with shared bathroom costs just US$2 to US$3 a double. A hot shower in such a hotel costs extra (up to 50 cents). In a one-star hotel, a room with its own bathroom costs around US$6 a double and will usually include hot water. For US$10 a double you are looking at semi-luxury.

Food is good and relatively cheap, and a standard meal of tajine or couscous costs around US$2, though the latter is usually slightly more expensive. European-style food costs more but rarely over US$4 a meal, so long as you aren't eating in an expensive restaurant or hotel. US$10 would buy you a Moroccan-style banquet.

The only things which are relatively expensive are alcoholic beverages (beer and wine). You will pay around US$1 for a small beer and US$5 and up for a bottle of Moroccan wine.

Transport is a bargain, particularly by bus or train (the latter even in 2nd class), though taxis cost up to half as much again. For instance, a long bus journey (eg 500 km) costs around US$12. So, adding on a few small tips here and there plus a few entry charges to museums and the like, you could get by on US$10 a day per person so long as you stay in cheap hotels, eat at cheap restaurants and are not in a hurry. If you'd prefer some of life's basic luxuries like hot showers, the occasional splurge at a good restaurant and don't mind taking a taxi if it's going to increase your enjoyment of a particular journey, then plan on US$15 to US$20 per day per person.

Obviously, some cities are more expensive than others, and the country is usually considerably cheaper than the cities, so your expenses will vary. The only other major expense which you need to bear in mind is the cost of all those crafts which you are going to buy when you get into the *souks*. Few people can resist purchasing at least two or three articles. There's no way of suggesting any approximate budget for these things, since it all depends on when and where you buy them, how good you are at haggling, whether you want quality or are happy with semi-trash, and the nature of the article. One thing's certain: money speaks and an empty pocket gets you nothing.

Stock up on petrol in Ceuta or Melilla if you have your own vehicle, as they are both duty-free ports; petrol will cost you more in Morocco.

TOURIST INFORMATION

Morocco is well geared for tourism. The national tourist body, ONMT, has offices in Agadir, Casablanca, El Jadida, Fès, Layoune, Marrakesh, Meknès, Ouarzazate, Oujda, Tangier and Tetouan.

Each office usually has a fair stock of glossy brochures and maps of the major places.

The offices of the national tourist body are complemented in many towns by local tourist offices, known as Syndicats d'Initiative. These have little printed information but the staff are usually more clued up on local matters.

The ONMT also maintains offices overseas and these are good places to contact if you need any info before you go.

Australia
    11 West St, North Sydney, NSW 2060 (tel 957 6717)
Canada
    2 Carlton St, Toronto, Ontario, M5B 1K2 (tel 6219760)
France
    161 Rue Ste Honoré, Place du Théâtre Français, Paris 1
Italy
    23 Via Larga, Milan 20122 (tel 860 927)
Switzerland
    Schifflände 5, Zürich 8001 (tel 252 7752)
UK
    174 Regent St, London W1R GHB (tel 437 0073)
USA
    20 East 46th St, New York, NY 10017 (tel 557 2520)
West Germany
    59 Graf Adolf Strasse, Düsseldorf 4000 (tel 370551)

GENERAL INFORMATION

Post

The Moroccan post is reliable, and you shouldn't have any problem receiving letters posted to you care of Poste Restante.

Parcels posted back to your home

address have to be inspected by customs (at the post office) before you seal the parcel and pay for the postage, so don't turn up at a post office with a sealed parcel – you'll just waste time and money. And although you will be handed what might appear to be a somewhat dubious receipt for a parcel, it will get there. The days when the contents might have been stolen or the stamps steamed off belong to the distant past. However, as in many countries around the world, it might not be a good idea to send money through the post.

Telephones

The telephone service is similarly reliable, and you shouldn't have to wait too long for an international connection. Telephone directories, on the other hand, are a different matter. Last time I was in Rabat, the only Rabat directory available at the main telephone office was 10 years out of date. In that time all the numbers had changed, as a new system had been installed, so it was completely useless.

The staff at the enquiry desk were about as useful.

Time

Moroccan time is one hour ahead of GMT all year round.

Banking Hours

Banking hours are Monday to Friday from 8.30 to 11.30 am and 3 to 5.30 pm, except during the month of Ramadan when the hours are 8.30 am to 2 pm. When the banks are closed you can usually change cash or travellers' cheques at larger hotels, travel agents and tourist shops, though they'll probably charge commission.

FILM & PHOTOGRAPHY

Colour negative and slide film are readily available in all large Moroccan cities and towns, but they're usually Kodak or Fuji. If you prefer Agfa bring your own because you won't find it in Morocco.

Kodak or Fuji film of 64, 100 and even 200 ASA is available in most photography shops, but don't expect to find 400 or 800 ASA film. They'd probably order it for you, but if you're not going to be hanging around for several weeks then forget about it.

As prices go, there's not a great deal in it, but if you want to be sure, bring your own supply with you.

As with most hot, dry countries, remember that photographs are best taken in the early morning or late afternoon. Unless you know a lot about photography and your camera has manual override, most photographs taken in the middle of the day will be 'washed-out', especially in summer.

The reverse is true of photographs taken in the medinas of places like Fès, Marrakesh and Meknès. Even in the middle of the day it can be relatively dark in the narrow streets, and without fast film (400 to 800 ASA) you'll just end up with a lot of silhouettes or, more usually, nothing but indistinct rubbish.

Urban Moroccans are generally easygoing about foreigners taking photographs – most middle-class Moroccans, after all, own cameras. In the countryside, however, this isn't necessarily the case and you should ask permission beforehand or be very discreet. It isn't that country people are hostile to having their photographs taken: they just like to know who's taking them. And that can take half an hour of exchanging pleasantries, talking about where you come from and what life is like there, what you are doing in Morocco, or anything else they feel like asking you about. One thing is guaranteed: if you spare the time for this sort of exchange you'll end up with superb shots instead of furtive and very grainy garbage taken from a great distance with a zoom lens. Moroccan country people are very earthy and don't know how to pose, so you'll lose nothing, photographically speaking, by telling them what you want to do.

However, if you ever run into a situation where people don't want to be photographed, respect their right to privacy and don't take photos.

ACCOMMODATION
Youth Hostels

There are a number of youth hostels (auberges de jeunesse) in Morocco and, if you're travelling alone, they are among the cheapest places to stay. The charge is usually Dr 10 per night with a youth hostel card or Dr 12.50 without. If you buy a youth hostel card in Morocco it will cost you Dr 35. Generally, meals are not available at hostels and you have to pay extra for hot showers (cold showers are free). There are hostels at Asni, Azrou, Casablanca, Chechaouen, Fès, Ifrane, Marrakesh, Meknès, Mohammedia and Rabat.

Where there is no youth hostel, there is usually a Centre Sportif or a Centre de Jeunesse, where basic accommodation can be found for a small charge. Sometimes it's just floor space, at other times you get a bed.

Hotels

Youth hostels are fine if you don't mind dormitory accommodation and if you're carrying no valuables which might attract the attention of thieves. On the other hand, a cheap hotel will often not cost much more than a bed at a youth hostel. It's certainly cheaper to rent a room at a hotel if you are sharing, rather than paying for two (separate) beds at a youth hostel.

Only very rarely will you find a dirty room or dirty sheets, even in the cheapest hotels. The vast majority are remarkably clean and excellent value. The toilets and bathrooms are generally in the same state. Hot showers are the exception rather than the rule and, if you want one, there's usually a small additional charge for it (in most cheap hotels hot showers are run off bottles of propane gas).

Baggage left in hotel rooms is generally safe. I never had a single thing stolen and found the level of honesty to be very high indeed (Tetouan hustlers notwithstanding). For those wanting more comfort than a budget hotel there's usually plenty of choice, except in the very small places.

Camping

You can camp anywhere in Morocco so long as you have the permission of the site's owner, but there are a large number of official camp sites which vary in price depending on the facilities provided. Tourist offices have details of their location.

BOOKS

People & Society

Morocco - Its People & Places by Edmondo de Amicis, translated by C Rollin-Tilton (Darf, London, 1985). This book, first published in Italian in 1882, was written by a man who accompanied an Italian diplomatic mission to the sultan's court at Fès. It's a delightfully fresh and lively account of life in Morocco at that time and is illustrated with the original sketches executed by the artist who was attached to the mission. I'd nominate this book as one of the best travelogues I've ever read.

The Moors - Islam in the West by Michael Brett & Werner Forman (Orbis, London, 1985). This large-format book filled with superb colour photographs details the impact and development of Islam on Morocco and Spain when Moorish civilisation was at its height and follows through to the Spanish reconquista. It's not just a history book, however: it includes chapters on topics such as the social framework and the Muslim mind, and examines social, economic and political issues relevant to the times.

Doing Daily Battle by Fatima Mernissi, translated by Mary Jo Lakeland (The Women's Press, London, UK£5.95). This is a collection of interviews with eleven Moroccan women which gives a valuable insight into their lives and aspirations. Fatima Mernissi is also the author of the classic study Beyond the Veil: Male-Female Dynamics in a Modern Muslim Society.

History

The Conquest of Morocco by Douglas Porch (Cape, London, 1986) can be recommended. Another good book, also by Porch, is The Conquest of the Sahara (Cape, London, 1985).

Architecture

Islamic Architecture of North Africa by Antony Hutt (Scorpion, London, 1977). This book is mainly for those interested in the architecture of North Africa and is essentially a photographic essay. Unfortunately, most of the photographs are black and white, so much of the richness of the decoration is lost.

Cookbooks

The Taste of Morocco by Robert Carrier (Century, London, 1987) is a brilliant hardback on Moroccan cuisine; colour photos throughout.

MAPS

The only map which really makes the grade in terms of detail is the Michelin 'Morocco' No 169 (Scale 1:1,000,000).

For minute detail of routes within Morocco, you can't do better than buy the Michelin *Guide de Tourisme - Maroc*. The maps (and the descriptions of places) in this book are excellent.

Unfortunately for those who can speak only English, this guide is only published in French. You cannot buy it in Morocco, as it is banned there - apparently because certain regional maps mark the disputed border between Morocco and Algeria! - so you must buy it in Europe. Few bookshops in the UK stock it, since it's in French, but you may be able to find it in the bookshops along Charing Cross Rd or Tottenham Court Rd in London. Otherwise, it's available from Michelin, 46 Ave de Breteuil, 75341 Paris, France.

THINGS TO BUY

For centuries, Moroccan crafts have been justifiably world-famous both for their variety and their quality. There's probably no other country of a similar size which can boast so many different craft guilds. The sale and export of these crafts is an essential pillar of the Moroccan economy even though, in the 20th century, mining and agriculture have overtaken this in importance. Virtually no one returns home from a trip to Morocco without carrying with them one or more examples of the crafts which are produced here.

The extensive souks of Fès, Meknès, Marrakesh and, to a lesser extent, Rabat and Tangier offer a full range of crafts. Naturally, styles vary from region to region and the price of any particular object is usually lowest in its place of origin.

Wooden boxes, marquetry and chess boards are best bought in Essaouira, where the range is enormous. Cedar-wood screens assembled into intricate patterns are best sought in Fès or Meknès, whereas brightly painted chests and cradles are a speciality of Fès and Tetouan. Chased copper and brass trays, vases, candlesticks and the like are best bought in Casablanca, Fès, Marrakesh and Tetouan, and they range from items costing only a couple of dollars to trays on which you could literally stage a banquet.

Silver-inlaid sabres and muskets are best sought in Tiznit and Taroudannt. Tiznit, Rissani and Tantan are famous for their range of silverwork, since silver jewellery is worn by the nomads of the south. Gold jewellery, on the other hand, is at its best in Fès, Essaouira and Tangier.

Be careful when buying jewellery. At the cheaper end of the scale, what is sold as solid silver is nothing of the sort: it's merely plated. The same thing goes if you're offered cheap amber: put a lighted match to it and you'll quickly discover that it's plastic - albeit skilfully crafted to appear genuine.

Leatherwork is another of Morocco's famous crafts. Its quality and softness is legendary. The best wallets, desk sets, slippers (*babouches*) and embossed poufs are found in Fès, Meknès and Rabat, whereas elaborate leather bags are a speciality of the Riffian towns of Tetouan, Chechaouen and Taghzout. Camel saddles should be sought in Marrakesh.

Fès, Meknès, Marrakesh and Rabat all have their carpet souks, which stock a wide range of styles and sizes. You need to spend a considerable amount of time examining what is available before buying, as the quality varies and the colours in the cheaper examples have a tendency to fade rapidly. What was an extravaganza of colour when you first bought it can quickly lose its vividness. Enquire about the dyes used and make an effort to see the genuine article in a museum before doing the rounds of the carpet souks. Styles and patterns are as varied as the tribes and some are hard to find outside of their region of origin. You won't, for instance, come across many of the brightly coloured and delightfully

Rug

naive patterns which are found on the carpets woven in Ouarzazate and Zagora outside these areas.

Pottery – vases, plates, tajine dishes and the like – is best bought in Fès or Safi, where there are famous potteries.

Stoneware is at its best in Taroudannt, where you will find boxes, lamps and paperweights. Outside Taroudannt, along the mountain roads of the High Atlas, you will come across numerous stalls where semi-precious and ornamental stones are sold. These include amethyst, rock crystal, quartz and many others. Prices are very reasonable indeed.

Bargaining

Contrary to what a lot of people would like to believe, most prices in Morocco are more or less fixed. This includes hotel accommodation, meals at a restaurant or café and transport.

On the other hand, there is no such thing as a fixed price for crafts bought in the souks, where haggling is the name of the game. In some places, especially Marrakesh, this is becoming less and less the slow, relaxed process which it used to be: too many well-heeled tourists with more money than brains, no sense of values and little time to spare have been through before you. If you're not prepared to pay what local people would regard as ridiculous prices then there's always another mug around the corner who will. If you run up against this, go somewhere else.

Fortunately, there are still many places where you can enjoy the process of haggling and where it isn't just a charade put on to give you the illusion that you're getting a bargain. Traditionally, sellers would start off at around double the price they were actually prepared to accept and buyers would start off at less than half that amount. Gradually, over several glasses of mint tea, a mutually acceptable price would be reached.

These days it's no longer quite so predictable. Sellers frequently start at triple the price they are prepared to accept, so you need to start off at around one-quarter. The price will quickly drop to not far from what the trader is prepared to accept, so you'll mostly end up haggling over a few dirhams.

The major constraint on your bargaining power will be the guide who accompanies you around the souks. Unemployment amongst young people in Morocco is very high and tourists represent a temporary employment possibility. These 'guides' hang around the entrance to the souks and are incredibly tenacious. In some places – Marrakesh being notorious – it's virtually impossible at times to get past them without accepting one, until your face gets known. On the other hand, taking a 'guide' is probably a good idea for your first and second visits, as it's an opportunity to familiarise yourself with the layout of the souks. Agree on a price for the 'guide's' services before you set off. This shouldn't be more than a dollar or two.

The people who act as 'guides' make most of their income from commissions which they receive from shopkeepers when you buy something. This can be up to 40% of the price you pay, so they're naturally very keen to see you buy a lot of things, and your tour around the souks can rapidly degenerate into being hustled through an endless succession of shops. If you wish to maximise your bargaining powers, avoid buying anything whilst you are with a 'guide'. This isn't always easy, as you'll be subjected to high-powered sales tactics; some 'guides' actually get abusive once it appears you are not going to buy anything. Don't get sucked-in and react in the same manner: it's just a ruse to browbeat you, though many people fall for it. Even better, make it clear to the 'guide' before you set off that you may not be buying anything.

Refusing a 'guide's' services can be a harrowing experience. Many of them are expert at manipulating the conversation to suit their ends and in your own language. This is the major source of the bad news stories with which many travellers come away from Morocco. The trouble usually starts because the traveller doesn't want a guide, and eventually loses patience in the face of the extreme persistence of the guide who wants to be taken on. There's no easy answer to this but anger isn't the solution: the guide will simply get angry too, and you'll end up having a full-on blue. Remember that one of the tenets of Islam is the giving of alms to the poor; you can generally assume that the guides who are trying to sell their services are otherwise unemployed. It helps if you can see things in this light, even if your sympathy is only verbal.

Marrakesh is probably the worst city in Morocco as far as 'guide' hassles go. I put the major cause for this down to the Club Méditerranée on the Djemaa el Fna. By comparison, Fès, Meknès and Rabat are a breeze.

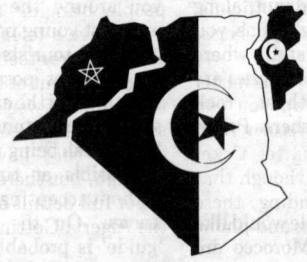

Getting There

AIR

Although most travellers arrive by ferry from Spain or Gibraltar, Morocco is well served by air from Europe, the Middle East and West Africa, and has international airports at Tangier, Casablanca and Agadir.

Airlines which fly to Casablanca, the country's main airport, include: Aeroflot, Air Afrique, Air Algérie, Air France, Alitalia, Iberia, KLM, Lufthansa, Royal Jordanian, Sabena, Saudia, Swissair and Tarom.

To/From Europe

Depending on the time of year that you want to travel, there may well be some incredibly cheap charter flight tickets available to Morocco from northern European cities such as Amsterdam, London or Paris. They're always return tickets and generally must be paid for in advance. However, some agents will sell you a one-way ticket a few days before the flight or even on the day itself if they have a deal with the charter companies and there are spare seats going.

The same goes for flights to Madrid and Malaga. These charter tickets are often tied to a minimum number of nights at a specific hotel and, in theory, you can't buy a ticket without also paying for the accommodation. In practice, most agents will sell you the air ticket and provide you with a bogus voucher for the accommodation so that it all looks normal in case you're questioned by officials. Naturally, you can't use the bogus voucher.

Even if you have to buy a return charter ticket, they're often so cheap you can afford to throw away the return half. A London/Agadir return charter ticket can cost as little as UK£40, though that would be exceptional. Finding these tickets can involve a lot of leg and phone work, and they get snapped up quickly. Trying to arrange them through provincial agents is usually a waste of time.

To/From North America

With no direct flights between the USA and Morocco, the cheapest way to go is on a cheap flight to London and then a separate flight to Morocco from there.

To/From Australia

As with the USA, there are no direct flights between Australia and Morocco. The cheapest fare quoted is A$1500 return and this is with Royal Jordanian going via Amman and Singapore. It wouldn't work out much more expensive to fly to London and then hunt around for a cheap ticket to Morocco from there.

OVERLAND

To/From Algeria

There are two crossing points between the two countries: between Oujda and Tlemcen in the north near the coast and between Figuig and Beni Ounif some 300 km further south.

It is possible to enter Morocco on foot via either point, but if you are heading for Algeria you must use the Figuig-Beni Ounif crossing.

People with their own vehicle can use either crossing in either direction. However, Moroccan regulations are such that people bringing vehicles into Morocco must have a telex from their embassy in Rabat guaranteeing that they will take the vehicle out of the country. It takes up to a couple of weeks to organise this telex, so plan ahead. People with just a carnet or a green card have been known to get through, but there is no guarantee.

For full details of the two crossings, see the Algeria Getting There chapter.

BOAT

To/From Spain

There's a whole variety of car ferries operated by Compania Transmediterranea and the Compagnie Marocaine de Navigation. The most popular of these is the Algeciras-Tangier route; the others are Algeciras-Ceuta (Spanish Morocco), Almeria-Melilla (Spanish Morocco) and Malaga-Melilla. All ferries are of the drive-on and drive-off type.

There are also hydrofoil services, operated by Transtour, between Tarifa and Tangier, and high-speed catamarans from Gibraltar to Tangier.

Algeciras to Tangier On this route there are a minimum of three daily departures in each direction. This rises to six in the peak season from the beginning of July to mid-September.

The crossing takes about 2½ hours and the minimum fares are 2550 Ptas or Dr 170. A car up to six metres long costs 11,200 Ptas or Dr 740; a motorcycle costs 2400 Ptas or Dr 160.

Tarifa to Tangier The Transtour hydrofoil service operates daily as long as the weather isn't too rough. At only 30 minutes, it's by far the quickest way to make the crossing.

The hydrofoil leaves Tarifa at 9 am and returns from Tangier at 4.30 pm. The one-way fare is 2400 Ptas, Dr 150 or UK£12.

Algeciras to Ceuta (Spanish Morocco) In summer this Compania Transmediterranea service operates up to eight times daily, except Sunday when there are only three crossings.

The trip takes 1½ hours and the fare is 1100 Ptas or Dr 76 per person.

Almeria to Melilla (Spanish Morocco) A three-times-weekly Compania Transmediterranea service, this crossing takes 6½ hours. Ferries leave Almeria on Tuesday, Thursday and Saturday at 2 pm; they leave Melilla on Monday, Wednesday and Saturday at 11 pm.

The fare is 2000 Ptas per person.

Malaga to Melilla (Spanish Morocco) Also operated by Compania Transmediterranea, ferries leave Malaga on Monday, Wednesday and Friday at 1 pm; they leave Melilla on Tuesday, Thursday and Saturday at 11.30 pm.

The journey time is 7½ hours and the fare is 2000 Ptas per person.

To/From Gibraltar

Gibraltar to Tangier The only services between the two places are a hydrofoil and a high-speed catamaran, neither of which take vehicles.

The Transtour hydrofoils operate daily, leaving Gibraltar at 4 pm and Tangier at 9.30 am. The trip takes one hour and costs 3115 Ptas, Dr 180 or UK£15 per person.

The catamaran is operated by Gibline and there are up to three departures daily. The trip takes 75 minutes and the fare is UK£16.

Gibraltar to M'Diq This route is also operated by Gibline. At last report it ran only on Thursdays, leaving Gibraltar at 9 am and M'Diq at 4.30 pm. The fare is UK£16 per person.

I've never actually heard of anyone entering Morocco this way, but if it's possible it would be a good way to avoid the touts at Tangier and the chaotic border south of Ceuta.

M'Diq is just north of Tetouan and there are regular buses between the two.

To/From France

Sète to Tangier This car ferry service is operated by the Compagnie Marocaine de Navigation and the crossing is made between five and eight times per month, depending on the season.

The trip takes 38 hours and the minimum fare is UK£90 or FFr 720 per person one way, and a similar amount for a vehicle.

Addresses

The addresses of the major shipping companies are:

Compania Transmediterranea

Spain

Plaza Manuel Gomez Moreno, Esquina a Orense 4, Madrid 28020 (tel 455 0049)

Morocco

Intercona, 31 Ave de la Résistance, Tangier (tel 367 45)

France

Voyages Melia, 31 Ave de l'Opéra, Paris 75001 (tel (1) 42 61 56 56)

UK

Melia Travel, 12 Dover St, London W1X 4NE (tel (01) 499 6731)

West Germany

Karl Geuther GmbH, Heinrichstr 9, Frankfurt 6000 (tel (49) 69 730471)

Holland

Melia Travel Holland, Leiderstraat 27, Amsterdam 1017 (tel (31) 20 252552)

Switzerland

Voyages Melia Suisse, 13 to 17 Rue de Chantepoulet, Geneva 1201 (tel (41) 22 319491)

Transtour

Spain

Tourafrica, Estacion Maritima, Algeciras 11201 (tel 65 3706)

Tourafrica, Estacion Maritima, Tarifa (tel 68 4751)

Morocco

4 Rue Jabha al Ouatania, Tangier (tel 340 04)

Gibraltar

Batmar Ltd, The Arcade, 30 to 38 Main St, Unit L (tel 77 666)

Compagnie Marocaine de Navigation

Morocco

Comanav, 43 Ave Abou Alaa El Maari, Tangier (tel 326 52)

Comanov Voyages, 43 Ave des FAR, Casablanca (tel 31 20 50)

France

SNCM, 12 Rue Godot de Mauroy, Paris 75009 (tel (1) 42 66 60 19)

SNCM, 4 Quai d'Alger, Sète 34203 (tel 67 74 70 55)

UK

Continental Shipping & Travel Ltd, 179 Piccadilly, London W1V 9DB (tel (01) 491 4968)

West Germany

Karl Geuther GmbH, Heinrichstr 9, Frankfurt 6000 (tel (49069) 73 0471)

Switzerland

Gondrand Reisen AG, Tastrasse 66, Zürich 8021 (tel (01) 211 5938)

Gibline

Gibraltar

Gibline Ltd, Seagle Travel Ltd, 9B George's Lane, PO Box 480, Gibraltar (tel 71 415)

Getting Around

AIR

If your time is very limited and you want to see as much of Morocco as possible, it's worth considering the occasional internal flight offered by Royal Air Maroc. If you're 26 years of age or under it works out particularly cheap, as they offer 40% 'youth fare' discounts on the normal prices.

BUS

There is a good network of buses all over the country; departures are frequent, so a timetable is superfluous. Most Moroccan cities and towns now have a central bus terminal, though this isn't always the case (eg Meknès, Tangier). Where there is no central terminal, the various bus companies are usually clustered together in the same area.

CTM (Compagnie de Transports au Maroc) is the main company. Between the main centres of population they generally offer 1st-class buses plus 2nd-class buses along some routes. On minor routes the buses are usually 2nd class. CTM buses are slightly more expensive but no faster than those of the other companies such as SATAS, Maroc Express and FAK. CTM sometimes has its own bus terminal in the various cities, even if it also operates buses from the central terminal. Sufficient leg room is no problem on CTM buses but the width of the seats is another matter. On non-CTM buses you're usually looking at being squeezed both ways. On well-subscribed routes and those which have only one bus a day, try to book your ticket in advance.

Bus transport is cheap and isn't going to be one of your major expenses. Marrakesh to Ouarzazate, for example, is Dr 31.20 (about US$3.30) for the five to six-hour journey. Ouarzazate to Errachidia is Dr 36 for the nine-hour journey. Marrakesh to Essaouira is Dr 18 for the three-hour journey.

There are no official charges for baggage placed either on the roof or in the side compartments but, if it goes on the roof, the baggage handlers will demand a tip however much help you offer. They're usually happy with a dirham, though local people pay less. On dusty journeys your baggage is better placed on the roof, where it won't end up the colour of the road, since tarpaulins are pulled over baggage on the roof. You shouldn't have any problems with theft of baggage, though it might be wise to keep an eye on it if the bus is standing for any length of time at an intermediate terminal.

Don't expect even CTM buses to have heating, even on the journeys over the Atlas Mountains in winter; they often don't. Warm clothing is, therefore, essential and particularly if there's any chance of being stranded on the passes due to snow drifts. The Marrakesh-Ouarzazate road is prone to this. It's extremely unlikely you'll be stranded for longer than overnight, as snowploughs usually clear a path by early morning.

CTM also operates international buses from Casablanca and Rabat to Bordeaux and Paris, but at US$107 one-way and US$165 return they're poor value. You'd be able to do the same independently for less.

TRAIN

As with the bus system, there is a good network of railways connecting all the main centres of population. However, through services to Algeria were suspended many years ago because of political tension between Morocco and Algeria over the war in Western Sahara.

Trains are the best method of transport in Morocco if you have the choice. A lot of money has been spent on upgrading the railways and rolling stock in recent years, so trains are comfortable, fast and reliable. Also, even if you travel 2nd class the fares cost very little more than the equivalent bus fares would. Third class (known as Economique) is cheaper than going by bus, though it can be overcrowded. First class is definitely luxurious and an unnecessary expense. Second class consists of separate compartments with six seats and is usually air-conditioned. It would be the equivalent of 1st class on trains anywhere else in Africa and is the one most travellers seem to go for.

On the fringes of the railway system – Meknès or Fès to Oujda, for instance – you may come across 2nd-class carriages which are of the old type, in which case they won't be air-conditioned (or heated in winter). Third class is a community experience and perfectly adequate for short journeys. The Rabat-Casablanca line is an experience all of its own. The track is electrified and super fast, and the journey takes only 55 minutes (non-stop). It costs just Dr 22 (2nd class): a bargain.

Most trains offer a choice of all three classes, but there are some which offer only 1st and 2nd class. Sleepers are available on night trains. A refreshment trolley usually does the rounds of the carriages offering hot coffee, soft drinks and snacks and, on the longer journeys, there is a buffet car with lunch and dinner available.

Timetables are prominently displayed in the railway stations and are also available from the ticket offices, so you can plan ahead. At major stations it's also possible to buy, for Dr 1, a small booklet which lists the schedules of all the major trains in the country.

Advance booking is advisable for 1st class, though it's probably true to say that it would be rare for all the trains to be booked out on any particular day. For 2nd and 3rd class you just roll up and buy the ticket before departure. You can in fact buy the ticket in advance, but as there is no seat reservation there seems little point in this.

TAXI
Shared taxis (grands taxis) are worth considering on some routes – particularly along scenic routes which buses might cover partially after sunset. They cost about 50% more than the equivalent bus fare, but make sure you know what local people are paying beforehand. There's often an attempt to conceal this so that you end up paying more.

Shared taxis are a particularly good idea if there are enough of you to fill one and you'd like the driver to stop occasionally so you can take photographs or walk around for five or 10 minutes. It will cost you more if you want the driver to do this, so negotiate a price before you set off. They won't stop if you are sharing with local people. The Ziz and Drâa valleys and the Tiz-n-Test pass particularly lend themselves to shared taxis, and there are many other scenic routes.

Shared taxis are frequently older Mercedes-Benz, bought by their owners whilst they were 'guest workers' in France and Germany in the days when those countries were short of manual labourers.

City taxis (petits taxis) are very useful in urban areas and will save you a lot of time getting from one place to another. They're very cheap by European standards – rarely more than Dr 5 for an average journey – though a tip is appreciated.

DRIVING
There are many out-of-the-way places in Morocco which you simply won't be able to get to if you don't hire a taxi or haven't got your own transport. Car rental is not cheap, but with four people it's affordable. The cheapest cars are Renault 4 and Fiat 127. Charges vary slightly from company to company, and you may be able to do a bit of bargaining over the rates in the off season. Typical charges are Dr 1230 for three days and Dr 2170 for a week for unlimited mileage. However, you still have to pay the government tax of 19%; also, it's advisable to pay extra for the personal insurance (Dr 20 per day) and

the Collision Damage Waiver (Dr 30), otherwise you'll be liable for the first Dr 3000 of any damage. The estimated cost of the rental is payable at the time you take delivery (minimum deposit Dr 2000). Minimum age for drivers is 21 years with at least one year's driving experience. An international driving licence is usually required, though some agencies will accept your national driving licence.

Renting the car is the major cost, but fuel is not especially cheap and can mount up; super petrol costs Dr 6.05 per litre.

HITCHING

Hitching is OK, but demands a thick skin

and considerable diplomatic expertise in the north due to aggressive hustlers. They simply won't take 'no' for an answer or feign outrage if you express lack of interest in whatever it is that they're trying to sell you – usually drugs. It's particularly bad on the road between Tetouan and Tangier.

In the south, you can only travel by road without special permission as far as Tantan because of the war with Polisario in Western Sahara. In this area there are numerous army and police roadblocks where vehicles are searched for arms, though foreign-registered vehicles are often waved through.

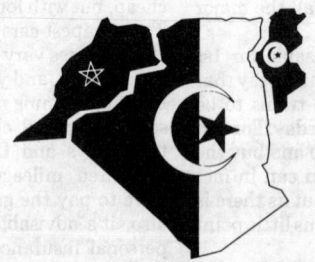

Top: Djemaa el Fna, Marrkesh, Morocco (GC)
Left: Water seller, Rabat, Morocco (HF)
Right: Dar el Makhzen, Tangier, Morocco (HF)

Top: Todra Gorge, Morocco (GC)
Left: Fès el-Bali, Morocco (HF)
Right: Tanneries, Fès, Morocco (HF)

The Mediterranean Coast & the Rif

Tangier & the Coast

TANGIER

All the various peoples who have settled here at one time or another have left their mark on the city, so it has an atmosphere which is very different from that of other Moroccan cities. However, there's little left of the sophisticated decadence for which it was notorious during the 1930s and 1940s.

As a result of Tangier being the major port of entry for tourists, the sleaze and the opulence have been replaced by hordes of the world's best hustlers. Pick any language, any situation, any time of day or night, and they'll find you like flies find shit. Nothing you say is going to make any difference to the persistent, superglue patter which will accompany you all the way from the ferry to the inside of the hotel room which you choose. Even if you know exactly which hotel you are heading for and its exact location, and require no 'help', they'll claim they found it for you. Naturally, you'll want to 'reward' them. Every subterfuge in the book will be used to get you to pay.

That unemployment in Morocco is high cannot be denied – hence there's some justification for this behaviour. But these hustlers are rivalled only by those who hang around the entrance to the medina in Marrakesh. There's no way through this cobweb that's guaranteed to succeed, but patience, politeness, minimal interaction and firmness can go a long way to reducing any 'claim' they have on you. You'll just have to treat it as your first introduction to Morocco. Things do get better!

History

Tangier has been coveted for millennia as a strategic site for a fortress commanding the Straits of Gibraltar. The area was certainly settled by the ancient Greeks and Phoenicians, for whom it was a trading port. The name which the latter gave to it – Tingis – has, more or less, remained the same. It also gave rise to the name of the citrus fruit tangerine, though the tree was imported by either the Romans or the Arabs at a later date.

Since those early days, the site has been one of the most contested in the Mediterranean world. Among those who have occupied it at one time or another are the Romans (1st to 5th century), Vandals (5th century), Byzantines (6th), Arabs (8th), Berbers (8th), Fatimids (10th), Almoravids (11th), Almohads (12th), Merenids (13th), Portuguese (15th and 16th), Spanish (16th), British (17th), and French (19th).

During the Roman period, Diocletian made it the capital of what remained of the province of Mauretania; incredible as it may seem, it was garrisoned by British (ie Celtic) cavalry. Not long after, it became part of the Christian episcopal see of Spain and may actually have been the seat of the bishops.

Following the break up of the Roman Empire and the arrival of the Vandals from Spain in 429 AD, there was a long period of strife between the barbarians and the Byzantine Empire for control of the site. Actually, the Byzantines only ever occupied Tangier for short periods of time, contenting themselves with their strongly fortified outpost at Ceuta.

The Byzantines remained for only a short while and, once they had withdrawn, little was recorded about the area until the coming of the Arabs in 705 AD. Possibly, one of the reasons for this is the smallpox epidemic which wrought havoc throughout Europe and North Africa not long afterwards; another may have been the continual warfare between the indigenous Berber tribes and the conquering Arabs.

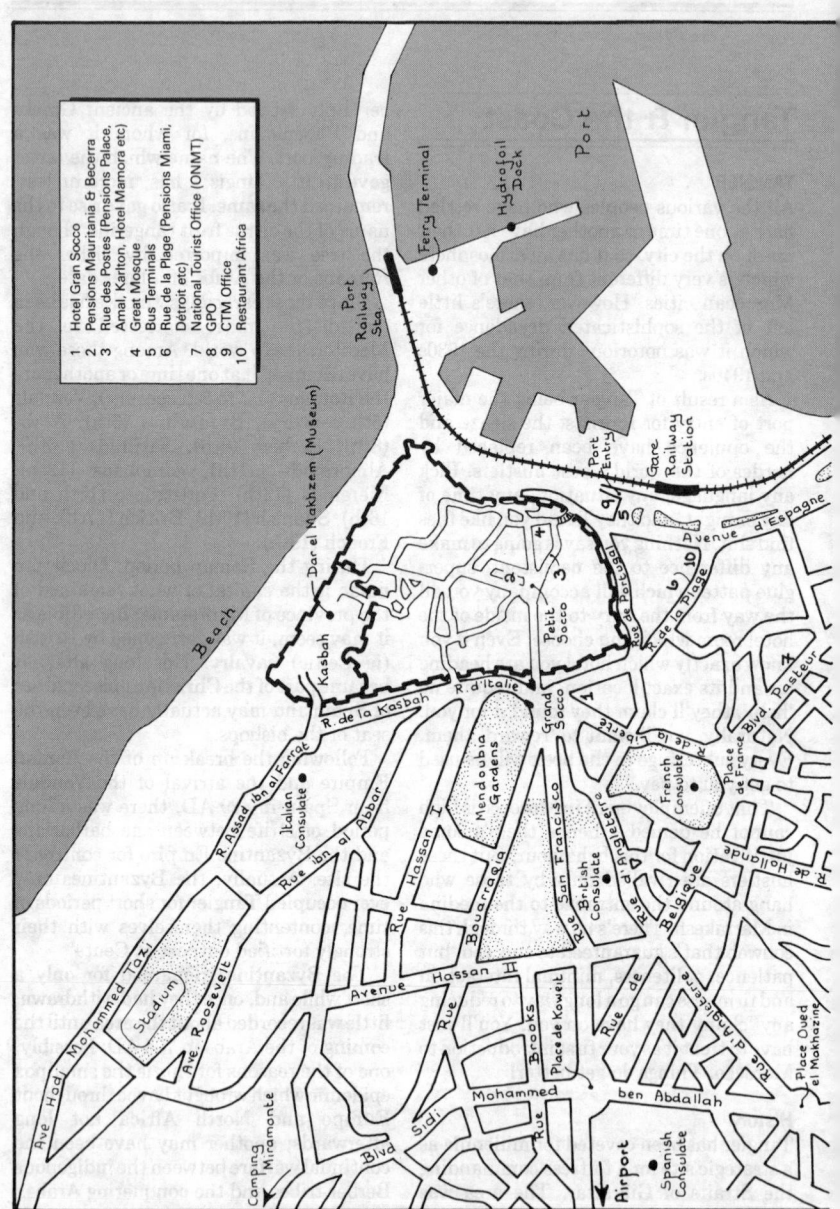

1 Hotel Gran Socco
2 Pensions Mauritania & Becerra
3 Rue des Postes (Pensions Palace,
   Amal, Kariton, Hotel Mamora etc)
4 Great Mosque
5 Bus Terminals
6 Rue de la Plage (Pensions Miami,
   Detroit etc)
7 National Tourist Office (ONMT)
8 GPO
9 CTM Office
10 Restaurant Africa

Once Arab supremacy had been established, however, Tangier became a bone of contention between the Omayyads of Spain and the Idrissids of Morocco, and was eventually occupied by the Fatimids of Tunis in 958. A little over 100 years later, the city was taken by the Islamic fundamentalist Almoravids as they swept across Morocco from their Mauretanian desert strongholds; it eventually passed to the Almohads in 1149. As the Almohad regime gradually reached its nadir the city elected to be ruled by the Hafsids of Tunis, but passed to Merenid control shortly afterwards in 1274.

A few centuries later, following the victories of the Christian armies in the Iberian peninsula, the Portuguese attempted to take Tangier in 1437. Unsuccessful at first, they finally made it in 1471. Tangier was passed to Philip II of Spain in 1580 when Spain and Portugal were united; it reverted to Portugal when that country regained its independence, only to be passed to England in 1661 as part of Catherine of Braganza's dowry to Charles II (she also brought with her the Portuguese enclave in India which would eventually become Bombay).

The English were not to remain long. Tangier was besieged by Moulay Ismail in 1679 but the English only abandoned the city seven years later (after destroying the port and most of the city), following a dispute between parliament and the king in which the former refused funding for the reinforcement of the garrison in Tangier.

From that point on, the Moroccans were left in control until the mid-19th century, when Tangier became the object of intense rivalry between the French, Spanish, Italians, British and Germans. The situation was partially resolved by the Treaty of Algeciras, whereby the British were bought off with Egypt and the Italians with Libya, leaving the remaining three European powers intriguing for the spoils. The status of the city was finally resolved only in 1923, when Tangier and the surrounding countryside was declared an 'international zone' controlled by the resident diplomatic agents of France, Spain, Britain, Portugal, Sweden, Holland, Belgium, Italy and the USA; however, Italy and the USA refused to recognise the arrangement for a while. Even the Moroccan sultan was represented by an agent, though the latter was appointed by the French Resident General (by this time France and Spain had divided Morocco between them).

Tangier was to remain an 'international zone' until a few months after Morocco became independent, when it was re-united with the rest of the country. In the meantime it became one of the most fashionable Mediterranean resorts, as well as a haven for free-booters, artists, writers, refugees, exiles and bankers; it was also renowned for its high-profile gay and paedophile scene. Each of the countries represented in Tangier maintained its own banks, post offices and currency, and took a share in the policing of the city. Banks, in particular, made fortunes out of manipulating the currency markets. All this came to an end in 1956, but the legend of notoriety lingers on.

Orientation

The square known as the Grand Socco is the centre of things and is the link between the medina and the new city. From here the medina covers the hillside below, and the crowded main street, Rue es Siaghin, leads down to the Petit Socco. This smaller square forms the heart of the medina. Below the medina, the port, bus and train stations are all within easy walking distance. The kasbah occupies the north-west corner of the medina and is built in a dominating position on the top of the cliff. The whole medina is fairly small and, although it is the usual tangle of twisting narrow lanes, it is very easy to find your way around in it.

The new city lies to the west and south of the medina and, as usual, it contains the bulk of the banks and middle and top accommodation.

Information

Tourist Information The tourist office, at 29 Boulevard Pasteur, is fairly well stocked with maps and brochures, bus and railway timetables; the staff speak several languages (you can usually rely on English, French, German and Spanish).

Post The main post office is on Blvd Pasteur, 15 minutes' walk from the Grand Socco.

Money There are plenty of banks along the main street, Blvd Pasteur. The travel agents near the port entrance will also change money but the rates are not always as good as the banks.

Outside banking hours, any of the big hotels should be able to help.

American Express The agent for American Express is Voyages Schwarz (tel 334 59), 76 Ave Mohammed V.

Thomas Cook The Thomas Cook office is at 86 Rue de la Liberté.

Consulates The following countries have consulates in Tangier: France (tel 320 39) Place de France; Portugal (tel 317 08) 9 Place Sahat Umame; Spain (tel 356 25) 85 Rue Sidi Boabid; and the UK (tel 358 95) Rue d'Angleterre.

Airlines The following airlines have offices in Tangier: Royal Air Maroc (tel 347 22) Place de France; Air France (tel 364 77) 7 Rue du Méxique; and Iberia (tel 361 77) 35 Blvd Pasteur.

Shipping Companies Comanov (tel 326 52) is at 43 Ave Abou Alaa el Maari. For boats to Algerciras, go to Comarit (tel 367 82) at 7 Rue du Méxique.

Books The *Rogue's Guide to Tangier* is a humorous and well-written alternative guide to the city. It's well worth buying but is only sporadically available from some of the larger hotels.

Medina

The Petit Socco, with its cafés and restaurants, is very much the centre of things; it's easy to sit for an hour or so, sipping a mint tea and watching the world go by. In the days of the international zone this was the sin and sleaze centre of the city and today it retains something of its seedy air. The whispers in your ear of 'Something special, my friend?' (or the equivalent phrase in French, German or Spanish) are amazingly constant.

The narrow Rue des Chrétiens takes you to the kasbah. When you take a walk along here you really have to run the gauntlet past the shopkeepers, who practically leap out and grab you to come and have a look.

Kasbah The kasbah is built on the highest point of the city; you enter from Bab el Assa at the end of Rue Ben Raissouli in the medina. The gate gives onto a large open courtyard which leads to the Dar el Makhzen, the former sultan's palace and now quite a good museum.

The palace itself was built by Moulay Ismail in the 17th century and enlarged at various stages by the later sultans. The interior has some beautifully carved wooden ceilings and a marble courtyard. You can leave via the garden and visit the Cafe Detroit on the 2nd floor in the walls. It was set up by Brian Gysin, the '60s writer and friend of the Rolling Stones, and was called The Thousand & One Nights. It became famous for the trance musicians who played here in the '60s and released a record produced by Brian Jones.

Musicians still play here, but today it's a tourist trap nonpareil. The tour groups all get brought here, and after the obligatory mint tea they file out while the musicians play European songs of the 'Roll Out the Barrel' variety. It's worth a trip up here just for the fantastic views over the port, but the tea and traditional cakes are expensive. The museum is open daily, except Tuesday, from 9 am to 3.30 pm in summer and 9 to 11.45 am and 3 to 6 pm in winter; entry is Dr 5.

Places to Stay – bottom end

The most interesting places (and some of the cheapest) are in the medina around the Petit Socco and along Rue des Postes, which connects the Petit Socco and the port area. They run the gamut from two-star to flea pits.

If you're arriving by ferry from Spain or Gibraltar, walk out of the port area until you pass through the main gates and arrive at a square with the railway station on your left and bus station on your right. Then take the road on the extreme right-hand side, which goes uphill until you get to a set of steps just past the junction with Rue du Portugal. Go up the steps and you'll find yourself at the bottom of Rue des Postes (see map).

If you'd prefer European-style hotels on your first night(s) then, once out of the port gates, carry on past the railway station and take the first street on your right (Rue de la Plage), where there are a half dozen or so such hotels (mainly one and two-star).

If you're staying in the medina area your local friendly hustler will undoubtedly recommend the *Hotel Mamora*, Rue des Postes. This is, however, a two-star hotel and, though it's very clean, has hot water and all the rooms have their own bathroom, it will cost you Dr 74 a double. Much cheaper and immaculately maintained is the *Pension Palace*, 2 Rue des Postes. The rooms here are spotlessly clean, spacious, secure and most of them front onto a cool, pleasant internal courtyard. It's excellent value at Dr 20 a single and Dr 35 a double. If it's full, try either the *Pension Amal*, the *Pension Marhaba* or the *Pension Karlton* further down the street, which are all similar.

For cheaper accommodation than these there's the *Pension Mauritania*, the

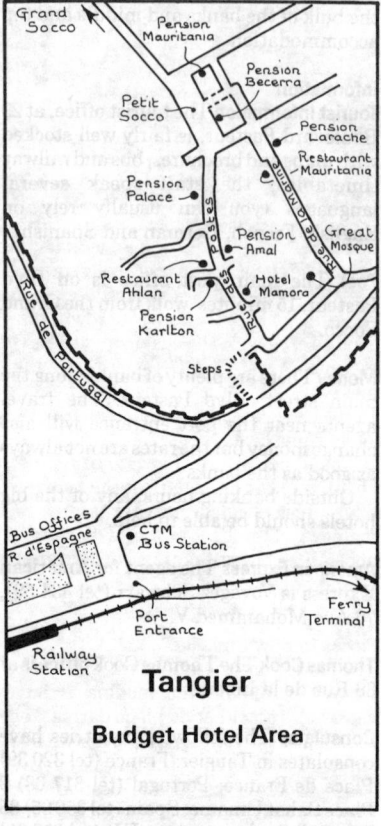

Tangier

Budget Hotel Area

Pension Fuentes and the *Pension Becerra* on the Petit Socco, and the *Pension Larache* just off the Petit Socco. They're all traditional, basic Moroccan hostelries.

If all these are full then head up to the Grand Socco (a very short walk) and try the *Hotel Gran Socco*. This has a variety of rooms but, if you're in a group of three to four people, the best deals are the large rooms overlooking the Socco.

If you are staying in a place with no showers there's a hammam at 80 Rue des Chrétiens, which runs off the Petit Socco by the Café Central. Dr 5 for a shower; open 8 am to 8 pm.

Going up in price, the hotels along Rue de la Plage will set you back Dr 40 and more a double excluding the cost of hot showers, depending on which one you choose. Two of the most popular are the *Pension Miami* and the *Pension le Détroit*. These hotels are both down at the bottom of the hill, near Avenue d'Espagne.

Camping Campers have a choice of two sites. The cheaper and more convenient of the two is *Camping Miramonte* about three km west of the centre of town. It's a good site, close to the beach, and there's a reasonable restaurant. To get there, take bus No 1, 2 or 21 from the Grand Socco. Don't leave valuables unattended at this site – things disappear.

The other site is *Caravaning Tingis* about six km to the east of the centre of town. This is much more expensive but includes a tennis court and swimming pool. To get there, take bus No 15 from the Grand Socco.

Places to Stay - middle

The *Hotel Continental* at the end of Rue Dar el Baroud in the medina is great value. It is an old-style place dating from the turn of the century and is not without charm. The view from the terrace out over the harbour is one of the best around. Rooms cost Dr 80 a double with bath and hot water.

The *Hotel el Muniria* on Rue Magellan is an English-owned one-star hotel and is good value at Dr 65 for a double. The *Tangerinn Bar* is part of the hotel and is a great place for a drink in the evening; open 9 pm to 2 am. Finding the place the first time can be difficult: from the Hotel Rembrandt on Blvd Pasteur, turn down Rue Rembrandt and take the steps down to the right next to the church; this is Rue Magellan. Or, from the port, go straight along Rue d'Espagne until you get to a service station on the right; take the steps next to it, and then take the second left and first right; the hotel is on the right.

The *Hotel Ibn Batouta* opposite the Muniria is also not a bad place.

Places to Stay - top end

As may be expected, there are several fancy hotels in Tangier. Among these is the five-star *Hotel el Minzah* (tel 358 85, 387 87) at 85 Rue de la Liberté; it has 100 rooms and all the amenities you'd expect in a luxury hotel.

The *Hotel Rif* (tel 359 08 to 12) on Avenue d'Espagne has 129 rooms and is similar to the Minzah. The four-star *Hotel Solazur* (tel 401 64 to 68), on Avenue des Forces Armées Royales, has 360 rooms and similar facilities.

Places to Eat

There are plenty of small rustic cafés and restaurants around the Petit Socco and the Grand Socco offering traditional fare for very reasonable prices. One of the cheapest is the *Restaurant Mauritania*, which might have the appearance of Lucifer's waiting room (if you've just come from Europe), but offers very tasty food at a price you can't beat elsewhere and has very friendly staff. Get there early, as they run out quickly as the night wears on.

For more substantial meals, try the *Restaurant Ahlan*, Rue des Postes. It's a popular place and offers excellent tajines with soup for around Dr 14 a meal. Also good value is the cosy *Restaurant Moderne* at No 21.

There are a couple of food stalls at the bottom of the stairs at the end of Rue des Postes. The one closest to the port looks a bit rough but does excellent fried fish with a tomato sauce and bread for Dr 1.50 each; three or four make a fair meal.

For a splurge or for food with a more European flavour head up to Place de France, around which there are several restaurants and cafés where you can get a good meal; however, you'll pay substantially more than you would at places around the Petit Socco.

At 83 Rue de la Plage, almost on the

corner of Rue d'Espagne, is the *Restaurant Africa*, which has good set menus for Dr 23 for three courses as well as good individual dishes. There are restaurants on either side of the Africa which are also worth investigating.

Things to Buy

Tangier is not the ideal place to buy souvenirs – the place sees too many people coming over from Spain on day trips and the prices are generally way over the top. It is possible to get things for a reasonable price but it involves a lot of hard work. If you have to buy something here, keep clear of Blvd Pasteur and shop in the medina.

Getting There & Away

Bus All buses leave from the square at the port entrance. The CTM office is just to the left of the port entrance. Other bus companies have their offices on Rue d'Espagne between Rue Portugal and Rue de la Plage.

Train There are two railway stations – Tangier Gare and Tangier Port. Most trains start from the Port station out at the port and stop at the Gare.

The main departures are to: Rabat & Casablanca (7.20 am (Gare only), 4.10 and 11.15 pm, four and 5½ hours); Marrakesh (11.15 pm, 10 hours); Meknès & Fès (8.10 am (Gare only), 4.10 pm, five and six hours); Oujda 8.10 am and midnight (both Gare only), 12 hours).

Taxi *Grands taxis* leave from around the square; regular departures to Tetouan (Dr 20), Asilah and Rabat.

Boat Ferry is the cheapest way to travel between Europe and Morocco. When arriving in Tangier, it's only a few minutes' walk from the ferry terminal to the medina; it will no doubt seem a lot longer, as you will be accompanied by persistent touts.

The ferry ticket offices are closed on weekends but you can buy tickets from any number of travel agents around town. The Wasteel agency by the port entrance is a popular one.

There are ferries to both Algeciras (Spain) and Sète (France). In summer there are also hydrofoils to Algeciras and Gibraltar. See the Getting There chapter for more details.

ASILAH

About 100 km south of Tangier along a magnificent sweep of Atlantic beach is the small port of Asilah. Small it may be but, over two millennia, it's had a tumultuous history far out of proportion to its size.

The first settlers here were the Carthaginians, who named the port Zilis. Next on the scene were the Romans. Faced with the prospect of having to deal with a population which had unfortunately backed the wrong side in the aftermath to the Punic Wars, the Romans forcibly moved the inhabitants to Spain and replaced them with people from that country.

Asilah featured again in the 10th century, when it successfully held Norman raiders from Sicily at bay; it was also prominent in the 11th century, when it became the last refuge of the Idrissids. Asilah's most turbulent period, however, followed the Christian victories over the forces of Islam on the Iberian peninsula in the 14th and 15th centuries. In 1471 it was captured by the Portuguese; the walls around the city date essentially from this period, though they have been repaired from time to time.

In 1578 King Sebastian of Portugal chose Asilah as the base for an ill-fated crusade against the Muslims. Despite the immense army which he landed, which included the flower of the Portuguese nobility, his forces were defeated by the Saadian sultan Abd el-Malik on the banks of a tributary of the River Makhazen. Some 26,000 Portuguese were killed or taken prisoner, Sebastian himself was killed and the sultan died of a heart attack in the early stages of the battle.

main street, Paseo del Revellin, and its continuation, Calle Camoens. It's sometimes possible to buy Moroccan dirhams, even though they're a non-exportable soft currency. Outside business hours you should be able to change small amounts of foreign currency at the four-star Hotel La Muralla at Plaza de Africa.

There are money-changing facilities at the border in the form of a bank on the Moroccan side and informal money changers on the Spanish side. The latter deal almost exclusively in dirhams and pesetas but the rate is only average. If you want to change other currencies, the rates are worse.

Post The main post office (*correos y telégrafos*) is the big yellow building at Plaza de España, a square just off Calle Camoens in the centre of town.

Archaeology Museum
This tiny museum set in a small park just off the busy Avenida de España is not really worth bothering with but it will kill five minutes if you are waiting for a ferry. There is just one tiny room, with a few bits and pieces from Palaeolithic times through to Spanish. There is a subterranean gallery beneath the museum but it has been closed off. Opening hours are 9 am to 1 pm and 5 to 7 pm; closed Monday.

Legión Museum
The Museo de la Legión is dedicated to this highly regarded special unit of the army created in 1920. It holds a staggering array of weapons, uniforms and other military paraphernalia – quite interesting if you like that sort of thing, although the glass-eyed dummies are a bit bizarre. The museum is on Paseo de Colón and is open only on Saturdays, Sundays and public holidays from 11 am to 2 pm and 4 to 6 pm.

Peninsula
If you have a couple of hours to spare it's easy to walk around the peninsula, which is capped by Monte Acho. From the

convent of Ermita de San Antonio there is an excellent view over the Mediterranean, and Gibraltar is plainly visible on a clear day.

At the convent itself, originally built in the 17th century and reconstructed in the 1960s, a large festival is held annually on 13 June to mark San Antonio's Day.

Places to Stay – bottom end
There is no shortage of *fondas* and *casas de huéspedes*, easily identifiable by the large blue-and-white F or CH on the entrances. Cheapest of these is the small *Charito* (tel 51 39 82) on the 1st floor at 5 Calle Arrabal, about 15 minutes' walk along the waterfront from the ferry terminal. The only indication that it is a guest house is the 'Chambres' sign above the footpath, and the CH sign on the wall. There are only eight rooms and they cost 500/900 Ptas for singles/doubles. There are no hot showers in this place but otherwise it is quite adequate. Just around the corner from the Charito, and right on the waterfront, is the *Marina* (tel 51 32 06) on the 3rd floor at 26 Marina Española. It is a tiny place with only three double rooms, which go for 1200 Ptas each. Basic but OK.

Conveniently situated right in the centre, the *Revellin* tel 51 6762) is on the 2nd floor at 2 Paseo del Revellin. The doorway is right in the middle of the busy shopping street but, again, can be identified by the CH sign. It is directly opposite the Banco Popular Español. Rooms cost 800/1500 Ptas for singles/ doubles, and hot showers are available for an extra 150 Ptas.

Youth Hostel The *Youth Hostel* is the cheapest place to stay, but unfortunately it only operates during the school vacation periods of July and August. It's hidden away on the Plaza Rafael Gilbert, just off Paseo del Revellin where you see a big red sign for the Restaurant China – stairs lead up through an arch to the Plaza, and the hostel is in the corner to the right.

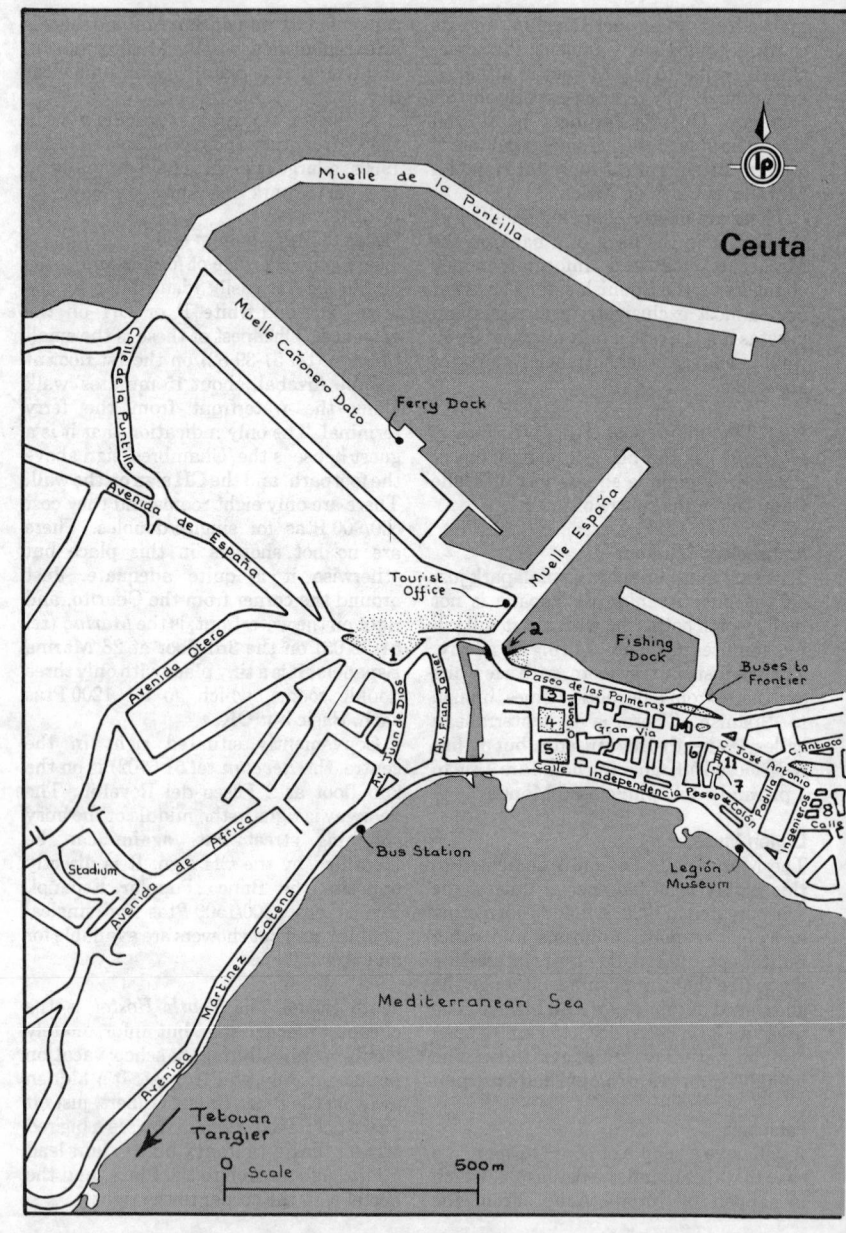

Ceuta

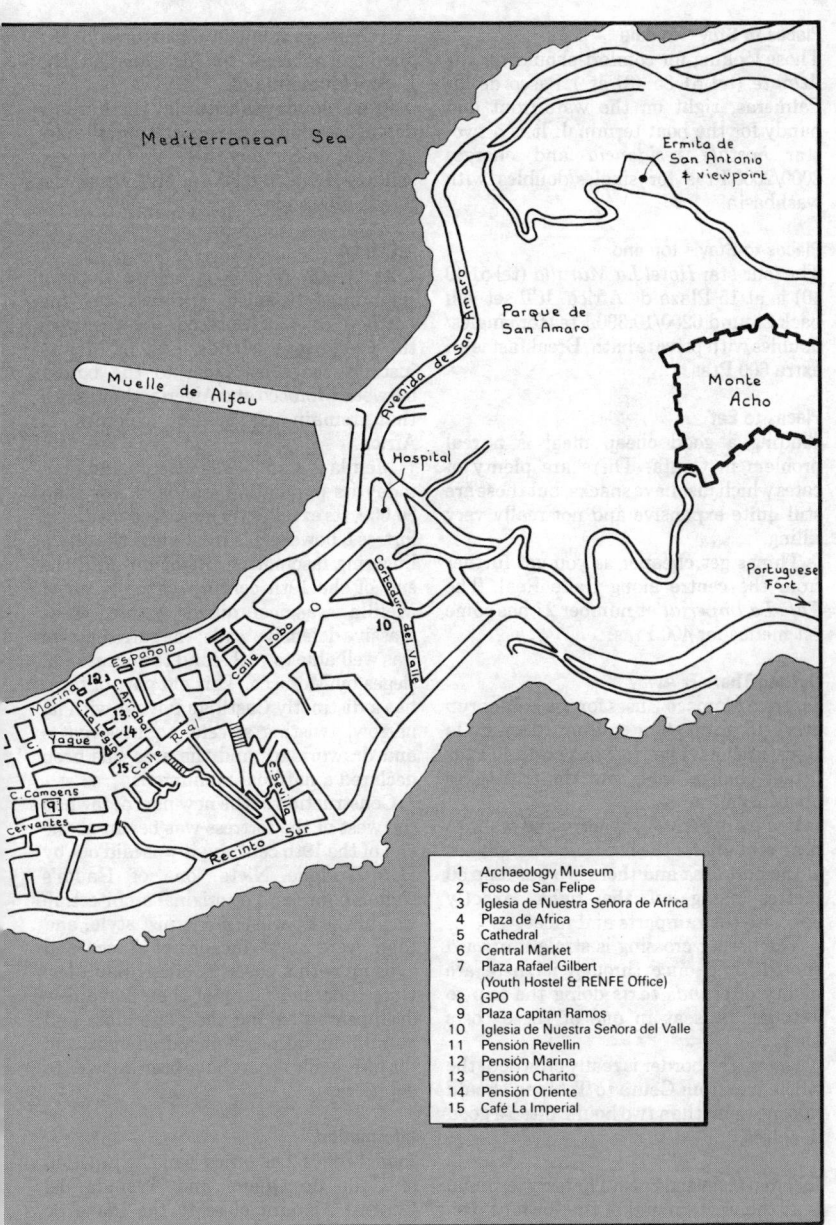

Mediterranean Sea

Ermita de
San Antonio
& viewpoint

Parque de
San Amaro

Muelle de Alfau

Monte
Acho

Avenida de San Amaro

Hospital

Cartagena del Valle

Portuguese
Fort

10

Española
Calle Lobo
Marina
Real
Yague
C. Camoens
Cervantes
Calle
Recinto Sur
Sevilla

12
13
14
15
9

1 Archaeology Museum
2 Foso de San Felipe
3 Iglesia de Nuestra Señora de Africa
4 Plaza de Africa
5 Cathedral
6 Central Market
7 Plaza Rafael Gilbert
   (Youth Hostel & RENFE Office)
8 GPO
9 Plaza Capitan Ramos
10 Iglesia de Nuestra Señora del Valle
11 Pensión Revellin
12 Pensión Marina
13 Pensión Charito
14 Pensión Oriente
15 Café La Imperial

Places to Stay – middle

Those looking for comfort should try the *Atlante* (tel 51 35 48) at 1 Paseo de las Palmeras, right on the waterfront and handy for the boat terminal. It is a two-star *hostale residencia* and charges 2000/2600 Ptas for singles/doubles with washbasin.

Places to Stay – top end

The four-star *Hotel La Muralla* (tel 51 49 40) is at 15 Plaza de Africa. It'll set you back around 6200/10,300 Ptas for singles/doubles with private bath. Breakfast is an extra 600 Ptas.

Places to Eat

Finding a good cheap meal is a real problem in Ceuta. There are plenty of cafés which just have snacks, but these are still quite expensive and not really very filling.

Things get cheaper as you get further from the centre along Calle Real. The *Café La Imperial* at number 27 has some set menus for 400 Ptas.

Getting There & Away

To/From Morocco Buses for the border run every 15 minutes or so from Plaza de la Constitucion. The No 7 bus costs 40 Ptas (exact change only) and the trip takes about 20 minutes.

If you are arriving by ferry and want to head straight for the border, turn right out of the port area and there is a bus stop 50 metres along on the right, exactly opposite the ramparts and moat.

The border crossing is straightforward enough, and once through it there are plenty of *grands taxis* doing the trip to Tetouan. A seat in one of these costs Dr 14.

Unless the border is really crowded, the whole trip from Ceuta to Tetouan should take no more than two hours; often a good deal less.

To/From Mainland Spain The ferry terminal is at the western end of the town centre,

and there are frequent departures for the one-hour journey to Algeciras on the European mainland.

From Monday to Saturday there are six departures daily, the first at 8 am, the last at 9 pm; on Sunday there are only three sailings between 9.30 am and 9 pm; the fare is 1100 Ptas.

MELILLA

Like Ceuta, Melilla is one of the two remaining Spanish enclaves on the northern coast of Morocco. Together with the Chafarinas Islands, east of Melilla just off the coast close to the border between Morocco and Algeria, they are all that remain of Spain's colonies in Africa.

Melilla is smaller than Ceuta and even today its population stands at less than 80,000. Its excellently preserved medieval fortress, however, is what gives the city a lingering fascination. Right up until the end of the 19th century virtually all of Melilla was contained within these massive defensive walls; the garrison here was well able to withstand the occasional sieges by Morocco. This old part of town has a distinctly Castilian flavour with its narrow, twisting streets, squares, gates and drawbridges and the area has been declared a national monument.

Construction of the new part of town to the west of the fortress was begun at the end of the 19th century; it was laid out by Don Enrique Nieto, one of Gaudi's contemporaries. The original architecture was in the Spanish modernist style, and there were many facades of stucco and gypsum with a covering of Sevillan tiles. Unfortunately, many of these have now disappeared behind the plate glass and aluminium frames of duty-free shops and the like, while others have been allowed to deteriorate.

Information

Tourist Office The office is at the junction of Calle de Querol and Avenida del General Aizpuru close to the Plaza de

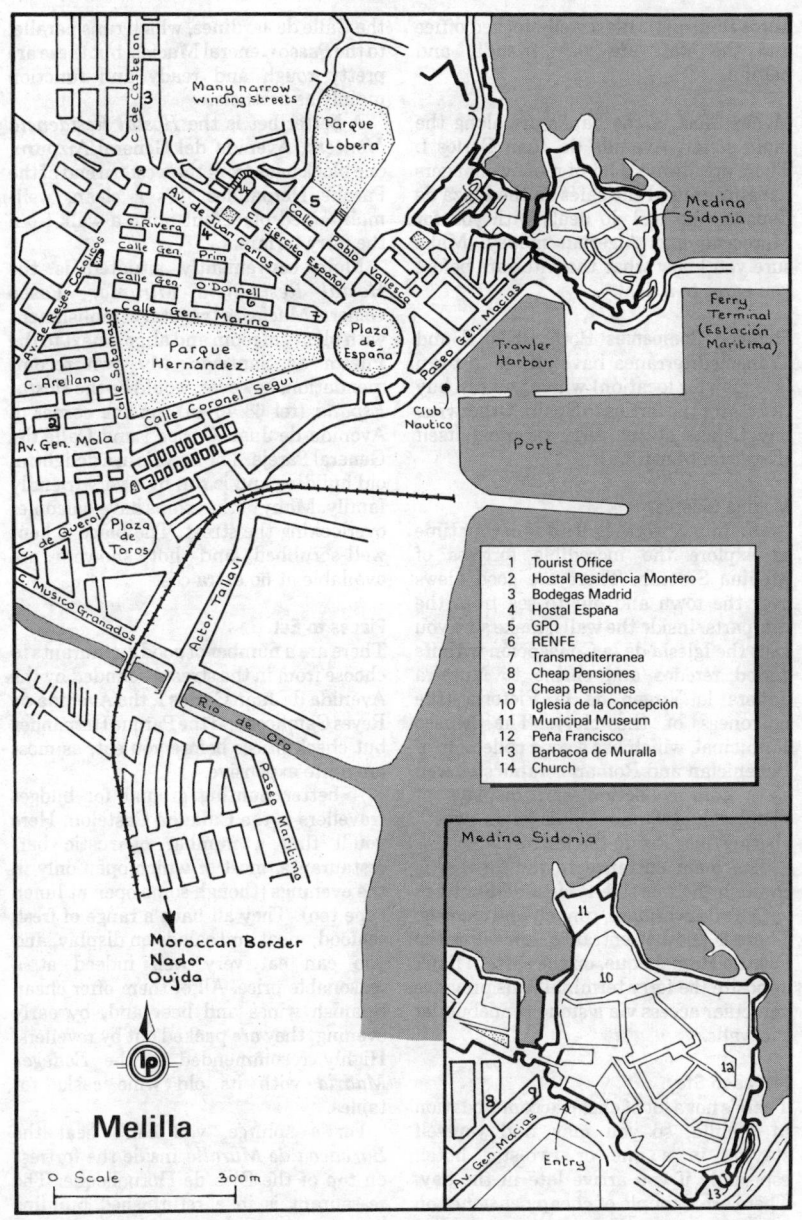

1 Tourist Office
2 Hostal Residencia Montero
3 Bodegas Madrid
4 Hostal España
5 GPO
6 RENFE
7 Transmediterranea
8 Cheap Pensiones
9 Cheap Pensiones
10 Iglesia de la Concepción
11 Municipal Museum
12 Peña Francisco
13 Barbacoa de Muralla
14 Church

Melilla

0   Scale   300m

Many narrow winding streets

Parque Lobera

Av. de Juan Carlos I

C. Rivera

Calle Gen. Prim

Calle Gen. O'Donnell

Calle Gen. Marina

Parque Hernández

C. Arellano

Av. de Reyes Católicos

Calle Coronel Segui

Av. Gen. Mola

C. de Querol

Plaza de Toros

C. Músico Granados

Actor Tallavi

Río de Oro

Paseo Marítimo

Moroccan Border
Nador
Oujda

Calle de Castellón

Calle Ejercito Español

Calle Pablo Vallego

Plaza de España

Paseo Gen. Macías

Club Nautico

Trawler Harbour

Port

Medina Sidonia

Ferry Terminal (Estación Marítima)

Medina Sidonia

11

10

12

8   9

Entry

Av. Gen. Macías

13

Toros (bullring). It's a well-stocked office and the staff are very friendly and helpful.

Money Most of the banks are along the main street, Avenida de Juan Carlos I. There are always a lot of money changers hanging around the cafés on the Plaza de España who will do deals with you for Moroccan and Algerian money. Make sure you know what the rates are before you agree to a deal.

Shipping Companies Both RENFE and Transmediterranea have offices in town (see map for location) where you can buy tickets for the ferries to Spain. Otherwise, buy tickets at the ferry terminal itself (Estación Maritima).

Medina Sidonia

It's definitely worth half a day of your time to explore the incredible fortress of Medina Sidonia. There are good views over the town and out to sea from the ramparts. Inside the walls, make sure you visit the Iglesia de la Concepción with its gilded reredos and shrine to Nuestra Señora la Virgen de la Victoria (the patroness of the city). The Museo Municipal, which has a good collection of Phoenician and Roman ceramics as well as a coin collection and displays of historical documents, is also worth visiting once inside the fortress.

The main entrance to the fortress is through the massive Puerta de Santiago with its drawbridges, tunnels and chapels. There is another entrance, known as the Foso de Hornabeque, on the eastern flank opposite the ferry terminal; this provides vehicular access via a stone tunnel under the walls.

Places to Stay

There's not a lot of cheap accommodation in Melilla, so you may find yourself staying in a one or two-star hotel, especially if you arrive late in the day. There are a couple of cheap *pensiones* on the Calle de Jardines, which runs parallel to the Paseo General Macías, but these are pretty rough and ready and function mainly as brothels.

A better bet is the *Hostal Residencia Montero*, Avenida del General Aizpuru, one block back from the western end of the Parque Hernández. It's a clean, well-maintained place but quite a walk from the ferry terminal.

More conveniently situated is the *Hostal Residencia Miramar*, Paseo General Macías, a two-star establishment with plenty of room and almost next to the Puerta de Santiago. My own recommendation, however, would be the *Hostal España* (tel 68 46 45), on the corner of Avenida de Juan Carlos I and Calle del General Pareja. The hotel is in a delightful old building and is run by a very friendly family. Many of the rooms have balconies overlooking the street. The place is kept well-scrubbed and hot showers are available at no extra cost.

Places to Eat

There are a number of good restaurants to choose from in the streets bounded by the Avenida de Juan Carlos I, the Avenida de Reyes Catolicos and the Parque Hernández but check prices before you eat, as most are quite expensive.

A better hunting ground for budget travellers is the Calle de Castelon. Here you'll find a number of rustic bar/restaurants, most of which open only in the evenings (though some open at lunch time too). They all have a range of fresh seafood, meat and salads on display, and you can eat very well indeed at a reasonable price. All of them offer cheap Spanish wines and beer and, by early evening, they are packed out by revellers. Highly recommended is the *Bodegas Madrid* with its old wine casks for tables.

For a splurge, you can't beat the *Barbacoa de Muralla* inside the fortress on top of the Foso de Hornabeque. The restaurant is in a refurbished building which retains all its original features, including the barred windows overlooking the port. If you're not sure you can afford a meal here, pop in first, order a beer and have a look at the menu.

Also inside the fortress are a number of small bar/restaurants where you can get simple meals and snacks and drink away to your heart's content. They're open lunch times and evenings.

Entertainment

You could spend your evenings in the many bars around town or promenading up and down the main street. Other than that, there's a folk music club – the *Peña Francisco* inside the fortress (see map) which is open in the evenings – as well as a number of discotheques (addresses in the tourist leaflet).

Getting There & Away

To/From Morocco There are local buses from the Plaza de España to the border which run from about 7.30 am to late evening. From where the buses stop, it's about 150 metres to the Spanish customs and then another 200 metres to the Moroccan customs. On the other side of the Moroccan customs there are frequent buses to Nador.

To/From Mainland Spain Melilla is connected to Spain by ferries from Malaga. There is usually at least one per day, though they are occasionally cancelled in the winter due to rough weather.

The Rif Mountains

TETOUAN

With its interesting medina, beautiful setting and nearby beaches, Tetouan isn't a bad place. However, if you have just come from Ceuta, the thing that will probably strike you most is the touts. They certainly aren't threatening at any stage but they are persistent enough for most people to be ready to leave after a day. As an introduction to Morocco it is not very encouraging, but things improve rapidly from here.

History

Tetouan was a Mauretanian city founded in the 3rd century BC; it was destroyed in the 1st century AD by the Romans, following a revolt against their annexation of the country. Other than a Roman military camp which remained for about 200 years, the site was not resettled until the advent of the Merenids in the early 14th century.

The Merenids needed Tetouan as a base from which to attack a rival claimant to the Moroccan throne who was supported by the Spanish. Though the town initially became prosperous, it was destroyed by the Christian king of Castille in 1399 and not re-occupied until the 16th century.

The new occupants of the town – mainly Arab-Berber and Jewish refugees from Spain – made their living from piracy in the western Mediterranean. They eventually incurred the wrath of the Spanish monarchy, which led to the blockading of the pirates' port of Martil on the coast. Tetouan entered another decline in its fortunes; it prospered once more under Moulay Ismail only to be captured again by the Spanish in 1862. The Spanish stayed for some three years and, although they evacuated the town, they effectively remained in control until they re-occupied the town in 1913 at the beginning of the Spanish protectorate.

Information

Tourist Office The tourist office is on Rue Mohammed V, just near the corner of Rue ben Tachfine. The guy here is helpful and speaks quite a bit of English. Don't be talked into hiring a guide (unless, of course, you want one), as the medina is small and manageable on your own. Even if you get lost it's never long before you come to the walls or a gate.

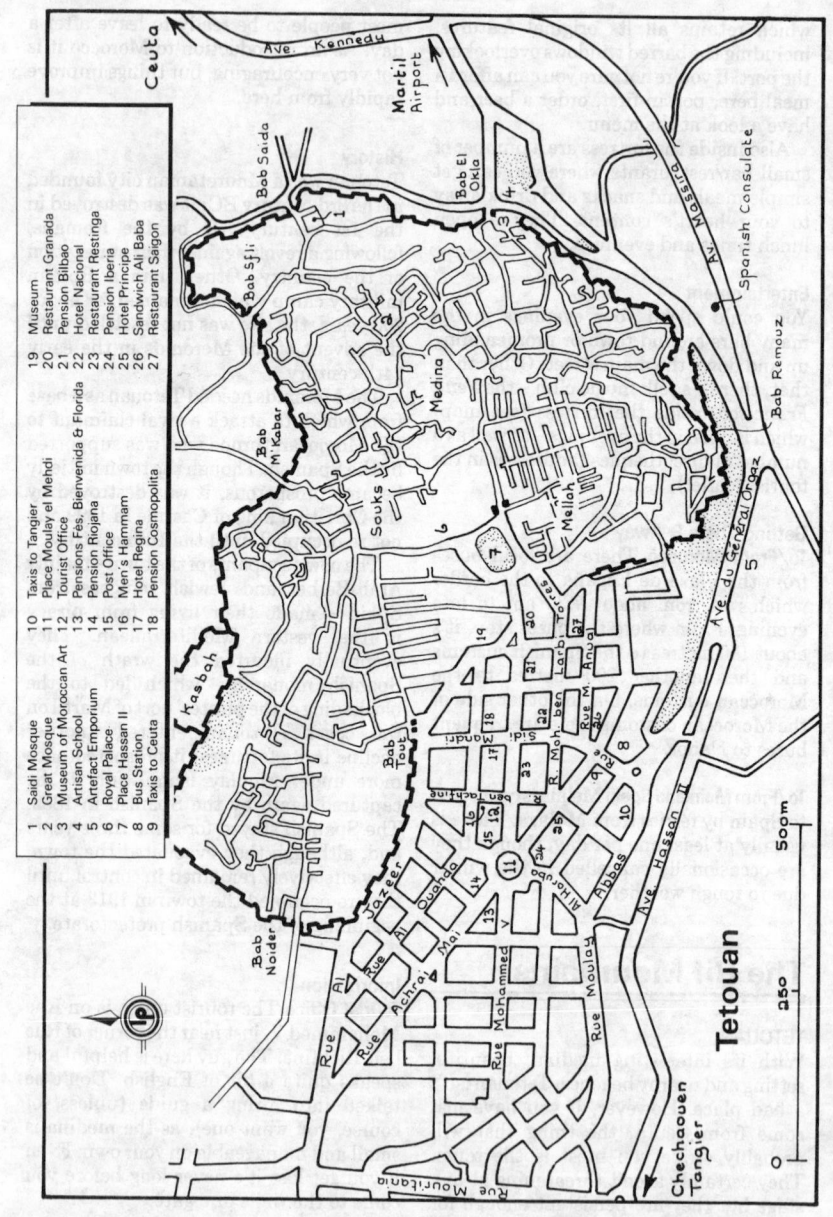

Tetouan

1 Saidi Mosque
2 Great Mosque
3 Museum of Moroccan Art
4 Artisan School
5 Artefact Emporium
6 Royal Palace
7 Place Hassan II
8 Bus Station
9 Taxis to Ceuta
10 Taxis to Tangier
11 Place Moulay el Mehdi
12 Tourist Office
13 Pensions Fès, Bienvenida & Florida
14 Pension Riojana
15 Post Office
16 Men's Hammam
17 Hotel Regina
18 Pension Cosmopolita
19 Museum
20 Restaurant Granada
21 Pension Bilbao
22 Hotel Nacional
23 Restaurant Restinga
24 Pension Iberia
25 Hotel Principe
26 Sandwich Ali Baba
27 Restaurant Saigon

Post The post office is on the roundabout known as Place Moulay el Mehdi in the Spanish-built new city.

Money There are plenty of banks along the main street, Rue Mohammed V, and around Place Moulay el Mehdi.

Spanish Consulate If you need a visa, the Spanish Consulate is on Ave Massira. Visas can be issued on the spot, although none of the staff speak English.

Medina & Around

As is often the case in Morocco, the place which links the old and new cities is the real centre of the city. In this case it is Place Hassan II, the town's showpiece. It has just undergone a massive 'beautification' project and is now resplendent with its four massive concrete pillars.

In the evenings Rue Mohammed V becomes a pedestrian precinct, and the place is thronged with hundreds of people promenading, mostly young men from the university campus in the town.

The busiest medina entrance is Bab er Rouah, to the right of the old Spanish Consulate. It's an interesting and surprisingly busy medina, great for just wandering at random. The area towards the eastern gate, Bab el Okla, was the up-market end of town; some of the fine houses built by the city's residents in the last century still stand here. At least one has been turned into a carpet showroom; there are plenty of touts hanging around who will take you to one if you want.

Museum of Moroccan Art Just inside Bab el Okla is the excellent Museum of Moroccan Art, built in an old bastion in the town wall – there are still cannon in place in the garden. The exhibits of everyday Moroccan and Andalusian life are well presented. It's a pity that the staff rush you through as fast as they can, switching lights off before you have finished and generally trying to hustle you through so they can go back to their seat at the door. It is open

daily, except Tuesday, from 9 am to 12 noon and 2 to 6 pm; entry Dr 3.

Artisan School Just opposite Bab el Okla is the artisan school, where you can see young kids being taught traditional crafts such as leatherwork, woodwork and the making of enamel *zellij* tiles. The building itself is worth a visit. The school is open from 9 am to 12 noon and 2.30 to 5.30 pm; closed Tuesday and Saturday; entry Dr 3.

Archaeology Museum There is a small archaeology museum opposite the end of Rue Prince Sidi Mohammed but it is only for the dedicated. They have a few prehistoric stones, some Roman coins, and a few small mosaics and bits and pieces from Lixus. It is open Monday to Saturday from 9.30 am to 12 noon and 2.30 to 5.30 pm; closed Sunday; entry Dr 3.

Places to Stay – bottom end

There are plenty of typical cheap hotels around Place Hassan II and the entrance to the medina but these places tend to be on the noisy side. The *Hotel Marrakesh* and *Hotel Seville* are typical.

There are a couple of dozen pensions dotted around, some representing good value for money. Many are run by women who speak only Spanish.

The *Pension Bilbao* (tel 79 39) at 7 Rue Mohammed V is close to Place Hassan II and is cheap at Dr 20 per person. There are no showers in the place but this is not a great problem, as there's a hammam about five minutes' walk away. Also on Rue Mohammed V, but down the other end past Place Moulay el Mehdi, the *Pension Fès* is on the 3rd floor – look for the sign over the street entrance. Beds cost Dr 20 and there are cold showers.

A bit more expensive but with a homely atmosphere is the *Pension Iberia*, on the 3rd floor above the Banque Marocaine du Commerce Extérieur (BMCE) on Place Moulay el Mehdi. There are only a few rooms here; singles cost Dr 28, doubles

Dr 40. Cold showers are free; hot showers are Dr 3.

Other cheap pensions include the *Bienvenida* and the *Floridal*, in the same building on Rue Achra Mai near place Moulay el Mehdi. Neither is especially friendly, but they'd do for one night.

There is a men's hammam on Rue ben Tachfine.

Camping The nearest camping ground is by the beach at Martil, eight km away. There's also a site not far from the Club Méd, about halfway between Tetouan and the border.

Places to Stay - middle
Going up in price, the best place in town is the *Hotel Regina* (tel 21 13) at 8 Rue Sidi Mandri. All rooms have a bathroom with hot water, the staff are friendly and at Dr 48/60 for singles/doubles it is excellent value.

The *Hotel Nacional* (tel 32 90/91) at 8 Rue Mohammed ben Larbi Torres is another reasonable one-star place with singles/doubles for Dr 69/81 with bath, Dr 54/71 without; however, unless the Regina is full, there's no real reason to stay here. Another similar place is the *Hotel Príncipe* (tel 27 95) at 20 Rue Youssef Touchfine, although the front rooms can be noisy because it is right by the place where the *grands taxis* queue up.

Place to Stay - top end
The four-star *Hotel Safir* (tel 70 44, 71 77) is on Avenue Kennedy. It has 98 rooms, a swimming pool, tennis courts and a nightclub.

Places to Eat
The best cheap place is *Sandwich Ali Baba* on Rue Mourakah Anual. Despite the name, they also do chicken, chips, soups and tajines. It's a very popular place, and you practically have to fight through the crowd at the front to get to the seating area in the back.

For something a bit more formal try the *Restaurant Restinga*, which is in a small alley off Rue Mohammed V. It has a small open courtyard, but the menu is a bit limited and it closes early in the evening.

Despite the name, there's nothing Asian about the *Restaurant Saigon* on Rue Mourakah Anual. The food is OK as long as you are not put off by the glass display case by the door, which is full of rather old meat.

The *Restaurant Granada* on Rue Mohammed V at Place Al Jala is clean and cheap and serves the usual tajines, couscous and soups.

Things to Buy
To the south of the medina on Ave du Général Orgaz is a government-run artefact emporium, where you can get an idea of the real prices of things; however, bear in mind that what you would pay here is definitely the top end of the price scale. Upstairs and out the back downstairs you can see young men and women making all sorts of handicrafts. It is open daily from 9.30 am to 1 pm and 3.30 to 6.30 pm.

Getting There & Away
Bus The bus station for all buses is behind the municipality building on the corner of Rue Sidi Mandri and Rue Moulay Abbas. It is a dark and gloomy old place with the ticket windows upstairs and the buses downstairs.

There are at departures at least once a day to Al Hoceima, Casablanca, Rabat, Nador, Chechaouen, Ouezzane, Meknès, Fès and Tangier. Book in advance where possible and check around the different windows to find out all the possibilities.

Tickets for buses to the beaches at Martil and Cabo Negro are available from window 12 at the bus station.

Taxi There are literally dozens of blue Mercedes taxis in the two ranks, with frequent departures to Fnideq (for Ceuta, Dr 14) and Tangier (Dr 20).

To/From Ceuta (Spanish North Africa) The Spanish border is 33 km to the north at Fnideq. *Grands taxis* leave frequently from the corner of Rue de Mouquauama and Rue Sidi Mandri, just up from the bus station. A seat costs Dr 14 for the 20-minute trip. Although the border is open 24 hours, transport dries up from about 7 pm to 5 am.

On the Spanish side of the border, the No 7 public bus runs every half hour or so to the centre; 40 Ptas, exact change only.

This is a much easier way to enter Morocco than via Tangier. The border is fairly easy-going, although crowded at times. It is possible to visit Ceuta in a day trip from Tetouan but it's hard to think why anyone would want to, unless it's to buy a bottle of duty-free liquor. This is quite cheap and there's a good selection.

CHECHAOUEN

Also called Chaouen, Chefchaouen and Xauen, this delightful town in the Rif Mountains is a favourite with travellers – for obvious reasons: the air is cool and clear, the people are noticeably more relaxed (stoned?) than down by the coast, there's more *kif* than you can poke a stick at, and the town is small and manageable. All this makes it a great place to hang out for a few days.

Founded by Moulay Ali ben Rachid in 1471 as a base from which to attack the Portuguese in Ceuta, the town prospered and grew considerably with the arrival of Muslim refugees from Spain. It did, however, remain comparatively isolated until the occupation by Spanish troops in 1920.

Today the town sleeps beneath the Jebel ech-Chaouan ('the horns') and, although it sees its fair share of package-tour buses, it is still a remarkably easy-going town. The touts are relatively few and keep a fairly low profile – a blessed relief if you have just come from Tetouan or Tangier.

Information
Post & Money Both the post office and a branch of the BMCE are on Ave Hassan II – the main street, which runs from Place Mohammed V to Bab el Ain and curves around the south of the medina.

Market
The market is on Ave Al Khattabi, one block south of Ave Hassan II. It is very much the centre of things on market days (Monday and Thursday), when merchants come from all over the Rif to trade. The emphasis is on food and second-hand clothes, although there are sometimes a few things of interest in the way of souvenirs.

Medina
The old medina is small, uncrowded and very easy to find your way around in. For the most part, the houses and buildings are a blinding blue-white and, on the northern side especially, you'll find many with tiny ground-floor rooms crowded with weaving looms. The guys working these looms are often as not bored out of their brains and may well invite you in for a smoke and a chat to break the monotony. There is also a fair smattering of tourist shops, particularly around Place de Makhzen and Place Outa el Hammam – the focal points of the old city.

Place Outa el Hammam & Kasbah The shady, cobbled Place Outa el Hammam with the kasbah along one side is at its busiest in the early evening, when everyone starts to get out and about after the inactivity of the afternoon. It's a great time to sit in one of the many cafés opposite the kasbah and relax. The atmosphere is sedate and almost medieval; it's a pity that cars are still allowed in. The ruins of the 15th-century kasbah dominate the square and its walls now enclose a beautiful garden. An entrance fee of Dr 1 is charged but this gives you access to the museum, where you'll get shown the cells, complete with neck chains at floor level,

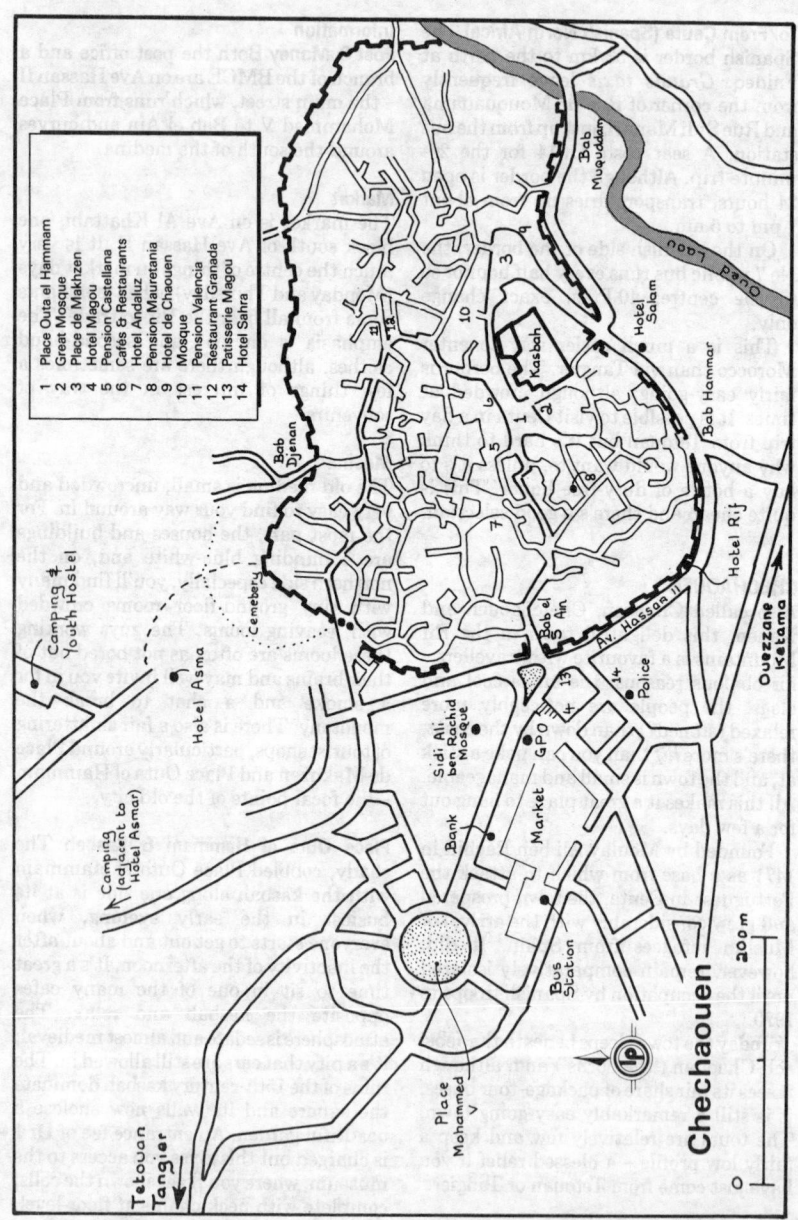

Chechaouen

Tetouan
Tangier

Ouezzane
Ketama

1 Place Outa el Hammam
2 Great Mosque
3 Place de Makhzen
4 Hotel Magou
5 Pension Castellana
6 Cafés & Restaurants
7 Hotel Andaluz
8 Pension Mauretania
9 Hotel de Chaouen
10 Mosque
11 Pension Valencia
12 Restaurant Granada
13 Patisserie Magou
14 Hotel Sahra

Bab Muquddam
Hotel Salam
Bab Hammar
Hotel Rif
Kasbah
Bab Djenan
Cemetery
Bab el 5 Ain
Av. Hassan II
Police
Camping & Youth Hostel
Camping (adjacent to Hotel Asmar)
Hotel Asma
Sidi Ali ben Rachid Mosque
Bank
Market
GPO
Bus Station
Place Mohammed V
Oued Laou

0   200m

where Abd el-Krim was imprisoned in 1926.

In the corner of the garden opposite the prison is a small pavilion, which has been restored to house a small display of traditional crafts, utensils, musical instruments and clothes.

Place de Makhzen The Place de Makhzen is the lesser of the two town squares; it has an enormous old gum tree in the centre. Instead of cafés, it has mostly tourist shops. However, on market days you still get people squatting under the tree selling bundles of mint and vegetables grown in the surrounding area.

If you take the lane heading east from the square you'll eventually come out at Bab Onsar; after this comes the river, with a couple of very agreeable shady cafés on its banks. This is also where the women come to slave away doing the washing while the men busy themselves drinking tea.

Places to Stay - bottom end

The cheapest places are the pensions in the medina. For the most part they are OK, if a little gloomy and claustrophobic at times.

The *Pension Castellana*, just off the western end of Place Outa el Hammam, is the cheapest of the lot at Dr 7 for a bed in rooms with two, three or four beds. A bit roomier is the *Hotel Andaluz*, which costs Dr 14 per person in double rooms; Dr 28 if you are alone and want the room to yourself, as there are no singles. The rooms all face an internal courtyard and so are poorly ventilated. Cold showers are Dr 2; hot showers Dr 4. The pension is signposted off to the left, about 50 metres inside Bab el Ain.

Another popular place with travellers is the *Hotel Mauritania*, which is unusual in that it has single rooms, although they would be better used as cupboards. It costs Dr 10 per person in singles, doubles or triples.

The best of the medina places is the *Pension Valencia* because it is up on the northern slope and gets some breeze and good views. It's a little more expensive than the others at Dr 15 per person but the rooms are larger and more airy. To find it, take the lane off to the north from Place Outa el Hammam; it twists back and forth up the hill but after a few minutes you come to the Restaurant Granada – the pension is around the back and to the right.

Going up in price, the *Hotel Sahra* close to the market lacks atmosphere but is quite good value at Dr 17 per person.

Better value is offered by the *Hotel Salam* (tel 62 39) at 39 Rue Tariq Ibn Ziad, the street which loops around the southern edge of the medina wall. The rooms are bright and clean and some look right out over the valley. Both the comfortable lounge and the shady rooftop terrace also have good views. Rooms are reasonable at Dr 42/64 for singles/doubles including hot shower. You can also take meals here, but at Dr 36 for a set menu they are not great value.

Youth Hostel & Camping Right up on the side of the hill, behind the ghastly Hotel Asma, is the camping ground and *Youth Hostel*. They are only really worth considering if you have your own vehicle, as it's quite a hike to get to them, especially if you have a rucksack. It's a 30-minute walk by the road (just follow the signs to the Hotel Asma), or a 15-minute scramble up the hill through the cemetery; you shouldn't attempt the latter on a Friday, as the locals don't take kindly to it.

The camping area is pleasantly shady, and cheap at Dr 2 per vehicle and the same per person. The hostel is extremely basic and, although it is cheap at Dr 5, you can do much better in the medina.

Places to Stay - middle

Further up the scale, the two-star *Hotel Magou* (tel 62 75) is close to the market and bus station at 23 Rue Moulay Idriss. It is often used by small tour groups and if you are looking for comfort it's not bad at Dr 80 for a double with bathroom.

Places to Stay – top end

The three-star *Hotel Asma* (tel 60 02, 60 65) has 94 rooms, a bar and a restaurant. You can make a reservation through Kasbah Tours Hotels (tel 311 11, 318 64 to 67), 9 Rue Patrice Lumumba, Rabat.

Places to Eat

Amongst the cafés on Place Outa el Hammam are a number of small restaurants which serve good local food. Up near the Pension Valencia the *Restaurant Granada* is run by a cheery character who cooks a variety of stuff at reasonable cost. Apart from these places, the only other restaurants are in the hotels and prices start at around Dr 35 for a set meal.

The *Patisserie Magou* on Ave Hassan II has OK pastries and fresh bread.

Most of the cafés on Place Outa el Hammam have seedy rooms upstairs where the hard smoking goes on – you can just about cut the air with a knife in some of them – and there are certainly worse ways to pass a few hours than to sit around playing dominoes with the locals.

Getting There & Away

Bus The bus station consists of an open yard next to the market. All buses leave from here and there are daily departures to Tetouan (four hours), Meknès (five hours) and Fès (seven hours).

It's well worth booking in advance as far as possible (at least 24 hours ahead), as transport from here, especially to Meknès, is in high demand. Buses coming from Tetouan are much quicker in getting to Meknès but there's no guarantee of getting a seat – in fact in summer you can be fairly well assured that there *won't* be seats.

Taxi *Grands taxis* also leave from the bus station to Tetouan, Meknès, Fès, Ketama, Al Hoceima and Ouezzane. Things are much busier in the mornings.

The Atlantic Coast

Rabat

All the different influences and building styles which have swept through Rabat have left an interesting legacy, and it's well worth spending a few days here.

Though it definitely retains a distinctive Moroccan flavour, the city is unlike many others in Morocco in that few of its people are involved in the tourist trade. Most are government and office workers. That being so, you are in for a treat – one of those rare Moroccan cities where there's no hassle. You can even walk through the souk without having to steel yourself against high-pressure sales tactics.

History

Rabat has been the capital of Morocco only since the days of the French protectorate. However, it has a long and interesting history which goes back over 2000 years to the days when the Phoenicians were exploring the North African Mediterranean and Atlantic coasts and setting up trading posts and colonies.

The Phoenicians were followed by the Romans, who built a settlement here known as Sala. This, like Volubilis, lasted long beyond the break-up of the Roman Empire and eventually gave rise to an independent Berber kingdom. This kingdom, though it quickly accepted Islam with the arrival of the Arabs in the 7th century, retained a high degree of independence both in secular and religious terms. Its unorthodox interpretation of the latter prompted the Arab rulers of the interior to build a ribat (a kind of fortified monastery) on the present site of the kasbah in an attempt to bring them into line.

The orthodox authorities were relatively successful in this venture; by the time a new settlement was established at Salé on the opposite side of the estuary in the 11th century, the original town had been all but abandoned.

Next on the scene were the Almohads, who arrived in the 12th century. They built a new kasbah on the site of the ribat and used it as their base for the conquest of Spain. The city was further expanded by Yacoub el Mansour, who was responsible for the building of the magnificent Oudaia Gate of the kasbah and for the Hassan Mosque which was never finished. This period of glory was, however, brief and, on the death of Mansour, the city declined rapidly in importance.

It was to remain that way until the early 17th century, when it was resettled by Muslims who had been expelled from Spain. Their numbers augmented by renegade Christians, Moorish pirates and adventurers of many nationalities, the settlement asserted its independence once more . The stage was set for the most colourful era of Rabat's history – that of the Sallee Rovers. The pirate corsairs which set sail from here attacked and plundered thousands of merchant vessels returning to Europe from Asia, West Africa and the Americas throughout much of the 17th century and were feared far and wide. Only towards the end of the century were the pirates finally subdued by the Alaouites under Moulay Ismail.

Orientation

Rabat is best approached by rail, since the railway station lies on the city's main thoroughfare, the wide, tree-lined Avenue Mohammed V, which becomes thronged with promenaders each evening. Arrival by bus is extremely inconvenient: the bus station lies several km outside the centre and you will need to take a bus or taxi into

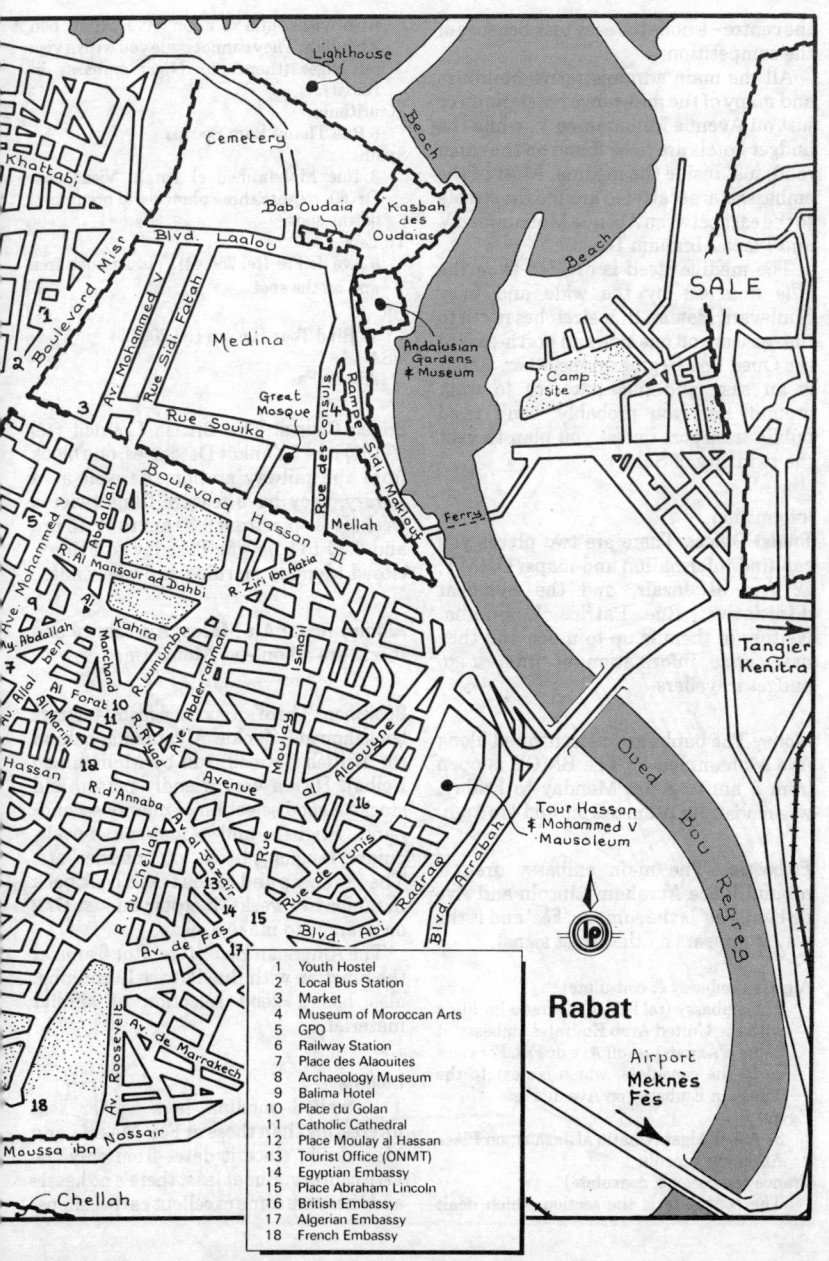

Rabat

1 Youth Hostel
2 Local Bus Station
3 Market
4 Museum of Moroccan Arts
5 GPO
6 Railway Station
7 Place des Alaouites
8 Archaeology Museum
9 Balima Hotel
10 Place du Golan
11 Catholic Cathedral
12 Place Moulay al Hassan
13 Tourist Office (ONMT)
14 Egyptian Embassy
15 Place Abraham Lincoln
16 British Embassy
17 Algerian Embassy
18 French Embassy

the centre – a none too easy task because of the competition.

All the main administrative buildings and many of the mid-range hotels lie on or just off Avenue Mohammed V, while the budget hotels are to be found on the same road, just inside the medina. Most of the embassies are scattered around the streets to the east between Avenue Mohammed V and Place Abraham Lincoln.

The medina itself is divided from the *ville nouvelle* by the wide and busy Boulevard Hassan II; it stretches north to the seashore on one side and north-east to the Oued Bov Regreg on the other. Rabat is an easy and pleasant city to walk around, and you probably won't need public transport unless you plan to visit the twin city of Salé.

Information

Tourist Offices There are two places you can find information and maps: ONMT, 22 Ave al Jazair, and the Syndicat d'Initiative, Rue Patrice Lumumba. Neither of them is up to much and they have little information of interest to budget travellers.

Money The banks are concentrated along Ave Mohammed V. The BMCE is open from 8 am to 8 pm Monday to Friday; weekends from 10 am to 2 pm and 4 to 8 pm.

Embassies The main embassy area is around Place Abraham Lincoln and Ave de Fas ('Fas' is the same as 'Fès' and is the way it appears on the street signs).

Algeria (embassy & consulate)
    The embassy (tel 242 15) shares a building with the United Arab Emirates embassy at 8 Rue d'Azrou, just off Ave de Fas. For visas go to the consulate, which is next to the Tunisian Embassy on Ave de Fas.
Egypt
    31 Ave d'Alger (Charia al Jazair), on Place Abraham Lincoln
France (embassy & consulate)
    The consulate is the section which deals

with visas and it's on Ave Allal ben Abdallah. They cannot issue you with a visa for Niger (there's no Niger embassy in Rabat).
Mauritania
    6 Rue Thami Lam Souissi
Spain
    3 Rue Mohammed el Fateh. Visas cost Dr 60, require three photos and are issued on the spot.
Tunisia
    6 Ave de Fas (tel 256 44). Visas issued free and on the spot.
UK
    17 Blvd Tour Hassan (tel 209 05)
USA
    Ave de Fas

British Council The British Council (tel 693 61) is at 3 Zankat Descartes, one block from the railway station. As well as a library, they have feature films twice a week. It is open from 9.30 am to 12.15 pm and 2.30 to 5.45 pm Tuesday to Friday; closed Monday morning and weekends.

Airlines Royal Air Maroc, Air France and Iberia are all on Ave Mohammed V.

Bookshops There's a good English-language bookshop at 7 Zenkat Alyamama, behind the British Council, run by Mohammed Belhaj. He's a very friendly person and stocks a good selection of mainly second-hand English and American novels, guides, language books, dictionaries, etc. They're cheap and, if you take a book back in under two weeks, it costs you just Dr 2 on average to make a swap.

The American Bookstore, Rue Tanja at the junction with Rue Patrice Lumumba, also has a good selection of similar material.

Medina

The walled medina here is far less interesting than those at Fès, Meknès and Marrakesh, since it dates from only the 17th century. But at least there's no hassle and there are some excellent carpet shops.

Kasbah des Oudaias

The Kasbah des Oudaias, built out on the bluff overlooking the estuary and the Atlantic Ocean, is much more interesting than the medina. The usual entry is via the enormous Almohad gate of Bab Oudaia built in 1195 AD. This is perhaps the only place in Rabat where you are likely to encounter hustlers. Say 'hello' but otherwise ignore them and don't believe a word they tell you about it being closed or anything else. It's a very pleasant place to wander around and there's only one main street, so you can't get lost.

Inside the kasbah is the 17th-century palace built by Moulay Ismail but now converted into the Museum of Moroccan Arts, which is well worth visiting. It's housed in two separate parts of the palace and is open daily, except Tuesday, from 8 am to 12 noon and 4 to 6 pm. The former palace encloses what are known as the Andalusian Gardens which, although laid out in the traditional style of that part of

Spain, were actually planted by the French during the colonial period.

Tour Hassan

Rabat's most famous landmark is the Tour Hassan, which overlooks the bridge which crosses the estuary to Salé. Construction of this enormous minaret – which was intended to be the largest and highest in the Muslim world – was begun by the Almohad sultan Yacoub el Mansour in 1195 but abandoned at his death some four years later. Though the tower still stands, little remains of the adjacent mosque. On the same site is the Mausoleum of Mohammed V, the present king's father. Entry is free, but you must be dressed in a respectful manner if you want to visit the mausoleum.

Chellah

Beyond the city walls, at the end of Ave Yacoub el Mansour at the junction with Blvd ad Doustour, are the remains of the ancient Roman city of Sala, which

Entrance to Chellah, Rabat

subsequently became the independent Berber city of Chellah. When abandoned in 1154, it was used by the Almohads as a royal burial ground. However, most of what stands today dates from Merenid times, when Sultan Abou el Hassan built the enclosing walls and gates. Entry is free, and although you'll run into a few touts offering to be guides you don't have to take one (nor do you need one).

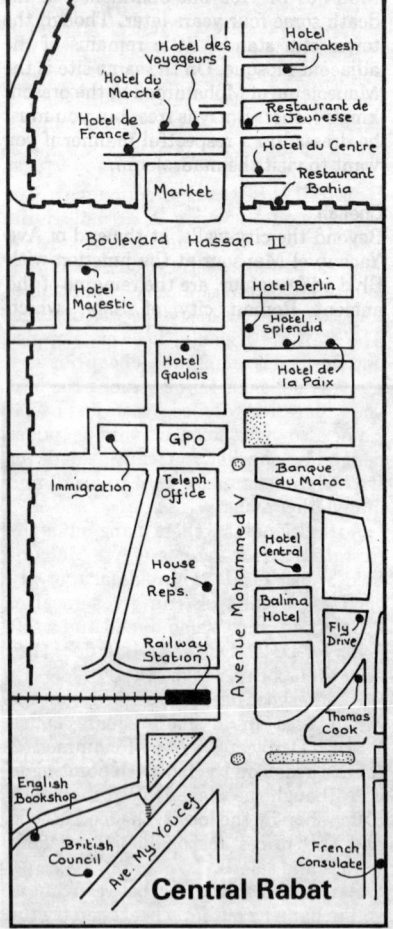

Central Rabat

Archaeology Museum

I would recommend a visit to the Archaeology Museum, which is close to the Great Mosque (*Grande Mosquée*) on Place Djemaa Assouna. It contains some excellent collections of Phoenician, Carthaginian and Roman relics. Some of the Roman exhibits were collected from Volubilis but others were found at Chellah. The museum is open daily, except Tuesday, from 8.30 am to 12 noon and 2.30 to 6 pm.

Places to Stay – bottom end

There are several rock-bottom budget hotels to choose from on or just off the continuation of Ave Mohammed V as it enters the medina. Few of them make any concessions to creature comforts and some of them don't even have showers, cold or otherwise, so they're not such good value for money. An extra dollar or two will buy you far better accommodation outside the medina.

Perhaps the best of the cheapies is the *Hotel Marrakesh*, Rue Sebbahi just off Ave Mohammed V, which costs Dr 25 a single, Dr 40 a double and Dr 45 a triple. The staff are friendly, but the communal showers have cold water only. The *Hotel des Voyageurs*, Rue Souika just off Ave Mohammed V, is similar. Two cheaper alternatives are: the *Hotel du Centre*, on the right just as you enter the medina, which costs Dr 30 a double (no singles); and the hotel with only an Arabic name on Rue Sidi M'Amed el Ghazi, just off Ave Mohammed V, which costs Dr 20 a single and Dr 30 a double. Neither of these last two have showers of any description.

Just outside the medina, the *Hotel Berlin*, Ave Mohammed V, is excellent value. It's on the 2nd floor, above the Vietnamese restaurant called Hong Kong. It's very clean, secure and friendly and the rooms cost Dr 25 a single and Dr 35 a double. Hot showers are Dr 3 extra. Get there early in the day if possible, as they have only a few rooms.

Also excellent value is the *Hotel*

Top: Moulay Idriss, Morocco (HF)
Left: Moulay Idriss, Morocco (HF)
Right: Todra Gorge, Morocco (GC)

Top: Berber kasbah, Drâa Valley, Morocco (GC)
Left: Chechaouen, Morocco (HF)
Right: Ruins of ancient granaries, Meknès, Morocco (HF)

there are regular connections to most of the countries of Western Europe, as well as to West Africa, Algeria, Tunisia, Egypt and the Middle East.

Bus The CTM bus terminal is between Avenue de l'Armée Royale and Rue Vidal, close to where these two streets meet the Boulevard Hassan Seghir, at the back of the Hotel Safir. There are other bus stations scattered around, but most of them use the terminal on the Rue Strasbourg, two blocks down from the Place de la Victoire. The latter terminal is some way from the centre of the city, so it might be better to take a taxi from the Place Mohammed V.

There are regular CTM departures to Marrakesh, Fès, Rabat and Tangier, but the trains are quicker and more comfortable.

Train Most departures are from Casa-Voyageurs station, which is a Dr 10 taxi ride from the centre, or 30 minutes' walk. Departures include: Tangier, 12.45 and 11.10 pm, seven hours; Fès, five daily from 6.00 am to 10 pm, 5½ hours; and Marrakesh, six daily from 1.20 to 7.13 pm, four hours.

Departures from the much more convenient Gare du Port ('Casa-Port' on the platform signs) at the bottom end of Boulevard Mohammed el Hansali are as follows: Tangier (7.15 am and 5.57 pm); Fès (8.04 am, 12.27 and 8.50 pm); Oujda (8.50 pm, 10½ hours); Marrakesh (1 pm); and Rabat (14 local trains daily from 6.50 am to 7.30 pm, 50 minutes; main-line departures as well).

Getting Around

Airport Transport The Mohammed V Airport is 35 km to the south of Casa and is well served by public buses, which leave the CTM station every 30 minutes from 5.30 am to 7 pm. The trip takes 45 minutes and costs Dr 20.

Taxi *Petits taxis* are red and there are

hundreds of them. Drivers are unwilling to use the meters, as they are out of date. Expect to pay Dr 10 for a ride in or around the city centre.

Central Coast

EL JADIDA
History
El Jadida was founded by the Portuguese in 1513, in the days when these seafaring people were undertaking their voyages of discovery around the world and pouring what meagre resources they had into establishing a maritime trading empire which quickly stretched as far as China and Japan. They were to hold on to El Jadida (which, in those days, was known as Mazagan) until 1769 when, following a siege by Sultan Mohammed ben Abdallah, the Portuguese were forced to evacuate the fortress. Although they took little more than the clothes they stood in, the ramparts were mined and, at the last moment, blown to smithereens taking with them a good part of the besieging army.

The walls of the fortress lay in ruins until 1820, when they were rebuilt by Sultan Moulay Abderrahman. The Moors who took over the town after the Portuguese withdrawal preferred to settle outside the walls of the fortress. The medina inside the walls was largely neglected until the mid-19th century, when it was recolonised by European merchants following the establishment of a series of 'open ports' along the Moroccan coast.

A large and influential Jewish community became established at this time. The Jews controlled trade with the interior and particularly with Marrakesh. Not only that but, contrary to practice in most Moroccan cities, the Jews of El Jadida were not confined to living within their own separate quarter (the mellah).

The massive bastioned fortress with its

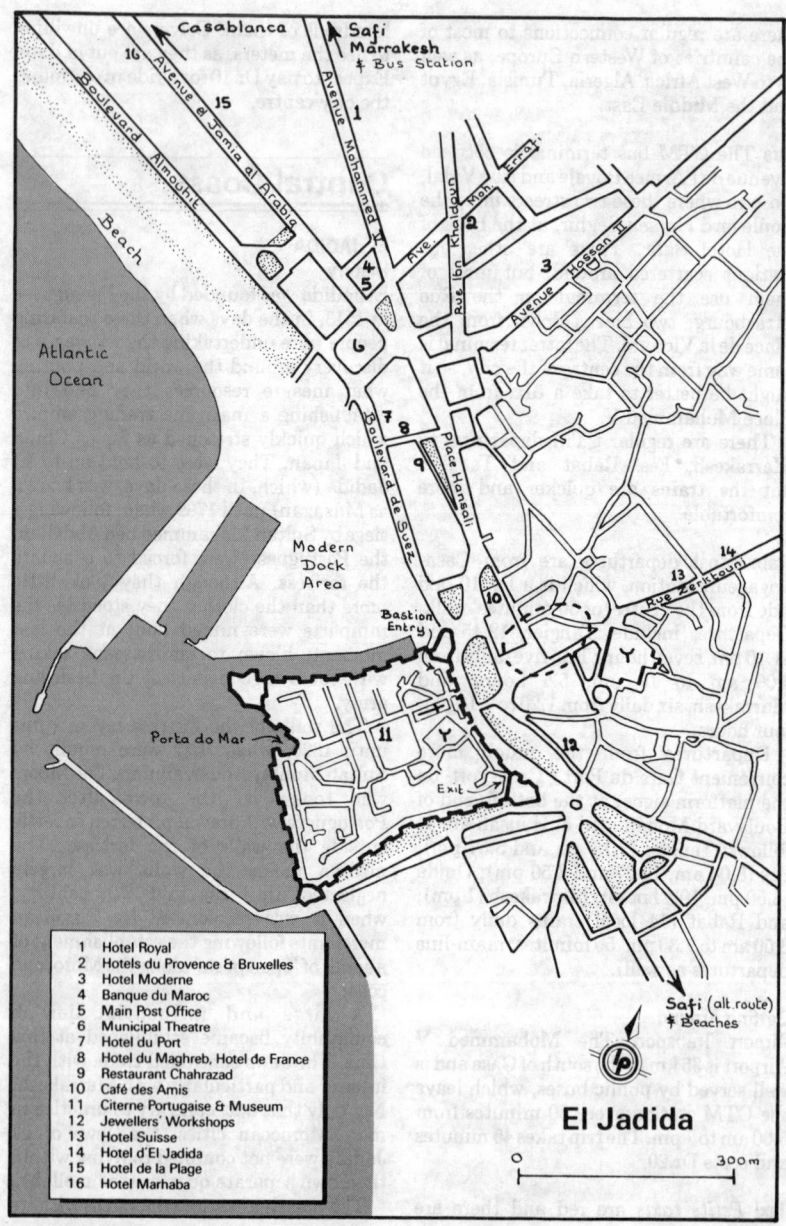

1 Hotel Royal
2 Hotels du Provence & Bruxelles
3 Hotel Moderne
4 Banque du Maroc
5 Main Post Office
6 Municipal Theatre
7 Hotel du Port
8 Hotel du Maghreb, Hotel de France
9 Restaurant Chahrazad
10 Café des Amis
11 Citerne Portugaise & Museum
12 Jewellers' Workshops
13 Hotel Suisse
14 Hotel d'El Jadida
15 Hotel de la Plage
16 Hotel Marhaba

El Jadida

0   300 m

enclosed medina, churches and enormous cistern is still remarkably well preserved. Indeed, despite having been reconstructed by the Moroccans, it's one of the most spectacular European-style medieval fortresses to be found anywhere in the world.

These days, El Jadida is a very popular Moroccan beach resort.

Portuguese Fortress

The old Portuguese fortress (known as the Cité Portugaise) is the focal centre of town. Although its enclosed medina has suffered from neglect, it's still inhabited and well worth exploring. There are two entrance gates to the fortress; the the northernmost one, which is more convenient, opens onto the main street through the medina. The street ends at the Porta do Mar, which is where ships used to discharge their cargo in the Portuguese era.

Citerne Portugaise About halfway down the main street is the famous Citerne Portugaise (Portuguese Cistern). Though the Romans built water collection and storage cisterns similar to this, it remains a remarkable piece of architecture and engineering which has stood the test of time and is still functional. The reflection of the roof and arched pillars in the water covering the floor creates a dramatic and beautiful effect. This hasn't escaped the attention of various film directors, who have staged scenes for several movies here. The cistern is open on weekdays from 8 am to 12 noon and 2 to 6 pm (sometimes later). Entry costs Dr 2 and includes a guide who will show you around. Photography is permitted at no extra charge. There's also a small museum next to the cistern (free) but it's not up to much.

Medina Being zealous Catholics, the Portuguese naturally constructed a number of churches within the medina. Unfortunately, they're all closed, except for what remains of one on top of the

ramparts at the extreme southern seaward side. Even if it were possible to visit them, however, it's unlikely that they would still retain their original features, since they were taken over and used for secular purposes long ago. The Great Mosque, adjacent to the largest former church close to the entrance, used to be a lighthouse.

Ramparts Entry to the ramparts, which you can walk all the way around, is through the large door at the end of the tiny cul-de-sac which is first on the right after entering the fortress. The man with the key for this is usually hanging around and, if not, he won't be far away. There's no charge, but he'll half expect a tip when he lets you out at the far side (you may have to hammer on the door for several minutes before he arrives).

Beaches

There are beaches to both the north and south of town, though the ones to the north occasionally get polluted by oil. They're pleasant enough out of season but can get very crowded during July and August, during which time you'd do better to head for Essaouira.

Places to Stay – bottom end

Hotel rooms can be very hard to find in the summer months, as there's heavy demand, so you may have to stay at a relatively expensive hotel if you arrive late in the day.

The best value of the budget hotels is the *Hotel du Maghreb* (which incorporates the *Hotel de France*), Rue Lescoul; it offers large, clean rooms without own shower and toilet for Dr 26 a single and Dr 35 a double. It's a huge place, and the staff are friendly and eager to please. Hot showers (gas-heated) cost extra. The *Hotel du Port*, around the corner on Blvd de Suez, isn't such good value at Dr 27 a single and Dr 36 a double with only cold water showers. Prices are negotiable, however, in the low season (Dr 30 a double, for instance).

Another budget hotel is the *Hotel Moderne*, Ave Hassan II, but it's nothing special and offers small, dimly-lit rooms for Dr 17 a single, Dr 26 a double and Dr 40 for a room with a double and a single bed.

Places to Stay – middle

Going up in price, there are two hotels adjacent to each other which are excellent value. They are the *Hotel de Provence* (tel 23 47), 42 Ave Mohammed Errafi, and the *Hotel Bruxelles* (tel 20 72), 40 Rue Ibn Khaldoun; they are both one-star hotels and are at the junction of these two streets. They're very clean and pleasant, and have a friendly staff and hot showers. Expect to pay Dr 38 a single and Dr 46 a double with own shower but without toilet; Dr 44 a single and Dr 56 a double with own shower and toilet. In the low season you can usually get a room with shower and toilet for the price you would normally pay for a room with just a shower.

Similar value may be found at the *Hotel Royal* (tel 28 39), 108 Ave Mohammed V; the *Hotel d'El Jadida*, Ave Zerktouni; and the *Hotel Suisse* (tel 28 16), 145 Ave Zerktouni.

Places to Stay – top end

The four-star *Hotel Le Palais Andalous* (tel 39 06, 37 45) has 36 rooms, a restaurant and a bar. The *Hotel Doukkala Salam* (tel 36 22, 35 75), on Ave el Jamiaa al Arabia, has tennis courts, a swimming pool and 81 rooms.

Places to Eat

There are very few cheap restaurants in El Jadida. One of the best is the *Restaurant Chahrazad*, 38 Place Hansali. This offers a variety of dishes (soup, salads, tajine, etc), and a meal costs around Dr 30. If it looks full, they have a mezzanine floor as well. Otherwise, try the *Café des Amis* at the southern end of Place Hansali.

There are quite a few restaurants opposite the post office and Teatro

Municipal, but you'd be well advised to check prices before ordering. They can be remarkably expensive.

For bars, check out the *Hotel de la Plage* and the *Hotel Marhaba*, both on Ave el Jamia al Arabia. There are others opposite the post office.

Getting There & Away

The bus terminal is at the northern end of town on Rue Abdelmoumen el Mouahidi, close to the junction with Ave Mohammed V. It's a 10-minute walk from here to the main hotel area, or 15 minutes to the fortress along Ave Mohammed V.

SAFI

Safi is largely a modern fishing port and industrial centre, which sits on the Atlantic coast in a steep crevasse formed by the River Châabah. It has a lively walled medina and souk, with fortresses dating from the Portuguese era. Also, it is well known for its traditional potteries.

Safi may not be the most attractive of Moroccan towns but it's definitely worth a day of your time if you are in the area.

History

Safi's natural harbour was known to the Phoenicians and was probably used by the Romans later on. However, involvement with Europeans really came with the arrival of the Portuguese in 1508. They began construction of a fortress, using Essaouira as their base. Though what they constructed at Safi was of monumental proportions (as all Portuguese military installations tended to be in those days), their stay at Safi was of limited duration and the town was voluntarily evacuated in 1541.

This event didn't herald the end of European contact. In the 17th century the French established a consulate at the port and were responsible for signing many trading treaties with the indigenous rulers. By the 19th century, however, the port had faded into insignificance. Its revival came in the 20th century, with the

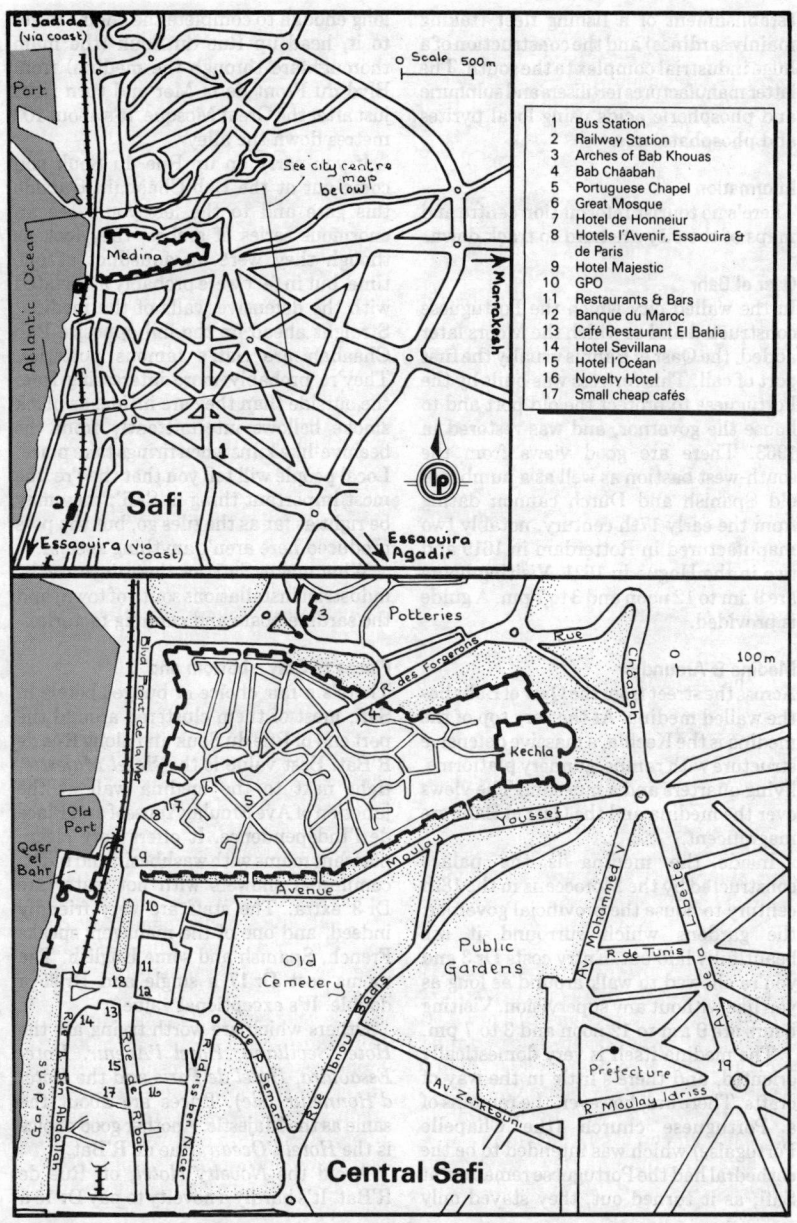

Safi

1 Bus Station
2 Railway Station
3 Arches of Bab Khouas
4 Bab Cháabah
5 Portuguese Chapel
6 Great Mosque
7 Hotel de Honneiur
8 Hotels l'Avenir, Essaouira & de Paris
9 Hotel Majestic
10 GPO
11 Restaurants & Bars
12 Banque du Maroc
13 Café Restaurant El Bahia
14 Hotel Sevillana
15 Hotel l'Océan
16 Novelty Hotel
17 Small cheap cafés

Central Safi

establishment of a fishing fleet (taking mainly sardines) and the construction of a huge industrial complex to the south. The latter manufactures fertilisers and sulphuric and phosphoric acids using local pyrites and phosphate ores.

Information

There's no tourist information centre and maps of the city are hard to track down.

Qasr el Bahr

In the walled city which the Portuguese constructed and to which the Moors later added, the Qasr el Bahr is usually the first port of call. This fortress was built by the Portuguese to protect the old port and to house the governor, and was restored in 1963. There are good views from the south-west bastion as well as a number of old Spanish and Dutch cannon dating from the early 17th century, notably two manufactured in Rotterdam in 1619 and two in the Hague in 1621. Visiting hours are 9 am to 12 noon and 3 to 7 pm. A guide is provided.

Medina & Around

Across the street from the Qasr el Bahr lies the walled medina. At the very top of the medina is the Kechla, a massive defensive structure with ramps, gunnery platforms, living quarters and a museum. The views over the medina and the Qasr el Bahr are magnificent.

Inside the medina is the palace constructed by the Moroccans in the 18th century to house the provincial governor; the gardens which surround it are beautifully laid out. Entry costs Dr 3 and you're allowed to walk around as long as you like without any supervision. Visiting hours are 9 am to 12 noon and 3 to 7 pm.

The medina itself is very domestically oriented, and there's little in the way of crafts. There are, however, the remains of a Portuguese church (the Chapelle Portugaise) which was intended to be the cathedral had the Portuguese remained at Safi; as it turned out, they stayed only

long enough to complete the choir. To get to it, head up Rue du Souk (the main thoroughfare through the medina) from Blvd du Front de la Mer and turn right just after the Great Mosque. It's about 100 metres down the alley.

If you carry on up Rue du Souk you come out at the Bab Châabah. Outside this gate and to the left you'll see an enormous series of arches; they look as though they were an aqueduct at one time, but in fact were probably associated with the defensive walls of the medina. Straight ahead on the hill opposite Bab Châabah are Safi's famous potteries. They're probably more interesting from the outside than they are inside, as black smoke bellows intermittently from the beehive-like kilns when firings take place. Local people will tell you that they're 'the most important thing in Safi'; they may be right as far as the tiles go, but the pots produced here aren't anything special.

What makes Safi tick these days are the industrial installations south of town, and the sardine boats and canning factories.

Places to Stay – bottom end

There's a fair choice of budget hotels in Safi, most of them clustered around the port end of Rue du Souk and along Rue de R'Bat. Best value is the *Hotel Majestic*, right next to the medina wall at the junction of Ave Moulay Youssef and Place de l'Indépendence. It offers very clean, pleasant rooms with washbasin and bidet; communal showers with hot water are Dr 3 extra. The staff are very friendly indeed, and one of the managers speaks French, Spanish and some English. The rooms cost Dr 17 a single and Dr 25 a double. It's exceptional value.

Others which are worth trying are the *Hotel Sevillana*, *Hotel l'Avenir*, *Hotel Essaouira*, *Hotel de Paris* and the *Hotel d'Honneiur* (*sic*). Prices are about the same as the Majestic. Another good choice is the *Hotel l'Océan*, Rue de R'Bat.

Avoid the *Novelty Hotel*, off Rue de R'Bat. It's hardly a novelty to pay Dr 15 a single and Dr 30 a double only to discover that the rooms are dark and dingy and there are no showers.

Places to Stay – top end
The three-star *Hotel Les Mimosas* (tel 32 08) is on Rue Ibn Zaïdoun. The four-star *Hotel Atlantide* (tel 21 60/61) has 50 rooms, a restaurant and a bar.

Places to Eat
There are plenty of small, traditional Moroccan cafés all the way up Rue du Souk; they offer cheap, tasty food which is usually displayed out front. This is probably the best area in which to eat – not only for the food, but also because it's a very lively and interesting street. Otherwise, a fairly cheap restaurant can be found on the left-hand side (about 10 metres down) of the only alleyway which branches off from the top of Place de l'Indépendence.

The *Café Restaurant El Bahia*, which takes up the whole top side of Place de l'Indépendence, is very much a tourist trap. The food is expensive and not exceptional. The same goes for the restaurants which line the other sides of the Place.

The most convenient bars are those on Place de l'Indépendence; beware of hustlers, though the locals will support you if you can't bite the bullet.

Getting There & Away
Both the bus terminal (which is on Ave du Président Kennedy) and the railway station (Rue de R'Bat) are quite some way from the centre of town, so it would be a good idea to either take a bus or share a taxi from these places to the centre (Place de l'Indépendence). A by-pass (Blvd Hassan II) circles the main part of town, so buses don't go through the centre.

The Middle Atlas

Fès

Fès is the oldest of the imperial cities of Morocco, having been founded shortly after the Arabs swept across North Africa following the death of the Prophet. It has been the capital of Morocco on a number of occasions and for long periods of time. Those periods of greatness and importance have left their mark not only on the city itself which, like Marrakesh and Meknès, is full of magnificent buildings reflecting the incomparable brilliance of Arab-Berber imagination and artistry, but also on the psychology of the inhabitants. Fassis (the name by which the people of Fès are known) justifiably look on their city as the cultural capital of Morocco and so consider themselves a cut above the rest of the inhabitants of the country. While Rabat may well be the modern capital of Morocco, no sultan would fare well or even survive very long without taking the wishes of Fès into consideration.

The medina of Fès el-Bali (Old Fès) is one of the largest in the world and the most interesting in Morocco. That it has survived intact and essentially unchanged over the centuries is, in itself, unique. With the exception of Marrakesh and a few ancient cities in the Middle East, there is nothing remotely comparable with this city in the Arab world. One day it will surely be nominated as a World Heritage Site. Its narrow winding alleys and covered bazaars are crammed with every conceivable sort of craft workshop, restaurants, meat, fruit and vegetable markets, mosques, medressas, and extensive dye pits and tanneries. What is more, the gates and walls which surround the whole are magnificent. But it's not just the sights that are going to draw you here. The exotic smells, the hammering of the metalworkers, the call of the muezzin

and the need to jostle through crowded bazaars and past teams of unco-operative donkeys all add up to an experience you're never going to forget. You can easily spend a week wandering through this endless labyrinth and still not be ready to leave.

Fès is the essence of a traveller's wildest dreams. Yet, relatively speaking, it is close to some of the world's most industrialised centres (on the northern shores of the Mediterranean). Times are changing rapidly, and this will undoubtedly affect the atmosphere of the city and the life styles of the inhabitants. Nevertheless, it is still mind-bogglingly different from Europe.

The city is certainly changing fast in response to the 20th century, and it would be wrong to assume that these changes have not affected Fès el-Bali and Fès el-Jedid (New Fès). They certainly have. Yet, although the city is definitely not a mere museum of medievalism, somehow the atmosphere of the past is intact. Since tradition runs so deep here, Fès will probably never come to resemble any of the medieval cities of northern Europe, or even Marrakesh or Meknès, which have been given over almost entirely to pulling in the tourist dollar. Indeed, Fès is one of the few Moroccan cities where hustlers are relatively hard to find, and where hardly anyone cares too much about attracting tourist trade. You'll be hard pressed to find American Express and Diners Club stickers in the souks here. Fassis are too proud to trade away their culture for such superficial symbols of international acceptability. Bargains are struck here in the way they have always been – slowly, over mint tea with an exchange of yarns. May it remain so!

History
Idriss I founded Fès on the right bank of the Oued Fès in 789, in what is now the

Andalous Quarter. His son, Idriss II, extended the city onto the left bank in 809; these two parts of the city are now known as Fès el-Bali.

The earliest settlers were mainly refugees from Córdoba (Spain) and Kairouan (Tunisia), the former favouring the right bank and the latter the left bank. Both groups were from well-established Islamic centres of brilliance. The skills which they brought with them were of inestimable value in laying the groundwork on which Fès would later draw, becoming one of the most important centres of Islamic intellectual and architectural development in the West.

These early days, however, were far from peaceful. As the Idrissid kingdom disintegrated, Morocco became the object of a a tug-of-war between the Omayyads of Spain and the Aghlabids of Tunisia. Fès experienced several changes of ruler, though both sides were responsible for improving the fortifications which enclosed the city.

The score was finally settled when the Islamic fundamentalist Almoravids swept out of the deserts of Mauritania and took Fès in 1069, going on from there to conquer Spain. This was the age of religious fundamentalism *par excellence*, and this affected not only the Muslims but the Christians on the other side of the Mediterranean. Probably no other age witnessed the formation of so many ascetic religious sects bent on the strict observance of scriptural laws. Like all the rest, however, once the fervour of conquest and purification waned, the Almoravids gradually succumbed to the pleasures of luxury and urban living. They were overthrown by the Almohads in 1146.

In their conquest of Fès, the Almohads destroyed the walls of the city and only replaced them when they were assured of the loyalty of the inhabitants. Large sections of the walls of Fès date from this period. Not only that, both the Almoravids and the Almohads preferred Marrakesh

as their capital; consequently Fès remained a backwater for many years.

The city finally entered its period of brilliance under the Merenids. This dynasty took the city in 1250 (after gaining and losing it again two years earlier), and it remained the capital of Morocco throughout the duration of their rule. Never absolutely sure of the loyalty of his subjects, the second Merenid sultan, Abu Youssef Yacoub (1258-1286), constructed a self-contained walled city outside the old one. This was known as Fès el-Jedid and was where the sultan stationed troops who could be relied upon to side with him in the event of a mutiny; foremost among these were Syrian and Christian mercenaries. Later on, in the 14th century, the Jewish community (itself originally descended from Spanish refugees during Idrissid times) was forcibly relocated from Fès el-Bali to the new city as an additional buffer. Though definitely regarded as second-class citizens and treated as such, the Jews were important economically in the life of the nation and were to become increasingly so. Because they enjoyed the protection of the sultan, they could be relied upon to side with the ruler in the event of an insurrection.

Few Jewish families remain in Fès these days. The great majority left for Israel during the '50s and '60s, and their synagogues have been converted into carpet warehouses and the like.

Following the rise to power of the Saadians in the 16th century, Marrakesh once again became the capital and Fès slipped into relative obscurity. However, the city enjoyed a revival under the Alaouite ruler Moulay Abdullah in the 19th century and, despite its period of decline, Fès remained one of the most important centres in the kingdom.

In 1916, following the establishment of the protectorate, the French began construction of the *ville nouvelle* on the plateau to the south-west of the two ancient cities. That Fès, in common with

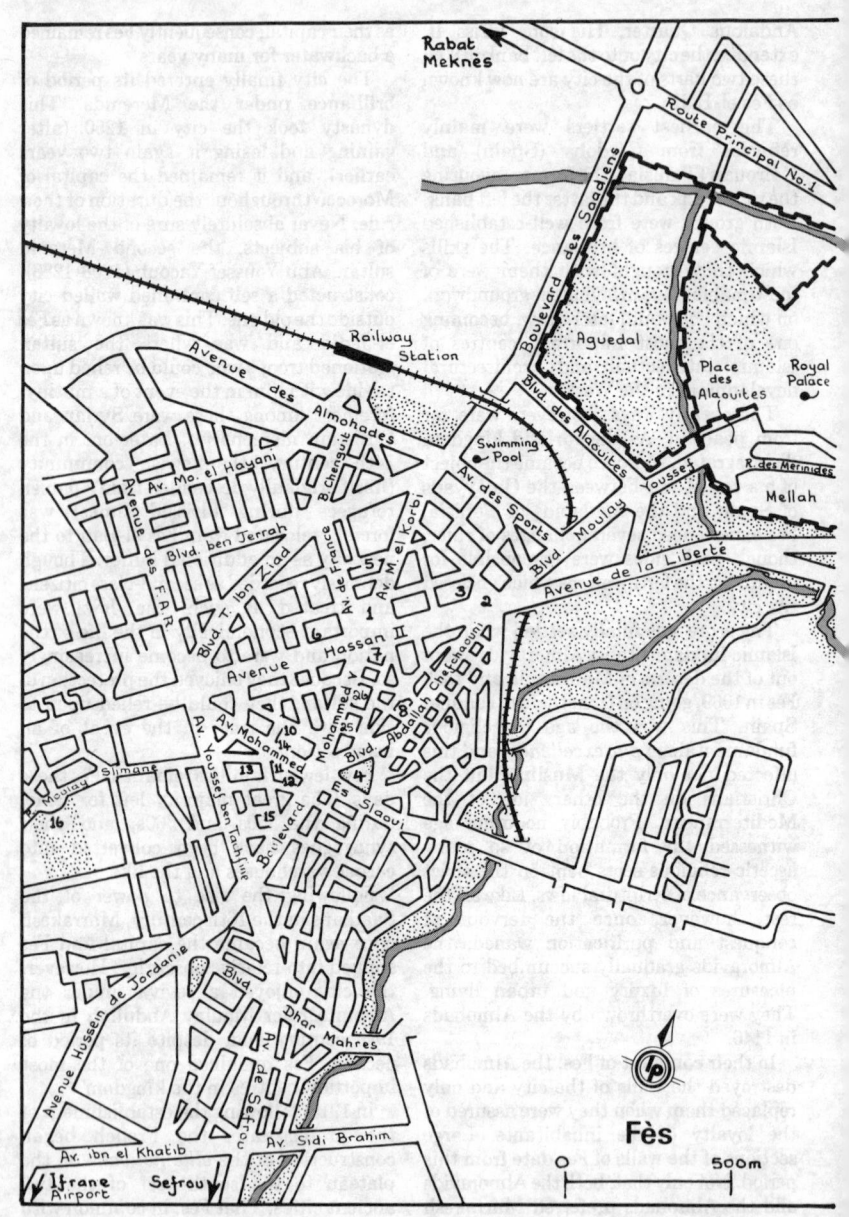

Rabat
Meknès

Route Principal No. 1

Boulevard des Saadiens

Aguedal

Place des Alaouites

Royal Palace

Blvd des Alaouites

Railway Station

Swimming Pool

Avenue des Almohades

Av. Ma. el Hayani

Avenue des F.A.R.

B. Chaquili

Av. des Sports

Av. des Sports

Blvd Moulay Yousset

R. des Mérinides

Mellah

Blvd ben Jerrah

Blvd T. Ibn Ziad

5

Av. M. el Korbi

Av. de France

3

2

Avenue de la Liberté

1

6

Avenue Hassan II

Moulay Slimane

Av. Mohammed

Av. Youssef ben Tachfine

10

11

13

12

Mohammed V

Blvd Abdallah Chefchaouni

8

9

2b

Es Siaoui

16

15

4

Boulevard Dhar Mahres

Avenue Hussein de Jordanie

Blvd de Sefrou

Av. de Sefrou

Av. ibn el Khatib

Av. Sidi Brahim

Ifrane Airport

Sefrou

Fès

0   500m

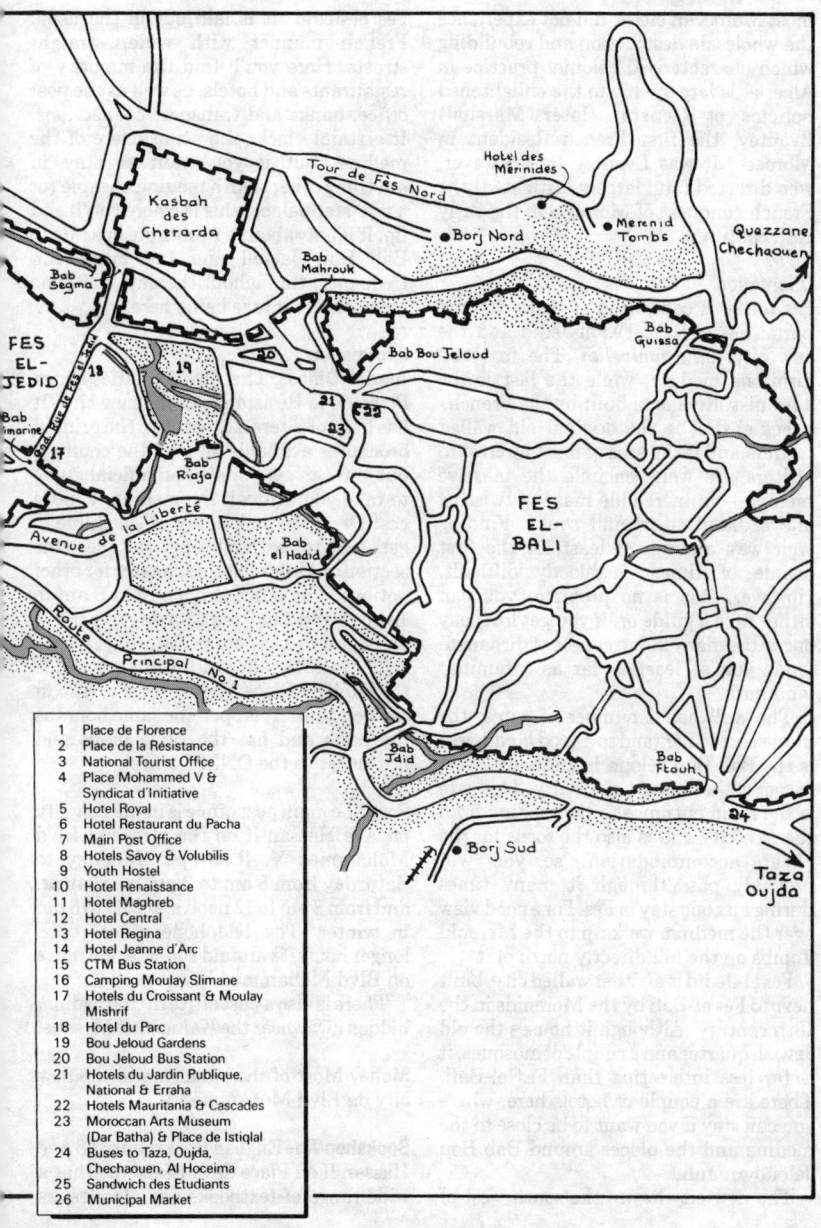

1 Place de Florence
2 Place de la Résistance
3 National Tourist Office
4 Place Mohammed V &
   Syndicat d'Initiative
5 Hotel Royal
6 Hotel Restaurant du Pacha
7 Main Post Office
8 Hotels Savoy & Volubilis
9 Youth Hostel
10 Hotel Renaissance
11 Hotel Maghreb
12 Hotel Central
13 Hotel Regina
14 Hotel Jeanne d'Arc
15 CTM Bus Station
16 Camping Moulay Slimane
17 Hotels du Croissant & Moulay
   Mishrif
18 Hotel du Parc
19 Bou Jeloud Gardens
20 Bou Jeloud Bus Station
21 Hotels du Jardin Publique,
   National & Erraha
22 Hotels Mauritania & Cascades
23 Moroccan Arts Museum
   (Dar Batha) & Place de Istiqlal
24 Buses to Taza, Oujda,
   Chechaouen, Al Hoceima
25 Sandwich des Etudiants
26 Municipal Market

most Moroccan cities, did not experience the wholesale destruction and rebuilding which characterised colonial practice in Algeria, is largely due to the enlightened policies of General (later Marshal) Lyautey, the first French Resident in Morocco. It was Lyautey too, however, who directed (and largely instigated) the French conquest of Morocco in the early 20th century.

Orientation

Fès today is comprised of three distinct parts: Fès el-Bali, Fès el-Jedid and the new city (*ville nouvelle*). The first two form the medina, while the last is the administrative area built by the French.

Fès el-Bali is the original old walled medina and is the area of most interest to visitors. Its walls encircle the massive medina – an incredible maze of twisting alleys, blind turns and souks. Finding your way around, at least for the first couple of times, is bloody difficult. However, this is no problem: you can either take a guide or, if you get lost, pay one of the many kids a couple of dirham to guide you at least as far as a familiar landmark.

The wall has a number of gates; the most spectacular (and so a good landmark) is the Bab Bou Jeloud in the south-west corner of the old part of the city. This gate is the main entrance to the medina from the new city and is also the focus for the cheap accommodation, so you will probably pass through it many times during any one stay in Fès. For a good view over the medina, walk up to the Merenid Tombs on the hill directly north of it.

Fès el-Jedid is another walled city, built next to Fès el-Bali by the Merenids in the 13th century. Although it houses the old Jewish quarter and a couple of mosques, it is far less interesting than Fès el-Bali. There are a couple of hotels here, where you can stay if you want to be close to the medina and the places around Bab Bou Jeloud are full.

The new city lies to the south-west of

Fès el-Jedid. It is laid out in the usual French manner with wide, straight streets. Here you'll find the majority of restaurants and hotels, as well as the post office, banks and transport connections. It certainly lacks the atmosphere of the medina, but if you want to stay in anything other than a medina cheapie (or a five-star palace) this is where you'll end up. It is only about a 10-minute bus ride to Bab Bou Jeloud and the buses run frequently throughout the day, so it's no great disadvantage being here.

Information

Tourist Offices The ONMT office is on Place de la Résistance in the new city. It has little of interest other than the printed brochures available all over the country, but you can get yourself an official guide to take you through the medina. Guides cost Dr 35 for half a day; it's possible to get around without one, but see the section on Guides in this chapter for other options. The office is open from 8 am to 12 noon and 2 to 6 pm Monday to Friday, and 8 am to 12 noon on Saturday.

The local Syndicat d'Initiative is inside the bank on Place Mohammed V, also in the new town. It is open the same hours as the bank and has the same maps and brochures as the ONMT office.

Post The main post office is in the new city on Ave Hassan II on the corner of Blvd Mohammed V. It is open Monday to Saturday from 8 am to 2 pm in summer, and from 8 am to 12 noon and 2.30 to 6 pm in winter. The telephone office (open longer hours) is around the side; entrance on Blvd Mohammed V.

There is also a post office in the medina, hidden away near the Kairaouine Mosque.

Money Most of the banks are in the new city on Blvd Mohammed V.

Bookshop The English Bookshop at 68 Ave Hassan II on Place de la Résistance has a wide range of textbooks and classics, as well as some others; it also has an excellent selection of books by African writers from all over the continent.

Car Rental All the major companies have offices here, including: Avis, 50 Blvd Chefchaouini; Budget (tel 209 19), cnr Blvd Hassan II & Rue Bahrein; Europcar (tel 239 47), Ave Essaouida; InterRent (tel 265 45), 41 Ave Hassan II; and Hertz (tel 228 12), Hotel de Fès.

Airlines Royal Air Maroc (tel 255 16) is at 54 Ave Hassan II.

Guides Official guides can be hired at the tourist office, but there are also plenty of unofficial hopefuls hanging around Bab Bou Jeloud. The latter *can* be good and are usually cheap (about Dr 10), but there are a few things you need to settle before agreeing to go with one. Make sure that you know exactly which sites you will be seeing, and if you don't want to be shown one craft shop after another make that clear at the beginning as well.

Although not strictly necessary, it's probably a good idea to take a guide for your first two or three visits to Fès el-Bali, if only to get an idea of the layout of the streets and the location of the activities that most interest you. However, if you don't take a guide and get hopelessly lost (which you will) it's no problem: for a couple of dirham, there are any number of street urchins who will lead you out of the maze to a familiar landmark.

If you do take a guide beware of the usual pitfalls. The way that guides make their money (apart from the fee you pay them to guide you around) is from commissions from shopkeepers into whose shops you are taken. Naturally, the guide's cut is built into the price of anything you buy, so if you see something you like, remember the shop and go back later without the guide. And, if you have acquired a hanger-on who won't leave you (very easy!), make this quite clear from the outset. One of their favourite tricks is

to tag along and get a commission, even though you haven't engaged them as a guide.

Another important point: make sure that you have a common language with anyone you hire – if you don't speak French, make sure the guide speaks your own language well enough for you to understand. Many of them speak enough to point out the obvious features of the things you're seeing, but not enough to be able to answer any questions.

Fès el-Bali

This is the original old walled medina and is the area of most interest to visitors. Its walls encircle the massive medina – an incredible maze of twisting alleys, blind turns, arches, mosques, medressas, shrines, fountains, workshops and every conceivable type of market. Because there are many cemeteries outside the walls and also because of the enlightened policies of General Lyautey (the first French Resident) in siting the *ville nouvelle* well away from the old city, building activity has not taken place immediately outside the walls. Finding your way around, at least for the first couple of times, is very difficult but a delightful way to get lost and found. Even if you do get the feeling that you're irrevocably lost simply keep walking – you'll eventually arrive at one of the enormous gates, though it might not be the one you expected!

There are innumerable sights in this incredible city, and it will take you several days and a great deal of walking to get around just some of them. And while notable buildings – mosques, medressas and the like – are interesting, they aren't really the essence of Fès; most of them, in any case, are closed to non-Muslims. You're much more likely to find the real Fès by letting your senses lead you slowly through the crowded bazaars, pausing wherever the mood takes you to watch something of interest, to rummage through the infinite variety of articles for

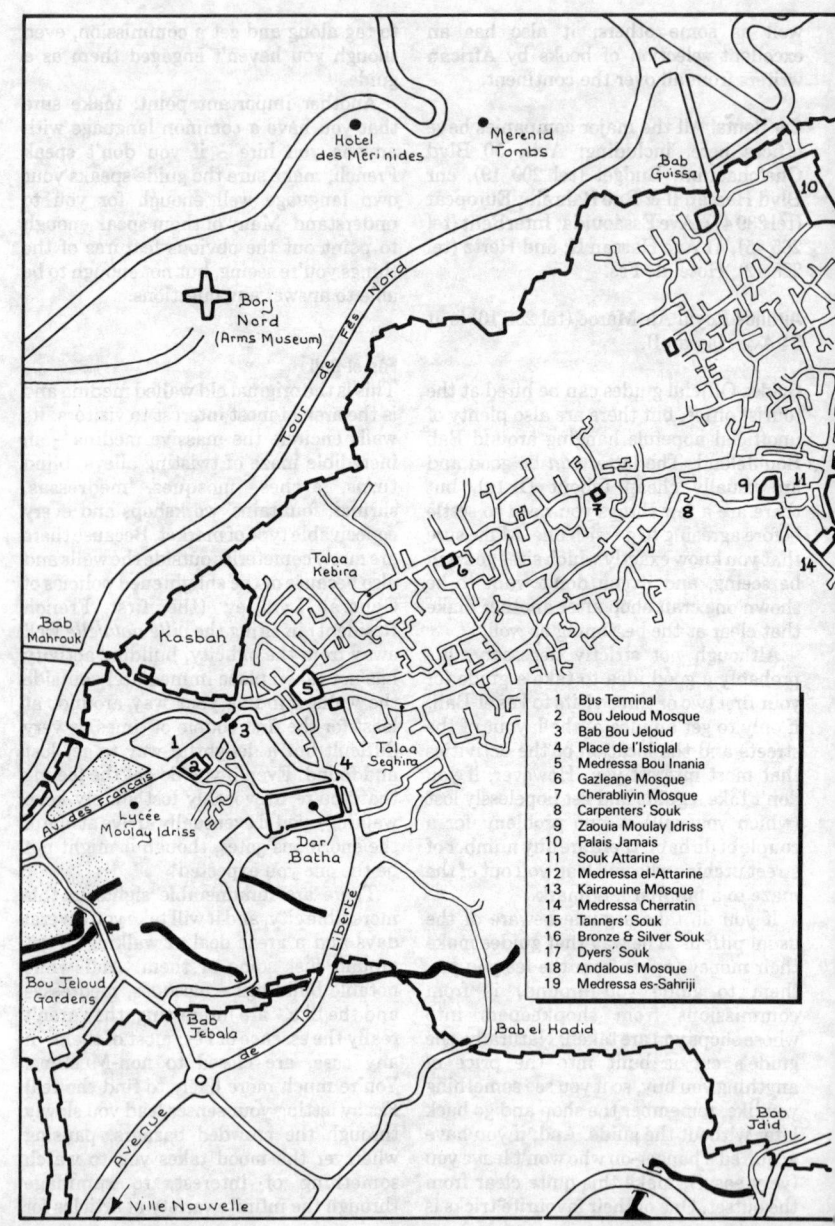

Hotel des Mérinides

Merenid Tombs

Bab Guissa

10

Borj Nord (Arms Museum)

Tour de Fès Nord

Bab Mahrouk

Kasbah

Talaa Kebira

9

11

7

8

14

6

5

Bab Jeloud Gardens

1

3

2

Talaa Seghira

4

Lycée Moulay Idriss

Av. des Français

Dar Batha

Bab Jebala

Avenue de la Liberté

Bab el Hadid

Bab Jdid

Ville Nouvelle

1	Bus Terminal
2	Bou Jeloud Mosque
3	Bab Bou Jeloud
4	Place de l'Istiqlal
5	Medressa Bou Inania
6	Gazleane Mosque
7	Cherabliyin Mosque
8	Carpenters' Souk
9	Zaouia Moulay Idriss
10	Palais Jamais
11	Souk Attarine
12	Medressa el-Attarine
13	Kairaouine Mosque
14	Medressa Cherratin
15	Tanners' Souk
16	Bronze & Silver Souk
17	Dyers' Souk
18	Andalous Mosque
19	Medressa es-Sahriji

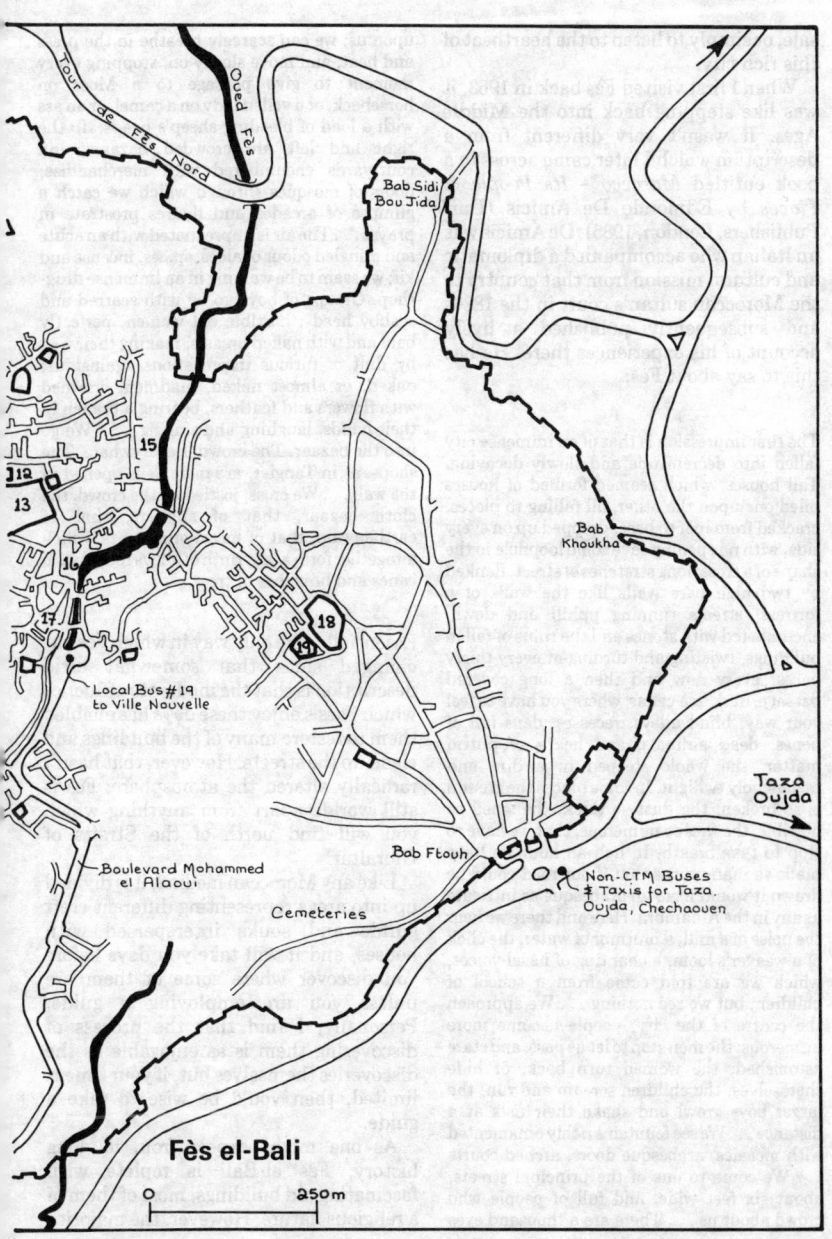

Bab Sidi Bou Jida

Bab Khoukha

Bab Ftouh

Taza
Oujda

Non-CTM Buses
& Taxis for Taza,
Oujda, Chechaouen

Local Bus #19
to Ville Nouvelle

Boulevard Mohammed
el Alaoui

Cemeteries

Tour de Fès Nord

Oued Fès

Fès el-Bali

250m

sale, or simply to listen to the heartbeat of this rich city.

When I first visited Fès back in 1963, it was like stepping back into the Middle Ages. It wasn't very different from a description which I later came across in a book entitled *Morocco – Its People & Places* by Edmondo De Amicis (Darf Publishers, London, 1985). De Amicis was an Italian who accompanied a diplomatic and cultural mission from that country to the Moroccan sultan's court in the 1880s and subsequently published a lively account of his experiences there. He has this to say about Fès:

The first impression is that of an immense city fallen into decrepitude and slowly decaying. Tall houses, which seemed formed of houses piled one upon the other, all falling to pieces, cracked from roof to base, propped up on every side, with no opening save some loophole in the shape of a cross; long stretches of street, flanked by two high bare walls like the walls of a fortress; streets running uphill and down, encumbered with stones and the ruins of fallen buildings, twisting and turning at every thirty paces; every now and then a long covered passage, dark as a cellar, where you have to feel your way; blind alleys, recesses, dens full of bones, dead animals, and heaps of putrid matter; the whole steeped in a dim and melancholy twilight. In some places the ground is so broken, the dust so thick, the smell so horrible, the flies so numerous, that we have to stop to take breath. In half an hour we have made so many turns that if our road could be drawn it would form an arabesque as intricate as any in the Alhambra. Here and there we hear the noise of a mill, a murmur of water, the click of a weaver's loom, a chanting of nasal voices, which we are told come from a school of children, but we see nothing . . . We approach the centre of the city; people become more numerous; the men stop to let us pass, and stare astonished; the women turn back, or hide themselves; the children scream and run; the larger boys growl and shake their fists at a distance . . . We see fountains richly ornamented with mosaics, arabesque doors, arched courts . . . We come to one of the principal streets, about six feet wide, and full of people who crowd about us . . . There are a thousand eyes upon us; we can scarcely breathe in the press and heat, and move slowly on, stopping every moment to give passage to a Moor on horseback, or a veiled lady on a camel, or an ass with a load of bleeding sheep's heads. To the right and left are crowded bazaars; inn courtyards encumbered with merchandise; doors of mosques through which we catch a glimpse of arcades and figures prostrate in prayer . . . The air is impregnated with an acute and mingled odour of aloes, spices, incense and kif; we seem to be walking in an immense drug-shop. Groups of boys go by with scarred and scabby heads; horrible old women, perfectly bald and with naked breasts, making their way by dint of furious imprecations against us; naked, or almost naked, madmen, crowned with flowers and feathers, bearing a branch in their hands, laughing and singing . . . We go into the bazaar. The crowd is everywhere. The shops, as in Tangier, are mere dens opened in the wall . . . We cross, jostled by the crowd, the cloth bazaar, that of slippers, that of earthenware, that of metal ornaments, which altogether form a labyrinth of alleys roofed with canes and branches of trees.

Essentially, the only way in which Fès has changed since that somewhat lurid description is that the moderate affluence which Fassis enjoy these days has enabled them to restore many of the buildings and clean up the streets. However, that hasn't radically altered the atmosphere; Fès is still worlds apart from anything which you will find north of the Straits of Gibraltar.

Like any Moroccan medina, it is divided up into areas representing different craft guilds and souks interspersed with houses, and it will take you days before you discover where some of them are unless you are employing a guide. Personally, I find that the process of discovering them is as enjoyable as the discoveries themselves but, if your time is limited, then you'd be wise to take a guide.

As one might expect from its long history, Fès el-Bali is replete with fascinating old buildings, most of them of a religious nature. However, the majority of them are unfortunately closed to non-Muslims and, because of the incredibly compact nature of this part of the city, little can be seen from the outside. No one particularly minds if you discreetly peer through the doorways, but that's the limit. And that being the case, there's no point in giving you long and detailed descriptions of places you can't visit. The ones which you are allowed to go into can easily all be seen in a day or less.

Bab Bou Jeloud The Bab Bou Jeloud is the main entrance to Fès el-Bali. Although, as at the main entrances to most large Moroccan cities, you will encounter people offering to be guides, there's very little hassle if you tell them you don't want their services. Should they be persistent, tell them you're staying at one of the cheap hotels just inside the gate. If they simply won't let go, sit down and have a mint tea at one of the numerous cafés just inside the gate and wait until they go away.

Medressa Bou Inania Not far from the Bab Bou Jeloud is the Medressa Bou Inania, built by the Merenid sultan Bou Inan between 1350 and 1357 and said to be the finest of the theological colleges built by the Merenids. It has been restored in recent years, and the skill which went into that restoration is proof that Moroccans have lost none of the talents for which they are justly famous. This is one of the few religious buildings which non-Muslims are allowed to enter, and there are excellent views over Fès from the roof. It's open between 8 am and 5 pm (except at prayer times); closed Friday mornings.

Kairaouine Mosque Right down in the guts of the city is the Kairaouine Mosque. This is the largest mosque in Morocco and is said to be capable of holding 20,000 people. It was built between 859 and 862 by Fatma bint Mohammed ben Feheri for her fellow refugees from Tunisia; it was enlarged by the first Fatimid governor and

brought to its present size by the Almoravid sultan Ali ben Youssef. The Almohads and Saadians also contributed to the detail. It contains one of the oldest universities in the world (with an average of 300 students in residence at any one time) and one of the finest libraries in the Muslim world. Unfortunately, non-Muslims are prohibited entry, and it's so hemmed in by other buildings that little can be seen of it from the outside.

Medressa el-Attarine The Medressa el-Attarine was built by Abu Said in 1325 and offers some particularly fine examples of Moroccan work. It's open from 9 am to 12 noon and 2 to 6 pm; closed Friday mornings. There are good views of the courtyard of the Kairaouine Mosque from the roof.

Andalous Quarter The only attractions here are the Andalous Mosque and the Medressa es-Sahriji. The latter was built in 1321. The basic structure of this college is very simple, but the inside is richly decorated and there are good views from the roof. Much of the structure lay in ruins until fairly recently, but restoration work is in progress.

Fès el-Jedid
Fès el-Jedid is the other walled city, built next to Fès el-Bali by the Merenids in the 13th century. Although it has the old Jewish quarter and a couple of mosques, it is far less interesting than Fès el-Bali. However, it does have some spectacular buildings and is much easier to get around. No one will hassle you for guide services here.

The entrance to the Dar el-Makhzen (Royal Palace) on Place des Alaouites is a stunning example of modern restoration work. The grounds cover some 200 acres and consist of palaces, pavilions, medressas, mosques and pleasure gardens; the complex was the site of a recent Arab League conference. It used to be possible to visit the palace with prior permission from the tourist office, but this is no longer possible unless you have political or cultural elbow.

At the northern end of the main street – Grande Rue de Fès el-Jedid – is the enormous Merenid gate of Bab Dekakene, which was formally the main entrance to the royal palace. Between this gate and Bab Bou Jeloud are the Bou Jeloud Gardens, which are very well maintained and a quiet place to relax. Through them flows the Oued Fès, which is still the city's main source of water.

The Grande Rue de Fès el-Jedid, though lined with shops and a few hotels and cafés, lacks the atmosphere of the main street in Fès el-Bali, so it's unlikely you will spend too much time here.

Museum of Moroccan Arts

One place on the border of Fès el-Jedid and Fès el-Bali, which you should not miss, is the Dar Batha, now the Museum of Moroccan Arts. It is on Place de l'Istiqlal, about five minutes' walk from the Bab Bou Jeloud. Built as a palace about 100 years ago by Moulay el-Hassan and Abd el-Aziz, it houses historical and artistic artefacts from ruined or decaying medressas, fine Fassi embroidery, tribal carpets, and ceramics dating from the 14th century to the present. It's open daily, except Tuesday, from 9 am to 12 noon and 3 to 6 pm.

Outskirts

For a spectacular overview of Fès, walk to the end of the Grande Rue de Fès el-Jedid and through the Bab Dekakene; then, instead of turning right towards the Bab Bou Jeloud, continue straight on through the old mechouar and out through the Bab Segma, taking the road which follows the left-hand wall of the Kasbah des Cherarda to the junction with the Tour de Fès Nord. Turn right here and walk down towards the Borj Nord. The whole of Fès lies before you in the valley below.

The Borj Nord itself was a former fortress, built in the late 16th century by the Saadian sultan el-Mansur, who used Christian slaves for labour. It now houses the Arms Museum, which consists mainly of endless rows of muskets and rifles, most of them taken from Riffian rebels in 1958.

Merenid Tombs Further along from here, near the Hotel des Mérinides, are the Merenid Tombs. These date from the time when the Merenids abandoned Chellah in Rabat as their necropolis. Unfortunately, they're in an advanced state of ruin and little remains of the fine work with which they were originally decorated. There are, however, good views over Fès from here.

Places to Stay

Fès is a large city, so where you stay on arrival will depend largely on the time of day and the season. In summer, when many of the smaller hotels tend to fill up towards the end of the day, there's not much point in heading for the far side of town if it's getting late. Take something close to where you are for the first night and have a look around the following morning. Also, in summer many of the cheapies in Fès el-Jedid and Fès el-Bali hike up their prices, and you end up paying the same as you would for far better accommodation in the *ville nouvelle* – not such good value. At this time, too, single rooms in the cheapies are almost impossible to find – hoteliers make more money by letting them out to two or three people at correspondingly double and triple prices.

Places to Stay – bottom end

Fès el-Bali The most colourful and interesting places to stay are the bunch of cheapies clustered around the Bab Bou Jeloud at the entrance to Fès el-Bali. They're all pretty basic and most of them don't have showers (or not a functioning shower), but that's no problem as there's a good hammam very close by with separate times for men and women. The best of the bunch here is the *Hotel du Jardin Public* down a side lane (signposted) just outside the Bab. It's clean, quiet, friendly and good value at Dr 30 a single, Dr 35 a double and Dr 42 a triple. There are a couple of rooms on the 3rd floor with windows in the outside wall; these are preferable to the more claustrophobic lower rooms, which face the internal courtyard, although the upper ones are hotter in summer. The hotel has cold showers.

If the Jardin Public is full, try the nearby *Hotel Erraha* or the *Hotel National* (the latter is down an alley, on the left going uphill from the Erraha). Just inside the Bab, on the right, are another couple of hotels: the *Hotel Mauritania* and the *Cascades*. The latter is probably the better of the two, as the rooms at the Mauritania are very basic and very small. Both charge Dr 25 a single and Dr 30 a double.

Fès el-Jedid If the preceding are full (which they often are late in the day during summer) or if you don't like what's offered but prefer to be as close as possible to the medina, there are three other cheap hotels in Fès el-Jedid. All of them are along the Grande Rue de Fès el-Jedid (the main street), and prices are similar to those at Bab Bou Jeloud. The one closest to the Bab Bou Jeloud, up near the end of the street, is the *Hotel du Parc*, which is clean and good value for money. At the bottom of the street just inside the Bab Smarine (Semmarin) are the *Hotel du Croissant* and the *Hotel Moulay Mishirf*.

New City The new city offers some bottom-end accommodation. The cheapest hotels here are the *Hotel Maghreb*, 25 Ave Mohammed es Slaoui, the *Hotel Regina*, 25 Rue Moulay Slimane and the *Hotel Renaissance*. The Maghreb and the Regina are basic but clean and have no showers. They cost Dr 20 a single, Dr 30 a double and Dr 38 a triple. The Renaissance is an old, cavernous place with an entrance lobby resembling an art gallery. It's friendly and clean, has no showers and

costs the same as the two previous hotels.

Better value than the rest and only slightly more expensive is the *Hotel Volubilis*, Blvd Abdallah Chefchaouni, and, just round the corner from it, the *Hotel Savoy*. At both you can get good, clean, airy rooms with hand basins; there are communal showers (cold water). Rooms cost Dr 30 a single and Dr 35 a double. Very similar is the *Hotel Jeanne d'Arc*, 36 Ave Mohammed es Slaoui, which costs Dr 30 a single and Dr 40 a double.

Youth Hostel The cheapest place in the new city is the *Youth Hostel*, 18 Rue Mohammed el Hansali. It costs Dr 10 per person and there are cold showers. It's a fairly new building, and they will allow you to sleep on the roof if there are no beds left.

Camping For campers, there's a good site at *Camping Moulay Slimane*, Rue Moulay Slimane, which costs Dr 4 per person plus Dr 2 per vehicle. The camp site is very popular with travellers having their own vehicles, so it's an excellent place to ask around for share-expenses lifts, especially if you intend to head off into Algeria and go down through the desert to Niger, Mali and the West African coast. Quite a lot of the people who stay here have vehicles which they intend to sell in Togo, Burkina Faso or the Ivory Coast. There are no tents for hire at the site and the showers have cold water only. There's a swimming pool (often empty) and a shop (expensive).

Places to Stay – middle
The new city also has quite a few middle-range hotels. One you might like to try in this bracket is the *Hotel Restaurant du Pacha*, 32 Ave Hassan II, which offers large, clean, airy rooms overlooking the avenue and has very friendly staff. A double room costs Dr 60 (less in winter).

Those looking for better amenities and hot showers should first check out the

Hotel Central (tel 223 33), 50 Rue Samuel Biarnay at the junction with Blvd Mohammed V, which is a one-star hotel offering excellent value for money. It's friendly, very clean, secure and easy-going. Rooms with own shower (hot water in the mornings and evenings), bidet and hand basin cost Dr 40 a single and Dr 48 a double. Baggage can safely be left in reception if you're catching a late bus or train. Also very comfortable, pleasant and friendly is the *Hotel Royal* (tel 246 56), 36 Rue d'Espagne, which costs Dr 51 a single and Dr 62 a double. All the rooms have their own shower and toilet; there's hot water all day, except occasionally in winter when there are not enough guests to warrant it.

Another hotel which has been recommended is the *Hotel CTM* (tel 228 11), Rue Ksar El Kebir, which charges Dr 57 a double.

The one-star *Hotel Excelsior* (tel 256 02) on Blvd Mohammed V has good doubles with bathroom and hot water for Dr 62, although it is not a good choice if you are catching a late bus or train and want to leave your baggage here during the day – they charge Dr 10 for that privilege!

Places to Stay – top end

There are several top-end places in the new city. These include the five-star *Hotel de Fès* (tel 250 02, 230 56), Ave des Forces Armées Royales, which has 295 rooms, and the four-star *Hotel Sofia* (tel 242 66/67/68), 3 Rue du Pakistan, which has 102 rooms. They both have the usual amenities.

Places to Eat

The best places to find a cheap meal in Fès el-Bali are at the restaurants clustered around the Bab Bou Jeloud and the Bab Guissa; however, the ones around the former are pretty indifferent to quality these days, as they get to see a few too many tourists. The best of the bunch is probably the *Restaurant Bouayad*, next to the Hotel Cascades, which offers reasonable tajine and is open until late at night. The *Restaurant des Jeunes* closer to the gate also has good set meals, although they have two menus and give you the one they think you can afford – one has Dr 25, the other Dr 35 for the same set meal! Good tajines for Dr 15, soup Dr 2 (with bargaining).

There are similar restaurants along the Grande Rue de Fès el-Jedid, close to the Bab Smarine. For something better check out the restaurant in the Bou Jeloud Gardens. This is popular with young Moroccans, but expect to pay considerably more for a meal here.

For a splurge in Fès el-Bali head for the *Palais Jamais*, close to the Bab Guissa, which has a terrace overlooking the medina. The food here is excellent, but you'll be up for a minimum of Dr 140 per person for the sumptuous buffet spread (it's a five-star hotel as well as a restaurant).

In the new city there's a good choice of relatively cheap restaurants along or just off the Blvd Mohammed V, with most of them clustered around the municipal market. Take your pick, but one of the best is the *Sandwich des Etudiants*. This is one block back from Place Mohammed V, on the right when walking towards the post office; it's next door to one of the few liquor stores in Fès. It's a popular place and cheap; a soup, salad, *kefta* and sauce costs about Dr 14. Another very good place (which apparently doesn't have a name) is the blue-and-white tiled restaurant on Rue 5, which is the second street on the left when walking away from Place Mohammed V towards the post office. It's very popular and has an extensive range of food. Prices are very reasonable.

The *Café Restaurant Mounia* at 11 Blvd Med Zerktouni, just around the corner from the Hotel Jeanne d'Arc, is a very stylish place (waiters with bow ties!), but the prices are reasonable and they have a decent wine list.

Something that you should try is the Fassi speciality pastilla (pigeon pie). It is available in some restaurants, where it is expensive, or from the small shops around Place Bou Jeloud, although it is sometimes difficult to find. One place that seems to have it regularly is the tiny shop right on the corner of the Talaa Kebira and the small 10-metre-long lane that connects it with Place Bou Jeloud. The pie is sweet and spicy, but very rich, so half a kg (Dr 15) should be plenty for two people.

Getting There & Away

Air The Fès airport is 15 km to the south of the new city. There are four flights weekly to Casablanca, two per week to Marrakesh and one to Tangier.

Bus - CTM The CTM station is in the new city on Blvd Mohammed V. Tickets can be bought up to five days in advance, and you should buy them as early as possible; demand is high, especially on the Fès-Tangier and Fès-Marrakesh runs, where there is only one bus per day.

There are departures to: Casablanca (seven daily); Marrakesh (one nightly, Dr 76); Rabat (six daily); Oujda (one daily); Tangier (one daily); and Tetouan (one daily).

Bus - non-CTM Private buses use a couple of different stations, both near Fès el-Bali. Buses for Oujda, Chechaouen, Al Hoceima and Taza leave from the station at Bab Ftouh, the south-eastern gate.

Buses to all other parts of the country leave from the station at Place Baghdadi, just up from Bab Bou Jeloud. There is a booking office where you can make reservations for the most popular runs.

Train The railway station is in the new city, 10 minutes' walk from the centre. Trains are the best bet if you are headed for Oujda, Tangier, Rabat, Casa or Marrakesh. The main direct departures are: Oujda (two daily, four hours); Tangier (two daily, 6½ hours); Casablanca (three daily, six hours); Rabat (one direct, and Casa

trains, 4½ hours); and Marrakesh (one daily, eight hours).

Taxi *Grands taxis* leave from a couple of locations: Bab Ftouh for Taza and east, and the streets around the CTM station for Meknès (frequent, fast and convenient, Dr 12) and elsewhere.

Getting Around

Bus Fès has a fairly good local bus service, although the buses are like sardine cans at certain times of the day. The bus number is displayed on the side of the bus, near the back door. Useful routes include: No 3 – Place de la Résistance to Bab Ftouh (for the Andalous Quarter); No 9 – Ave Hassan II to Place de l'Istiqlal (Dar Batha & Bab Bou Jeloud); and No 19 – Railway station to Place Baghdadi.

Taxi The red *petits taxis* are cheap and plentiful. The drivers use the meters without any fuss. Expect to pay about Dr 5 from the CTM station to Bab Bou Jeloud.

Meknès

Although a town of considerable size even in the days of the Merenids (13th century), it wasn't until the 17th century that Meknès experienced its heyday. In 1672, having fought for and won the succession to the throne, Moulay Ismail, the second Alaouite sultan, made Meknès his capital. Over the next 55 years an enormous palace complex surrounded by some 25 km of wall with 20 gates was completed by armies of slaves and workers, often whipped on by Moulay Ismail himself. By the time he died in 1727, Meknès had been transformed out of all recognition.

Yet this wasn't to last. After Moulay Ismail's death, the traditional balance of power between Fès and Marrakesh reasserted itself; two reigns later, under Sultan Sidi Mohammed, the capital was

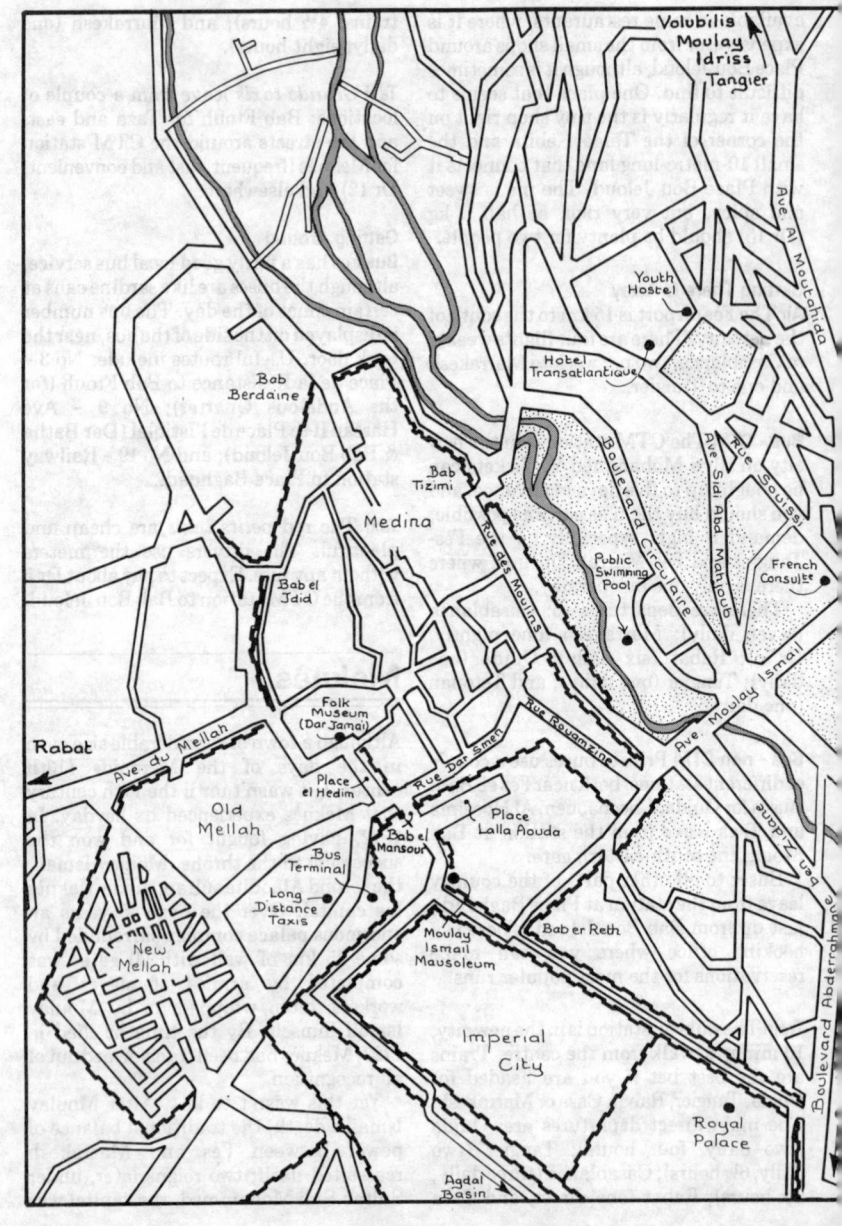

1 GPO
2 Hotel Palace
3 Hotel Touring
4 Hotel Moderne
5 Hotel Majestic
6 Abdelkadar Railway Station
7 Hotel Central
8 CTM Bus Terminal & Hotel Volubilis
9 Hotel Excelsior
10 Hotel Continental

Meknès

0   500m

moved back to Marrakesh. The disastrous earthquake in 1755 which destroyed Lisbon and severely damaged many Moroccan cities also took its toll on Moulay Ismail's constructions. No restoration was undertaken and the city has been allowed to crumble and decay ever since. Nevertheless, enough remains to make a visit to this city well worth while.

Orientation
The old medina and the French-built *ville nouvelle* are neatly divided by the small valley of the Oued Boufekrane. Train and CTM bus connections are in the new city, while the private buses, cheap hotels, camping ground and sights are in the old city. It's a 20-minute walk between the two, although there are regular (and very crowded) local buses as well as *petits taxis*.

Information
Tourist Office The Syndicat d'Initiative is just inside the gates of the Esplanade de la Foire at the top of the valley on Ave Hassan II. However, finding someone actually on duty is a bit of a hit-or-miss affair.

Post The main post office is in the new town on Place de France. In the medina there is another large post office on Rue Dar Smen, near the corner of Rue Rouamzine. Opening hours are Monday to Saturday from 8 am to 2 pm.

Money The banks are concentrated in the new city, mainly on Ave Hassan II and Ave Mohammed V.

Airlines Royal Air Maroc (tel 209 63) has an office at 7 Ave Mohammed V.

Medina
The focus of the old city is the massive gate of Bab el Mansour, the main entrance to Moulay Ismail's 17th-century Imperial City. The gate is exceptionally well preserved and is highly decorated, with (faded) zellij tiles and inscriptions which run right across the top.

The gate faces onto Place el Hedim. On the far north side of this square is the Dar Jamai, a palace built in the late 19th century which has recently been turned into a very good museum. As is often the case in museums housed in historic buildings, the building itself is as interesting as the exhibits. The domed reception room upstairs is fully furnished in the style of the time, complete with plush rugs and cushions. It is open daily, except Tuesday, from 9 am to 12 noon and 3 to 6 pm. Entry costs Dr 3.

The medina proper stretches away to the north behind the Dar Jamai. The most convenient access is through the arch to the left of the Dar Jamai. Though nowhere near as extensive or as interesting as the medina at Fès, it is, nevertheless, worth a visit and you won't be hassled by 'guides'. Most interesting, perhaps, are the carpet souks, which are just off to the left of the main medina street, about five minutes' walk from Dar Jamai. If you are looking for rugs to buy Meknès is not a bad place, as the shopkeepers are a little more relaxed than elsewhere. Bargains are still as rare as hens' teeth, but at least the bargaining starts at a reasonable level.

Further along the covered main street is the Bou Inania Medressa. Like the one of the same name in Fès, it was built in the mid-14th century. It is not all that conspicuous apart from the dome over the street, which is easy to spot. It has the same layout and features as the Fès medressas. It's about the only one where you are allowed up on to the roof, as it has all been restored at one time or another. The Bou Inania Medressa is open daily from 9 am to 12 noon and 3 to 6 pm. Entry costs Dr 3.

Imperial City
A visit to the Imperial City itself starts from the Bab el Mansour. Once through this gate, the road runs straight ahead and then round to the right. On the right here is an open grass area with a small white building, the *koubba*, which was once a

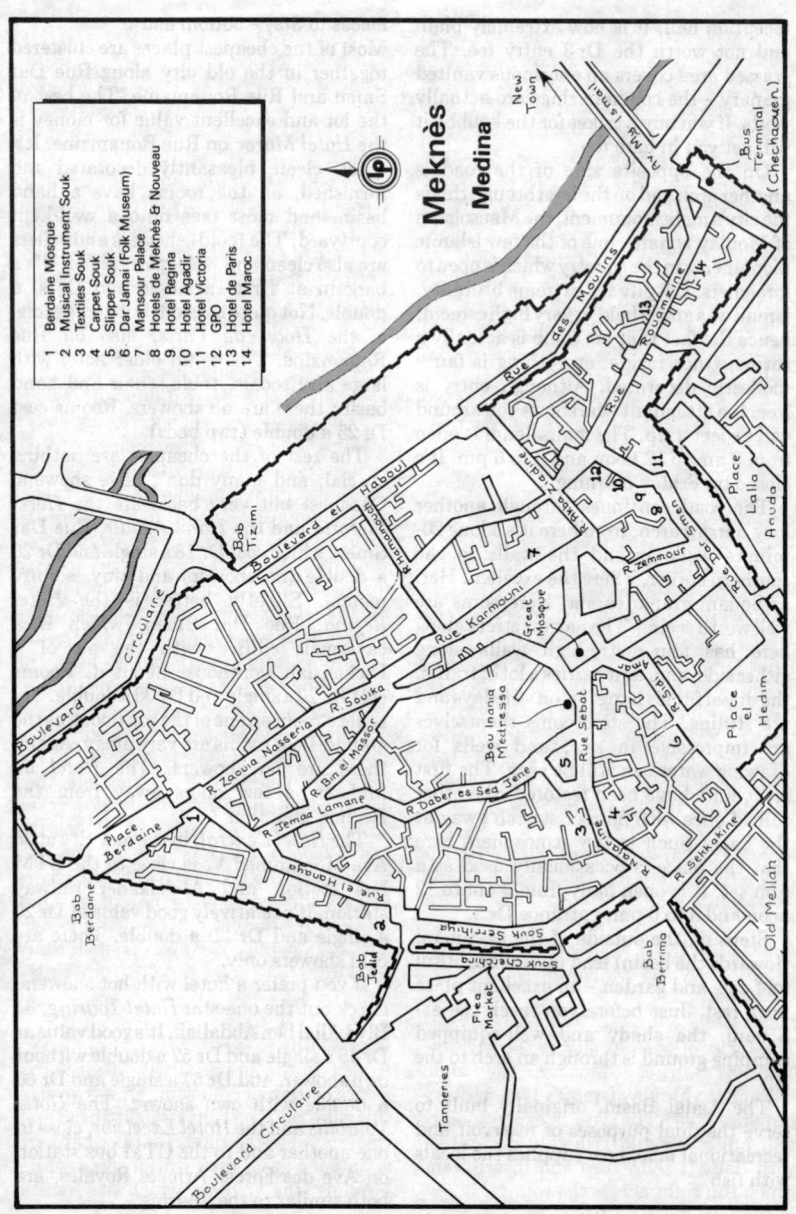

Meknès Medina

New Town

Bus Terminal (Chechaouen)

1 Berdaine Mosque
2 Musical Instrument Souk
3 Textiles Souk
4 Carpet Souk
5 Slipper Souk
6 Dar Jamai (Folk Museum)
7 Mansour Palace
8 Hotels de Meknès & Nouveau
9 Hotel Regina
10 Hotel Agadir
11 Hotel Victoria
12 GPO
13 Hotel de Paris
14 Hotel Maroc

reception hall. It is now extremely plain and not worth the Dr 3 entry fee. The grassed area covers an enormous vaulted granary – the concrete rings are actually vents. If you buy a ticket for the koubba it will get you in here too.

On the opposite side of the road is another arch and on the left through this is the city's main monument, the Mausoleum of Moulay Ismail – one of the few Islamic monuments in the country which is open to foreigners. Despite his extreme brutality, Ismail was and is held in very high esteem; hence the fact that his tomb is actually a shrine. Once inside, everything is fairly modestly decorated. Although entry is free, the attendant who shows you around will expect a tip. The mausoleum is open from 9 am to 12 noon and 3 to 6 pm. It's closed on Friday morning.

The road continues through another long narrow arch; from here it's a long 20-minute walk around the walls to the southern corner, where the excellent Heri as-Souani granaries and storerooms are well worth seeing. The narrow street along here has four-metre-high walls along either side, and, as it carries a lot of traffic, the diesel fumes hang low on still days and are stifling. The storerooms themselves are impressive in size, and wells for drawing water can still be seen. The first few vaults have been restored; the other ruined ones with no roof stretch away at the back. Such is the atmosphere here that the place is occasionally used as a film set. It is open daily from 9 am to 12 noon and 3 to 6 pm; entrance Dr 3.

Steps on the outside of the as-Souani (towards the basin) lead up to a beautiful roof café and garden – an excellent place for a rest. Just before you reach the as-Souani, the shady and well-equipped camping ground is through an arch to the left.

The Agdal Basin, originally built to serve the dual purposes of reservoir and recreational lake, now supplies the locals with fish.

Places to Stay – bottom end

Most of the cheapest places are clustered together in the old city along Rue Dar Smen and Rue Rouamzine. The best of the lot and excellent value for money is the Hotel Maroc on Rue Rouamzine. It's quiet, clean, pleasantly decorated and furnished, all the rooms have a hand basin, and most face onto a well-kept courtyard. The (cold) showers and toilets are also clean and well-maintained. It's a bargain at Dr 20 a single and Dr 30 a double. Not quite as good, but acceptable, is the Hotel de Paris, also on Rue Rouamzine. This is an older hotel with large airy rooms, table, chair and hand basin; there are no showers. Rooms cost Dr 25 a double (two beds).

The rest of the cheapies are nothing special, and many don't have showers. Cheapest but very basic are the Hotel Victoria and the Hotel Agadir, Rue Dar Smen, which cost Dr 18 a single and Dr 20 a double (no showers and tiny, scruffy rooms). Slightly better is the Hotel Regina, Rue Dar Smen, which is a cavernous edifice with the air of a Dickensian workhouse about it. Rooms cost Dr 20 a single and Dr 30 a double. Try to get a room on one of the top floors, as the ground-floor rooms are very dingy. Again, there are no showers. The Hotel de Meknès, a few doors away from the Regina, is similar.

The Hotel Central, in the new city at 35 Ave Mohammed V, is close to the CTM bus station and Abdelkader railway station. It's relatively good value at Dr 20 a single and Dr 30 a double. There are cold showers only.

If you prefer a hotel with hot showers, check out the one-star Hotel Touring, 34 Blvd Allal ben Abdallah. It's good value at Dr 45 a single and Dr 57 a double without own shower, and Dr 57 a single and Dr 66 a double with own shower. The Hotel Volubilis and the Hotel Excelsior, close to one another and to the CTM bus station on Ave des Forces Armées Royales, are both similar to the Touring.

The unclassified *Hotel du Marché* is on Zankat Abou Hassan M'Rini, which is on the corner of the main street, Ave Hassan II. It's reasonable value at Dr 50 a double but it fills up early.

Youth Hostel The *Youth Hostel* is very close to the large Hotel Transatlantique in the new town. You'll see signs for the latter in several places in Meknès, so just follow them to get to the hostel (about a km from the centre). It is open from 8 to 10 am, 12 noon to 3, and 6 to 10.30 pm.

Camping There is an excellent camp site on the south side of the Imperial City right up against the walls, though it's quite a walk if you are on foot. A taxi from the railway station or the CTM bus station costs Dr 10. The camp site is fairly expensive at Dr 10 per person, Dr 5 per vehicle, and Dr 5 for a tent space. However, it has very clean toilets and showers, washing facilities, a shop and a restaurant (three-course meals for Dr 30). Hot showers are Dr 5 extra. The site is open 24 hours.

Places to Stay – middle
Further up-market and more expensive accommodation can be found at the following two-star hotels: the *Hotel Palace* (tel 223 88) Rue de Ghana; the *Hotel Majestic* (tel 220 35), 19 Ave Mohammed V; and the *Hotel Panorama* (tel 227 37) and the *Hotel Continental* (tel 202 00), both of which are on Ave des Forces Armées Royales.

Places to Stay – top end
The five-star *Hotel Transatlantique* (tel 200 02/03) is on Rue El Mériniyine. It has 122 air-conditioned rooms, tennis courts and a swimming pool. The four-star *Hotel Rif* (tel 225 91 to 94) on Zankat Accra has a swimming pool and 120 rooms with air-conditioning.

Places to Eat
Meknès isn't an outstanding city for gastronomic delights, but there are a few cheap places to eat which stand out above the rest. If you are staying in the old town, there's a fair choice of simple restaurants doing standard fare along Rue Dar Smen between the Hotel Regina and Place el Hedim. One of the best is the *Restaurant Economique* at number 123, one of the few with a sign. It's right opposite Bab Jama en Nouar, the gate which takes the traffic, just up from Bab el Mansour. There are a few others along Rue Rouamazine.

In the new town, check out the *Rotisserie Karam* at 2 Ave Ghana near the corner of Ave Hassan II. They do some of the best chips in the country, and the set meal of salad, meat and dessert is good value at Dr 24.

The *Restaurant Walima* at 2 Ave Hassan II near Ave Mohammed V does mostly takeaway stuff, but you can sit upstairs and eat quite cheaply.

For something a bit up-market, try the *Restaurant Gambrinus* on Rue Loubnane opposite the market.

Getting There & Away
Bus – CTM The CTM terminal is on Ave Mohammed V near the junction with Ave des Forces Armées Royales. There are six departures daily to Fès; two to Oujda; seven to Casa and Rabat; and one to Tangier.

Bus – non-CTM Other buses use the terminal just below Place el Hedim in the old city. Regular departures to Fès and elsewhere.

Train The main train station is some way from the centre of the new city, on Ave du Sénégal. It's much more convenient, however, to use the Abdelkader station, one block down and parallel to Ave Mohammed V, as all trains stop here. All trains to or from Fès also stop in Meknès.

Taxi All the *grands taxis* leave from opposite the bus station in the old town, down from Bab el Mansour. There are regular departures to Fès (Dr 12) and Moulay Idriss (for Volubilis) Dr 5.

Getting Around
Bus There are local buses which run between the medina and the new city, but they are invariably chocker and hard to get on at times. Useful routes include: No 2 – Bab Mansour to Blvd Allal ben Abdallah, returning to the medina along Ave Mohammed V; and No 7 – Bab Mansour to CTM station.

Taxi A useful *petit taxi* route, which connects the new and old cities, starts in the new city from Rue de Ghana near the corner of Ave Hassan II, right opposite the Rotisserie Karam. The *petits taxis* are always silver Mercedes with black roofs. Fare is Dr 1.50 per person.

AROUND MEKNES
Volubilis
About 33 km from Meknès is the site of the largest and best-preserved Roman ruins in Morocco. Volubilis dates largely from the 2nd and 3rd centuries AD, though excavations have revealed that the site was originally settled by Carthaginian traders in the 3rd century BC.

Volubilis was one of the Roman Empire's most remote outposts, and capital of the province of Mauretania (as North Africa was then known). Direct Roman rule lasted for only 240 years after the area was annexed by Claudius in 45 AD. Its population of Berbers, Greeks, Jews and Syrians continued to speak Latin and practise Christianity right up until the coming of Islam. The city was finally abandoned only in the 18th century, when its marble was plundered for the building of Moulay Ismail's palaces in Meknès.

If you like ancient ruins, Volubilis is worth a visit. It is an easy day trip from Meknès, and you can also take in the nearby town of Moulay Idriss.

The whole site has been well excavated. Its most attractive feature are the stunning mosaics, made even more so by

Roman mosaic

the fact that they have been left *in situ*. A few officious men in blue coats with whistles patrol the site, making sure you don't do what you shouldn't (ie walk on the mosaics); this is good to see, but they tend to take themselves a bit too seriously at times. The site is open daily from sunrise to sunset and entry is Dr 15.

The major points of interest are in the northern part of the site, although it's convenient to start at the south. Once over the Oued Fertassa, the path from the entrance takes you through an unremarkable residential quarter. The House of Orpheus, a little higher up and identifiable by the three pine trees growing in the corner, was a sumptuous mansion for one of the city's wealthier residents. Its two mosaics, one representing the Orpheus myth and the other the chariot of Amphitrite, are still in place.

The basilica, capitol and forum are, typically, built on a high point. The

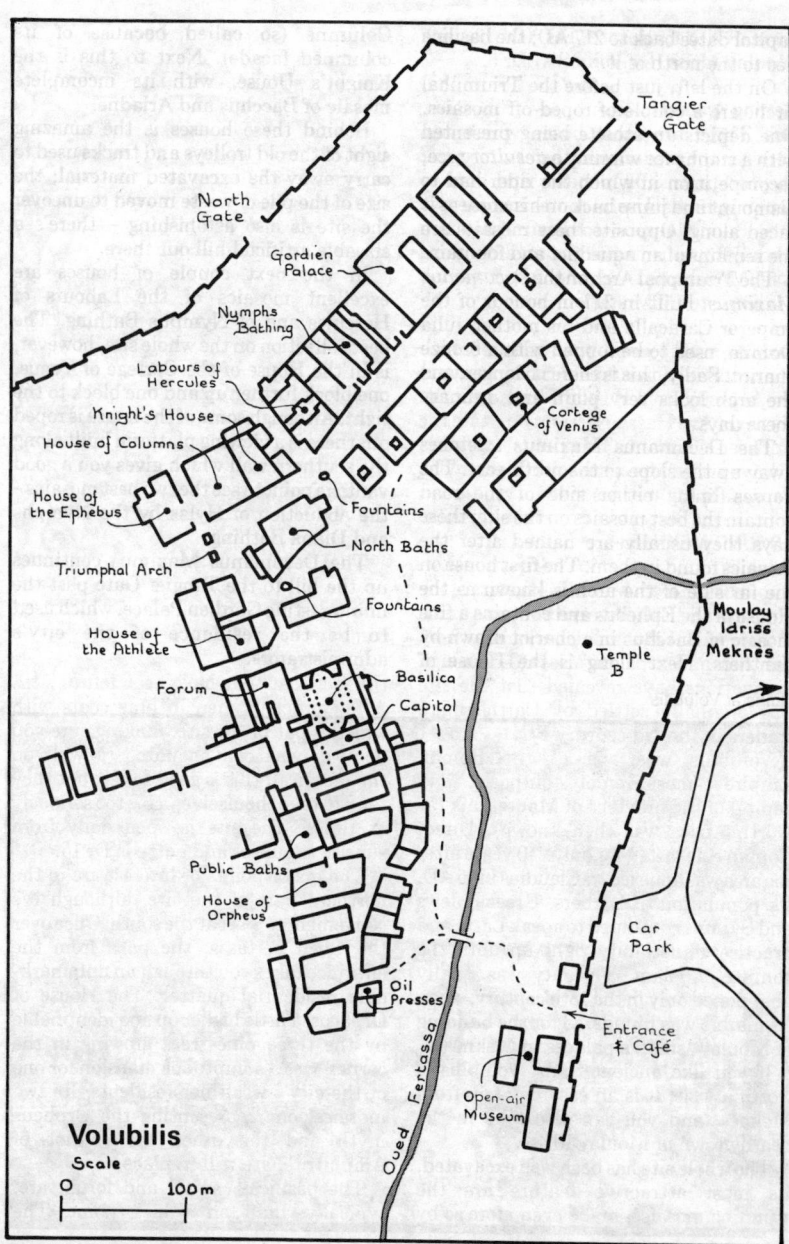

North Gate

Gordien Palace

Nymphs Bathing

Labours of Hercules

Knight's House

House of Columns

House of the Ephebus

Triumphal Arch

House of the Athlete

Forum

Public Baths

House of Orpheus

Oil Presses

Tangier Gate

Cortege of Venus

Fountains

North Baths

Fountains

Moulay Idriss Meknès

Temple B

Basilica

Capitol

Car Park

Entrance & Café

Open-air Museum

Oued Fertassa

Volubilis

Scale

0   100 m

capitol dates back to 217 AD; the basilica lies to the north of it.

On the left, just before the Triumphal Arch, are a couple of roped-off mosaics. One depicts an athlete being presented with a trophy for winning a *desultor* race, a competition in which the rider had to dismount and jump back on his horse as it raced along. Opposite these mosaics are the remains of an aqueduct and fountain.

The Triumphal Arch on the *Decumanus Maximus*, built in 217 in honour of the emperor Caracalla and his mother Julia Domna, used to be topped with a bronze chariot. Sadly, this is there no longer, and the arch looks very plain and ordinary these days.

The Decumanus Maximus stretches away up the slope to the north-east. The houses lining either side of the road contain the best mosaics on the site; these days they usually are named after the mosaics found in them. The first house on the far side of the arch is known as the House of the Ephebus and contains a fine mosaic of Bacchus in a chariot drawn by panthers. Next along is the House of Columns (so called because of its columned facade). Next to this is the Knight's House, with its incomplete mosaic of Bacchus and Ariadne.

Behind these houses is the amazing sight of the old trolleys and tracks used to carry away the excavated material; the size of the pile of waste moved to uncover the site is also astonishing – there's a sizeable artificial hill out there.

In the next couple of houses are excellent mosaics of the Labours of Hercules and of Nymphs Bathing. The best collection on the whole site, however, is in the House of the Cortege of Venus, one block further up and one block to the right. Although some of the house is roped off, there is a viewing platform built along the southern wall which gives you a good vantage point to see the two best mosaics – the abduction of Hylas by the Nymphs and Diana Bathing.

The Decumanus Maximus continues up the hill to the Tangier Gate past the uninteresting Gordien Palace, which used to be the residence of the city's administrators.

Ruins at Volubilis

Back at the entrance, there is a good café where you can rehydrate yourself.

Getting There & Away To get to Volubilis from Meknès it's best to get a small group together and hire a taxi from just below Place el Hedim in the old city (about Dr 6 per person each way, not including waiting time).

Alternatively, there are buses to nearby Moulay Idriss which leave when full from the same place and cost Dr 3.50 each way. There are also *grands taxis* to Moulay Idriss, which are more frequent than the buses. If you take the bus or a *grand taxi*, ask the driver to drop you off at the turn off (signposted) about two km from Moulay Idriss at the bottom of the hill, and walk from there (a further 2½ km). As long as it's not stinking hot, it is a pleasant one-hour walk. There is a good chance of being able to hitch a lift back to Meknès with tourists from the car park at the site.

Moulay Idriss
The other main place of interest outside Meknès is Moulay Idriss, about 4½ km from Volubilis. The town is named after its founder, Morocco's most revered saint, a great-grandson of the Prophet and the founder of the country's first Arab dynasty. Moulay Idriss fled Damascus in the late 8th century AD after the great civil war which split the Muslim world into the Shia and Sunni sects.

Moulay Idriss is certainly a very attractive town when seen from a distance, as it nestles in a cradle of lush mountains. It is heavily promoted in the tourist literature, but the town itself is a profound disappointment.

For Moroccans it's a place of pilgrimage, and non-Muslims can well get the feeling that they are only grudgingly tolerated (it's been open to infidels only for the last 70 years or so). You cannot visit any of the mosques or shrines and you are not allowed to stay overnight. This being so, it's hardly worth the effort. However, if you do want to check it out take a taxi

(Dr 6) or bus (Dr 3.50) from just below Place el Hedim in the old city. These are the same taxis and buses which you take from Meknès to Volubilis.

If you do decide to go, the best day to do so is Saturday; this is market day and the place is a lot more lively than at other times. There are also many more buses and *grands taxis* making the trip, in the morning at least.

AZROU

Azrou is a primarily Berber town. It's a very pleasant place in which to relax in the mountains surrounded by pine forests, when you've had enough of souks and handicraft hustlers down on the plains. There's not a great deal to do other than trek into the mountains, but the people are very friendly and there is absolutely no hassle. It's another dimension of Morocco.

Places to Stay - bottom end
Behind the main street is a small square around which you'll find four budget hotels – the *Hotel Ziz*, the *Hotel Atlas*, the *Hotel Beau Séjour* and the *Hotel Salam*. The first three are all about the same standard, and cost Dr 17 single and Dr 20 to Dr 25 a double. None of them have hot water (and it's cold in the mornings at this altitude - 1250 metres). The Ziz is parsimonious with blankets, too, and it's a hassle to get more out of the management. The Hotel Salam, which is more modern, is slightly better and costs Dr 30 a double.

For only a little more you can stay at the one-star *Hotel des Cèdres* (tel 23 26), Place Mohammed V, which has large, airy, comfortable and spotlessly clean rooms with hot showers at no extra cost at any time of day. The staff are very friendly and it costs Dr 30 a single and Dr 40 a double without own bathroom; Dr 55 a single and Dr 64 a double with own bathroom. Meals, however, are expensive at Dr 35.

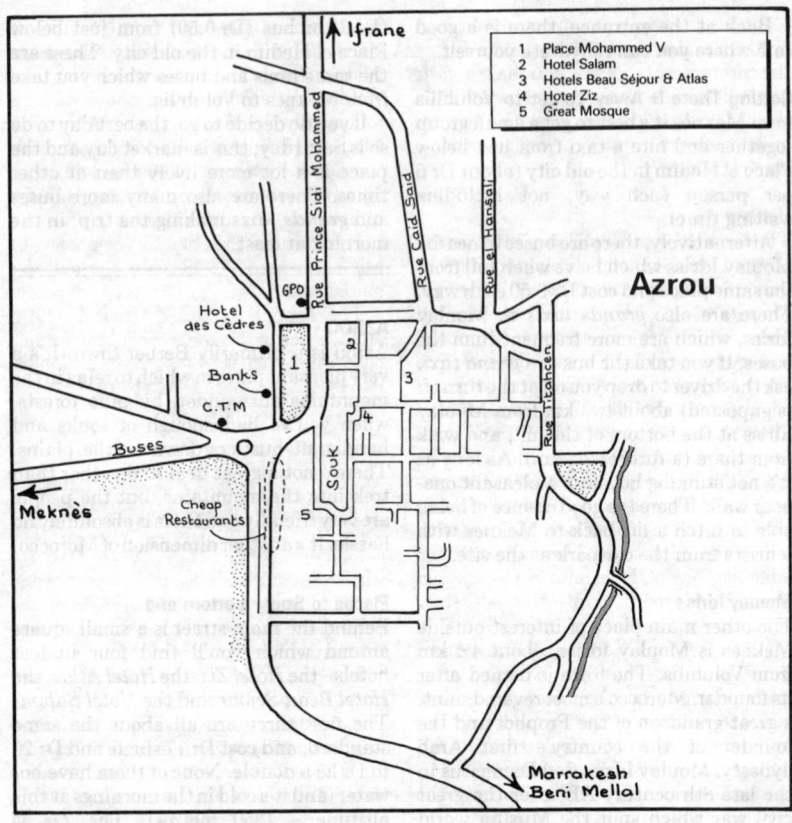

1	Place Mohammed V
2	Hotel Salam
3	Hotels Beau Séjour & Atlas
4	Hotel Ziz
5	Great Mosque

Youth Hostel The *Youth Hostel* is on the Route du Midelt and has 40 beds.

Places to Stay – middle

The two-star *Hotel Panorama* (tel 20 10) has 36 rooms with heating.

Places to Eat

The cheapest restaurants are those clustered on the street opposite the park below the main roundabout. You can get a good meal here for around Dr 10 to Dr 15. Two pieces of fish, sauce, salad, bread and tea at one of these restaurants costs Dr 15 and is very tasty.

Things to Buy

A visit to the Co-opérative Artisanale on the right-hand side on the road to Khenifra (signposted) is well worth while. Here you can find work in cedar and iron, as well as Berber carpets typical of the Middle Atlas.

TAZA

Despite its tempestuous history, Taza is a relatively quiet city these days. Nevertheless, it is worth a visit if you are passing through the area going to or coming from Algeria, if only for the views and the crumbling fortifications.

Since it was an important French military and administrative centre during the protectorate, Taza too has a *ville nouvelle* which, as usual, is separate from the old town. However, here the two are quite some distance from each other – three km in fact.

History

The fortified citadel of Taza, built on the edge of an escarpment overlooking the only feasible pass between the Rif Mountains and the Middle Atlas, has been important throughout Morocco's history as a garrison town from which to exert control over the eastern extremities of the country. The Taza Gap, as it is known, has provided the traditional invasion route for armies moving west from Tunisia and Algeria. The Romans and the Arabs entered Morocco via this pass, and the town itself was the base from which the Almohads, Merenids and the Alaouites swept down onto Fès to conquer lowland Morocco and establish their respective dynasties.

All the various Moroccan sultans had a hand in fortifying Taza. Nevertheless, their control over the area was always tenuous, since the fiercely independent and rebellious local tribes were always willing to exploit any weakness in the central power in order to overrun the city.

Taza's most notable inhabitant, however, was Bou Hamara, who lived here at the end of the 19th century and who almost succeeded in usurping the Moroccan throne. Accused of intrigues by the Alaouite sultan, he was imprisoned and later went into exile in Algeria. Several years later he returned disguised as a devout traveller and quickly established a widespread reputation as a marabout (saint).

Taking advantage of the unpopularity of Sultan Abd el-Aziz, who was accused of conspiring with the Christians, Bou Hamara had himself proclaimed sultan, raised the standard of revolt among the neighbouring tribes and for the next seven years fought a successful campaign against the central authorities. With final victory within his grasp, however, his followers were trounced by the army of Moulay Hafid, who had succeeded his brother as sultan. Thousands of his followers were butchered and Bou Hamara himself was captured, brought to Fès in a cage and there, jeered at by the people, he was thrown to the lions in the sultan's menagerie.

The French occupied Taza in 1914, after which it became the main French base from which they fought the prolonged rebellion against their rule by the tribes of the Rif and Middle Atlas.

City Walls

Most of the city walls, which have a circumference of about three km, date from the time of the Almohads (12th century). Since they have had to withstand many sieges, they are ruined in parts. There's also a solid bastion at one corner of the town, which was built by the Saadians in the 16th century.

The most interesting part of a trip around the walls is the Bab er Rih (Gate of Winds), from which there are incredible views over the surrounding countryside. On the extreme left you can see the wooded slopes of Mt Tazzeka and before that, across the Oued Taza, the terraced gardens and dry ravines of the foothills of the Rif. On the right, below the park, is the *ville nouvelle*, with the Rif Mountains in the distance.

Great Mosque

Not far from the Bab er Rih is the Great Mosque, which was begun by the Almohads in 1135 and added to by the Merenids in the 13th century. Non-Muslims are not allowed to enter. Stretching from here down to the far end of the old town is the main thoroughfare (Rue Kettanine/Rue Nejjarine/Rue Koubet/Rue Sidi Ali Derrar). This is perhaps the most interesting part of town: there are many

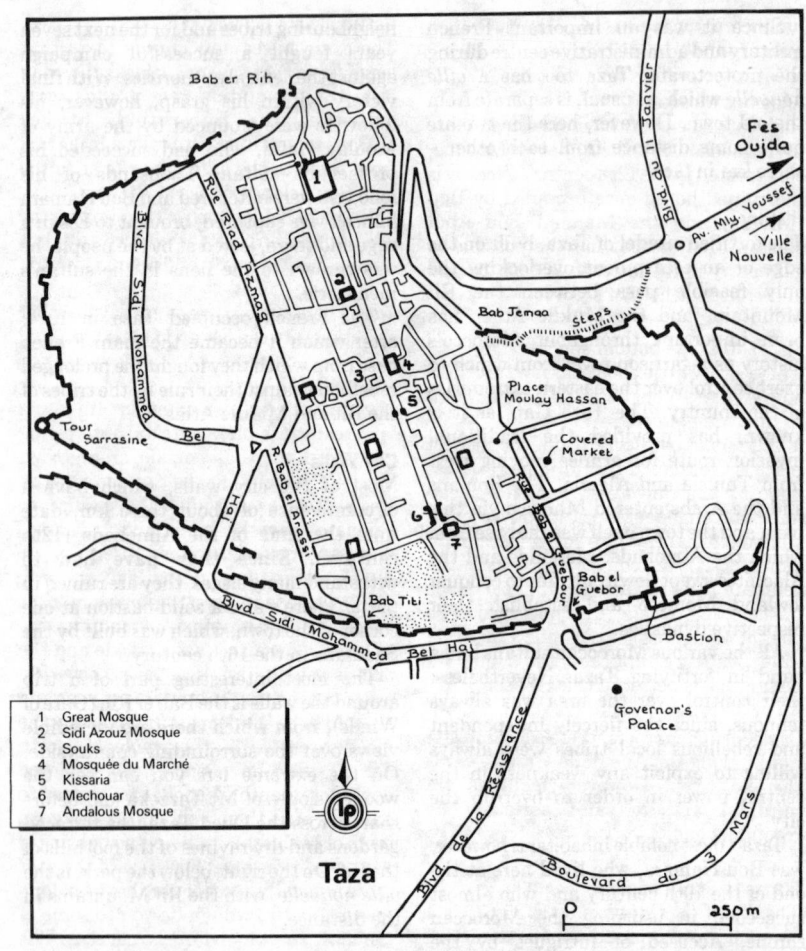

1 Great Mosque
2 Sidi Azouz Mosque
3 Souks
4 Mosquée du Marché
5 Kissaria
6 Mechouar
7 Andalous Mosque

Taza

examples of richly decorated doorways and, occasionally, windows high up in the walls are guarded by very old, carved cedar screens.

Souks

The souks are about halfway down the street, around the Mosquée du Marché; they are of minor interest unless you are searching for second-hand European clothing. However, there are a few shops which offer mats and carpets woven by the Beni Ouarain tribe in the surrounding mountains.

Most of the shops cater for household necessities and foodstuffs as do the ones in the nearby *kissaria*. Whilst in this part of the city don't miss the minaret of the Mosquée du Marché, which is perhaps unique in Morocco in that its upper part is wider than its base.

Andalous Mosque

Right at the end of the main street, close to the mechouar, is the Andalous Mosque, constructed in the 12th century. Nearby is the ruined house once occupied by Bou Hamara, and the Merenid Bou Abul Hassan Medressa. It may be possible to gain entry to the latter if you ask around and enlist the help of a guide.

Places to Stay – bottom end

There's very little choice, as few travellers stop off here. What hotels there are, are all in the *ville nouvelle*.

If arriving by bus or train, the nearest place is the *Hotel de la Gare*, more or less opposite the railway station. It's cheap and plain but adequate, and convenient if you want to be near the transport terminals. However, it is not convenient as far as the centre of town – Place de l'Indépendence in the *ville nouvelle* – is concerned. The cheap unnamed hotel on Place de l'Indépendence, opposite the Hotel du Dauphine, is better in this respect.

Camping For campers, there's a camp site uphill along the Ave de la Gare towards the old town. However, facilities are minimal and it can't seriously be recommended.

Places to Stay – middle

The *Hotel du Dauphine* (tel 35 67) is a two-star hotel housed in an attractive colonial-style building and is the best place to stay if you have the money. It has its own very good restaurant and bar. There's a three-star hotel, the *Hotel Friouato* (tel 25 93), further out of town but it's quite a walk away and not worth the extra expense.

Places to Eat

All the main restaurants are along Ave de Tetouan off Place de l'Indépendence.

Getting There & Away

There are buses and *grands taxis* that leave for Fès several times the day from the bus station. The *grands taxis* arrive at the Bab Ftouh in Fès el-Bali, so you'll need to take a local taxi from there to the *ville nouvelle* or to the Bab Bou Jeloud.

Buses to Nador and Al Hoceima on the Mediterranean coast leave twice a day but usually between 4.30 and 5 am.

Train There are four trains per day in either direction between Fès and Oujda via Taza.

AROUND TAZA

If you have your own transport (hitching isn't really feasible), there's an interesting day trip you can make around Mt Tazzeka, which takes in the Cascades de Ras el-Oued (waterfalls), the Gouffre du Friouato (caves), Daïa Chiker (a lake), and the gorges of the Oued Zireg.

The waterfalls and the lake are only really worth visiting in the winter months since, during the dry summer months, the falls are reduced to just a trickle and the lake is usually dry. The caves, however, are worth visiting at any time of year and are said to be the deepest and possibly the most extensive in the whole of North Africa; they have only been explored down to a depth of about 200 metres to date. To visit them you will need a good torch or flashlight, as there's no lighting of any sort down there. For most of the year there is usually a local guardian who, for a reasonable tip, will guide you to some of the most spectacular of the caverns. The caves are about 45 minutes' walk up the hillside to the right of the main track – signposted 'Gouffre'. You may be able to get a lift from Taza with tourists visiting the caves but don't count on it. The alternative is to get a small group together and hire a taxi to take you there.

Lake Chiker is a geological curiosity associated with fault lines in the calciferous rock structure; it is connected to a subterranean reservoir whose water is

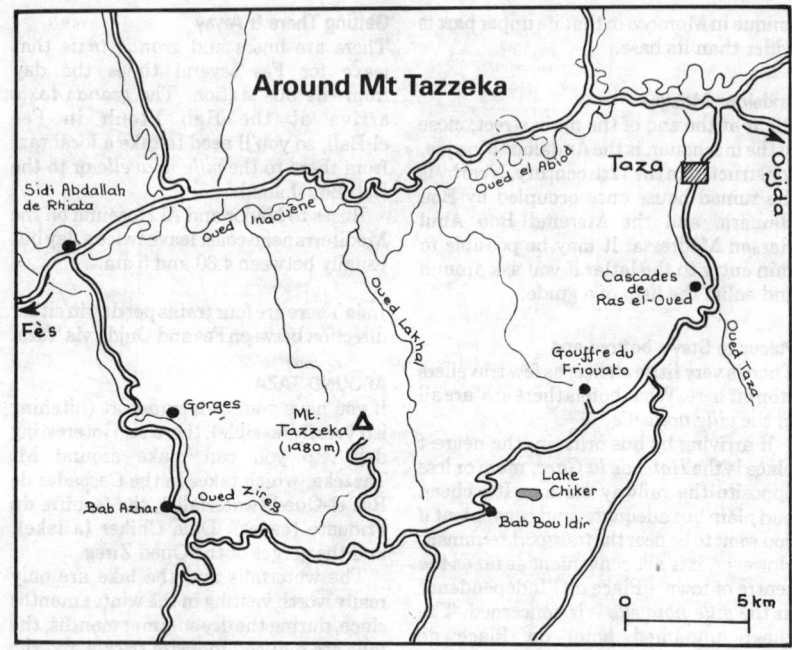

Around Mt Tazzeka

Taza

Oujda

Oued el Abiod

Sidi Abdallah de Rhiata

Oued Inaouène

Fès

Oued Lakhal

Cascades de Ras el-Oued

Oued Taza

Gouffre du Friouato

Gorges

Mt. Tazzeka (1980 m) ▲

Lake Chiker

Bab Azhar

Oued Zireg

Bab Bou Idir

0   5 km

highly charged with carbon dioxide. Depending on the season and the state of affairs in the subterranean reservoir, the surface of the lake can change dramatically. The nearby Grottes du Chiker (caves) at the northern end of the lake have been explored and are said to give access to a five-km-long underground river, but they are not open to casual visitors.

The other main attraction of this route is, of course, an ascent of Mt Tazzeka itself (1980 metres), from the summit of which there are incredible views over the surrounding countryside. While it can be done by those with little mountain experience, it helps if you have done this sort of thing before. There is a *piste* as far as a TV relay station, about nine km off to the right from the main track, where cars can be left. Unlike with Mt Toubkal outside Marrakesh, there are no guidebooks available to help you with information

about this mountain; all that's available are a few hard-to-find articles in French mountaineering publications.

OUJDA

This is the last town before the Algerian border and, if you have just come from Algeria, make the most of the very relaxed, un-Moroccan atmosphere – there is no hassling, apart from the occasional offers to change money.

The town itself is of little interest – the medina is quite small and the French new city lacks character. If you arrive from Tlemcen during the day and are heading for Fès, there are evening trains which will get you there early the next morning.

Information

Post The main post office is in the centre on the main street, Ave Mohammed V.

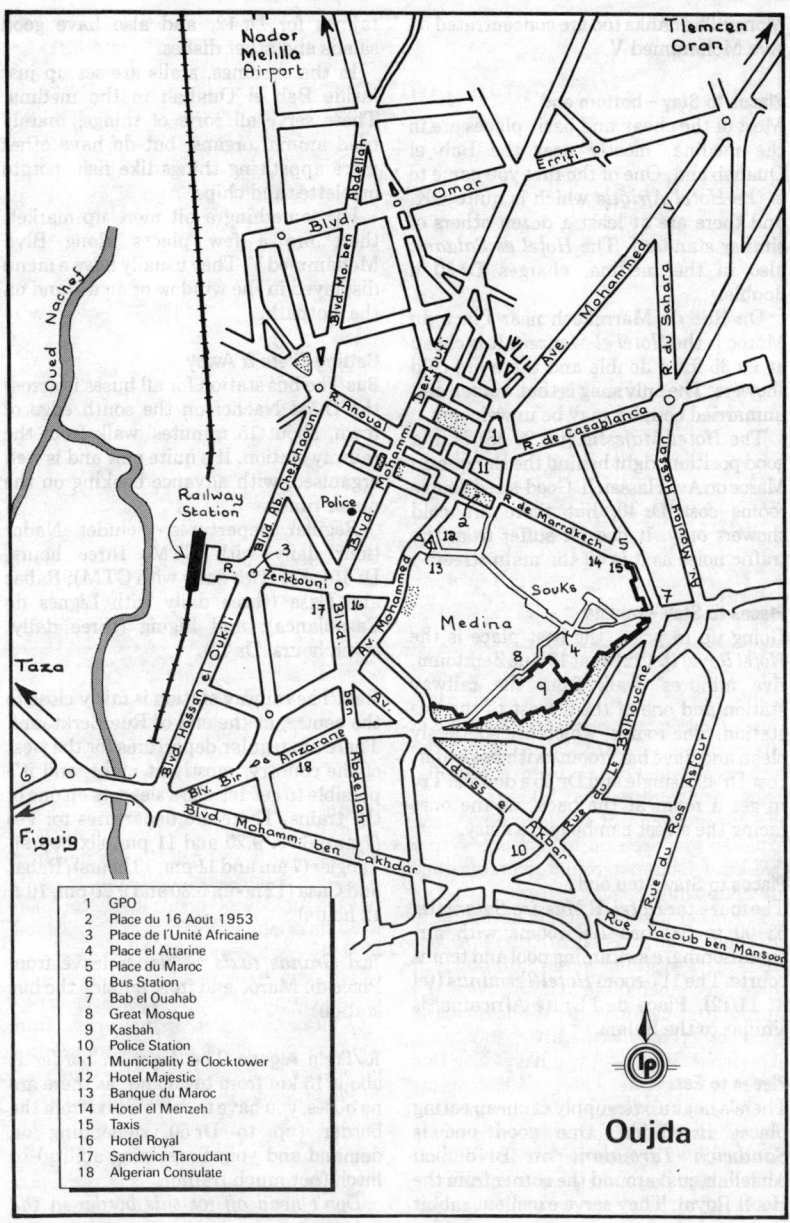

Nador
Melilla
Airport

Tlemcen
Oran

Blvd. ben Abdellah

Omar

Erciti

Blvd. Mo hammed

Ave. Mohammed

R. de Sahara

R. Derkoui

R. Anoual

R. de Casablanca

Gare d'Oujda

Blvd. Ab Chechaouni

R. Moh med

Blvd.

R. de Marrakech

Railway
Station

Police

Hassan II

R. Zerktouni

Souks

Medina

Av. Mohammed

ben

Abdellah

Av.

Idriss el

Oued Nachef

Taza

Figuig

Blvd. Hassan el Oukili

Blvd. Bir Anzarane

Blv.

Blvd. Mohamm. ben Lakhdar

Rue du Ras Astour

Rue Yacoub ben Mansour

Rue du Rt. Belhoucine

Balhoucine

1 GPO
2 Place du 16 Aout 1953
3 Place de l'Unité Africaine
4 Place el Attarine
5 Place du Maroc
6 Bus Station
7 Bab el Ouahab
8 Great Mosque
9 Kasbah
10 Police Station
11 Municipality & Clocktower
12 Hotel Majestic
13 Banque du Maroc
14 Hotel el Menzeh
15 Taxis
16 Hotel Royal
17 Sandwich Taroudant
18 Algerian Consulate

Oujda

Money The banks too are concentrated on Ave Mohammed V.

Places to Stay - bottom end

Most of the cheap and basic places are in the medina, mostly near the Bab el Ouahab end. One of the first you come to is the *Hotel Afrique* which is quite OK, and there are at least a dozen others of similar standard. The *Hotel es Salaam*, also in the medina, charges Dr 30 a double.

On Rue de Marrakech near Place du Maroc is the *Hotel el Menzeh*. It is cheap at Dr 35 for a double and there are cold showers. The only snag is that women and unmarried couples may be unwelcome.

The *Hotel Majestic* (tel 29 48) is in a good position, right behind the Banque du Maroc on Ave Hassan II. Good-sized double rooms cost Dr 40, but there are cold showers only. It doesn't suffer from the traffic noise as it is off the main street.

Places to Stay - middle

Going up in price, the best place is the *Hotel Royal* (tel 22 84) at 13 Rue Zerktouni, five minutes' walk from the railway station and one of the closest to the bus station. The rooms, which are spotlessly clean and have bathrooms with hot water, cost Dr 49 a single and Dr 65 a double. Try to get a room at the back, as the ones facing the street can be quite noisy.

Places to Stay - top end

The four-star *Hotel Al Massira Salam* (tel 53 00 to 03) has 108 rooms with air-conditioning, a swimming pool and tennis courts. The 117-room *Hotel Terminus* (tel 32 11/12), Place de l'Unité Africaine, is similar to the Salam.

Places to Eat

There's not an oversupply of cheap eating places in Oujda. One good one is *Sandwich Taroudant* on Blvd ben Abdellah, just around the corner from the Hotel Royal. They serve excellent rabbit

tajines for Dr 12, and also have good salads and other dishes.

In the evenings, stalls are set up just inside Bab el Ouahab in the medina. These serve all sorts of things, mainly fried animal organs, but do have other more appetising things like fish, potato omelettes and chips.

For something a bit more up-market, there are a few places along Blvd Mohammed V. They usually have a menu displayed in the window or on a stand on the footpath.

Getting There & Away

Bus The bus station for all buses is across the Oued Nachef on the south edge of town, about 15 minutes' walk from the railway station. It's quite new and is well organised, with advance booking on the major runs.

Regular departures include: Nador (four daily with CTM, three hours, Dr 15); Fès (two daily with CTM); Rabat and Casa (three daily with Lignes de Casablanca); and Figuig (three daily, seven hours, Dr 42).

Train The railway station is fairly close to the centre, at the end of Rue Zerktouni. There are regular departures for the west of the country, mostly at night, and it's possible to get 1st-class sleepers on one of the trains. There are departures to: Fès (7 am, 6.30, 9.20 and 11 pm, six hours); Tangier (7 am and 11 pm, 13 hours); Rabat and Casa (12 noon, 6.30 and 9.20 pm, 10 & 12 hours).

Taxi *Grands taxis* to Nador leave from Place du Maroc and from outside the bus station.

To/From Algeria The Algerian border is about 13 km from town and, as there are no buses, you have to catch a taxi from the border (up to Dr 50, depending on demand and your bargaining ability) or hitch (not much traffic).

Don't head off for this border in the

hope of being allowed to cross on foot – the Algerians don't allow it!

People with their own vehicles face no such difficulties and the crossing is straightforward in either direction. The only thing you should be aware of when taking a vehicle to Morocco from Algeria, is that you must have a telex from your embassy in Rabat stating that you will be exporting the vehicle. These letters usually take a couple of weeks for your embassy to organise, so don't leave it till the last minute. The telex gets sent to the border post where you will be entering the country. Although this telex is supposedly compulsory, it is often possible to get through with just a green card or carnet.

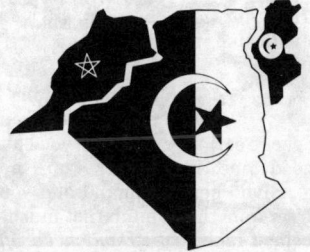

The High Atlas

The Coast

AGADIR

Agadir was destroyed by an earthquake in 1960 and, although it's now been rebuilt, it's hardly a typical Moroccan city any longer. Most of the activity here centres around catering for the short-stay package tourists from Europe, who flock in by the plane-load daily in search of sun, sand and an acceptably sanitised version of the mysteries of the Barbary Coast.

The reek of Ambre Soleil and the rustle of *Paris Match*, *Der Spiegel* and the airmail *Sunday Times* fills the air. Not that it's unpleasant – it's just that it could be any resort town on the northern Mediterranean coast. Agadir is also one of the more expensive cities in Morocco.

However, it's the take-off point for visits east and further south, so you'll probably have to stay here overnight at least.

Information

Tourist Office The national tourist office is on Ave Prince Sidi Mohammed; there's also a Syndicat d'Initiative on Blvd Mohammed V at the junction with Ave du Général Kettani. Both places offer a free map of Agadir but are otherwise not much help to budget travellers.

Consulates There are consulates for Belgium, Finland, France, Italy, Norway and Spain.

Places to Stay – bottom end

Most of the budget hotels and a few of the

Ruined village near Ait-Baha

142

Selling baskets beside the road

mid-range hotels are clustered around the bus terminal area and along Rue Allal ben Abdallah. In the high seasons you must get into Agadir early in the day if you want to be sure of a room. If you arrive late you may have to sleep out or pay through the nose at an expensive hotel. Disappointed backpackers wandering around with nowhere to go are a common sight by 8 pm.

Best value is the *Hotel Amenou*, a fairly new hotel, which is very clean and has a really pleasant decor and furnishings. It costs Dr 31 a single and Dr 42 a double without own bathroom. The communal bathrooms have hot showers and, although you're supposed to pay an extra Dr 3 for this, they rarely ask.

If the Amenou is full, try the *Hotel Tifaut*, which costs Dr 35 a single and Dr 50 a double, or the *Hotel Excelcior*, which costs Dr 30 a single and Dr 42 a double without own bathroom, and Dr 60 a double with own bathroom. Both these hotels will tell you they have hot water but it's sometimes a long time coming at the latter.

Going down Rue Allal ben Abdallah, try the *Hotel Select*, the *Hotel Diaf* or the *Hotel de la Braie*. The latter costs Dr 29 a single and Dr 38 a double without own bathroom, and Dr 44 a single and Dr 50 a double with own bathroom. It's a clean place and there's hot water in the showers.

Similar to these is the *Hotel de Paris*, Ave du Président Kennedy, which is clean and comfortable but has no hot water. It costs Dr 32 a single and Dr 44 a double. Breakfast is available for Dr 6.

Avoid the *Hotel Hassa* if possible. It's

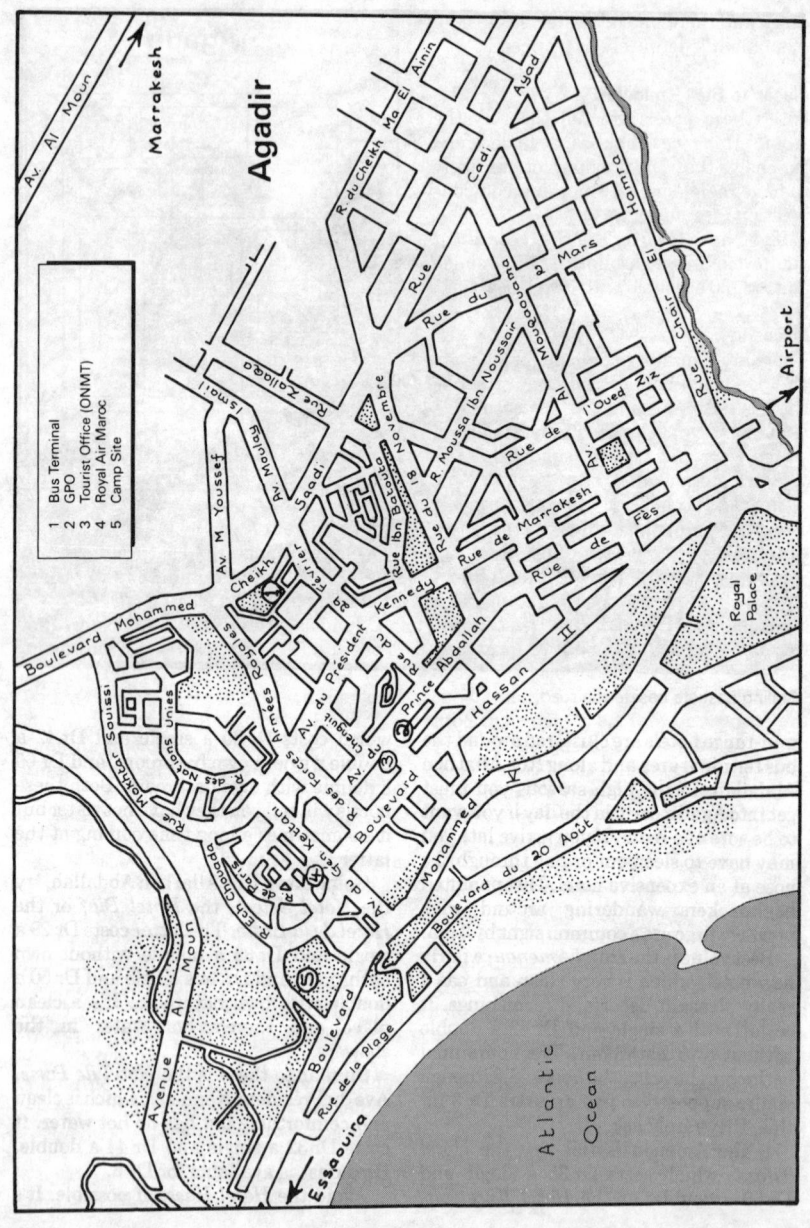

Agadir

Marrakesh

Essaouira

Airport

Atlantic Ocean

1 Bus Terminal
2 GPO
3 Tourist Office (ONMT)
4 Royal Air Maroc
5 Camp Site

dingy and there's no hot water, so at Dr 40 a double it's definitely overpriced.

Places to Stay - middle

If all these hotels are full then try the *Hotel Moderne*. This is a little more expensive than the previous lot but likely to have room, since it's not in an obvious position (see map).

If you have to go for the *Hotel Sindibad* you're looking at around Dr 95 a single and Dr 130 a double with own bathroom.

Places to Eat

There are a number of cheap restaurants and sandwich bars on the same street as the bus terminals and they're reasonable value. You can get almost anything from seafood to kebabs to sandwiches to yoghurt.

Just at the back of the bus terminal street is a small plaza where there are two restaurants next to each other; these are very popular with travellers and night strollers from the tourist district in search of a change. They are the *Restaurant Chabib* and the *Restaurant Mille et Une Nuit (sic)*. They might look expensive (judging from some of the clients) but they're not and the food is very good. Both offer you a choice of sitting inside or at tables in the open air. A three-course meal of bread, soup, tajine and a sweet costs just Dr 13 to Dr 15. It's excellent value.

If you're looking for a cleansing ale or a bottle of Moroccan wine, the tourist palaces on Blvd Mohammed V are going to empty your pockets and the clientele is going to regard you with disdain unless you have just emerged from the laundromat. There are much livelier Moroccan-style bars if you take the trouble to wander around.

For takeaways go to one or other of the two supermarkets on the opposite side of the street from the Hotel Erfoud, Blvd Hassan II. There's an excellent choice of local and imported beers, wines and spirits.

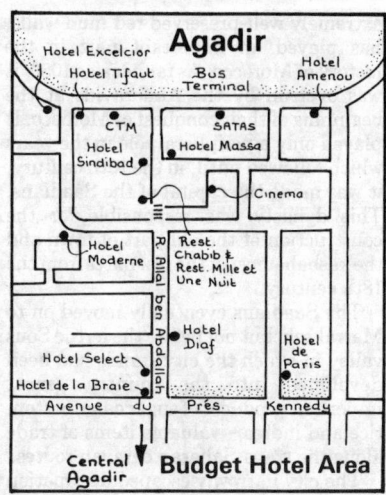

Getting There & Away

The bus terminals are all at the junction of Rue Allal ben Abdallah and Blvd Mohammed Cheikh Saadi.

CTM has buses to Tiznit (3.30 pm) and Essaouira (7.30 am, 7.30 and 9 pm) daily but, strangely, doesn't have buses to Marrakesh.

SATAS has buses to Marrakesh (8 am and 6.30 pm), Tiznit (3, 5, 6, 9 am and 2 pm) and Goulimime (6 am and 2 pm) daily. Express Sud-Est has a bus to Marrakesh daily at 9.30 am.

AROUND AGADIR
Beaches

For beaches head north of Agadir. There are plenty of beautiful sandy coves every few km. Most of the ones nearer Agadir have been heavily colonised by obviously affluent Europeans who have built their winter villas here. Further north this gives way to a sea of campervans, but by the time you are 20 to 25 km north of Agadir you might find something resembling space and even peace and quiet.

TAROUDANNT

Taroudannt, with its magnificent and

extremely well-preserved red mud walls, has played an important part in the history of Morocco. As far back as 1056, it was overrun by the Almoravids at the beginning of their conquest of Morocco. It played only a peripheral role in the years which followed until, in the 16th century, it was made the capital of the Saadians. This dynasty was responsible for the construction of the old part of town and the kasbah; most of the rest dates from the 18th century.

The Saadians eventually moved on to Marrakesh, but not before the fertile Sous valley in which the city stands had been developed into the country's most important producer of sugar cane, cotton, rice and indigo – valuable items of trade along the trans-Saharan caravan routes.

The city narrowly escaped destruction in 1687 at the hands of Moulay Ismail, after it became the centre of a rebellion opposing his rule. Instead, Moulay Ismail contented himself with a massacre of its inhabitants. It regained some of its former prominence when Moulay Abdallah was proclaimed sultan here at the end of the following century. It was to remain a centre of intrigue and sedition against the central government throughout much of the 19th century though, by then, its importance in the overall scheme of things had begun to decline rapidly.

Unlike many Moroccan towns of its size and importance, Taroudannt was never chosen as a French administrative or military centre; consequently, there is no 'European' quarter of wide boulevards and modern buildings tacked onto the original city. Perhaps this is one reason why, despite its proximity to Agadir, you'll see very few well-heeled tourists here.

Information

Most of the city's hotels and banks are grouped on Place Assarag.

Ramparts

You can explore the ramparts of Taroudannt on foot if you like, but it is better to hire a

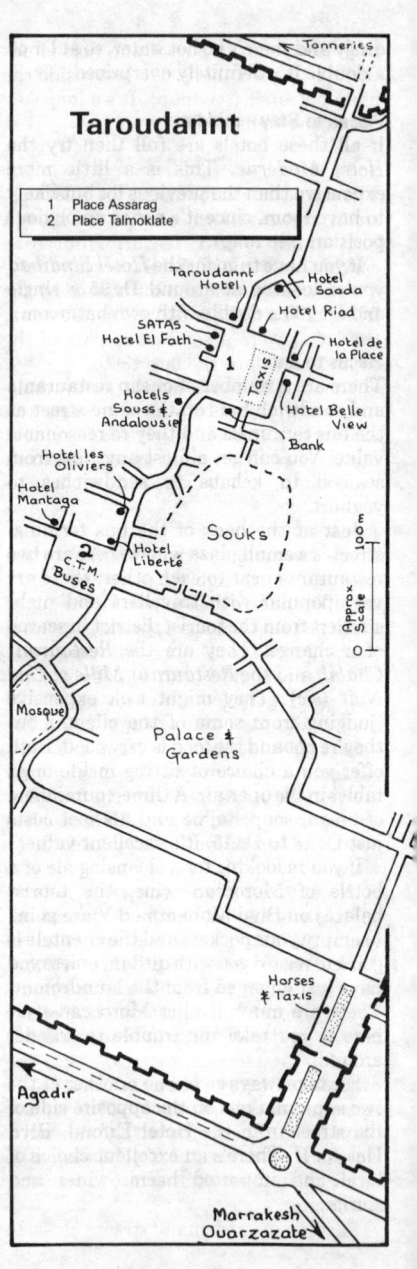

Taroudannt

1 Place Assarag
2 Place Talmoklate

Tanneries

Taroudannt Hotel
Hotel Saada
Hotel Riad
SATAS
Hotel El Fath
Hotel de la Place
Taxis
Hotels Souss & Andalousie
Hotel Belle View
Bank
Hotel les Oliviers
Hotel Mantaga
Souks
Hotel Liberté
C.T.M. Buses
Approx Scale
100 m
0
Mosque
Palace & Gardens
Horses & Taxis
Agadir
Marrakesh Ouarzazate

bicycle or engage one of the horse-and-cart drivers who hang out just inside the main entrance (see map). It's a long way round the walls!

Souk

The souk at Taroudannt is relatively small. However, the items for sale are of a high quality and feature limestone carvings and traditional Berber jewellery. This jewellery has been influenced by the tribes of the Sahara as well as the Jews; the latter were a significant part of the community until the late 1960s.

You might come across a few half-hearted attempts by youths to press you into engaging their services as 'guides', but this isn't Marrakesh and a guide isn't necessary.

Tanneries

There are tanneries here similar to the ones at Fès, though smaller. You get to them by following the main street out of Place Assarag (on the opposite side from the bank) and continuing down until you reach the ramparts. Turn left as you come out of the gate, continue for about 100 metres and then take the first right. Let your nose guide you from there.

Most of the skins (which you can buy) are from sheep and cattle, but the tanneries also cater for those who couldn't care less about the extermination of wildlife.

Places to Stay – bottom end

Most travellers like to stay as close to the centre of activity as possible, and in Taroudannt you can do this without paying a lot of money. There are many hotels around Place Assarag. One of the cheapest is the *Hotel de la Place*, which is pleasant and clean, though basic; the owner is friendly and eager to please. A rooftop double overlooking the square costs Dr 30. There are cold showers only. The *Hotel Souss* and the *Hotel Andalousie*, on the main street coming into the square, are similar.

Further up the main street, close to

Place Talmoklate, is the *Hotel Les Oliviers*, which is also good value at Dr 25 a double. It's pleasant, clean, friendly and has a rooftop terrace but, like the other hotels in this range, has cold showers only. The *Hotel Liberté* on Place Talmoklate is very similar.

If you're looking for something better, I can recommend the *Hotel Taroudannt* on Place Assarag. This is a one-star hotel with its own bar, which is owned by a garrulous and somewhat eccentric but thoroughly agreeable Frenchwoman. It's a great place to stay: it's clean, has hot water, and costs Dr 43 a single and Dr 55 a double. If it's full try the *Hotel Belle View* on the same square but expect to pay a little more.

Places to Stay – middle & top end

The two-star *Hotel Saada* (tel 25 89) has 57 rooms, mostly without private bath or shower. The four-star *Hotel Salam* (tel 23 12) has 75 rooms, a swimming pool and tennis courts. The five-star *Hotel La Gazelle D'Or* (tel 20 39/48) has 23 rooms, all with private bath, and a swimming pool and tennis courts.

Places to Eat

There are quite a few small cafés along the main street just before you get to Place Assarag, where you can get traditional food like tajine, salads and soups. The terrace of the *Hotel Belle View* is also a popular place to eat or have a snack, but is relatively expensive.

For a splurge, have a meal at the *Hotel Taroudannt*, which offers very good French cuisine at reasonable prices.

Getting There & Away

CTM buses arrive in Place Talmoklate, whereas SATAS and Ait M'Zal Express buses have their depot in Place Assarag.

AROUND TAROUDANNT
Tizi-n-Test Pass

The road between Taroudannt and Marrakesh goes over the spectacular Tizi-n-Test pass – one of the highest in Morocco. It's a good road all the way, though it twists and turns endlessly and, in some places, is hair-raising. The views from many points are magnificent. If you can't arrange a lift with tourists, SATAS has buses daily at around 5 am which arrive in Marrakesh at around 2 pm. Towards the end of the journey the road passes Asni, which is the starting point for treks up Mt Toubkal, the highest mountain in North Africa.

ESSAOUIRA

Essaouira is the most popular of the coastal towns with independent travellers, and you hardly ever see package tourists here. Not only does the town have a magnificent beach which curves for miles to the south, its atmosphere is in complete contrast to the souk cities of Marrakesh, Fès, Meknès and Tangier. It can be summed up in one word: relaxation.

Essaouira was founded in the 16th century by the Portuguese, who continued to occupy it until the mid-18th century when the trans-Saharan trade routes fell apart. The present town dates from 1765, when Sultan Sidi Mohammed ben Abdallah re-established it to serve as a fortress town and base from which to suppress a revolt at Agadir.

The fortifications are thus an interesting mixture of Portuguese and Berber military architecture, though the walls around the town date mainly from ben Abdallah's time. They're certainly very impressive and their massiveness lends a powerful mystique to the town; yet inside the walls it's all light and charm. You'll find narrow, freshly whitewashed streets, painted blinds, tranquil squares, artisans in tiny workshops beavering away at fragrant thuya wood, friendly cafés – and there's not a hustler in sight. It's one of the few places in Morocco where you can feel that local people aren't thinking of you as a tourist, with everything that that normally implies elsewhere.

Information

Tourist Office There is a tourist office in the square between Place Prince Moulay Hassan and the fishing harbour. It's often closed during the winter months.

Ramparts

You can walk along most of the ramparts on the seaward part of town and visit the two main forts (*skalas*) during daylight hours; however, the Skala du Port is locked at lunch times. There's no charge and no one will hustle you to act as a guide. The Skala de la Ville is particularly impressive, with its collection of 18th and 19th century brass cannon from various European countries.

Just off the coast to the south-west is the Ile de Mogador, on which there's another massive fortification. It's actually two islets; they were known as far back as Phoenician and Roman times, when they served as an entrepôt for Mediterranean merchants and were known as the Isles Purpuraires. These days the island is a sanctuary for a particular species of falcon as well as other birds, and visits are normally prohibited.

Museum

On Rue Laalouj is a museum which has displays of jewellery, costumes and weapons. Given the history of this town it could be better. It's open daily except Tuesday from 8.30 am to 12 noon and 2 to 6 pm; entry is Dr 3.

Beach

The beach stretches some 10 km down the coast to the sand dunes of Cap Sim. On the way you'll pass the ruins of an old fortress and pavilion partially covered in sand.

Close to Cap Sim and inland about a km through sand dunes and scrub is the Berber village of Diabat, which became a legend among hippies in the 1960s as the result of a visit by Jimi Hendrix. It subsequently became a freak colony similar to those on the beaches of Goa in

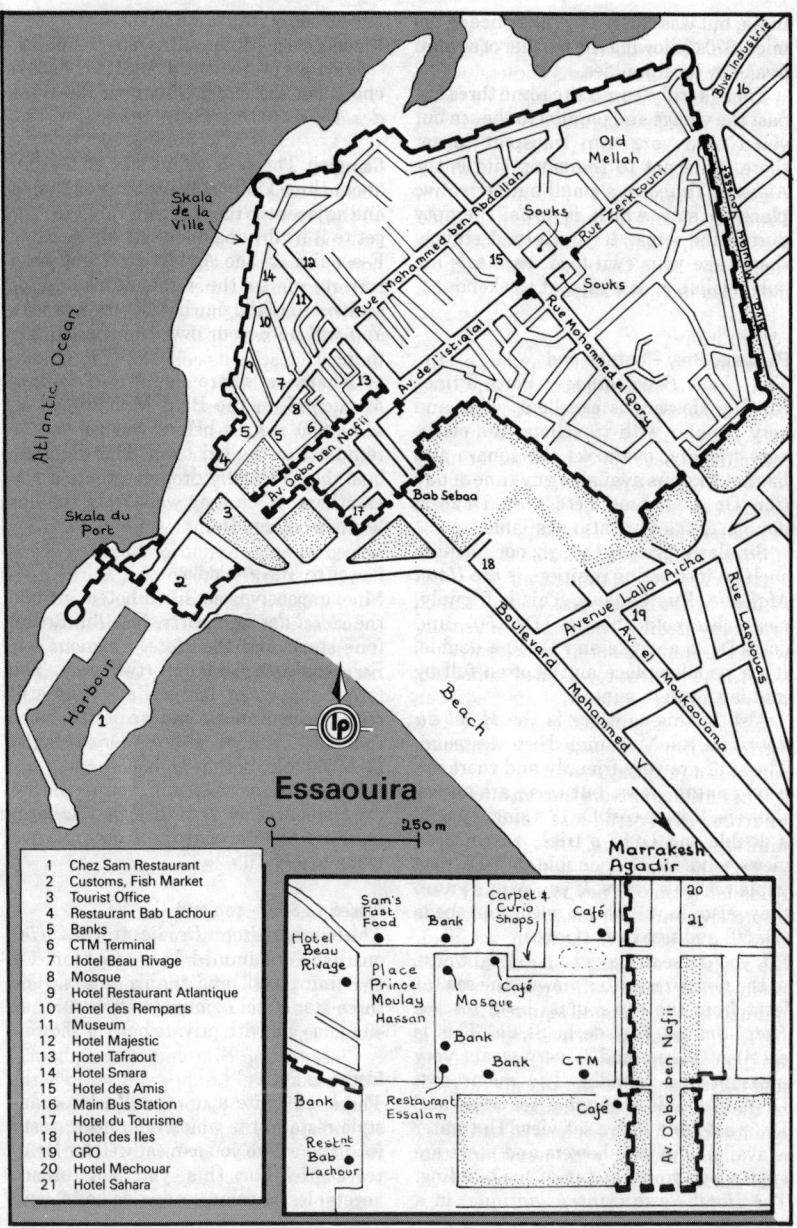

Essaouira

0   250 m

Marrakesh
Agadir

1   Chez Sam Restaurant
2   Customs, Fish Market
3   Tourist Office
4   Restaurant Bab Lachour
5   Banks
6   CTM Terminal
7   Hotel Beau Rivage
8   Mosque
9   Hotel Restaurant Atlantique
10 Hotel des Remparts
11 Museum
12 Hotel Majestic
13 Hotel Tafraout
14 Hotel Smara
15 Hotel des Amis
16 Main Bus Station
17 Hotel du Tourisme
18 Hotel des Iles
19 GPO
20 Hotel Mechouar
21 Hotel Sahara

India, but was cleared by the police in the mid-1970s following the murder of several freaks by local junkies.

There's still a camp site some three km past the village and parallel to the sea but you'd need your own transport to get there. Adjacent to the camp site is the *Auberge Tangaro*, a small but attractive place to stay which is usually empty during the week. If you intend staying there take your own food, as meals are only available, as a rule, at weekends.

Places to Stay – bottom end

The *Hotel Beau Rivage*, Place Prince Moulay Hassan, is excellent value and very popular with travellers. It's clean, very friendly, overlooks the square and has hot showers available any time of day (for Dr 3). Rooms here cost Dr 28 a double. Singles are also available.

Similarly priced, though not in quite such an interesting position, is the *Hotel Majestic*, Rue Laalouj. This is friendly, clean, has cold showers (Dr 1.50), and costs Dr 25 a single and Dr 40 a double. It's a popular place and is often full by midday, even in winter.

Also in this category is the *Hotel du Tourisme*, Rue Mohammed ben Messaoud. The staff are very friendly and there are good rooftop views, but there are no hot showers. Rooms cost Dr 17 a single, Dr 25 a double and Dr 37 a triple without sea views, and Dr 27 a double and Dr 40 a triple with sea views. If you're in a group they also have rooms with four beds (Dr 50) and five beds (Dr 60).

If you'd like to stay in a hotel right next to the ramparts with a view of the sea (at least from the top rooms) head for the *Hotel Smara*, Rue de la Skala. This is excellent value, and is very clean, very pleasant and friendly. The rooms cost Dr 42 a double without a sea view and Dr 52 a double with a sea view. Hot water is available in the showers and there are great views from the top of the building. The *Hotel Restaurant Atlantique*, in a

cul-de-sac off the same street but closer to Place Prince Moulay Hassan, is similar.

For a simple room in a hotel in the souks check out the *Hotel Chakir* or the *Hotel des Amis*.

Camping The best camp site is the one about three km past the village of Diabat and adjacent to the Auberge Tangaro. You get to it by driving about six km south of Essaouira on the Agadir road and then turning off to the right. It should be signposted (if the sign hasn't disappeared). You will need your own transport to get there.

Otherwise there is the *Camping Municipal* on the Blvd Mohammed V, some 600 metres before you get to the ramparts of the old town. If arriving by bus, they'll usually drop you there if you ask them. It's a long walk from the bus terminal otherwise.

Places to Stay – middle

More expensive, classified hotels include the *Hotel des Remparts*, Rue Ibn Rochd (one star), and the *Hotel Tafraout*, off Rue Allal ben Abdallah (two star). The former has seen better days, but still retains a lot of charm and is a better choice than the Tafraout. It costs Dr 45 single, Dr 60 double, both with bath.

If the Remparts is full then try either the *Hotel Mechouar* or the *Hotel Sahara*, more or less adjacent to each other on Ave Oqba ben Nafii.

Places to Stay – top end

The four-star *Hotel Des Iles* (tel 23 29/74) on Blvd Mohammed V has 77 rooms, a swimming pool and tennis courts. The three-star *Hotel Tafoukt* (tel 25 04/05) has 40 rooms, all with private bath or shower.

Places to Eat

There are quite a few small Moroccan-style restaurants which offer good, tasty food and where you can eat well for Dr 10 to Dr 15. For this you get bread, vegetables, a salad, tajine or kefta, and chips. All these little places display what they have for sale in the front window. There's a cluster of them about three-quarters of the way up Rue Allal ben Abdallah, walking away from Place Moulay Hassan, where the road begins to narrow. There are others in the narrow street and small square between the mosque on Place Moulay Hassan and the ramparts which flank Ave Oqba ben Nafii. The restaurant in the small square is a popular hang-out with travellers.

The *Restaurant Bab Lachour*, next to the bank at the bottom of Place Prince Moulay Hassan, is also worth checking out. It looks expensive but offers four-course set-menu meals for Dr 50. You can also order à la carte. Diagonally opposite is the *Restaurant Essalam*, which is similar.

For a splurge on seafood, head down to *Chez Sam* in the harbour area. This restaurant is in a somewhat eccentric building, which looks rather like a cross between an old wooden boat and an antique shop, and the atmosphere is delightful. You can have a fish meal for as little as Dr 20 to Dr 30. Four-course, set-menu meals cost Dr 35 and a three-course meal with lobster as the main dish will cost Dr 80. The restaurant also offers local (Dr 7) and imported (Dr 10) beers and Moroccan wines (Dr 35).

The *Hotel Beau Rivage* with its outdoor tables and chairs is a very popular place to sit and have coffee or mint tea; you can watch the world go by at any time but particularly in the evening. It's frequented by visitors and local people equally.

For cheap, fresh barbecued fish, try the stalls with umbrellas just past the Restaurant Bab Lachour. Don't be put off as the owners rush up to you and try to coax you into their stall. Just pick one and sit down to five large sardines, a chunk of bread, hot sauce and lemon for Dr 4 for the lot – great value.

Bars If you're looking for a bar there's not much choice. *Chez Sam* serves beer and wine, but otherwise it's down to the bar at the *Hotel des Remparts* or the *Chalet de la Plage* (on the promenade opposite the Hotel des Iles). Else there's the bar at the *Hotel des Iles* itself; you don't have to be a resident to drink there.

Things to Buy

Essaouira is a centre for thuya carving, and the quality of the work is superb. Most of the carvers have workshops under the Skala de la Ville and they're very laid-back, so you can walk around and look at what they are doing without any pressure to buy. It's unlikely that you won't want to buy something but, because there's no pressure, don't expect to be able to reduce their stated prices by anything but a small fraction. Nevertheless, you won't find this sort of craftwork cheaper anywhere else in Morocco. There are also quite a few craft shops with an equally impressive range of goods in the immediate vicinity.

Carpet and rug shops, as well as bric-a-brac, jewellery and brassware shops, are clustered together in the narrow street and the small square between Place Prince Moulay Hassan and the ramparts which flank the Ave Oqba ben Nafii.

Getting There & Away

The CTM bus terminal is in the square opposite the tourist office, round the corner from Place Prince Moulay Hassan. All other bus companies have their terminals at Bab Doukkala, just outside the ramparts at the northern end of town.

Go to ticket office No 6 for CTM buses to Casa (9.30 am, Dr 48) and Agadir (12 noon, Dr 28), and to office No 2 for Marrakesh.

Marrakesh

There can be few travellers who have not heard of Marrakesh. During the 1960s and 1970s it was the travellers' mecca, along with Istanbul and Kathmandu – and rightly so! This turn in the fame and fortunes of Marrakesh is only the most recent of the Scheherazadian sagas which this city has experienced.

Sitting against the snow-capped backdrop of Morocco's highest mountains, the city has a scenic setting that is hard to surpass.

History

Once one of the most important artistic and cultural centres in the Islamic world, Marrakesh was founded in 1062 AD by the Almoravid sultan Youssef Ibn Tachfin. It experienced its heyday under Youssef's son, Ali, who was born to a Christian slave mother. It was Ali who was responsible for constructing the extensive underground irrigation canals (the *khettara*), which still supply the city's gardens with water. Later, as a result of the Almoravid conquest of Spain, Fès became more prominent; yet Marrakesh remained the southern capital, and much of the wealth which flowed to the kingdom was lavished on extending and beautifying the city.

The city was razed by the Almohads in 1147, though the walls and the gateway to Ali's huge palace were spared. It was rebuilt shortly afterwards in the Omayyad style and became the capital of Almohad Empire until its collapse in 1269. For the next 300 years the focus of Moroccan brilliance in the arts was Fès, but after the defeat of the Merenids by the Saadians in 1536 Marrakesh once again became the capital of the empire. However, the Saadian takeover of the city was preceded by hard times. Even the Portuguese made a vain attempt to capture Marrakesh in 1515, and in the following years there were famines which reduced activity in the city and surrounding countryside to a low level.

Saadian control brought prosperity once again. During their reign the Portuguese were forced to abandon all their coastal enclaves with the sole exception of El Jadida. The mellah, the

huge mosque of el-Mouassine and the mosque of Ben Youssef with its adjacent medressa were all built in these times. The Saadians also set up a customs house for the Christian colony which had been established in Marrakesh. The el-Badi palace, constructed using Muslim-Spanish designs and techniques, was also a creation of the later Saadian sultans.

In time, decadence set in and Morocco was taken over by the Alaouites, who made Meknès their capital. Marrakesh could not be ignored, however. Although Moulay Ismail was responsible for tearing apart the el-Badi palace for building materials, his successor, Sidi Mohammed ben Abdallah, poured resources into rebuilding or restoring the walls, the kasbah, the palaces, mosques and mechouars of the city as well as creating new gardens (such as the Menara Gardens).

By the 19th century, Marrakesh was again on the decline, though it did regain some of its former prestige when Moulay Hassan was crowned there in 1873. Its most recent return to fame and fortune is largely the result of French activities during the protectorate period, when the *ville nouvelle* was built, the medina was revitalised and resettled, and Place Foucauld was created below the Djemaa el Fna. Increasing tourism since then has ensured Marrakesh's continued prosperity.

Orientation

As in Fès and Meknès, the old city and the *ville nouvelle* of Marrakesh are about the same size; you'll find it convenient to use public transport to get from one to the other.

The main thoroughfare connecting the two is Avenue Mohammed V. Along this road in the *ville nouvelle* is the main post office, the tourist office and many of the mid-range hotels. The railway station lies to the west of Avenue Mohammed V along Avenue Hassan II, which joins the former at Place du 16 Novembre.

The heart of the old city is the Djemaa

el Fna, a large, irregularly-shaped square overlooked by the city's most prominent landmark, the Koutoubia. Most of the budget hotels are clustered in the narrow streets branching off the eastern and south-eastern sides of the square. The souks lie to the north of the Djemaa el Fna and the palaces to the south. The main bus station lies just outside the old city walls and is within 10 to 15 minutes' walk of the Djemaa el Fna.

Information

Tourist Office This is at the junction of Ave Mohammed V and Ave du Président Kennedy. They have the usual range of leaflets, but it's a long walk from the budget hotel area.

Money There is a branch of the Banque du Maroc on the south side of the Djemaa el Fna next to the post office. There are others in the *ville nouvelle*.

Post Office The main post office is on Place 16 du Novembre in the *ville nouvelle*. There is a branch office on the Djemaa el Fna.

Djemaa el Fna

The focal point of Marrakesh is the Djemaa el Fna, a huge square in the old part of town where many of the budget hotels are located. Other than the souks, this is where everything happens; visitors are destined to spend a lot of time here. Although it's a lively place at any time of day, it really comes into its own in the late afternoon and evening. There's no place quite like it anywhere else in Morocco.

Almost without warning, the curtain goes up on one of the world's most fascinating and bizarre spectacles. Rows and rows of open-air food stalls are set up and mouth-watering aromas quickly fill the square. Jugglers, story-tellers, snake charmers, magicians, acrobats and benign lunatics quickly take over the rest of the space, each of them surrounded by an audience of jostling spectators who listen or watch intently and then fall about laughing. In the meantime, assistants hassle them for contributions. In between the groups weave hustlers, thieves, knick-knack sellers and bewildered tourists. And, on the outer edges, kerosene lanterns ablaze, are the fruit and juice stalls. Overlooking one end of the square are the huge, eerily-lit Berber tents on the terrace of the Club Méd hotel; you will occasionally hear snatches of folk music being played for the well-heeled up there. Down below the medieval pageant presents its nightly cornucopia of delights; Breughel would have had a field day here!

Souks

Just as the Djemaa el Fna is justifiably famous for its energy and life, the souks of Marrakesh are some of the best in Morocco, producing a wide variety of high-quality crafts. The streets here are just as labyrinthine as those in Fès and every bit as busy. There is a difference, however: it's a long time since *Marrakesh Express* was written but it sure as hell put the place in the limelight.

There is no way you can get within even sniffing distance of any of the entrances to the medina these days without being besieged by 'guides'. And there is no way you can shake them off – they'll pursue you every inch of the way. Not only that, shake one off, and there will be another there within seconds.

Until your face gets familiar, attempting to go to the medina without a 'guide' is a total waste of time and extremely frustrating. Forget trying and take a guide. Just remember that the only thing they' are basically interested in is the commission they make by getting you to buy things in the shops. Some are better than others, of course, but that's the bottom line.

The tourist blurb raves on benignly to the effect that 'Merchants sit cross-legged on heaps of merchandise, a fan waving indolently in the hand'. Nothing could be further from the truth. You are about to

Casablanca

El Jadida

Hospital

Railway
Station

Essaouira

Bus
Stat?

Bab
Doukk

Bab
Larissa

Camping

Youth
Hostel

Olive
Groves

1   Hotel Oasis
2   Tourist Office (ONMT)
3   Hotel Renaissance
4   GPO
5   Place du 16 Novembre
6   Place de la Liberté
7   Hotel des Almoravides
8   Club Méditerranée
9   Djemaa el Fna
10   Koutoubia
11   Hotel Foucauld
12   Hotel Tazi
13   Hotel Chems
14   Hotel Mamounia
15   Kasbah Mosque & Saadian Tombs
16   Public Swimming Pool

Marrakesh

0   500 m

confront high-pressure sales tactics, high prices and contempt bordering on abuse if you refuse to buy anything or balk at the quoted prices. Never spend a lot of time in any one shop unless you are seriously interested in the merchandise, otherwise you may well be in for a traumatic experience. Almost every one of the shops in the souks here have stickers displaying the fact that they will accept American Express, Diners Club, Visa and often many other credit cards.

This is *not* Fès! It's more like Barter Town in *Mad Max Beyond Thunderdome*!

Never believe a word you are told about anything relating to silver, gold or amber. The gold and silver are always plated, never solid, and the amber is plastic (put a lighted match to it and smell it). Anything claimed to be 'authentic', 'tribal' or 'antique' is nothing of the sort. Techniques for ageing anything whatsoever are well known here. Thousands, perhaps hundreds of thousands, of tourists are conned here every year and waste their money on trash.

Having said that, there are, of course, some things which can't be faked such as brass plates, leatherwork, woodwork and, up to a point, carpets. There are, also, some merchants who do offer genuine jewellery, though they take some finding.

Mosques & Medressas

Like their counterparts elsewhere in Morocco, the mosques and medressas in Marrakesh are generally closed to non-Muslims; this being so, a detailed description of them is largely pointless. And, as in Fès, the ones inside the medina are generally so hemmed in by other buildings that little can be seen from the outside.

Ali ben Youssef Mosque The largest of the mosques inside the medina is the Ali ben Youssef Mosque, first built in the second half of the 12th century by the Almoravid sultan of the same name. It's the oldest surviving mosque in Marrakesh. However, the building itself is of fairly recent date, as it was almost completely rebuilt in the 19th century in the Merenid style in response to popular demand. When first constructed it was about twice its present size but it was severely damaged when the Almoravids were overthrown by the Almohads. The Almohads restored it later on; the Saadians, too, had a hand in the restoration work.

Medressa ben Youssef Adjacent to the Ali ben Youssef Mosque is the Medressa ben Youssef, the largest theological college in the Maghreb, built by the Saadians in 1565. There is accommodation here for more than 100 students and teachers. Of the annexes to the ben Youssef Mosque only the Koubba Ba'adiyn survives, the fountain having disappeared during the last century when the kissaria was constructed. The koubba is said to be one of the finest examples of Maghrebi work in existence but was only rediscovered in 1947. Both the mosque and the medressa are closed to non-Muslims.

Mouassine Mosque The other large mosque in the medina is the Mouassine Mosque, built in the 16th century by the Saadians on land formerly occupied by the Jewish community. Its most notable features are the three huge doorways and the intricately carved cedar-wood ceilings. The fountain attached to this mosque still survives and is quite elaborate, with three sections – two for animals and one for humans. The mosque is closed to non-Muslims.

Ben Salah Mosque Of the other mosques in the medina, the Ben Salah Mosque (also known as the Zaouia ben Salah) is the most prominent; its brilliant green-tiled minaret can be seen from many places. It was built by the Merenid sultan, Abu Said Uthman, between 1318 and 1321. Again, it's closed to non-Muslims.

Koutoubia The only mosque whose perspective you can really get an idea of is

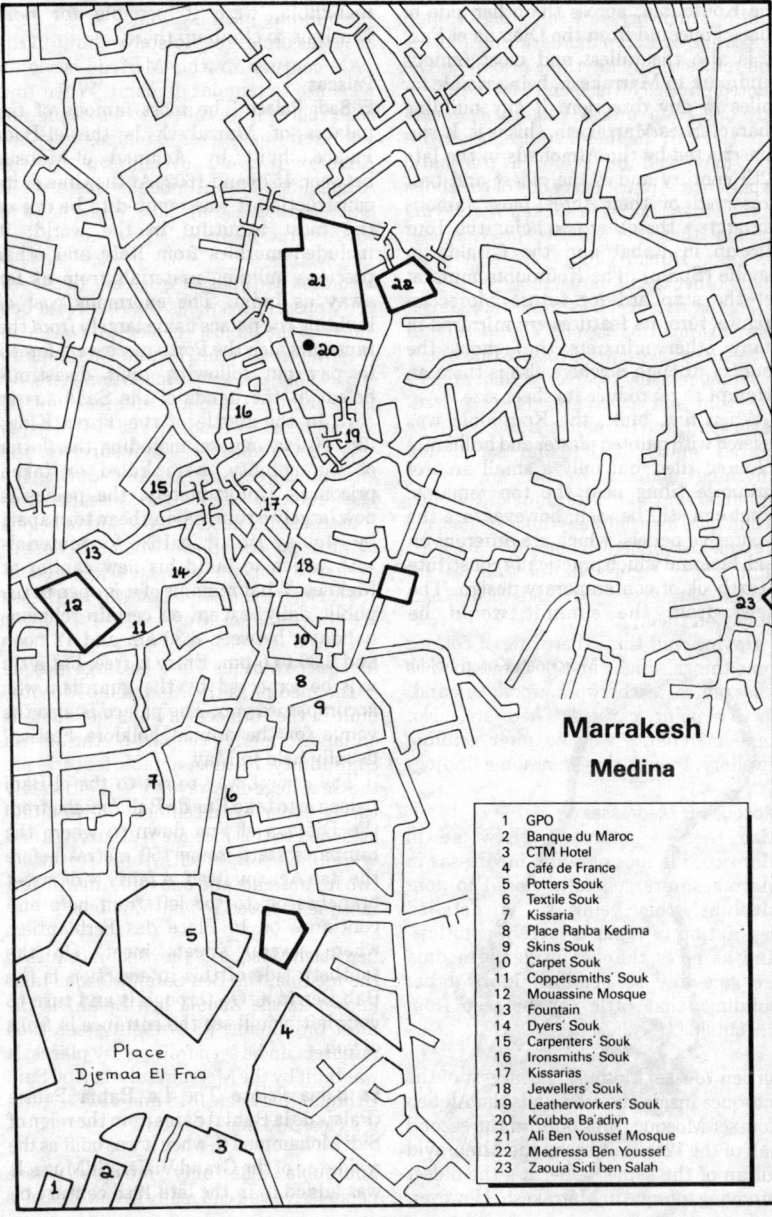

Marrakesh

Medina

Place
Djemaa El Fna

1 GPO
2 Banque du Maroc
3 CTM Hotel
4 Café de France
5 Potters Souk
6 Textile Souk
7 Kissaria
8 Place Rahba Kedima
9 Skins Souk
10 Carpet Souk
11 Coppersmiths' Souk
12 Mouassine Mosque
13 Fountain
14 Dyers' Souk
15 Carpenters' Souk
16 Ironsmiths' Souk
17 Kissarias
18 Jewellers' Souk
19 Leatherworkers' Souk
20 Koubba Ba'adiyn
21 Ali Ben Youssef Mosque
22 Medressa Ben Youssef
23 Zaouia Sidi ben Salah

the Koutoubia, across the other side of Place Foucauld from the Djemaa el Fna. It is also the tallest and most famous landmark in Marrakesh, being visible for miles in any direction. If any building characterises Marrakesh, this is it. It was constructed by the Almohads in the late 12th century and is the oldest and best preserved of their three most famous minarets – the other two being the Tour Hassan in Rabat and the Giralda in Seville (Spain). The Koutoubia minaret set the standard for future Moroccan architecture; its features are mirrored in many other minarets throughout the country, though nowhere else is there an attempt to reproduce its sheer size.

When first built, the Koutoubia was covered with painted plaster and brilliantly coloured tiles, but only a small area of turquoise tiling near the top remains. What can still be seen, however, are the decorative panels, which are different on each face and which practically constitute a textbook of contemporary design. The views from the summit would be

Moroccan Koran holder

incredible, were it possible for non-Muslims to climb up there.

Palaces

El-Badi Palace The most famous of the palaces of Marrakesh is the el-Badi Palace, built by Achmed el-Mansur between 1578 and 1602. At the time of its construction it was reputed to be one of the most beautiful in the world; it included marbles from Italy and other precious building materials from as far away as India. The enormous cost of building the palace came largely from the ransom which the Portuguese were forced to pay out following their disastrous defeat at the hands of the Saadians in 1578 in the Battle of the Three Kings (26,000 Portuguese, including the flower of the nobility, were killed or taken prisoner). Unfortunately, the palace is now largely a ruin, having been torn apart by Moulay Ismail in 1696 for materials with which to build his new capital at Meknès. What remains of it is open to the public daily, except on certain religious holidays, between 8.30 am and 12 noon and 2.30 to 6 pm. Entry is free, but a tip will be expected by the guardian who accompanies you. The palace is also the venue for the annual Folklore Festival usually held in May.

The easiest way to get to the el-Badi palace is to take Rue de Bab Agnaou from the Djemaa el Fna down to where the ramparts start, some 150 metres before the Bab Agnaou itself. A fairly wide street branches off to the left from here and continues on to Place des Ferblantiers where several streets meet. On the southern side of this intersection is the Bab Berrima. Go through it and turn to your left: you'll see the entrance in front of you.

La Bahia Palace The La Bahia Palace (Palais de la Bahia) dates from the reign of Sidi Mohammed II, when it was built as the residence of the Grand Vizier, Si'Musa. It was added to in the late 19th century by

Moulay Hassan and Abd el-Aziz. It's a rambling structure with fountains, living quarters, pleasure gardens and numerous secluded, shady courtyards, but it lacks architectural cohesiveness. The palace was ransacked by the sultan in 1900 and left to rot, but has been partially restored in recent years. It's open daily, except on certain religious holidays, from 9.30 am to 1 pm (11.45 am in winter) and 4 to 7 pm (2.30 to 6 pm in winter). Entry is free, but you must take a guide and he will expect a tip at the end.

Dar Si Said The other palace which is definitely worth a visit is the Dar Si Said, which these days is the Museum of Moroccan Arts. It was built towards the end of the 19th century by Sidi Said, Moulay Hassan's Grand Vizier, as his town house. The museum houses one of the finest collections in the country, including jewellery from the High Atlas, the Anti-Atlas and the extreme south; carpets from the Haouz and the High Atlas; oil lamps from Taroudannt; blue pottery from Safi and green pottery from Tamegroute; leatherwork from Marrakesh; and many other art objects from various epochs. It also has an extensive display of Berber muskets, pistols and daggers. It's open from 9 am to 12 noon and 4 to 7 pm (2.30 to 6 pm in winter); closed Tuesday.

Saadian Tombs
Adjacent to the Kasbah Mosque is the necropolis begun by the Saadian sultan Achmed el-Mansur, who also built the el-Badi palace. Unlike the palace, however, the tombs escaped Moulay Ismail's depredations – possibly because he was superstitious about plundering the dead. Instead, he sealed the tombs; as a result, even though they are partially in ruins, they convey some of the opulence and superb artistry which must have been lavished on the palace. Sixty-six of the Saadians, including el-Mansur, his successors and their closest family members, lie buried under the two main

structures, and over 100 more outside them. The tombs – particularly the so-called 'Chamber of the Twelve Columns' – display a fine balance between brilliantly-coloured and plain surfaces which is hard to match anywhere else (though the style was obviously influenced by that of the Alhambra in Spain).

Though the mad sultan, Moulay Yazid, was also laid to rest here in 1792, the tombs essentially remained sealed following Moulay Ismail's reign. They were not 'rediscovered' until 1917, when General Lyautey (the first French Resident), his curiosity awakened by an aerial survey undertaken of the area, ordered the construction of a passageway to them. Since then they have been restored and are now open to the public every day, except Friday morning, from 8 am to 7 pm (6 pm in winter). The guardian who accompanies you will expect a tip at the end of the visit.

To get to the tombs, take Rue de Bab Agnaou to the Bab Agnaou itself (the only surviving Almohad gateway in Marrakesh), which is on the left and almost adjacent to the Bab er Rob (outside which there is a dirt patch which serves as the terminus for local buses and taxis to Ourika and other nearby destinations). Go through the Bab Agnaou and walk straight on until you come to the Kasbah Mosque. Turn left here down Rue de la Kasbah and, when you get to the end of the mosque, you'll see a narrow alleyway on the right. Go down it, and the entrance to the tombs is at the end.

Places to Stay – bottom end
The best deals in accommodation are found in the area between Rue Oqba ben Nafaa and Rue Riad Zitoun el Kedim, where there are scores of reasonably priced hotels. There's not a lot to choose between most of them, other than whether they offer hot showers or not (not important in summer but definitely so in winter). Most of the cheapies will charge extra for hot showers (usually Dr 5). Average prices for cheapies are Dr 15 to

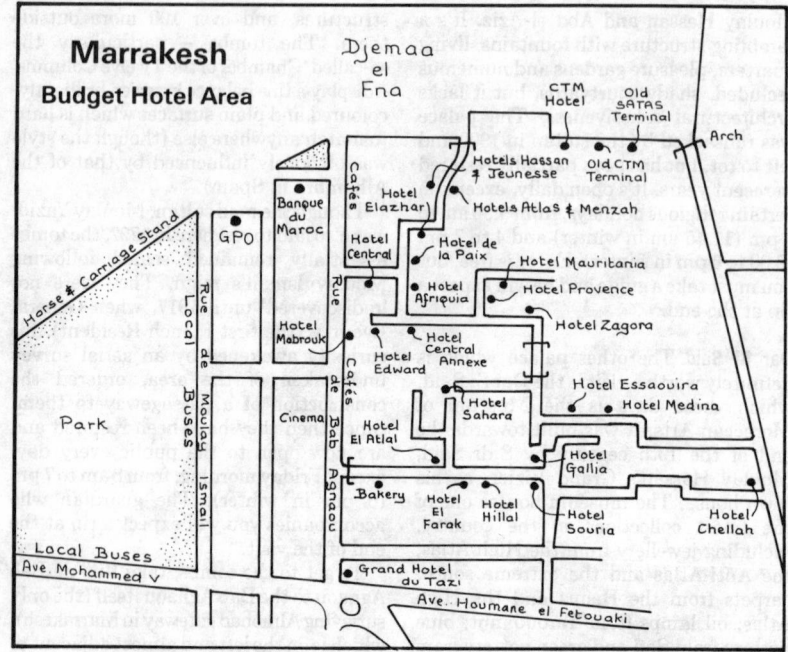

Marrakesh
Budget Hotel Area

Djemaa el Fna

CTM Hotel
Old SATAS Terminal
Arch

Hotels Hassan & Jeunesse
Old CTM Terminal

Cafes

Hotel Elazhar

Hotels Atlas & Menzah

Banque du Maroc

GPO

Horse & Carriage Stand

Rue de Moulay Ismail

Local Buses

Hotel Central

Hotel de la Paix

Hotel Mauritania

Hotel Afriquia

Hotel Provence

Hotel Zagora

Hotel Mabrouk

Hotel Central Annexe

Hotel Edward

Rue de Bab Agnaou

Cafes

Park

Cinema

Hotel El Atlal

Hotel Sahara

Hotel Essaouira

Hotel Medina

Hotel Gallia

Bakery

Hotel El Farak

Hotel Hillal

Hotel Souria

Hotel Chellah

Local Buses
Ave. Mohammed V

Grand Hotel du Tazi

Ave. Houmane el Fetouaki

Dr 25 a single and Dr 25 to Dr 40 a double depending on the season, their standard and your haggling ability.

Most of the ones available are marked on the detailed map of this area. Which one you choose may very well depend on where there is room. Take your pick.

The *Hotel El Atlal* is a very friendly, family-run place with clean showers and toilets. It offers rooms with own washbasin for Dr 40 a double (Dr 10 extra during holidays); hot showers are Dr 5 extra. Baggage left in the rooms is secure. The *Hotel Afriquia* is also very pleasant, friendly and has a quiet courtyard. Rooms cost Dr 25 a double with own hand basin, but there are cold showers only.

The *Hotel Central* has good rooms on the upper floors, but the lower ones are dark and dingy. It costs Dr 20 a single and Dr 30 a double; cold showers only. The *Hotel de la Paix* is similar.

If you're prepared to pay a little extra the *Hotel Gallia* is excellent value. This is a beautiful and spotlessly clean place with a quiet courtyard, luxurious TV lounge and hot showers. It costs Dr 38 a single and Dr 47 a double without own bathroom, and Dr 47 a single and Dr 58 a double with own bathroom. It's a gem!

Very popular with travellers who want to stay on the Djemaa el Fna is the *CTM Hotel*. This costs about Dr 45 a single and Dr 60 a double without own shower, Dr 54 a single and Dr 65 a double with own shower (hot water); a tax of 10% is charged as well. The rooms are pleasant, and there's a courtyard on the 1st floor; there's also a rooftop terrace, where you can watch the activity in the square below. Don't complain about anything here or they may throw you out – they have, after all, a guaranteed clientele.

The *Hotel de France* (tel 223 19), also on

the Djemaa el Fna, is another popular place, since it too overlooks the square. There are no singles, but doubles cost Dr 25 to Dr 30, triples Dr 45 and rooms with four beds cost Dr 60 – all without own bathroom. The hotel has cold showers only. There is both a ground-floor and a roof-terrace restaurant.

Youth Hostel For the die-hards there's a *Youth Hostel*, close to the railway station, which costs Dr 10 a night. It's clean and pleasant and, although the warden is something of a strange character, he's harmless. Youth hostel hours are strictly maintained.

Places to Stay – middle
Among the two-star hotels is the *Grand Hotel Tazi* (tel 221 52/53), at the corner of Ave Houmane el Fetouaki and Rue Bab Agnaou. This has 61 rooms with either bath or shower, and a swimming pool. Three-star hotels include the *Hotel la Renaissance* (tel 312 31/33/34) at 89 Ave Mohammed V and the *Hotel Sun* (tel 311 39) at 25 Rue Moulay Ali. Both hotels have rooms with private bath or shower, and the Sun has a swimming pool.

Places to Stay – top end
There are several top-end hotels in Marrakesh, but there's not much point in staying in them unless you need a touch of luxury. If you do, a couple of four-star hotels are the *Hotel Agdal* (tel 336 70) at 1 Blvd Mohammed Zerktouni and the *Hotel Siaha* (tel 342 52) on Ave du Président Kennedy. Five-star hotels include the *Hotel Sofitel* (tel 346 26), also on Ave du Président Kennedy, and the *Hotel Palais El Badia* (tel 330 77) on Ave de la Ménéra. All these hotels have the usual top-end facilities.

Places to Eat
There are cheap restaurants all around the Djemaa el Fna and along Rue Oqba ben Nafaa which offer a mixture of Moroccan and European-style food.

Many of them do their cooking on the pavement outside the café, so you can see what they have on offer. Some of the cooks and waiters can be very entertaining in at least five or six languages. Take your pick. There's not a lot to choose between them, though, naturally, you get what you pay for. The average cost of a meal would be around Dr 10 to Dr 15.

In the evenings, between 5 and 9 pm, you can't beat eating at the food stalls in the Djemaa el Fna. There's an incredible range of food to choose from – tajine, kebabs, soup, fish and even chips – and you're looking at just Dr 10 for a meal. Just about everyone eats here in the evening.

Getting There & Away
Bus Even though CTM and SATAS still have garages on the Djemaa el Fna, there is now a centralised bus station from which all buses (regardless of the company) leave. It is just outside the walls of the medina, close to Bab Doukkala, and is a 20-minute walk or a Dr 5 taxi ride from the Djemaa el Fna.

Train The railway station is on Ave Hassan II and is a long way from the Djemaa el Fna. Take a taxi or bus into the centre.

AROUND MARRAKESH
Ourika
There is an incredible donkey market every Monday in the nearby valley of Ourika. Buses to here leave Marrakesh from the patch of dirt outside the Bab er Rob.

High Atlas Trekking
If you'd like to do some trekking in the High Atlas, ask for either Houssein or Lacem Izahan at the Café Azagya, about two km before the village of Setti Fatma in the Ourika Valley. These two young guides know the Atlas like their pockets. They can take you for half-hour walks or treks lasting three to 10 days (or more), and they're reliable.

Mt Toubkal

Mt Toubkal (4165 metres) is Morocco's highest mountain. Getting there from Marrakesh takes you through spectacularly beautiful countryside. First take a bus from Marrakesh to Asni – they leave every hour. If you want to stay at Asni, there's a *Youth Hostel* which costs Dr 10 per person.

From Asni you take a taxi to Imlil, where there is a hostel known as the *CAF Refuge*; you need to bring your own food unless you are happy with omelettes, cheese, bread and oranges, which you can get in Imlil. The hostel costs Dr 17 per night and has beds but no sheets or blankets, so you'll need a sleeping bag. There are cooking facilities, pots and pans, crockery and cutlery, and the warden takes good care of the place. This is the best place to hire guides. If it's full, there's another pension opposite, where you can put your head down for Dr 10 per person.

It's possible to buy maps of the hiking trails up Mt Toubkal in Imlil; however, it might be a good idea to come to Morocco equipped with the guide *Atlas Mountains* by Robin G Collomb (West Col Productions, UK, 1980), since this covers the region comprehensively. Some of the general comments in the book, however, might leave you wondering how much time the author spent in lowland Morocco as opposed to gazing at snow-capped peaks. Remarks such as 'All Berbers are beggars by nature' and, ' . . . couscous – a sort of Lancashire hot pot cooked in a basin of semolina' stretch the bounds of credibility. Otherwise it's an excellent book.

Guides can be hired in Imlil, but you don't need one as far as the first refuge if you are just going up the normal route to the summit via the Mizane valley. You may need one, however, for the climb from the refuge to the summit. The guide's fees are usually fixed, though he'll probably expect a tip at the end as well.

On the first day of the trek you walk from Imlil to the Neltner Hut (3207 metres) via the villages of Aroumd and Sidi Chamharouch. This takes about five hours. Bottled drinks are usually available at both these villages. The Neltner Hut is a stone cottage built in 1938 and has beds for 29 people in two dormitories, though you have to provide your own sheets and blankets. There's also a kitchen with Calor Gas stove, and a range of cooking utensils and hot water is available. The charge is Dr 17 per person per night, plus an extra charge if you use the cooking facilities or need hot water. There's a resident warden, who'll let you in. You must bring all your own food with you – there's none for sale here – though the warden may, if you give him plenty of notice, prepare meals for you.

The ascent from the Neltner Hut to the summit should take you about four hours and the descent about two hours. It's best to take water with you in summer, but this isn't generally necessary in winter. It can be bitterly cold at the top even in summer, so bring plenty of warm clothing with you. On clear days, there are incredible views in all directions but especially south into the Sahara.

OUARZAZATE

Ouarzazate was created by the French as a garrison and regional administrative centre. The town did not exist prior to this, though the Glaoui kasbah of Taourirt at the far end of town on the road to Tinerhir had been here for a long time.

Except for the kasbah, it's a pretty nondescript town with little of interest, though Club Méditerranée has seen fit to build a huge hotel/resort on the hill overlooking the town. The best thing about Ouarzazate, in fact, is getting here from Marrakesh over the Tizi-n-Tichka pass. There are superb views over the mountains and down into the valleys below from many points on this journey.

Most travellers spend the night in Ouarzazate en route to or from Zagora in the Drâa Valley or the Todra and Dadès

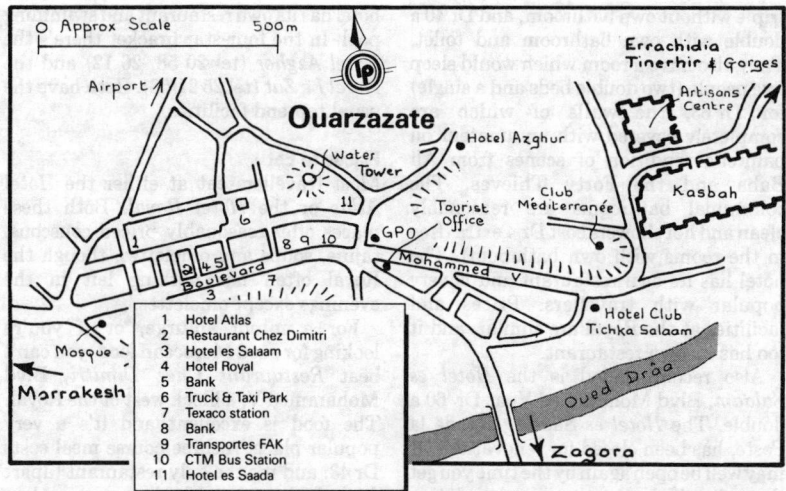

gorges. If you're here in winter make sure
you have plenty of warm clothes. Bitterly
cold winds whip down off the snow-
covered High Atlas Mountains at this
time of year.

Information

Tourist Office The tourist office is in the
centre of town, opposite the post office.
The staff are helpful, but they have
precious little other than a useful bus
timetable chart.

Kasbah & Around

The only place worth visiting in Ouarzazate
itself is the kasbah at the eastern end of
town. In the heyday of the Glaoui chiefs
during the 1930s this was one of the largest
kasbahs in the area. In those days it
housed numerous members of the Glaoui
dynasty along with hundreds of their
servants and workers, but it appears to
have been largely abandoned after the
government took it over at independence.

Wandering through the narrow streets
of this kasbah, you'll be struck by how
deserted it all feels and how derelict it has
become. Indeed, part of the outer walls
facing the River Drâa appear to be ready

to collapse. The actual 'palace' which the
Glaouis occupied consists of courtyards,
living quarters, reception rooms and the
like, and is open from 9 am to 12 noon and
3 to 6 pm; closed Sunday. A guide is
provided. It's worth a visit, but you'll only
be shown a part of the complex. The rest of
the kasbah can be visited at any time.

Opposite the entrance to the kasbah is
another building in the same style, which
today houses an artisans' centre. Here you
can find stone carvings, pottery and woollen
carpets woven by the region's Ouzguita
Berbers. It's open Monday to Friday from
8.30 am to 12 noon and 1 to 6 pm, and on
Saturdays from 8.30 am to 12 noon.

Places to Stay – bottom end

It can sometimes be difficult to find cheap
accommodation in Ouarzazate if you
arrive late in the day, since there are not
too many hotels in the budget category.
Two of the cheapest are the *Hotel Atlas*
and the *Hotel Royal*. The latter fills up
earlier because it's more prominently
placed, on Blvd Mohammed V (the main
road). They're both clean, have hot water
and the staff are friendly. The Atlas costs
Dr 15 a single, Dr 30 a double and Dr 35 a

triple without own bathroom, and Dr 40 a double with own bathroom and toilet. They also have a room which would sleep five people (two double beds and a single) for Dr 63, the walls of which are completely covered with an amateur oil painter's rendition of scenes from Ali Baba and the Forty Thieves. The communal bathrooms are reasonably clean and hot showers cost Dr 4 extra (free in the rooms with own bathroom). The hotel has its own restaurant and is very popular with travellers. Prices and facilities at the Royal are similar, and it too has its own restaurant.

Also recommended is the *Hotel es Salaam*, Blvd Mohammed V, at Dr 60 a double. The *Hotel es Saada*, Rue de la Poste, has been closed for renovations. It may well be open again by the time you get there, in which case the accommodation prospects will be better. There's also the *Hotel La Vallée*, on the road to Zagora about two km from the centre of Ouarzazate, which has similar prices to the Atlas and Royal.

Camping There is a camp site past the kasbah on the road to Tinerhir, but it's very run-down, inconvenient and almost the same price as a hotel.

Places to Stay – middle
Going up-market, there is the *Hotel La Gazelle* about 1½ km out of town on the road to Marrakesh. If you're coming in from Marrakesh on the bus, ask the driver to drop you there. It's well lit, so you can't miss it. It's a two-star hotel with its own swimming pool and restaurant. The rooms are very clean and comfortable and there's hot water in the showers. Quite a few tourists with their own cars stay here, so there's a good chance of fixing up lifts to nearby places of interest.

Places to Stay – top end
The three-star *Hotel Tichka* (tel 22 06) has 113 rooms with either private shower or bath. The rooms have heating, and the hotel has its own restaurant and swimming pool. In the four-star bracket there's the *Hotel Azghor* (tel 20 58, 26 12) and the *Hotel Le Zat* (tel 25 21/58). Both have the usual top-end facilities.

Places to Eat
Most travellers eat at either the *Hotel Atlas* or the *Hotel Royal*. Both these places offer reasonably priced couscous, tajine, soups and omelettes, though the Royal often has nothing left in the evenings except omelettes.

For a minor splurge, or if you're looking for good Moroccan food, you can't beat *Restaurant Chez Dimitri*, Blvd Mohammed V, a block west of the Royal. The food is excellent and it's a very popular place. A three-course meal costs Dr 43, and it's the only restaurant (apart from the large hotels) where you can buy beer, wine (Dr 18 to Dr 35 per bottle) and spirits. It's definitely the only place to go on a winter's evening, as they have a pot-belly stove from which you can soak up enough heat to keep you warm all night. Get there early if you don't want to wait for a table.

Getting There & Away
The main bus companies (CTM and Transportes FAK) have their terminals on the main street (Blvd Mohammed V), close to the post office. The taxi and truck park is in a small square behind the main street, below the water tower.

CTM has buses to: Agadir (3, 8 and 10 pm, nine hours, Dr 42.50); Errachidia (1 pm, nine hours, Dr 36); Marrakesh (6 and 10 am, 12 noon, 2 and 4 pm, five hours, Dr 31.20); Taroudannt (3, 8, 10 and 10.30 am, eight hours, Dr 35); Tinerhir (6 am and 12 noon, 4¼ hours, Dr 27.75); and Zagora (12 noon, four to five hours, Dr 27.65).

Some of the Zagora buses continue on to M'Hamid but you can't go there on the same bus, as you must first get permission to go to M'Hamid from the authorities in Zagora.

AROUND OUARZAZATE

Tifoultoutte

From any vantage point in Ouarzazate you can look out south across the valley of the Drâa and see another magnificent mud-brick fortress. This is the kasbah of Tifoultoutte which, like the one in Ouarzazate, formerly belonged to the Glaouis.

It certainly looks romantic from a distance. However, in the 1960s, it was converted into a hotel for use by the cast of *Lawrence of Arabia* and has since become somewhat kitsch. Package-tour groups are ferried in here regularly for supposedly authentic tribal music and dance evenings. If that doesn't deter you, take the road to Zagora for about nine km and then turn off (the road by-passes the kasbah). You'll probably have to take a taxi.

Ait Benhaddou

In the opposite direction from Tifoultoutte, off the road to Marrakesh 31 km from Ouarzazate, is the village of Ait Benhaddou. This has some of the most exotic and best-preserved kasbahs in the whole Atlas region. This is hardly surprising, since it has had money poured into it as a result of being used for various film sets, notably *Lawrence of Arabia* and *Jesus of Nazareth*. Much of the village was rebuilt for the filming of the latter. It's fame lives on, but the population has dwindled.

Getting There & Away To get there, take the main road to Marrakesh and turn off after 22 km when you see the signpost for the village; Ait Benhaddou is another nine km down a good bitumen track. There are occasional local buses there from Ouarzazate, but it's a lot easier to get there by sharing a taxi. Otherwise, ask around among tourists in the restaurants or at La Gazelle. Hitching is difficult.

Skoura

There are also some very impressive kasbahs in the oasis town of Skoura, some 38 km east of Ouarzazate on the road to Tinerhir.

TINERHIR & THE TODRA GORGE

Some 14 km from Tinerhir (Tineghir on some maps), at the end of a lush valley full of *palmeraies* and mud-brick villages hemmed in by barren, craggy mountains, is one of Morocco's most magnificent natural sights. This is the Todra Gorge: some 300 metres high but only 10 metres wide at its narrowest, and with a crystal clear river running through it. It's a magnificent sight, especially in the mornings, when the sun penetrates to the bottom of the gorge. In the afternoons it gets very dark and cold (in winter), cool (in summer).

It's well worth making the effort to get here. Although most of the gorge can be explored in just a morning or an afternoon, those with more time might like to explore further up the gorge or walk through the palmeraies on the way to Tinerhir (people are very friendly). There are numerous ruined kasbahs flanking the palmeraies.

There's little of interest in Tinerhir itself.

Places to Stay

At the Gorge At the entrance to the gorge or just inside it are three places to stay. The cheapest is the *Hotel Restaurant El Mansour*, right at the entrance to the gorge. It's a friendly place, has sun for most of the day, a good selection of western music and costs Dr 30 a double for a clean, basic concrete box. The toilets are clean but primitive and there's neither hot water nor electricity – kerosene lamps light the night's activities. The hotel has its own restaurant, and although the food is a little expensive it's very good. Tajine and salad costs Dr 25 to Dr 30, a salad on its own is Dr 8, omelette Dr 7 and tea or coffee Dr 2.50. The staff try hard to make you welcome.

A little further, inside the gorge itself, are two other places, the *Hotel Yasmina* and the *Hotel Les Roches*; most of the package tourists or the well-heeled stay here. Both places have hot water and wood fires at night in winter (demand permitting). Despite this, they charge only Dr 35 a double in the winter (more in summer) and offer a good set menu for Dr 35 (soup or salad, tajine and dessert). Both have Berber tents in the grounds with tables, chairs and divans, which makes them an excellent place to eat in the summer; you won't be using them in winter or you'll freeze your butt off. Both places are good for finding lifts with tourists who have their own transport.

Neither of these hotels would have been built in a country where environmental impact studies are required before construction. What is more, while they keep a clean image around their doorsteps, they treat the rest of the upper gorge as their private garbage tip. Take a walk up there and have a look at the trash that has been strewn around. Incredible!

Camping Along the main road, some four km back from the gorge towards Tinerhir, are three camping sites. They're all next to each other in the palmeraies and they cost Dr 3. They all have showers and toilets, and there's a small shop in the village nearby which sells basics (but no cigarettes – get these from Le Lac). The sites are *Camping Les Poissons Sacrés*, *Camping Le Lac* and *Camping La Source Sacrée*. Take your pick.

Tinerhir If you decide not to stay at the gorge itself or need somewhere to stay in Tinerhir, there are three hotels, all of them around the main square. The two cheapest are the *Hotel Oasis* and the *Hotel Salam*. The Oasis is Dr 25 a single and Dr 30 a double without own bathroom, or you can sleep on the roof for less. It's basic and there's no hot water.

The Salam, which also houses the CTM office, is similar. The restaurant here is good value. The most expensive place is the *Hotel du Todra*, which sports bizarre concrete fantasies of monkeys and the like around the balcony and costs Dr 57 a single and Dr 68 a double with own shower and toilet (hot water). Meals here cost Dr 9 (breakfast) and Dr 35 (three-course dinner).

Getting to the Gorge
There are no buses from Tinerhir to the gorge but there are frequent shared taxis from the main square for Dr 5.50 per person which will take you right to the entrance to the gorge. It is possible to hitch if you can't afford a taxi. Simply walk out of Tinerhir in the direction of Errachidia until you get to the bridge across the river. Turn left here and wait for a lift (the only sign here is in Arabic). Unless tourists come along you may have to pay for a lift in any case.

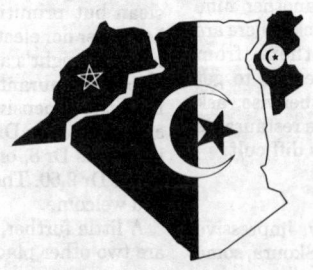

Southern Morocco

Anti-Atlas Mountains

TIZNIT

In an arid corner of the Sous Valley at the very end of the Anti-Atlas range, Tiznit has the appearance of being a very old town, with its six km of encircling red mud walls, yet it is a fairly recent creation.

The best time to be in Tiznit is when the package-tour buses from Agadir have all departed (mid to late afternoon). It then reverts to normality and is a pleasant place to hang around and explore. This is also the best time to have a look at the silver jewellery which is reputedly some of the best in the south.

History

Though there was a settlement of sorts here previously, the town dates substantially from 1881. In that year it was chosen by Sultan Moulay Hassan as a base from which to assert his authority over the semi-autonomous and rebellious tribes of the Sous and Anti-Atlas, as well as the nomadic Touareg further to the south. He was only partially successful in this quest; it wasn't until the 1930s – 20 years after Spain and France had partitioned Morocco between themselves – that the tribes were finally 'pacified'.

In the first decade of the 20th century, Tiznit became a focal point of resistance against foreign incursions. The resistance was led by El Hiba, an Idrissid chief from Mauritania who was regarded as a saint and credited with performing miracles. In 1912 he had himself proclaimed sultan at the mosque in Tiznit and succeeded in uniting the tribes of the Anti-Atlas and the Touareg in a fanatical effort to repel the French invaders.

Places to Stay - bottom end

The best hotels are on Place Almachouar.

Many have rooftop terraces where you can escape the tourist hordes during the middle of the day. They're all much the same price and offer similar facilities. Where you stay will largely depend on what you take a fancy to and which hotel has room.

Most travellers stay at the *Hotel Atlas*, which has one of the best and liveliest restaurants. It's clean and costs Dr 30 a double. The *Hotel des Amis* and the *Hotel de la Jeunesse* are almost identical to the Atlas.

Next best are the *Hotel Voyageur* and the *Hotel du Bon Accueil* on the opposite side of the square. For something up-market, try the *Hotel Massa*. Another hotel nearby, which is worth checking out if the others are full, is the *Hotel Sahara*, at the start of Rue de l'Hôpital.

Off Place Almachouar is Rue Bain Maure, along which there are several other cheapies. Perhaps the best of them is the *Hotel Al Mourabitine*; this is clean and costs Dr 30 a double but has only one hand basin and toilet for the whole hotel. It's adequate and secure, but poor value on the whole. There's a tea room on the 1st floor.

Outside this immediate area is the *CTM Hotel*, next to the CTM bus terminal, which is clean and costs Dr 30 a double in the upstairs rooms or Dr 25 a double downstairs. The staff are friendly, and there's a bar and restaurant on the 1st floor.

None of these hotels have hot water in the showers but this is no problem: about halfway down Rue Bain Maure, at the end of a cul-de-sac, is a public showerhouse (the *Douche Atlas*). This costs Dr 3.50 for as much hot water as you want to use. There are separate showers for men and women.

Places to Stay - middle

The three-star *Hotel De Tiznit* (tel 24 11,

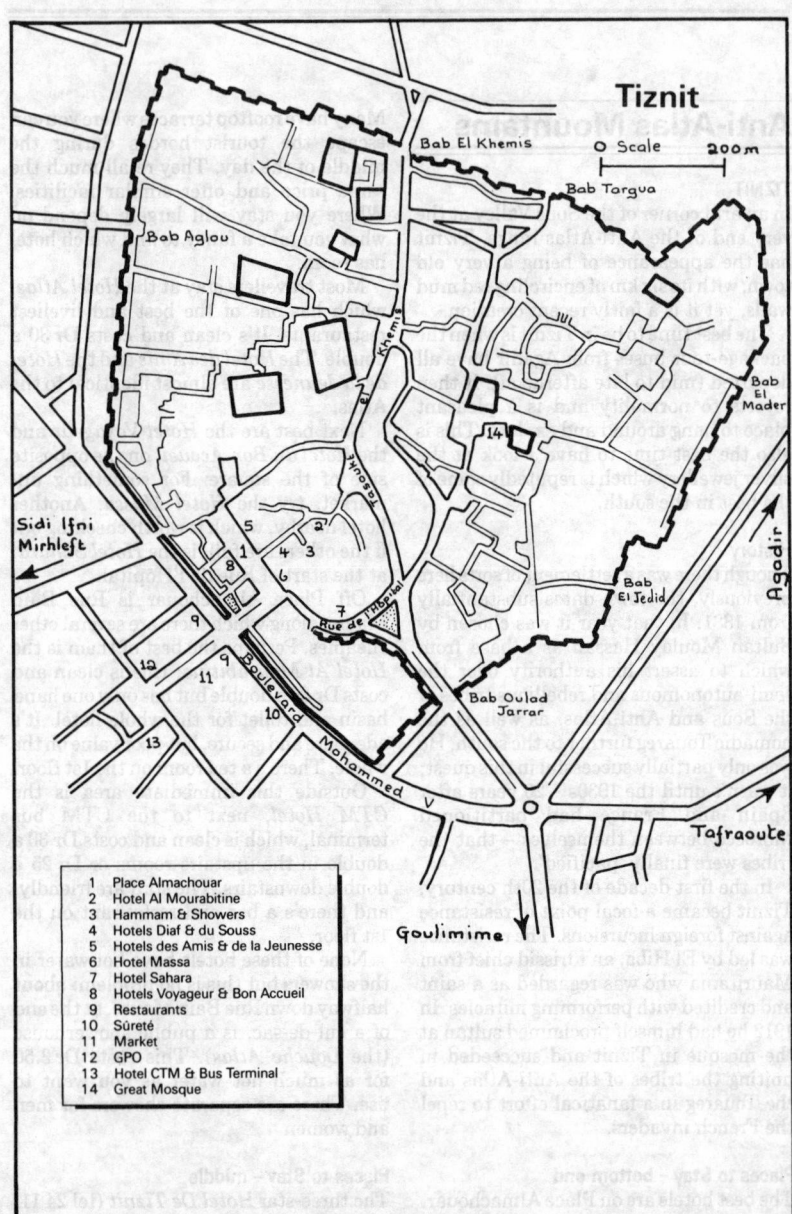

Tiznit

Bab El Khemis

Bab Targua

Bab Aglou

Bab El Mader

Sidi Ifni
Mirhleft

Bab
El Jedid

Bab
El Jedid

Bab Oulad
Jarrar

Agadir

Tafraoute

Mohammed V

Goulimime

O Scale   200 m

1   Place Almachouar
2   Hotel Al Mourabitine
3   Hammam & Showers
4   Hotels Diaf & du Souss
5   Hotels des Amis & de la Jeunesse
6   Hotel Massa
7   Hotel Sahara
8   Hotels Voyageur & Bon Accueil
9   Restaurants
10   Sûreté
11   Market
12   GPO
13   Hotel CTM & Bus Terminal
14   Great Mosque

21 19) has 40 air-conditioned rooms, all of which have either private shower or bath. The hotel has its own restaurant and swimming pool.

Places to Eat

There are several good cafés just outside and also opposite the main entrance (Les Trois Portes) to Place Almachouar on Blvd Mohammed V. Take your pick.

In the evening, the best place is the restaurant at the *Hotel Atlas*. Those wanting to put together their own food should go to the market, which is just over Blvd Mohammed V from Les Trois Portes (see map). There's an excellent selection of meat, vegetables, fruit (fresh and dried) and many other foodstuffs.

TAFRAOUTE

The attraction of Tafraoute, like a number of places in southern Morocco, is not so much in the town itself but in its setting and the journey there. Its setting is spectacular. Hemmed in on all sides by massive boulder-strewn mountains, its nearest equivalent is Hampi in India, except that here the prevailing colour is pink instead of grey. The boulders are smooth and well-weathered – quite a contrast to the craggy *jebels* (hills) elsewhere in Morocco.

Palmeraies and small cultivated areas hog the river courses. There are plenty of mud-brick villages nearby, though the economy is based on the almond trees. It's good walking country, and the town itself is very laid-back. Stay here a few days and you'll find it hard to leave.

The road between here and Agadir is spectacular, and there are excellent photographic possibilities – abandoned Berber mud-brick villages and kasbahs perched on hair-raising precipices, others, inhabited, built on the summits of conical rock outcrops and, of course, the vistas from the summits of passes. Some of the roads are rough in parts, but there's nothing which an ordinary car can't handle. The road south to Tiznit is also

spectacular, though much more forbidding and barren, particularly towards the end; you may get the feeling that you've taken the wrong turning and won't see another village until you get to Timbuktu.

Market day is Wednesday.

Places to Stay – bottom end

There are three budget hotels in the centre which offer much the same facilities and they all have their own restaurants. They are the *Hotel Tanger*, the *Hotel Redduane* and the *Hotel Salama* and they all charge the same – Dr 25 a double with communal bathrooms and toilets. None have hot water.

Camping Camping is the cheapest way to stay in Tafraoute *if* you have a tent (there are none for hire). It costs Dr 3 per person plus Dr 2.50 for a tent (one person) or Dr 3 for a tent (two people) and Dr 3 per car. The camp site has hot showers, electricity and is a very friendly, pleasant place to stay.

Places to Stay – top end

Those seeking comfort should check out the four-star *Hotel Les Amandiers* (tel 8), an amateur architect's travesty of a kasbah, which sits on the crest of the hill overlooking the town. It does, however, have the only bar in town. A good case for abstinence.

Places to Eat

All three budget hotels have their own restaurants. Prices at all three are reasonable, though the one at the *Hotel Tanger* definitely appears to be the most popular.

For a splurge, try the *Restaurant Etoile du Sud* opposite the post office. The *Restaurant Atlas*, further up the square, purports to be of the same standard but is a nasty rip-off at around Dr 40 per person for what amounts to essentially salad and a mediocre tajine.

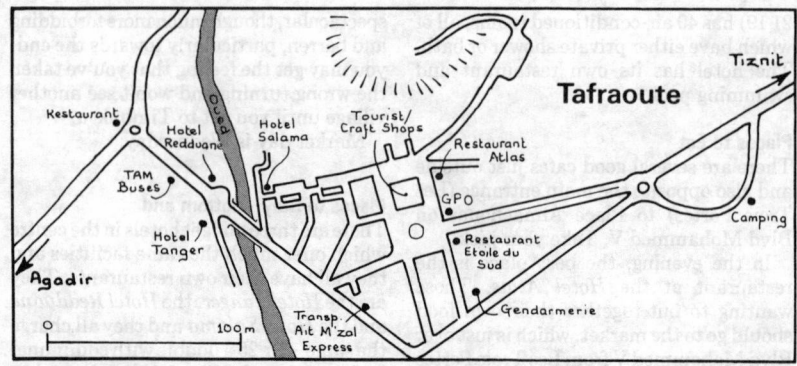

The South Coast

SIDI IFNI

Those of you who collected postage stamps in the dim and distant past may recall coming across the occasional one from Sidi Ifni. Finding out where on earth this place was required a good atlas. It turned out to be a tiny Spanish colony on the southern coast of Morocco. But why here? The motivation for colonising Western Sahara (then known as Río de Oro) was fairly obvious (phosphates), but what was so special about Sidi Ifni? It was this which drew me to the place, along with a lingering fascination to visit tiny esoteric colonies and ex-colonies (Macau, Goa, Daman and Diu, East Timor and Pitcairn Island, for instance). Sidi Ifni turned out to be quite delightful in a strange sort of way.

It was acquired by the Spanish at the Treaty of Tetouan in 1860, following Morocco's defeat by Spain – the first such defeat the Moroccan armies had suffered at the hands of a European power in hundreds of years. It was finally evacuated only in 1969, after the Moroccan government had sealed all land borders into the colony for the previous three years. The town dates largely from the early 1930s and is an eclectic mixture of Spanish art deco and traditional Moroccan styles.

The church just off the main plaza and the building (built to imitate a ship) on the edge of the cliff next to the Hotel Suerte Loca shouldn't be missed! There's even a Spanish Consulate on one corner of the plaza, which is, apparently, still staffed, though it's rarely open for business. Elsewhere in the Spanish quarter, many of the houses are locked and boarded up and in various states of decay. The former port no longer functions.

So why come here? If decay can be described as delightful, that's it in a nutshell. The prevailing atmosphere is a very relaxing one of enigma, abandonment and lethargy. The beaches are virtually deserted, but they're not up to much and are used as a rubbish tip unless you get well away from the town. I didn't expect to see more than one or two travellers here, yet there was a steady stream of them.

Information

There's a bank (fast and efficient and no commission on travellers' cheques), a post office and a gendarmerie, as well as a lively market (fish, fruit and vegetables) and a number of fairly well-stocked shops.

Places to Stay – bottom end

The most popular budget hotel by far is the *Hotel Suerte Loca*, which is run by a very friendly old man (who speaks Spanish and French) and his family (two

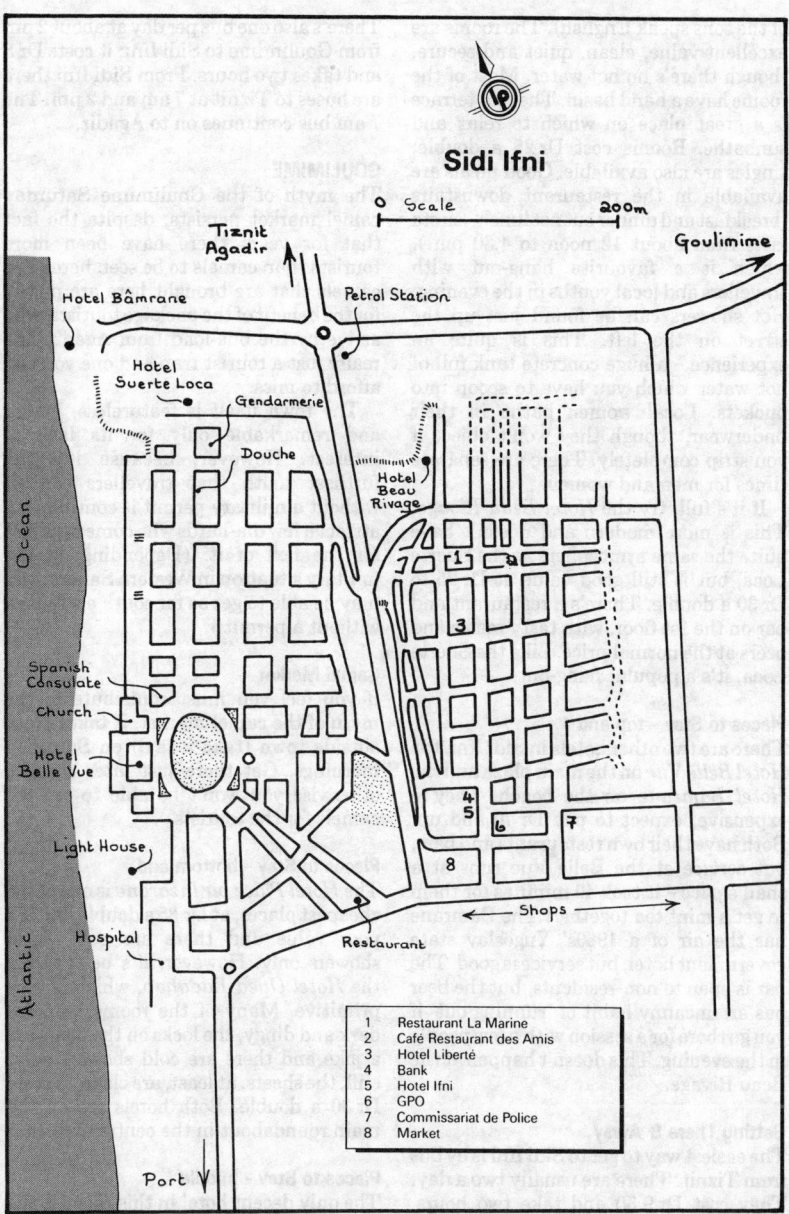

Sidi Ifni

0 ——— Scale ——— 200m

Tiznit
Agadir

Goulimime

Petrol Station

Hotel Bâmrane

Hotel Suerte Loca

Gendarmerie

Douche

Hotel Beau Rivage

Spanish Consulate

Church

Hotel Belle Vue

Light House

Hospital

Restaurant

Shops

Ocean

Atlantic

Port

1   Restaurant La Marine
2   Café Restaurant des Amis
3   Hotel Liberté
4   Bank
5   Hotel Ifni
6   GPO
7   Commissariat de Police
8   Market

of the sons speak English). The rooms are excellent value, clean, quiet and secure, though there's no hot water. Most of the rooms have a hand basin. The roof terrace is a great place on which to relax and sunbathe. Rooms cost Dr 25 a double; singles are also available. Good meals are available in the restaurant downstairs (breakfast and dinner but not lunch – siesta lasts from about 12 noon to 4.30 pm!), which is a favourite hang-out with travellers and local youths in the evening. Hot showers can be found just up the street on the left. This is quite an experience – a huge concrete tank full of hot water which you have to scoop into buckets. Local women bathe in their underwear, though they won't object if you strip completely. There are separate times for men and women.

If it's full, try the *Hotel Beau Rivage*. This is more modern and doesn't have quite the same atmosphere as the Suerte Loca, but is still good value at Dr 25 to Dr 30 a double. There's a restaurant and bar on the 1st floor, with tasty meals and beers at the normal price. Like the Suerte Loca, it's a popular hang-out.

Places to Stay – top end

There are two other hotels in Sidi Ifni, the *Hotel Belle Vue* on the main plaza and the *Hotel Bâmrane* on the beach. They're expensive: expect to pay Dr 70 and up. Both have their own restaurants and bars, but service at the Belle Vue runs at a snail's pace – it took 40 minutes for them to get a mint tea together! The Bâmrane has the air of a 1960s' Yugoslav state government hotel, but service is good. The bar is open to non-residents, but the beer has an uncanny habit of 'running out' if you go there for a session with a few people in the evening. This doesn't happen at the Beau Rivage.

Getting There & Away

The easiest way to get to Sidi Ifni is by bus from Tiznit. There are usually two a day. They cost Dr 9.50 and take two hours.

There's also one bus per day at about 2 pm from Goulimime to Sidi Ifni; it costs Dr 8 and takes two hours. From Sidi Ifni there are buses to Tiznit at 7 am and 2 pm. The 7 am bus continues on to Agadir.

GOULIMIME

The myth of the Goulimime Saturday camel market persists, despite the fact that for years there have been more tourists than camels to be seen here. The camels are brought here purely for the benefit of the package tourists, who arrive by the bus-load from Agadir. It's really just a tourist trap and one you can afford to miss.

The town itself is featureless, boring and remarkable only for its lack of interest. However, because it's the furthest south that travellers can go without a military permit it continues to attract a few die-hards who come here just for the hell of it. (Depending on the military situation in Western Sahara, you may be able to get as far south as Tantan without a permit.)

Camel Market

If you feel you must contribute to the myth of the camel market, it takes place outside town (take a taxi) on Saturday mornings. Get there just after sunrise, otherwise you won't be able to see the camels for the tourists.

Places to Stay – bottom end

The *Hotel Place bir Inzarane* is one of the cheapest places, at Dr 35 a double, but it's poor value and there are cold water showers only. However, it's better than the *Hotel Oued Eddahab*, which is very primitive. Many of the rooms here are dark and dingy, the locks on the doors are a joke and there are cold showers only; still, the sheets, at least, are clean. It costs Dr 30 a double. Both hotels are on the main roundabout in the centre of town.

Places to Stay – middle

The only decent hotel in this range is the

Hotel Salam (tel 20 57), but the management knows it and charges Dr 70 to Dr 80 for a single.

Places to Eat
For a cheap but basic meal of fried fish, chilli sauce and bread, go to the café a few doors up from the Hotel Place bir Inzarane as you walk away from the roundabout. A meal here costs Dr 6.

The only two decent restaurants in town are the *Café de la Poste* and the *Café Jour et Nuit*, opposite the post office where the main road from Tiznit and the road from the bus terminal meet. Here you are looking at about Dr 35 for a three-course meal.

Getting There & Away
The bus terminal is about one km from the centre of town which you get to by turning right after coming out of the terminal.

There are a few daily buses in either direction between Tiznit and Goulimime, and one bus a day from Goulimime to Sidi Ifni at around 2 pm. The latter costs Dr 8 and takes about two hours. The countryside you pass through on this journey is interesting.

The Drâa Valley

ZAGORA
The journey down through the Drâa Valley, with its innumerable crumbling red-mud kasbahs and lush green palmeraies hemmed in by its forbidding, barren and craggy cliffs on either side, has to be one of the world's most colourful and exotic experiences. It's pure magic from what feels like another world. All the more reason to expect something special of Zagora.

Unfortunately, Zagora, like Ouarzazate, is largely a fairly recent creation, dating from French colonial times when it was set up as an administrative centre. Nevertheless, there are plenty of interesting

places to explore in the vicinity and the town does have its moments, particularly when a dust storm blows up out of the desert in the late afternoon and the lighting becomes totally surreal.

Information
Market days are Wednesday and Sunday. Fruit and vegetables, herbs, hardware, handicrafts, sheep, goats and donkeys are brought in to be bought and sold.

Things to See
The spectacular jebel (hill) which rises up across the other side of the river is worth climbing for the views – if you have the stamina and you set off early in the morning.

Places to Stay – bottom end
In Zagora itself there are just four hotels to choose from all up. The cheapest is the *Hotel des Amis*, which costs Dr 18 a single, Dr 30 a double and Dr 35 a triple without own bathroom; and Dr 20 a single, Dr 30 a double and Dr 37 a triple with own bathroom. It's popular with travellers and the staff are friendly, but many of the rooms are very small and dark and there's no hot water.

Slightly better, especially if you can get a front room, is the *Hotel Vallée du Drâa*. This costs Dr 32 a single and Dr 42 a double without own bathroom, and Dr 57 a single, and Dr 65 a double with own bathroom.

Both these hotels are on Blvd Mohammed V.

Camping
Campers have a choice of two sites. The most convenient is *Camping d'Amezrou*, about 400 metres past La Fibule along the dirt track which runs alongside the irrigation channel.

The other site is *Camping Montagne*, which is at the foot of the jebel that you get to by crossing the bridge over the irrigation channel immediately past La Fibule and then turning right. Follow the dirt track for about two km. It's run by friendly

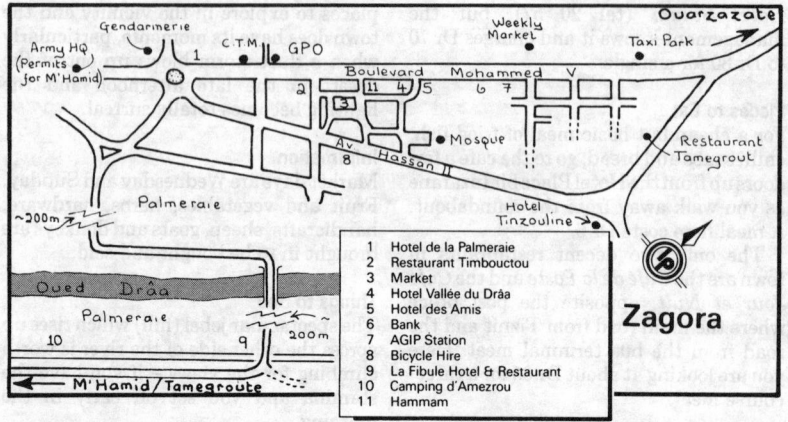

1 Hotel de la Palmeraie
2 Restaurant Timbouctou
3 Market
4 Hotel Vallée du Drâa
5 Hotel des Amis
6 Bank
7 AGIP Station
8 Bicycle Hire
9 La Fibule Hotel & Restaurant
10 Camping d'Amezrou
11 Hammam

people; cold drinks are available, but you're advised to bring your own food.

Places to Stay – middle

Better than either of the two cheaper places is the *Hotel de la Palmeraie* (tel 08), also on Blvd Mohammed V, where the staff are very friendly. The rooms – most with their own balcony – cost Dr 59 a double and Dr 83 a triple with own shower; Dr 68 a double and Dr 92 a triple with own shower and toilet. There are no singles. The showers have hot water. They also have one room on the ground floor for Dr 43 a double, but it's very stuffy and not worth the money. The best place of all, however, if you're prepared to walk a km (or hire a taxi), is *La Fibule* (tel 4, Boîte Postale 11) across the other side of the River Drâa. Set in the palmeraie, with its own shady garden and restaurant, it's a beautifully-converted mud-brick Berber house. It's delightfully cool during the day, and on cold nights there is a fire burning in the restaurant/bar. The rooms cost Dr 45 a double, Dr 60 a triple and Dr 75 for a room with four beds. Bathrooms and toilets are shared, but there's hot water. There's a 15% reduction if you stay for a minimum of two nights with full board. Since there are so few rooms, it's advisable to book in advance.

It's excellent value and a much pleasanter place to stay than in the town itself.

Places to Stay – top end

The only other place in town is the *Hotel Tinsouline*, which has 90 rooms and its own bar, restaurant and swimming pool. Obviously, it's expensive – forget it if you're on a budget.

Places to Eat

All the hotels have their own restaurants, and it's probably true to say that they all try hard to produce tasty Moroccan-style dishes – soups, tajine, salad etc – though the quality does vary from day to day.

The *Hotel des Amis* offers the cheapest meals at Dr 25, but the service can be excruciatingly slow and the tajine is of minimal size, though great play is made of clean plates for each course. It's often better to eat at either the *Hotel Vallée du Drâa* or the *Hotel de la Palmeraie*, both of which offer excellent meals at Dr 35; nor will you have to wait ages between each course. These last two hotels stock beer and wine.

For a change from the hotels try a meal at the *Restaurant Timbouctou*, which offers excellent food and is popular with local people. The complete menu costs Dr 25, or you can buy items separately –

soup (Dr 1.50), salad (Dr 5), tajine (Dr 14).

Even if you are not staying at *La Fibule* you should try to make it there for a meal one day. The food is excellent and the surroundings very relaxing, although you don't want to be in a hurry because the service can be painfully slow at times. La Fibule also has its own bar, where beer and wine are available (you don't necessarily have to eat here to use the bar).

The *Café Restaurant Essahara* in the market square has a good complete menu of soup, tajine and salad for Dr 20.

Getting There & Away
There's a CTM bus once daily in either direction between Zagora and Ouarzazate,

but if you want to stop here and there to take photographs or briefly explore a kasbah get a group together and hire a taxi. It can be very frustrating to catch only brief glances of these places as you speed through on a bus. Make sure you fill the taxi – they won't stop if you are sharing it with local people. Negotiate the price before you set off and make sure the driver understands what you intend to do.

Getting Around
Bicycles can be rented from a repair shop on Ave Hassan II. They cost Dr 5 per hour but the price is negotiable. They're ideal for visiting Amezrou and Tamegroute to the south, or Tinezouline to the north, without going to the expense of hiring a taxi.

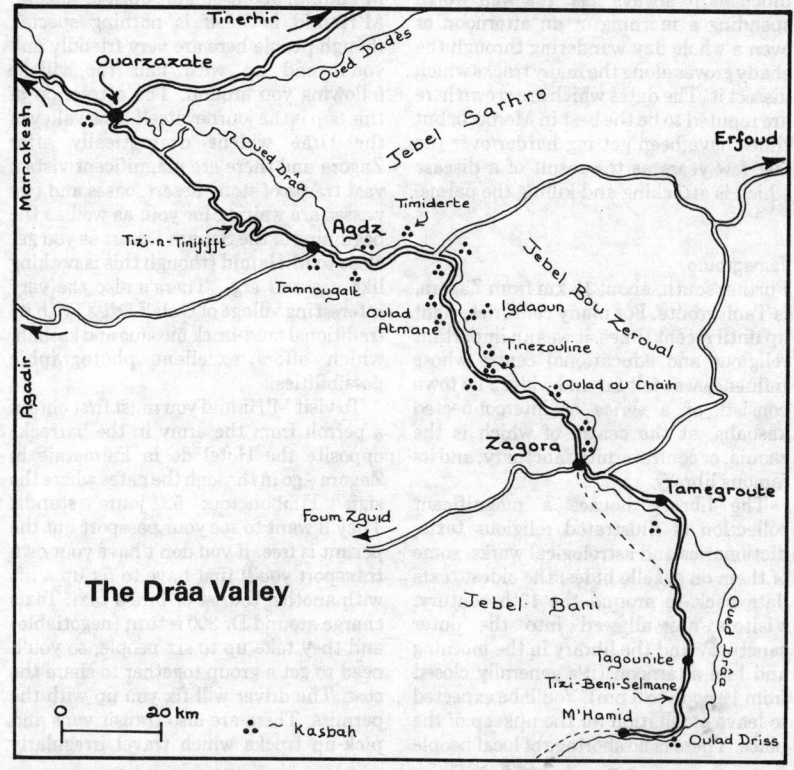

The Drâa Valley

AROUND ZAGORA
Amezrou

Across the other side of the River Drâa, about three km south of Zagora, is the village of Amezrou. It has an interesting old Jewish kasbah, which is still a centre for the casting of silver jewellery. Jews lived here for centuries and formerly controlled the silver trade, but they all took off for Israel in 1948 leaving the Berbers to carry on the tradition. If you look like you might buy something, the locals will be willing to show you the whole process. Because the village is so close to Zagora local children will leap on you offering to be guides, but it's fairly low-key hassle.

Elsewhere in the palmeraie life goes on much as it always has. It's well worth spending a morning or an afternoon or even a whole day wandering through the shady groves along the many tracks which dissect it. The dates which are grown here are reputed to be the best in Morocco, but times have been getting harder over the last few years as the result of a disease which is attacking and killing the palms.

Tamegroute

Further south, about 18 km from Zagora, is Tamegroute. For many centuries, right up until recent times, it was an important religious and educational centre whose influence was felt far and wide. The town consists of a series of interconnected kasbahs, at the centre of which is the zaouia, or confraternity sanctuary, and its famous library.

The library houses a magnificent collection of illustrated religious texts, dictionaries and astrological works, some of them on gazelle hides; the oldest texts date back to around the 13th century. Visitors are allowed into the outer sanctuary and the library in the morning and late afternoon (it's generally closed from 12 noon to 3 pm). You'll be expected to leave a donation for the upkeep of the place. There is no shortage of local people willing to act as guides. Also in Tamegroute is a small potters' souk.

About three km south of Tamegroute you can get your first glimpse of the Sahara Desert. Off the road to the left are a number of isolated sand dunes which, if you've never seen the desert proper or are not intending to go there, might be worth a visit. Otherwise, it's hardly worth the effort. There are the inevitable craft tents selling everything from silverware to carpets, but the guys who own them are very pleasant and will invite you in for mint tea. Sales pressure is at a minimum.

M'Hamid

Most people who come to Zagora try to make it to the end of the road at M'Hamid, about 95 km south of Zagora. M'Hamid in itself is nothing special, though people here are very friendly and you'll end up with half the village following you around. The attraction of this trip is the journey itself. The valley of the Drâa widens dramatically after Zagora and there are magnificent vistas; vast tracks of stony desert, oases and two passes are waiting for you, as well as the beginning of the Sahara Desert as you get close to M'Hamid (though this is nothing like a *grand erg*). There's also the very interesting village of Oulad Driss, with its traditional mud-brick mosque and kasbah, which offers excellent photographic possibilities.

To visit M'Hamid you must first obtain a permit from the army in the barracks opposite the Hotel de la Palmeraie in Zagora – go in through the gates where the sign 'Timbouctou: 52 jours' stands. They'll want to see your passport but the permit is free. If you don't have your own transport you'll first have to fix up a lift with another tourist or hire a taxi. Taxis charge around Dr 300 return (negotiable) and they take up to six people, so you'll need to get a group together to share the cost. The driver will fix you up with the permits. There are also transit vans and pick-up trucks which travel irregularly

Top: Glaoui chiefs' kasbah, Ouarzazate, Morocco (HF)
Left: Carpet shop, Agdz, Morocco (HF)
Right: Unusual building materials, Moulay Idriss, Morocco (HF)

Top: Souvenir stall at Ait Benhaddou, Morocco (HF)
Bottom: Portuguese fortress, El Jadida, Morocco (HF)

between Zagora and M'Hamid and they're much cheaper than taxis. Ask around.

Tamegroute is the furthest south you are allowed to go without a permit.

The Ziz Valley

ERRACHIDIA
Formerly known as Ksar es Souk, Errachidia is a large town and an important cross-roads south of the High Atlas Mountains. However, it's a modern town and holds little of interest for the traveller; it usually serves as an overnight stop to and from the Ziz Valley.

Information
Tourist Office There is a Syndicat d'Initiative in the square opposite the covered market on the main road through town. It's rarely open.

Places to Stay - bottom end
The *Hotel Royal* and the *Hotel Les Oliviers*, both on Rue Mohammed Zerktouni close to the taxi park, and the *Hotel Restaurant Renaissance*, Rue Moulay Youssef, are the only budget hotels in town. They're all basic, spartan, concrete boxes which are all right for a night, but you wouldn't want to stay any longer. (The Hotel Royal is the same as the Hotel Marhaba though the signs suggest otherwise.) The Renaissance is the best of the three but none of them are particularly good value for money. Expect to pay about Dr 25 a single, Dr 35 a double and Dr 50 a triple without own bathroom. None have hot water.

Places to Stay - middle
If you have the money it's worth thinking about staying at the two-star *Hotel Oasis* (tel 25 19/26) Rue Sidi Bou Abdellah, which offers very attractive, warm, carpeted rooms with their own shower and toilet and hot water. It costs Dr 70 a single and Dr 90 a double. If hot water is not

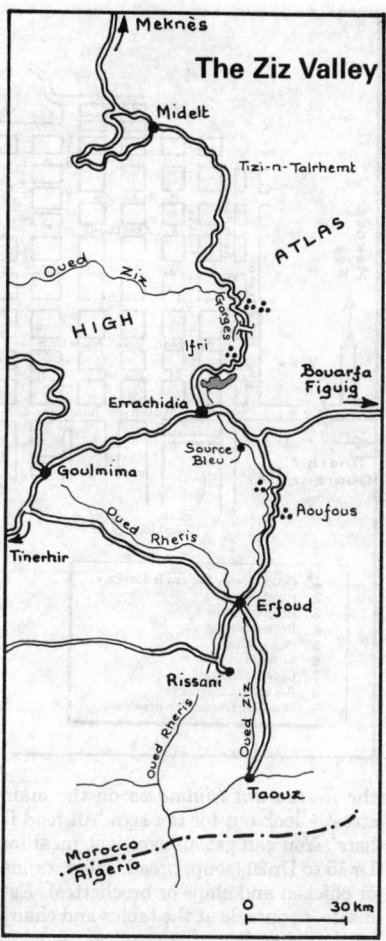

available, a complaint usually secures a Dr 20 reduction in the room rates.

Places to Stay - top end
The four-star *Hotel Rissani* (tel 21 86, 25 84) has 60 rooms, all with private bath. It also has its own restaurant, bar and swimming pool.

Places to Eat
One of the most popular places to eat is

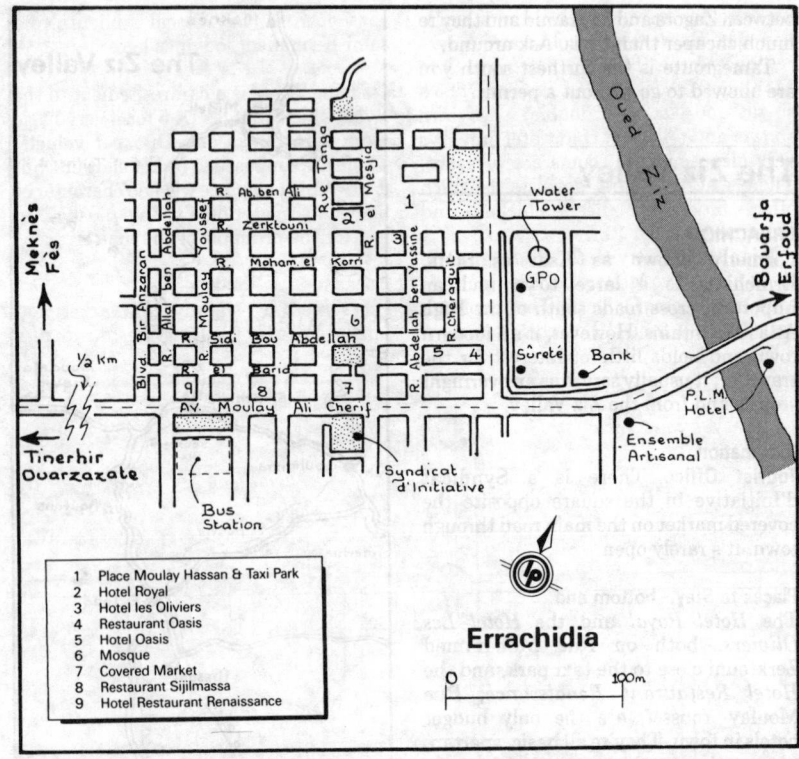

1 Place Moulay Hassan & Taxi Park
2 Hotel Royal
3 Hotel les Oliviers
4 Restaurant Oasis
5 Hotel Oasis
6 Mosque
7 Covered Market
8 Restaurant Sijilmassa
9 Hotel Restaurant Renaissance

Errachidia

0   100m

the *Restaurant Sijilmassa* on the main street – look out for the sign 'All food is here'. You can get an excellent meal for Dr 15 to Dr 20 (soup, bread, salad, tajine or chicken and chips or brochettes). Eat inside, or outside at the tables and chairs on the sidewalk.

The restaurant at the *Hotel Oasis* is expensive at Dr 40 for a meal, but beer and wine are available (drink in or take away).

Those wishing to put their own food together should have a look around the covered market, where a wide variety of food is available.

ERFOUD

Erfoud is the principal town in the Ziz Valley south of Errachidia but, like many small and modern Moroccan towns, it offers little of interest to the traveller. There is no labyrinthine souk – just a small square with fruit and vegetable stalls and three or four handicraft shops with super-aggressive owners. The town is the take-off point for visits to Rissani and Merzouga further into the desert.

Places to Stay – bottom end

The best of the cheapies is the *Hotel Bar Ziz*, 3 Ave Mohammed V, which offers basic but clean and pleasant rooms for Dr 20 a double downstairs and Dr 35 a double or triple upstairs including own sink and toilet. There are no singles. The triple rooms have a double and a single bed. The showers have cold water only.

The *Hotel Les Palmeraies*, Ave Mohammed V, is similar. It costs Dr 25 a single and Dr 30 a double, with own shower and toilet but cold water only. It's very clean and the rooms are pleasant. There's a restaurant downstairs which offers brochettes, beef, chicken and couscous all at Dr 13.

It is also worth trying the *Restaurant de la Jeunesse*, Ave Mohammed V, which has a few basic rooms for Dr 20. The people are very friendly indeed but the restaurant

isn't open all day. Local students find semi-permanent lodgings here.

Camping There is a camp site next to the river, which charges Dr 5 for a very basic room with bunks and Dr 5 per vehicle. There are supposed to be hot showers, but it's a dump of a place with no character or life whatsoever. Some people must camp just for the principle of the matter.

Places to Stay - middle
For something slightly up-market you might like to try the *Hotel Restaurant La*

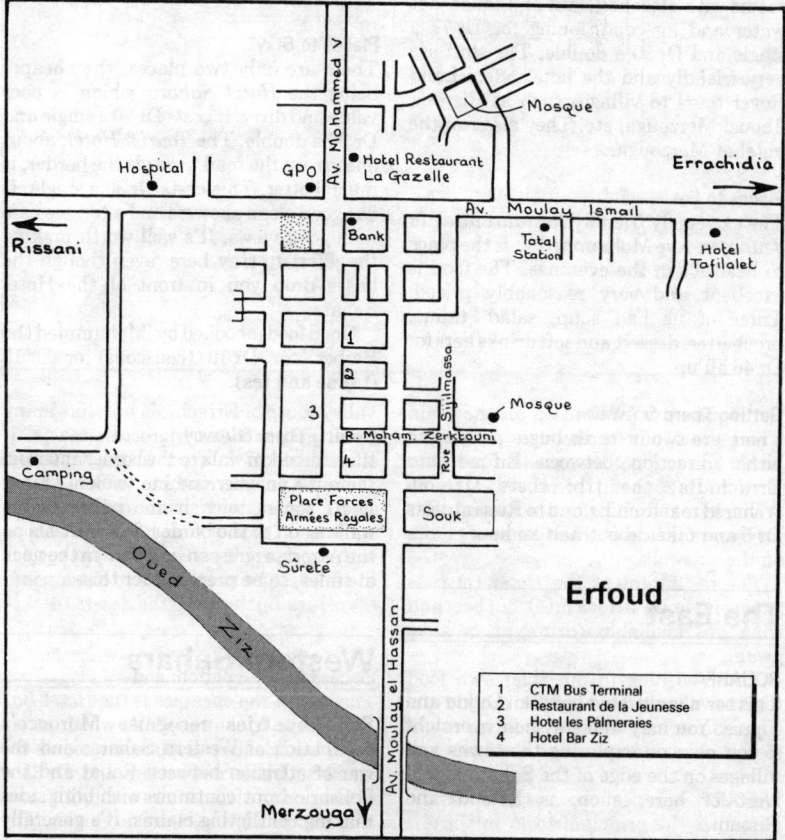

Erfoud

1 CTM Bus Terminal
2 Restaurant de la Jeunesse
3 Hotel les Palmeraies
4 Hotel Bar Ziz

Gazelle, Ave Mohammed V, which has clean pleasant rooms with attached shower and bathroom. However, the manager is very reluctant to rent rooms unless you want to have breakfast and dinner there. This works out at Dr 54 per person. The dinner is priced at Dr 30 (three courses), so that makes it Dr 24 per person for bed and breakfast – a good deal. Hot showers cost an extra Dr 2.

Places to Stay – top end
Those looking for luxury should head for the *Hotel Tafilalet* (tel 30), Ave Moulay Ismail, which is a two-star hotel. It offers rooms with attached bath and toilet, hot water and air-conditioning for Dr 77 a single and Dr 90 a double. The staff are very friendly and the hotel offers Land Rover tours to villages such as Rissani, Taouz, Merzouga, etc. They also run the hotel at Merzouga.

Places to Eat
The extremely friendly *Restaurant de la Jeunesse*, Ave Mohammed V, is the place to head for in the evenings. The food is excellent and very reasonably priced. Three of us had soup, salad, tajine, brochettes, dessert and soft drinks here for Dr 46 all up.

Getting There & Away
There are two or three buses per day in either direction between Erfoud and Errachidia; the trip costs Dr 8.50. A shared taxi from Erfoud to Rissani costs Dr 5 and takes about half an hour.

The East

BOUARFA
This town is situated between Oujda and Figuig. You may well stay here overnight if you plan on exploring the towns and villages on the edge of the Sahara southwest of here, such as Erfoud and Rissani.

Places to Stay
There's only one hotel in the town: *Hotel Hauts Plakas* on the main street. It is very basic and costs Dr 30 a double.

FIGUIG
This is a beautiful old Berber village and the last Moroccan town before you get to the Algerian border. It's the only crossing point possible for those without vehicles if going *from* Morocco *to* Algeria. Palm trees blanket the ruins of the old city.

There's no black market here for Algerian dinar and you cannot reconvert excess dirham into hard currency.

Places to Stay
There are only two places, the cheaper being the *Hotel Sahara* which is poor value and dirty. It costs Dr 20 a single and Dr 30 a double. The *Tourist Hotel*, about one km up the road towards the border, is much better. This costs Dr 30 a single. It has good clean showers and a terrace café with good views. It's well worth making the effort to stay here, even though the buses drop you in front of the Hotel Sahara.

Good food is cooked by 'Mohammed the Berber' for Dr 10 (couscous) or Dr 15 (tajine and tea).

Getting There & Away
It's a three-km walk to the border and from there it's another one km to Beni Ounif. Don't forget to visit the police before walking off to the border. The officials on the Algerian side can be a pain in the neck at times, so be prepared for this.

Western Sahara

Few countries recognise Morocco's occupation of Western Sahara, and the war of attrition between Rabat and the Polisario front continues with both sides making conflicting claims. It's generally

acknowledged, however, that the Moroccans have the upper hand and that Polisario's activities have been drastically restricted. The 1600-km-long sand wall which the Moroccans have constructed, from their previous border west of Tindouf (Algeria) to the coast south of Dakhla, and which is protected by some 100,000 Moroccan regular soldiers has made sure of that.

It's probably true to say that the Moroccans are in complete control between this sand wall and the coast (except for the occasional rebel incursion into the Smara region). That being so, permits to visit the area are becoming increasingly easy to obtain. These permits have to be obtained from military headquarters in Tantan.

Assuming you get one, it will allow you to take a bus from Tantan to Tarfaya (Dr 45, about five hours if there's not much sand on the road) and another from there to Layoune (Dr 12, about one hour). There are other buses from there to Dakhla if your permit allows you to go so far.

TARFAYA

Tarfaya was described recently by travellers who went there as, 'a real hole and very noisy when the desert wind is blowing; a quiet desert town with only one hotel'.

The same travellers described the beach as very good if the wind isn't too strong, and that it was well worth walking to one or other of the four shipwrecks which lie within seven km of the town.

Places to Stay & Eat

The hotel doesn't even have a sign but it's only Dr 30 a double. There are no restaurants as such but there are a couple of simple cafés which sell soup, omelettes and salads. The best of them is the one opposite the hotel to the left. It sells harira and bread, which is very filling, for Dr 1, but make sure you are there around 5.30 pm – otherwise they'll have sold out.

LAYOUNE

Layoune is another quiet desert town, where you can walk along the streets without the usual beggars, guides and dealers hassling you. It's a modern town with some attractive buildings and a bird sanctuary.

Places to Stay & Eat

The best budget hotel is the *Hotel Marhaba*, Ave Hassan II, which is very clean and offers large rooms for Dr 42 a double. On the roof there are good washing facilities and excellent views of the town and the surrounding sand dunes.

There are numerous places to eat along the Ave Hassan II, especially around the place where the bus from Tarfaya stops.

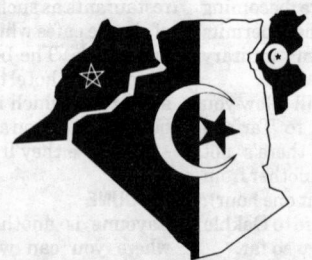

◐ ALGERIA

The French presence in North Africa dates in particular in 1541 when they blockaded and attacked Algiers, supposedly became the dey of Algiers, usually held French consul. The final motive however was the idea of Charles X... to revive the flagging...

Charles X.

Within three weeks...
dey had captured...
weeks later Oran...
overthrown...
Expelled or...
the greater...
behaved...
Algeria...
that even...
been up...
Abdelkader...
control...
Abdelkader...
exiled local...
with the...
he led them...
the French forces...
effectively every...
and imprisoned...
won further concessions...
for not 1847. Such was...
still... fiercely people competed...
late 1848 the area saw its... was the...
stretching from France to the Moroccan border in the north and from the Atlas to Oran in the south. This was virtually... a multitude's apparatus state, with its own modern and educational system.

After a six-year struggle against the French followed their freedom in November 1954. Abderahm... Morocco where he... Abdul al-Rahman... for support. This was provided, but this time was supported by the French as key forces loyal in 1844.

French in 1518... allowed to live by the 'Middle East'. Despite this he was imprisoned in Turkish... and Ambrose... until 1876 he was finally allowed to settle in Damascus where he died in 1883 after 25 years of... when by now a Muslim leader in a... movement and is a... city, with many streets... him, many...

It was decided that... was reached in 1851 when the... commander of the Kabylie (or... region of Algeria) were finally reached.

During the next 80 years of French occupation land was misappropriated and European settlers — mainly of French, Italian, Maltese and Spanish origin — exploited and took domination of the local inhabitants. Local culture was actively suppressed and the Arab interests were replaced with those that certain elite... Many Algerians worked for France, particularly in the factories supporting the war effort from 1914 to 1918, and it was among these expatriate workers that...

Facts about the Country

HISTORY SINCE 1830

The French presence in North Africa started in earnest in 1830, when they blockaded and attacked Algiers, supposedly because the dey of Algiers insulted the French consul. The real motive, however, was the need at home for a military success to revive the flagging fortunes of Charles X.

Within three weeks of the French landing on July 5 the government of the dey had capitulated and, a couple of weeks later, Charles X himself had been overthrown; his successor, Louis Philippe, favoured colonisation.

By 1845, General Bugeaud had conquered the greater part of the country and had been proclaimed governor-general of Algeria. However, it wasn't until 1847 that the west of the country, which had been under the control of the famous Abdelkader, finally came under French control.

Abdelkader was a *sherif*, who had been elected locally as the leader in the conflict with the invading European Christians. He had been recognised by the French by the Desmichels Treaty of 1834, which effectively gave him control of western and inland central Algeria. His position was further strengthened by the Treaty of Tafna in 1837. Such was his charisma and ability to rally people around him that, by late 1938, the area under his control stretched from Biskra to the Moroccan border in the south, and from the Kabylie to Oran in the north. This area virtually constituted a separate state, with its own judicial and administrative system.

After a six-year struggle against the French following their breaking of the treaty in 1839, Abdelkader was forced into Morocco where he called on the sultan, Abd er Rahman, for support. This was provided, but the army was trounced by the French at Isly (near Oujda) in 1844.

Abdelkader finally surrendered to the French in 1846 on condition that he be allowed to live in the Middle East. Despite this he was imprisoned in Toulon, Pau and Amboise until 1852; he was finally allowed to settle in Damascus, where he died in 1883 after 36 years of exile. He was by far the greatest figure in Algeria's nationalist movement and is a national hero today, with many streets named after him and a major statue in central Algiers.

Abdelkader

French domination of the entire country was complete in 1871, when the people of the mountains of the Kabylie (to the east of Algiers) were finally subdued.

During the next 50 years of French occupation land was appropriated and European settlers – mainly of French, Italian, Maltese and Spanish origin – established their domination of the local inhabitants. Local culture was actively eliminated, and the Arab medinas were replaced with streets laid out in grids.

Many Algerians worked in France, particularly in the factories supporting the war effort from 1914 to 1918, and it was among these expatriate workers that some of the first stirrings of nationalism occurred. This led to the formation of the Parti du Peuple Algérien, which was followed by the establishment of the Association of Algerian Ulama, a largely religious body, in Algeria itself.

After WW II the French president, Charles de Gaulle, offered citizenship to certain categories of Muslims. This was considered inadequate, and an uprising near Sétif saw the massacre of more than 80 Europeans. By 1947, however, all Muslims had been given full French citizenship rights and the right to live and work in France.

The Algerian war of independence really began on October 31 1954 with an outbreak of violence in Batna. This was led by young men who had formed the new National Liberation Front (FLN) – a body whose stated aim was the bringing down of the French administration by military means at home and diplomacy abroad. The bitter and bloody fight which was to continue for the next seven years cost at least a million Algerian lives.

By 1956, the fight for Algerian independence was being actively supported by the country's neighbours, both former French protectorates. This led to the construction by the French of a series of massive barbed-wire fences and observation posts which separated Algeria from both Morocco and Tunisia. The fence along the Moroccan border was over 1000 km long, and the remnants can still be seen today. The fences were actually some distance in from the border, and the buffer zones were patrolled day and night by Algerian forces. The idea (successful, as it turned out) was to cut off the revolutionaries from Tunisian and Moroccan support.

As Algeria was in fact a part of metropolitan France, there were over three million French settlers living there. They were obviously unwilling to see the country lose touch with France and, in an uprising in early 1958, thousands of these settlers called for continued integration with France; it was largely these people

(*colons*) who voted de Gaulle back in to power, using the slogan *Algérie Française*.

These same settlers became increasingly troubled when it became obvious that de Gaulle was thinking about granting Algerian independence. In 1961 some of them even went to the extent of forming what amounted to a settler terrorist organisation, the Organisation de l'Armée Secrète (OAS). De Gaulle was unmoved and, on March 18 1962, agreement was reached for a referendum in Algeria which, if the vote went the right way, would grant the country independence. In the event, the vote was six million in favour and only 16,000 against. The trickle of French settlers returning to France turned into a flood, with only some 40,000 staying on after independence.

The cost of the war to Algeria had been tremendous – over a million Algerians had lost their lives, and a further two million had been displaced in an effort by the colonial authorities to disrupt all attempts to organise an effective nationalist movement.

Ahmed ben Bella was the first elected premier; he pledged a 'revolutionary Arab-Islamic state based on the principles of socialism and collective leadership at home and anti-imperialism abroad'. Although popular, his leadership style did not foster orderly administration and he was overthrown in 1965 by the defence minister and FLN Chief of Staff, Colonel Houari Boumedienne. Ben Bella now lives in Switzerland, where he is involved in Islamic fundamentalism.

Boumedienne was a cautious pragmatist. He set about rebuilding the country's economy, which had come unstuck at the time of independence with the departure of the majority of the country's administrators and technical experts, all of whom were Europeans. Unemployment and underemployment remained serious problems and many Algerians were forced to work in France, despite the ill feeling which existed there towards them.

Large gas and oil reserves in the Sahara

were developed and, despite the fact that over 70% of the workforce were employed on the land, agriculture was neglected in favour of industry in the 1970s. As a result, agricultural production fell below levels achieved under the French.

Colonel Boumedienne died in December 1978 and, at a meeting of the FLN in Algiers, Colonel Chadli Benjedid was elected president, a post he has held ever since. He was re-elected in 1984.

There has been very little political change in Algeria since independence. The FLN continues to be the sole political party and it pursues socialist policies. Bad planning by the lumbering centralised bureaucracy is largely responsible for the poor state of the agricultural sector. The last few years have seen President Chadli undertaking a certain amount of cautious reform with the aim of reducing Algeria's dependence on imported food, clothes and medical supplies.

The most radical reform since independence came in late 1987 when Chadli abolished the central planning authority, the bastion of socialist economic control. The new legislation removed most public companies from direct government control and freed up the banking system. Such reform is encouraging private-sector participation but Chadli has been careful not to move too fast for fear of opposition within the ruling FLN, where the old-timers regard any moves away from central control of the economy with deep suspicion.

Algeria is often seen as being anti-western in its foreign policy but it is an active member of the Non-Aligned Movement, and in fields such as gas exports it is in direct competition with the Soviet Union.

The country has become well respected on the world stage for its strong stand on a better deal for the Third World and in its support of liberation struggles. It is a staunch supporter of the Polisario struggle against the Moroccan occupation of Western Sahara and the Polisario base

is in fact at Tindouf. The two countries have come close to war over the issue on a couple of occasions, and the border situation does change from time to time. In 1988 there was a rapprochement between the two countries so hopefully now the position will remain more stable.

Until 1988 there was little real opposition to the government, although there were a number of minor incidents. In 1985, a group of Muslim extremists attacked a police barracks, and in the Kabylie region Berber activists staged a 24-hour strike following the arrest of a number of members of the cultural rights group, Enfants des Martyrs. In December of the same year several members of a newly formed human rights group were also detained without trial.

The most serious challenge to President Chadli's rule came in October 1988, when thousands of people took to the streets in protest against government austerity measures and food shortages. The army was called in to restore order and in the ensuing violence between 160 and 500 people were killed, depending on whose figures you believe. More than 3000 were held in detention without trial. As a result of the riots, a referendum was called and constitutional changes were made.

GEOGRAPHY

The greater part of the country is occupied by the Sahara, while the Tell region in the north makes up the rest.

The Tell accounts for only about 15% of the land area but has the vast majority of the population and all the arable land. It is broken up by a few mountain ranges. The first of these is the Tell Atlas, which is a continuation of the Moroccan Atlas Mountains and cuts right across the north and into Tunisia. It is not an unbroken chain: it consists of a number of separate ranges, and so doesn't constitute an impenetrable barrier. There is some fantastic mountain scenery here, particularly in the Kabylie region to the east of Algiers.

To the south of the Atlas lie the high plateaus (Hauts Plateaux). Further south again, the Saharan Atlas (Atlas Saharien) is the last mountain range before the Sahara takes over.

The Sahara occupies the other 85% of Algeria as well as large slabs of half a dozen other countries. It is absolutely enormous and statistics tend to be incomprehensible – there are just too many zeros! It covers more than nine million square km and stretches from the Atlantic Ocean to the Red Sea.

Despite the common misconception, the Sahara is not just one big expanse of sand. Such expanses certainly do exist, but it also has mountain ranges (such as the Hoggar, which peak at around 3000 metres), dead-flat plains (where the most prominent feature for miles around is a rock the size of a tennis ball) and numerous oases, which support small numbers of people and produce the most delicately-flavoured dates in the world.

The vegetation of the desert varies from esparto-grass plains in the M'Zab to areas the size of England where not a thing grows. Absolutely nothing.

As might be expected, the only major river systems are in the north of the country, and even many of these are only seasonal. The main reservoirs for irrigation are in the mountains to the west of Algiers, while those in the north-east produce the 5% of the country's power which is generated by hydroelectricity.

Distances

With an area of some 2.4 million square km (about the size of Western Australia, or five times the size of California or France), Algeria is the second-largest country in Africa, smaller only than Sudan.

Distances are great: from Algiers to Tamanrasset, for example, is more than 2000 km – greater than the distance from Algiers to Paris.

CLIMATE

Algeria's geography, vegetation and, therefore, its settlement pattern are dominated by climate rather than relief.

Rainfall ranges from 1000 mm annually in the Kabylie region to virtually nil in some places in the Sahara; in fact, some Saharan towns go for up to 20 years without any rainfall at all!

Summer in the north is generally hot (around 32°C), with high humidity along the coast. In the Sahara the temperature is regularly 45°C, and it's not that uncommon for the mercury to climb to 50°C and above.

Winter in the north is wet and cold, with snow common on the peaks south of Algiers; in the Sahara it never really cools down that much, and daytime temperatures are about 25°C.

Tamanrasset in the Hoggar Mountains has a milder summer and a colder winter, as it has an elevation of over 1500 metres, and at nearby Assekrem the temperatures drop to below freezing at night.

The following table gives the average daily minimum and maximum temperatures in °C.

	Algiers	Ghardaia	Tamanrasset
January	7-15	6-19	4-19
April	13-20	18-31	13-30
July	21-29	25-37	21-35
October	17-25	19-31	15-30
December	4-19	8-20	6-21

When to Go

The ideal time for a visit is in the spring. Autumn is the next choice, but the only hassle is that for most of the time the skies are very hazy due to a heat and dust haze that builds up over the summer.

If you are only going to be in the north summer is also a possibility, although the high humidity of the coastal areas can be very tiring.

Travellers intending to take in the Sahara shouldn't even consider heading off in summer. It can be done, but you need to spend quite a few hours of each day indoors, out of the heat, and the rest of the time trying to keep up your intake of fluid to match what is being lost through perspiration. For the rest of the year, and especially in winter, the temperatures are pleasant and make for comfortable travelling.

GOVERNMENT

Officially known as the Democratic and Popular Republic of Algeria, the country is governed by the FLN. Executive power is in the hands of the president, as laid down in the original National Charter of 1976. President Chadli had a new Charter approved by referendum in 1986.

Legislative power is vested in the 261-member National Assembly which is elected to a five-year term by universal adult suffrage.

Directly below the central government is the *wilaya* (province). There are 48 wilayas, each of which is headed by an elected executive council and a member of the central government, known as the *wali*.

On the bottom of the administrative ladder are the local collectives. These are financed predominantly by local taxes, although the state does intervene with funds to meet the commune's needs.

ECONOMY

Since independence the emphasis has been on industry rather than agriculture (it was the other way round during the French colonial days).

The country relies almost exclusively on oil and gas for exports (98%) and was hit hard by the slump of 1986. Until this time the Algerian economy recorded a yearly trade surplus. Although the hydrocarbons industry still receives the major portion of annual government expenditure, increasing importance is being placed on agriculture (15% of spending) and associated medium and light industry such as farm equipment and fertilisers.

In an effort to streamline the public sector, 60 of the country's national

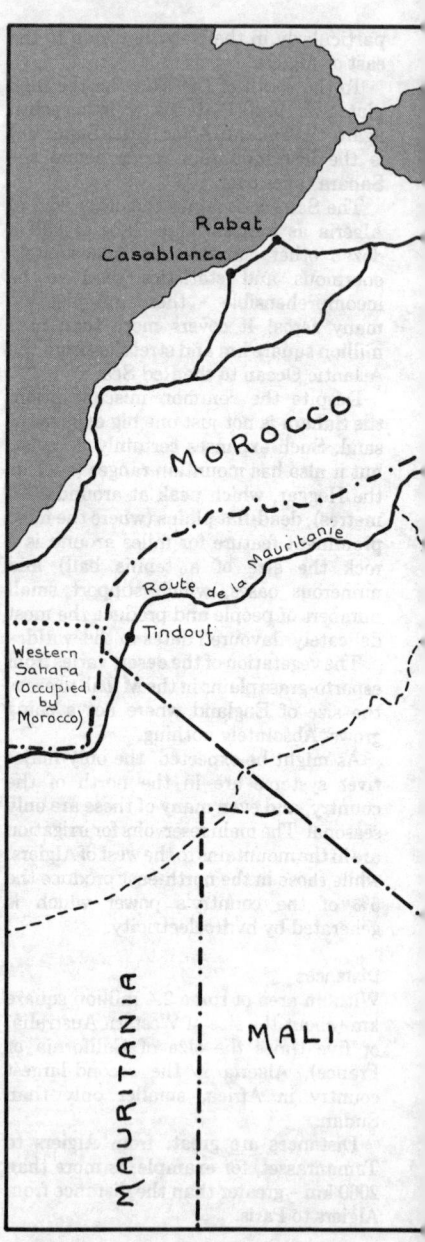

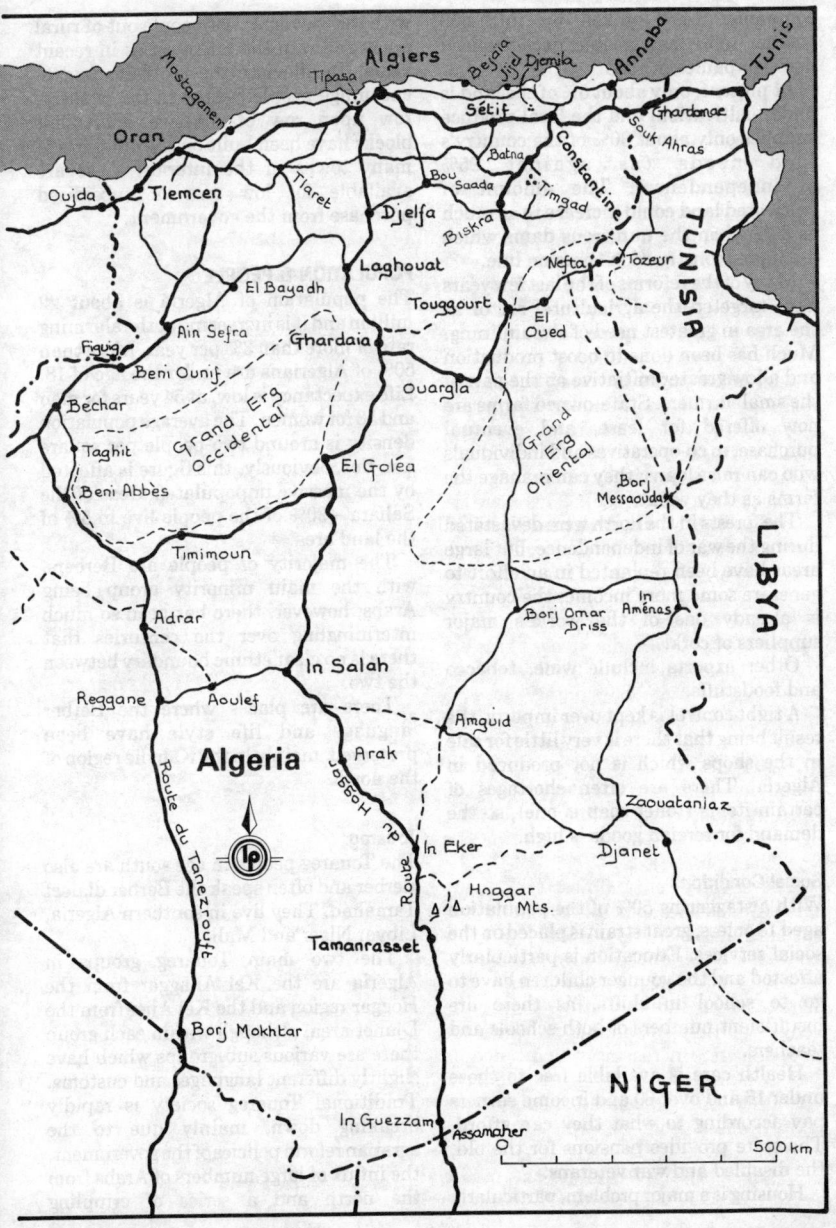

companies were broken up into 400 smaller, more manageable, decentralised new companies in 1985.

At present, only about 5% of the land is under cultivation, and the local produce supplies only about 30% of the country's food needs (as against 95% at independence). The amount of cultivated land could increase to as much as 30% when the numerous dams which are under construction come on line.

Many of the reforms of the last few years have targeted the agricultural sector as the area in greatest need of streamlining. Much has been done to boost production and allow greater initiative on the part of the small farmers. State-owned farms are now offered for lease, and eventual purchase, to co-operatives and individuals who can raise loans; they can manage the farms as they want.

The forests in the north were devastated during the war of independence, but large areas have been replanted in an effort to generate some more income; the country is already one of the world's major suppliers of cork.

Other exports include wine, tobacco and foodstuffs.

A tight control is kept over imports, the result being that there is very little for sale in the shops which is not produced in Algeria. There are often shortages of certain items (toilet soap is one), so the demand for foreign goods is high.

Social Conditions

With a staggering 50% of the population aged 18 or less, great strain is placed on the social services. Education is particularly affected and the younger children have to go to school in shifts, as there are insufficient numbers of both schools and teachers.

Health care is available free to those under 16 and over 60 and income earners pay according to what they can afford. The state provides pensions for the old, the disabled and war veterans.

Housing is a major problem, particularly with the movement of people out of rural areas and into the larger cities in recent years. To alleviate the problems and to encourage people to stay in the country, row upon row of massive apartment blocks have been built on the outskirts of many towns in the interior; these are available for low rent or subsidised purchase from the government.

POPULATION & PEOPLE

The population of Algeria is about 22 million and it is increasing at the alarming rate of more than 3% per year. More than 50% of Algerians are under the age of 18. Life expectancy is low, at 54 years for men and 56 for women. The average population density is around two people per square km, but, obviously, this figure is affected by the massive unpopulated areas of the Sahara – 90% of the people live in 5% of the land area.

The majority of people are Berbers, with the main minority group being Arabs; however, there has been so much intermingling over the centuries that there is no clear ethnic boundary between the two.

There are places where the Berber language and life style have been preserved, mainly in the Kabylie region of the north.

Touareg

The Touareg people in the south are also Berber and often speak the Berber dialect Tamahaq. They live in southern Algeria, Libya, Niger and Mali.

The two main Touareg groups in Algeria are the Kel Ahaggar from the Hoggar region and the Kel Ajjer from the Djanet area, although within each group there are various sub-groups which have slightly different languages and customs. Traditional Touareg society is rapidly breaking down, mainly due to the agrarian reform policies of the government, the influx of large numbers of Arabs from the north and a series of crippling droughts which have forced many people into the towns to search for work.

Touareg women play a much more active role in the organisation of the society than do their Islamic counterparts. The fact that they generally go unveiled has led to some misunderstandings about their morals.

The men often wear a blue or white head cloth (*tagelmoust*), tied in such a way that it covers most of the face; in the past this cloth was usually dyed with indigo – these days it is imported and synthetically dyed.

RELIGION

Islam is the predominant religion and is one of the few things which unites a variety of fairly disparate groups. There are also small Christian and Jewish communities.

Algeria is by far the most conservative of the three Maghreb countries. Apart from those in Algiers, a high proportion of women wear veils. These vary from the white, lacy, handkerchief-type ones worn in the north which cover just the lower half of the face, to the robes worn by the women of the M'Zab (the area around Ghardaia) which are held together in such a way that only one eye is visible – a bizarre sight.

For a full rundown on Islam, see the Religion section in the Facts About the Region chapter.

HOLIDAYS & FESTIVALS

Most public holidays are connected with important events in the Islamic year. For a list of these, see the section in the Facts About the Region chapter.

There are also a number of holidays which are related to events and people important in the formation of the modern state.

New Year's Day
1 January
Labour Day
1 May
Anniversary of the Overthrow of Ben Bella
19 June
Independence Day
5 July
Anniversary of the Revolution
1 November

There are numerous fêtes and festivals held throughout the year, the principal function of which is to attract tourists. The main ones are:

March-April
Spring Festivals in Biskra, Djanet, Ghardaia and Timimoun.
March-May
Tomato Festival, Adrar.
Cherry Festival, Tlemcen.
Carpet Festival, El Oued.
Old Ksar Festival, El Goléa.
May
International Fair, Algiers.
December-January
Folklore Festival, Tamanrasset.

Facts for the Visitor

VISAS

The Algerian visa situation is pretty straightforward for nationals of most countries. People from the following countries do not require a visa for a stay of up to three months: Denmark, Finland, Italy, Norway, Sweden, Switzerland and the UK. All other nationals require visas and these must be obtained before you show up at a border, as they are not issued on the spot.

For some obscure reason, West Germans often have hassles when applying for a visa in Africa. The best bet seems to be to apply for it in Germany well in advance in case there are any hitches. On the other hand we have had letters from Germans saying that they had no difficulty in getting a visa, so there are no hard and fast rules.

Nationals of South Africa and Israel are banned from entering.

For most people, the most convenient place to get an Algerian visa is in neighbouring Tunisia or Morocco. In Tunis they are issued without fuss on the same day, cost TD 9.500 and require two passport photos. In Morocco they can be more trouble, as the consulate in Oujda has the nasty habit of sending people back to Rabat. Once again, the situation is unpredictable and, to be on the safe side, you are better off getting the visa in Rabat (or elsewhere in Europe) unless you are prepared to backtrack. If you do apply in Rabat, it costs Dr 50, requires four photos and is issued the same day.

All tourists entering Algeria are required to declare all their foreign currency (cash and cheques) on a declaration form, and change the equivalent of AD 1000 (about US$200). These forms are important and *must* be kept in order if you want to avoid hassles when leaving. The idea is that you change your money at the official rate and don't use the black market, which pays something over three times the official rate. For the full story on how to play the black market for fun and profit, see the Money section.

Embassies

Visas can be obtained from the following Algerian embassies and consulates:

Benin
Les Cocotiers Lot H 27, (PO Box 1809), Cotonou (tel 30 0454)

France
50 Rue de Lisbonne, Paris 75016 (tel 42 25 70 70)

West Germany
Rheinalee 32, 5300 Bonn, Bad Godesberg (tel 35 6054)

Greece
Vassileos Constantinou 14, Athens 78 (tel 751 8625)

Italy
Via Barnaba Oriani, 2600197 Rome (tel 87 8680)

Jordan
3rd Circle, Jebel Amman, Amman (tel 41 271)

Morocco
8 Rue d'Azrou (PO Box 448), Rabat (tel 654 74)
1 Blvd Bir Amzarane, Oujda (tel 37 40; unreliable)

Niger
Blvd du Sahel (PO Box 142), Niamey (tel 72 3164)

Nigeria
26 Maitama Sule St, SW Ikoyi, (PO Box 7288), Lagos (tel 68 3153)

Senegal
5 Rue Mermoz (PO Box 3233), Dakar (tel 22 3509)

Sierra Leone
Premier Boulevard opposite Armed Forces Building, (PO BOX 1004), Conakry (tel 41 503)

Spain
12 Calle General Oraa, Madrid (tel 411 6065)

Switzerland
74 Wallading, WEG 3006 Berne (tel 44 6961)
Tanzania
35 Upanga Rd (PO Box 2963), Dar es Salaam (tel 20 846)
USA
2118 Kalorama Rd NW, Washington SCN 20008 (tel 32 8530)

Visa Extensions

Tourist visas are valid for one month and are easily extendable for a further two months in Algiers at the Département des Etrangers, Blvd Zeroud Youssef 19A. To get the extension, however, you need to show bank receipts to prove that you have been changing money legally and not playing the black market. If you have changed the equivalent of the AD 1000, the receipts which prove this are sufficient.

Visas can also be extended at the capital of any wilaya, although the process is likely to be simpler in Algiers.

Extensions cost AD 60 (payable only in fiscal stamps available from the post office), require two photos and take 24 hours to issue.

You may also be asked for a certificate from the hotel you are staying at. Often a receipt is sufficient; if not, bear in mind that it may take a couple of days to get the hotel manager to sign a declaration stating that you are staying at that hotel. The whole thing is a bit of a farce, but hopefully you won't have to go through it.

The staff at the foreigners' office do not speak English but are very helpful and polite. As usual, the forms are all in French.

Other African Visas

Algiers is not a bad place for picking up visas, but as Mali and Niger both have embassies in Tamanrasset, it is easier to pick those ones up on your way south.

For a full list of foreign embassies, see the Tourist Information section in this chapter. The visa situation often changes here, and, as the embassies are mostly out in the suburb of Hydra, it pays to make a phone call first. The best way to get out to Hydra is to catch a No 31 bus from Place Audin, get out at the big marketplace just before the end, and from there catch a No 44 bus to Hydra.

Burkina Faso The embassy (tel 61 3897) is at 12 Rue Mouloud Belhouchat. Visas are issued without fuss.

Cameroun The embassy (tel 78 8195) is at 60 Blvd Colonel M'Hamed Bougara, El-Biar. It usually refers applications to Douala, so a visa can take up to four weeks.

Central African Republic The French embassy here (tel 60 4488) is at 6 Ave Larbi Alik, Hydra. It issues only 48-hour transit visas.

Mali The embassy (tel 60 6118) is at Cité DNC Villa 15, Chemin Ahmed Kara, Hydra. Visas issued here are slightly cheaper than those issued at Tamanrasset. They cost AD 60, require two photos and take 24 hours.

Niger The embassy (tel 78 8921) is way out in the suburbs, at 54 Rue du Vercos, Rostomia, Al-Hamadya, Bouzaréah. A taxi there costs at least AD 40, or else take a No 59 bus from Place des Martyrs. Telephone ahead to make sure it is open.

Visas take up to three days to issue, cost AD 40, and you need a yellow fever vaccination certificate and sometimes your Algerian currency form.

It is easier to get visas from the consulate in Tamanrasset, where you need to have three passport photos and AD 64. Visas there take three days also.

Nigeria The embassy (tel 60 6050) is at 27b Rue Ali Boufelgued. If you can avoid using this embassy, do so.

Visas cost up to AD 60, depending on your nationality, and they will keep you hanging around for up to a week.

MONEY

US$1	=	AD 4.98	(official)
	=	AD 15.00	(black market)
FFr 1	=	AD 0.82	(official)
	=	AD 2.00	(black market)
UK£1	=	AD 8.20	(official)
	=	AD 20.00	(black market)

The local currency is the Algerian dinar, which is divided into 100 centimes. Coins in use are 5, 10, 20 and 50 centimes, and 1, 5 and 10 dinars. The coins have only Arabic writing and numbers. The 10 dinar coin is very distinctive, as it is 10 sided and the colour of brass. Notes in circulation are 5 (rare), 10, 20, 50, 100 and 200. Again, they have only Arabic writing but, unlike the coins, they have familiar numerals, so are a bit easier to identify. There used to be a AD 500 note, but this has been taken out of circulation in order to make it harder to smuggle large amounts of cash in or out of the country. If you buy dinars

in Morocco or elsewhere don't accept any AD 500 notes, as some people will try to off-load these onto unsuspecting foreigners.

The fact that prices are sometimes expressed in French can be confusing. For instance, AD 20 is *deux milles* (2000 centimes).

The AD 1000 Catch

The bad news about Algeria is that all foreigners entering the country must change the equivalent of AD 1000 on arrival. There are no exceptions to the rule and, if it makes you feel any better, even Algerians themselves have to change AD 700 if they have been away.

Not only must you change AD 1000, you must do so at the official rate; this means you are looking at changing around US$200. It is quite possible that on arrival you will not be compelled to change on the spot, but will just be told to change at the first bank. In this case there is then nothing to make you change the money and you could use the black market the whole time; however, if you haven't

changed the right amount you can expect hassles when you leave, particularly if you cross from In Guezzam into Niger.

The likely penalty is that you will have to change AD 1000 and then hand it straight over to the officials. This is not always the case; some people have got away with changing only half that amount, but it's most unlikely that you will get out without having to hand over some money. You might just as well change it officially to start with and get something for your money, rather than see it go to a customs official who then does who-knows-what with it.

It is supposed to be possible to re-exchange dinars back to hard currency if you have receipts, but in practice it is extremely difficult.

Currency Declaration Form

Everyone entering the country has to fill in one of these forms. On it you must list all your foreign currency in both cash and cheques, and the officials may demand to see and count it. All official transactions are then recorded on the form during your stay. On departure, the money you are carrying must tally with what you brought in minus exchanges recorded on the form. It is important to keep this form in order and get bank receipts to back up any official transactions.

If you lose the form you are in deep shit and can expect to spend a week or so learning the ins and outs of Algerian bureaucracy. You may even get sent back to the point of entry at which the form was issued, so look after it.

If you can't show the right amount on leaving, expect a 'fine' which might be as much as (or more than) your shortfall.

It's also a good idea to declare any valuables, particularly cameras, and get them put on the form. It has happened in the past that travellers have had such items confiscated when leaving because they were not listed on the form. The same thing applies if you are bringing in a vehicle and are carrying lots of big spare parts.

Exactly how thoroughly you and your form get scrutinised on leaving varies from day to day and border to border, but as long as you keep a cool head and adopt a non-confrontationist approach things should be OK.

It is also necessary to prove that you have changed the compulsory AD 1000 if you need to get a visa extension, buy an internal plane ticket or an international plane or ferry ticket.

Black Market

There is a thriving black market in hard currencies and goods which are hard to obtain in Algeria. By far the best currency is French francs, as most people are familiar with them. You can also use US dollars and pounds sterling, but in many places people are reluctant to take anything other than francs.

The rate is triple (or more) what you get officially; however, because you will get AD 1000 to start with, you need to be staying in the country for more than just a week or so to be able to make much use of it.

Obviously, if you want to change money on the black market, it must be with money that is over and above the amount listed on your form. It is easy enough to smuggle it in (and out), but as searches at some borders are thorough (particularly Figuig-Beni Ounif), make sure it is very well hidden. Any extra money which is found will be confiscated.

The black market is usually not that hard to find, especially in places which are on the tourist route, such as it is. Algiers is one place where it is not that easy to change money unofficially.

The best people to deal with are the owners of souvenir shops, as they are used to dealing with foreigners and are the most ready to change money. The most discreet way of bringing up the subject is to express interest in an item and then ask if they take dollars or francs. If you get no response, try another shop. It is really very straightforward and the risks are minimal, but tact and common sense are necessary. Hotel owners are also often willing to change. The bottom line is that the risk is greater for the locals than for you.

The people not to change with are the ones who approach you in the street. Some may be OK, but others definitely are not.

The government keeps tight control on imports, and with the recent severe austerity measures they were one of the first things to suffer. Items in demand are jeans, T-shirts, sunglasses (Raybans), running shoes, instant coffee, cameras (as long as they are not on your currency form), car parts and jerry cans (metal or plastic). At the official rate it will appear that you are being offered outrageously high prices for things, but keep in mind that it is the black-market rate which reflects the true value of the dinar; the official rate is there only to get more out of you (and the locals) when entering the country.

If you are only going to be in the country for a week or 10 days the chances are that the black market will be of little use to you until you have spent your AD 1000, although it is often possible to exchange goods for handicrafts or for services (such as a mechanic).

Credit Cards
Plastic money is not used at all in Algeria, so you need to carry all you will need in cash and travellers' cheques.

COSTS
If you are staying just a short time and are using up your AD 1000, costs are high. The longer you stay in the country and take advantage of the black market, the less it costs comparatively.

At the official rate, a double room in an average hotel is going to cost about US$20, but this drops to around US$6 unofficially.

Generally speaking, your AD 1000 should last you about 10 to 14 days, more if you stay in the cheapest hotels and hitch a lot.

If you have your own vehicle and are not paying for accommodation it is possible that you will have trouble spending all of your AD 1000, especially if you pay for fuel with second-hand clothes or other items.

TOURIST INFORMATION
Local Tourist Offices
With less than 300,000 foreign tourists annually, Algeria does not have much of a tourist industry and this is reflected in the amount of tourist information available.

Inside the country, the national tourist body, Office National de l'Animation de la Promotion et de l'Information Touristique (ONAT), has offices in just about every major town. However, they are more like travel agencies for Algerians travelling overseas than offices for foreign tourists looking for info. The exception is the office at Annaba, where the tourist officer speaks reasonable English and is exceptionally helpful.

Of more use are the local tourist offices run by the wilayas. The ones at El Oued, Oran and Tamanrasset are all reasonably helpful.

Overseas Reps
You can try writing to the following addresses before you go if you really want some information. West Germany: Algerisches Verkehrsburo (tel 230 7641), Taunustrasse 20, 6 Frankfurt; France: ONAT, 28 ave de l'Opéra, Paris 75002; UK: Algerian National Tourist Office (tel 493 7494) Time-Life Building, New Bond St, London W1.

Foreign Embassies
The following countries have diplomatic representation in Algeria:

Australia
12 Djenane Malik, Hydra, Algiers (tel 60 1965)

Austria
Les Vergers, Rue No 2 Lot 9, Bir Mourad Rais, Algiers (tel 56 2699)
Benin
16 Lotissement du Stade, Birkhadem, Algiers (tel 56 6271)
Burkina Faso
12 Rue Mouloud Belhouchat, Algiers (tel 61 3897)
Burundi
22 Lotissement du Carrefour, El-Biar, Algiers (tel 79 4729)
Cameroun
60 Blvd Colonel M'Hamed Bougara, El-Biar, Algiers (tel 78 8195)
Canada
27b Rue Ali Messaoudi, Hydra, Algiers (tel 60 6190)
Congo
179 Lotissement Cadat, Ben Omar, Kouba, Algiers (tel 58 3888)
Denmark
29 Blvd Zighout Youcef, Algiers (tel 63 8871)
France
6 Ave Larbi Alik, Hydra, Algiers (tel 60 4488)
Rue Gouta Sebti, Annaba (tel 82 6391)
3 Square Cayla, Oran (tel 33 1012)
Gabon
80 Rue Ali Remli, Al-Hamadya, Bouzaréah, Algiers (tel 78 0264)
Ghana
62 Rue des Frères Benali Abdallah, Hydra, Algiers (tel 56 2332)
Guinea
43 Blvd Said Hamdine, Hydra, Algiers (tel 60 0059)
Guinea Bissau
Cité DNC Villa 17, Chemin Ahmed Kara, Hydra, Algiers (tel 60 0151)
Japan
1 Chemin Al-Bakri, El-Biar, Algiers (tel 78 6200)
Mali
Cité DNC Villa 15, Chemin Ahmed Kara, Hydra, Algiers (tel 60 6118)
Blvd Emir Abdelkader, Tamanrasset (tel 74 4115)
Mauritania
107 Lot Baranès, El-Hamadya, Bouzaréah, Algiers (tel 79 2044)
Morocco
16 Rue Dr Khaldi Abdelaziz, El Mouradia, Algiers (tel 56 2752)

Niger
54 Rue du Vercos, Rostomia, Al Hamadya, Bouzaréah, Algiers (tel 78 8921)
Blvd Emir Abdelkader, Tamanrasset
Nigeria
27b Rue Ali Boufelgued, Algiers (tel 60 6050)
Rwanda
30 Rue Doukdouk Abdelkader, Rostomia, Algiers (tel 78 7769)
Senegal
1 Rue Mahieddine Bacha, El Mouradia, Algiers (tel 56 9043)
Spain
10 Rue Ali Azil, Algiers (tel 61 7062)
Tunisia
11 Rue du Bois de Boulogne, Algiers (tel 60 1388)
UK
7 Chemin Capt Hocine Sliman, Algiers (tel 60 5038)
USA
4 Chemin Cheikh Bachir El Ibrahimi, El-Biar, Algiers (tel 60 1186)
14 Square Bamako, Oran (tel 33 4509)
Zaire
104 Lot Cadat, Djenane Ben Omar, Kouba, Algiers (tel 58 0679)

GENERAL INFORMATION
Post

The Algerian postal system is slow but, in the end, the mail gets through. Allow at least three weeks for letters posted from Algeria to reach their destination, and about the same for letters to arrive in Algeria from overseas.

It is far better to hang onto letters and send them from a major town than from a smaller centre, where it's likely to take a week or more for the letter to reach even Algiers.

There are yellow post boxes all over the country but, although I have never actually had anything go astray from one of them, letters posted at them take even longer than from a post office.

Parcel Post Sending a parcel is simple enough, but is best done at one of the bigger post offices such as in Algiers, Constantine or Tlemcen.

Take your parcel to the post office for

problem but there are far too few public phones, so where they do exist there are usually long queues outside them.

It can take a couple of hours to get long-distance calls connected. These can be dialled direct but it is more reliable to go through the telephone office at one of the post offices.

International calls can be made with ease from Algiers. Calls to Europe can be dialled direct, and connections to most other countries take less than 15 minutes. International calls from other towns have to go through Algiers, so they suffer the same fate as long-distance calls: it can take forever to get a line to Algiers.

All post offices have a telephone office, easily recognised by the yellow-and-red PTT symbol. These offices are often open longer hours than the regular post office. The Algiers office is open 24 hours a day.

To give you an idea of the cost, a call to Australia costs AD 70 for three minutes.

inspection before you wrap it. Parcels posted by surface mail to Australia usually take up to four months to arrive; they take a bit less to get to Europe.

Receiving Mail All post offices in the larger towns operate a poste restante service where you can have mail sent. Make it clear to people writing to you that it is important that they write your surname clearly in block letters, preferably putting only the initial for the given name to avoid confusion.

Mail is held for a period of one month before being returned to the sender (or chucked out, I suspect), except at Tamanrasset where they hold mail for 15 days only .

American Express is not represented in Algeria, so there are no card-holder services available.

Telephones
The Algerian telephone system is badly overloaded. Local calls are usually no

Electricity
Algeria uses both the 240 and 120-volt systems, so check before using any appliances.

Time
Time in Algeria is GMT plus one hour all year round.

Business Hours
To a certain extent, business hours are dictated by the climate. In summer, shops tend to close up for most of the afternoon, and a lot of businesses are closed altogether after about 2 pm.

The working week is from Saturday to Thursday morning. During the month of Ramadan businesses are open for only a few hours in the mornings; shops open up again late in the evening.

Government Offices & Businesses These are open Saturday to Wednesday from 8 am to 12 noon and 2 to 5.30 pm; only in the morning on Thursdays.

Banks Saturday to Thursday from 9 am to 3 pm; however, some banks are shut on Saturday as well.

Shops Shops are open from approximately 8.30 am to 12 noon and 2.30 to 6 pm, but these hours are quite flexible.

MEDIA

There are no English-language newspapers or magazines published in the country, nor can you find any of the international current affairs magazines such as *Time* and *Newsweek*.

The closest you can come to some news in English is the back page of the daily *Horizons* newspaper; this is printed in English, but one page doesn't exactly keep you well informed.

The major French-language daily is the *El-Moudjahid*, with a circulation of over 350,000 copies daily.

Papers printed in Arabic include *An-Nasr* and *El-Djoumhouria*.

HEALTH

If you are arriving from a yellow fever zone (West Africa) you will need to show a vaccination certificate.

Make sure that you have an up-to-date International Health Certificate with a valid cholera stamp. Despite the fact that the vaccination is less than 100% effective, officials will not allow anyone to enter the country from the south without a cholera jab; they may even demand that you have one on the spot.

Malaria

There is a small risk of catching malaria, but it is so small that it is not worth worrying about.

If you are heading for West Africa you will have to start taking anti-malarials at some stage, so you may as well do it sooner and save yourself getting it in Algeria.

Water

Tap water throughout the country is safe to drink, although at times it tastes pretty awful.

The water in the southern oases comes from underground and varies from sweet (El Goléa) to hard and saline (In Salah).

Bottled water is sporadically available for those with troublesome guts. Don't bother buying it in El Goléa, however, because it is the ground water here which goes into the 1½ litre plastic bottles anyway! When buying bottled water, check the plastic seal to make sure it is intact; otherwise you may be paying for plain old tap water.

Mineral water is also available, mainly in Algiers where it known by the generic name of Vichy.

FILM & PHOTOGRAPHY

Agfa and Fuji film is sold everywhere and prices are reasonable, although the expiry date should be checked – some of it looks like it has been lying around for years.

There are facilities for getting film developed in all the major towns of the north, but this is not especially cheap and takes a couple of days.

With the variety of scenery and people within the country, there are some fantastic photographic possibilities. Use a bit of discretion when photographing people – particularly women, who usually object to having a camera pointed at them.

The Touareg in the south, both men and women, are also often touchy about photos, so ask first.

ACCOMMODATION
Youth Hostels

Although there is a system of youth hostels, they are well hidden and of little use to the budget traveller.

The main exception is the hostel at Zeralda, 40 km west of Algiers on the coast. This is also the place to head for if you want to camp near the capital.

Hotels

In most towns there is a fair selection of hotels, particularly in the budget range. A room in a basic hotel costs about AD 50 to AD 80 for a double.

In the north most of the hotel buildings date back to the colonial days and still have the original fittings and furnishings: window shutters, washbasin, bidet, wardrobe and a bed which is so old it wouldn't be out of place in a museum. Occasionally, breakfast is added to the price and, although it is tacked on as an extra, it will usually be compulsory: no breakfast – no room.

Even in the cheapest hotels the rooms are often cleaned daily, and the general standard of cleanliness is very high.

For men the option at the very bottom of the range is the hammam (*bain maure* in French). Although hammams are not spectacularly appointed and are usually hot and damp, they are an option when everything else is full. They are certainly not a realistic choice for very long, as you always have to vacate early in the morning and then find somewhere to put your gear all day. Just ask around in the centre of any town.

Top-end accommodation is in fairly short supply, but there is always at least one hotel in each town which offers above-average accommodation. These hotels are often government run and suffer from indifferent service and the couldn't-give-a-stuff attitude (from both management and staff) that frequently goes with state-run hotels. It often happens that these places check your currency form.

Places fill up early in the day in summer and it's not uncommon to find a couple of places full before you strike it lucky.

Camping

There are a number of camp sites in the country, particularly in the Sahara where there are relatively large numbers of tourists with vehicles and camping gear. In the north the sites are limited to a few low-key resorts along the coast.

In the south it is possible to sleep under the stars for much of the year, so if you have a sleeping mat or groundsheet this is the way to go. It's the cheapest way to travel and, if you are hitching, the camping grounds are the best places to hunt around for lifts with other travellers.

Camping facilities range from primitive (Tlemcen and In Salah) to above average (Ghardaia), and the cost is about AD 10 to AD 20 per person and a similar amount for a vehicle.

In the south of the country the best camp sites are in the middle of nowhere but, obviously, these are an option only if you have your own vehicle.

If you have your own campervan and are looking for a place to stay in towns in the north, it is usually possible to park in the corner of a Naftal service station for the night. Always ask permission and leave a packet of cigarettes or other small gift.

BOOKS
People & Society

Adventures in Algeria by Alexandre Dumas. In 1846 Dumas was asked by the Ministry of Public Instruction in France to travel in Algeria and write a book on it, so that French people could learn a bit about the new acquisition. The result is *Adventures in Algeria* (or *Tangier to Tunis*), and it provides a good insight into the life of both the colonists and the locals in the early days.

The Passionate Nomad by Isabelle Eberhardt (Virago, London, 1987). Early this century Eberhardt went to North Africa, became a Muslim and spent years travelling in Algeria on horseback, dressed most of the time as a man, before she drowned in a flash flood in Ain Sefra in 1904. She was the illegitimate daughter of a French woman and an ex-pope of the Russian Orthodox Church. The diaries she kept have been translated into English and are interesting reading, as she had a deep understanding of Arab culture and politics.

Other Guidebooks

For a complete coverage of the African continent, *Africa on a shoestring* is the definitive guide. It's written by Geoff Crowther and published by Lonely Planet.

If you are taking your own vehicle across the Sahara, there are several excellent books available. One of the best is the *Sahara Handbook* by Simon and Jan Glen (Lascelles, London, 1987, UK£17.95). Despite the hefty price tag this book is worth carrying, as it has detailed descriptions of all the navigable routes in the Sahara.

Other good books are the Hachette guide (French) and the Polyglott book (German). Both are similar to the Sahara Handbook, so if you are fluent in French or German they may be worth having as well.

The best overall guide to the country's attractions is the French *Algérie* (Hachette Guides Bleus, Paris, 1986). It is expensive at FFr 165, but compact and well worth carrying if your French is up to it.

None of these guidebooks are available in Algeria itself; get the ones you want before setting off.

Periodicals

The *Africa Review* and *Middle East Review* are published annually by World of Information (21 Gold St, Saffron Waldon, Essex CB10 1EJ, UK) and are a useful source for recent developments within the individual countries of the region. They include a business guide and directory for each country with some useful addresses, so it may be worth consulting one before setting off.

MAPS

The most detailed map available is the Michelin map No 172 of Algeria and Tunisia. It has excellent, detailed coverage of the north of the country but doesn't include the bulk of the Saharan region. For this you have to go to the Michelin map No 153, which covers the whole of West and North Africa and so doesn't have the depth of detail which some people may require.

Another quite good map which covers the same region is the Baedeker's map of North and West Africa.

Unfortunately, there is no decent map of Algeria alone. The state oil company, SONATRACH, published an excellent map of the country in the 1970s, but there are very few copies floating around now.

There is a National Mapping Office on Rue Abane Ramdane, not far from the Touring Club d'Algérie office. They have topographic maps covering large areas of the country, but you need to give 24 hours notice and fill in a form to get hold of any of these.

Finding your way around cities can present problems, as a lot of the bilingual street signs have had the French writing painted over, leaving only the Arabic.

THINGS TO BUY

As usual, carpets make an excellent souvenir but, unless it's possible to buy and post in the same place, their sheer bulk make them an impractical purchase.

Ghardaia is the main centre for carpets, and there are a dozen or so shops selling them. Designs vary from region to region and many of the rugs you see displayed are actually from another region.

In Algiers there are a couple of large shops in the centre which sell nothing but carpets and, although prices are high, they have some good stuff. One of these shops is on Rue Ali Boumendjel near Square Port Said just up from the Hotel des Etrangers.

Tamanrasset also has a lot of stuff in the way of souvenirs, most of it of Touareg origin. At the market across the *oued* (river) there are always Touareg from the whole region selling jewellery, bags and other knick-knacks. Much is made purely for the tourist market but there is still some genuine stuff for sale. Unfortunately, the reason why a lot of these guys are selling this stuff is that the drought conditions have deprived them of their traditional income.

El Oued is another big centre for handicraft buying but, again, most items are made with the tourist industry in mind and the prices asked are often ridiculous.

Bargaining

Bargaining is an integral part of the buying process; don't just pay the asking price, as this is usually inflated. Basically, the more time you are prepared to spend, the more likely you are to get a realistic price.

It is often possible when buying souvenirs to trade them for goods which you are carrying. Things such as jeans, running shoes and cameras are good items for barter.

Getting There

You can enter Algeria by air from Europe, the Middle East and West Africa, by sea from France or Spain, or overland from Morocco, Tunisia, Niger or Mali.

Regardless of where and how you enter the country, it is compulsory to declare your foreign currency on a declaration form and to change the equivalent of AD 1000 (about US$200). Read the Money section in the Facts for the Visitor chapter before entering Algeria.

AIR

Algiers is the main international airport but there are others at Oran, Tlemcen, Constantine, Ghardaia and Annaba as well. Most of the flights from these other towns go only to places in France.

Airlines serving Algiers include Air Algérie (the national flag carrier), Aeroflot, Air France, Air Mali, Alitalia, Egyptair, Libyan Arab Airlines, Royal Air Maroc and Tunis Air.

Air Algérie flies to the following cities: Athens (weekly); Bamako, Nigeria (weekly); Barcelona (three times weekly); Berlin (three times weekly); Cairo (twice weekly); Dakar (weekly); Frankfurt (three times weekly); London (four times weekly); Lyons (twice daily); Marseilles (twice daily); Niamey, Niger (weekly); Nouakchott, Mauritania (weekly); Ouagadougou, Burkina Faso (five times weekly); Paris (at least twice daily); Tunis (daily).

To/From Europe

There are frequent connections with all the major cities in Europe but, as there is not a great volume of traffic, you will be up for the full economy fare.

To/From North America

There are no direct flights. The best way would be a flight to London or Paris and then another flight from there.

To/From Australia

Again, there are no direct flights and the best way is probably via London or Athens. If you want to fly straight from Australia you will have to go via Athens and pay the full fare of A$1585 one way or A$2366 return (low season).

OVERLAND

To most people a trip to Algeria means a trip across or into the Sahara. However, there are many places in the north of the country which are well worth a visit, particularly if you are interested in Roman history.

Whether you are going south from Tunisia or Morocco to West Africa, or are doing a trans-Maghreb trip across the top of North Africa, it is easy to spend at least a month exploring Algeria. Remember that once you have changed the mandatory AD 1000 at the official rate you can start to make use of the black-market rates and travelling becomes much, much cheaper.

Overland through Algeria

Tunisia to Niger Most people enter Algeria at El Oued, but the more interesting crossing is up in the north between Tabarka or Ain Draham and Annaba. From here you can then go along the coast and the Corniche Kabyle, and then cut south to Sétif and the Roman ruins at Djemila.

From Sétif you can head east again to Constantine, Batna and the exceptionally well-preserved Roman city at Timgad, going on to the El Abiod Gorges and Biskra, and then through the desert to El Oued, Ghardaia, In Salah and south to Tamanrasset and the Hoggar Mountains.

Morocco to Niger The options are a bit limited here because of the ridiculous border situation between Oujda and Tlemcen, which means that, unless you

203

have your own vehicle, you have to cross further south at Figuig-Beni Ounif.

A loop around the southern edge of the Great Western Erg should take in Taghit, Beni Abbès and Timimoun. From here you have the choice of heading south for Adrar and then across to the main N1 route south at In Salah, or continuing around the erg to El Goléa and possibly nipping up to Ghardaia (recommended) before heading south again from there. Both routes are served by public transport but the latter is the more reliable if you are hitching, although even then you will probably end up on the bus between In Salah and Tamanrasset.

Morocco to Tunisia (or vice versa). These routes can be done easily in either direction on public transport or by hitching. If you are going from east to west you can easily take in Tlemcen (well worth a look) in the north-west corner of Algeria before crossing into Morocco. If travelling in the opposite direction this is not practical, because the Morocco/Algeria border situation doesn't allow you to cross on foot; however, if you are a vehicle I would recommend this trip.

My ideal route would be from Beni Ounif (or Tlemcen if you have a car), around the Great Eastern Erg up to Ghardaia and then Algiers. From Algiers head east through the mountains of the Kabylie region to Bejaia; from there go south to Sétif and Djemila through the Kherrata Gorge (although you now don't see a lot of the best scenery in the gorge because of a new tunnel) and then to Constantine.

If you want to see more of the desert, head south from Constantine through Batna (and Roman Timgad) and Biskra to El Oued, from which there are good connections to Tozeur in Tunisia. Alternatively, take the northern route from Constantine through Annaba to Tabarka on the north coast of Tunisia, or Ain Draham up in the mountains behind the coast.

To/From Morocco

There are two crossing points between the two countries: between Oujda and Tlemcen not far from the coast in the north, and between Figuig and Beni Ounif 300 km to the south.

Although relations between Morocco and Algeria have been strained at times, things have been fairly stable in the last few years. However, as long as the war in Western Sahara continues, with Algeria supporting the Polisario movement, the border situation could change.

Oujda-Tlemcen The strange quirk with this border post is that it is not possible to cross on foot if you are entering Algeria from Morocco. It *is* possible, however, if you are going in the opposite direction, (*from Algeria to Morocco*). It's a ridiculous situation and may change but, for the meantime, check the situation in Oujda before heading out to the border.

The problem lies in the fact that the Algerian officials will not let people in on foot, but the Moroccan officials don't tell you this and will let you through. The Algerians then turn you back and you have to go through the rigmarole of Moroccan customs again. Very funny.

If you do try to cross and get knocked back, it's a simple matter to catch a bus down to Figuig. The most direct route from Fès to Figuig is via Oujda anyway.

From Tlemcen there are five buses to the border between 7.40 am and 2.10 pm. The trip takes about an hour and costs AD 12.30. The buses stop in Maghnia, so you could jump on there.

The two border posts are right on either side of the fence, so there is no enormous tract of neutral territory to cross.

From the Moroccan side there are taxis in to Oujda, 13 km away. Hiring the vehicle should cost no more than Dr 50.

Vehicle drivers face no such nonsense at the border and can cross easily in either direction. They do, however, face a problem of a different kind if travelling *from* Algeria *to* Morocco: before you can import a vehicle into Morocco you must have a letter or telex from your embassy in Rabat confirming that you will indeed re-export the vehicle. This can take a week or so to come through, so contact your embassy in good time or be prepared to hang around in Oujda until it does come through.

People with vehicles have been known to get through the border here with just a carnet or a green card, but there is no guarantee of this.

There are banks on both sides of the border.

Figuig-Beni Ounif This border crossing is straightforward enough, although you will have to walk a total of about four km. In summer make sure you have some water and a hat, as this is an extremely hot place at that time of year.

This crossing is renowned for the thoroughness and surliness of the Algerian officials who search your baggage, as they are looking for Algerian dinars and undeclared foreign currency. Hide any excess cash very well.

Don't bother setting off from Figuig late in the afternoon, as the formalities and walking take up to three hours.

To/From Tunisia
There are several crossing points between Algeria and Tunisia, not all of them always open. The most popular crossing points are between El Oued and Nefta, and up in the north between Souk Ahras and Ghardimao.

Because there are far fewer tourists crossing into the country from Tunisia than Morocco, the border crossings with Tunisia are far more relaxed and the Algerian officials are not as surly as those who staff the posts on the other side of the country.

Bus There is a daily air-conditioned bus

from Tunis to Annaba run by the Tunisian national bus company, SNTRI. It is a popular run and you need to book 24 hours in advance at the Tunis South Bus Station or the Annaba Bus Station. The trip takes about eight hours (depending on the border crossing) and costs TD 6.

A similar bus connects Tunis and Constantine every second day, also leaving from the Tunis South Bus Station.

These buses are by far the easiest way to cross between the two countries; the drawback is that you have to get on at the point of origin, as they don't stop en route to pick up passengers.

Train There is a daily train, the Trans-Maghreb Express, which connects Algiers and Tunis. In happier days it used to continue on from Algiers to Rabat in Morocco, but this service has been discontinued.

The train leaves Algiers daily at 7 pm and Tunis at 1.50 pm, and you can also get on at Constantine, Annaba or Souk Ahras. The trip between the two capitals takes about 24 hours.

Taxi From El Oued there are infrequent taxis to and from the border. There's a four-km walk between the two posts and from the Tunisian side there are *louages* (large taxis which seat four or five passengers) and a daily bus to Nefta.

To/From Niger
The border post between the two countries is between In Guezzam (Algeria) and Assammaka (Niger), a bit over 400 km south of Tamanrasset.

When leaving Algeria it is no longer necessary to clear immigration in Tamanrasset, as this is now taken care of in In Guezzam; however, you must still check with customs when leaving Tamanrasset.

There is a weekly truck/bus from Tam to In Guezzam on Mondays, returning from there the next day. Although it does get you 400 km further along the way it is next to useless, as you still have to wait around in In Guezzam for a lift further on. As any vehicle leaving Tam will be going through In Guezzam anyway, you may as well wait in relative comfort at Tam and try and get a lift right through.

Hitching south from Tam is relatively easy, although you may have to wait for a few days before you find a lift. The camping ground is the best place to try.

To/From Mali

There is a crossing on the Route de Tanezrouft between Algeria and Mali at a place called Borj Mokhtar. This isolated outpost is 660 lonely km south of Reggane.

There are twice-weekly buses from Adrar to Borj Mokhtar, but you are better off trying to hitch out of Reggane or Adrar than catching the bus down to the border and then having to wait a week for a lift going further.

There are trucks doing the run from Adrar to Gao, a further 800 km south of the border, but it may take a few days to get a lift. The trip takes up to a week, so stock up with supplies before setting off.

It is necessary to clear customs at Adrar and you will be checked again in Borj Mokhtar. There are no banking facilities between Adrar and Gao, so make sure you have what you need.

If you are driving, the road south is surfaced as far as Reggane; from there on it is *piste*, although 4WD is not necessary and the route is in fact easier on vehicles than the Route du Hoggar from Tamanrasset. You need to carry enough fuel to get from Reggane to Gao; although there is a station at Borj Mokhtar, you might have to wait for a few days for some fuel to arrive.

If you are coming up from the south, Gao is the place to find a lift to Adrar. From Borj Mokhtar there is a *piste* direct to Tamanrasset. It is a lonely stretch of road, and it was along here that Maggie Thatcher's little dear, Mark, managed to

get himself lost during the 1985 Paris-Dakar Rally.

BOAT

To/From France

The Compagnie Nationale Algérienne de Navigation (CNAN) operates regular services between Marseilles and Oran, Algiers, Bejaia, Skikda and Annaba, and between Sète and Oran.

In summer these services are very heavily subscribed; if you intend bringing a vehicle across, make a reservation as far in advance as possible.

These are the most expensive of the Mediterranean ferries. Those to Morocco and Tunisia are cheaper.

Algiers to Marseilles This is the most popular (and therefore most crowded) route. In summer there are departures almost daily but this drops to about two per week in winter. Fares from Algiers are AD 409/748 (FFr 730/1318) one way and return per person, and about AD 1250 (FFr 2100) one way for the average 4WD vehicle.

Oran to Marseilles Six sailings per month in summer dropping to one weekly in winter. Fares are AD 461/832 one way/return for passengers and AD 1250 for a vehicle.

Bejaia to Marseilles Seven per month in summer, once weekly or less in winter. Fares as for Oran.

Annaba to Marseilles Four per month in summer, twice monthly in winter. Fares as for Oran.

Skikda to Marseilles Three per month in summer, monthly in winter. Fares as for Oran.

Oran to Sète One of the less crowded routes, but only three per month in summer, fewer in winter. Fares are the same as from Oran to Marseilles.

To/From Spain

There are regular sailings from the Spanish port of Alicante to Oran and Algiers. The port of Palma on the Balearic island of Majorca is also served by ferries from Algiers.

Oran to Alicante Eight sailings monthly in summer, two in winter. The economy class fare is AD 270/474 (FFr 428/752) one way/return per person. For a vehicle you are up for AD 942 (FFr 1600) one way.

Algiers to Alicante Only two sailings per month in summer, nothing in winter; AD 325/596 one way/return; AD 1058 for a vehicle.

Algiers to Palma This is another popular route. The boats stop in Palma and continue on to Marseilles. Four per month in summer, one per month in winter; fares as between Oran and Alicante.

Addresses

CNAN has the following offices in France and Spain:

Marseilles
    29 Blvd des Dames, Marseilles 13002 (tel 91 90 64 70)
Paris
    25 Rue St Augustin, metro Opéra, Paris
Sète
    4 Quai d'Alger, Sète 34203 (tel 67 74 70 55)
Lyons
    3 Rue Président Carnot, Lyons 69002 (tel 78 42 22 70)
Palma
    Agencia Schembri, Plaza Lonja 2 to 4, (PO Box 71; tel 72 7141)
Alicante
    Agencia Romeu, Plaza 18 Julio 2, Alicante (tel 20 8333)

Madrid
    Romeu Y Cia SA Cristobal Bordiu 19 to 21 (tel 234 7407)

In Algeria there are offices in all the major towns and cities along the coast; these are listed in the appropriate sections on each city.

The head office (tel 63 2697) is in Algiers at 6 Blvd Khemisti, near the main post office.

LEAVING ALGERIA

One thing to be aware of if you are buying a ferry or plane ticket (local or international) is that you have to change money specially (at the official rate) to do it. Even if you have receipts to prove that you have already changed AD 1000, these are not sufficient. It is sometimes possible to get around this regulation by trying a different agency (if there is another in the city), so try this before changing more money.

When changing money for an international ticket, ask for a paper called 'Attestation de Cession de Devises', which the bank fills out in triplicate. You then give one copy to the office where you buy the ticket and you keep another to show when leaving the country, if asked. The issue of the form is also noted on your currency declaration form.

It does sometimes happen that when the bank issues an Attestation they want to keep your bank receipts. In this case make sure you get photocopies to show the border officials when leaving. In fact, if possible, it is better to give the bank the photocopies and keep the originals.

Getting Around

AIR

Algeria has a well-developed internal air network, and there are regular connections between Algiers and other major centres. One of the main problems is that most of the flights radiate from Algiers, so although two towns might have good connections with Algiers there will be no direct flight between them.

Air fares are heavily subsidised by the government, so the locals look on the internal flights rather like a bus service. Don't expect any in-flight comforts such as food or drinks; this is basic, no-frills people transport, and you'll be lucky if you even have a safety belt which works.

These flights are not such a bargain for foreigners, because all air fares must be paid for with dinars bought at the official rate, and with a special receipt ('Attestation de Cession de Devises') to prove it. It is sometimes possible to get around this regulation in Algiers by trying at a second Air Algérie agency, and in the country centres they may be less strict about it. If you can get away with it and use black market money, flights are a real bargain.

All flights are usually heavily booked, so you need to make a reservation as far in advance as possible. Air Algérie has a computerised booking system, but unless you are making a reservation in Algiers you still have to wait a couple of days before you can get a confirmation.

Air Algérie operates the following flights (fares quoted are one way and include a tax of AD 40):

From Algiers
Adrar, three times weekly; AD 295
Annaba: three times daily; AD 331
Béchar: daily; AD 330
Constantine: three times daily; AD 258
Djanet: three times weekly; AD 410
El Goléa: twice weekly; AD 302
El Oued: daily; AD 225
Ghardaia: twice daily; AD 226

Hassi Messaoud: three times weekly; AD 279
Illizi: three times weekly; AD 343
In Amenas: twice weekly; AD 319
In Guezzam: once weekly; AD 513
In Salah: three times weekly; AD 299
Tamanrasset: at least daily; AD 424
Tindouf: twice weekly; AD 409

From Adrar
Borj Mokhtar: twice weekly; AD 220
Tamanrasset: twice weekly; AD 236
Ghardaia: twice weekly; AD 197
In Salah:weekly; AD 108

From Djanet
Ghardaia: twice weekly; AD 300
Illizi: three times weekly; AD 108
In Amenas: once weekly; AD 144
Ouargla: four times weekly; AD 271
Tamanrasset: once weekly; AD 410

From Ghardaia
Constantine: twice weekly; AD 234
Tamanrasset: four times weekly; AD 305

From Tamanrasset
Constantine: once weekly; AD 410
Borj Mokhtar: once weekly; AD 162
In Guezzam: once weekly; AD 240
In Salah: four times weekly; AD 182

BUS

All buses in the country are operated by the national bus company. This is known by various initials, most commonly TVE but also SNTV and TVSE. The buses are usually bright orange but the newer ones are white.

The larger towns have a purpose-built bus station while the smaller towns have, at the very least, an office where you can make reservations and from which the buses leave.

Bus travel is fast and comfortable throughout the north with frequent departures connecting all the towns. In the south things are much the same on the good roads, except that there are fewer services. Points as far south as Adrar, El

Top: Old appartment block, Algiers (HF)
Left: Martyrs' Monument, Algiers (HF)
Right: The main square, Constantine, Algeria (HF)

Goléa and Hassi Messaoud are all served daily by regular buses.

There are public buses even on the bad roads, although they are buses with a difference – they are usually Mercedes trucks, with a passenger cabin with seats for about 20 people built on to the chassis. As you can well imagine, these are real bone shakers: 18 hours on of them along roads which defy description leaves you feeling more than just a tad knackered.

These truck/buses operate on the route south from In Salah to Tamanrasset and In Guezzam, and from Adrar to Borj Mokhtar and across to In Salah. The incredibly tough conditions that these buses have to endure day after day mean that they are prone to breakdowns. The main routes are usually kept serviced, but services on the less frequented ones, such as from In Salah to Adrar, may be suspended if there aren't enough buses in one piece at any one time.

From Tamanrasset there are no buses out to the Hoggar Mountains or to Djanet, nor are there any services south of In Aménas on the route to Djanet from Touggourt.

Booking in advance is advisable, particularly in the summer. It is only possible to book 24 or sometimes just 12 hours in advance; this varies from one place to the next. Fares are reasonable (AD 97 for Annaba to El Oued, or AD 81 for Adrar to Beni Abbès, for example); there is usually a AD 5 or AD 10 charge made for any bag which goes in the luggage compartment.

TRAIN
There is a limited rail network in the north of the country, but the trains are slow and frequency is not that great. Buses are a better (and faster) bet if you prefer not to hitch.

Passenger services run as far south as Béchar in the west and Touggourt in the east.

TAXI
Louages (large shared taxis) operate only in the northern part of the country. They go as far south as Adrar on the Route du Tanezrouft, Ghardaia in the centre and Hassi Messaoud in the east.

They don't run to any schedule but just leave when full. For this reason they can be more convenient than the buses but they are considerably more expensive. Count on about AD 30 per 100 km.

All taxis are yellow Peugeot station wagons, either the old 404, or the newer 504 or 505.

DRIVING
Car Rental
It is possible to rent cars but the tariffs are astronomically high, especially as you have to show that you have changed money officially.

The main rental company is Algérie Auto Tourisme and they have offices in Algiers, Annaba, Oran and Constantine.

The tariff for the smallest category (Renault 4) is AD 218 per day, plus AD 2 per km, plus insurance and fuel.

Fuel
Fuel is fairly cheap in Algeria, particularly in comparison with neighbouring Tunisia and Morocco.

The hydrocarbons industry is wholly owned and run by the state company SONATRACH. Naftal is the brand name given to the state's petrol and service stations.

Particularly in the south it is sometimes possible to pay for your fuel with goods which you don't want, especially vehicle spare parts and jerry cans.

The price of petrol (*essence*) is set at AD 3.20 per litre for super, AD 2.70 per litre for regular. Diesel ('Gasoil') is much cheaper at only AD 0.80 per litre.

It is obviously much more economical to be driving a diesel-powered vehicle, and an added advantage is that diesel is more widely available than petrol.

When buying petrol check whether you

are getting super or regular, as there is often a shortage of super.

Vehicle Insurance

When you are bringing your own vehicle into Algeria, insurance has to be purchased at the port or border post. It costs AD 50 for 10 days; AD 60 for 20 days; AD 90 for 30 days; and AD 130 for 45 days.

There is also a vague tax of about AD 40 that has to be paid on top of the insurance.

HITCHING

This is one of the joys of Algeria. In the north it is really a dream come true. No sooner have you got your pack off and the thumb out than a car stops, and you can even be choosy about which cars you pick. Lifts are always free and often lead to an invite to someone's house for a meal or even overnight, especially if you can converse in French.

The only real problem with hitching is that you need to get yourself to the outskirts of the town before you start, as most traffic is only local and it's a waste of time trying to get a ride in the centre of town. The best plan in the bigger towns is to catch a local bus to the first small town along your route. Otherwise, a taxi to the edge of town can save an hour's hard slog and usually only costs a few dinar.

In the south it's a different story. Yes, you can still hitch all the way to Tamanrasset for free, but it is becoming increasingly difficult. A lot of the vehicles on the roads are trucks, many of which belong to the state-owned transport company (SNTR) and have a large 'D' on top of the cabin. Drivers of these trucks are forbidden to carry passengers and risk losing their jobs if they are caught with someone else in the cab. Some drivers will pick people up if they know there is no police checkpoint along the road they will be using.

Hitching south from Ghardaia to Tamanrasset is generally a lot easier than hitching in the opposite direction, mainly because there are a fair number of foreigners in vehicles heading south, but very few going north. They will usually give lifts where possible but most are so loaded to the eyeballs with gear that there is just no room for an extra body or two. Nevertheless, people still do get to Tam (and beyond) for free, although waits of two or three days to get out of places like In Salah are not unheard of.

Registration Plates The last two numbers of the licence plates of Algerian vehicles identify the wilaya (province) that the vehicle is from. It can sometimes be useful, especially when hitching, to know whether the vehicle is local or from somewhere else and therefore likely to be travelling further. It could also help to pass the time . . .

The main wilaya numbers are:

Adrar	01
Batna	05
Bejaia	06
Biskra	07
Béchar	08
Tamanrasset	11
Tlemcen	13
Algiers	16
Annaba	23
Constantine	25
Ouargla	30
Oran	31
Illizi	33
Tindouf	37
El Oued	39
Ghardaia	47

LOCAL TRANSPORT
Bus

Most cities and towns have a local bus network but, other than in Algiers, usually only the route number is intelligible to non-Arabic speakers.

In Algiers the system is well organised and there are route maps at all the main stops. In other places it is less easy to get a grasp of the system and you need local advice on which bus to catch. Local people will generally go out of their way to help.

Taxi

Local taxis are yellow, just the same as the long-distance ones. Fares should be negotiated in advance, although in Algiers drivers will use the meter.

Metro

There is a metro system under construction in Algiers but it is unlikely to open in the near future.

Algiers

Known as Alger in French and El Djazair in Arabic, Algiers is the capital of Algeria; with a population approaching three million, it is also far and away the largest city in the country.

As a city it is not all that fantastic but it's still a pleasant enough place to spend a few days in. It's especially good if you need to pick up visas, as just about every African country has diplomatic representation here.

As is the case in most countries in the developing world, what you find in the capital is hardly typical of the whole country – in Algiers the pace is faster, the hemlines higher and veils are few and far between. Most of the buildings in the medina (and indeed in the rest of the city) date back only to the time of the French occupation – nearly all the local buildings were pulled down to make way for the French buildings. There are a few magnificent mansions and palaces built by the Turks but, with a couple of exceptions, you can look at these from the outside only.

History

Known as Icosium in Phoenician and Roman times, Algiers was definitely overshadowed by the main North African capital, Cesare (Cherchell), about 100 km to the west.

It fell to the Vandals in the 5th century, but its fortunes revived under the Byzantines. Icosium remained a commercial outpost until the 10th century, when the town was revived by a Berber dynasty of the Sanhaja federation under the name of El Djazair.

Piracy became a major occupation on the Barbary coast and, in the 16th century, the famous pirate Barbarossa (from whose name Barbary is derived) occupied the city. After he defended it against Spanish invasion the title of

beylerbey was conferred on him by the sultan of Constantinople.

During the years of Ottoman occupation the city prospered, and the large kasbah built on the hill overlooking the bay became the beylical residence.

On June 14 1830 the French landed at Sidi Fredj, and by July 5 the last governor of Algiers capitulated to them. Algiers became the administrative and military capital of the French colony.

During WW II the city became the headquarters of the Allied forces in North Africa. During the late '50s and early '60s it was the focal point in the nationalist struggle against the French. In 1962 Algiers became the capital of independent Algeria.

Orientation

The city centre is hemmed in against the bay by the mountains which rise steeply from the coast. The skyline of the city is dominated by two structures, both impossible to miss. To the south of the centre is the Martyrs' Monument (Makam ech Chahid), a 92-metre-high concrete memorial in the shape of three highly stylised palm fronds. Closer to the city centre, the box shape of the four-star Hotel Aurassi is dominant.

The commercial and business centre is the area directly south of the medina. Here you'll find all the major shops, banks, hotels and the post office. The railway station and ferry terminal are only five minutes' walk from this area, and the bus station is 15 minutes away.

Everything in the centre is within walking distance, and nothing is far from the main street, Rue Larbi Ben M'Hidi. This is a tree-lined pedestrian precinct running north from Place Grande Poste to the medina. Place Grande Poste is a major square, where you'll find the post office and local bus terminal; at present, with the new metro under construction, it is also a building site.

The medina itself is fairly run down and has become something of a slum area, although there has been a concerted effort in the last few years to clean up the place a bit.

In the centre, the buildings along the waterfront road, Blvd Zighout Youcef, provide a grand architectural sweep as they look out over the docks and the bay; the boulevard itself is popular among evening promenaders. Below this road, almost at water level, is another road running parallel to the waterfront; on this reclaimed strip of land is the railway station and ferry terminal.

Out in front of Place Port Said, a small square on Blvd Zighout Youcef, there is what looks like a water tower. It is in fact an *ascenseur* (passenger lift), which for 50 centimes will take you from one level to another – handy if you have just got off the train and have a heavy pack to lug up the ramps which connect the two road levels. On the lower level the lift is right by the railway station entrance.

The embassies are nearly all out in the suburb of Hydra, five km south of the centre, or in the suburbs of El Biar and Bouzaréah. All these places are easily reached by taxi. Else take bus No 31 from Place Audin to a large marketplace, and a bus No 44 from there to Hydra; to get to Bouzaréah, take bus No 59 from Place des Martyrs (Martyrs' Square).

Just to make life easier for foreigners, all the bilingual Arabic-French street-name signs have had the French painted over leaving only the Arabic, which is of very little use to the average visitor. This is a practice which has been pursued throughout the north.

Information
Tourist Offices For what it's worth, there are branches of ONAT (Office National Algérien du Tourisme; tel 64 1550), behind the Hotel Safir, and at 2 Rue Didouche Mourad (tel 63 1066). Neither of these offices has any information, but the staff do try to help.

The Touring Club d'Algérie (tel 64 6276) has an office at 21 Rue Abane Ramdane, which runs off Place Port Said. The people staffing this office are helpful and can sometimes supply maps of the country. If you have a vehicle and need assistance, these are the people to see.

A good map of Algiers is available from the bookshops along Rue Larbi Ben M'Hidi for AD 10.

Also extremely helpful are the city maps on signboards on the footpath at various places around town. Two handy ones are at Place Port Said and behind the town hall, right near the entrance to the Safir Hotel.

Post The main post office is on Place Grande Poste, at the southern end of the main street, Rue Larbi Ben M'Hidi. It's an imposing neo-Moorish building complete with arches and mosaics and is worth a look inside even if you have no business to do there.

The poste restante counter is well organised and is in the telex office, around to the left of the main entrance. It's the doorway at the top of a short flight of steps, at the end of the small alley on the left of the post office. There is a charge of AD 1 for every letter collected.

The parcel-post counter is in the main hall of the post office, as is the philatelic section.

The post office is open Saturday to Wednesday from 8 am to 7 pm, Thursday 8 am to 1 pm; closed on Fridays.

Telephones The international telephone office is by Place Grande Poste on the corner of Rue Asselah. It is open 24 hours a day and you can dial direct to most countries in Europe.

To ring Australia or the USA you have to go through the operator, and calls cost AD 70 for three minutes.

Connections are very quick; a wait of 15 minutes is unusually long.

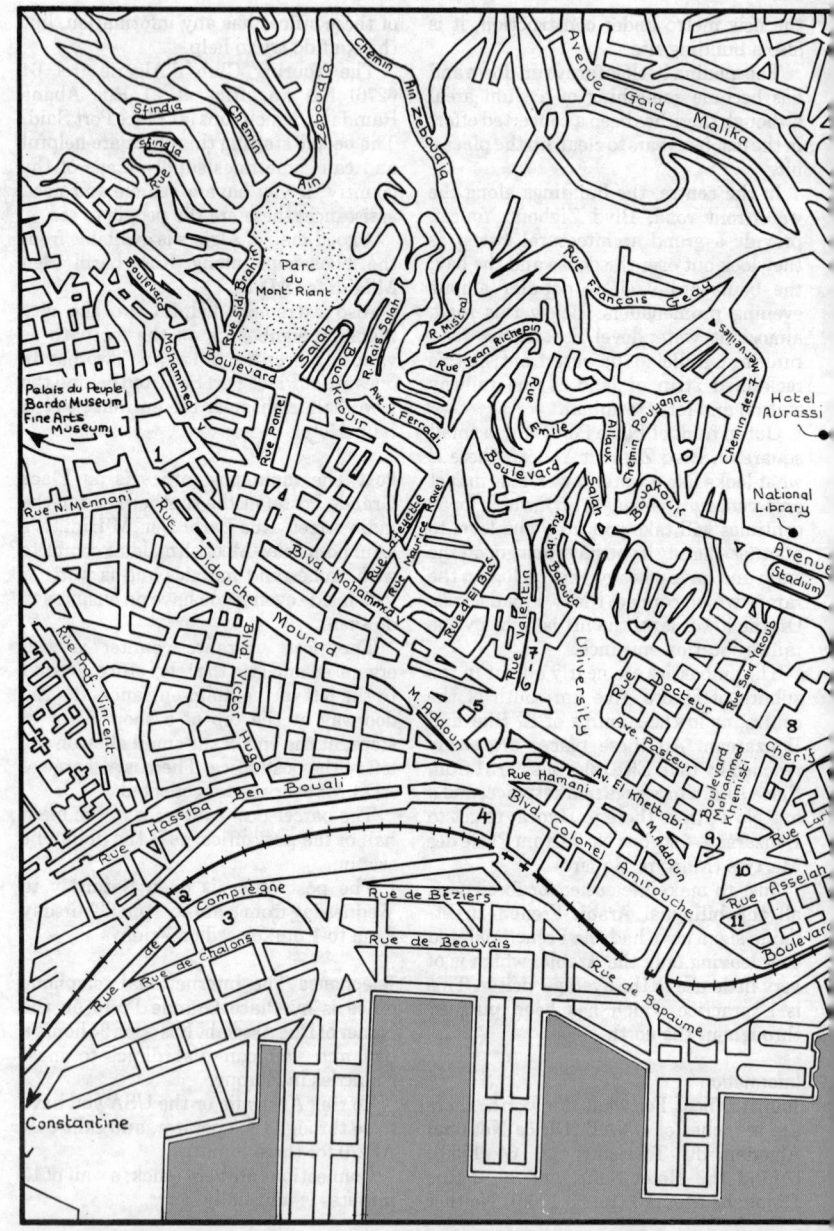

Palais du Peuple
Bardo Museum
Fine Arts
Museum

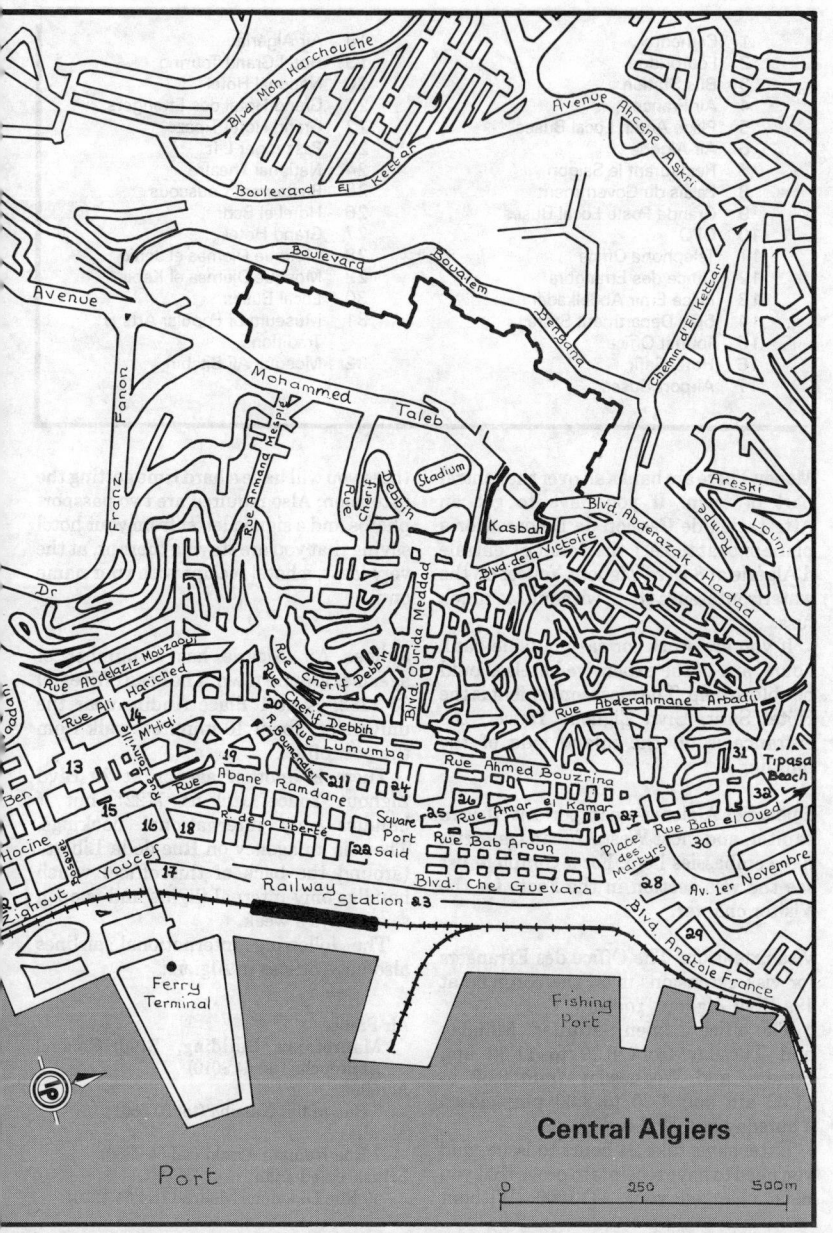

Central Algiers

0   250   500m

Blvd. Moh. Harchouche

Avenue Ahcene Askri

Boulevard El Kettar

Boulevard Bouzrem

Avenue

Franz Fanon

Mohammed Taleb

Bendada

Chemin d'El Kettar

Dr

Stadium

Kasbah

Areski Louni

Blvd. Abderazak Hadad

Blvd. de la Victoire

Rue Amar Mepre

Rue Cherif Debbih

Rue Abdelaziz Mouzaoui

Rue Ali Hariched

Rue Cherif Debbih

Blvd. Ourida Meddad

Rue Cherif Debbih

Rue M'Hidi

Rue Bouardite

Rue Lumumba

Rue Abderahmane Arbadji

13   Rue

Abane Ramdane

19   21   24

Rue Ahmed Bouzrina

31   Tipasa Beach

32

15   Square Port Said

Rue de la Liberte   25   Rue Amar el Kamar

27

16   18   22   26   37   Rue Bab el Oued

Ben Hocine

Rue Bab Aroun   Place des Martyrs   30

Zighout Youcef   17   23   Blvd. Che Guevara   28   Av. 1er Novembre

Railway Station

29

Blvd. Anatole France

Ferry Terminal

Fishing Port

Port

1	Cathedral	18	Air Algérie
2	Footbridge	19	Hotel Grand Touring
3	Bus Station	20	National Hotel
4	Air France	21	Grand Hotel des Etrangers
5	Place Audin Local Buses	22	Grand Hotel Tipaza
6	Air Algérie	23	Passenger Lift
7	Restaurant le Saigon	24	National Theatre
8	Palais du Government	25	Restaurant Couscous
9	Grande Poste Local Buses	26	Hotel el Badr
10	GPO	27	Grand Hotel
11	Telephone Office	28	Mosque Djemaa el Jedid
12	Office des Etrangers	29	Mosque Djemaa el Kebir
13	Place Emir Abdelkader	30	Local Buses
14	501 Department Store	31	Museum of Popular Arts & Traditions
15	Tourist Office		
16	Hotel Safir	32	Mosque Ali Bitchin
17	Airport Buses		

Money There are banks all over the central part of town. If you have to get an Attestation de Cession de Devises (for a plane or boat ticket), the Banque Centrale d'Algérie at 8 Blvd Zighout Youcef on the waterfront issues them without too much fuss.

If you are stuck for cash outside bank hours, any of the expensive hotels should be able to help. The most convenient is the Hotel Safir, Blvd Zighout Youcef; the entrance is on the inland side of the building.

Embassies Algiers is an important African capital, and most West African countries have embassies here. For a complete list see the visa section in the Facts for the Visitor chapter.

Visa Extensions The Office des Etrangers for visa extensions is on the corniche at 19a Blvd Zighout Youcef.

The office is open Saturday, Monday and Tuesday from 8.30 to 11.30 am, Sunday and Wednesday from 8.30 to 11.30 am and 1.30 to 3.30 pm; closed Thursday and Friday.

Extensions take 24 hours to issue, and you need to have receipts to prove that you have changed your AD 1000. Without these you will have a hard time getting the extension. Also required are two passport photos and a signed letter from your hotel saying that you are staying there or, at the very least, a hotel receipt with your name on it.

Airlines Air Algérie has a number of agencies around town. The head office (tel 63 1282) is at 1 Place Audin, near the university, about 10 minutes' walk from the post office.

There is another agency at 29 Blvd Zighout Youcef (tel 64 7722), but it handles only international bookings. There is an agency on Rue de la Liberté (around the back of this office) which handles only internal flights and is open seven days a week.

The following international airlines also have offices in Algiers:

Air France
    Mauretania Building, Blvd Colonel Amirouche (tel 64 9010)
Aeroflot
    7 Rue Malki Nassiba (tel 60 5661)
Alitalia
    7 Rue Hamani Arezki (tel 64 6860)
British Caledonian
    40 Rue Didouche Mourad (tel 64 1220)

Egyptair
    4 Rue Didouche Mourad (tel 63 0505)
Lufthansa
    10 Rue Didouche Mourad (tel 64 2736)
Swissair
    19 Rue Didouche Mourad (tel 63 3367)
Tunis Air
    6 Rue Emir El-Khettabi (tel 63 2573)

Car Rental Algérie Auto Tourisme has offices at 5 Rue Professeur Curtillet (tel 59 4304), at the Hotel Aurassi (tel 64 8252) and at the airport (tel 75 1209).

Shipping Companies The Compagnie Nationale Algérienne de Navigation (CNAN) sells tickets for the ferries to France and has offices at 6 Blvd Mohammed Khemisti (tel 63 2698) and at 7 Blvd Colonel Amirouche (tel 63 8932).

There is also an office at the ferry terminal, at Quai 9, Nouvelle Gare Maritime (tel 57 9312).

Bookshops There are a number of shops along Rue Larbi Ben M'Hidi which have an excellent range of French and Arabic books but not a thing in English.

The only shop with anything much in English is the one at Place Audin, right at the end of the road tunnel which goes under the university.

Maps There is a government mapping office on Rue Abane Ramdane, almost opposite the Hotel Grand Touring, and they have topographic maps of all regions of the country. To get copies of them you need to fill in a form and then wait 24 hours for it to be approved.

Photo Shops If you need passport photos there are a couple of small shops around Place Emir Abdelkader on Rue Larbi Ben M'Hidi which can do them in a couple of hours.

Left Luggage There is a left-luggage office (*consigne*) at both the bus station and the railway station. The one at the railway station is more convenient and cheaper. It

costs AD 1 per day, and there is no limit as to how many days you can leave stuff for.

Vaccinations It is possible to get vaccinations from the Pasteur Institute, not far from the Museum of Fine Arts.

Medina

The best place to start a wander around the medina is Place des Martyrs, at the northern end of the corniche (which is called Blvd Che Guevara at this end). The large open square is a terminus for local buses and is busy throughout the day. The square was created in the 1860s when the government knocked down a large number of old houses.

The medina is largely a tangle of narrow streets, which still follow the ancient plan but which are lined with French buildings; many of these have decayed badly in the last 25 years and look like they may not last another 25. The area is definitely seedy but is not dangerous.

Mosques Near the waterfront side is the Djemaa el Jedid mosque, also known as the Mosquée de la Pêcherie. As the name suggests (*jedid* means new) it is a relatively new mosque, built in 1660 for the Hanefite Turks.

Two blocks further along, past the Chamber of Commerce, is the Great Mosque, the Djemaa el Kebir. This one dates back to the 11th century and was built by the founder of Tlemcen, the Almoravid Youssef Ibn Tachfin, on the site of a Christian church from Icosium. Both these mosques are closed to non-Muslims.

Just a short way along Rue Ave Bab el Oued lies the Mosque of Ali Bitchin, built in 1623 by an Italian pirate.

Rue Omar Hadj opens out at Place Cheikh Ben Badis and the Ketchaoua Mosque. Dating originally from 1162, the mosque was completely rebuilt in 1794 by Hassan Pacha (dey of Algiers). It was converted to a church in July 1930, and then back to a mosque after independence. No entry to non-Muslims.

Museum of Popular Arts & Traditions

Cunningly concealed in the tangle of streets up behind the Ali Bitchin Mosque is the Museum of Popular Arts & Traditions. It is housed in one of the finest Turkish palaces in the city, construction of which was started in 1570. After the French took Algiers in 1830 this building became the city's first town hall. To find it, take the first left up the hill beyond the Ali Bitchin Mosque (alongside the high iron fence blocking off the metro constructions), then take the first left again (Rue Hadj Omar, at a café), and then turn right up the stairs of Rue Mohammed Akli Malek, which is partly obscured by wooden constructions; the museum is 30 metres up on the right at No 9.

Today the museum houses excellent displays of rugs, jewellery, costumes and pottery. The palace itself is still in good condition; the reception room on the 3rd floor has a beautiful stucco ceiling and parquet floor (the latter is in fact a French addition). It is open daily, except Saturday, from 10 am to 12 noon and 2 to 5 pm; entry is AD 1.

Mansions

Mansions Back towards the centre along Rue Hadj Omar there are some more fine Turkish mansions, easily recognisable by the small windows and the way the upper floors hang over the street. At No 10 is the building (known as Dar Ahmed) which houses the administration headquarters of the Algerian National Theatre. It was occupied by the dey Ahmed from 1805 to 1808.

Two other mansions are found at No 12 and 17 in the same street. The relatively plain exteriors of these places belies the opulence within: faïence tiles from Europe, marble columns and doorways, stucco ceilings and mirrors.

Next door to the Ketchaoua Mosque is another Turkish palace, Dar Hassan Pacha; this was built in 1790 and now houses the ministry responsible for religious matters. Up the small side street, Rue Cheikh el Kinai, is yet another mansion (at No 5); this one is now home to the Wilaya Committee, and they may let you wander around.

New City

From Place Cheikh Ben Badis, Rue Ahmed Bouzrina leads to the market up behind the National Theatre on Place Port Said, and eventually to the main street, Rue Larbi Ben M'Hidi. This street is now a pedestrian precinct and is crowded at any time of day.

About a third of the way along is Place Emir Abdelkader, which has an enormous statue of Abdelkader on horseback. There is an expensive pavement café here. The street is lined with some fancy shops, one of the most amazing being the cavernous '501' department store one block back towards the medina.

On the other side of the metro excavations at Place Grande Poste, Rue M Addoun leads up to Rue Didouche Mourad and Place Audin – a busy intersection and another local bus terminus.

Rue Didouche Mourad, which heads up the hill to the south, has several airline offices and some fancy restaurants. About 500 metres along it starts to twist and curve up the hill, and then it's not long before you come to an absolutely dreadful concrete church, the Sacred Heart Cathedral.

Continuing up the hill you come to another pocket of Turkish palaces, all three of which house museums. To save your legs, take bus No 35 or 40 from the Grande Poste and get off at the Palais du Peuple stop.

Bardo Museum

Bardo Museum The first museum you come to along Rue Didouche Mourad is the Bardo Museum, which has a collection that's a strange combination of prehistory and ethnography. The prehistory section has literally thousands of stone hand-tools and arrow heads, and seemingly every piece of ancient bone and stone ever dug up in the country. Pride of place goes to a 20-cm-long elephant tooth and the two-metre horn of a long-extinct type of buffalo.

Upstairs, the ethnography museum has a very peaceful courtyard. The rooms around it have displays of costumes and and handicrafts of the various Algerian ethnic groups, including the Touareg and the Kabylie. One of the most impressive displays is the collection of coral-studded jewellery.

The museum is open in summer from 9 am to 12 noon and 2.30 to 5.30 pm, in winter from 9 am to 12 noon and 2 to 5 pm; closed on Friday morning and all day Saturday; entry is AD 1.

National Museum of Antiquities Further up the hill, on the right, is the National Museum of Antiquities; it's actually in the small Parc de la Liberté, on the corner of Ave Franklin Roosevelt (right by the Palais du Peuple bus stop). It houses a collection of various bits and pieces from all over the country. The display of coins must be among the best anywhere, and the 5th-century Vandal manuscripts on wooden tablets are priceless. Both these displays are in the antiquities room, to the left inside the entrance. Other rooms contain Roman statuary and Islamic art. The museum is open the same hours as the Bardo, and entry is free on Friday afternoon.

Palais du Peuple Another 100 metres up Ave Franklin Roosevelt, on the left, are the vast luxuriant grounds of the Palais du Peuple. This is the former residence of the Algerian head of state and, before him, of the French governor.

In 1987 the palace did finally become a 'people's palace', as the whole place is now open to the public. There are a few museums on the site. The History Museum is in an incredibly ornate and luxurious Turkish palace, with gold leaf everywhere, mosaics on the floors and walls, monstrous chandeliers and carved wood; a classic example of Turkish opulence. In any other place the exhibits would stand out; here they are totally outclassed by the building itself. There is a fantastic collection of old jewel-encrusted swords, but unfortunately all the exhibits are labelled only in Arabic.

The Flora & Fauna Museum has three floors of plants, trees, insects and stuffed birds and animals from all over the world – a good display if that's your interest.

At the top of the site is a house full of 19th-century photos, which give a good insight into the country as it was in the 1850s – well worth the visit.

Entrance to the palace is from either down the bottom near the Museum of Antiquities or up at the top at Place Addis Ababa. To get there catch a No 35 or 40 bus from Grande Poste or No 32 from Place Audin to either of the two stops. The palace grounds are open from Monday to Saturday from 9 am to 9 pm, and the museums are open from 9 am to 12 noon and 2 to 6 pm; closed Friday. Entry to the grounds is AD 10, and this pays for entry to all the museums.

Musée National du Jihad Beneath the Martyrs' Monument is the Musée National du Jihad, which covers the 'holy war' – the struggle for independence from 1955 to 1962. The museum is exceptionally well set out and has excellent displays of equipment used in the war. A major drawback is that because this place is the centre of nationalistic pride everything is labelled in Arabic, which makes it hard for most foreigners to gain a full understanding of the Algerian viewpoint. The museum is open from 9 am to 6 pm Monday to Friday; Sunday from 2 to 6 pm; closed Saturday. Entry is AD 5.

Army Museum At the opposite end of Riad El Fet'h from the Martyrs' Monument is the Army Museum. Looking more like a five-star hotel, it is another expensive

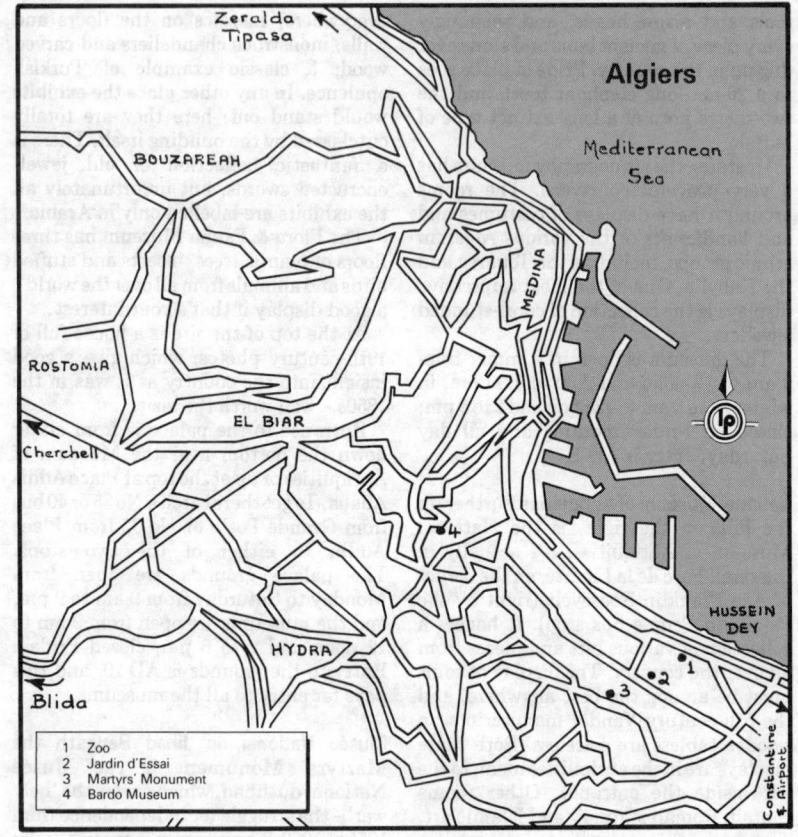

Algiers

Mediterranean Sea

BOUZAREAH

MEDINA

ROSTOMIA

EL BIAR

Cherchell

HUSSEIN DEY

Blida

HYDRA

Constantine & Airport

Zeralda
Tipasa

1 Zoo
2 Jardin d'Essai
3 Martyrs' Monument
4 Bardo Museum

reminder of the war for independence. The interior too would do justice to an international hotel – piped classical music, chandeliers, fountains, white marble floors, polished granite stairways, the works. The displays are all of a military nature and are quite interesting, although the building is so large that they tend to get lost in the open spaces. It is open the same hours as the Jihad Museum.

Museum of Fine Arts At the foot of the hill below the Martyrs' Monument is the Museum of Fine Arts (Musée des Beaux Arts). It has a small collection of sculpture, and one floor of paintings with some minor works by some major artists of the 19th century – Renoir, Monet, Courbet and Degas, to name a few. You may have to wake the attendants up to get the lights switched on.

The museum is open Monday to Thursday from 10.30 am to 12.30 pm and 1.30 to 5.30 pm, Friday and Sunday from 2.30 to 5.30 pm, closed Sunday. To get there from the centre, catch a No 9 bus from Place des Martyrs; the trip takes about 20 minutes. Get out directly below the Martyrs' Monument, or ask the conductor for the Musée des Beaux Arts.

Jardin d'Essai Across the road from the Museum of Fine Arts is the entrance to the somewhat overgrown botanical gardens. They must have been amazing at one stage but are sadly neglected now. At the far side, towards the sea, is a small zoo with a motley collection of animals, most of them kept in depressingly small cages. The gardens are open from 10.30 am to 6.30 pm Sunday to Friday, closed Saturday. To get there, follow the directions for the Museum of Fine Arts.

Martyrs' Monument From Place Audin (or Place Addis Ababa on the hill directly above the Palais du Peuple), a No 32 bus goes within a few hundred metres of the Martyrs' Monument, which is on top of the hill to the south of town. Get off at the stop where the bus goes under the overpass, right on the top of the hill.

This is a concrete monstrosity of truly gargantuan proportions, but somehow it works. It was built as a memorial to all those who died in the struggle for independence and was opened in 1982, to mark the 20th anniversary of Algerian independence. It is now seen as the true heart of this developing country and represents everything the Algerian people have struggled for. It all sounds like good propaganda but it really is hard not to be impressed by the monument, although one wonders whether the millions of dinar couldn't have been spent in a way which would directly benefit a lot more people.

In the area beneath the three stylised palm fronds is an eternal flame guarded night and day by two armed soldiers. The views out over the city from the edge of this area are the best you'll get.

Riad El Fet'h Stretching away from the monument is a massive concrete concourse known as Riad El Fet'h (Victory Park).

This is a major gathering point for people, especially on weekends. In the centre is a round sunken courtyard with three levels of fancy shops, boutiques and restaurants. This place, known as the Bois des Arcades, has been a resounding success and is always packed with people. In the centre of the courtyard is the Théâtre du Verdure – an open-air theatre given over to various performances.

Places to Stay – bottom end
The centre of things as far as accommodation is concerned is Place Port Said. The square itself is the hangout of some fairly seedy characters, but the hotels in the area are quite OK. There are a few cheap places close by, as well as up near the medina and along the main street Rue Larbi Ben M'Hidi.

The best cheap hotel in the city is the enormous *Hotel El Badr* (tel 62 0812) at 31 Rue Amar el Kamar. It is just off Place Port Said and, with over 80 rooms, it is rarely full. Rooms are cleaned daily and cost AD 70 for a double with breakfast; hot showers are AD 10 (a bit expensive, but the hammam round the corner charges the same). The staff are extremely friendly and helpful, and all in all it's one of the best hotels in the country. Rue Amar el Kamar is a narrow street running off the north-west corner of the square. The hotel has no sign in English, but is about 50 metres along on the left and has a green-and-black tiled doorway.

A little further back towards Place Port Said and on the other side of the road is the *Hotel Tunis* (tel 62 7509), at 38 Rue Amar el Kamar. It's not as good as the El Badr and has no showers, but charges the same. It too has no English sign and, because it is much smaller, it fills up early.

Up by the medina near the Ketchaoua Mosque is the *Grand Hotel* (tel 62 8413), at 4 Rue Aoua Abdelkader. It isn't too bad; the only problem here is that couples may have their marital status questioned. The hotel is just above Place des Martyrs, towards the Ketchaoua Mosque. The mosaic on the footpath dates back to the French era and says Grand Hotel d'Hiver. The rooms are clean and, at around AD 44/55 for singles/doubles, are about the cheapest available.

Right in the thick of things, off Rue Larbi Ben M'Hidi, there are a couple of places on Rue des Tanneurs, but these should only be tried if all else fails. The street runs west off the main street, not far from Place Port Said. The *Hotel Club* (tel 64 9987) and the *Hotel es Saada* (tel 63 6505) are at numbers 2 and 1 respectively. The es Saada is the cheaper at AD 60 for a double, while the Club has the nerve to charge AD 75 and AD 10 for a cold shower! As mentioned, leave these until last.

At the other end of the main street, about five minutes' walk past the Grande Poste, is the *Hotel du Soleil*, at 29 Rue Ferroukhi Mustapha, the street which runs from the Air France building diagonally up the hill to Rue Didouche Mourad. Rooms cost AD 44 for a large single, and AD 60 for a double.

Youth Hostel & Camping The closest hostel and camping are at Zeralda, 40 km west of Algiers on the coast. Zeralda is easily reached by bus, which takes about an hour, although you then have to walk roughly three km. It is probably the best bet for people with their own vehicles who don't want to pay for a hotel. Buses run from the central bus station throughout the day, until about 6 pm. Any bus going to Cherchell or Tipasa will take you through Zeralda.

Places to Stay – middle
There is a wide choice in this category and, again, Place Port Said is a good place to start looking. Right on the south side of the square is the one-star *Grand Hotel Tipaza* (tel 63 0040). Rooms cost AD 118 for a double with breakfast. The green fluorescent sign that has only 'Hotel' written in English, all the rest is in Arabic.

Also on the square and of a similar standard is the *Grand Hotel des Etrangers* (tel 63 3245); this is a couple of doors along from the National Theatre at 1 Rue Ali Boumandjel, the street which connects Place Port Said with Rue Larbi Ben M'Hidi. Rooms here cost AD 120 with breakfast and shower.

Also well located is the one-star *Hotel National* at 1 Rue Lumumba, a street which is actually the northern continuation of Rue Larbi Ben M'Hidi.

Moving up the price scale a bit, these few places charge more but don't really give you much extra. The best of the bunch is the *Hotel Grand Palais* on Rue Abane Ramdane, a street off Place Port Said to the south. Here rooms cost AD 139 with bath and breakfast.

Parallel to Rue Ben M'Hidi Larbi and one block towards the waterfront is Rue Ben Boulaid, which has two two-star hotels, the *Hotel Regina* and the *Hotel d'Angleterre*; both hotels are staffed by the most unfriendly and unhelpful people you're ever likely to come across. Just a shade better is the *Hotel Grand Touring*, opposite the Hotel Grand Palais; you might even get a smile here if you're lucky.

Places to Stay – top end
Right on the corniche, the four-star *Hotel Safir* (tel 63 5040) actually has its entrance around the back in Rue Asselah Hocine. It is the most central of the de luxe places and charges AD 215/280 for singles/doubles.

Another over-the-top place is the *Hotel Aurassi* (tel 64 8252) on Ave Dr Frantz Fanon; it's that great blot on the landscape which towers over the city.

Less pretentious than both these last two is the three-star *Hotel Albert I* (tel 63 0020) at 5 Avenue Pasteur, just 100 metres uphill from the main post office.

Places to Eat
Local Food For local Algerian food, there is a stack of places in the web of streets

between Rue Larbi Ben M'Hidi and Rue Abane Ramdane, between Place Emir Abdelkader and Place Port Said. They all sell the usual stuff – soup, brochettes, chicken, chips and salads.

One place that stands out is the tiny restaurant at 7 Rue du Coq, a small street running to the right off Rue Larbi Ben M'Hidi at the northern end. Here AD 14 gets you a good omelette and plate of excellent *salade variée*, which makes a decent meal with a bit of bread. The restaurant is popular with locals and is right opposite a driving school.

In the north-west corner of Place Port Said, near the beginning of Rue Amar Kamar, the *Restaurant Couscous* does the usual couscous, chicken, rice, salad and chips fairly cheaply.

Speciality Restaurants There is an excellent place for Chinese food: *Restaurant Le Saigon* (tel 64 0623), near Place Audin. It serves all sorts of dishes, priced between AD 30 and AD 60, and is so popular with expatriates living in Algiers that you need to make a reservation by phone or get there at 7 pm to get a a seat without waiting. The restaurant closes early at 9.45 pm. It is at 10 Rue Valentin, the street which runs uphill along the left-hand side of the Air Algérie head office at Place Audin.

There's another Chinese place, *Le Chinois*, at 5 Rue Abane Ramdane, but this is expensive and the food is very mediocre. Close by on the same street are a few other restaurants, including the *Pizzeria* at No 17 and the *Restaurant Europe*; all these places sell alcohol.

For a minor splurge, the air-conditioned *Restaurant Marivaux* at 5 Rue du Coq does a four-course set menu for AD 60; it also has fish dishes for AD 70 and meat ones for AD 60.

Up at the Martyrs' Monument on the top if the hill is a whole bunch of restaurants in the Bois des Arcades; however, none of them are particularly cheap. They have everything from western-style fast food to the local cuisine offered by a three-star Algerian speciality restaurant, *El-Boustane*.

Seafood There's a curious little pocket of restaurants, almost beneath Martyrs' Square, which specialise in seafood. To get to them, go down the stairs next to the Djemaa el Jedid mosque on Martyrs' Square. The entrance to the stairs is through two arches which have been incorporated into the facade of the mosque and is known as the Rampe de la Pêcherie.

There are half a dozen or so restaurants here and the atmosphere is good, although the prices are high. Cheapest of the lot is the first restaurant on the right, *La Porte de la Mer*, where you can get a plate of prawns for AD 18 and the usual chicken and chips.

Further along the prices start to rise. *Restaurant Le Sindbad* is the best-known seafood restaurant in Algiers, and this is reflected in the prices; expect to pay around AD 200 *per kg* for any seafood. The produce is all laid out on a table and after you have made your selection it is weighed and then cooked.

Just down from the Sindbad, the *Sirène de la Mer* is marginally cheaper at AD 160 per kg.

All the restaurants here have a reasonable selection of local wines but, again, the prices are high.

In the Bois des Arcades up at the Martyrs' Monument there is the excellent *Soltan Ibrahim Restaurant*; here too the prices are way up.

Getting There & Away

Air Air Algérie flies to just about every major city in the north and all the far-flung oases in the Sahara. Even at the official rate, fares are relatively cheap (US$80 to Tamanrasset, for example) and if, as sometimes possible, you get them at black-market rates, they are ridiculously cheap – Algiers to Tamanrasset for US$26, would you believe?

For full details of flights and fares, see the Getting There and Getting Around chapters.

Bus The main bus station is down at the waterfront, south of the centre, about 15 minutes' walk from the Grande Poste. Take the road heading towards the water from Grande Poste and then go down the road ramp to the right. There is a small bus station at the bottom but ignore this, as the main station is another 300 metres further on.

There are buses to just about every major town in the country as far south as Béchar, Ghardaia and El Oued. The station is well organised and all the ticket windows have the destination and departure time displayed. There is an information booth in the centre of the hall.

For most of the year there are enough departures to satisfy demand but things get a bit hectic in the summer months. Buy tickets the day before for all trips.

From Place des Martyrs the blue-and-white city buses No 72, 77 and 05 go past the bus station.

The left-luggage office (*consigne*) is on the left inside the entrance and is open from 1 am to 10 pm. It costs a hefty AD 5 per article per day.

Train The railway station is also on the lower street level but is much closer to the centre, being directly below Place Port Said, just a couple of minutes' walk from the hotel area.

The main departures are to: Annaba, Souk Ahras and Tunis (daily at 7 pm); Constantine (8.30 am, 7 and 9 pm); and Bejaia (5.30 and 8.30 am, 2.45 and 3.45 pm).

Departures for Oran, Tlemcen and places west of Algiers are from the Gare de l'Agha station near the main bus station.

Taxi The long-distance taxis leave from the ramps which connect the upper and lower street levels in front of Place Port Said. At any one time there are up to 100 taxis in the queues, and it's easy to find the one you want – just ask the drivers.

There are departures at all hours to Sétif, Bejaia, Tébessa, Oran, Constantine, Tizi-Ouzou, Batna, Biskra and many other places.

Boat The CNAN line operates ferries from Algiers to Marseilles and Sète in France. For details of departures, see the Getting There chapter.

The passenger terminal is at the Nouvelle Gare Maritime, right in the centre of town in front of the Hotel Safir. you can enter from either the upper or lower street levels.

Getting Around

Airport Transport Blue-and-white buses leave for the 45-minute run out to the Houari Boumedienne Airport from Blvd Zighout Youcef, right across the road from the Air Algérie office near the Hotel Safir.

At the terminal building, the buses leave from an area to the right of the exit. They leave approximately every half hour from 5 am to 11.30 pm; the fare is AD 10.

Bus There are buses which serve all parts of the city. The four major stations for these buses are Place des Martyrs, Place Grande Poste, Place Audin and Place 1 Mai.

At each of the platforms (and at most stops en route) there are signboards giving the destination and the route taken. Entry is through the back door, where you pay the conductor.

From Place des Martyrs take Nos 5, 72 or 77 for the main bus station; take No 59 to get to Bouzaréah (for the Niger Embassy).

From Place Grande Poste take No 35 or 40 for the Bardo and other museums. From Place Audin take No 32 for the

Martyrs' Monument via the Bardo and other museums.

Taxi There are taxis everywhere, and you just flag them down – there are no taxi stations. All taxis have a meter, and you should ensure that the driver uses it.

Around Algiers

ZERALDA
Situated some 40 km along the coast to the west of Algiers, Zeralda has a reasonable beach. It's about the closest you can get to the capital if you want to camp; there is a youth hostel here as well.

Places to Stay
The *Youth Hostel*, where you can also camp, is down by the beach right behind the Complexe Touristique – just follow the signs to the latter. It's inconvenient, as it is about 20 minutes' walk from Zeralda itself; also, there are no restaurants in the immediate vicinity. The hostel is on the right just before the entrance to the resort. There is no sign in English, but the driveway is right beside an electrical sub-station with the letters EGA on it.

During the summer months the youth hostel has tents set up on permanent frames. In winter the frames are still there, but the tents are gone; however, at this time the hostel is usually empty and you can sleep inside. If you stay here you need to bring all your own supplies.

Getting There & Away
Buses leave from the main bus station in Algiers throughout the day, until about 6 pm. Any of the buses going to Tipasa, Bou Ismail and Cherchell go through Zeralda.

TIPASA
Further around the coast is the village of Tipasa. The ruins of this Phoenician and Roman trading post are right on the edge of the sea; these days they are accompanied by two modern vacation villages, but fortunately these don't intrude too much.

The site itself does not really compare with Djemila or Timgad south-east of Algiers, but it is unusual in that it is right on the coast and is set in quite thick bush. If you can't make it to either of the other sites or feel like a day trip out of Algiers, this is the place to come.

The new village of Tipasa is right by the ruins, so access is easy. Being only 70 km from Algiers, Tipasa can easily be seen in a day trip from the capital; else there are a few accommodation possibilities in the immediate vicinity.

The streets right by the entrance to the Parc Archéologique have been made into pedestrian malls, and are lined with shady peppercorn trees and a few up-market restaurants.

History
The ancient town prospered until the time of the Vandal invasion in 430. The majority of the inhabitants were Christian; when the invaders brought with them the heresy of Arianism, townspeople who refused to give up their orthodox Christian faith were persecuted and fled to Spain.

The town revived briefly during the Byzantine occupation in the 6th century, but by the time the Arabs arrived the town was derelict; hence the Arabic name, Tefassed, which translates roughly as 'badly damaged'.

The Ruins
The entrance to the ruins is one block from the main road, towards the water. The ruins are open from 9 am to 12 noon and 2 to 5.30 pm daily, except Saturday; entry is AD 1.

On the right as you enter is the amphitheatre, and beyond that are two temples. The first is known as the Anonymous Temple and the second, on

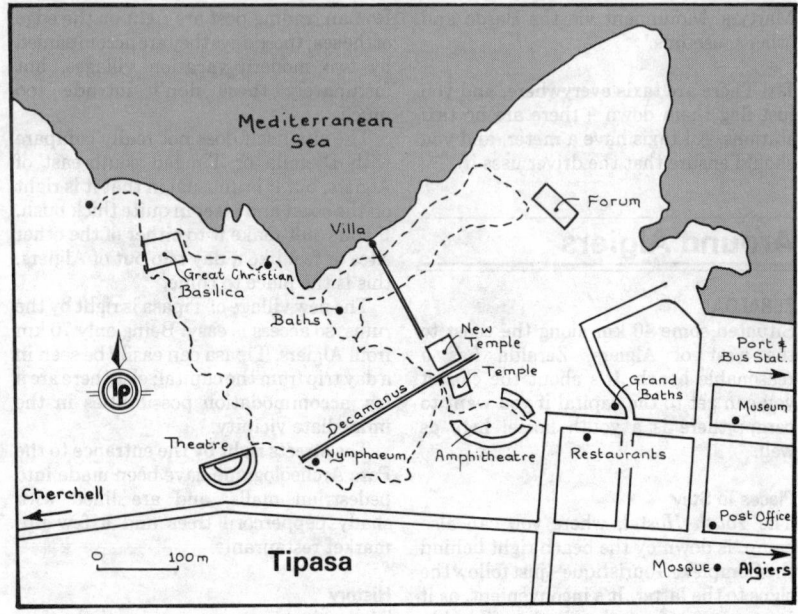

the other side of the Decumanus Maximus, as the New Temple.

The Decumanus Maximus here is actually the old Cherchell to Icosium (Algiers) road. It is more than 14 metres wide, and there is a stretch of about 200 metres which is not in bad condition.

From the New Temple the road continues through a residential area to the Villa of Frescoes on the water's edge. This villa, which must have belonged to one of the town's wealthiest residents, was named after the finds which were made in it during the course of excavations.

Up on a small rise to the right are the ruins of the Judicial Basilica, which dates from the 2nd century. Above the basilica is the well-preserved forum and, towards the lighthouse, you'll find a small Christian chapel.

Along the waterfront to the left of the Villa of Frescoes, the path leads past the ruins of a *garum* factory (garum was a spicy, fish-based sauce), a bath complex and a cavalry station; it eventually comes to a hemispherical well-cover, on which the rope marks can be clearly seen.

From the well, the track heads steeply up the small cliff to what is left of the Great Christian Basilica; you can reach this more easily by backtracking a bit until you come to a sandy path leading up to the right. The nine-nave basilica measures more than 40 by 50 metres and dates back to the 4th century.

Back near the entrance, the Decumanus Maximus leads past the Nymphaeum, complete with marble fountain, to the theatre.

Other Attractions

Outside the entrance to the ruins, the street leads past the ruins of another baths complex to the museum (on the left-hand side) of the road. Although very small, the museum does have some excellent pieces, including some particularly fine glass exhibits. It is open the same hours as the ruins and costs AD 1.

Further along the same street is the old Punic port, which is now a small fishing harbour, and a Phoenician tomb.

Places to Stay & Eat

The only hotel in the town is the *Hotel Sindbad*, on the main road near the start of town as you arrive from Algiers. There is no sign, but it is on the left and is the only building that looks remotely like a hotel. Rooms here cost AD 120 for a double with breakfast.

The only alternative (apart from camping) is one of the expensive resort hotels. In summer these are completely booked out by holidaying Algerians, but the rest of the time there should be no problem. The *Tipasa Plage* resort (tel 46 1820) is 1½ km west of town, and the enormous *Tipasa Village* (tel 46 1761) with its 600 bungalows is three km to the east along the Algiers road.

Camping At the village of Chenoua, a couple of km along the beach to the west (or about four km by road), is a camping ground with permanent tents for hire. It costs a pricey AD 70 for a four-bed tent, but is not a bad place if you have your own tent. The beach here is not bad at all either. To walk there from Tipasa, get to the beach through the tourist complex and walk around from there. A taxi between the two places costs about AD 10, or else you can hitch.

Getting There & Away

There are buses to Cherchell and Algiers. They leave regularly from the open space down by the fishing harbour.

CHREA & BLIDA

The ski resort of Chréa lies 1510 metres above sea level, in the mountains 70 km south of Algiers. The resort is not that well developed by European standards, but there are a few runs.

In summer too it is a popular vacation spot, and there are numerous walking trails in the area.

The ascent to the resort starts at the the town of Blida, 20 km back towards Algiers, and the views are spectacular as you climb up the Atlas from the fertile Mitidja plains.

Blida, the capital of a wilaya of one million inhabitants, is the centre of an important agricultural region that grows oranges, lemons and olives. The town's connection with agriculture and irrigation goes back to the 16th century, when Andalusian immigrants settled there and began using the water from the Oued el Kebir river.

Today the town is of little interest to the traveller.

Places to Stay

The only hotel in Chréa is the small, one-star *Hotel Des Cèdres* (tel 13), which is likely to be fully booked in summer. Rooms cost AD 120 for a double with breakfast.

It is unlikely that you would want to stay in Blida but, should the need arise, there are a couple of possibilities. The cheapest of these is the *Hotel Royal* (tel 49 2801), which is on the main square, Place 1 November.

Getting There & Away

Bus The main bus station for buses to Algiers, Ghardaia and towns to the west is about 1½ km from the centre of Blida. Local buses run from outside the gate into the centre.

Buses for Chréa leave from south of the main street in Blida; ask to be shown where it is.

Train The railway station is near the bus station. There are departures for Algiers and Oran.

North-East Algeria

The north-east region of the country is sadly neglected by visitors to Algeria. It stands out as a tourist destination in its own right but most people pass it by, as it is the Sahara that they have come to conquer.

The mountains of the Kabylie region, in the area directly to the east of Algiers, are spectacular and the stretch of coastline between Bejaia and Jijel, known as the Corniche Kabyle, is one of the most rugged and scenic in North Africa.

Inland lie the ruins of the Roman city of Cuicul, present-day Djemila, with its beautiful setting in the mountains. A little further on is Constantine, seat of the ancient kings of Numidia, built right on the edge of the deep and precipitous Gorges of the Rhumel – not to be missed.

Further east lies Annaba, Algeria's third city, site of the ruins of the Roman city of Hippo Regius and seat of the great Christian reformer St Augustine. Today it is largely an industrial town but it is the main northern gateway to Tunisia, as there are good transport connections all the way to Tunis.

South of Constantine are the Aurès Mountains, part of the Saharan Atlas, which run from Morocco in the west right through into Tunisia. The range roughly marks the boundary between inhabited, arable land in the north and desert in the south. The Aurès Mountains are quite barren and spectacular, but the real draw card is the fantastically preserved Roman city of Thamugadi (present-day Timgad). For once the ruins are well served by public transport, and there is accommodation close by. It's a place well worth visiting if you are passing through the area.

The Kabylie

The range of mountains known as the Grande Kabyle run from south of Algiers across to Bejaia in the west. The region is home to the country's largest Berber minority, the Kabylie. These people speak Berber first, French second and Arabic third; over the years the government has not been at all sympathetic to their demands for a separate cultural identity, and this led to serious disturbances in the area in the early 1980s.

Because of the mountainous terrain, it may be difficult to use many of the high roads for about six months of the year over winter. In spring and summer the region is cool and colourful – a blessed relief from the heat and humidity of the coast.

There is a reasonable beach at Tigzirt, which has the only accommodation along this stretch of coast.

The area around Tikjda, south of Tizi-Ouzou and in the centre of the forests of the Djurdura Mountains, is now a ski resort. During the war for independence the forests were decimated by French napalm bombs (these days the French play with their bombs in the Pacific arena instead, but that's another kettle of radioactive fish altogether).

TIZI-OUZOU

With a population of about 300,000, the city of Tizi-Ouzou is the capital of the wilaya of the same name. It is not a particularly riveting place but is the best base for any explorations in the area, and the setting is pleasant.

Places to Stay & Eat

The only budget choice is the relatively new *Hotel Olympia*, up a side street one block north of the main street, Rue Larbi Ben M'Hidi, and about 10 minutes' walk from the bus station. Rooms are cleaned daily and cost AD 50/90 for a single/double with washbasin. There are no showers in the place but this is not a problem, as there is a public hammam right across the street. To find the hotel from the bus station, walk uphill along the main street, turn left at the roundabout (Place Lamari Meziane) and then take the first street on the right. The hotel is on a corner about two blocks along on the left. It is above a pharmacy and has only the word 'Hotel' painted on the building. Ask the locals, as they all know it.

Next up is the two-star *Hotel Beloua* (tel 40 4612) at 16 Rue Larbi Ben M'Hidi, only 100 metres or so from the roundabout and five minutes from the bus station. Rooms cost AD 120/160 for singles/doubles with breakfast.

There are a couple of restaurants in the same street as the Hotel Olympia. Almost directly opposite is the *Restaurant Mediterranean*, which caters more for drinkers; beer is AD 10 for a small bottle and local wine is AD 40. The food is not bad, but it's cheaper and just as good elsewhere. There are also a few cheap restaurants in Rue Larbi Ben M'Hidi.

Getting There & Away

Bus The bus station is on Rue Larbi Ben M'Hidi (the Algiers road), 300 metres down the hill from the main roundabout at Place Lamari Meziane. It is a large blue building; the ticket offices are upstairs and the buses downstairs, where there is also a helpful information office.

This is about the only area in the country where private buses augment the government services.

There are buses for Algiers almost every hour, and less frequently to other towns in the region such as Tigzirt, Azazga, Beni Yenni (great name!), Dellys and Bouira.

There is no direct connection to Bejaia; you have to catch a bus to Azazga, then a taxi to Hammam Keria, and then another bus from there. This is a spectacular trip and well worth the effort involved. It can

easily be done in a day, but there are hotels at Hammam Keria, Adekar and Azazga should you decide to linger.

Taxi Taxis also run from the bus station and there are always a few in the parking area. There are regular departures for Algiers and Bouira from here.

For towns to the east of Tizi-Ouzou and places up in the mountains, the taxi station is on the main road, 500 metres in the opposite direction from the main roundabout.

TIGZIRT

This is a small town on the coast. Although it sees a few tourists in summer, it is very much off the track and is likely to remain that way. The town never seems to get out of first gear; it just rolls slowly along, and nothing much disturbs the sleepy atmosphere that pervades the whole place.

Surprisingly, it is a town with a history, as is testified by the ruined Christian basilica (5th or 6th century) which is right in the middle of the town. The town site was in fact inhabited in prehistoric times and eventually became the important Roman trading port of Iomnium.

The beach is only average, as it is quite stony; however, it is sheltered, as the town is tucked right in under the hills which separate it from Tizi-Ouzou.

There is a local tourist office on the main street but this is open only during the summer months.

Places to Stay & Eat

The only place which is halfway reasonable is the *Hotel el Awres* (tel 42 8094) on the main street. The staff are extremely indifferent, not giving a stuff whether you stay or not. Rooms cost AD 80 for a double; those at the front have views of the water and catch what breeze there is.

The up-market alternative is the two-star *Hotel Mizrana* (tel 42 8085), a couple of km above the town to the east.

Getting There & Away

Buses terminate at a small square just near the waterfront. There is no office but there are always people hanging around. There are several departures daily for the short trip to Tizi-Ouzou (AD 5.40, one hour).

The trip over the mountains from Tizi-Ouzou is quite spectacular in itself, with the road winding up and over the range.

There are also infrequent departures to Dellys, further along the coast to the west, from where there are buses back to Tizi-Ouzou.

BENI YENNI

The town of Beni Yenni is 760 metres above sea level, up in the mountains 50 km south of Tizi-Ouzou.

Places to Stay

The only hotel is the two-star *Hotel Le Bracelet D'Argent* (tel 59), which charges AD 120/160 for singles/doubles with breakfast.

In summer it should be possible to camp in the area, although you would need to be pretty well self-sufficient, as there is no equipment available locally.

Getting There & Away

In summer there are regular buses between Beni Yenni and Tizi-Ouzou.

Bejaia & the Corniche Kabyle

BEJAIA

Bejaia is a port town with a population of 150,000. It is built in a beautiful spot: it's on the flank of Jebel Gouraya, at the eastern end of the Gulf of Bejaia.

The city itself is very pleasant, although things have been spoiled to a great extent by the construction of a petrochemical complex on the edge of the town, which has resulted in pollution of both the air and water.

The centre of the town is a congested mess of very narrow streets which wind up the hillside. The view out over the harbour, the bay and the mountains from Place 1 November is really something (when the pollution is not too bad, that is).

Despite its long history, there is really very little to see in the town itself. However, the beach at Tichi (17 km to the east) is one of the best in the country, and there is some good walking out to Cap Carbon and around.

History

In Roman times the town was called Saldae. When it became a major town of the Hammadid chief Emir En Nasser it really prospered and was renamed En Nassria.

En Nasser's son, El Mansour, built a beautiful palace within the fortifications built by his father. The last Hammadid ruler, Yahia, ruled over a town which flourished on the trade in goods across the Sahara and grew to over 100,000 inhabitants.

The downfall of the Hammadid empire came in 1152, when the Almohad ruler Abd el Moumane invaded from Morocco. In the 13th century the town became part of the Hafsid empire, when that dynasty came to power in Tunis.

Piracy was a major occupation along the Barbary coast in the years up to the beginning of the 16th century. About this time the activities of the pirates in Bejaia brought the town to the attention of the Spanish, who besieged it in 1509. The Spaniards were followed by the Turks in 1555 and the French in 1833, by which time the population had dwindled to a meagre 2000.

Orientation

The centre of the town is actually up on the side of the hill but, because of the terrain, the transport connections are all at the bottom, about 20 minutes' walk from the centre.

Suburban buses run up as far as the impossibly small and busy square, Place Chérif Medjahed, which has an unusual sculpture in the centre. Around the square you'll find the post office, shipping office, Air Algérie and banks. The hotels too are close by.

Place 1 November is a beautiful open terrace 100 metres towards the water along Rue Ben M'Hidi, a small pedestrian street. It is flanked by two old colonial buildings – the Banque Centrale d'Algérie and the Hotel de l'Etoile (the place to stay if money permits). The view from here is excellent, and a stairway near the hotel entrance leads down to the museum below.

To help you get your bearings, there is a map of the town on the wall of the cinema, on the right at the entrance to Place Chérif Medjahed as you come up from the bus station.

Information
Tourist Office The ONAT office (tel 92 8001) on Place Chérif Medjahed is staffed by helpful people but, as usual, they have very little in the way of information.

This office is also the CNAN booking office (tel 92 0360) for the ferries to France.

Post The post office is also on Place Chérif Medjahed. The telephone office is through the door to the left of the main entrance. The post office steps are a gathering point for the local youths.

Money The main bank is on Place 1 November.

Airlines Air Algérie has an office (tel 92 1845) on the west side of Place Chérif Medjahed.

Museum
The museum is one of the town's more peculiar sights. The entrance itself is strange enough: you can go down the

stairs from Place 1 November but, as these have been used as a *pissoir* about a thousand times too often, it is preferable to walk around to the bottom street entrance and go in there. The museum is on the 1st floor, and there is no sign on the various doors at street level – ask for help if you can't find the stairs.

Once inside things get stranger: the museum has an enormously varied collection, ranging from paintings by local artists to hundreds of stuffed birds in various stages of decay – a real mish-mash of exhibits. Entry costs AD 1 and the museum is closed from 12 noon to 2 pm.

Other Attractions
There are a few remnants from the past but they are all either run down, closed or both. The kasbah (closed) is down near the waterfront, straight down from Place Chérif Medjahed, and dates from the time of the Spanish occupation.

About 10 minutes' walk up the hill behind the square along Rue Fatima is the small 16th-century Sidi Soufi Mosque with its square minaret. Further on up the hill is the marketplace. Higher still is Fort Moussa, which also dates from the 16th century; it was built by the Spaniard Pedro Navarro, possibly on the site of the palace built by the Hafsids. This building too is closed.

The walk out to Cap Carbon takes a solid couple of hours, as it is over seven km from the centre. From the end of the road it is a further 30 minutes on foot to the lighthouse near the tip of the cape.

If you are really keen, there is a road up to the Spanish fort on top of Jebel Gouraya behind the town. To get to this, follow Rue Fatima up to Fort Moussa and then take Rue Gouraya; this goes past an Islamic institute, which was opened in 1972 and was built on the site of an Islamic university established by the saint Sidi Touati.

Places to Stay
The best cheapie you'll find is the friendly

Hotel Touring (tel 92 0383) at 6 Rue Hocine Hihat, the street which slopes gently uphill directly opposite the post office. Rooms cost AD 60 for a double and those at the back are quieter than the ones on the street. Cold showers only.

Similarly priced but not as good is the *Hotel Saada* on the pedestrian street, Rue Ben M'Hidi, which connects the two squares.

The best place for the money is the one-star *Hotel l'Etoile* (tel 92 9895) on Place 1 November. Some of the large rooms have great views from the balconies out over the bay and the coast to the east. It's not all that expensive at AD 88/120 for a single/double with breakfast.

Places to Eat

The cavernous *Restaurant de la Soummam* is right next to the Hotel Touring at 4 Rue Hocine Hihat. It sells all the usual stuff and does a good-value, two-course lunch for AD 22.

There is another restaurant almost opposite, but this place serves alcohol as well and the atmosphere is just a shade seedy.

There are a couple more places on Rue Ben M'Hidi near the Hotel Saada.

Getting There & Away

Air The airport is three km south of town, off to the left of the road to Tichi and Jijel.

There are daily flights to Algiers; the trip takes 50 minutes.

Bus The bus station is at the bottom of the hill, south of the city centre. It is about 20 minutes away on foot; else, all the local buses from the terminal halfway down the hill go past it.

There is a booking office, where a reasonably up-to-date timetable is on display.

There are regular departures to Algiers, Bouira, Jijel, Sétif and Constantine. There are no direct buses to Tizi-Ouzou. The best you can get is a bus to Hammam Keria and then local transport on to Azazga and Tizi-Ouzou.

Taxi The taxis depart from the intersection of the Algiers and Jijel roads, about two km past the bus station.

Hitching This intersection is also where you will have to get yourself to for hitching, either to Algiers or Tizi-Ouzou in the west, or to Jijel and Sétif to the east. There is plenty of traffic in both directions and hitching is easy.

TICHI

The beach at Tichi, 17 km east of Bejaia, is not too bad at all. The beach right in the town itself gets quite crowded, but you only have to walk a few hundred metres back towards Bejaia and the crowds thin out.

The only problem here is that the pollution from the oil refinery at Bejaia is sometimes so bad that the water line is dotted with dirty great globs of tar. It makes life mighty unpleasant to have your feet stained black while walking along the beach. This may have been an isolated incident, but I have my doubts.

Places to Stay

There are a couple of places, but neither represents fantastic value. In fact the *Hotel du Golfe* (tel 92 6806) must be someone's idea of a joke. The rooms are incredibly small and dingy, and the bar/restaurant, although right on the edge of the beach, is completely caged in, either to keep stray people from the beach out, or to keep the drunks in. Either way it's a dump, which is best avoided.

Up on the rise towards the eastern edge of the town is the *Hotel Bar Restaurant Les Hammadites* (tel 92 6680). This has quite a good terrace bar with views around the bay to Bejaia. Pity the rest of the place isn't up to much. Rooms cost AD 120 for a double with breakfast.

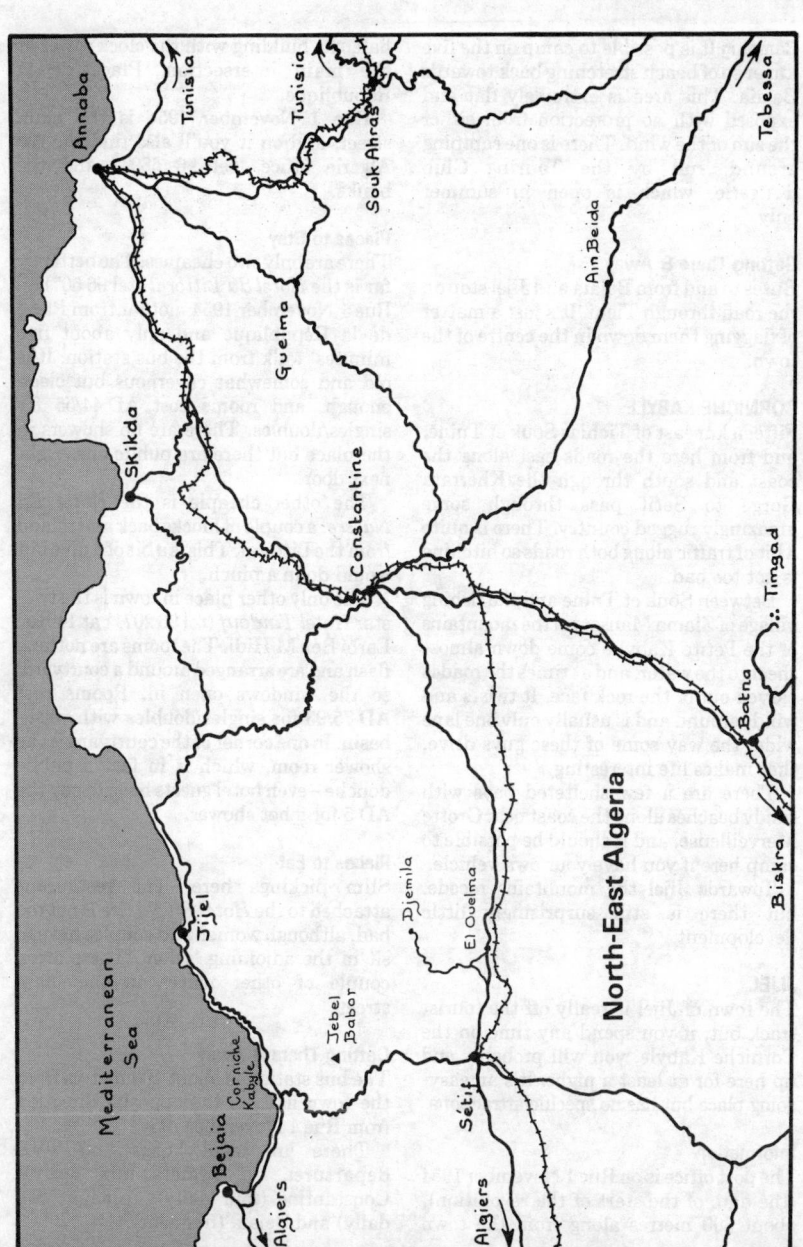

Camping It is possible to camp on the five km or so of beach stretching back towards Bejaia. This area is extremely flat and exposed with no protection from either the sun or the wind. There is one camping ground, run by the Touring Club d'Algérie, which is open in summer only.

Getting There & Away
Buses to and from Bejaia and Jijel stop on the road through Tichi. It's just a matter of flagging them down in the centre of the town.

CORNICHE KABYLE
Fifteen km east of Tichi is Souk et Tnine, and from here the roads east along the coast and south through the Kherrata Gorge to Sétif pass through some amazingly rugged country. There is quite a bit of traffic along both roads so hitching is not too bad.

Between Souk et Tnine and the fishing village of Ziama Mansouria the mountains of the Petite Kabylie come down almost sheer to the water, and at times the road is carved out of the rock face. It twists and winds around and is usually only one lane wide; the way some of these guys drive, that makes life interesting.

There are a few sheltered bays with sandy beaches along the coast near Grotte Merveilleuse, and it should be possible to camp here if you have your own vehicle.

Towards Jijel the mountains recede, but there is still surprisingly little development.

JIJEL
The town of Jijel is really off the tourist track but, if you spend any time on the Corniche Kabyle, you will probably end up here for at least a night. It's an easy-going place but has no specific attractions.

Information
The post office is on Rue 1 November 1954 (the date of the start of the revolution), about 300 metres along from the town hall, the building with the clock tower at the main intersection, Place de la République.

Rue 1 November 1954 is the main street, and on it you'll also find the Air Algérie office (tel 96 5894) and the banks.

Places to Stay
There are only two cheapies. The better by far is the *Hotel du Littoral* (tel 96 507) on Rue 1 November 1954, not far from Place de la République and only about five minutes' walk from the bus station. It is old and somewhat cavernous but clean enough, and rooms cost AD 44/55 for singles/doubles. There are no showers in the place but there are public ones right next door.

The other cheapie is the *Hotel En Nassre*, a couple of blocks back and inland from the Littoral. This is a bit of a dive but would do in a pinch.

The only other place in town is the two-star *Hotel Tindouf* (tel 96 2071) at 14 Rue Larbi Ben M'Hidi. The rooms are nothing flash and are arranged around a courtyard, so the windows open in. Rooms cost AD 75/93 for singles/doubles with wash-basin. In one corner of the courtyard is the shower room, which is in fact a public douche – even hotel guests have to pay the AD 5 for a hot shower.

Places to Eat
Slim pickings here. The restaurant attached to the *Hotel En Nassre* is not too bad, although women and couples have to sit in the adjoining 'salon'. There are a couple of other places in the main street.

Getting There & Away
The bus station is about 100 metres from the town hall, in the opposite direction from Rue 1 November 1954.

There are local buses and TVE departures for Algiers (six daily), Constantine (four daily), Annaba (two daily) and Bejaia (frequent).

KHERRATA GORGE

The narrow road which connects the coast with Sétif crosses the Petite Kabylie range of mountains through this narrow gorge. It is most likely, however, that by the time you read this the most spectacular (and dangerous) part of the gorge will have been by-passed (under-passed?) by a new tunnel which cuts right through the guts of the mountain range.

If that is the case it will be a shame. It may still be possible to use the old road but this seems unlikely, as it was chronically prone to rock falls. It would make an excellent walk but you would need to carry all your gear, as there is no accommodation between Sétif and Tichi.

The tunnel, built by an Italian company, is an impressive piece of engineering and the approach to the northern end of it is even more so. The tunnel entrance is some 50 metres up the side of the mountain, so a bridge 1½-km long has had to be built to gain access. It is being touted as the longest bridge in Africa.

The village of Kherrata on the inland side of the gorge is huddled beneath Jebel Babor, which at 2004 metres is up there amongst the highest in the country. In the village it is possible to hire guides who will take you up some of the peaks in the area – it is not technical climbing, just bloody hard slogging.

The waters of the Oued Agrioun have been dammed here by the Ighil Emda Dam to form a small lake, which is used to generate hydroelectricity.

Sétif & Djemila

It's not the town of Sétif itself which is the attraction in this area inland from the Corniche Kabyle and west of Constantine, but the surrounding region. This is because the ruins of Roman Cuicul, present-day Djemila, are tucked away in the hills to the east.

SETIF

The town of Sétif is largely a product of the French colonial era. Until the French occupation in 1838 nothing much had happened in the town, other than the establishment of a veterans' colony by the Roman emperor Nerva; the ruins of this are still visible.

In 1945, however, the town became the focus of the emerging nationalist feeling. The raising of nationalist flags led to a uncontrolled riot in which 84 Europeans were massacred. French reprisals were both quick and indiscriminate; by French estimates at least 2000 Muslims lost their lives, so you can be fairly well assured that the figure was a good deal higher. Similar events were reported in nearby Kherrata and Guelma; Algerian estimates go to the opposite extreme and put the total number of deaths at 45,000.

Today the town has a population of about 200,000 and, at 1096 metres above sea level, is the second-highest wilaya capital in the country. Now how's *that* for trivia!

This town, with it's tree-lined streets, fountain and theatre, still has a very French feel to it.

Information

The main street, Ave 8 May 1945 (the date of the massacres), runs east-west through the centre of town. On it you'll find the banks, post office and the offices of Air Algérie and Air France.

Everything is within walking distance.

Things to See

The town's pride and joy is the huge amusement park (Parc d'Attraction), a couple of blocks north of the main street. Here there are rides of all sorts, giant slides and dodgem cars, and the whole thing seems to be just a tad out of place. The park itself is enormous: it has an artificial lake and fountains, and a small zoo with animals in tiny cages. There is even a coffee shop set up in a traditional

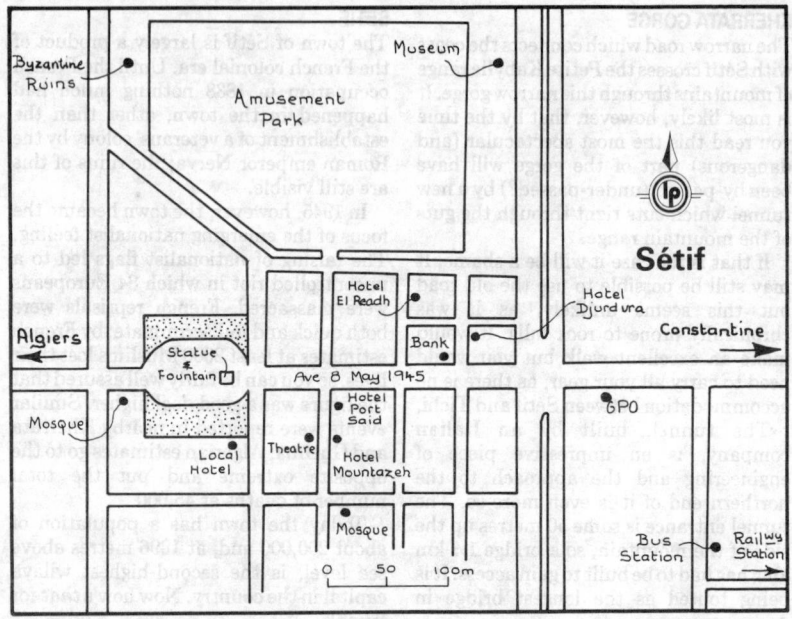

Sétif

Byzantine Ruins · Museum · Amusement Park · Algiers → · Mosque · Statue & Fountain · Local Hotel · Theatre · Mosque · Ave 8 May 1945 · Hotel El Readh · Bank · Hotel Port Said · Hotel Mountazeh · Hotel Djurdura · Constantine → · GPO · Bus Station · Railway Station · 0 50 100m

Bedouin tent. It is a popular place in the evenings, but people come here to stroll rather than to actually use the rides.

On the western edge of the park are the ruins of a Byzantine fortress, while at the eastern end is the modern museum, accessible only from Blvd de la Palestine (outside the park). It has a collection of bits and pieces from prehistoric to Islamic times, including a couple of good mosaics. The museum is open from 9 am to 12 noon and 2 to 6 pm; closed Friday morning and all day Saturday.

Places to Stay – bottom end

The best place is the relatively clean and friendly *Hotel Port Said* (tel 90 7183) at 6 Ave Ben Boulaid. Large rooms with shower cost AD 44/55 for singles/doubles and come complete with resident cockroaches (nothing unusual), although they are only small ones! As is often the case, there is no sign in English, just 'Hotel'

painted on the wall next to the entrance, which is in between two restaurants.

The *Hotel Djurdura* (tel 90 4655) is on Rue des Frères Habbèche, the side street next to the Banque Centrale d'Algérie. Rooms cost AD 50 for a double but they are not very private.

There is also a local hotel on Place de l'Indépendance. This is a place for males only; expect to pay about AD 30 for a bed.

Places to Stay – middle & top end

On Rue Frères Meslem the *Hotel El Readh* (tel 90 4778) is a one-star hotel that charges AD 120 for a double with breakfast.

Just a couple of doors up from the Hotel Port Said is the featureless two-star *Hotel Mountazeh* (tel 90 4828) at 12 Ave Ben Boulaid. Prices are the usual AD 120/159 for singles/doubles.

The town's top-end place is the three-star *Hotel El Hidhab* (tel 90 4043) in the north-eastern corner of the park, north of the museum.

Places to Eat

There's a restaurant on either side of the entrance to the Hotel Port Said; both are quite good, but the one on the south side is marginally better.

There are the usual patisseries all over the place, with the standard array of cakes and coffee.

The restaurant at the *Hotel Readh* does a four-course set menu for AD 40.

Getting There & Away

Bus The bus station is south of Ave 1 November 1954, 50 metres along the street which runs down beside the post office. There are daily connections to Algiers, Bejaia, Constantine, Ghardaia and Batna.

Buses for El Ouelma, which is 17 km east and is the turn off for Djemila, leave regularly from outside the railway station.

Train The railway station is another 150 metres from the bus station. Turn left past the bus station and then take the second street on the right.

There are infrequent trains to Algiers and Constantine.

Hitching The road to the north coast runs alongside the Byzantine ruins. It's about a two-km walk to the edge of the town along this road.

For Constantine, the best bet is to take a local bus from the railway station to El Ouelma (AD 2.50) and then hitch from there.

DJEMILA

Ho hum, another Roman site? Well, yes, but this one is really something. The setting is superb and the major buildings are remarkably well preserved.

Although there is no accommodation here, the transport connections are good and it is easy enough to visit the ruins in a

leisurely day using Sétif as a base. There are a few spartan restaurants where you can get a bite to eat and a cold drink.

As well as the ruins themselves, Djemila has an incredible museum which is absolutely chocker with mosaics found on the site. The 10-metre-high walls are covered in them, and the effect is in fact a bit overpowering.

The site is open daily from 7 am to 6 pm in summer, 5 pm in winter. The museum is open only from 9 am to 12 noon and 2 to 5 pm; closed Saturday.

History

Ancient Cuicul was built as a military garrison on a narrow triangular plateau in amongst some fairly rugged country at the confluence of two rivers. The site was chosen largely because of the rich arable land surrounding it.

The town was built to the standard pattern of a forum at the centre with two main streets, the Cardo and the Decumanus Maximus, forming the major axes. During the reign of Caracalla in the 3rd century, however, the town's administrators pulled down some of the old ramparts and built a new forum, surrounding it with even bigger and more grandiose edifices than graced the old one.

The building and expansion pattern was so limited by the terrain that the theatre had to be built *outside* the town walls – a very unorthodox move.

When Christianity became all the rage in the 4th century, a basilica and baptistry were built on the slope to the south of the town; they are among the major attractions of the ruins today.

The Ruins

The museum is right by the entrance to the ruins. Inside, among other things, is a good model of the site; one of the major attendants can point out the major features. The mosaics here are just superb, particularly the one showing gladiators doing battle with wild animals in an amphitheatre. There is also a very

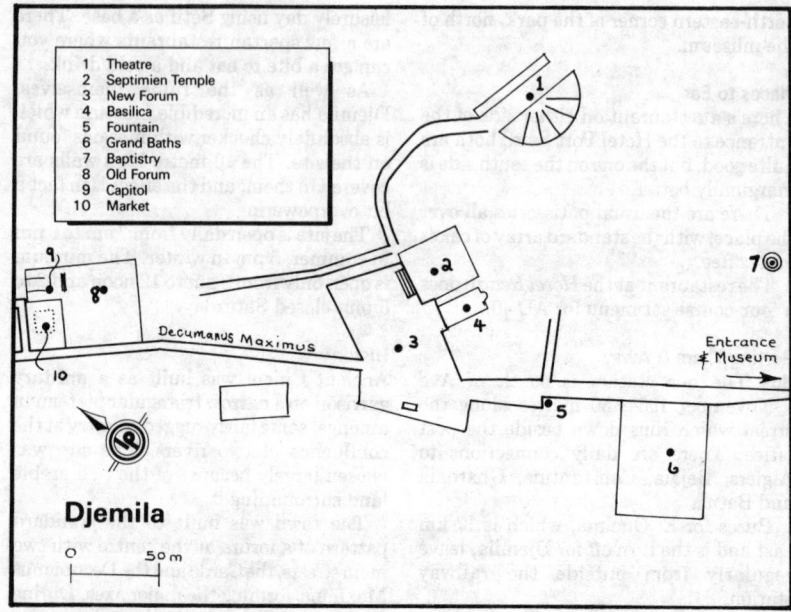

1	Theatre
2	Septimien Temple
3	New Forum
4	Basilica
5	Fountain
6	Grand Baths
7	Baptistry
8	Old Forum
9	Capitol
10	Market

Djemila

0 50 m

impressive collection of everyday items found during excavations; these simple things such as surgical instruments, door locks, glass and jewellery give a much better insight into the life of these people than a hundred mosaics or marble statues ever could – fascinating stuff.

From the museum the path leads down the slope; along here you will no doubt be hounded by unofficial guides and people selling bits of carved marble and other bits and pieces. Some of this stuff is obviously genuine, and some is just as obviously not.

The new dome of the baptistry is visible up to the right. The building is kept locked to ensure that the mosaics inside don't come to any harm. It's a bit of a scramble down to the enormous Grand Baths, which cover an area of over 2500 square metres. The walls of some rooms are still standing, and in places it is still possible to see the channels and pipes which used to carry the water and direct the steam.

The road continues past a marble fountain on the left to the new forum, officially called Place Serverus after the emperor Septimus Serverus, who was from Africa. The road to the west spanned by the highly decorative Triumphal Arch (built in 216 and dedicated to the emperor Caracalla) was the road to Sétif. The Decumanus Maximus, to the north, was the road to Jijel; to the east, the road led to Constantine, while the southern route was to Timgad.

The Temple Septimien stands on the south-eastern corner of the forum; in it were found statues of Septimus Serverus and his Syrian wife, Julia Domna.

The road leads downhill, past the town brothel on the right (easily identifiable by the phallic symbol carved in the stone by the entrance), to the old forum. There is a 3rd-century altar in the centre; on the western side, the bas reliefs of the sacrificial animals and a man with a mace are still amazingly clear.

The market backs onto the forum and is entered through an arch on the Cardo. This market is one of the delights of Djemila. The tables for vendors around the walls are still in position and, at about shoulder height in the wall which backs onto the forum, there are six holes which used to hold the poles for measuring scales. In front of these is a small stone table with three cavities with holes in the bottom. These were standard measures for produce: when you bought your oil or grain, a cavity was filled and you placed your receptacle underneath. The market was named after its donator, Cosinius Primus.

Next to the market entrance on the Cardo, under the civil basilica, is the old town prison.

The theatre is actually outside the original city walls and is set in the side of the valley, which is quite steep at this point.

Getting There & Away

Buses do run to Djemila but very infrequently, so you are much better off catching a taxi from El Ouelma on the main Sétif-Constantine road. They operate frequently and cost AD 12 per person. Be warned that Friday is not a good day to see the ruins, as there is very little traffic, especially in the afternoons. It is still possible, just a bit more difficult.

There is usually enough traffic to make hitching an option, at least on the stretch from Sétif to El Ouelma.

From El Ouelma, the taxis gather in a parking lot near the multi-storey apartment blocks, 300 metres along the signposted road to Arbaoun and Djemila, just on the edge of town towards Sétif. The bus station is in a spare block on the other side of the apartment buildings, five minutes' walk away.

Constantine

'An eagle's nest perched on the summit of a crag' was how Alexandre Dumas described Constantine when he travelled through here in the 19th century. A fit enough description.

The main part of the town is built on a neck of land with precipitous drops on one side to the plains below. On two other sides the cliffs drop down into the Rhumel Gorge and rise equally sheer on the other side, only 100 metres away.

The setting is stunning, especially with the four bridges across the gorge, all of different types. Closer inspection of the gorge, however, reveals a national disgrace – it has become little more than a massive rubbish dump. It is all too easy for residents of the medina to just chuck their rubbish over the edge; at one point there is a Naftal service station which has its waste outlet at the edge of the cliff, so there is a dirty black stain right down one side at this point. The Oued Rhumel at the bottom is now little more than a trickle of black water.

Pollution aside, this city of 600,000 inhabitants is well worth a visit, although there is little to see other than the gorge itself.

History

The Punic town of Cirta Regia became the capital of Numidia. The Numidian king Massinissa, who reigned in the 2nd century BC, allied himself with the Romans in their battles against the Carthaginians.

Jugurtha, the grandson of the famous Massinissa, ended up doing battle with the Romans soon after the fall of Carthage and came off second best.

In the early years of the Christian era, the colonial Cirta became the capital of a confederation of cities in the region and then, in the 2nd century, became a colony of Cuicul (Djemila) to the west. In this era it became one of the richest cities in Africa.

After an uprising in the town in 311, it was destroyed by Maxence. Its fortunes were revived under the emperor Constantine and the city took on the name Constantina.

From the 8th century on, the city fell to various regional Islamic dynasties – the Fatimids, Zirids, Hammadids, Almohads and the Hafsids. It was conquered again in the 16th century, by the Ottoman Turks (who were already based in Algiers), and became the important *beylik* of Qacentina.

The city finally fell to the French in 1937, on their second attempt to take it; they had been successfully repelled in an initial attack on the town the year before.

Orientation

The city has two squares, Place des Martyrs and Place 1 November. The latter is the main focus, and around it is the post office, theatre and banks; the hotel and restaurant area is right behind it. The square is always busy during the day but takes on a slightly aggressive atmosphere at night, when all the university students hang out with nothing to do and there is an air of expectancy around, as though something is about to happen.

The streets of the medina are narrow and congested and, due to the terrain, the transport services are all some distance from the centre. The railway station is across the gorge while the bus station is a few km south of the city, by the river.

Getting around on foot is no problem and in fact is the most interesting way to go.

Information

Tourist Office There is a very helpful Syndicat d'Initiative (tel 93 2661) at 32 Rue Abane Ramdane, the street which runs uphill south from Place des Martyrs, right alongside the Air Algérie office.

The guys running it may even take the time out to show you around.

Post The post office is one of the large edifices around Place 1 November. The telephone office is adjacent to it and is open 24 hours.

Money There are a couple of banks on Place 1 November. The Banque Nationale d'Algérie takes only cash. For travellers' cheques you need to go to the Banque Centrale d'Algérie, just along Blvd Zighout Youcef.

Consulates There is a French Consulate (tel 93 7602) at 28 Blvd M Belouizdad.

Airlines Air Algérie has an enormous office (tel 93 9211) at Place des Martyrs, right in the centre of town. Air France (tel 93 6661) is at 8 Rue Abane Ramdane.

Sonacom This national company, which is the spare-parts dealer for all foreign vehicles, is at 2 Ave Bidi Louiza.

Touring Club d'Algérie There is an office (tel 94 6129) at 6 Rue Zabaane.

Things to See

For the best view of the city, walk along Blvd Zighout Youcef from Place 1 November. This road takes you along the edge of the precipice, and winds around the cliff face to the edge of the old kasbah and the spectacular Sidi M'Cid Bridge. This suspension bridge, built in 1912, is 168 metres long and a towering 175 metres above the bottom of the gorge; it is one of the many good vantage points around the city.

There is another excellent view of the old city from the war memorial (to those who died in WW I) on the hill above the far end of the Sidi M'Cid Bridge. It's only about a 10-minute walk; take the stairs to the left on the far side of the bridge.

Top: Town theatre, Sétif, Algeria (HF)
Left: Great Mosque, Tlemcen, Algeria (HF)
Right: Kabylie Mountains, Algeria (HF)

Top: Music store, Beni Abbès, Algeria (HF)
Left: Kids in old town, Timimoun, Algeria (HF)
Right: Oasis swimming pool, Beni Abbès, Algeria (HF)

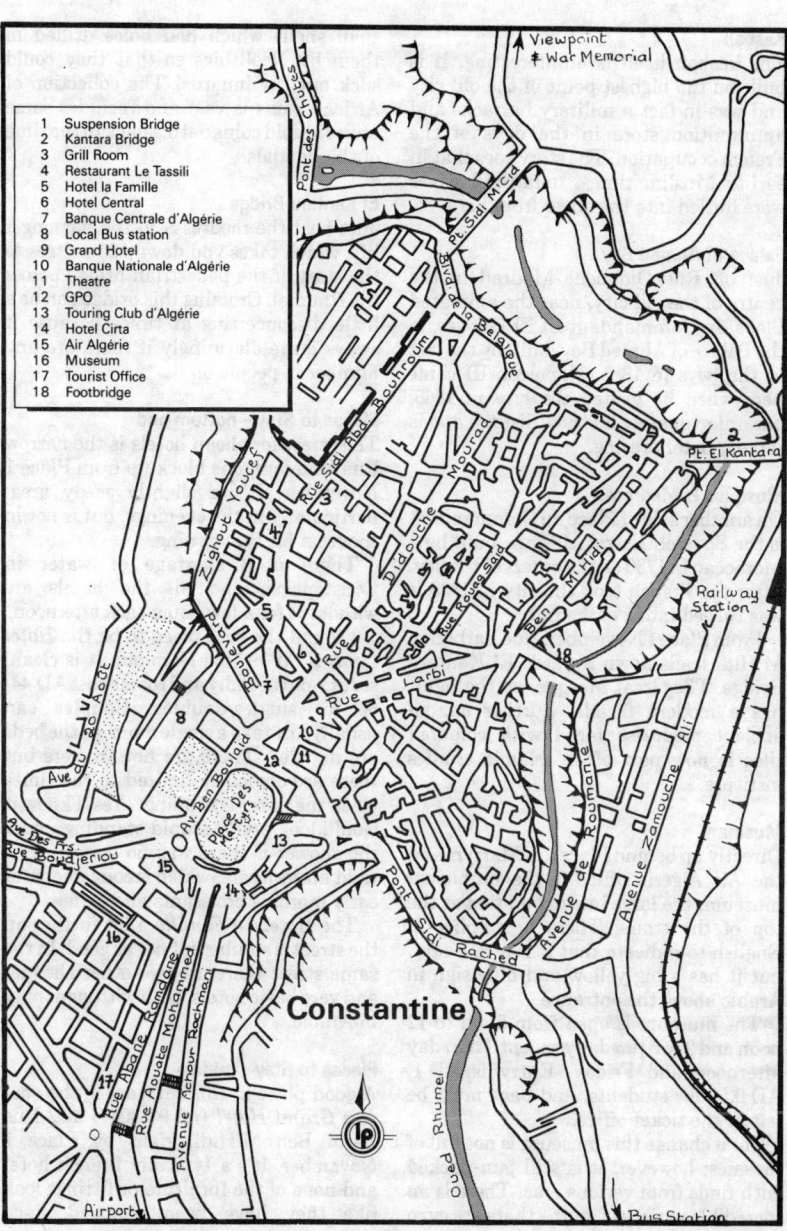

1   Suspension Bridge
2   Kantara Bridge
3   Grill Room
4   Restaurant Le Tassili
5   Hotel la Famille
6   Hotel Central
7   Banque Centrale d'Algérie
8   Local Bus station
9   Grand Hotel
10 Banque Nationale d'Algérie
11 Theatre
12 GPO
13 Touring Club d'Algérie
14 Hotel Cirta
15 Air Algérie
16 Museum
17 Tourist Office
18 Footbridge

Constantine

Kasbah

The kasbah itself is uninteresting. It is built on the highest point of the old city and was in fact a military barracks and ammunition store in the days of the French occupation. The story goes that in earlier Muslim times, unfaithful wives were hurled into the abyss from here.

Palace of Ahmed Bey

Just off Rue Didouche Mourad in the centre of the old city, near the animated Place du Commandant Si El Haouès, is the Palace of Ahmed Bey, built by the last of the beys in 1835. Napoleon III came here when he visited the city in 1865, but unfortunately it is now disused and is rapidly deteriorating.

Mosques & Medressa

On another side of Place du Commandant is the Souk el Ghazal Mosque, built by a Moroccan in 1730 on the orders of the bey. After the French took the city in 1838 it was turned into a cathedral.

From Place 1 November, Rue Larbi Ben M'Hidi leads down towards El Kantara Bridge. The Great Mosque, on the right, has a modern facade. Further on, an ancient medressa faced with coloured tiles is now part of an Islamic studies institute.

Museum

Directly up behind Place des Martyrs and the Air Algérie office is the municipal museum, the large brown building at the top of the stairs. There is nothing in English to indicate that it is a museum, but it has a big yellow-and-blue sign in Arabic above the entrance.

The museum is open from 8 am to 12 noon and 2 to 5 pm daily except Thursday afternoon and Friday. Entry is AD 1, AD 0.50 for students, and bags must be left at the ticket office.

For a change this museum is not full of mosaics; however, it is still jam-packed with finds from various eras. There is an incredible variety of stuff – there are even

snail shells which had holes drilled in them by Neolithics so that they could suck out the innards! The collection of African coins is vast and includes some unusual gold coins dating back to the time of the Vandals.

El Kantara Bridge

Just past the medressa in the passenger lift, which takes you down 125 metres to the start of the pedestrian bridge across the Rhumel. Crossing this bridge can be a little disconcerting at times because it sways quite alarmingly if there are any number of people on it.

Places to Stay – bottom end

The street for cheap hotels is the narrow Rue Hamloui, one block up from Place 1 November. It's a slightly seedy area, particularly in the evenings, but is not in the least bit threatening.

There is a shortage of water in Constantine, and all the hotels are without it for a few hours each afternoon.

I found the best place to be the *Hotel Central*, at 19 Rue Hamloui. It is clean, secure and friendly and rooms cost AD 44/66 for singles/doubles. Couples can usually just take a single room, as the beds are doubles. There are hot showers but these are obviously limited to the times when the water is running. (Yes, I know it would look pretty stupid standing under the shower if there was no water!) It is right above a café, which is convenient for early morning croissants and coffee.

The *Hotel La Famille* a bit further up the street is similar but not as good. In the same street there are two other cheaper and very basic hotels, both with signs only in Arabic.

Places to Stay – middle

A good place in this category is the one-star *Grand Hotel* (tel 93 3047) at 2 Rue Larbi Ben M'Hidi, right by Place 1 November. It's a typically French hotel and none of the furniture or fittings look like they have been changed since

Sidi M'Cid suspension bridge

independence. It's quite good value at AD 80/108 for a single/double with breakfast.

Places to Stay – top end

If you can afford it, the place to stay is the grand old *Hotel Cirta* (tel 94 3033) at 1 Ave Achour Rachmani, right on the edge of Place des Martyrs. It is another remnant of the colonial era, with a grand entrance and decor that could best be described as quaint. Room rates are AD 119/194 for singles/doubles with bath and breakfast.

Places to Eat

Again, Rue Hamloui is a good place to start. The *Restaurant el Baraka* at No 23 is not bad and does all the standard stuff. Rice and meat, or couscous, for AD 20, salads for AD 6.

Further down the street at No 29 is the *Restaurant Dounyazed* and, although it looks interesting with its fish bowl and fountain and fluted columns, it should be avoided – unless of course you like

watching dozens of tiny cockroaches walk all over your bread and up and down the table legs. The problem is not unique to this restaurant, but things are just a little out of control here. The tables against the walls are the worst affected.

Right at the very bottom of Rue Hamloui is a small network of narrow streets, and here you'll find a dozen or so snack eateries, all with their food on display. Just take a wander around and choose what you like.

At 31 Rue Meriem Bouatoura up from Place 1 November, the *Restaurant Le Tassili* provides a bit of welcome variety: good pizzas from AD 15, hamburgers AD 16, sandwiches AD 16, mushroom omelettes for AD 10 and two crèpes for AD 6. Further up, in Rue Sidi Abdelleh Bouhroum, is the *Grill Room*, which is also OK.

Getting There & Away

Air Constantine's Ain-el-Bey airport is seven km south of the city.

There are flights to Algiers (at least twice daily, AD 218), Ghardaia (twice weekly, AD 194), Oran (four times weekly, AD 464), Tamanrasset (once weekly, AD 370) and Tindouf (once weekly, AD 415).

Bus The bus station is a few km south of the centre, right by the river at the bottom of the ravine, which widens out considerably not far from the centre of town.

Because it is a major city, there are buses to just about anywhere. Timetables are displayed at the bus station, and tickets for longer journeys should be bought in advance.

Destinations include Annaba, Sétif, Algiers, Tébessa, Oran, Ghardaia, Jijel and El Oued.

There is a bus every second day for Tunis, and seats on this must be booked 24 hours in advance.

There is another bus station for towns in the immediate area, and this is almost opposite the railway station.

Train It is about a 15-minute walk from the centre to the railway station, which is on the other side of the gorge. The most direct access is via the footbridge.

There are four trains to Algiers every day, one to Tunis, two to Skikda and two to Touggourt.

Taxi Taxis also leave from the main bus station. Departures for Sétif, Algiers, Souk Ahras and Annaba.

Getting Around
Bus The city bus system has its main terminus just off to one side between Place des Martyrs and Place 1 November.

The only bus you are likely to need is the No 18 to the bus station. Tickets cost AD 1.50 and must be bought from the green ticket booth at the terminus. The trip takes about 10 to 20 minutes depending on the traffic, which varies a lot but is rarely light.

Taxi Yellow taxis are everywhere and can be flagged down. Fare is by negotiation and should be established before you take off. To the bus station from the centre should cost AD 10 for the cab, not per person.

Annaba

Set on one of the few coastal plains in the country, the city of Annaba is one that has been booming, as is attested by the massive steel works south of the city.

With almost 500,000 inhabitants, it is now the fourth-largest city in the country; it boasts a university and Algeria's third-largest port.

The heart of the city is the wide main street, Cours de la Révolution, and this broad avenue, with it's central shady strip, is just so French it's ridiculous. It is also the focus of activity in the evenings, when the dozen or so pavement cafés and ice-cream kiosks which line the central strip come to life.

The city is ringed by hills. The skyline to the south-west is dominated by the incredibly ugly Basilica of St Augustine, while the opposite direction boasts a full complement of even uglier apartment blocks.

The city is a pleasant enough place in which to pass a day or two on the way to or from Tunisia.

History
The site of the Roman town of Hippo Regius is just to the south of town, and it was here that St Augustine was a bishop for 34 years.

Augustine was very influential in Christianity in Africa and was one of the main opponents of the Donatist movement in the latter half of the 2nd century. He also developed a theory which gave orthodox Christian rulers the right to move forcefully against heretics; this eventually led to the crushing of the

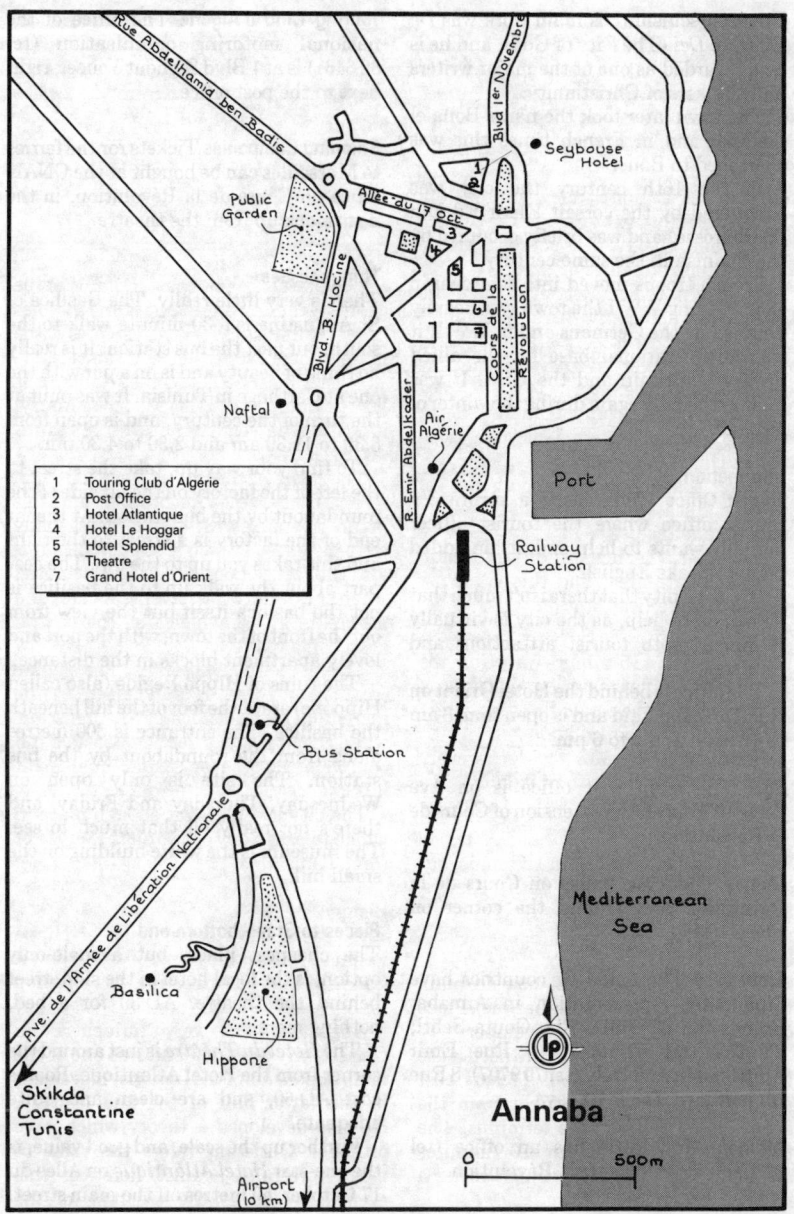

1   Touring Club d'Algérie
2   Post Office
3   Hotel Atlantique
4   Hotel Le Hoggar
5   Hotel Splendid
6   Theatre
7   Grand Hotel d'Orient

Rue Abdelhamid ben Badis

Blvd 1er Novembre

Seybouse Hotel

Allée du 17 Oct.

Public Garden

Blvd B Hocine

Cours de la Révolution

Naftal

R. Emir Abdelkader

Air Algérie

Port

Railway Station

Bus Station

Ave. de l'Armée de Liberation Nationale

Basilica

Hippone

Mediterranean Sea

Skikda
Constantine
Tunis

Annaba

0   500m

Airport
(10 km)

Donatist schism. His main work was *De Civitate Dei* (The City of God), and he is now regarded as one of the major writers and thinkers of Christianity.

The town later took the name Bona el Hadida, and in French times this was shortened to Bône.

In the 16th century the city was conquered by the corsair Khair Ed Din (Barbarossa) and was briefly occupied by the Spanish in the same century.

French troops moved into the town in 1832. During WW I the town was heavily bombed by the Germans and in WW II it was an operational base for the allied armies of Britain and the USA. It was bombed heavily again during the winter of 1942-43.

Information
Tourist Office Well, this is a surprise: a tourist office where the tourist officer actually wants to help and, as an added bonus, speaks English.

It's just a pity that there isn't much that he can do to help, as the city is virtually devoid of both tourist attractions and tourists.

The office is behind the Hotel Orient on Rue Tarik Ibn Zaid and is open from 8 am to 12 noon and 2 to 6 pm.

Post The main post office is on Ave Zighout Youcef, the extension of Cours de la Révolution.

Money There are banks on Cours de la Révolution and around the corner on Place 1 May.

Embassies The following countries have diplomatic representation in Annaba: France (tel 82 6391), Rue Gouta Sebti; Tunisia (tel 82 4447), 6 Rue Emir Abdelkader; and Italy (tel 70 9707), 8 Rue Mohammed Tahar Rkhaya.

Airlines Air Algérie has an office (tel 82 1906) at 2 Cours de la Révolution.

Touring Club d'Algérie The office of the national motoring organisation (tel 82 6461) is at 1 Blvd Zighout Youcef, right next to the post office.

Shipping Companies Tickets for the ferries to Marseilles can be bought at the CNAN office on Cours de la Révolution, in the next block up from the theatre.

Things to See
There's very little really. The Basilica of St Augustine is a 30-minute walk to the south, out past the bus station. It is really no thing of beauty and is on a par with the one at Carthage in Tunisia. It was built at the turn of the century, and is open from 8.30 to 11.30 am and 2.30 to 4.30 pm.

To find your way up, take the street to the left of the factory on the far side of the roundabout by the bus station. At the far end of the factory is a street to the right and this takes you up to the top. The best part about the walk up to the basilica is not the basilica itself but the view from out the front of the town, with the port and lovely apartment blocks in the distance.

The ruins of Hippo Regius (also called Hippone) are at the foot of the hill beneath the basilica. The entrance is 300 metres along from the roundabout by the bus station. The site is only open on Wednesday, Thursday and Friday, and there's not really all that much to see. The museum is the white building on the small hill.

Places to Stay – bottom end
The cheapest place, but a male-only option, is the local hotel in the side street behind the theatre. AD 30 for a bed, nothing more.

The *Hotel du Théâtre* is just around the corner from the Hotel Atlantique. Rooms cost AD 60, and are clean and quite adequate.

Further up the scale, and good value, is the one-star *Hotel Atlantique* on Allée du 17 October, 50 metres off the main street.

Breakfast is included in the price of AD 118 for a double.

Places to Stay – middle

There are a couple of two-star places around a small square just off Cours de la Révolution. The one to avoid is the *Hotel Le Hoggar*, which can really only be described as a bloody filthy rip-off. The rooms are absolutely infested with cockroaches and look as though they haven't been cleaned in ages, the water rarely works and the whole place is a bad joke.

The hotel further up towards Allée du 17 October on the same side is a better bet.

Places to Stay – top end

In the main street is the *Grand Hotel d'Orient* (tel 82 2051), which is left over from colonial days and still has all the period touches like chandeliers and a grand piano in the café. It is right next to the theatre. Double rooms cost a hefty AD 200 including breakfast and douche.

Top of the range is the *Hotel Seybouse International* (tel 82 3577) on Rue 24 Février 1966 (the date of the foundation of the UGTA trade union), where you'll pay a mere AD 500 for a double for the night. The main reason you are likely to want to come here is to change money outside banking hours.

Places to Eat

There's nothing very special here. On the square near the Hotel Le Hoggar is a small restaurant run by a great old character who used to be shoe-shine boy when the British and American troops were here in WW II. He speaks excellent English, loves to reminisce and starts singing all the old war-time songs! His food isn't bad either. Excellent briks with potato, shakshuka and salads.

In the middle of the Cours de la Révolution there are cafés and ice-cream kiosks which open up in the evenings.

Getting There & Away

Bus The bus station is 500 metres along Ave de l'Armée Libération Nationale from the centre – it's about a 20-minute walk. From the outside the station looks very modern and efficient but inside it is pretty dirty and gloomy. The ticket windows are upstairs, and a timetable of arrivals and departures is displayed.

Most long-distance trips can be booked in advance, but trying to find out when the ticket window is open is an exercise in persistence.

There is a daily departure to Tunis at 5 am for the eight-hour journey. Tickets for this service definitely have to be bought in advance, particularly in summer.

Other destinations include: Ouargla, Algiers (three daily), Ghardaia (two daily), Constantine (six daily), Tébessa (two daily), El Oued (daily) and Souk Ahras (five daily).

Train The railway station is right in the centre on Place 1 May. It is in fact closed most of the time and only opens up when there is a train arriving or departing. If you need information, there are offices around the left-hand side where you can find out about things.

Departures are at 10 pm for Constantine and Algiers, 9.30 pm to Tunis.

Taxi There are long-distance taxis to Constantine for AD 60 from a couple of blocks west of the hotel area – just ask around.

Boat The ferry port is right in the centre of town.

There are sailings about four times a month in summer to Marseilles, dropping to one per month in winter. The journey takes about 23 hours.

The one-way fare is AD 409 in a Pullman seat. For the average-size 4WD the cost is AD 1251.

EL KALA

From Annaba the road heads inland

before joining the coast again at El Kala, a beautiful small town hemmed in against the sea by the forested mountains of the Kala National Park.

The beach here is fairly reasonable and the town is a minor summer resort for holidaying Algerians.

It is possible to hitch from El Kala to Tabarka, the first town on the Tunisian Mediterranean coast. There is less traffic along the road which heads up through the mountains and across the Tunisian border at Babouch. The best way to get along this road is to catch the daily Annaba-Tunis bus. It is not possible to pick the bus up en route.

Places to Stay

The town has the two-star *Hotel El Morjane* (tel 82 0242), which is not especially cheap at AD 159 for a double with breakfast.

Other than that, it may be possible to camp on the beach in the summer months at Plage de la Messida, 10 km to the east.

SOUK AHRAS

This town is built in rugged country and is the last large town before the Tunisian border. There is really no reason to stop here, but if you get stuck there is the one-star *Hotel d'Orient*.

The bus station is at the top of the hill, on the road to Annaba, about 15 minutes' walk from the centre.

The only train through here each day is the Trans-Maghreb Express from Tunis to Algiers, which passes through at about 6 pm on the journey west.

Aurès Mountains

These mountains are part of the Algerian Saharan Atlas range, which is an extension of the Moroccan Atlas and runs south-west to north-east clear across Algeria into Tunisia.

The ruins of Roman Thamaguadi, or Timgad, some 40 km east of the unexciting provincial capital of Batna, are the area's main attraction.

Between Batna on the north side of the mountains and Biskra on the south, two roads wind through some spectacular country. The northern route is the faster of the two and has more transport while the southern one is the more interesting, mainly because of the gorges of the Oued El-Abiod and the local mud-brick villages.

Biskra is an important regional centre and is really the gateway to the desert in this part of the country.

The people of the Aurès are Chaouias, a Berber tribe who have retained their original language and culture much like the Kabylies have further north.

BATNA

There is not really much of interest in Batna. However, the setting in the wide valley is pleasant, and the altitude of over 1000 metres keeps the air clear and the temperatures bearable.

Batna also boasts one of the biggest collections of the ugly apartment blocks which blot the skyline in most Algerian towns.

When visiting Timgad you can use Batna as a base; alternatively, you can stay at one of the hotels out by the ruins itself, which is probably the better bet.

Information

There is a very well organised and helpful local tourist office here on Ave de l'Indépendence, the main street.

The banks, post office and Air Algérie office are all in the compact central area, about five minutes' walk from the bus station.

There are public showers for men and women just around the corner from the Hotel Laverdure, towards the bus station. AD 7 for a shower only or AD 10 complete with soap, towel and shampoo.

Places to Stay & Eat

There are a couple of cheapies here. The *Hotel Laverdure* (tel 55 1163) is at 3 Ave de l'Indépendance, only a couple of minutes' walk from the bus station. It doesn't win any prizes for friendliness or value for money, but is clean and not too bad. Rooms cost AD 80 for a tiny double. From the bus station, go straight on past the fountain roundabout and take the first street left; the hotel is on the right above a café.

Also near the bus station is another hotel, without a name, although it does have 'Hotel' on it. It costs AD 30 for a bed in a shared room or AD 90 for the whole room, as there are no doubles and you have to pay for the three beds regardless of how many you use. From the bus station, turn right at the roundabout and the hotel is on the right after 100 metres.

For something better, the *Hotel el Hayat* (tel 55 2601) is a good two-star place on a small square, 10 minutes' walk from the bus station. Rooms cost AD 119/159 with breakfast and there is a good patisserie and restaurant on street level. From the bus station go straight across the roundabout and take the second on the right, which leads you past the market to the square.

The *Restaurant el Atik* is upstairs on the corner, a couple of blocks north of the Hotel Laverdure and on the opposite side of the road. They do an excellent chicken, chips and salad for AD 32.

On the cross-street here, heading towards the market and the mountains, there are a number of small restaurants which do chicken and rotisseried sheep heads – fine if you like that sort of thing I suppose.

There is an excellent patisserie diagonally opposite the Hotel Laverdure.

Getting There & Away

Bus The enormous bus station is right in the centre of town in a spot where one would normally expect to find the town hall or some other public building. Opposite the station is a big government supermarket and next to it is a large roundabout complete with fountain.

Timetables are displayed inside the station, and tickets can be bought in advance for longer journeys. There are daily departures to Algiers, Annaba, Constantine and Biskra.

For Timgad, there are four regional buses daily which drop you off right at the entrance to the ruins. The first bus is supposedly at 9 am, the last at 5 pm, but the schedule seems to be very flexible. The Timgad buses are grey with a red stripe and they park up to the right of the station building (as you face it). The local people and the drivers of other buses are helpful and will point you in the right direction. The trip takes 40 minutes and costs AD 4.

Taxi The taxi station is a couple of blocks from the bus station, in the opposite direction to the fountain. There are departures to all surrounding towns (including Timgad) and to Algiers.

Hitching Batna is a difficult place to hitch out of because there is a ring road around the city and the through-traffic doesn't come anywhere near the centre of town.

From the centre, it's about a 30-minute walk to the outskirts in the direction of Constantine, and a similar distance to the south for Biskra.

TIMGAD

The old Roman town of Thamugadi is 40 km east of Batna in rolling countryside. Even in mid-summer the temperature here is mild and walking around becomes a pleasure rather than an endurance test.

The ruins are unusual in that the desert sands have perfectly preserved everything up to a height of about half a metre. From there up there is little left, but the result is that the layout of the town and the buildings is exceptionally clear.

It's one of the most laid-back little

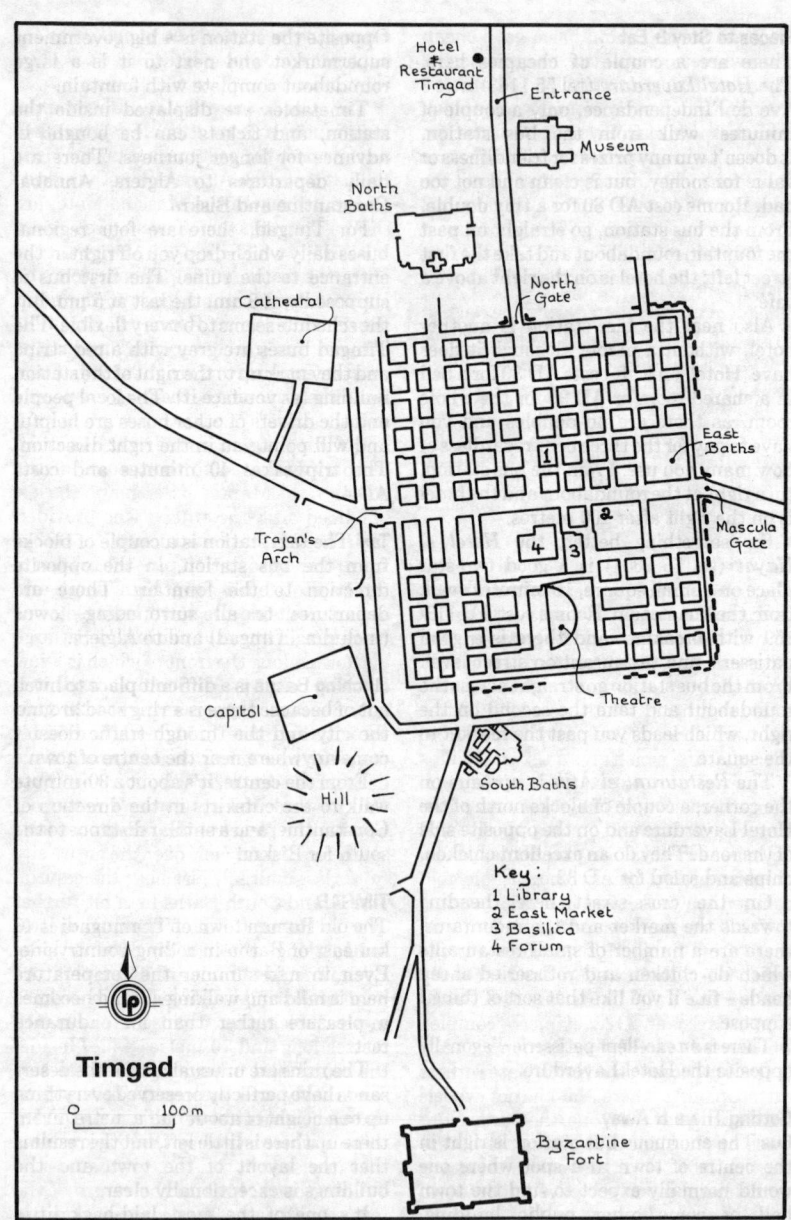

Timgad

0   100 m

Hotel
* Restaurant
Timgad

Entrance

Museum

North
Baths

North
Gate

Cathedral

East
Baths

1

Mascula
Gate

Trajan's
Arch

4   2
  3

Capitol

Theatre

Hill

South Baths

Key:
1 Library
2 East Market
3 Basilica
4 Forum

Byzantine
Fort

towns in the north and has a good cheap hotel where you can stay, or camp in the shady garden. Well worth the detour.

The entrance to the site is just one block from the main road. If you come on the bus it drops you right at the gate. The site is open every day from 7 am to sunset; the museum only from 8 am to 12 noon and 2 to 6 pm; closed Saturday.

History

The town was founded during the reign of Trajan in the 1st century AD as a place where retired legionnaires were given land.

The town prospered during the Roman era but was destroyed by Berbers during a revolt in the 6th century. It was rebuilt in part by the Byzantines, only to be destroyed again during the Arab invasion.

The Ruins

The museum is just inside the entrance on the left. For once the display of mosaics is not too overpowering; however, the other exhibits, although good, are poorly labelled.

These other exhibits include an extraordinary array of bits and pieces from everyday life, which give a very vivid idea of how the people used to live. There are items such as jewellery, geometry and surgery instruments, coins, locks and keys, bone clothes pins and fibulas, and a amazing glob of barely recognisable gold coins which were fused in a fire.

The town itself was small, covering an area of only about 12 hectares. On the right, past the museum and actually outside the town limits, are the Grand North Baths, an 80 by 66 metre complex which used to have over 30 rooms.

Once in through the North Gate with its rutted paving where the chariot wheels have worn away the stone, the Cardo Nord leads up the slope and passes the library on the left. This has columns and a semicircular room; the paved floor is still intact, apart from a couple of slabs

which have been removed to make way for lighting (which looks like it hasn't worked for years).

The Cardo meets the Decumanus Maximus at a T-junction. If you turn left it leads past the east market on the right (up a few stairs). At the end of the street, on the left before the Mascula Gate, are the east baths, which were erected in 146 AD.

To the right of the T-junction the Decumanus Maximus leads to the main monument, Trajan's Arch. It was built early in the 3rd century and marks the western extremity of Trajan's town. Once again the stones in the roadway are deeply rutted.

Outside the gate, on the right, is a small temple (dedicated to the 'genius of the colony'); the Market of Sertius on the left is named after the official who provided the money for its construction.

Further up to the left past the market is the capitol, built on a high point and actually outside the town limits. It was built late in the 2nd century on a large platform, along the front of which is a row of small columns. The temple itself was enormous and there was a flight of 28 steps up to the entrance. It originally had six 14-metre-high columns, two of which have been reconstructed. The size of these columns really hits you when you see just how big the pieces of the fallen ones are.

There's a good view over the entire site from the small hill just near the capitol. The Grand South Baths lie a bit further over to the east. Three hundred metres south along a rough track is a large Byzantine fort, built in 539 during the reign of Justinian. The walls are over 2½ metres thick and enclose an area 110 metres long and 70 metres wide. Inside, the rooms and other structures are still remarkably well preserved. To the right through the entrance is a pool, and a terrace which still has the brick paving tiles in place.

The theatre, back in the centre of the town, could seat 3500 people; it now has modern accretions for the performances held here every May.

The forum lies almost directly opposite the end of the Cardo.

Places to Stay & Eat

Right outside the entrance is a small post office, and next to this is the *Hotel & Restaurant Timgad*. It's a nice, quiet, old-fashioned building and rooms are a reasonable AD 60 for a double; you can camp in the shady garden for AD 10 per person. If you stay here you are more or less obliged to use the restaurant, as there is nothing else nearby. A four-course set menu is AD 40 and bottles of weak beer are AD 10.

Next door to the Hotel Timgad is the characterless *Hotel El Kahina* (tel 68). Air-con rooms cost AD 150 for a double with breakfast.

There is absolutely nothing to eat in the village of Timgad, so either bring what you want from Batna or be prepared to shell out at one of the hotels.

Getting There & Away

Bus There are four buses daily to Batna from the main street, 100 metres from the entrance to the ruins.

The trip takes 40 minutes and costs AD 4.

Taxi Taxis run more frequently from near the entrance to the town, about 10 minutes' walk from the ruins; AD 10 for a seat.

OUED EL-ABIOD

The gorges of the Oued El-Abiod are worth seeing, either as a day trip from Batna, or en route from Batna to Biskra or vice versa. Three roads connect the two towns. The northern one goes through some spectacular country, including the steep gap in the ranges, the Défilé, near the village of El Kantara. This is the route taken by the Batna-Biskra buses.

The central one is a minor road and has little of interest.

The southern route is the most interesting but is less well served by public transport.

The Oued El-Abiod runs north-east to south-west alongside the road, and there are a few viewing points along the way. The best one is at the village of Rhoufi, just off the road 90 km from Batna. The view into the gorge from here is magnificent, with the palm trees in the bottom and the old village of Rhoufi.

It's possible to explore along the oued in either direction. It would take a couple of hours to walk south of the next main village of Baniane, or about five hours to M'Chounceche, another beautiful oasis, five km off the main road.

Places to Stay

There is no official accommodation between the two major towns of the area, Batna and Biskra, but if you have the gear and ask around camping should be no problem.

Getting There & Away

There are no direct buses between Batna and Biskra along the southern road. Buses from Batna go as far as Arris, but there are then buses and taxis to Biskra and the villages en route.

Traffic along this road is fairly light but hitching shouldn't be too much of a problem.

BISKRA

This is the beginning of the desert and is the first of the real oasis towns, although those further south are much more interesting.

There is really no reason to stop here but if you want to stay the night there are a few choices.

The Air Algérie office (tel 71 2371) is on Ave Ben Badis.

Places to Stay

As well as a *Youth Hostel*, there is a cheap hotel in the bus station building in the north of town.

In the main part of town, the *Hotel Guendouz* is on Blvd Emir Abdelkader and charges AD 159 for a double with breakfast.

Camping The Touring Club d'Algérie runs a site south of the palmeraie near the small village of Bab Ed Darb.

Getting There & Away
Air There is a daily flight at 5.30 pm connecting Biskra with the capital. The one-way fare is AD 250.

Bus The bus station is in the north of the town, about 300 metres' walk from the main street. It is a modern complex, complete with hotel, restaurant and separate waiting rooms for men and women.

There is a timetable displayed above the ticket windows and there are regular departures for Algiers, Batna, Constantine, El Oued, Ghardaia, In Aménas (once weekly), Ouargla and Touggourt.

Train There is also a daily train from Constantine to Touggourt and vice versa which passes through Biskra.

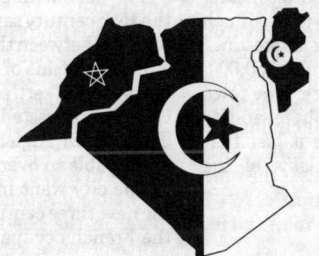

Apart from the city of Tlemcen (the capital of the central Maghreb for three centuries from the 12th century), the area to the west of Algiers holds little of interest to the visitor.

The coast has some beaches but there is little accommodation, while the interior is just a collection of nondescript industrial and dormitory towns.

Oran is worth a brief visit but don't lose any sleep if you can't get there. Tlemcen, on the other hand, should not be by-passed.

If you do want to take your time crossing the region, there are hotels of one-star standard (AD 120 double) or cheaper in Sidi-Bel-Abbès, Oran, Mostaganem, Relizane, Tiaret, Ténès and Cherchell.

Tlemcen

More than other cities in northern Algeria, Tlemcen is a curious blend of Islamic and French-colonial architecture. The mosques of the city are the country's finest, while the main tree-lined square with the town hall on one side is very French.

It's unfortunate that the city is off the main route for most people, chiefly because it is not possible to cross *from* Morocco to Algeria here unless you are in a vehicle. If you are coming up from the Sahara and heading for Morocco consider going via Tlemcen, as it is not a much longer route but is vastly more interesting.

With a population of only 150,000, Tlemcen is a manageable size. The town has a very easy-going atmosphere, and its altitude of 830 metres make it just that little bit cooler than the plains of the coast.

History

Although the area around Tlemcen was occupied from prehistoric times, it is only after the Arab invasion that things start to get interesting. Idriss I established a town here (called Agadir) late in the 8th century.

It wasn't until the 11th century that Tlemcen itself was founded by the Almoravid Youssef Ibn Tachfin, who named it Tagrart ('the camp'); it was under Almoravid rule that the Great Mosque was built.

The town became the capital of the central Maghreb and reached its peak under the Berber Abd el Wadids, or Zianids, whose leader, Yaghmoracen, founded a dynasty here in 1236. The city thrived on the trans-Saharan trade and became an important link between Black Africa and Europe.

The Zianids' Berber cousins, the Merenids, ruled in Morocco and the rivalry between the two was the only threat to Tlemcen's prosperity. The Merenids fought for control of the city three times and each time occupied it briefly.

The first siege came at the end of the 13th century. It was during this siege that the Merenids built the walled city of Mansourah on the western outskirts of the city, under the leadership of Abou Yakoub. The second and third sieges came in 1337 and 1353.

The decline in power of the Zianids in the 15th century saw the control of the city oscillate between the Merenids in the west and the Hafsids of Tunis in the east. The Spanish had settled in Oran and they too were an interested party, but it was the Turks from Algiers who, in 1555, were finally able to overrun Tlemcen.

The city went into a long decline over the next three centuries, and at the time of the French occupation of Algiers in 1830

Tlemcen was divided once again. This time the Turks and Kouloughlis (an important ethnic minority descended from Turkish men and local women) sided with the French, while the Moors and Berbers favoured union with the Alaouite sultans of Morocco. The French won out, and in 1842 Tlemcen officially became part of French Algeria.

Tlemcen was an important centre in the nationalist movement. Before the French takeover, Emir Abdelkader was very active in the area; and in 1924 the city saw the foundation by Ahmed Messali Hadj of the MTLD (Mouvement pour le Triomphe des Libertés Démocratiques), the forerunner of the FLN.

Information

Tourist Office There is a local tourist office (tel 20 3456) on Ave Commandant Faradj, just near the entrance to the mechouar. A good hand-out map is available here, and the people staffing the office are helpful.

Post The post office is in the main street, the tree-lined Ave Colonel Lotfi. It is open Saturday to Wednesday from 8 am to 6.30 pm, Thursday from 8 am to 4 pm, and Friday (for stamps only) from 8 to 11 am.

The parcel post counter is in the room to the left of the entrance, and the telephone office is at the rear of the building – entry is through the car park.

Money There are banks all over the centre, the main one being the Banque Centrale d'Algérie next to the post office.

Outside banking hours it is possible to change money at the four-star Hotel Les Zianides.

Airlines The Air Algérie office (tel 20 4518) is on Rue Dr Damerdji Tedjini.

Air France (tel 20 3901) has an office on Rue de la Paix, the street parallel to and one block south of Rue Colonel Lotfi.

Shipping Companies For ferry tickets, there is a CNAN office (tel 20 0071) on the corner of Rue 1 November and Blvd Gaouar Hocine.

Market Tlemcen has an excellent produce market just off the central Place Emir Abdelkader.

Hammams The cheap hotels here have no bathing facilities, so the hammams are the answer.

For men only, there is a public showerhouse on Rue d'Ibn Khamis, not far from Place Emir Abdelkader. It is open from 7.30 am to 5.30 pm.

For more traditional hammams, the most convenient is the one just off Rue 1 November, which is open for women from 9.30 am to 4.30 pm, and for men from 5.30 to 9 am and 5 to 9 pm; AD 10 for a wash, which includes towel and soap.

Things to See

The best place to start is Place Emir Abdelkader. This is very much the centre of the city and is very pleasant with it's fountain and cafés. It's a popular place in the early evenings, and this is the best time to sit at one of the cafés and sip on a mint tea or a coffee. At this time you can also witness the local phenomenon of literally thousands of small birds screeching in the trees overhead. For obvious reasons, it is best not to sit at a table directly under one of the branches. The eastern half of the square is actually called Place Khemisti.

On the south side of the square is the town hall, which dates back to 1843.

Great Mosque

The Great Mosque backs onto the square. This is one of the few important mosques in the whole of the Maghreb where visitors are allowed to wander around inside the prayer hall. The entrance is down the side alley on the right; the mosque is open to non-Muslims from 8 to 11 am daily, except Friday.

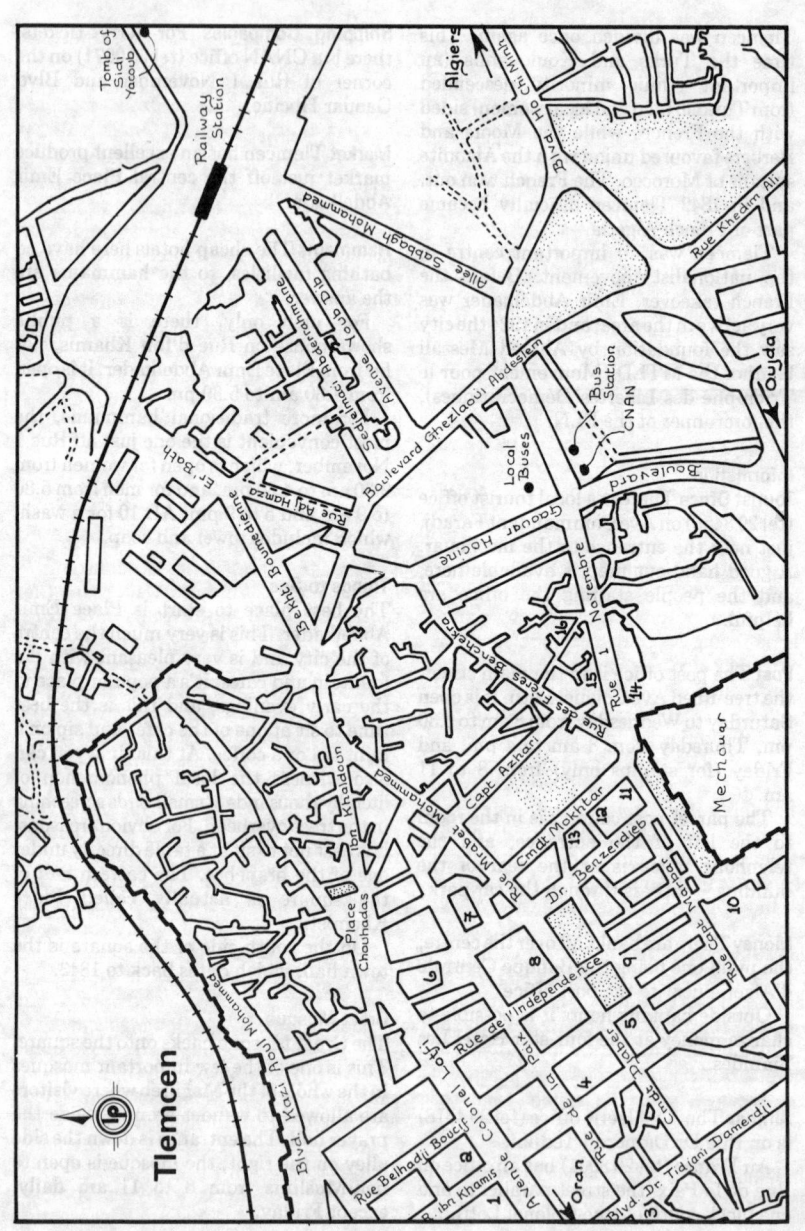

1	GPO
2	Banque Centrale d'Algérie
3	Air France
4	Public Douche (Showerhouse)
5	Mosque Sidi Bel Hassan
6	Snack Shop
7	Market
8	Great Mosque
9	Banque Nationale d'Algérie
10	Tourist Office
11	Hotel Maghreb
12	Hotel Majestic
13	Restaurant
14	Restaurant du Coupole
15	Hotel Restaurant Moderne
16	Hammam

The mosque was built by the Almoravid Ali Ben Youssef in 1135 and was later added to by the Zianid sultan Abou Ibrahim Ben Yahia Yaghmoracen, who was responsible for the polychrome-tiled minaret. The entrance leads straight into the prayer hall, which has 13 naves and six rows.

The dome above the mihrab (prayer niche facing Mecca) has some excellent stalactite decoration and the mihrab itself, although heavily restored, is covered with delicate stucco work. The wooden minbar (pulpit) slides on tracks into a niche next to the mihrab.

The monstrous wooden and brass chandelier which holds literally dozens of candles is a relatively modern piece and replaces a much older one, remnants of which are in the museum. Also of interest is the collection of grandfather clocks around the walls, and the ablutions fountain out in the small courtyard,

Tradition has it that Yaghmoracen is buried in the mosque, beneath the first nave to the right of the mihrab. All the other Zianid sultans are buried in the domed koubba in the south-west corner of the mosque, which is visible from the square.

Mosque Sidi Bel Hassan/Museum of Antiquities

At the western end of Place Emir Abdelkader is the small Mosque Sidi Bel Hassan, which has been turned into the Museum of Antiquities. The mosque itself was built in honour of Yaghmoracen at the end of the 13th century. It is named after a famous theologian who taught here in the early 14th century.

The arch of the mihrab, which is supported by onyx pillars, and the surrounding stucco decoration represent the peak of Zianid art. Amongst the museum pieces themselves are some beautiful carved wooden panels (12th to 14th century) and faïence mosaic tiles (14th century).

The museum is open Sunday to Thursday from 9 am to 12 noon and 2.30 to 6 pm; closed Friday am and all day Saturday. Entry is free.

Mansourah

Further out of town, about a km to the west, are the ruins of ancient Mansourah. It is about a 20-minute walk from the centre. The four km of walls date from around the end of the 13th century and mark the perimeter of the walled Merenid town, which covered an area of about 100 hectares. The only ruins left inside the walls are the minaret and the mosque. Of the minaret, only three sides are left standing and even these were restored in the late 19th century. On the inside you can see where the stairs used to lead up to the top.

Mansourah was only used during the Merenid invasions; after that time it was deserted and became a handy source of building materials for structures in Tlemcen.

Mosque & Tomb of Sidi Bou Mediène

Out in the opposite direction from Mansourah, two km east of the centre, is the mosque and tomb of Sidi Bou Mediène, also known as El Eubbad. This is an important example of Merenid architecture.

Sidi Bou Mediène, a mystic born in Spain who taught in Seville, Fès and

Bejaia, died here on his way from Bejaia to Marrakesh. His real name was Ibn Hussein El Andalousi, but his surname was Bou Mediène El Ghouts and from this came his popular name. It is no coincidence that the name is remarkably similar to that of the former president of Algeria: in 1956, Mohammed Boukharouba took on the name Houari Boumedienne in honour of the famous teacher.

The present koubba was built in 1339, but the original decoration suffered during restorations in the 18th century. With its bronze-clad cedar doors and cupola with stalactites, the monumental porch to the mosque is as fine a monument as you'll see anywhere in the Maghreb.

There is an adjoining medressa dating from 1347 which was visited by the great Islamic historian Ibn Khaldoun in the 14th century.

To get there, walk out along the road to the left above the Hotel Les Zianides.

Other Attractions

Back in town, Rue Mrabet Mohammed has been turned into a pedestrian mall and is now one of the main shopping streets. It's a good place to go looking if you want to buy a *burnous*, the brown full-length robes worn by the men in winter. These are of varying quality, and prices range from about AD 150 for rough cheapie up to about AD 800 for a good camel-hair one. This area to the east and north of the square is the old Andalusian part of town and is known as the Hadar Quarter.

One block south-east of the main square is the mechouar, the site of the residence of the palace of the early Almohad governors. The present walls date only from the time of the French occupation; as the buildings inside are occupied by a cadet school, it is off-limits to visitors.

To the north of Ave Colonel Lotfi are the old city ramparts, and from these there is a good view of the industrial area of town!

Places to Stay – bottom end

For such a large town, the accommodation is surprisingly limited. Pick of the very small bunch here is the *Hotel Majestic* (tel 20 0786) on the shady Place Cheikh Bahir Ibrahimi, one block south-east of Place Emir Abdelkader. It is the grey building on the corner. There is no English sign, only a small blue-and-white one in Arabic above the entrance, which is in the side street. Rooms cost AD 80/120 for singles/doubles, but couples pay only for a single. The beds are almost museum pieces and there are no showers.

The *Hotel Moderne* (tel 20 8796) at 20 Rue 1 November is a good deal cheaper at AD 70 for a double, but it is a bit gloomy and none too friendly.

Camping The *Camping Municipale* is amongst the olive groves at Mansourah. It is a solid 20-minute walk from the centre and more from the bus or railway station.

The facilities are extremely basic to say the least but the security is good, as the place is guarded by two large and noisy German Shepherd dogs. It costs AD 7.50 per person, AD 10 for a tent and the same again for a vehicle.

If you are coming from the border by car or bus, the camping is on the right just after you pass the large ruined minaret at Mansourah. From the centre of town, follow the signs for Maghnia; just after the arch over the road by the hospital the road forks, and the camp site is 100 metres along the right-hand fork.

Places to Stay – middle

The *Hotel Maghreb* (tel 20 3571) is on Place Commandant Faradj, just along from the Hotel Majestic. It is expensive at AD 121/161 for singles/doubles with breakfast and bath. It is possible to change money here out of banking hours.

Places to Stay – top end

If you have the money and the inclination,

the *Hotel Les Zianides* (tel 20 7118) will relieve you of AD 183/246 for a single/double with breakfast. The building is a charmless monolith in an inconvenient location, 10 minutes' walk from the centre.

Places to Eat

As with the accommodation, there is no over supply of restaurants. One good little place is on the next corner up from the Hotel Majestic (although it is often closed on Friday and Saturday). Here a good meal of half a chicken, chips and salad will set you back AD 25.

For snacks such as Spanish omelette (*tortilla*) and chips, there is a tiny place on a small square just to the north of the market.

On Rue 1 November, the *Restaurant du Coupole* has a reasonable set menu for AD 45, while across the road the *Restaurant Moderne* attached to the hotel of the same name charges AD 35 for soup, salad, *côtelette* (chop) and chips.

For a splurge, the restaurant of the *Hotel Maghreb* is not bad. The spaghetti entree is big enough for a main course and with a salad you have a decent meal for AD 45. Bottles of a cheeky local red wine cost AD 50.

Getting There & Away

Air The Zénata airport is 24 km to the north and there are buses and taxis into the centre of town.

There is at least one flight daily to Algiers (AD366).

Air Algérie also operates direct flights to Lyons, Marseilles and Paris.

Bus The main bus station is on the basement level of the building on the corner of Rue 1 November and Blvd Gaouar Hocine, about 10 minutes' walk from the centre. There are stairs down from both streets.

There is a timetable on display, and tickets are sold from numbered windows. Any of the uniformed staff who seem to drift aimlessly around the whole time can usually help.

The main departures are: Moroccan border (five daily, AD 12.30); Oran (11 daily from 5 am to 4.30 pm, AD 19); Algiers (three daily, AD 103); Tiaret (daily, AD 62); Béchar (daily, AD 108); and Sebdou (four daily, AD 5.60).

If you are staying at the camp site and are heading for the border, you can flag down the buses from the stop outside the hospital, just by the arch on the main street, 100 metres back towards town from the camping ground.

Train The railway station is a grand white building, about 15 minutes' walk east of the town centre.

Although the buses are more convenient, it is possible to catch a train to the Moroccan border; it leaves daily at 10 am. The train from the border leaves at 12 noon for the return trip.

Hitching For the route south, the best plan is to take a bus to Sebdou (AD 5.60), 30 km to the south, as most of the traffic heading south from Tlemcen is just local traffic coming here anyway.

Oran

Not the most fascinating city in the country and certainly not worth a special detour, but if you are passing through there are enough things to see to keep you occupied for a day or so. It's also a possible entry point to the country, as there are direct ferries from Alicante (Spain) and Sète (France).

With a population of 700,000, Oran is the second-largest city in the country. It is situated on a crescent bay, which is dominated by the west by Jebel Mudjadjo, with the 16th-century fort of Santa Cruz and the basilica clearly visible on its flanks.

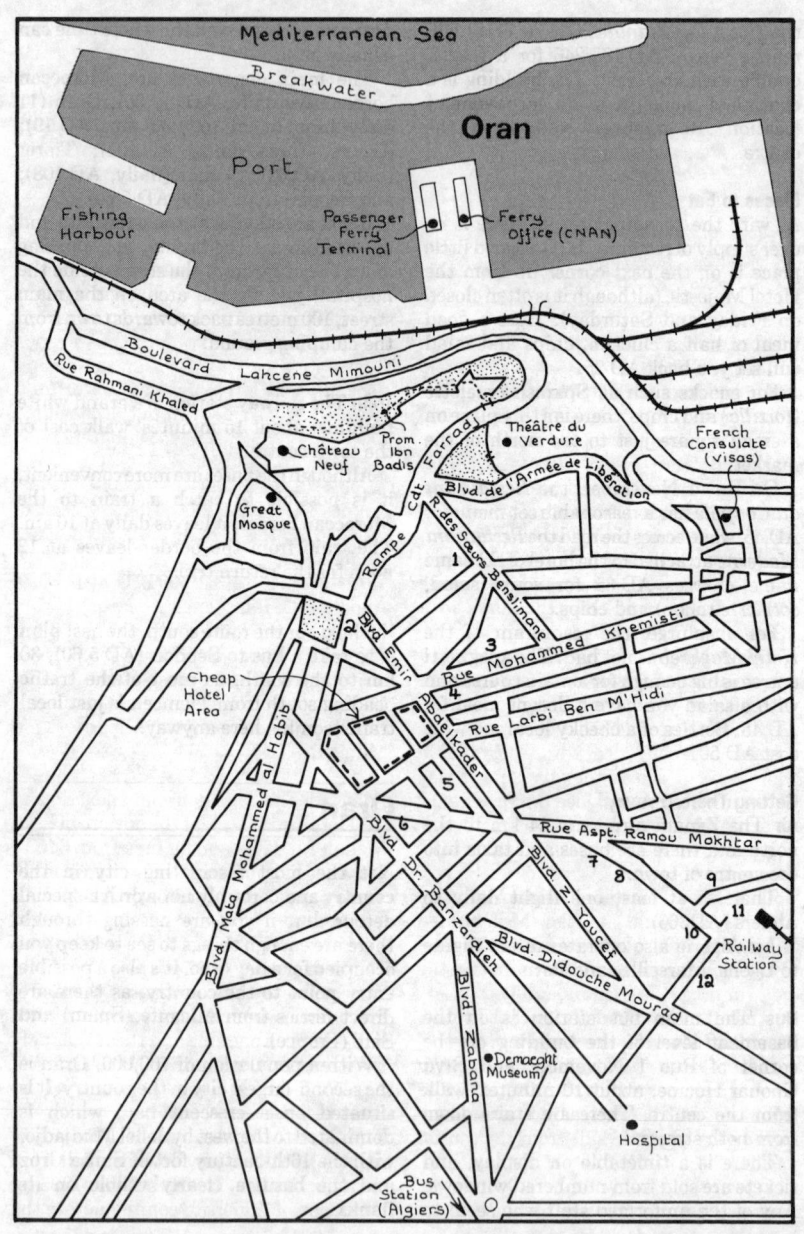

Mediterranean Sea

Breakwater

Oran

Port

Fishing Harbour

Passenger Ferry Terminal

Ferry Office (CNAN)

Boulevard Lahcene Mimouni

Rue Rahmani Khaled

Château Neuf

Prom. Ibn Badis

Théâtre du Verdure

French Consulate (visas)

Great Mosque

Rampe Cdt. Farrad

Blvd. de l'Armée de Libération

Rue des Sœurs Benalimone

1

2

Blvd. Emir

3

Rue Mohammed Khemisti

4

Rue Larbi Ben M'Hidi

Cheap Hotel Area

Abdelkader

5

Blvd. Mata Mohammed al Habib

6

Rue Aspt. Ramou Mokhtar

7 8

Blvd. Dr. Banzardieh

Blvd. Z. Youcef

9

10

11

Railway Station

12

Blvd. Didouche Mourad

Blvd. Nabara

Demaeght Museum

Hospital

Bus Station (Algiers)

1	Banque Centrale d'Algérie
2	Air Algérie
3	Post Office
4	Tourist Office
5	Cathedral
6	Pizzeria Hamburger
7	Hotel de l'Ouest
8	Hotel Meliani
9	Market
10	Hotel Riad
11	Bus Station (for Tlemcen)
12	Bus Booking Office

History

Oran is one of the more recent towns in the country, having been founded only in the 10th century by Andalusian Arab sailors. It was relatively prosperous during the Almohad and Zianid dynasties, and maintained good relations with Spain and other Mediterranean countries.

The Spanish occupied the city from early in the 15th century until 1792, when they left following a massive earthquake in 1790. It was occupied by the Turks until 1831, when the French moved in.

Development of the city suffered a major setback following a cholera outbreak in 1849, but after that many people from Spain and France settled here.

After independence, a massive 200,000 Europeans deserted the city, and it was some time before it regained the appearance of actually being inhabited.

Information

Tourist Office There is a local tourist office (tel 39 5130) at 4 Rue Mohammed Khemisti, right in the centre of the city. They have a good hand-out map, and the guy running it is friendly and helpful.

The office is open daily, except Friday, from 8.30 am to 12 noon and 2 to 5 pm.

Post The post office is also on Rue Mohammed Khemisti, a bit further along and on the opposite side from the tourist office.

Money The main branch of the Banque Centrale d'Algérie is on the corner of Rue des Soeurs Benslimane and Blvd de la Soummam.

Outside banking hours it is possible to change money at the four-star Hotel Timgad, just around the corner from the tourist office, on Blvd Emir Abdelkader.

Embassies Since Oran is a major city, a few countries have diplomatic representation here. These include France (tel 33 5300), 3 Square Émile Cayla, and Spain, 7 Rue Mohammed Benabdeslem.

The visa section for the French Consulate is actually inside an anonymous door in a side street near the waterfront, 100 metres or so away from the consulate itself. It is open only from 9 am to 12 noon Saturday to Wednesday.

Airlines The Air Algérie office (tel 39 1206) is right in the centre at 2 Blvd Emir Abdelkader.

Air France (tel 33 5906) is at 5 Place Abdelmalek Ramdane.

Shipping Companies There is a CNAN office at 13 Blvd Abane Ramdane, near the French Consulate, where you can buy tickets for ferries to Alicante and Marseilles.

Hammam There is a hammam next door to the Hotel de l'Ouest, at the bottom of Blvd Mellah Ali. It is open for men from 6 to 10 am and 6 to 10 pm, and for women from 10 am to 6 pm; AD 12 for a bath, AD 20 with a massage.

Things to See

The centre of the new city is Place 1 November, which has the enormous town hall (1888) on one side and the rather ugly theatre (1906) on another.

Great Mosque

The Great Mosque, or Pasha Mosque, is on Rue Boutkhil, just down the hill from the main square. It was built in 1796 by the pasha of Algiers to commemorate the expulsion of the Spanish and was restored heavily in 1900. It is possible to enter the small semicircular courtyard and peek into the highly decorated prayer hall. It is open from 8 am to 12 noon daily, except Friday.

Château Neuf

Not far from the mosque, up the hill, is the old Château Neuf, whose fortifications date from various periods. Inside the large gate a four-star hotel is in the process of being built (and has been for the last five years at least), and the area is off-limits.

Promenade Ibn-Badis

Heading downhill from Place 1 November, Rampe Commandant Faradj leads to the port past the open-air theatre on the right, and the Promenade Ibn-Badis on the left. The latter is a small garden and walk created in 1847 by General Létang (and still signposted as Promenade de Létang) and planted with various exotic trees. From the top there is an excellent view out over the port and back along the promenade to the east. It is open daily from 8 am to 12 noon and 2 to 5 pm.

Demaeght Museum

The Demaeght Museum is on Blvd Zabana, about 15 minutes' walk from the centre. Downstairs is the prehistory section with case upon case of fossils, while the natural history section has its full complement of stuffed animals and birds. It does give a good insight into the fauna of North Africa, although the bizarre collection of preserved deformed animal foetuses is a bit off-putting. Upstairs is the ethnography section, with bits and pieces from Africa and Asia.

The museum is open from 8 am to 12 noon and 1.30 to 5 pm Sunday to Thursday; closed Friday afternoon and all day Saturday. Entry is AD 2.

Other Attractions

The old Sacré Coeur Cathedral in the centre of town has been deconsecrated

and turned into the city library. It is grotesquely decorated on the outside. At one time, churches outnumbered mosques in Oran.

The only way to get up to Jebel Mudjadjo is to take a taxi. Expect to pay around AD 50 for the round trip.

Places to Stay – bottom end

The best place is the *Hotel Riad* (tel 36 3846) at 46 Blvd Mellah Ali, right opposite the railway station and one of the bus stations. There is no sign in English, but it is next door to a driving school. Rooms cost AD 75/93 with bath, and there is hot water in the evenings and clean sheets every day. It's a friendly place in a good location.

Further down the street is the *Hotel Meliani* (tel 34 3845) at No 14. Double rooms cost AD 87 including breakfast, and there are cold showers.

There is a whole stack of cheaper places down closer to the centre in an area just off Blvd Emir Abdelkader, but none are fantastic value. Rue Ozanam has plenty of hotels and is easy to find, as it is the street which runs down off Blvd Hamou Boultélis directly in front of the cathedral.

The *Hotel Takadoum* (tel 39 4102) at 5 Rue Ozanam is friendly and the rooms are OK at AD 60 for a double, but there are no showers. There is no sign in English but there's a large yellow one in Arabic above the footpath.

Opposite the Takadoum, at No 6, is the *Hotel Baalabek* (tel 39 2324), which is unspectacular at AD 87 for a double.

If all these places are full (unlikely), there are plenty of others in the vicinity.

Places to Stay – middle

At the bottom of Blvd Mellah Ali is the *Hotel de l'Ouest* (tel 36 4698) at No 6. It charges AD 150 for a double with breakfast, but the rooms have their own bathrooms, and heating and air conditioning.

Places to Stay – top end

Top of the range is the *Hotel Timgad* (tel 39 4797), right in the thick of things at 22 Blvd Emir Abdelkader. It's a four-star hotel, so you can expect to pay in the range of AD 180/250 for singles/doubles; but if you are likely to be staying in a place like this you probably don't give a bugger how much it costs!

Places to Eat

For cheap local food, there's a good little restaurant at 14A Blvd Mellah Ali, right next to the Hotel Meliani.

On Rue Ozanam in the cheap hotel area is a similar but larger place, on the first corner on the right as you face downhill.

Other than that you have a choice of any number of three-star restaurants on Blvd Emir Abdelkader and Rue Mohammed Khemisti.

Getting There & Away

Air The airport is at Tafraoui, 20 km south-east of Oran. There are local buses from Place 1 November.

There are flights with Air Algérie to: Adrar (four times weekly, AD 254); Algiers (at least twice daily, AD 295); Annaba (three time weekly, AD 584); Béchar (five times weekly, AD 220); Constantine (four times weekly, AD 504); Ghardaia (twice weekly, AD 250); Ouargla (weekly, AD 306); Tamanrasset (weekly, AD 420); and Tindouf (three times weekly, AD 319).

International destinations from Oran include: Geneva, London, Lyons, Marseilles, Paris, Toulouse and Zurich, all with either Air Algérie or Air France.

Bus There are two bus stations. The one right outside the railway station is for regional buses and destinations to the west, including Tlemcen. The booking office is in Rue Tenazet, 100 metres from the station.

The other bus station is a solid 10-minute walk south of the museum. This one is much larger (and more crowded) and handles destinations to all parts of the country not served by the smaller station.

Train The railway station is on Blvd Mellah Ali at the top of the hill. It is the large white building with the clock tower.

There are departures to: Algiers (three daily, seven hours); Mohammedia (for Béchar, once daily); and Tlemcen (four daily, one continues to the Moroccan border).

Boat The ferry terminal is directly in front of the centre of town at the bottom of Rampe Commandant Faradj. Tickets for the ferries to Alicante and Marseilles can be bought at the CNAN office at 13 Blvd Abane Ramdane, near the French Consulate. There is another CNAN office in the passenger terminal.

There are departures for Alicante eight times per month in summer, falling to four per month in winter. The fare per person is AD 325 one way and AD 942 for an average 4WD; the trip takes 12 hours.

There are also six departures per month to Marseilles in summer, fewer in winter. The one-way fare is AD 461 per person and AD 1251 for a 4WD; the trip takes 24 hours.

The French town of Sète is also served by ferries from Oran, although there are only three per month in summer. Fares are the same as between Oran and Marseilles and the crossing takes 29 hours.

The Algerian Sahara

The Sahara Desert, the greatest desert on earth, stretches right across the countries of northern Africa, but the lion's share lies in Algeria. A full 85% of the country is occupied by it, and yet this area accounts for only 10% of the country's population.

The Sahara offers the traveller the ultimate challenge. To get out there and cross it is one of the last great adventures left in a world which is rapidly shrinking. It is definitely not a trip for those who love their creature comforts, as the transport is usually uncomfortable, conditions often primitive, the climate extreme and the range of food limited.

In Algeria the Saharan road network is fairly well developed, and there is public transport to the southern border with both Mali and Niger. It is still possible to hitch across the Sahara for free, but this is the exception rather than the rule these days.

Basically, without a vehicle you can take any of the routes normally followed by the overland crowd by using a combination of public transport and hitching. However, on some of the routes transport is infrequent, so you need to be prepared to take a plane to get you out or else sit around for a week or more waiting for a lift. This applies mainly to the eastern route from Hassi Messaoud down through In Aménas and Djanet to Tamanrasset. The Route du Hoggar presents no such problems, although you may end up on a bus between In Salah and Tamanrasset.

It is essential that you are prepared for this sort of travelling, particularly if you hitch and end up for three days on the top of a truck, exposed to the elements. The two essential items to have are a decent hat with a brim, and a water bottle that will hold at least a couple of litres. Travellers do set out without these things and do survive, but why make things more uncomfortable than need be?

History

The prehistoric rock paintings in the Hoggar and Tassili N'Ajjer clearly show that at that time, the Sahara was a much more hospitable place than it is today. The paintings depict mainly men hunting and women and children playing. They suggest that the Sahara of 6000 years ago must have been much like the savanna lands of East Africa today.

Before the 5th century BC, the area was inhabited by hunter-gatherers. From the 4th to the 2nd century BC the people began herding animals and took up a more settled existence.

The horse was first seen in the desert around 1000 BC; an indication that the area was getting drier was the introduction of the camel in the early years of the Christian era.

Trans-Saharan trade became well established, and it was due to this that many of the Punic and Roman towns in the north flourished. The Berbers were the ones who controlled this trade, however, as they were the ones who knew the desert and were able to make the trips across it.

With the Arab invasions in the north in the 7th century, the indigenous Berbers, keen not to be assimilated, retreated to the desert as well as the mountains of the north.

Today the towns and villages of the Algerian Sahara are populated largely by Touareg, who are themselves Berber. However, there have been large numbers of Arabs coming down from the north, in search of work or as civil servants who have been sent here to fill administrative posts.

The towns are relatively prosperous. Nevertheless, with the crippling droughts that have hit the Sahel (the semi-desert area directly south of the true desert) they are being increasingly surrounded by slums (*bidonvilles*) inhabited by destitute nomadic Touareg, who have gravitated to the population centres in the hope of something better. At Tamanrasset in the market you'll see Touareg men selling jewellery; some of it is obviously made for tourists, but other pieces are genuine tribal jewellery which they hope will make them a few dinars.

Grand Erg Occidental

One of the two great sand seas (*ergs* in Arabic), the Grand Erg Occidental (Great Western Erg) occupies an enormous area south of the Saharan Atlas mountains in the west of Algeria. Anywhere else this would constitute a sizeable desert in its own right, but in the Sahara things are a bit different.

On the fringes of the erg are some of the most beautiful oases in the country; these are all relatively accessible, as the erg is flanked on two sides by good, tar-sealed roads. The N6 is the main road from Oran on the north coast to Adrar and this skirts around the western edge of the erg, passing through Ain Sefra, Beni Ounif (for the Moroccan border), Béchar and Beni Abbès. North of Adrar the N51 forks off to the north-east and follows the edge of the dunes to El Goléa, which is on the eastern edge. El Goléa is also on the main N1 road, which connects Algiers and Tamanrasset, a distance of over 2000 km.

If you are coming from Morocco and Beni Ounif, the places to stop are Taghit and Beni Abbès; then head for Timimoun and El Goléa if you want to hitch south. It's easy enough to get to Adrar, but the traffic from there across to the main road at In Salah is negligible. There is supposed to be a weekly bus across this route but it always seems to be the first route to be axed when there is a shortage of buses due to breakdowns, and that happens quite often because of the pounding the desert bus/trucks take on the *pistes* of the south.

The best sand dunes are at Taghit, Beni Abbès and Kerzaz, so make sure you see at least one of these places. Timimoun is a beautiful town in itself, while El Goléa has some good dunes but not much else.

AIN SEFRA
This town in the Saharan Atlas mountains is the gateway to the desert from the north-west.

This is about as far north as you will find sand dunes on this side of the country, and they are quite a sight blown up against the foot of the mountains.

There is little of interest in the town itself and, with the only accommodation being a flash three-star place with air-con and pool, it's best to move on. The trouble is that all along the Western Erg the accommodation is not that cheap. Sleeping out in the camping grounds is the best option, but these are to be found in Beni Abbès, Timimoun and El Goléa only.

Perhaps the most famous thing about the town is that it was here that the young writer and adventurer Isabelle Eberhardt was drowned in a flood in 1904. She was a Russian born in Switzerland who spent most of her adult life in the Algerian Sahara. She became a Muslim, dressed as a man and spent most of her time travelling on horseback. She had a particularly good understanding of Arab culture and politics, and her diaries make interesting reading. (*The Passionate Nomad*, Virago, 1987). She is buried in the town's Muslim cemetery.

The town has a Cultural Week from the 13th to the 19th of May.

As you come into the town from the north, the most striking feature is the modern architecture by the side of the road. These multi-coloured apartment blocks must rate as some of the worst eyesores in the country.

Places to Stay
There's no choice here. The only place is the *Hotel el Mekhter* (tel 31 1417). Rooms

cost AD 140/180 for singles/doubles with breakfast and, since the hotel is more than 1½ km out of town, you have to pay AD 90 for dinner as well.

The hotel is signposted past the military barracks, which you are advised not to photograph unless you want to take a closer look at the inside of a cell.

Getting There & Away

Bus There are buses north to Tlemcen, Algiers and Oran, and south to Béchar.

Hitching The town lies just to the east of the main road, and there is still enough traffic as far south as Béchar to make hitching fairly easy.

BENI OUNIF

Still in the Saharan Atlas, this is a totally unremarkable little town; however, for many travellers it is their first taste of Algeria. Don't worry, things get a lot more interesting before very long.

The town is small and is only about half a km from one end to the other, so there is no difficulty in finding anything.

There is a bank here but it is not authorised to exchange travellers' cheques; you are unlikely to want to use it, as they will probably have just made you change about US$200 at the border.

The road between here and Béchar still has some of the few remaining signs of the battle for Algerian independence. Right along this border, some distance in from the actual line, the French built a continuous barrier of barbed wire some five metres wide. The whole section was patrolled by soldiers stationed at forts, each built in sight of the next, and the line was over 1000 km long on this side of the country. The idea, largely successful, was to isolate the Algerian nationalists from any support from Morocco. Most of the forts are still there today; so is much of the barbed wire, although most of it has been rolled up into large bundles, which you see every few hundred metres.

Places to Stay & Eat

The only hotel in town is the *Hotel Afrique*, on the main road near the turn off for Figuig. It has been recently repainted and rooms cost AD 60/100 for a single/ double.

If you miss out here it's a fairly easy hitch or bus ride to Béchar, 114 km to the south.

The *Restaurant el Feth* is on the corner of the main road at the main intersection and has spaghetti and salad for AD 25, or omelette and chips for AD 15.

Getting There & Away

Bus There is no bus station here; all the buses just stop outside the Hotel Afrique. You have to be lucky to get a seat at times, as these buses are all going through Beni Ounif in transit and are often full.

Train The railway station is just near the shops in the centre of the town. There is one train daily in either direction: at 7.15 am for Béchar, and at 7.40 pm to Mohammedia for Oran and Tlemcen.

Hitching There is enough traffic here to make hitching an option. Just walk to the edge of town and stick out the thumb.

To/from Morocco The road to Morocco leaves the main road in the south of town, just near the customs house – you can't miss it. You can see the Algerian border post, about 1½ km distant in the gap in the mountains. A taxi from the town will cost around AD 30.

From here it's another few hundred metres to the Moroccan side, from where it's a further few km to Figuig.

The whole crossing takes about half a day, and you can expect very heavy searches on the Algerian side. Patience and a smile go a long way, although when it's 45° and some arsehole starts hassling for a 'gift' it's a real effort to be anything less than hostile – hang in there.

BECHAR

This is a modern, sprawling, administrative town and capital of the Saoura region (as this corner of the Sahara is known). It has nothing at all to recommend it but you will probably find yourself stopping for a night here on the way through.

There are a couple of banks here, and it is the last major town in which you can stock up on things for the road south. The Air Algérie office (tel 23 9469) and the tourist office are on the Ain Sefra side of Place de la République. The tourist office has very little info, and the woman staffing it is well meaning, friendly and totally useless.

Right next to the mosque with the large minaret on Ave Colonel Lotfi in the centre is a good market with a fair selection of fruit, vegetables and meat.

From Béchar the road heads south-west for 100 km before curving around the western corner of the Great Western Erg. Here the N50 heads straight on for the 800 km journey to Tindouf in the far west of the country. This route into Mauritania is at present closed, due to the war in Western Sahara; Tindouf is the main base for the Polisario fighters, who are actively supported by Algeria.

Places to Stay

The best place here is the friendly *Grand Hotel de la Saoura* (tel 23 8007) at 24 Rue Kada Belahrech, just around the corner from the post office near the main square, Place de la République. It's a clean place but not all that cheap at AD 60/100 for singles/doubles without breakfast.

The other choice is the *Hotel de la Paix* (or *Hotel Salaam*) in the same area. Although it looks locked, just knock on the side door. It's none too friendly a place, and rooms cost AD 105 for a double.

For men only there is also a cheaper local hotel close by, but it has no signs of any sort and is rough as guts. Ask around.

As there are only the two cheapish

hotels, they tend to fill up by about noon.

Béchar also has a three-star place, the *Hotel Antar* (tel 23 7161), signposted just off the main road one km towards Beni Abbès. Rooms cost AD 120/150 with breakfast and it's quite likely that your currency form will be checked.

Getting There & Away

Air The airport is seven km north of town and local buses make the trip out there.

There are flights to: Adrar (twice weekly, AD 140); Algiers (daily, AD 330); Ghardaia (twice weekly, AD 262); Oran (five weekly, AD 220); Timimoun (twice weekly, AD 130); and Tindouf (twice weekly, AD 218).

Bus The bus station, a busy place, is in the street next to the market, on the opposite side to the mosque. Timetables are displayed, and tickets should be bought in advance whenever possible. Most of the buses heading north travel in the late afternoon and evening, as this is one of the hottest areas in the country.

The main destinations are: Tlemcen (daily, AD 108); Adrar (daily); Taghit (daily, AD 13),; Tindouf (three times weekly, AD 141),; Algiers (twice daily, AD 169),; Beni Abbès (daily, AD 44); and Timimoun (daily, AD 117).

Train There is a daily train to Mohammedia, departing at 5.40 pm and taking something over 14 hours to cover the 650 km – an average of a lightning-fast 45 kmh.

Taxi Taxis to Adrar leave from outside the bus station. Taxis to Beni Ounif leave from a corner of Place de la République.

Hitching Béchar is the sort of town which hitchers could easily get to hate. It is extremely spread out, so getting to the edge of town is a pain. If you're heading towards Beni Abbès there are local buses which run along the main drag the few km to the edge of town. If you're heading towards Ain Sefra you have to walk.

TAGHIT
Pronounced 'Ta-rit', this small oasis village 90 km south of Béchar has some of the most spectacular dunes in the Western Erg. The dunes tower over the eastern edge of the town, and the view as you come over the hill is really something.

The old mud-brick part of the village is dominated by the old *ksar* (fortified stronghold), which is still occupied by the military. This section of the village is a real maze of winding lanes, and the architecture is typical of this part of the Sahara.

There is no bank here, but there is a post office, a fuel station and a few general stores.

A climb up the dunes is a must, as the view from the top is magnificent: the sand sea stretches endlessly to the east, while the oasis and the Oued Zousfana are spread out before you to the west.

Because of the limited transport and accommodation, if you are coming from Beni Abbès the best idea is to take the morning bus from there to Taghit, and then the afternoon bus on to Béchar.

Places to Stay & Eat
The only hotel is the expensive *Hotel Taghit* (tel 0 07). You can't miss it, as it's the only big building in the village. As far as such places go, this one is not bad; it has a nice garden and swimming pool (probably empty). Air-con rooms cost AD 120/150 for singles/doubles with breakfast.

There is a makeshift camping ground on the road heading south of town, out past the shops, on the edge of the palmeraie. There are no facilities to speak of and no charge.

Apart from the AD 65 set menu at the hotel, there is only a small restaurant near the entrance of the old village. Otherwise it's a case of buying tinned food and bread

from the bakery (near the bus stop) and putting your own food together.

Getting There & Away
There is one bus daily to Beni Abbès and another to Béchar. It should be possible to hitch in either direction, although the traffic is very thin. The road to both Béchar and Beni Abbès has been surfaced, so the amount of traffic using the road has increased.

Taxis go to Béchar a couple of times a day and there may be one to Beni Abbès if the demand warrants it.

BENI ABBES
Another beautiful oasis town. This one is built on the edge of an escarpment, so it looks down on the palmeraie and the oued. The town is backed by high dunes, and the favourite occupation of the local kids is sliding down these on pieces of tin and plastic.

From the top of the dune, there is nothing but sand out to the east. If you are taking a camera up here, make sure it is well protected, as the wind really whips the sand up and it wouldn't take much to ruin the mechanism. On a really windy day, leave cameras behind.

Information & Orientation
On entering the town across the oued, the track to the right just before the shops leads to the palmeraie, which has an ancient ksar and an excellent swimming pool.

To the left the road leads to the good little museum and zoo run by the Centre National de Recherches sur les Zones Arides.

The road straight ahead leads up the escarpment past a small row of shops, and then forks. Up to the right lies the market, bus station, post office and Hotel Grand Erg, while to the left is the Hotel Rym, the bank and the dunes.

There are two bakeries in town, one at the market and one along the road to the museum. Neither is open on Fridays, so stock up the day before.

Also up by the market is the town supermarket in the large blue building. Don't get your hopes up at the idea of a supermarket – this one has the usual collection of about six different products, but hundreds of each!

Things to See

The track into the palmeraie leads past the old abandoned mud-brick ksar off to the right. This dates from the last century and is now gradually returning to the earth.

Beyond the ksar and beneath the stone water tower on the edge of the escarpment, is a small swimming pool. It is a cool, green retreat from the blinding desert all around. A few trees give shade to the pool which is filled by beautifully clear spring water and is in a paved enclosure. The pool is maintained by a caretaker and is open during daylight hours.

The other obvious sight is the dunes. Take a scramble up them in the late afternoon when the light is at its best.

The museum is about 100 metres along the track to the left along the oued, and then up the first street on the right. It has an interesting selection of the desert fauna and flora. Someone has spent a lot of time and effort putting together the display that has samples and descriptions of more than 70 different types of dates.

The zoo is in the same compound and, although the birds and animals displayed are interesting, once again the cages are depressingly small.

Both are open from 7 am to 12 noon and 2 to 5 pm daily, except Friday; entry is AD 3.

Places to Stay

The *Hotel Grand Erg* (tel 23 3439) is expensive at AD 120 for a double. However, the best thing about it is that they let you camp in the garden, although even that is not cheap at AD 20 per person and AD 5 for a shower. If you are sleeping

out without a tent there is plenty of shelter here, as you can sleep under the verandahs (not that it's likely to be raining!). The staff are exceedingly surly but it's this or nothing. The view from the terrace is fantastic in the early morning.

The only other hotel is the *Hotel Rym* (tel 23 3203), at the foot of the large dune. It was built with tour groups in mind, and they charge AD 140/180 for singles/doubles with bath and breakfast.

Places to Eat

Meagre pickings indeed: there are only two restaurants in town. The one up by the bus station has a menu which is limited to meat, omelettes and chips.

Down on the corner of the main road and the track to the museum is another small place, which does much the same stuff but also has occasional vegetables. Other than that it's a case of putting your own food together or paying out at the *Hotel Rym* – AD 83 for a four-course set menu.

The *Hotel Grand Erg* has the only bar in town, so it gets fairly raucous some evenings.

Getting There & Away

The bus station is up by the market. There are twice-daily departures to Béchar, and buses leave once a day for Adrar and Timimoun. All these buses pass through en route from somewhere else, so seats are not guaranteed.

There is also a bus to Taghit every day in the morning.

ADRAR

Adrar is a major regional capital 120 km south of the road which rings the Great Western Erg. Where this road branches off to the south is a café, where you can wait for a lift if necessary.

The town has very little in the way of formal attractions but its uniform brick-red colour is interesting. The centre of town is an absolutely enormous main square (Place des Martyrs) – you could

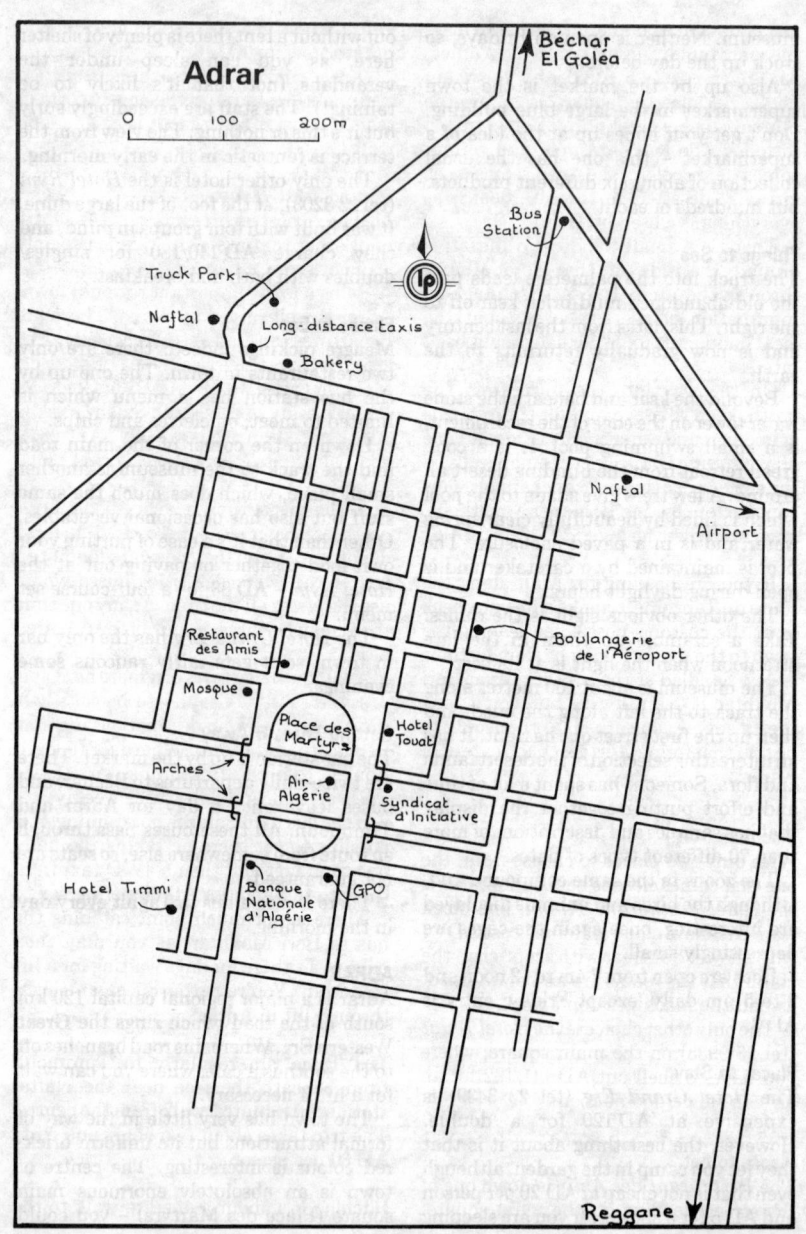

just about land a plane on it! Around it are the main buildings: the banks, post office, Air Algérie (tel 25 9365) and the main hotel. Because the square is so big the midday sun here is blinding, and you need to follow the local example and retreat somewhere cooler – the town seems to be virtually deserted in the afternoons, as everything is closed up tight.

There is a small Syndicat d'Initiative around the side of the Hotel Touat, through the arch. It has absolutely no information of use to tourists, but the local handicraft items for sale might be of interest.

On the way into the town from the north, keep your eyes out for the *foggaras* or underground water channels, identifiable above ground by the lines of small wells on the surface. This system of channels, now superseded by more modern methods, once stretched for over 2000 km in this area.

If you are heading for Mali along the route du Tanezrouft, make sure you check in at the customs post when leaving the town to the south. It may be that customs is now handled at the border post at Borj Mokhtar 800 km away, but you'd look pretty silly if you turned up there only to be told that formalities are taken care of in Adrar!

Places to Stay

With only two places to choose from, the one that comes close to being affordable is the *Hotel Restaurant Timmi*, one block from the main square. Rooms cost AD 87 with shower but treat with scepticism the claim that the rooms are air conditioned, as half the machines don't work.

The only other choice is the *Hotel Touat* (tel 25 9933) on the main square, where you have to shell out AD 141/192 for an air-con single/double room.

Places to Eat

The *Restaurant des Amis* is down one of the streets leading off the main square.

Here you can get an excellent chicken and potato stew for AD 16.

Out at the bus station there is quite a reasonable restaurant, the best in town in fact. It's just a pity that it is such a long walk.

Getting There & Away

Air The airport is three km from the centre and, other than walking, taxi is the only way out there.

Being a fairly important regional town, Adrar is well served by plane. There are departures to: Algiers (three weekly, AD 295); Béchar (three weekly, AD 156); Borj Mokhtar (twice weekly, AD 220); Ghardaia (twice weekly, AD 197); In Salah (weekly, AD 108); Oran (four weekly, AD 254); and Tamanrasset (twice weekly, AD 236).

Bus The bus station is about 500 metres north of the main square. It is a large depot, and is also the graveyard for quite a few of the Mercedes truck/buses which use the *pistes* all the time. At any one time there may be three or four being repaired here.

As all the departures originate here, it is possible (and advisable) to book tickets the day before. Main destinations include: Béchar (daily, 6 pm); Ghardaia (5 pm); Aoulef (daily); Borj Mokhtar (twice weekly); and In Salah (twice weekly).

If the bus to In Salah is not running, it is possible to get there by taking the daily bus to Aoulef and then a 4WD taxi from there to In Salah for AD 50 per person.

There is not much point catching the bus to Borj Mokhtar, as you may then have to sit there for days waiting for a lift into Mali. You're better off organising a through lift in Adrar.

Taxi Taxis run regularly to Timimoun from beneath the tree near the Naftal station, 10 minutes' walk from the centre. The trip takes about two hours and costs AD 60 per person.

Hitching It's about a one-km walk to the

northern edge of town for the road to Béchar and Timimoun.

There is an SNTR depot up by the Naftal station and it may be possible to arrange a lift in a truck from here; however, as always with these government trucks, you need to be discreet, as it's illegal for the drivers to take passengers.

TIMIMOUN

If you can stop at only one of the oases around the Great Western Erg, make it Timimoun. It's an enchanting place, built very much in the Sudanese red-mud style, and the residents are very friendly – it's one of the best places in the Sahara.

The town is built on the edge of an escarpment, and there are fantastic views out over an ancient salt lake to the sand dunes in the distance; on a bright, moonlit night the effect is just magic.

If you have access to a vehicle the Gourara Circuit is an absolute must. This is a 70-km loop through a few oasis villages to the north of Timimoun and takes in the finest of the desert scenery. The ideal way to see this area would be to hire a camel and guide for a few days and do it at a leisurely pace. The guy at the tourist office may be able to fix you up, or more likely the sharp young lads who run the camping ground. They seem to have good contacts, but women alone may have to set them straight about exactly where they stand. There is a map of the circuit in the tourist office.

The population of the town and the area is a real mix: the Haratine (non-Negroid blacks), the Zénète Berbers, the Chaamba Arabs (originally from the east) and the Black Africans (descendents of Malian slaves). The predominant language of the region is Zénète, a Berber dialect similar to those spoken in the Kabylie and the M'Zab.

Information

Tourist Office The tourist office is in the municipality building, near the roundabout on the main street. Here you can see a copy of the Gourara Circuit map.

Post The post office too is close to the roundabout, on the road that connects the main street with the main Adrar-El Goléa road.

Money There is a branch of the Banque Nationale d'Algérie by the market square, about halfway along the main street.

Airlines The Air Algérie office (tel 23 4555) is also on the main square.

Things to See

The town lends itself well to photography; just walking up and down the main street you'll see plenty of possibilities, with the red buildings and the koubba in the middle of the road. The Hotel Rouge de l'Oasis is a fine old building and, although it is now only partially open, it is worth a wander around inside to see the walls, which are decorated with traditional designs.

The administrative buildings of the town are also built to a similar design but are hidden behind a high wall.

Down towards the palmeraie, along the road to the camping, the old section of town is a maze of dusty alleys and red-mud houses. The palmeraie itself is cool and shady, and the individual plots are divided by mud-brick walls. Enter by the road which leads from the main roundabout down past the high school to the camping and Hotel Gourara.

Places to Stay – bottom end

The cheapest place is the *Hotel Ighzer* on the southern end of the main street. Spartan rooms cost AD 60/80 and these are adequate. It is also possible to camp in the backyard for AD 10 per person, but there is no shade.

Camping Although you can camp in the grounds of the Hotel Ighzer, a much better alternative is the *Camping la Palmeraie*

Top: Main street, Tamanrasset, Algeria (HF)
Bottom: Dunes encroaching on In Salah, Algeria (HF)

Top: Bus in the Algerian Sahara (HF)
Left: Municipality buildings, Timimoun, Algeria (HF)
Right: Ghardaia medina, the M'Zab, Algeria (HF)

on the edge of the escarpment. It is more expensive at AD 20 per person and AD 15 per vehicle, but there is plenty of shade, hot showers and the guys running it are eager to help.

Places to Stay – middle & top end

The *Hotel Rouge de l'Oasis* (tel 23 4417) may or may not be open. It suffered a minor collapse a few years ago and, although the bar is still open, there is some doubt as to whether the hotel will remain open. At the time of writing, rooms were AD 90 for a double. It will be a real crime if this place is allowed to fall into ruin, as it is one of the most colourful hotels in the whole country.

The alternative is the government-run *Hotel Gourara* (tel 23 4451) right on the edge of the escarpment, just past the camping. It has fantastic views over the salt lake and dunes, but rooms are not cheap at AD 141/192 for singles/doubles with breakfast. Even if you are not staying here it's not a bad place to come for a beer on the terrace at sunset.

Places to Eat

The choices are strictly limited here. Other than putting your own food together with bread and whatever you can find in the market, there is only one restaurant. It's just off the main street, in the street between the Hotel Rouge de l'Oasis and the gardens opposite the municipality building. It's the place to come if you want to try camel stew, although this is nothing special.

The *Café November 1* on the main square is the main hangout, but they don't serve food.

There is a bakery in the street which runs off the main street, alongside the gardens.

Things to Buy

For souvenirs, the Artisanat du Grand Erg shop is on the road down to the camping and has a small selection of locally made goods.

Getting There & Away

Air The airport is eight km to the south-east of town.

There are flights to: Algiers (twice weekly, AD 255); Béchar (twice weekly, AD 130); and Ghardaia (three times weekly, AD 160).

Bus The TVE station is on the main street, almost opposite the mosque.

It is possible to book in advance on only some of the services, as most are just passing through and don't originate in Timimoun.

The services from Timimoun are to: Béchar (7 am, AD 118.50); Adrar (daily at midnight, Fridays only at 8.30 am, AD 37.40); and Ghardaia (5.15 pm, AD 118.60).

Taxi Taxis leave from just next to the bus station. The only main destination is Adrar. The trip takes two hours and costs AD 60 per person.

Hitching The town itself is only a five-minute walk from the main highway connecting El Goléa and Adrar, so getting out onto the road for hitching in either direction is easy enough.

EL GOLEA

The most easterly oasis of the Great Western Erg, El Goléa is a major stop on the route south. With over 180,000 palm trees, it is one of the biggest oases of the south.

The town is dominated by the old ksar, El Menia, built on a rocky knoll in the east of town. It was built by the Zénète Berbers in the 10th century and is now in a sad state.

The water here is some of the sweetest in the whole Sahara; fill up your tanks if you're driving, especially if you are heading south, as the water at In Salah is absolutely foul. It is possible to buy bottled water in the supermarket here but this seems a bit pointless, as all you

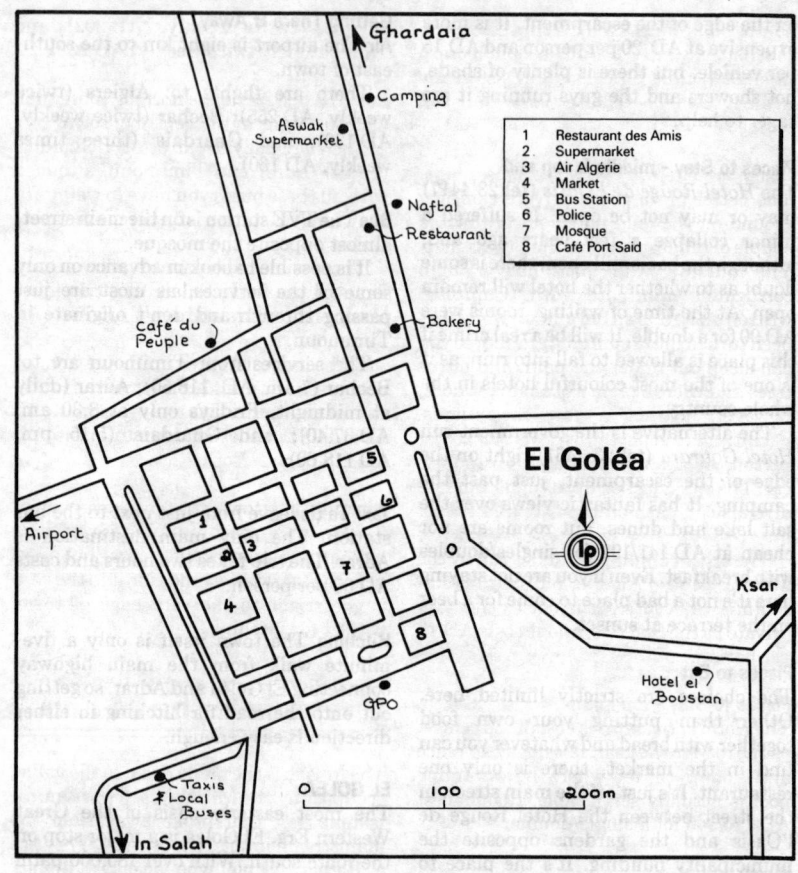

1	Restaurant des Amis
2	Supermarket
3	Air Algérie
4	Market
5	Bus Station
6	Police
7	Mosque
8	Café Port Said

El Goléa

Ghardaia

Camping

Aswak Supermarket

Naftal

Restaurant

Café du Peuple

Bakery

Airport

Ksar

Hotel el Boustan

GPO

0   100   200m

Taxis
Local Buses

In Salah

are getting is exactly the same as what's in the tap.

El Goléa has a bank, post office and Air Algérie office (tel 73 6100). Accommodation is limited to a fancy three-star hotel, an inconveniently-located hotel and one of the best camping grounds in the country.

Right opposite the camping ground is a supermarket, which is not at all well stocked.

The oasis itself is very lush and, apart from palms, supports a large variety of fruit trees including plum, peach, apricot, cherry, orange and fig. The market here has the last decent produce (apart from potatoes and onions) on the southward route, so stock up.

Just near the ksar is a cemetery, where Charles de Foucauld (who was responsible for the hermitage in the Hoggar) was buried in 1929.

Places to Stay – bottom end

The only reasonably priced place is the new *Hotel Vieux Ksar* on the road to the south, 30 minutes' walk from the centre. It's not bad at AD 90 for a double with breakfast, but it's location is really against it. There are some air-con rooms.

Camping There are two choices here. The better place is the private camping ground on the road north out of town, a couple of hundred metres from the centre. The outside wall just has a high corrugated iron gate with 'Camping' written on it. It is an old garden which has been turned into a camping ground, so you can sleep out under the palm and citrus trees and there's plenty of shade; it does, however, attract a few mosquitoes. Facilities are good and it costs AD 20 per person, AD 12 for a tent and AD 15 for a car. The site is locked up at night, but late arrivals can bash on the gate and get let in.

The other camping ground is run by the Touring Club d'Algérie and is three km south of the centre. It is not as shady or private as the first one, and it costs AD 15 per person.

Places to Stay – top end
The *Hotel el Boustan* is east of the centre, on the road to the ksar. It is not a bad place and is one of the few where the swimming pool is actually serviceable. Rooms cost AD 120/140 for a single/double.

Places to Eat
There's a little restaurant, almost opposite the Naftal station on the road out to the north, and this place has good chicken, chips and salad.

Other than that, the *Restaurant des Amis* in the centre has very mediocre food but is open late, as it caters for the bus passengers who stop here for a meal break on the Ghardaia-Adrar run.

Getting There & Away
Air The airport is three km to the west of town.

There are flights with Air Algérie to

Algiers (twice weekly, AD 302) and Tamanrasset (twice weekly, AD 262).

Bus The bus station is nothing more than an office right in the centre of town.

There are daily departures for Ghardaia (3 pm), Adrar and Timimoun, although with all these buses you have to wait until they arrive to see if there are spare seats.

There is also a departure every second day at 4 pm for In Salah. The trip takes about eight hours and costs AD 72.

Taxi The long-distance taxis leave from an area just a few minutes' walk to the south-west of the centre. The main destination is Ghardaia but they also run to Timimoun (AD 120 per person).

Hitching The town stretches away about five km to the south, so if you are hitching in that direction catch a local bus from near the taxi station and ride it to the end; it goes right to the very edge of town, perfect for hitching.

Ghardaia & the M'Zab

The M'Zab is the name given to the valley occupied by the Mozabites, a puritanical Islamic sect that broke away from the mainstream in the 11th century. They are a Berber people who speak a dialect similar to that spoken by the people of the Kabylie in the north.

The 100,000 inhabitants of this deep narrow valley live in a pentapolis – five villages which have developed independently of the rest of the country. Ghardaia is the main town and the others, which surround it, are Melika, Beni Isguen, Bou Noura and El Ateuf. The Mozabites are well known for being astute merchants; many of them have migrated to Algiers and now own businesses there and in France. Those who have remained in the M'Zab are still fairly conservative, particularly the older generation. Traditions are strong here, and most of the people still wear traditional dress – baggy pants for the men, white garments of hand-woven wool for the women.

One of the main reasons why the towns have retained their character and traditions is that the Mozabites were not involved in the fight for independence, so the French left them alone.

Each town is built on a knoll in the valley and each is crowned by a distinctive, unadorned minaret. The town centres, particularly Ghardaia, Melika and Beni Isguen, consist of narrow winding streets and are excellent places to explore. Beni Isguen ('the pious') is the religious town of the M'Zab; foreigners can't enter unless accompanied by a guide and they cannot stay overnight.

The oasis is massive, stretching for some 10 km along the valley, and the 3000-plus wells support over 270,000 palm trees.

This is the most interesting area in the country, so be sure to put aside a few days to explore it. There is a good range of accommodation including a very well-run camp site.

GHARDAIA

The largest and most important of the five towns, Ghardaia is very much the hub of the M'Zab; it's also the only one with facilities for catering to tourists. As well as a number of hotels and restaurants, there are a dozen or so shops which sell souvenirs of all kinds but mainly rugs, which are a speciality of the area.

Information
Tourist Offices There are two ONAT offices in Ghardaia, one in the Hotel Rostimedes and the other on the main street, Rue Emir Abdelkader. Both are fairly useless, but the one at the Rostimedes does organise (expensive) tours if you are interested.

Post The main post office is also on the main street, which becomes Ave 1 November south of the main side street, Rue Ahmed Talbi; the latter leads to the Oued M'Zab and the bus station.

The post office is open in summer from 7.30 am to 12 noon and 4 to 7 pm Saturday to Wednesday, and 7 am to 1 pm Thursday, closed Friday. Winter hours are from 8 am to 6.30 pm Saturday to Wednesday and 8 am to 4 pm Thursday; closed Friday.

If you buy any rugs in Ghardaia it is possible to post them from this office; however, take them along unwrapped, as the officials need to see the contents first. A 10-kg parcel to Australia costs AD 108.

Money There are banks on the main street. You can change money at the Hotel Rostimedes too.

Market The daily market is held in the cobbled marketplace, an open square in the middle of the old part of the town.

Airlines The busy Air Algérie office (tel 89 4550) is on Ave 1 November.

Hammam If your hotel doesn't have showers, there is a hammam in the central area, to the right of the entrance to the Hotel es Saada. It is open for women from 8.30 am to 1 pm, and the women's entrance is in the side lane to the left. An orange rag is hung in the doorway to indicate that it is the women's time.

Things to See
The entrance to the old city is along Rue Ibn Rosten, which leads to the marketplace. The market takes place daily, mainly in the morning, and is a colourful affair. As well as agricultural produce, there is all manner of other stuff for sale. Around the market square are a number of souvenir shops.

Off to the right of the square and leading up to the Great Mosque is the Souk Ed Dellada, where on Wednesdays

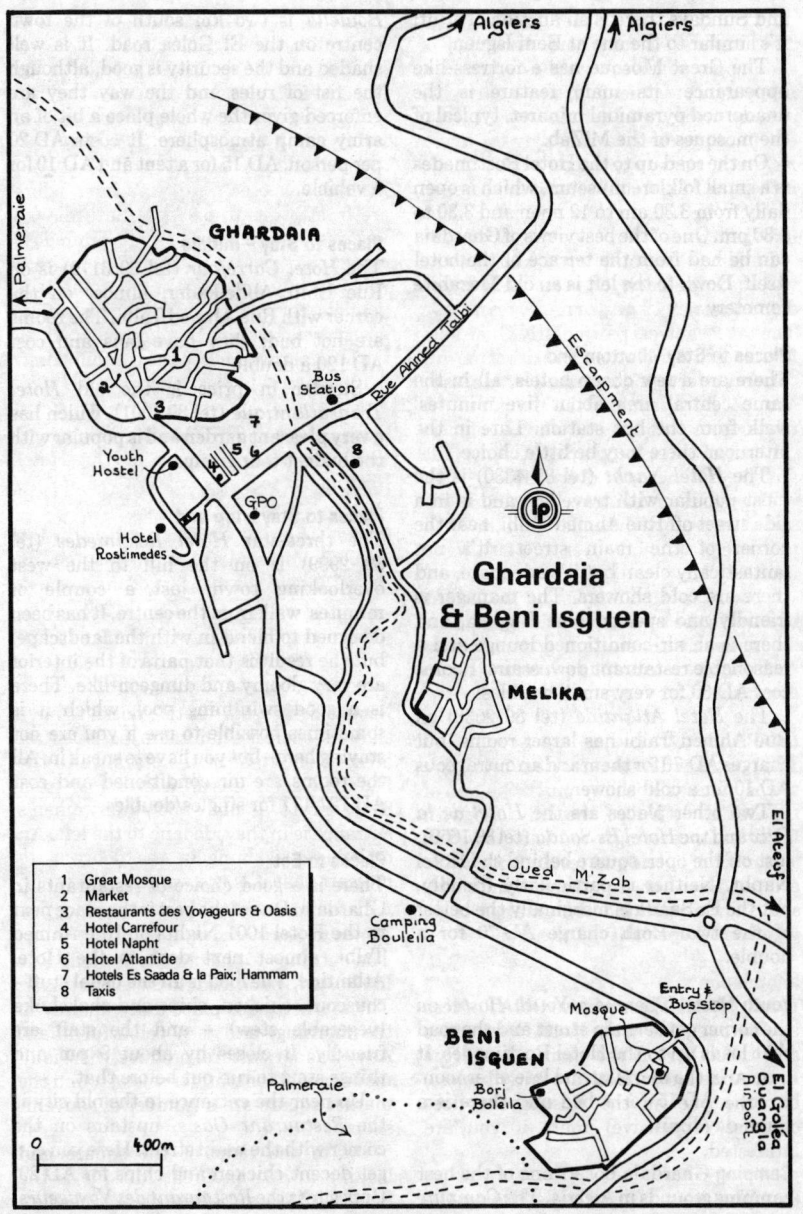

GHARDAIA

Palmeraie

Bus
Station

Rue Ahmed Talb

Escarpment

Youth
Hostel

GPO

Hotel
Rostimedes

Ghardaia
& Beni Isguen

MELIKA

El Ateuf

Oued M'Zab

1 Great Mosque
2 Market
3 Restaurants des Voyageurs & Oasis
4 Hotel Carrefour
5 Hotel Napht
6 Hotel Atlantide
7 Hotels Es Saada & la Paix; Hammam
8 Taxis

Camping
Bouleila

Entry &
Bus Stop

Mosque

El Goléa
Ouarga
Airport

BENI
ISGUEN

Borj
Boleila

Palmeraie

0   400m

and Sundays there is an auction of stuff; it's similar to the one at Beni Isguen.

The Great Mosque has a fortress-like appearance; its main feature is the unadorned pyramidal minaret, typical of the mosques of the M'Zab.

On the road up to the Hotel Rostimedes is a small folklore museum, which is open daily from 8.30 am to 12 noon and 3.30 to 6.30 pm. One of the best views of Ghardaia can be had from the terrace of the hotel itself. Down to the left is an old Mozabite cemetery.

Places to Stay – bottom end

There are a few cheap hotels, all in the same central area about five minutes' walk from the bus station. Late in the afternoon there may be little choice.

The *Hotel Napht* (tel 89 4330) is the most popular with travellers and is in a side street off Rue Ahmed Talbi, near the corner of the main street. It's not fantastically clean but it's adequate, and there are cold showers. The manager is friendly and speaks some English, and there is an air-conditioned lounge and a reasonable restaurant downstairs. Rooms cost AD 60 for very small doubles.

The *Hotel Atlantide* (tel 89 2536) on Rue Ahmed Talbi has larger rooms, but charges AD 70 for them and an outrageous AD 10 for a cold shower.

Two other places are the *Hotel de la Paix* and the *Hotel Es Saada* (tel 89 1659), just off the open square behind the Hotel Napht. Neither is particularly friendly, but the Es Saada is marginally the better of the two. Both charge AD 70 for a double.

Youth Hostel There is a *Youth Hostel* on the corner of the main street and the road that leads up to the Hotel Rostimedes. It is open in the morning and late afternoon. It costs AD 15 for a bed and there is a three-day limit.

Camping Ghardaia boasts one of the best camping grounds in Algeria. The *Camping Bouleila* is two km south of the town centre on the El Goléa road. It is well shaded and the security is good, although the list of rules and the way they are enforced gives the whole place a bit of an army camp atmosphere. It costs AD 20 per person, AD 15 for a tent and AD 10 for a vehicle.

Places to Stay – middle

The *Hotel Carrefour* (tel 89 3179) is on Rue Emir Abdelkader, almost on the corner with Rue Ahmed Talbi. The rooms are not bad; they have fans and cost AD 120 a double.

Similar in price is the old *Hotel Transatlantique* (tel 89 1001), which has a very pleasant garden and is popular with the budget tour groups.

Places to Stay – top end

The three-star *Hotel Rostimedes* (tel 89 2999) is on the hill to the west overlooking town, just a couple of minutes' walk from the centre. It has been designed to blend in with the landscape, but the result is that parts of the interior are very gloomy and dungeon-like. There is a good swimming pool, which it is sometimes possible to use if you are not staying here – but you have to sneak in. All the rooms are air conditioned and cost AD 127/177 for singles/doubles.

Places to Eat

There is a good choice of restaurants in Ghardaia. One of the best is the place next to the Hotel 1001 Nights on Rue Ahmed Talbi, almost next door to the Hotel Atlantide. The food is all the usual stuff – couscous, chicken, chips and shakshuka (vegetable stew) – and the staff are friendly. It closes by about 9 pm and things start to run out before that.

Up near the entrance to the old city is the *Restaurant Oasis*, upstairs on the corner with the main street. Here you can get decent chicken and chips for AD 20. Opposite is the *Restaurant des Voyageurs*, which is also not bad but is not as popular with the locals.

The restaurant at the *Hotel Napht* does quite decent food but, almost directly opposite, the *Restaurant Zahia* does possibly the worst couscous in North Africa. The other meat dishes are not so bad, and it's pleasant sitting outside. Behind it there is a tiny snack shop which does very good shakshuka.

The restaurant of the *Hotel Atlantide* offers slightly better fare and has a four-course set menu for AD 40.

Things to Buy

If you are interested in buying any of the beautifully colourful rugs here check the quality closely, as they vary enormously. The better quality ones have more knots per square cm. The greatest concentration of shops is around the market square.

You need to haggle over the prices; these may seem outrageously expensive, but when you think in real (black-market) terms, are actually very reasonable. It is also possible to do a bit of bartering with some of the shopkeepers, using any surplus goods which you may have.

As an example of prices, a 1½ by one metre rug will cost anything from AD 500 to AD 1000; officially that's US$100 to US$200, but on the black market it's only US$30 to US$60. If you are paying in undeclared foreign currency you can get a better price again, but be discreet.

Getting There & Away

Air The airport is 10 km south of town on the road to El Goléa.

As this is a major centre, it is well served by Air Algérie. There is a weekly flight direct to Paris. The internal flights are to: Adrar (twice weekly, AD 197); Algiers (daily, AD 226); Annaba (twice weekly, AD 276); Béchar (twice weekly, AD 262); Constantine (twice weekly, AD 234); Djanet (twice weekly, AD 300); In Salah (weekly, AD 184); Oran (twice weekly, AD 250); Tamanrasset (four times weekly, AD 305); and Timimoun (three times weekly, AD 160).

Bus The main station is on Rue Ahmed Talbi, just across the Oued M'Zab, only five minutes' walk from the centre. The ticket office can be a bit of a shambles and demand for tickets is often high, so make reservations in advance. A timetable is displayed.

The main destinations are: Adrar (daily); Algiers (three times daily); Oran (three times daily); Biskra (daily), Constantine (twice daily); El Goléa (three times daily); and Timimoun (daily).

Taxi Taxis for El Goléa and Algiers leave from over the oued, opposite the bus station. As with everything in Ghardaia, there is very little activity here in the afternoons.

Hitching For hitching south out of town, catch a local bus heading for El Ateuf and get off at the main roundabout near Beni Isguen. The El Goléa road heads off south up the escarpment from here.

Getting Around

The station for the local buses is just opposite the entrance to the old city. There are buses for Beni Isguen, El Ateuf and Bou Noura.

AROUND GHARDAIA
Beni Isguen

This is the most important religious town in the M'Zab. The people here hang on very firmly to their traditional ways, and the amount of outside influence is kept to an absolute minimum. One of the major restrictions in this direction is that the residents must marry within the town.

The town itself is built on the slope of the hill, 2½ km south of Ghardaia. It is closed to outsiders from noon to 3.30 pm for prayer. The best time for a visit is in the late afternoon, when the market square comes alive with the daily auction. Here locals sell hand-made cloth, rugs and other general items. It is interesting to watch: there are no cafés in the town, so this becomes the social event of the day, and all the men sit out around the square.

The narrow streets are entered from the main road from Ghardaia, and here you have to pick up a guide. It is compulsory for all non-Muslims entering the town to have a guide, and this will cost you AD 10 per person. There are plenty of guides, so make sure you get one with whom you have a common language; many of the older men speak no English. Photography and smoking are forbidden in the town, and there are signs up at the entrance to remind you.

The guide will show you all the interesting bits and pieces around the town. The highlight is the Turkish tower, Borj Cheikh el Hadj (also known as Borj Boleila), in the eastern corner of the town. The view from the top of the tower is excellent and you are allowed to take photos. Your guide will probably leave you at the marketplace, around which there are a few shops selling the colourful local rugs; the prices here are a bit more negotiable than in Ghardaia.

The palmeraie at Beni Isguen is probably the best in the M'Zab. It stretches for a couple of km behind the town. Just continue on the road, past the entrance to the town, and it winds around to the back of the palmeraie. The gardens here are green havens, veritable Gardens of Eden; however, they are difficult to see properly, as they are mostly behind high walls. It is usually not long before someone invites you in to sit in the shade of their fruit trees. Once behind the wall, the contrast is vivid – fruit trees of all kinds battling each other for room. You'll find every kind of fruit here, from grapes and figs to bananas and dates.

Getting There & Away Local buses leave Ghardaia from outside the entrance to the old city. They drop you outside the gates to Beni Isguen; alternatively, it's a half-hour walk.

Melika
It is from Melika that you get the best overall views of the Oued M'Zab and Ghardaia itself. The town is about a km to the south-east, high above the oued.

The main point of interest is the curious cemetery on the northern side, although the town itself is interesting to wander around.

Getting There & Away The easiest way up to Melika is on foot. It takes about 30 minutes to make the climb, and the best route is the road which leads south opposite the bus station. It is also possible to cross the oued anywhere and just scramble up the side of the hill.

Grand Erg Oriental

The Great Eastern Erg is much larger than its western counterpart. From central-eastern Algeria it stretches north and east into Tunisia.

Close to its northern edge is the oasis of El Oued, in the centre of the Souf region. This is a series of oases dotted throughout a small triangular area. For many people El Oued is their first Algerian town, as there is a good road connecting it with Nefta and the towns of the Chott el Jerid in Tunisia. It is worth spending a couple of days here before moving on.

In the Souf region an ingenious method of agriculture has been developed, which allows for the growing of dates and fruits in one of the hottest areas of the Sahara. Great depressions are excavated with hand tools and the sand piled up on all sides; palm fronds are then stuck along the ridges to stop the sand blowing back into the dip. Palms and other plants are planted in the bottom, from where their roots can reach the subterranean water. It is not uncommon to see just the tip of a palm tree sticking out of the top of an excavated pit.

Touggourt is another oasis town, right

on the western edge of the erg, south of El Oued; the road that connects the two towns passes through some magnificent sand-dune country. At times the dunes are actually creeping across the road and it is a constant struggle to keep it clear.

Further south again is oil country, from where the majority of Algeria's exports come. Hassi Messaoud is the heart of the oil industry, although Ouargla on the edge of the erg is as close as most people will need to go, unless they are heading for Djanet.

EL OUED

El Oued has been dubbed 'The Village of a Thousand Domes' and it doesn't take long to work out why: virtually all the buildings use vaults and domes in an effort to alleviate the incredible summer heat. Temperatures as high as 60°C are not unknown here and for days on end it will hit 45° or more with monotonous regularity, so be prepared for it if you are here then. It gets so bloody hot in this place that everything is hot to touch – even the handrails inside the buses and the door handles of the hotel rooms! The town is also famous for its carpets, many of which bear the brown Cross of the Souf motif on a white background. There are simpler designs on the rough black

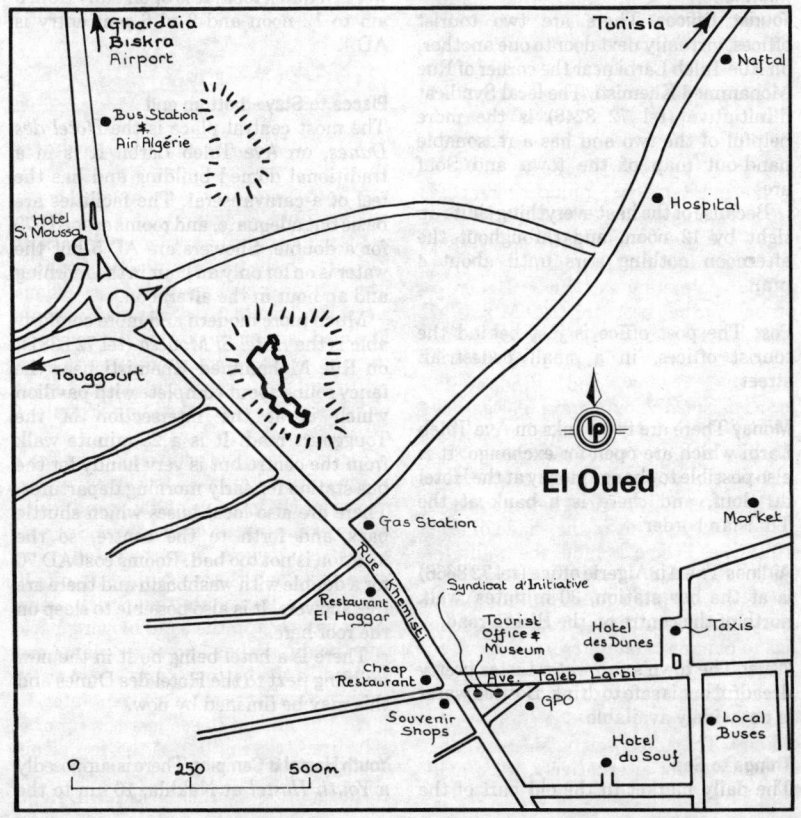

rugs with red and white lines through them. Many of the carpets sold in Ghardaia are actually made in El Oued and, obviously, the prices at the source are better.

The dozen or so villages around El Oued are worth a poke around, particularly Nakhla, 15 km to the south-east, and Guemar, 18 km along the Biskra road.

In the entire Souf region the women wear a single robe/veil which covers everything except for one eye. This makes them a truly bizarre sight; if ever a garment has had a dehumanising effect, it has to be this one.

Information

Tourist Offices There are two tourist offices, virtually next door to one another, on Rue Taleb Larbi near the corner of Rue Mohammed Khemisti. The local Syndicat d'Initiative (tel 72 8248) is the more helpful of the two and has a reasonable hand-out map of the town and Souf area.

Because of the heat everything shuts up tight by 12 noon, and throughout the afternoon nothing stirs until about 4 pm.

Post The post office is just behind the tourist offices, in a small pedestrian street.

Money There are two banks on Ave Taleb Larbi which are open for exchange. It is also possible to change money at the Hotel du Souf, and there is a bank at the Tunisian border.

Airlines The Air Algérie office (tel 72 8666) is at the bus station, 30 minutes' walk north of the centre on the Biskra road.

Water The town's tap water tastes pretty dreadful but is safe to drink. Bottled water is not widely available.

Things to See

The daily market in the old part of the town is a colourful and animated affair. It is at its busiest on Fridays. Most of the stuff for sale is food and everyday items, but there are a few stalls which cater to the tourist trade.

The museum in between the two tourist offices consists of just one room. However, it has some good displays including old aerial photos of the area, a collection of the various insects and animals of the region, some good sand roses and other geological curiosities. There are also a couple of traditional rugs, and the boots with wool-and-camel-hair soles which are used to walk on the burning hot sand. The whole thing is bit dusty and moth-eaten but is worth a quick look. It is open daily from 9 am to 12 noon and 3 to 6 pm; entry is AD 1.

Places to Stay – bottom end

The most central place is the *Hotel des Dunes*, on Ave Taleb Larbi. It is in a traditional domed building and has the feel of a caravanserai. The facilities are basic but adequate, and rooms cost AD 70 for a double. Showers are AD 5 but the water is on for only an hour in the morning and an hour in the afternoon.

Much more modern and more comfortable is the *Hotel Si Moussa* (tel 72 8381), on Rue Mohammed Khemisti near the fancy roundabout complete with pavilion which is at the intersection of the Touggourt road. It is a 25-minute walk from the centre but is very handy for the bus station for early morning departures. There are also local buses which shuttle back and forth to the centre, so the location is not too bad. Rooms cost AD 70 for a double with washbasin and there are free showers. It is also possible to sleep on the roof here.

There is a hotel being built in the new building next to the Hotel des Dunes and this may be finished by now.

Youth Hostel & Camping There is supposedly a *Youth Hostel* at Nakhla, 16 km to the south, where you can stay or camp, but this hasn't been confirmed.

The camping ground north of town on the Tunis road, next to the Naftal station, is very much a thing of the past.

Places to Stay - top end

The only other place is the *Hotel du Souf* (tel 72 8170), a couple of blocks south of the tourist office, complete with swimming pool and tower. Rooms cost a mere AD 141/192 for a single/double with breakfast.

Places to Eat

There is a local restaurant on Rue Mohammed Khemisti, diagonally opposite the tourist office. It does the usual stuff, although the choice is a bit limited – salad, soup or spaghetti for AD 8. In the shop attached to it they sell tins of beautifully cold grapefruit, orange or apricot juice for AD 7.

Halfway along the main street, the *Restaurant El Hoggar* is about the best place in town. It is one of the few places which doesn't close up in the afternoons and is a cool retreat from the heat outside. The food is good, but a bit expensive at AD 10 for salad or soup, AD 25 for a meat main course and AD 5 for watermelon.

The *Hotel Si Moussa* also does food, but you have to wait an eternity to get it.

Getting There & Away

Air The airport is at Guemar, 18 km to the north, and can be reached by local bus.

There are flights to Algiers (three times weekly, AD 225) and Annaba (three times weekly, AD 186).

Bus The main bus station is about three km north of the town centre; a 30-minute walk, or there are local minibuses which take you to the centre.

There are departures to: Algiers (two nightly); Constantine (two daily); Ouargla (two daily); Ghardaia (daily); Annaba (daily); Touggourt (daily); Biskra (daily); and Tébessa (two daily).

Taxi Yellow long-distance taxis leave when full from just next door to the Hotel des Dunes.

The main destination is Touggourt (two hours, AD 60 per person), but they also run to the Tunisian border and towns in the Souf area.

Getting Around

Local bus services for the surrounding towns leave from opposite the taxi station. Not much happens after 7 pm.

Indian Tata minibuses also leave from here, and run back and forth to the bus station.

TOUGGOURT

A totally unremarkable oasis town, Touggourt is perhaps most famous as the starting point of the first motorised crossing of the Sahara. The Citroen half-track vehicles of the Haardt and Audouin-Debreuil expedition set off from here in 1922 for Timbuktu via Tamanrasset. The event is marked by a simple pillar in the town square.

Today the town is a regional administrative centre, with a large palmeraie and a couple of vaguely interesting old mud-brick villages to the south. There are a couple of banks, a post office and an Air Algérie office (tel 72 6096).

Market day is Friday; in winter especially, the town is full of itinerant merchants who've come for the market. The marketplace is just off the road to El Oued, near the taxi station.

From the main square, the road to the right curves around past the cinema to the bus stop for buses to Temacine. The road straight ahead leads past the old hotel on the left to the Hotel Oasis and Temacine.

If you have a day to spare you could do worse than spend it here, but don't lose any sleep if you miss it.

Places to Stay - bottom end

The *Hotel Marhaba* is right by the taxi station and costs AD 70 for a double, although this is negotiable. The best idea is to follow the local custom and sleep on the roof in summer, as the rooms become intolerably hot. The showers and toilets are cockroach infested but that's nothing new. In summer you'll be lucky if you can stand under the shower, as the water pipes are above ground and get incredibly hot.

Between the market and the main street is the *Hotel de la Paix*, but it is no different from the Marhaba.

Places to Stay – top end

The only improvement on these places is the expensive *Hotel Oasis*, one km south of town on the road to Temacine, although even this place seems to suffer from the general malaise that grips the rest of the town. Rooms cost AD 192 for a double with breakfast. The swimming pool is only just useable, as the water is a sickly shade of green. The most useful thing in the hotel is the map of the town on the wall in the lobby.

Places to Eat

Between the taxi station and the market are a couple of ultra-basic restaurants. The one closest to the Hotel Marhaba serves food that doesn't exactly make the mouth water but is at least edible.

Getting There & Away

Air The airport is five km east of town along the El Oued road. There are daily flights to Algiers (AD 225).

Bus The bus station is just an office by the railway line. The competition for seats can be high, as most of the buses are coming through en route from somewhere else.

There are buses to: Algiers (two daily); Biskra (three daily); Constantine (two daily); El Oued (daily); Ghardaia (three daily); Hassi Messaoud (four daily); and Ouargla (three daily).

Local buses for Tamelhat and Temacine leave from a stop along the road that curves around to the right at the end of the main street – just ask around.

Train There is only one passenger train daily, and that is to Biskra. It leaves at the ridiculous time of 12.50 am.

Taxi The taxi station is just off the main El Oued road, five minutes' walk from the centre, past the marketplace.

There are departures for El Oued, Ouargla and Biskra, but very little happens after about 1 pm.

AROUND TOUGGOURT

Tamelhat

On the edge of the palmeraie 12 km south of Touggourt, the village of Tamelhat is a traditional mud-brick village which, although it is inhabited, has the air of a place that has been abandoned. There are large open spaces where buildings have collapsed completely.

The narrow lanes wind between high walls, and in places the houses actually span the lanes. The occasional open door reveals a small courtyard where the family donkey is kept and where the women work spreading chillies out to dry.

In the centre of the town is the mosque and mausoleum of Sidi El Hadj Ali; the cupola above the latter is decorated with some coloured tiles and stucco.

Chances are one of the local kids will latch onto you as a guide, although what they can actually show you is limited. One thing they will try and drag you along to is the 'sea'. This is a small brackish lake between Tamelhat and Temacine – forget it.

Getting There & Away

There are local buses from close to the centre of Touggourt and these drop you at an intersection a couple of km from the main road. Tamelhat is directly on the right; Temacine a few km to the left. Taxis run back to Touggourt via Temacine and the Hotel Oasis.

Temacine

Temacine is much the same as Tamelhat. However, it is more picturesque, as the houses are built around a ksar on top of a small hill. Palm tree trunks have been used extensively in the construction of the fortifications.

The mosque here dates from 1431; all the building materials used in its construction were imported from Tunisia.

OUARGLA

The town of Ouargla has even less attractions than Touggourt, although if you find yourself stuck here there are a couple of hotels (neither of them cheap) and a camping ground.

The town is very much a modern oil town; if you are driving in the area at night the horizon is bright orange with the glow of the flares.

Places to Stay

The *Hotel de Tassili* (formerly the *Transatlantique*) (tel 70 0154) and the *Hotel El Mehri* (tel 70 2066) are both two-star and cost AD 120/150 for a single/double with breakfast.

Camping The camp site is called the *Motel et Camping Tahost* (tel 70 5032). It's clean and the people are very friendly. There are bungalows for AD 95, rooms for AD 80, tents for AD 20 and *zeribas* (grass huts) for AD 25. Hot showers are included in the price.

Route du Tassili N'Ajjer

This route heads south from Hassi Messaoud along the Gassi Touil, a large oued between two sections of the Great Eastern Erg, to In Aménas, 730 km to the south-east and very close to the Libyan border.

The road is bitumen as far as In Aménas but turns to *piste* between there and Tamanrasset.

There is a weekly bus along here between Biskra and In Aménas but very little other traffic – just the occasional

truck. If you are heading for Tamanrasset, the easiest and quickest way is to hitch to Ghardaia and then head down the N1. If you have the time and don't mind running the risk of getting stuck for a few days in some tiny backwater it is possible to get to Djanet and then on to Tamanrasset this way, but it's not a trip which should be undertaken lightly. In winter there is a trickle of tourist vehicles but there's no guarantee that they'll be able to pick you up.

If you get really stuck there are flights from In Aménas and Illizi to Ouargla, and from Illizi to Djanet.

IN AMENAS

This is a modern, characterless town built to service the oil industry. There is a post office, petrol station and SNTR truck depot, where it may be possible to get lifts.

On arrival you must check in at the *daira* (municipal headquarters) and give them the details of your trip to Djanet.

Places to Stay

The only formal accommodation is the *Hotel Cash*, which charges AD 120 for a double. Other than that it is possible to camp outside the police station.

Getting There & Away

Air The airport is 16 km south-east of town.

There are flights to: Algiers (twice weekly, AD 319); Djanet (weekly, AD 144); Oran (weekly, AD 356); and Ouargla (AD 186).

Bus The bus station is south-west of the centre of the town. There is just the one bus per week to Biskra. There used to be a weekly bus to Illizi, but we haven't heard about this for some time.

ILLIZI

Nearly 300 km south of In Aménas, Illizi is the main settlement between there and Djanet.

The town boasts a fuel station, hospital, basic shop, customs post (where you have to check in) and a hotel (of sorts).

If you really get stranded here there are flights to: Algiers (twice weekly, AD 343); Djanet (four times weekly, AD 108); and Ouargla (six times weekly, AD 204). The 'airport' is five km north of town and there's not a building at the place – just a graded runway.

DJANET

The main town of the Tassili, Djanet is a pretty place built on the edge of a palmeraie.

Here you'll find all the facilities including post office, bank, Air Algérie office, shops and basic restaurants.

The main attraction are the rock paintings in the Tassili National Park, around Tamrit. Without a vehicle the only way to get out to these places is on a tour (expensive) or by hitching with other tourists. Even if you do have a vehicle, it is not possible to go into the park unless accompanied by an official guide.

Places to Stay

The only place is the *Camping Zeribas* in the centre of town. The zeribas (grass huts) cost AD 50 per person. There is a restaurant attached.

It is prohibited to camp in the palmeraie.

Getting There & Away

Air The airstrip is five km along the Tamanrasset road.

There are flights to: Algiers (three times weekly, AD 410); Ghardaia (twice weekly, AD 300); Illizi (four times weekly, AD 108); In Aménas (weekly, AD 144); Ouargla (four times weekly, AD 271); and Tamanrasset (weekly, AD 148).

Hitching There is no public transport into Djanet other than plane. It's a matter of hitching with trucks or tourists. There are a fair number of vehicles running between here and Tamanrasset, so hitching shouldn't be a great problem.

Route du Hoggar

From El Goléa, Route N1 continues south across the amazingly flat Tademait Plateau, where in places the largest thing in sight is a rock the size of a tennis ball. The road is surfaced for the most part, and where it's not the *piste* is not too bad.

After 410 km you hit In Salah, the last town of any size before Tamanrasset. The latter is another 710 km further south, along a road which ranges from beautiful stretches of brand new bitumen to one-km-wide *piste*, all of it a mass of sand and corrugations, but still easily negotiated by conventional vehicles.

Tamanrasset is a good place to rest up for a while and a base from which to explore the Hoggar Mountains, which shouldn't be missed.

From Tam the *piste* heads south again for another 410 km to In Guezzam, 10 km before the Algerian border crossing with Niger. The road is fairly punishing on vehicles but 4WD is not necessary.

Right along this route there's a fair amount of traffic, mostly trucks and travellers in vehicles, and hitching is possible; however, it is a lucky traveller who can get all the way to Tamanrasset without having to catch a bus.

IN SALAH

Built in the red Sudanese style, In Salah is really a very pleasant friendly town but one overlooked by most travellers, who spend as little time here as possible. The name means 'salty source' and refers to the terrible water. Bring as much water with you as you can from Tamanrasset or El Goléa, as the water here really is foul. Even the local soft drinks are made from it and bottled water is only sporadically available.

The most interesting feature of the

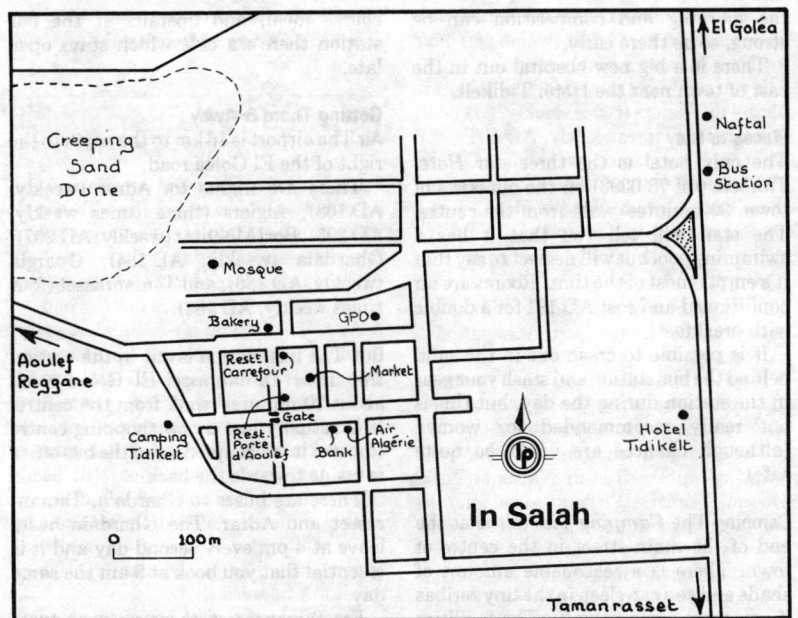

town is the creeping sand dunes on the western edge by the Aoulef road. Behind the mosque you can see how the dune is gradually encroaching on the town. From the top of the dune it becomes apparent that the town has actually been cut in two.

The dunes move at the rate of about one metre every five years. The amount of sand on the move actually remains fairly constant, so while it is swallowing up a building on its leading edge it is uncovering one behind it which may have been under the sand for a generation or two.

Once the ruins of a house have been uncovered, it is established who it used to belong to and then that person's relatives rebuild the place and move in.

The view from the top of this dune is great at sunset, although you will no doubt be pestered by the local kids with *'Donnez-moi stylo!'*.

There is a local Touareg English teacher by the name of Mohammed who is very friendly and hospitable. He often hangs out around the camping ground and is keen to talk.

To the west of town along the Aoulef road is the palmeraie, with its 225,000 trees. Date-growing has become the major occupation of the people of In Salah, a town which used to be important as a place of barter between European goods from the north, and gold, ivory and slaves from the south.

Information

There is a bank in the main street, the Air Algérie office is next door and the post office is one block to the north.

The market is in the centre and has very little – just a few spuds and onions, and the occasional tomato or chilli.

The sole bakery in town is just up from the Restaurant Carrefour. It bakes only in the morning and competition can be strong, so be there early.

There is a big new hospital out in the east of town near the Hotel Tidikelt.

Places to Stay

The only hotel is the three-star *Hotel Tidikelt* (tel 73 0393) on the outskirts of town, 30 minutes' walk from the centre. The staff will tell you that it has a swimming pool but will neglect to say that it's empty most of the time. Rooms are air conditioned and cost AD 191 for a double with breakfast.

It is possible to crash out in the sand behind the bus station and stash your gear in the station during the day, but this is not really recommended for women (although chances are you'd be quite safe).

Camping The *Camping Tidikelt* is at the end of the main street in the centre of town. There is a reasonable amount of shade and you can sleep in the tiny zeribas if you want some privacy. The facilities are totally inadequate: they consist of a couple of toilets and showers which are part of the old market square adjacent to the camping ground. You share these facilities with the guys who staff the fire station. It costs AD 15 per person to sleep here.

Places to Eat

The *Restaurant Porte d'Aoulef* is just by the arched gate over the street. It does very average food, which is, however, as good as you'll find anywhere.

Just along the street behind the gate, on the left where the footpath is raised, is another small place which does a fair *ragoût* (stew) and chips.

The *Restaurant Carrefour* used to be the place to eat but now, sadly, the standards have reached rock bottom. Most of the food comes straight out of tins.

The *Hotel Tidikelt* has a fancy restaurant where AD 42 gets you a four-course meal, and upstairs at the bus station there's a café which stays open late.

Getting There & Away

Air The airport is 16 km to the north to the right of the El Goléa road.

There are flights to: Adrar (weekly, AD 108); Algiers (three times weekly, AD 295); Borj Mokhtar (weekly, AD 207); Ghardaia (weekly, AD 184); Ouargla (weekly, AD 186); and Tamanrasset (four times weekly, AD 182).

Bus The bus station is out in the east on the main Tamanrasset-El Goléa road, about 20 minutes' walk from the centre. It is actually just a new shopping centre (most of it unoccupied), and the bus office is inside towards the back.

There are buses to Ghardaia, Tamanrasset and Adrar. The Ghardaia buses leave at 4 pm every second day and it is essential that you book at 9 am the same day.

For Tamanrasset, there are departures in Mercedes truck/buses on Tuesday, Thursday and Sunday at 4 am. Tickets are sold in the afternoon the day before and, again, booking in advance is crucial. On these buses there are no numbered seats, and it is important to get there at least half an hour before departure if you don't want to end up in a seat behind the rear wheels (or, worse, in the aisle with no seat at all), as the ride is incredibly rough. The trip takes about 19 hours and costs AD 120 and AD 10 for a rucksack. There are stops made along the way (including a meal at Arak), but basically you need to be prepared with a bit of food and water.

The buses to Adrar are scheduled to run twice weekly but they are often suspended. Ask (persistently) at the bus station to try and track them down. They usually leave not from the bus station but from the street to the right of the gate in the centre of town.

Taxi Taxis run regularly from In Salah to Aoulef (AD 50 per person), 170 km west along the road to Adrar, and from there you can catch a daily bus to Adrar. This In Salah-Adrar road is surfaced, except for about 90 km of *piste* between In Salah and Aoulef.

Hitching From the main road you can hitch north from just by the Naftal station, or south from past the Hotel Tidikelt. I met two guys who sat by the road for three days trying to get to Tamanrasset before they ended up catching a bus.

There is very little traffic to Adrar, but you can stand on the road down near the Camping Tidikelt and try your luck.

There is an SNTR depot not far from the Hotel Tidikelt and it may be possible to organise a lift with one of the drivers. They sometimes park overnight by the road from the centre to the bus station.

ARAK

Although the gorges around Arak are quite spectacular, the little settlement itself is very humble. It doesn't have the altitude that Tamanrasset has and subsequently is as hot as all hell.

There is a camping ground with zeribas, a restaurant where you can get a reasonable meal, and a fuel station.

If you are on the bus it will stop here for a meal break.

TAMANRASSET

Despite the increase in tourism over the years, Tamanrasset (known locally as Tamenghest) is still quite an appealing Touareg town. It now has a population approaching 30,000, although many people have been driven here by the droughts in the Sahel and now live in the *bidonville* (slum) on the far side of the oued.

With an altitude of nearly 1400 metres, it has a climate which stays relatively moderate all year round. Even in mid-summer the temperature rarely gets above 35°C.

The town is the centre of the Hoggar region and, despite the number of Arabs from the north, the Kel Ahaggar Touareg men can be seen all over the place, often riding a camel down the main street.

Tamanrasset is also the place from which to arrange trips up into the Hoggar Mountains to the east, something which should not be missed on any account. If you can't hook up with other travellers with vehicles in the camping ground, it is possible to get a group together and hire a vehicle and driver from one of the travel agencies around town.

The town is one of those places where virtually all trans-Saharan travellers stop for a few days to rest up and make repairs to equipment, so at any time there may be a dozen vehicles coming and going each day from the camping ground. With such a high turnover you rarely have to wait longer than a few days for a lift.

If you are heading south, make sure you clear customs on the southern edge of town when you leave. They will scrutinise your currency form (which gets handed in at In Guezzam) and check over your gear. Passport control is handled at the border post, 10 km south of In Guezzam.

If you have just arrived from Niger, check with the authorities at the daira (in the military fort), even though you have already been checked at the border.

Information

Tourist Office There is a small Syndicat d'Initiative in one of the main streets, Ave Emir Abdelkader. It is of little use, but the staff may be able to help if you have a specific enquiry.

Post The post office is in between the two main streets. It has a telephone office where it's possible to make international calls, although you may have to wait a while. If you are sending a telegram make sure to ask for a receipt, or your message

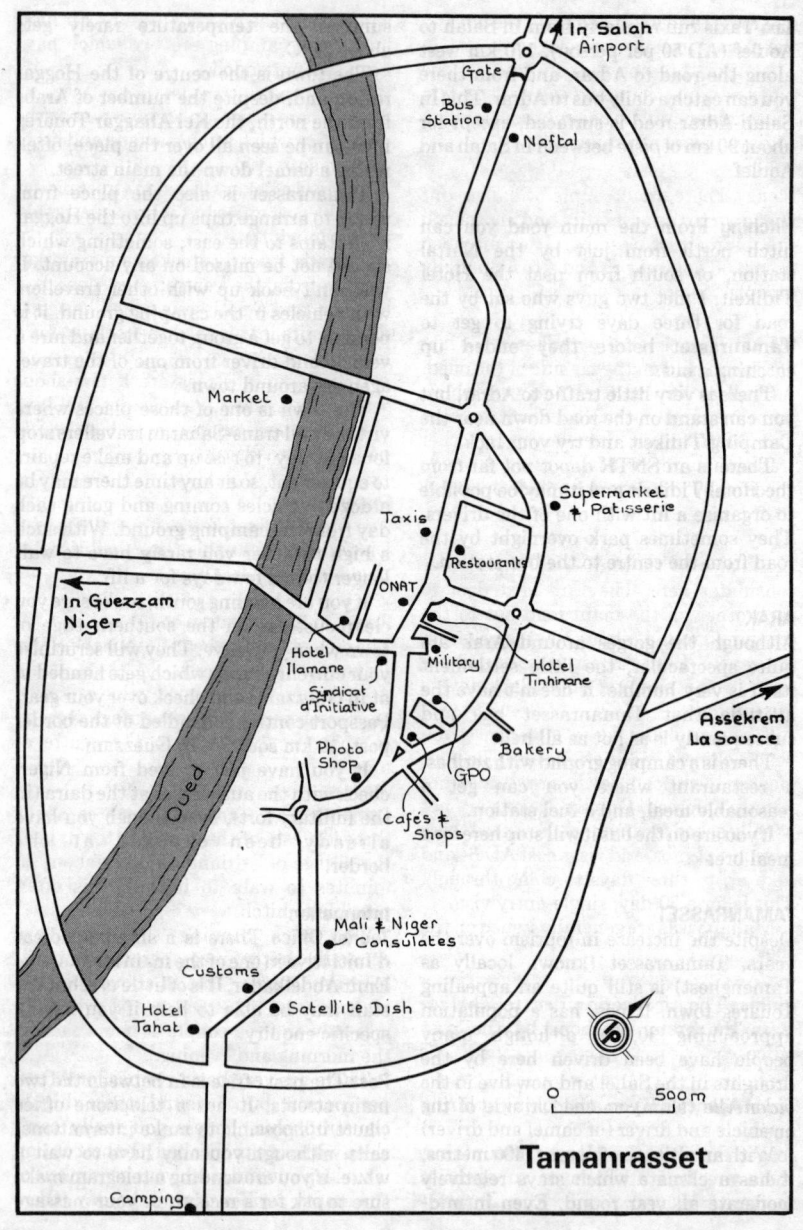

In Salah
Airport

Gate

Bus
Station

Naftal

Market

Supermarket
Patisserie

Taxis

Restaurants

ONAT

In Guezzam
Niger

Hotel
Ilamane

Military

Hotel
Tinhinane

Assekrem
La Source

Syndicat
d'Initiative

Photo
Shop

Bakery

GPO

Cafés &
Shops

Oued

Mali & Niger
Consulates

Customs

Satellite Dish

Hotel
Tahat

0   500 m

Camping

Tamanrasset

will more than likely end up in the bin and the money in someone's pocket.

It's worth noting that in the past the poste restante counter (open all day, in the telephone office) has only held mail for 15 days before returning it.

Money There are a couple of banks, one next door to the post office and another on the main street close by. They are open from 8.30 am to 1 pm and 4 to 5 pm daily except Friday.

Market There is a daily market in the late afternoon held on the far side of the oued. As well as limited fruit and vegetables, there are usually a few Touareg from Niger and Mali selling jewellery and other traditional items. Much of it is made specifically for the tourist trade but other stuff is genuine.

Consulates Both Mali and Niger have consulates here. They are next door to each other on the main road out to the camping ground, about 500 metres from the centre. Both can issue visas and are open in the morning only, Saturday to Wednesday.

When applying for a Niger visa you need a cholera vaccination stamp on your Health Certificate, although this is not strictly enforced. Onward tickets are not usually asked for anymore. You need three passport photos, and visas cost AD 64 and take up to three days to come through. This is for a 30-day, single-entry visa.

Malian visas are generally issued on the spot.

Airlines The Air Algérie office (tel 73 4174) is in the group of shops by the post office.

Travel Agencies If you are looking at hiring a vehicle and driver (or camel and driver) to get out into the Hoggar Mountains, there are half a dozen or so agencies scattered around town. The Tarahist agency near the post office and Akar Akar out at the camping are two which have been recommended.

Shops There is a group of shops just by the post office which sell basic food and other general supplies.

There is a bakery in a side street not far from the post office but it has usually sold out by lunch time.

There is a poorly stocked supermarket not far from the centre; next door is a butcher, and a patisserie which has good dry biscuits if you need to stock up for a long bus ride.

On the main street are a few shops selling souvenirs of various descriptions. Nothing is particularly cheap but they do have some good stuff.

Festivals
The Tamanrasset Festival is held in late December and at this time facilities are strained to the maximum.

Places to Stay – bottom end
The only remotely cheap hotel is the *Hotel Ilamane*, just south of Ave Emir Abdelkader. It is not good value at AD 50 per person and its only advantage over the camping is that it is in the centre of town.

Camping The *Camping Zerib* is about three km east of the centre of town, near the village of Adriane. It takes about 40 minutes to walk to it, but it is often possible to hitch.

The guys running the place are generally pretty unco-operative but will help grudgingly. This is about the only place in town to get water, and even then it is only on for a couple of hours each in the morning and evening.

There are very basic zeribas for AD 40 per person but I found these highly claustrophobic. Unless you really can't sleep without a proper bed, the best option is to sleep out and stash your gear in one of the empty zeribas during the day (there are always spare ones, except during the festival).

It costs AD 15 per person to camp and AD 10 for a vehicle. This is the best place in town to stay if you want to meet other travellers and try and arrange lifts onwards or up to Assekrem. Most people with vehicles base themselves here and make a two-day trip up into the mountains; they will often take an extra person or two.

There is another camping ground, *La Source*, 15 km from Tam along the road to Assekrem. This is only an option if you have a vehicle, but it is an alternative place to fill up with water and the people running it are a good deal more pleasant than those at the Tam camping ground. It's not all that difficult to hitch to and is run by friendly West Africans.

Places to Stay – middle & top end
In the centre of town, the *Hotel Tinhinane* is as good as you need and costs AD 120 for a double with breakfast. This is the town watering hole, and all the local beer drinkers come here during the day and evening to get their fill.

The other choice is the expensive *Hotel Tahat* (tel 73 4474), on the eastern edge of town. It charges AD 121/141 for a single/double with breakfast. It is the usual government-run place and suffers accordingly. The paper shop in the lobby has a few three-day-old newspapers from Algiers and a few scruffy French novels.

Places to Eat
There is a string of six or so restaurants down at the western end of Ave Emir Abdelkader. Very much the pick of the bunch is the very pleasant *Restaurant Le Palmier*, which has good food and service. Main courses are AD 20 and good soup is AD 10.

The other places are all much the same and serve the usual stuff.

There is another small place on the north side of the group of shops near the post office. It is just around the back of the

Air Algérie office and has a couple of umbrellas outside, where you can sit.

The restaurant of the *Hotel Tinhinane* has a three-course set menu for AD 60 per person.

Getting There & Away
Air The airport is 12 km north of town, off to the left of the main road. Yellow taxis meet all incoming flights and seats cost AD 10 per person for the trip into town. You may have to abandon your bags and grab hold of a door handle when a taxi rolls up, as demand for seats can be high.

There are flights from here to: Adrar (twice weekly, AD 236); Algiers (at least one daily, AD 424); Borj Mokhtar (weekly, AD 162); Constantine (weekly, AD 411); Djanet (weekly, AD 148); El Goléa (twice weekly, AD 262); Ghardaia (four times weekly, AD 305); In Guezzam (weekly, AD 240); In Salah (four times weekly, AD 182); Oran (weekly, AD 420); and Ouargla (three times weekly, AD 290).

Bus The bus station is in the northern part of town. It is a 20-minute walk from the centre of town and a solid hour from the camp site. If you arrive late at night, or are heading out early in the morning, it is standard practice to doss down at the station, which is quite safe. It is a modern building but gets very little use. The bus schedule (which differs slightly from time to time) is displayed on a board inside the building.

Make sure you reserve your ticket the day before departure. They usually go on sale at 4 pm but it is worth checking earlier in the day, as things vary and demand is sometimes high.

The main destination is In Salah. There are three departures weekly, on Monday, Wednesday and Saturday at 4 am (5 am in winter). The trip takes a gruelling 19 hours (barring breakdowns) and, for the privilege of having yourself tossed around inside a tin box on a truck chassis, you pay AD 120 and AD 10 for your bag – what a travel bargain!

There is also a weekly departure to In Guezzam (Monday morning) but there is little point in catching this bus, as you still have to get across the border to Agadez. It's better to arrange a lift all the way from Tam.

There are also weekly buses to Idelès (Thursday, 9 am) and Silet (Thursday, 11 am).

AROUND TAMANRASSET
Assekrem

Without your own transport, getting out into the Hoggar can be difficult. However, it's worth making the effort to get to Assekrem, 73 km north-east of Tamanrasset by the shorter of the two routes.

The scenery around here is absolutely incredible and a sunrise in the these mountains is an experience you're likely never to forget. Words can't even come close to doing the place justice – get up there and see it for yourself.

Charles de Foucauld, a dedicated Christian who came to the Hoggar early this century, built a hermitage up here in 1910; this is still lived in and maintained by Fathers. The hermitage is on top of the Assekrem Plateau and can only be reached on foot. It takes about 30 minutes to walk up from below and it is the place to come for the sunrise.

Places to Stay & Eat It is possible to stay at the refuge below the hermitage but you need to bring all your own food.

Getting There & Away The only way to get up to Assekrem is to get a lift. If you can't strike it lucky at the camping ground in Tam, the only other alternative is to hire a 4WD and driver from one of the agencies in Tam. It is not possible to hire a vehicle without a driver.

This is only an option if you have five or six people, as it costs between AD 900 and AD 1100 per day for vehicle and driver. There are sometimes enough backpackers at the camping ground to arrange a trip like this, but it may take a few days to organise. If you want extras such as food the agency will charge an additional fee for this, typically about AD 150 per person per day.

If you want to keep the expense to a minimum, it is best to hire a vehicle from about 2 pm for a 24-hour period . The drive up there takes about three hours, so this arrangement makes best use of the time and means you get to see the sunrise.

If you do manage to get out to Assekrem with someone who is going on to Djanet and you want to go back to Tam, you will probably have to spend anything up to a few days in Assekrem waiting for a lift back. You definitely can't walk there, although the agencies will organise trips with camels from Tamanrasset if you want to do it this way.

If you are driving up and have some spare room, you can do the restaurant owner a favour and take him up some water, as he has no regular supply.

IN GUEZZAM

What was a collection of half a dozen huts a few years ago has grown into a tent settlement of about 3000 people today. Unfortunately, most of the people aren't here by choice but, because of the droughts in the Sahel, have gravitated to the nearest place where they are likely to get food.

The town is 416 km south of Tamanrasset and is the last place in Algeria before you cross into Niger. The Algerian border post is 10 km south of In Guezzam, so there is really no need to stop here for long.

This border post used to be worst in the country, with drunken guards and the like, but recent reports suggest that things are considerably more manageable here now. This doesn't mean that you won't be searched thoroughly or get your currency form scrutinised closely, but at least you're not likely to get harassed. The morning is the best time to go through. The guards are generally gruff and indifferent, but as long as you are polite, firm and friendly (no need to grovel) there should be no problem. Don't arrive there between 12 noon and 4 pm, as the border is closed and you have to sit it out in the heat without a scrap of shade. They don't even let you go back to In Guezzam.

Places to Stay & Eat

Really the only place is *Le Restaurant des Dunes chez Omar*. Apart from a good collection of western music, you can get OK food and stay overnight.

Getting There & Away

Air There is a weekly flight between In Guezzam and Tamanrasset but I can think of no reason to take it.

Bus The same goes for the bus. It leaves Tam on Monday morning and In Guezzam on Tuesday morning for the return journey, but you are far better off arranging a through lift at least as far as Arlit or Agadez from Tamanrasset.

TUNISIA

Facts about the Country

HISTORY SINCE 1830

In Tunisia, the struggle for independence didn't take the violent course that it did in Algeria. The Huseinid ruler Ahmed Bey, who governed from 1837 to 1855, encouraged westernisation and brought in military and other advisors to this end. In 1861, during the reign of Mohammed Sadiq, a constitution, the first in the Arab world, was proclaimed.

These western reforms, however, exacted a heavy toll on the country's limited finances and there was heavy borrowing in the form of high-interest loans from European banks. Proposed higher taxes led to internal revolt, and by 1869 the country was in such a financial shambles that control of its finances was given to an international commission.

The last attempt to hold off European control came in a short-lived effort from 1873 to 1877 by the reformer Khaireddin, but he was forced from office and his plans were scuttled. At the Congress of Berlin in 1878, the major European powers divided up the southern Mediterranean region, and the only challenge to French dominance in Tunisia came from the Italians.

In order to consolidate their position, the French announced in 1881 that Tunisian tribesmen had made incursions into Algeria and that they, the French, would retaliate. Some 30,000 troops were sent into Tunisia; before long they had occupied Tunis, and in 1883 the bey signed the Convention of La Marsa, which gave the French control over Tunisian affairs. The bey was answerable to a French Resident who presided over both domestic and foreign affairs.

Until WW I the protectorate prospered under French rule, although it was at the expense of local interests. Unlike in Algeria, land was not sequestered on any scale, but the best of the fertile land (in the Medjerda Valley and Cap Bon Peninsula) passed into European hands. Mineral and phosphate reserves were tapped and a railway network was constructed to service them. Tunisians were totally denied any say in Tunisian affairs, and agitation and resistance wasn't long in coming.

In 1920 the first nationalist political party, the Destour Party, was formed (*destour* means constitution in Arabic; the party was named after the constitution of 1861). Its demands for democratic government, despite being supported by the bey, were ignored by the French and the nationalist movement lost its way for some years.

In the early 1930s, a young Tunisian lawyer, Habib Bourguiba, led a breakaway movement from the Destour Party; in 1934 he founded the Neo-Destour, which soon totally replaced the old guard of the Destour. Thanks to the tireless efforts and popular appeal of Bourguiba, the party was quick to gain popular support. The French, keen to put down any potential threat, outlawed the party and jailed Bourguiba.

With the fall of France during WW II, the Neo-Destour leaders, who had been imprisoned there, were handed over to the Italians by the Germans. Although they were well treated in Rome, they refused to support Italy.

In 1942 the Germans landed in Tunis in the hope that they could turn back the Allied advances from east and west; the Americans were on the way from Algeria, and the British forces led by Field Marshal Montgomery were driving back Rommel's Afrika Korps in Egypt. The campaign in Tunisia raged for six months; only after the loss of over 15,000 men were the allies able to take Bizerte on 7 May 1943.

In the same year the Neo-Destour

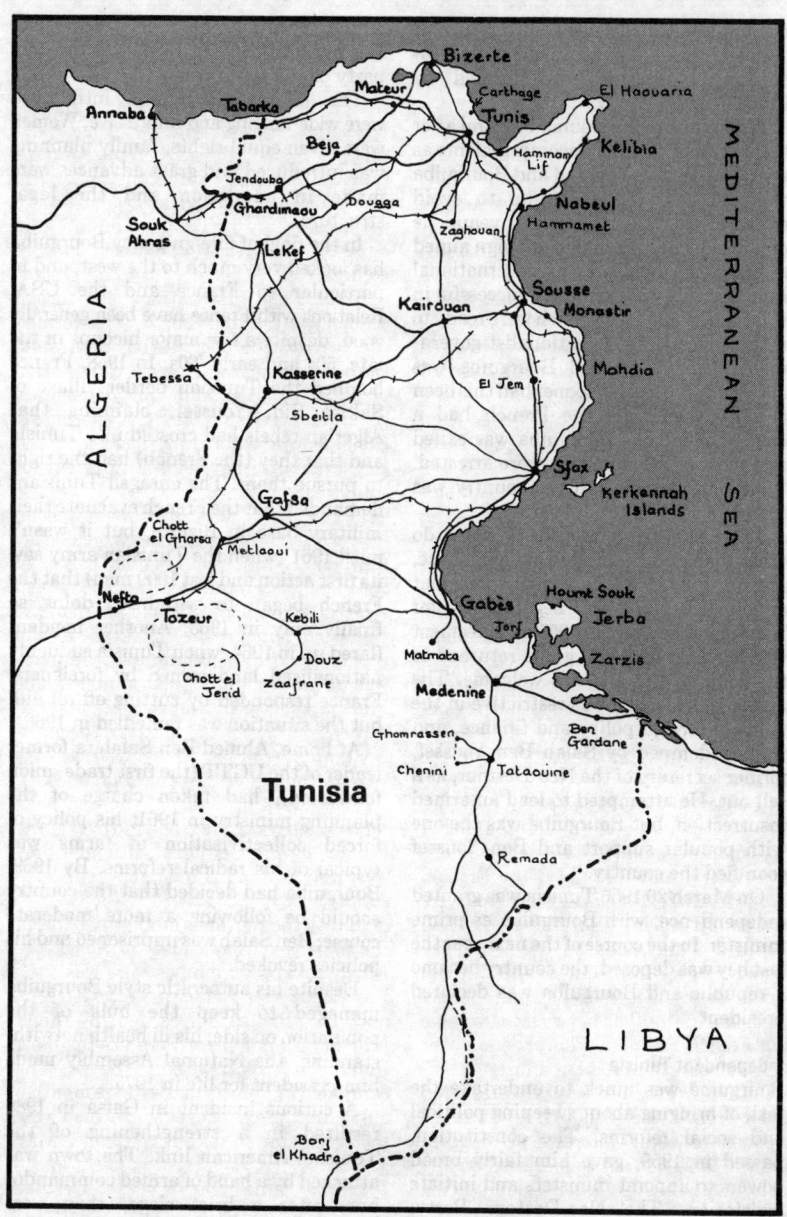

MEDITERRANEAN SEA

ALGERIA

LIBYA

Tunisia

Annaba
Tabarka
Bizerte
Mateur
Carthage
El Haouaria
Tunis
Kelibia
Beja
Jendouba
Hammam Lif
Souk Ahras
Ghardimaou
Dougga
Nabeul
Hammamet
Le Kef
Zaghouan
Zaghouan
Kairouan
Sousse
Monastir
Tebessa
Kasserine
El Jem
Mahdia
Sbeitla
Sfax
Kerkennah Islands
Gafsa
Chott el Gharsa
Metlaoui
Houmt Souk
Jerba
Nefta
Gabès
Jorf
Tozeur
Kebili
Zarzis
Chott el Jerid
Douz
Matmata
Zaafrane
Medenine
Ghomrassen
Ben Gardane
Chenini
Tataouine
Remada
Borj el Khadra

leaders were finally allowed to return to Tunisia, where a government with Neo-Destour sympathies was formed by Moncef Bey.

When the French resumed control after the war, they were as uncompromising as ever; the bey was deposed and Bourguiba was forced to flee to Cairo to avoid capture. In the next few years he organised a propaganda campaign aimed at bringing Tunisia into the international limelight. He was extremely successful in this, and by 1951 the French were ready to make concessions. A nationalist government was set up and Bourguiba was allowed to return. No sooner had this been accomplished than the French had a change of mind – Bourguiba was exiled and most of the ministers were arrested. Violence followed, and the country was soon in a state of total disarray.

There was little left for the French to do other than grant complete independence, and in July 1954 the French president announced plans for negotiations for Tunisian autonomy. In 1955 an agreement was reached, and Bourguiba returned to the country and a hero's welcome. The agreement reached was restrictive in the fields of foreign policy and finance, and was condemned by Salah Ben Youssef, former secretary of the Neo-Destour, as a sell out. He attempted to lead an armed insurrection, but Bourguiba was the one with popular support and Ben Youssef soon fled the country.

On March 20 1956 Tunisia was granted independence, with Bourguiba as prime minister. In the course of the next year the last bey was deposed, the country became a republic and Bourguiba was declared president.

Independent Tunisia
Bourguiba was quick to undertake the task of bringing about sweeping political and social reforms. The constitution, passed in 1959, gave him fairly broad powers to appoint ministers and initiate legislation. The Neo-Destour Party,

which became the Parti Socialiste Destourien (PSD) in 1964, was the only party of any significance.

The reforms Bourguiba introduced were wide-ranging and impressive. Women were given equal rights, family planning was introduced and great advances were made in education and the legal structure.

In the field of foreign policy Bourguiba has looked very much to the west, and in particular to France and the USA. Relations with France have been generally good, despite a few major hiccups in the late '50s and early '60s. In 1958, France bombed the Tunisian border village of Sakiet Sidi Youssef, claiming that Algerian rebels had crossed into Tunisia and that they (the French) had the right to pursue them. The enraged Tunisians demanded that the French evacuate their military base in Bizerte, but it wasn't until 1961 (when the Tunisian army saw its first action and lost 1000 men) that the French began to withdraw, doing so finally only in 1963. Another incident flared up in 1964, when Tunisia suddenly nationalised land owned by foreigners. France responded by cutting off all aid, but the situation was remedied in 1966.

At home, Ahmed Ben Salah, a former leader of the UGTT (the first trade union federation), had taken charge of the planning ministry in 1961; his policy of forced collectivisation of farms was typical of his radical reforms. By 1969, Bourguiba had decided that the country should be following a more moderate course; Ben Salah was imprisoned and his policies revoked.

Despite his autocratic style Bourguiba managed to keep the bulk of the population on side; his ill health notwithstanding, the National Assembly made him president for life in 1975.

A curious incident in Gafsa in 1980 resulted in a strengthening of the Tunisian-American link. The town was attacked by a band of armed commandos but, after a brief siege, they were overpowered. Tunisia claimed that the men came from Libya and the Americans, keen to see the Libyans discouraged, became the major supplier of equipment to the Tunisian army.

After promising more political freedoms, the government persuaded Bourguiba to call the first multi-party elections in 1981. The outcome was a total letdown for the newly formed opposition parties, as the National Front (the alliance formed between the TSD and the UGTT) took all of the 136 seats on offer. There were in fact cries of foul play from the opposition.

The bread riots of 1984 were a spontaneous backlash to the announcement that the bread subsidy was being withdrawn. They died out only after about six days, when Bourguiba resumed the subsidy.

As the '80s progressed, Bourguiba was increasingly seen to be more and more out of touch with both the people at home and Tunisia's position in the Arab world. At home he would build up the career of a possible successor, only to later cut the ground out from under his feet. An example was Prime Minister Rachid Sfar, appointed in July 1986 to replace Mohammed Mzali (who was the scapegoat for the economic crisis in 1986) and deposed only 12 months later. Sfar was replaced by the tough minister for the interior and former general in the armed forces Zine el-Abidine Ben Ali, who eventually orchestrated the ousting of Bourguiba.

On November 7 1987, a group of doctors was assembled by Ben Ali and were asked to examine the 83-year-old president, who was, predictably, declared unfit to carry out his duties. It seems that, despite a heart condition, his physical health was not too bad for a man of his age; it was his mental health that was causing the concern.

In ousting Bourguiba, Ben Ali acted on two things: firstly, he had heard that Bourguiba intended to get rid of him; and, more importantly, the appeal of five of the Muslim radicals, members of the outlawed MTI (Islamic Tendency Movement) who had been sentenced in September, was coming up on November 9. One of these radicals had been given the death sentence and the others heavy jail terms. It is known that Bourguiba was unhappy with this and wanted heavier terms, which went totally against popular opinion within the country. He was in fact becoming less and less the people's leader. As it turned out, the jailed radicals' appeal was upheld and they were retried.

Bourguiba was held for some time in detention in his palace in Carthage before being shunted off to 'retirement' in another palace outside Sfax.

All in all it was a popular coup within the country, and one which many people felt was long overdue, although many also felt that it could have been done with a little more decorum. At any rate it removed the uncertainty which had surrounded Bourguiba's succession for the last five or so years.

On taking power Ben Ali appointed some new ministers but, significantly, retained the defence minister, indicating that he had made sure the army was on side before he moved against Bourguiba and had kept them informed as to what he was doing.

The downfall of Bourguiba saw the demise of one of the world's great rulers and the longest-serving Third-World leader. Undoubtedly his greatest achievements were the fostering of a strong national identity and the development of a standard of living which puts the country at the top of the pile in the developing world.

The challenge for the new government is to overcome the economic crisis facing the country, brought about largely by the 1986 collapse in oil prices. It is only too well aware that increased austerity measures are likely to aggravate the already high unemployment problem, leading to popular opposition along the lines of the bread riots of 1984.

The country occupies an important position in the Arab world. Since 1979, when Egypt signed a peace treaty with Israel, Tunisia has been home to the Arab League. The PLO has its headquarters just outside Tunis, although these were badly damaged by an Israeli bombing raid in 1985 in retaliation for the killing of three Israelis in Cyprus. In a deplorable incident in 1988 an Israeli hit squad was sent in to assassinate the PLO second-in-command, Khalil Al-Wazir (also known as Abu Jihad), at his home in Sidi Bou Said, as an act of retaliation against the Palestinian uprising in the Occupied Territories.

GEOGRAPHY

The main topographical feature in the north of the country is the Tunisian Dorsale, a range of mountains which runs south-west to north-east and tapers off towards the Gulf of Tunis. These mountains are actually a continuation of both the Algerian Saharan Atlas and the High Atlas Mountains of Morocco. The highest mountain in the country, Jebel Chambi (1544 metres), rises in this range just west of Kasserine, near the Algerian border.

North of this range is the Medjerda Valley, the principal river system in the country, which drains into the Gulf of Tunis. This was the granary of ancient Rome and is still the major grain growing area in the country. The waters of the river are used for irrigation and the generation of hydroelectricity.

Directly south of the range is a 200 to 400-metre-high treeless plain, which drops down to a series of *chott* (salt lakes) before the country gives out completely to desert in the south. Although this is only the very edge of the Sahara, it attracts up to two million tourists to the country each year. Abundant artesian water makes cultivation possible in places, and from these green oases come some of the finest dates in the world.

The sand sea which completely covers the southern tip of Tunisia is the eastern extremity of the Great Eastern Erg (Grand Erg Oriental), which covers a large area of Algeria.

The country borders on Algeria to the west and Libya to the south-east. The ragged and irregular 1400-km coastline forms the eastern and northern boundaries.

Distances

With an area of 164,000 square km, Tunisia is by far the smallest of the Maghreb countries; it's about half as big as Italy, or about the same size as Washington State in the USA or Victoria in Australia.

Its long narrow shape means that it measures 750 km from north to south but only 150 km from east and west.

CLIMATE

Tunisia basically has a Mediterranean climate, which features mild wet winters and hot dry summers. Winds are generally mild and from the west, but at times in summer the sirocco wind can blow in hot and strong from the Sahara for days on end, and the temperature can hover around 45°C in Tunis and even higher in the south.

Rainfall is extremely variable, but the averages range from 1500 mm annually in the north right down to 150 mm (and less) in the south.

When to Go

Summer is the most popular time for visiting Tunisia, mainly because that is the European holiday season, but it is far from being the ideal time to see the country. Even in Tunis the mercury regularly hits 40°C and more, and in the south and interior it is usually hotter. You really have to have a masochistic streak to be able to enjoy trudging around a ruined Roman city getting your brains baked in weather like this.

At this time of year it is sheer madness to try and do anything between about 1 and 4 in the afternoon. Despite the heat, summer is the high season, so it is also the time when transport is stretched to the limit and hotel rooms can be hard to find after midday. Archaeological sites can also be crowded and, all in all, it's a good time to avoid if at all possible.

The best time of all to visit is in spring, when the north is still green, the south is pleasantly warm and the summer hordes have yet to arrive. Autumn is the next choice, the only drawback being the fact that throughout most of the country the skies can be very hazy, due to the heat and dust build-up over the summer.

Winter can be downright cold and unpleasant in the north. Tunis becomes a cold, rainy and somewhat dreary place, while places up in the hills, such as Ain Draham and Le Kef, often get snow.

The celsius temperatures in the box below are, obviously, only averages and in no way indicate how fierce the summer can be (and usually is), especially in the south, nor how cold the winter.

FLORA & FAUNA

The climate largely dictates which plants and animals can exist in any region. With the mild conditions in the north, cork forests flourish there and these are home to many wild boar.

The semi-arid Sahel region in the east-central part of the country is where olives are grown; when you are driving through, the rows upon rows of olive trees seem to stretch on for ever. If you fly to Jerba in daylight you can see the lines of trees covering enormous areas.

The treeless plains of the south support large areas of esparto grass, which is gathered for use in the production of high-quality paper. It is also woven into donkey-harness straps and reed mats by the local inhabitants.

Further south the vegetation gives way altogether to desert, and, apart from at the occasional oasis, there is barely a single bush or even blade of grass to be seen. There was widespread hunting for gazelle in the past but fortunately this has been banned – only just in time, as the animals were in danger of extinction.

GOVERNMENT

The 1959 constitution of the Republic of Tunisia gives legislative power to the Chamber of Deputies, which consists of 136 members elected directly by universal suffrage to a five-year term.

The president has executive power and is the head of both the state and the government. The constitution states that the president must be a Muslim and can serve for no more than three consecutive terms; however, the first president of independent Tunisia, Habib Bourguiba, was elected president for life in 1974 before being ousted in 1987.

The country is governed under a one-party system, even though opposition parties were introduced in 1981. The Neo-Destour Party holds all the seats in the Chamber of Deputies.

ECONOMY

The mixed Tunisian economy, in which both the public and private sectors participate, relies heavily on tourism and remittances from nationals working in the Gulf states. The hard times that the country is going through at present are

	Tunis	Bizerte	Hammamet	Sousse	Tozeur	Jerba
January	11.1	11.3	11.0	11.2	11.7	12.1
April	15.8	15.4	16.0	16.1	20.1	18.5
July	26.0	25.2	25.5	25.7	32.3	26.5
October	20.4	20.5	20.9	21.3	22.4	23.1
December	12.2	12.4	12.6	12.6	11.5	13.6

Average temperatures in degrees celsius

due in no small part to the fact that tourism figures have been down in recent years, and that in 1985 Libya expelled thousands of Tunisian nationals who were working there (which is why the border between the two countries is closed).

The economy sees a regular (and increasing) trade deficit and, although it is not on the scale of most developing countries, it is serious enough for the government to turn to the World Bank and the IMF for help in alleviating the deficit problem.

Petrol and petroleum products account for about 40% of exports, but the lack of refining capacity within the country means that most of the country's heavy petroleum needs have to be met with imports. The oil slump in 1986 has drastically reduced Tunisia's exports.

Other important exports include textiles, fertilisers and chemicals, with the main destinations being France, the USA, Italy and West Germany. Imports are chiefly food, raw materials and capital goods.

The agricultural sector has become smaller in the last 20 years and now provides work for only 30% of the workforce; almost 40% of food required has to be imported. Despite the fact that large areas of the south of the country are desert, over 55% of the land in the country is cultivated. The main crops are wheat, barley, maize, sorghum, olives and dates.

Major industries are concentrated in the fields of processing agricultural produce and minerals, and include textiles, foodstuffs, cement, steel and phosphate processing.

The mining industry is also important to the economy and Tunisia is the world's sixth-largest producer of phosphate.

Unemployment is widespread and the situation is exacerbated by the fact that most manufacturing is small scale and most businesses employ no more than five people.

Social Conditions

Living standards are generally good and are considered high by developing-world standards.

Education is free and, thanks to the high government spending (typically 25% of total expenditure), the number of schools has increased rapidly since independence. Literacy is fairly high, at about 60% in males and 40% in females. School attendance is not compulsory, but the primary schools especially are well attended. It seems that, no matter which town you are in, at any time during daylight hours there are hundreds of young kids in their school tunics on their way to or from school.

Health care is also free, and low income earners are eligible for extra benefits such as free milk for newborn babies and free school lunches. Although there are still shortages of trained personnel and modern facilities, general health conditions have improved dramatically in the last 20 years. This has led to infectious diseases such as typhoid and diphtheria being brought under control.

The social security system also provides old age and disability pensions, and compensation for sickness and injury.

POPULATION & PEOPLE

The people of Tunisia, who number over seven million, are basically Arab Berber. The vast majority are Muslims, and in fact the non-Muslim population numbers less than 40,000 (down from over 300,000 in the 1950s).

The country has a fairly high growth rate of about 2.5%. Almost half the population is under the age of 15, which places a great strain on social services. Another problem is the population distribution, as it varies from over 2000 per square km in Tunis to less than 10 in the south.

The Berbers were the original inhabitants of the area, but waves of immigrations over the centuries have brought Phoenicians, Jews, Romans, Vandals and Arabs. There was a major influx of Spanish Moors in the 17th century, while

In the medina

over the last 300 years the Ottoman Turks have added their bit to the great ethnic mix.

RELIGION

Islam is the state religion in Tunisia and, with the amount of westernisation and reform, it is not surprising that it takes a fairly liberal form.

Bourguiba was very keen on liberalisation and it is largely because of this that religious observance has decreased markedly in the last 20 years.

Recently there has been a definite resurgence of religious adherence, particularly among the young and unemployed, in the form of the outlawed Islamic Tendency Movement (MTI); it was partly Bourguiba's firm opposition to *any* activity in this direction which led to his ousting in 1987.

Minority religious groups include Christians and Jews, and account for about 40,000 people.

HOLIDAYS & FESTIVALS

Public holidays and festivals are primarily religious celebrations, or festivities which mark the anniversary of various events in the creation of the modern state.

As the Gregorian (western) and Islamic calendars are of different lengths, the Islamic holidays fall 11 days earlier every western calendar year. For the Islamic holidays see the section in the chapter on Facts about the Region. Ramadan is the main one to watch out for, as for an entire month the opening hours of everything are disrupted.

Other public holidays in Tunisia are:

New Year's Day
1 January
Anniversary of the Revolution
18 January
Independence Day
20 March
Martyrs' Day
9 April
Labour Day
1 May
Victory Day
1 June
Republic Day
25 July
Women's Day
13 August
Anniversary of the PSD
3 September
Evacuation of Bizerte
15 October

Some of these holidays, such as Women's Day and the Evacuation of Bizerte, pass without notice. On others everything comes to a halt, and there is absolutely nothing happening (although transport still runs). On some long weekends such as the Eid el Fitr (celebrating the end of Ramadan) transport is strained, as people return home for the festival.

There are a number of festivals held at various times throughout the year. Most of them are fairly touristy and the 'folkloric' events are tacky, but they are worth a look if you are in the area. The main ones are:

January
  Sahara Festival, Douz. Everything from
  camel races to traditional marriages.
April
  Nefta Festival. Parades and folkloric events.
May
  Monastir Festival
June
  Dougga Festival. Classical performances at
  the Roman theatre.
July-August
  Carthage Festival. Main cultural event of
  the year; performances at the Roman theatre.
  El Jem Festival
  Siren Festival, Kerkennah Islands.

Hammamet Festival. Musical and cultural
events.
Tabarka Festival. Music and theatre, coral
exhibition.
Ulysses Festival, Jerba. Strictly for the
tourists this one, right down to the Miss
Ulysses competition.
August
  Baba Aoussou Festival, Sousse.
October
  Carthage Film Festival (biennial).
December
  Sahara Festival, Tozeur. The Douz festival
  all over again.

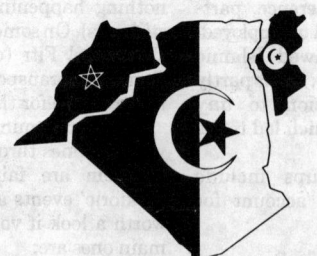

Facts for the Visitor

VISAS

Nationals of European countries, the USA, Canada and Japan need no visa for a stay of up to three months: you just roll up and get a small stamp in your passport – simple.

Australians and New Zealanders (and anyone else not covered above) do need one-month tourist visas, and these can be obtained wherever Tunisia has diplomatic representation overseas. Even though you can obtain a one-week extendable visa on arrival, it is strongly recommended that you get a tourist visa before arriving; the extension process is complicated beyond belief and can take anything up to 10 days, during which time you have to remain in Tunis.

Nationals of Israel and South Africa are not allowed to enter the country.

Embassies

Visas can be obtained from the following Tunisian diplomatic representatives abroad.

Algeria
   11 Rue de Bois De Boulogne, Algiers (tel 60 1388)
   6 Rue Emir Abdelkader, Annaba (tel 82 4448)
   Post Box 280, Tébessa (tel 97 4480)
Austria
   Chegastr 3, 1030 Vienna (tel 78 6552)
Belgium
   278 Ave de Tervuesen, 1150 Brussels (tel 762 1448)
Canada
   515 Oscannor St, Ottawa (tel 237 0330)
Egypt
   26 Rue El Jazirah, Zamalek, Cairo (tel 69 8940)
France
   17 Rue de Lubeck, Paris
   3 Blvd d'Athènes, 13001 Marseilles
Italy
   7 Via Asmara, Rome (tel 839 0748)
   Piazza Ignazio Florio 24, Palermo (tel 32 8996)

Jordan
   Ave el Aksa, 4th Circle, Amman (tel 67 4307)
Libya
   Rue Bechar El-Ibrahimi, Tripoli (tel 30 331)
Mauritania
   BP 681, Nouakchott (tel 52 871)
Morocco
   Cnr Ave du Fas & Rue d'Ifrane, Rabat (tel 305 76)
Senegal
   Rue el Hadj Seydou, Nourou Tall-Dakar (tel 31 261)
Spain
   Plaza Alonzo Martinez 3, Madrid (tel 447 3508)
Syria
   6 Jaddet Al Chaffi, Damascus (tel 66 0356)
UK
   29 Prince's Gate, London SW7 (tel 584 8117)
USA
   2408 Massachusetts Ave NW, Washington DC 20008 (tel 234 6644)
West Germany
   Godesberger Allee 103,53, Bonn 2 (tel 37 6981)

Transit Visas

These are available on arrival at Tunis port and airport and at the land border posts for TD 2.500. They are valid for one week only but can be extended (with difficulty).

Visa extensions

If you are one of the poor unfortunates who has to go through this convoluted process, here's how you go about it.

First of all, wait until about the fourth day of your one-week visa before even bothering to apply for the extension; they won't entertain your request before that.

Arm yourself with two passport photos, bank receipts showing that you have changed enough money to support yourself during your stay, and a 'Certificat d'Aubergement' from your hotel. This certificate is simply a declaration from the hotel owner stating that you are in fact staying in that hotel. It's a totally meaningless document but without it you cannot get the extension. You need to let the hotel know a couple of days before you need one, as hotel employees won't usually do it and the owner is more often than not somewhere else. If for some reason you can't get one, a simple receipt should be adequate. It's also a good idea to photocopy the bank receipts, so that if you want to exchange dinar back to hard currency when you leave you have some proof of exchange.

The next step is to take all these goodies along to the appropriate office of the Ministry of the Interior, which happens to be a nondescript wooden shed down by the old port in Tunis at 30 Avenue de la République. Here you'll be given a form to complete which you hand in along with your passport, upon which you get told to come along in a couple of days to collect it. This couple of days can turn into a week,

as you go back to the office every day and get told 'perhaps tomorrow'. When you go to collect, make sure you buy fiscal stamps to the value of TD 2.500 in advance. These are available from the Recette des Finances office at 22 Avenue de la République, another nondescript office, near the beginning of the flyover.

If you are lucky, you will have your extension within three days; mine took 12 and involved an interview (interrogation might be a better word) at the Ministry of the Interior, so be prepared for a wait.

MONEY

US$1	=	TD 0.900
A$1	=	TD 0.770
UK£1	=	TD 1.600
C$1	=	TD 0.750
DM 1	=	TD 0.500
Y100	=	TD 0.710

The Tunisian currency is the dinar, which is divided into 1000 millimes. Coins in circulation are 5, 10, 20, 50, 100, 500 millimes and one dinar. Notes in use are 1

(rare), 5, 10 and 20 dinars. The 20 dinar note is too big for everyday use, and even the 10 can be a pain to change.

The dinar is a soft currency, so import or export thereof is prohibited. There is no black market and it is not necessary to declare your foreign currency on arrival.

Foreign currency is exchangeable only at banks and flash hotels. When leaving the country you can reconvert only up to 30% of the amount you have changed to dinars (up to a limit of TD 100), so hang on to exchange receipts and don't change too much towards the end of your stay. If you don't have any receipts to show you won't be able to reconvert *any* dinars.

Credit Cards
Major credit cards such as Visa, Amex and Mastercard are accepted widely throughout the country at large shops, tourist hotels, car rental agencies and banks. If you want to get a cash advance you can get only local currency.

COSTS
Tunisia is not all that cheap a country to travel in. Its generally high standard of living and the fact that it is certainly not a Third-World country are reflected in the cost of everyday items.

Accommodation costs for an average presentable hotel are around US$8 for a double and US$5 for a single. By the time you add food and transport costs, you are looking at around US$15 to US$20 per day all up.

Obviously you could spend a lot more than this; you could also spend quite a bit less if you are prepared to rough it a bit, staying in hotels with cold showers (or no shower at all), and hitching or taking buses rather than trains or louages (shared taxis).

TOURIST INFORMATION
Local Tourist Offices
The government-run Office National du Tourisme Tunisien has offices dotted around the country in Tunis, Bizerte,

Sousse, Nabeul, Kairouan, Sfax, Tozeur, Gabès and Jerba. The staff in these offices are generally helpful but speak little or no English.

The government doesn't put out a great deal of printed information, but does issue some glossy hand-out stuff in various languages.

There are also quite a few local tourist offices, usually called Syndicats d'Initiative, which have a limited amount of information on a particular area.

The main tourist office (tel 341 077) is at 1 Avenue Mohammed V, Tunis.

Overseas Reps
Overseas offices include:

Germany
    Fremdenverkehrsamt Tunisien, Am Hauptbahnhof 6, 6000 Frankfurt (tel 23 1891)
Austria
    Tunesisches Fremdenverkehrsamt, Landesgerichstr 22, 1010 Vienna (tel 48 3944)
France
    Office National du Tourisme Tunisien, 32 Ave de l'Opéra, 75002 Paris
England
    Tunisian National Tourist Office, 7A Stafford St, London W1 (tel 499 2234)
Italy
    Ente Nazionale Tunisino Per il Turismo, 10 Via Baracchini, 20123 Milan (tel 87 1214)
Holland
    Tunesisch National Verkeersbureau, Leidsestraat 61, 1017 Amsterdam (tel 22 4971)

Foreign Embassies
Countries which have diplomatic representation in Tunisia include:

Algeria
    136 Ave de la Liberté, Tunis
Australia
    Australian affairs are handled by the Canadian embassy in Tunis.
Canada
    Rue du Sénégal, Tunis (tel 286 577)

Egypt
  16 Rue Essayouti, El Menzeh, Tunis (tel 230 004)
France
  Place de l'Indépendence, Ave Bourguiba, Tunis (tel 245 700)
Ivory Coast
  6 Rue ibn Charaf, Tunis (tel 283 878)
Jordan
  4 Rue Didon, Tunis (tel 288 401)
Libya
  48 Rue du 1 Juin, Tunis
Morocco
  39 Rue du 1 Juin, Tunis (tel 288 063)
Senegal
  122 Ave de la Liberté, Tunis (tel 282 393)
UK
  5 Place de la Victoire, Tunis (tel 245 100)
USA
  144 Ave de la Liberté, Tunis (tel 282 566)
West Germany
  18 Ave Challaye, Tunis (tel 281 246)

GENERAL INFORMATION
Post

The Tunisian postal service is a little slow, but you will find that your things do arrive eventually.

Letters from overseas generally arrive in good time (up to a week), but mail can take much longer when going from Tunisia to other countries. Allow up to three weeks for letters to the USA and Australia, somewhat less to Europe.

Postal Rates Airmail letters to Australia and the USA cost 300 mills; slightly less to Europe. Postcards cost 200 mills.

Parcels are not particularly cheap; the rate for a 10-kg parcel to Australia is TD 21.600.

As well as at post offices, stamps are available from some general stores, major hotels and some news-stands.

Sending Mail Post office hours are different in summer and winter, and can also vary a bit from town to town. Generally, they are open in summer from 8 am to 12 noon and 3 to 6 pm Monday to Friday, and from 8 am to 12 noon

Saturday. Winter hours are 7.30 am to 1.30 pm Monday to Saturday. During Ramadan the hours are 8 am to 3 pm Monday to Saturday. The main post office in Tunis is open seven days a week.

Parcel Post The best place to send parcels from is the parcel post office in Tunis on Avenue de la République. You have to take the parcel there *unwrapped* so that it can be inspected; if you want to send something surface mail make sure you stress the fact or you may find yourself getting charged for airmail.

There is a separate parcel post office at Bizerte too.

Receiving Mail Mail can be received at any post office in the country. It should be addressed clearly and, if the clerks will co-operate, get them to check under your given name if you think you are missing mail.

Telephones

The phone system is quite sophisticated and functions smoothly. The international telephone office in Tunis is open 24 hours and you can dial direct to most countries. Making an international call from any other city may take longer, mainly because it can take a while to get a line to Tunis. Calls can also be made from major hotels but these are considerably more expensive.

Local calls cost 100 mills and there are public phones in most hotels and some cafés. Calls within the country can be made from all phones. The area codes are: Tunis region – 01; Bizerte, Hammamet & Nabeul – 02; Sousse & Monastir – 03; Sfax – 04; Gabès & Jerba – 05; Tozeur & Gafsa – 06; Kairouan – 07; Tabarka & Le Kef – 08.

Electricity

Most of the country is on 220 volts, but the occasional hotel in Tunis and some of the smaller towns in the south are still on 110 volts. Check before plugging in any appliance. The supply is reliable and uninterrupted. Wall plugs are of the two-round-pin variety, as in Europe.

Time

Tunisia is one hour ahead of GMT from October to April; two hours ahead of GMT from May to September.

Business Hours

Government Offices & Businesses These are open Monday to Thursday from 8.30 to 1 pm and 3 to 5.45 pm, Friday and Saturday 8.30 am to 1.30 pm; in summer offices do not open in the afternoon at all.

Banks Banking hours are from 8 to 11 am and 2 to 4 pm Monday to Thursday, and 8 to 11 am and 1 to 3 pm Friday. As with the government offices, banks are not open in the afternoons in summer.

In Tunis there are banks which are open outside these hours.

Shops Generally, shops are open Monday to Friday from 8 am to 12.30 pm and 2.30 to 6 pm, Saturday from 8 am to 12 noon. Summer hours are usually 7.30 am to 1 pm. These hours vary slightly from place to place, especially in the south where the weather is more extreme in summer.

Hammams

These are the modern equivalent of the old Turkish bath and are a great way to relax for an hour or two. Every town has at least one; the bigger towns have separate ones for men and women, or else there are separate times for each sex. It is usually possible to have a massage as well.

Hammams can also be used for a cheap place to stay, but this is a men-only option; also, as you can well imagine, they are damp and hot. An added inconvenience is that you have to be out by about 6.30 am, which is when they open.

MEDIA

Understandably, the media in Tunisia are dominated by the French and Arabic languages. There are no English-language newspapers or broadcasts. However, in Tunis and Gabès you can buy two-day-old English newspapers; international current affairs magazines such as *Time* and *Newsweek* are readily available from the kiosks in the dividing strip of Avenue Bourguiba in Tunis.

The local French-language papers, *La Presse* and *Le Temps*, had toed the party line and been very light on overseas coverage until Bourguiba's unceremonious removal from office in late 1987, but with the new regime they may have improved. Inside its back page *La Presse* has lists of exchange rates, aircraft departures and arrivals, useful phone numbers and air-con bus and train departures.

French newspapers such as *Le Monde* are also widely available.

FILM & PHOTOGRAPHY

Name-brand film such as Kodak and Fuji is widely available but don't expect any bargains: it will cost you at least as much as it does at home.

People are often a bit touchy about having their picture taken. Always ask before taking photos of people and respect their decision if they say no.

Islam and photos of women don't go together and, although Tunisia is a relatively liberal country, photographing women is still a no-no in parts of the country. On the other hand, you may well find some people who are more than happy to have their 'mug shot' taken.

ACCOMMODATION

Tunisia is well geared for tourism, and the accommodation available runs the whole gamut from basic Tunisian hotels to five-star luxury resorts. Such resorts are totally isolated from the local communities; they cater to tourists who want to spend time on the beach and not trouble themselves with what the local culture might have to offer.

Youth Hostels

There are hostels in just about every major town, but they are almost without exception characterless concrete structures (usually near the local stadium) which have the spartan feel of an army barracks. Two notable exception are the hostels at Bizerte and Houmt Souk (Jerba).

The usual cost is TD 1.500 for a bed and the hostels are open all year. For the most part, you can do just as well at one of the local hotels, where you won't have the inconvenience of being out of the town centre.

There are hostels at Ain Draham, Beja, Bizerte, Gafsa, Houmt Souk, Kelibia, Nabeul, Radès (Tunis), Sfax, Sousse and Tozeur.

Hotels

Tunisian hotels are almost always clean and very well kept. Most come under the government's rating system and so have a maximum price that they can charge.

These hotels, rated from one-star

through to four-star, must display the tariff by the reception desk, so you can always see what the top price should be. Most hotels stick to these prices and in fact, out of season, they often knock the prices down a bit. Often the ratings seem to make no sense at all, as you can find a well-kept one-star place that is far more comfortable than a run-down two-star.

The approximate highest charges for each classification (and they do vary a bit from town to town) are: one-star TD 7.500/11 for singles/doubles including breakfast (often compulsory); two-star TD 9.500/14; three-star TD 10.500/16; four-star TD 57/70. In the cheaper places, showers often cost extra, usually about 500 mills.

Looking at these prices you may think it's going to be impossible to find a cheap bed, but below the one-star rating there are many unclassified hotels which are more than adequate and often better value than the rated places.

Medina hotels are usually unclassified; they are basic, often with no showers, and you pay for a bed in a shared room. These cost around TD 2 per person and vary from quite good cheap hotels to filthy flop-houses where even a dog would hesitate to bed down.

On average you can find a good, clean double room for around TD 8, although in summer places tend to fill up early and you may have little choice.

In many places, usually two-star and above, breakfast will be included; although it will be listed as an optional extra it is usually compulsory and consists of French bread, butter, jam and coffee.

Camping

At the bottom of the scale, there are a few official camping grounds in the country. Most of them have only basic facilities and charge about TD 1 per person. Camping grounds apart, it should be possible to camp anywhere as long as you get the permission of the landowner.

On the beaches in the north at Raf Raf and Ghar el Melh sleeping out on the beach or renting one of the grass huts is the accepted thing. The same applies to the remote beaches of the north coast, although you won't find any grass huts there. In the resort areas of the Cap Bon Peninsula and Sousse this would definitely be frowned on.

The official sites are at Nabeul, Hammamet, Hammam Lif, Tozeur and Degache (near Tozeur); the youth hostel just outside Bizerte is also a popular place to camp.

BOOKS

The following are a few books which may help give you a better understanding of the country and its people. If you can read French, you'll find that there is a much greater range of material available in that language than there is in English.

People & Society

The Arabs by Peter Mansfield (Penguin, Harmondsworth) offers an excellent insight into the Arab psyche and is the most accessible text for the newcomer to the topic.

The Koran may seem like a strange recommendation, but it makes interesting reading for those who want to know more about the foundations on which Islam is based.

History

Africa in History by Basil Davidson (Paladin, 1974) is a very readable account of the history of the whole continent by one of the most knowledgeable Africa hands.

General

Salammbô by Gustave Flaubert (Penguin Classics) is really a pretty dreadful book, but this 19th-century novel is set in 3rd-century Carthage. It has a more than adequate quota of sex and violence.

Fountains in the Sand by Norman Douglas (OUP, 1986). This is an entertaining account of Douglas' trip through south-western Tunisia early this century,

so long as you ignore his intolerance of Arabs and everything Tunisian.

Middle East Review, published by World of Information, is a yearly digest of events in the Middle East and North Africa. It goes into a fair amount of detail on the economies and politics of each country, and has some basic tourist information as well.

Bookshops

These are fairly rare throughout the country and no shop stocks anything much in English. In Tunis there is a small bookshop in the lobby of the Africa Hotel which has a few junk novels, but that is about the limit of it.

MAPS

The Michelin map of Algeria & Tunisia (No 172) is the best map of the region and is quite adequate. The Hildebrand's Travel Map of Tunisia (No 1-19-1) is much bigger than the Michelin map and gives more detail, but it is weak on place names.

Neither of these maps is available inside the country, but the tourist office in Tunis sometimes has a reasonable map which it gives out free of charge.

THINGS TO BUY
Rugs & Carpets

These are amongst the most readily available souvenirs and, although they are not cheap, there are some really beautiful ones for sale. The main carpet-selling centres are Tunis, Kairouan, Tozeur and Jerba.

There are two basic types: knotted carpets and *mergoums* (Berber rugs). The former follow traditional designs and are highly decorative, while the latter are much more functional, more geometric in design and use brighter colours.

The ONAT office inspects all carpets for sale, classifies them by quality and affixes a label and seal on the back of each one.

The different qualities are Ordinary (*Deuxième Choix*), Fine (*Première Choix*) and Superfine (*Qualité Supérieure*), and they have up to 40,000, 90,000 and 250,000 knots per square metre respectively. Approximate prices per square metre for Fine quality are:

knots	dinars
10,000	38 to 50
40,000	57 to 75
90,000	85 to 140
160,000	150 to 210
250,000 (wool)	220 to 290
250,000 (silk)	430 to 600

Mergoum prices range from TD 37 to TD 50 per square metre.

These prices are the official ONAT prices and so are definitely at the top end of the scale, but they are at least an indication of the maximum prices to pay.

Of course there are many carpets for sale which have not been inspected and classified by ONAT, and in these cases you are on your own as far as what you are getting for your money is concerned. The prices will be cheaper but the quality may be suspect – the only safeguard is to know your product.

Pottery

Tunisia has a long connection with the art of pottery, as the Romans were making the stuff here nearly 2000 years ago. The main centre is Nabeul, partly because of the number of tourists that pass through there; Guellala (on Jerba) is another.

Leather

There is plenty of leatherwork for sale in the souk in Tunis, and some of it is really fine work. Most of it comes from Morocco, however, and is not all that cheap.

Leatherwork that originates in Tunisia often comes from Kairouan. Articles for sale include traditional pieces such as camel and donkey saddles, waterskins and cartridge pouches, as well as more mundane stuff like wallets and belts.

Copper & Brass

Beaten copper and brass items are also popular and are widely available. Beaten plates, ranging in size from saucer to coffee table, make good souvenirs, although transporting the larger ones can be a problem.

A lot of the stuff is mass produced by the shopowners in the souk in Tunis and quality varies enormously.

Jewellery

Arabic jewellery (and particularly gold jewellery) is often too gaudy and ornate for western tastes, but there are some styles which are attractive.

The Hand of Fatima (daughter of the Prophet) is a traditional Arabic design; it can be found in varying sizes, from small earrings to large neck pendants, and is usually made of silver. In pre-Islamic times this same design represented Baal, the protector of the Carthaginians, and is also known today as the *khomsa*.

Other traditional pieces of jewellery include:

Hedeyed These are finely engraved wide bracelets made of gold or silver.
Kholkal Similar to the hedeyed but worn around the ankle. In Carthaginian times they were a sign of chastity; today they are still a symbol of fidelity and are often part of a bride's dowry.

The quality of pure silver and gold jewellery can be established by the official stamps used to grade all work. The quality of unstamped items is immediately suspect.

The stamps in use are:

Horse's Head Used to mark all 18-carat gold jewellery; the horse's head is the Carthaginian symbol for money.
Scorpion This is used on all 9-carat gold jewellery.
Grape clusters Used on silver graded at 900 mills per gram.

Negro Head Used on the poorer quality silver graded at 800 mills per gram.

Obviously, the price of jewellery depends to a large extent on the quality of the work, but the following prices give an indication of cost: TD 15 to TD 20 per gram for 18-carat gold; TD 7 to TD 12 per gram for 9-carat gold; 750 mills to 950 mills per gram for 900 mills silver; 650 mills to 800 mills for 800 mills silver .

Articles which weigh less than 50 grams are sold not by weight but by quality.

Miscellaneous

Chechias These are the small red felt hats worn by Tunisian men, although it is unusual to see young men wearing them these days.

The chechia souk in Tunis is the obvious place to look; you can see the poor blokes making them in sweat-shop conditions.

Quality varies, but an average price is around TD 3.

Straw Goods The rectangular woven straw baskets with patterns on them are practical and cheap. Some are pretty bloody awful, with camels and 'typical desert scenes' woven into the patterns, but there are plenty of other more simple designs.

Hats and fans are other popular goods. Most of the straw stuff comes from Gabès and Jerba in the south of the country.

Perfume Cheap oil scents are sold everywhere. Bottle sizes range from a tiny five ml for TD 1 up to whopping half litres.

Sand Roses You'll find these for sale all over the country, and in fact all over the entire Maghreb. They are formed of gypsum, which is present in the sand and has been dissolved and then dehydrated many times. When it crystalises, the crystals form some beautiful patterns.

They are most prominent in the area from Ghardaia in Algeria right through

Medina rug shop, Kairouan

into southern Tunisia, and range in size from about a five-cm diameter up to the size of a large watermelon.

They do make good souvenirs, but unless you have a vehicle I can't imagine that you would be prepared to cart around a couple of kilos of gypsum for days or weeks on end.

Stuffed Camels Well, much as I hate them I have to mention them. It seems that in Arabic desert countries you can tell how well developed the tourist industry is by the number of stuffed camels for sale – Tunisia is way out in front in this field. Every souvenir shop has a selection, ranging from pocket size right up to about one-third full size!

Markets
Town and village life often revolves around the weekly markets. It is a good day to be in the town, as it will be far more lively than usual and, apart from the itinerant merchants selling fairly mundane household goods, there are other local people from the outlying districts who come into town just for the market.

Some markets have become real tourist traps, and for that reason are crowded and worth avoiding; nevertheless, it is on market days that there is the best selection of stuff for sale. Nabeul is one that fits into this category.

Market days throughout the country are as follows:

Monday	Tataouine, Houmt Souk, Kairouan and Ain Draham
Tuesday	Ghardimao, Kasserine and Beja
Wednesday	Sbeitla, Nefta and Jendouba
Thursday	Gafsa, Tebersouk and Douz
Friday	Mahdia, Zaghouan, Tabarka, Mateur, Sfax, Nabeul and Zarzis
Saturday	El Fahs and Ben Ghardane
Sunday	Sousse, Hammam Lif and El Jem

Getting There

AIR

To/From Europe

With over 1½ million tourists arriving every year, Tunisia has three international airports to cater for them: Tunis, Jerba and Monastir.

A large percentage of the flights using the Jerba and Monastir airports are charter flights from Europe; these can be incredibly cheap if you don't mind the restrictions on the tickets. These are usually to do with the minimum and maximum permitted length of stay. The tickets must be bought well in advance, although you can often buy them heavily discounted at the last minute.

The best source of information are the overseas branches of the Tunisian National Office, which have a list of all holiday operators.

If you want to fly back to Europe it's going to cost you, as you will have to take a regular scheduled flight. If money is your main consideration, take the ferry to Italy and go overland from there.

Airlines which serve Tunis include: Tunis Air, Aeroflot, Air Algérie, Air France, Royal Jordanian, British Caledonian, Egypt Air, Iberia, KLM, Lufthansa, Royal Air Maroc, Sabena and Swissair.

One of the cheapest scheduled airlines out of the country is Tunisavia, which flies regularly to Malta. They have agencies in the larger cities in Tunisia.

To/From North America

There are no direct flights between Tunisia and the USA. The cheapest option would be a cheap fare to London and then a charter flight or bucket shop deal from there.

To/From Australia

As with the USA, there are no direct flights to or from Australia, so London is a good transit point.

A more direct route is to fly with Royal Jordanian to Singapore (via Amman) and then fly from there to Australia. A return flight from the Australian east coast to Tunis costs around US$1200; but you may get stuck in Amman for a few days, as the connections are not that frequent.

Buying the same ticket in Tunisia would cost considerably more than buying it in Australia.

To/From Morocco

Royal Air Maroc and Tunis Air fly regularly between the two countries. The standard economy fare is about US$400 return.

OVERLAND

To/From Algeria

There are numerous crossing points between Algeria and Tunisia, not all of them always open. The most popular points are at Babouch (connecting Annaba and Ain Draham), Ghardimao (Jendouba and Souk Ahras), Sakiet Sidi Youssef (Le Kef and Souk Ahras), Bou Chebka (Kasserine and Tebessa) and the desert post between Nefta and El Oued.

None of the crossing points suffer from the obnoxious Algerian officials you encounter when entering Algeria from Morocco (particularly at the Figuig-Beni Ounif crossing), and you even get the occasional smile.

It is quite possible that if you have only travellers' cheques you won't be compelled to change the mandatory AD 1000 when entering Algeria. Instead they will tell you that you have to do it at the first town you get to. Although you could then travel through Algeria without changing at the bank, you run the risk on departure of being forced to change the money, only to have it confiscated straight away. See the

315

Money section in Algeria for more details.

Bus There is a direct air-con SNTRI bus daily at 6 am from Tunis to Annaba which goes via the border at Babouch. The officials on the Algerian side here are polite, you are not compelled to change money (but see the warning in the Algeria Money section) and there is only the most cursory baggage search. The return bus leaves Annaba at 6 am also. You need to book 24 hours in advance at the south bus station in Tunis or the Annaba bus station; TD 6.00.

There are also air-con SNTRI buses between Tunis and Constantine, departing every second day. Again, book in advance at the Constantine bus station or the south bus station in Tunis.

These buses are the easiest way to cross between the two countries; the only drawback is that you have to get on at the point of origin, as they don't stop en route to collect passengers.

Train The advantage of crossing by train is that, unlike crossing by bus, you can get on en route (in Ghardimao in Tunisia, or Souk Ahras or Constantine in Algeria) instead of at the point of origin. In summer it can be hellishly hot on the train and it takes a good deal of time to process everyone through customs. Women get preferential treatment.

The daily train is the Trans-Maghreb Express. In the days of better relations between Algeria and Morocco it used to run all the way from Rabat to Tunis, but these days it only runs from Algiers to Tunis, taking about 24 hours between the two cities. The best bet is to take it from Jendouba to Constantine (or vice versa), as there is not much in between. It leaves from Tunis daily at 1 pm and from Algiers at 7 pm.

Taxi The crossing in the desert between Nefta and El Oued is the most popular. There are a few louages (shared taxis) daily from Nefta to the border at Hazoua; from there it's a four-km walk to the Algerian post known as Bou Aroua. From here there are irregular taxis to El Oued, 27 km away. There is a good deal of tourist traffic on this road outside of the summer months, so hitching shouldn't be too difficult.

From Le Kef there are regular louages to the border at Sakiet Sidi Youssef.

To/From Libya
There is a border crossing between the two countries on the coast at Ras Ajdir, but at the time of writing it was most definitely closed.

BOAT
To/From Italy
There are frequent crossings throughout the year between Tunis and the Italian port of Trapani in Sicily. Some boats go on to (or start from) Cagliari in Sardinia and Genoa on the Italian riviera.

In summer the boats are heavily booked, and if you are taking a vehicle it is essential that you book well in advance. If you are on foot you may get on without a booking, but it can be torrid.

The Sicilian and Sardinian services are operated by the Tirrenia Line (see Addresses).

Trapani to Tunis The service from Trapani is weekly; officially, the boat departs at 9 am on Wednesdays, but you'll be lucky if it goes before midday. It arrives in Tunis at 4.30 pm; the trip costs 65,000 lire (about US$55). In the other direction, the boat leaves Tunis at 8 pm on Wednesday and arrives in Trapani at 6 am on Thursday.

Cagliari to Tunis This run is actually a continuation of the Trapani to Tunis service. It leaves Cagliari (Sardinia) at 7 pm on Tuesday, and arrives back at 8 am on Friday.

The fare is about UK£40 per person.

Genoa to Tunis The Compagnie Tunisienne de Navigation (CTN) regularly operates a boat between Tunis and Genoa. Service varies between four per month in winter to 11 per month at the height of summer. The one-way fare is TD 47 (FFr 560) and the trip takes about 24 hours.

Catania to Tunis From Catania on the southern coast of Sicily CTN operates a weekly car-ferry service. This leaves Catania at 9 pm on Saturday, arriving in Tunis at 3 pm on Sunday.

Departure from Tunis is at 6 pm on Thursday, arriving back in Catania at 6 am on Saturday. This service goes via Valletta in Malta on the way back to Italy.

To/From France

Marseilles to Tunis Also operated by CTN, this ferry service is also packed in summer; vehicle owners will need to book ahead. They operate nine services per month in summer, four in winter; the trip takes 22 hours and the fare is TD 65.000.

Addresses

There are CTN offices in:

Tunisia
   122 Rue de Yougoslavie, Tunis (tel 242 801)

Italy
   Tirrenia Line, Ufficio Passeggeri, Ponte Colombo, Genoa 16100 (tel 25 8041)
   Rione Sirignano 2, 80121 Naples, (tel 721 662)
France
   SNCM, 61 Blvd des Dames, 13002 Marseilles (tel 91 91 92 20)
UK
   Serena Holidays, 40/42 Kenway Rd, London, SW 5 (tel 373 6548)
West Germany
   Karl Geuther GmbH, Heinrichstr 9, Frankfurt 6000 (tel 730 4711)

There are Tirrenia Line offices in:

Tunisia
   CTN, 122 Rue de Yougoslavie, Tunis, (tel 242 801)
Italy
   Via Roma 385, Palermo (tel 58 5733)
   Corso Italia 52, Trapani
   Stazione Marittima, Molo Angiono, Naples (tel 551 2181)
   Agenave, Via Campidano 1, Cagliari, Sardinia (tel 66 6065)
France
   SNCM, 12 Rue Godot de Mauroy, Paris 75009 (tel 42 66 60 19)
Switzerland
   Avimare Ltd, Oerlikonerstr 47, Zürich 8057 (tel 311 7650)
UK
   Serena Holidays, 40-42 Kenway Rd, London SW5 0RA (tel 373 6548)
West Germany
   Karl Geuther GmbH, Heinrichstr 9, Frankfurt 6000 (tel 730 4711)

Getting Around

The transport network is fairly well developed and, with the short distances, just about every town in the country has daily connections of some sort with Tunis.

For most of the year there is ample public transport to meet the demand. However, in the summer months, particularly August and September, there are many more people travelling, both locals and tourists, and competition for seats is high. At these times booking in advance is highly recommended.

AIR

Being such a small country there is very little call for a domestic network, but Tunis Air does operate the following services: Tunis to Jerba (at least one per day; TD 22 one way); Tunis to Tozeur (Mondays); Tunis to Sfax (Thursdays); Tunis to Monastir (Mondays); Monastir to Jerba (Fridays); and Tozeur to Jerba (Mondays).

BUS
SNTRI Bus

The national bus company operates daily air-con buses to just about every town in the country. To the smaller places there is only one departure per day, while to major places there are three or four. The green-and-yellow buses run pretty much to schedule, are fast, comfortable and are not too expensive. For long-distance travel, they are the way to go.

In summer many of the departures are at night to avoid the heat of the day, so if you want to see something of the country you are travelling through you will have to go by louage, local bus or hitch.

Booking in advance, especially when leaving from Tunis, is advisable, particularly in the summer months.

There are departures from Tunis to:

Jerba; five daily, 11 hours
Medenine; two daily, eight hours
Tataouine; one daily, nine hours
Zarzis; one daily, 11 hours
Gabès; four daily, six hours
Matmata; one daily, seven hours
Tozeur; three daily, nine hours
Gafsa; five daily, 7½ hours
Douz; one daily, 10 hours
Nefta; one daily, 10 hours
Le Kef; six daily, four hours
Kasserine; five daily, six hours
Sfax; five daily, five hours
Sousse; seven daily, two hours
Kairouan; eight daily, 2½ hours
Bizerte; several daily, one hour
Tabarka; four daily, five hours
Jendouba; eight daily, four hours

All these buses stop en route to pick up and set down passengers, so you don't have to be going all the way to or from Tunis to use them; however, there is no guarantee that seats will be available if you want to pick one up en route.

Regional Buses

In addition to the national company, there are regional bus companies which operate services in a particular region, to other nearby cities just outside the region and often to Tunis as well.

The buses are reliable enough but are often getting on a bit, are slow and are never air conditioned. Coverage of routes is good and is enough to meet demand most of the time. Booking in advance is not necessary and, in fact, just finding out when buses actually leave can be a major exercise in persistence, as you'll often get conflicting answers. The best you can hope for is that you will be able to confirm that there will be at least one bus sometime that day. Most depots do not have timetables displayed. Louages are usually a better bet but are a good deal more expensive.

TRAIN

The rail network is not all that well developed, and the services are often slow and inconvenient. The exception is the coastal route from Tunis to Sfax and Gabès, where there are frequent air-con express services going via Sousse. To the south-west, a line goes to Tozeur, but passenger services have been discontinued and now go only as far as Metlaoui.

Lines run from Tunis to Ghardimao, Tozeur, Sousse (Monastir and Mahdia), Sfax and Gabès (this is being extended to Medenine). There are quite a few other lines in the country but they are either obsolete or carry freight services only.

Train fares are generally slightly more than what you would pay for a bus, and on the air-con services you pay a supplement which hikes up the cost. Demand for seats is high during the summer, so book in advance if possible.

There are services from Tunis to: Nabeul (12 daily, two direct and the others involve a change at Bir Bou Rebka, 1½ hours); Sousse (eight daily, two hours); Mahdia (one daily, 3½ hours); El Jem (four daily, three hours); Sfax (six daily, 3½ hours); Gabès (three daily, five to six hours); Metlaoui (one daily via Sfax, 8½ hours); and Ghardimao (five daily, one continuing on to Algeria, 3 hours).

TAXI

Louages are long-distance taxis, nearly all of them old, white Peugeot 404 station wagons with an extra seat in the back. They take five passengers and leave when full. They are the fastest way to get around, as it never takes long for one to fill up, and they are generally quite comfortable, as the five-person limit is always adhered to.

The louage 'station' in most towns is usually just a convenient gathering point – a vacant lot or other open space – close to the town centre. In Tunis there are at least half a dozen of these and they tend to change from time to time as new buildings are put up and others come down. If you are asking locals for directions to the louage station (or anywhere else for that matter) always get a second (and even third) opinion, as it's quite possible you'll inadvertently be led astray.

The louages themselves are instantly recognisable by their roof-racks with white identification sign on the front and back. These have a town name on them – in Arabic or English or both – but, unfortunately, these do not tell you where the vehicle is going – just where it's licensed.

At certain times, particularly during the summer, public transport is in high demand and competition for seats on louages can be fierce. You may find it necessary to be fairly ruthless when it comes to the battle for a seat or you will simply not get on. Fortunately, this situation does not arise that often.

BOAT

There are two regular scheduled ferry services in the country.

The first connects Sfax with the Kerkennah Islands, which lie about 25 km off the coast. In summer there are five crossings daily, dropping to three in winter. The trip takes 1½ hours and costs 500 mills per person and TD 4.500 for a vehicle. If you are taking a vehicle across you need to get in the queue well before the first departure at 7.30 am to be assured of getting across that morning.

The second service runs from Jorf on the mainland to Ajim on the island of Jerba. The crossing takes only a few minutes and the ferries run throughout the day and night.

DRIVING

Tunisia's roads are mostly excellent and are tar surfaced. The minor roads in the north are usually just a single narrow strip of bitumen.

In the south there are more unsurfaced roads but these are usually easily negotiated. The worst road you are likely to encounter is the one from Matmata direct to Medenine; though people will tell you it's for 4WDs only, it can be negotiated with caution in even the small Fiats and Citroens that the car rental companies have. Everywhere else the roads are surfaced.

Tunisian drivers are generally well behaved, and drive fairly safely and predictably. For someone used to driving in Europe, the worst thing is not the cars but the thousands of moped riders who weave suicidally in and out of the traffic, and the pedestrians who think that it is their inalienable right to walk on the road regardless of traffic conditions. Don't expect them to move, even when it is blindingly obvious that they are a hazard to everyone, especially themselves.

Car Rental Hire cars can be a great way to see the country in a bit more detail, but unless you have a fat wallet they're not a realistic option. All the major international operators have offices in the larger towns. You need four people before it starts to become affordable.

Rental conditions are fairly straight-forward. If you are paying by cash, a deposit of roughly the equivalent of the rental is required. Credit cards don't have the same restriction.

Typical rental charges for the smallest cars (Citroen LNA or Fiat Uno) are about TD 12 per day plus 120 mills per km. It is cheaper to take an unlimited-km deal, which works out to around TD 270 per week and includes insurance and the mandatory government tax of 14.3%. With the price of fuel being set at 470 mills per litre the costs mount up.

In summer, particularly in Jerba and Tunis, it's almost impossible to get a car straight away. You may have to wait up to a week unless you are prepared to take a larger and more expensive model. Book as early as possible and check with the company every day to make sure that they don't forget your booking, as this does happen. Out of season when things are much quieter you can easily get a small car and it is even sometimes possible to bargain a bit on the rates, especially if you are paying cash.

When you hire the car make sure there is an accident report form with the car's papers. If you have an accident while driving a hire car, both parties involved in the accident must complete the form. If you don't you may be liable for the costs, regardless of whether you have paid for insurance or not.

There are military checkpoints all over the country and, although they are not too bothered with checking foreigners, make sure you have your passport handy at all times.

MOTORCYCLE
The short distances and fair road conditions make motorcycling an ideal way of making the most of Tunisia. Unfortunately, unless you bring your own motorbike you won't be enjoying it, as there is no motorcycle rental in the country.

It is, however, possible to rent mopeds, but only on Jerba. This is by far the best way to see the island, and is affordable at TD 8 for a half day (six hours) or TD 12 for a full day. There is no insurance or licensing of any sort, so you have to ride to survive.

If you are bringing your own motorbike, make sure you are carrying some basic spare parts; these are virtually impossible to find within the country, as people just don't own motorbikes in Tunisia.

BICYCLE
Also an excellent way to see the country. In the height of summer it would be uncomfortably hot and winter is bleak, especially in the north, but for the rest of the year conditions are ideal. It's also possible to put a bike on the train, if you want to skip a long stretch or get yourself back to Tunis.

There are a few places where bicycle rental is possible and you pay about TD 2 per day. A lot of the bikes are horrible old rattlers that leave you tired and sore at the end of the day. Where possible, check the bikes available for the best one and make sure that the brakes work. The locals are only really concerned that the bike goes, and aren't too bothered about how to stop it. Maintenance is done on a very casual basis – when something stuffs up it gets patched up, but nothing is done that might prevent the thing from failing in the first place.

Where there is no set up for renting bikes, it is worth asking at one of the many local bike repair shops in each town to see if they will rent you one for a few hours – they often will.

HITCHING

Hitching is a definite possibility for one person, but is more difficult (though not impossible) for two.

Conditions for hitching vary throughout the country. The south is easiest, as there is a great deal more tourist traffic, either people who hire cars in Jerba or overlanders heading for Tozeur and the Sahara. You shouldn't have to wait more than a couple of hours for a lift. In the north people seem less inclined to pick up hitchers, particularly in the summer when there are so many tourists in the country.

Between small towns the Peugeot 404 pick-up is the usual means of transport and hitching on these is standard practice, although you may well be asked to pay something. If in doubt, check before you get in as to whether the driver expects payment or not and try to establish what the locals are paying if you think you are being ripped off.

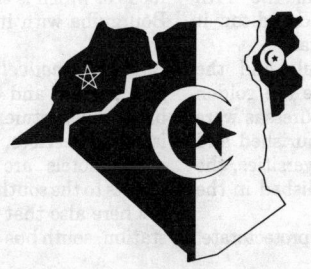

Tunis

Despite the claims made in the tourist literature, Tunis is not a wildly exciting city. The medina is only mildly interesting, and the French *ville nouvelle* (new city) is plain and functional in the extreme with few redeeming features. It is the places surrounding the city, rather than Tunis itself, which are interesting.

As far as capital cities go, however, Tunis has an easy-going, unhurried air about it. It is quite easy to spend a few pleasant days here wandering in the medina, exploring the nearby ruins of Carthage and sitting on the beaches.

Tunis is many people's first introduction to Africa and the Arabs, and in this respect it is an easy place to make the adjustment from west to east. In fact, wandering around the new city it is hard to tell that you are in a Muslim country, let alone in Africa. Islam takes a fairly liberal form in the country, and the capital leads the way as far as western trends go.

History

With Carthage as a neighbour, Tunis remained in the background for centuries. In fact it wasn't until the Aghlabid ruler Ibrahim Ahmed I made it his residence and built the Great Mosque there that it took on any significance.

Its glory was shortlived, for the Fatimids chose Mahdia as their capital in the 10th century. However, the ravages of the Beni Hilal invasion in the 11th century left Tunis untouched and saw it once again become the capital.

The period of Hafsid rule and the following two centuries were the golden age of Tunis: souks and medressas were built, trade with Europe flourished and one of the great Islamic universities, the Zitouna Mosque, was established in the heart of the medina.

Until the time of the French protectorate,

the medina remained very much the centre of things. However, when the French arrived they wasted no time in stamping their influence on the place by building a *ville nouvelle* directly to the east of the medina.

This new city, laid out on a grid, is today very much the heart of Tunis; it has a distinctly European feel with its wide main boulevard, street cafés and buildings complete with cast-iron balconies and wooden shutters.

Orientation

The city lies at the western end of the shallow and often smelly Lake of Tunis, which opens to the sea at La Goulette (the gullet). This is the first of a string of beach suburbs which stretch away to the north and it's here that the city's port is located. This coast area includes the ruins of Carthage and the picturesque coastal suburb of Sidi Bou Said (both dealt with in the Around Tunis section).

The lake itself is certainly not a thing of beauty and pollution is an increasing problem. However, in November there are often pink flamingoes on the edge of the causeway, resting up on their way from Europe to the lakes of Kenya. The causeway carrying both motor vehicles and the light-rail TGM line runs clear across the centre of the lake and connects the beach suburbs, Carthage and the port with the centre of the *ville nouvelle*, the focus of which is the wide, tree-lined Ave Bourguiba with its shady central paved strip.

The *ville nouvelle* is laid out on a formal grid pattern and contains all the major banks, department stores and administrative services. Virtually all the mid-range hotels are concentrated in the streets to the south of Ave Bourguiba, and it's here also that you'll find the railway station, south bus station and most of the louage stations. Most of these streets are one way only, and it can be very frustrating getting to where you want to be if you are driving.

At the western end of Ave Bourguiba is the Place de la Victoire and the entrance to the medina, where you'll find the cheap hotels, souvenir shops and points of interest.

The airport is only eight km to the north-east.

Information

Tourist Office The tourist office is on Ave Bourguiba, at Place de l'Afrique with its chevalier statue. This is the head office of the tourist authority, but the staff have only a limited amount of printed information, are none too clued up about things in Tunis and do not speak English. Getting information out of them can be like pulling teeth. The printed information in English is all of the glossy brochure type, full of flowery descriptions of places of interest.

The office is open from 8 am to 1.30 pm Monday to Saturday in summer, and 8 am to 12 noon and 3 to 6 pm in winter; closed Sundays and public holidays.

There is another branch of the tourist office at the railway station, which hands out train timetables among other things; yet another branch can be found on the mezzanine level at the airport.

Post The main post office is the cavernous old building on Rue Charles de Gaulle, between Rue d'Espagne and Rue d'Angleterre. The poste restante counter is efficient and well organised. Postage stamps can often be bought from the small booths just inside the doors, which saves queuing with the mobs.

The post office is open in summer from 7.30 am to 12.30 pm and 5 to 7 pm Monday to Thursday, 7.30 am to 1.30 pm Friday and Saturday, and 9 to 11 am on Sunday.

Telephone, Telegram & Telex The tele-communications office is in the same building as the post office, but the entrance is around the other side in Rue Jamel Abdelnasser.

It is open 24 hours and, although it can be crowded at times, making international calls is straightforward; you can dial direct to Europe and many other countries.

Money There are branches of the major banks along Ave Bourguiba, most of which are open longer than normal hours. The branch of the STB next to the Africa Hotel is one such bank.

There is another branch of the STB at the airport inside the arrivals hall, before you clear customs, which is open to meet incoming flights; however, if you arrive late at night you will probably have to wait for someone to come and open it up.

American Express American Express is represented by Carthage Tours (tel 254 605) at 59 Ave Bourguiba.

Thomas Cook Thomas Cook is represented by Wagon-Lits Tourisme (tel 347 622), 3rd floor, International Hotel, cnr Ave Bourguiba and Ave de Paris.

Embassies & Consulates Tunis is a good place to pick up visas, as most countries in West Africa are represented here. The embassy area is up around the northern end of Ave de la Liberté. Buses No 5 and 35 go along the parallel Rue de Palestine, or a taxi costs about 500 mills from Ave Bourguiba.

The Algerian Consulate is open for visas from 8.30 to 11.30 am Monday to Saturday. One-month tourist visas cost TD 9.500, require four photos and are issued on the same day if you apply before 10.30 am.

For a list of countries which have diplomatic representation here see the Facts for the Visitor chapter for Tunisia.

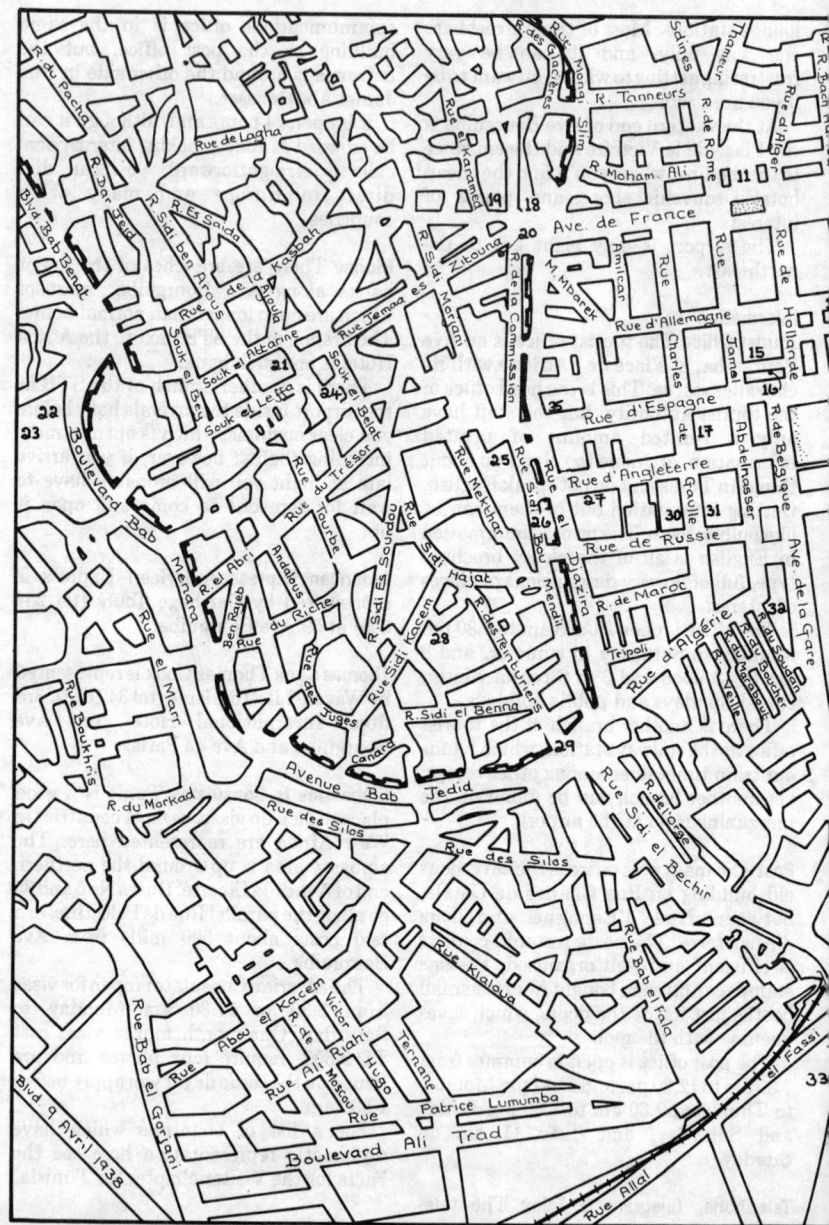

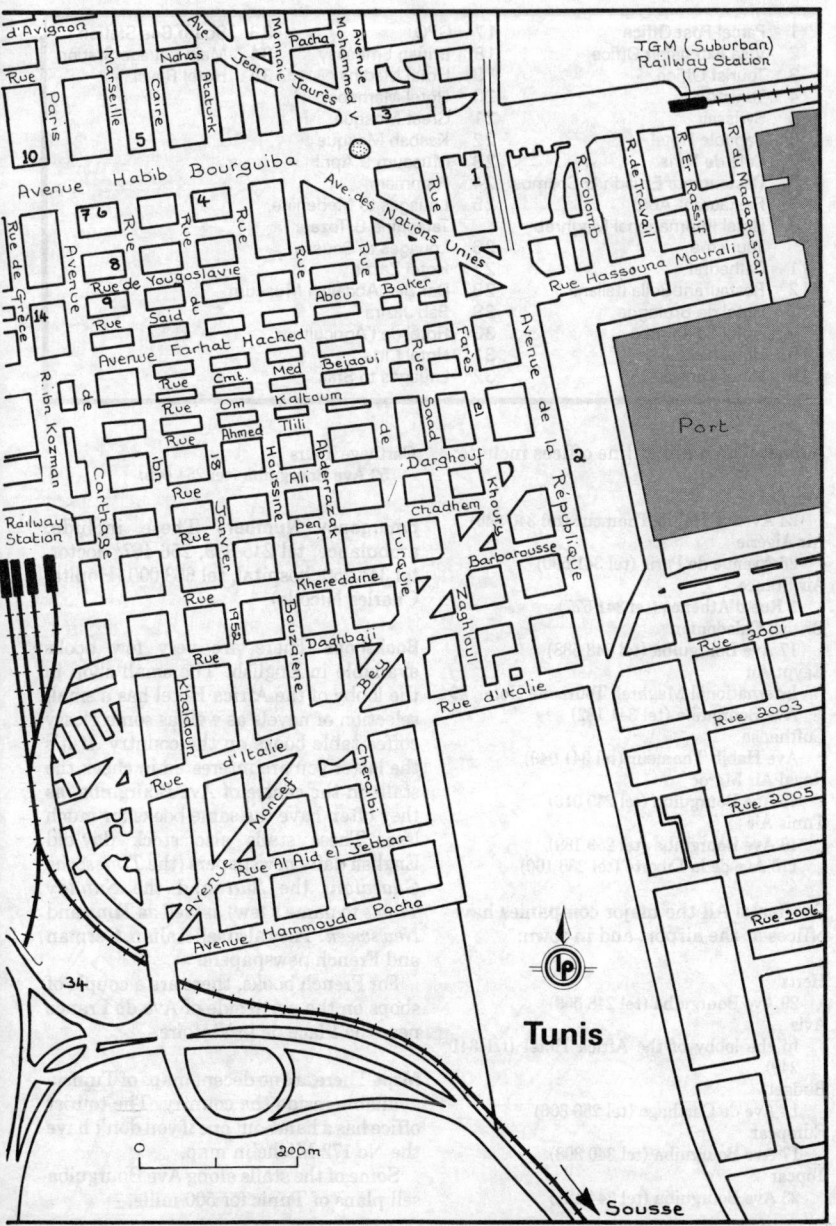

1	Parcel Post Office	17	GPO	33	South Bus Station
2	Visa Extension Office	18	British Embassy	34	Main Louage Station
3	Tourist Office	19	Hotel Medina	35	Hotel Royal
4	Tunis Air	20	Hotel Marhaba		
5	Swissair	21	Great Mosque		
6	Capitole Hotel	22	Kasbah Mosque		
7	Café de Paris	23	Museum 9 April		
8	Restaurants Erriadh & Cosmos	24	Hammam		
9	Restaurant Abid	25	Louages to Medenine,		
10	Hotel International Maghreb		Tataouine & Tozeur		
	Tourisme	26	Louages to Sousse		
11	Cathedral	27	Hotel Zarzis		
12	Restaurant Bella Italiana	28	Dar Ben Abdallah Museum		
13	Hotel de Bretagne	29	Bab Jazira		
14	Hotel Salammbô	30	Hotel de l'Agriculture		
15	Hotel de Suisse	31	Hotel Cirta		
16	Hotel Central	32	Louages to Sfax		

Airlines The main airline offices include:

Aeroflot
24 Avenue Habib Thameur (tel 340 845)
Air Algérie
26 Avenue de Paris (tel 341 590)
Air France
1 Rue d'Athènes (tel 341 577)
British Caledonian
17 Ave Bourguiba (tel 248 588)
Egypt Air
International Maghreb Tourisme Hotel, 49 Ave Bourguiba (tel 341 182)
Lufthansa
Ave Habib Thameur (tel 341 049)
Royal Air Maroc
45 Ave Bourguiba (tel 249 016)
Tunis Air
48 Ave Bourguiba (tel 259 189)
113 Ave de la Liberté (tel 288 100)

Car Rental All the major companies have offices at the airport and in town:

Hertz
29 Ave Bourguiba (tel 248 559)
Avis
In the lobby of the Africa Hotel (tel 341 249)
Budget
14 Ave de Carthage (tel 256 806)
Europcar
17 Ave Bourguiba (tel 340 308)
Topcar
23 Ave Bourguiba (tel 344 121)

Carthage Tours
59 Ave Bourguiba (tel 254 605)

Emergency Numbers These include: ambulance, tel 245 339, 256 467; doctor, tel 341 250; hospital, tel 663 000 (Hôpital Charles Nicolle).

Bookshops There are very few books available in English. The small shop in the lobby of the Africa Hotel has a small selection of novels as well as some glossy coffee-table books on the country. If it's the latter you are interested in check the stalls in the centre of Ave Bourguiba, as they often have the same books for much less. These stalls also stock day-old English daily newspapers (the *Times*, the *Guardian*, the *Sun* and the *Sunday Times* to name a few) as well as *Time* and *Newsweek*. They also sell Italian, German and French newspapers.

For French books, there are a couple of shops on the north side of Ave de France near the Place de la Victoire.

Maps There are no decent maps of Tunisia available inside the country. The tourist office has a hand-out one if you don't have the No 172 Michelin map.

Some of the stalls along Ave Bourguiba sell plans of Tunis for 500 mills.

Film & Photography There are shops dotted all over the centre which sell and process print film. The one on the corner of Ave Bourguiba and Rue de Rome also does cheap black-and-white passport photos on the spot.

Handicrafts To get an idea of what the best stuff available is like, visit the ONAT showroom on the corner of Ave Bourguiba and Ave de Carthage. There is a large selection of crafts from all over the country; both the quality and prices are high.

Hammams If you are staying in a hotel without washing facilities, or if you just feel like a hot sauna and bath, there are a couple of hammams in the medina. One of the best is at 30 Souk des Libraries; enter through the barber shop.

There's another at 11 Rue el-Methira, not far from the Rue des Teinturiers, but you'll have to ask for directions. It's open all day but is reserved for women between 1 and 3 pm.

The hammam at 64 Rue des Teinturiers is for men only; a bath here costs between 500 and 650 mills.

Beaches The beaches of Tunis are all accessible by TGM. La Marsa, at the end of the line, is the best of them and is less crowded than those at Amilcar and La Goulette.

Medina

The medina in Tunis certainly doesn't compare with those in Cairo or Fès, but then again it is a whole lot more manageable and hassle free. If you have just come from Europe it is the ideal place to get a feel for the way of life, as the medina, with it's mosques, cafés and hammams, is the focal point of any Arab city.

With the building of the *ville nouvelle* by the French on reclaimed land by the east gate early this century, the medina lost its importance as the centre of the city; a lot of what remains would also go, if it weren't for the thousands of tourists who pour through here each summer.

The most usual entry is through (or around) the old Porte de France gate at the end of Ave de France. From this paved square, Place de la Victoire, which is something of an assembly point in the evenings, there are two roads which lead off in a 'V' to the heart of the medina and the Great Mosque. The one to the right, Rue de la Kasbah, is of little interest but is lined fairly solidly with shops catering to all tourist tastes. The street to the left, Rue Jemaa es Zitouna, is the one along which most tourists get led into the medina, and so contains the bulk of the souvenir shops and the most aggressive storekeepers (although these guys are really not too bad). If you just want to get an idea of prices, or have to do a bit of last-minute shopping, this is the place to do it. If you are going to other parts of the country you can buy the same stuff for quite a bit less elsewhere.

Great Mosque Rue Jemaa es Zitouna eventually comes out at the entrance to the Great Mosque. Built by the Aghlabids in the 9th century, it was an important centre of theological study right up to the 1950s. Today it is just an ordinary mosque, and non-Muslims are allowed in as far as the courtyard between 8 am and 12 noon daily, except Friday; modest dress is compulsory.

Souks The street to the left of the Great Mosque, the Souk des Libraries, has several medressas (old Islamic colleges). Through the barber shop at number 30 is a fairly clean and spacious hammam.

To the right of the Great Mosque are more souks named after the main business activity which used to be carried on there. To a certain extent these names are still appropriate, but the medina is gradually decreasing in importance as the commercial area.

One of the most interesting souks is the

Souk des Chechias, where you can see the traditional red felt hats being made. They are now being made in various other lairy colours for the tourist trade. This souk runs between Rue Sidi ben Arous and Souk el Bey, just to the right and behind the Great Mosque.

Dar el Bey & Kasbah Mosque The prime minister's office is now housed in the Dar el Bey, a former palace guest house on Souk el Bey. The guards are a real sight in their fancy red uniforms.

The Dar el Bey is on the the western edge of the medina at the Place de la Kasbah, and on the rise above this stood the kasbah; this is now an enormous building site. The Kasbah Mosque here dates from the 13th century. The call to prayer is signalled by a white flag hung from the pole on the minaret. You have to be quick to spot it, as they hang it out for only a minute or two.

Museum 9 April Just beyond the Kasbah Mosque is the Museum 9 April, which is housed in an old prison where Bourguiba was once interned for a while. It is full of photos and other memorabilia related to the fight for independence. Unfortunately, what could be an interesting display is rendered totally meaningless to non-Arabic speaking (and reading) people, although the tiny cells speak for themselves.

Rue des Teinturiers & Dar Ben Abdallah Museum Back at the bottom of the medina the Rue des Teinturiers, one of the main thoroughfares, is off to the left of Rue Jemaa es Zitouna; it takes you to the southern gate, Bab Al Jazira. Along its length are a few points of interest. The street itself is named after the dyers who used to carry on their business here. There are a few still left in a couple of small alleys leading off to the right of the street about halfway along.

One of the finest sights in the old city, the Dar Ben Abdallah Museum, is

signposted off the Rue des Teinturiers along Rue Sidi Kacem. Once an old palace, it now houses a collection of traditional costumes and everyday items. The building itself is probably of more interest: it has the usual highly ornate entrance way leading to the marble courtyard complete with fountains and sculptures. Part of the entrance hall has been shored up and looks none too safe, although I was assured it was not in danger of imminent collapse. In one room is a very detailed map of the medina with all the hammams shown on it. Exactly why it is there I don't know, but it can be handy to know the location of the one nearest to your hotel if you are staying in a medina cheapie without showers.

At Bab Jedid the street opens out onto the busy Place Bab Al Jazira; this section of the old city has a more Arab feel to it than most, probably because it is just left to get on with things and doesn't have a constant parade of tourists through it.

New City

There are very few points of interest in the ville nouvelle. The only unusual building is the cathedral on Ave Bourguiba, and that is remarkable only for its ugliness. It was built by the French in 1882.

The streets are lined with French buildings complete with louvre windows and balconies with wrought-iron railings. This gives the whole place a very European air, which is heightened by the numerous patisseries selling all manner of both sweet and savoury pastries, and the pavement cafés.

Bardo Museum

The best museum in the country, the Bardo is in an outer suburb to the west of the medina and is housed in an old palace set in a large garden. Even if you are normally bored shitless by museums, you'll be missing out badly if you don't pay at least a brief visit to the Bardo.

It is organised in sections, which cover

the Carthaginian, Roman, Palaeo-Christian and Arab-Islamic eras.

The most interesting and by far the most impressive display is that of mosaics from the Roman era. It is no exaggeration to say that the Bardo has one of the best collections anywhere in the world, and just when you think you have seen the best, another room reveals something bigger and better. There are so many mosaics, in fact, that they are overwhelming, and excellent pieces that would stand out on their own elsewhere get lost in the floor-to-ceiling displays. It is worth making a couple of half-day trips here if you are keen, rather than trying to do it all in one hit and becoming so saturated that it is hard to look at yet another mosaic.

The best mosaics include the one of the poet Virgil flanked by the muses of literature and drama (room 15) and that of the monumental triumph of Neptune (room 10). The statues in room 6 from Bulla Regia are also worth a look.

Not to be missed is the haul from the wreck of a boat which came to grief off the coast at Mahdia in the 1st century BC. It was carrying a load of marble and bronze statuary, which adds some welcome variety to the museum. They are displayed in rooms 17 to 22.

The Islamic section would be more interesting were it not for the fact that it is totally overshadowed and outclassed by the other exhibits.

The Bardo is open from 9.30 am to 4.30 pm Tuesday to Saturday; the only public holiday on which it is not open is the Eid festival at the end of Ramadan. Entry is TD 1 and there is a further charge of TD 1 if you want to take photos. To get there take a No 3 bus from opposite the Africa Hotel. It terminates right opposite the museum grounds, but the entrance is a couple of hundred metres further on and around the corner to the right.

Places to Stay

All hotels display a chart, both at reception and on the back of the door in the rooms, listing the maximum price they can charge. In the off season the prices are definitely negotiable, but in summer just finding an empty room can be a major job if you are searching late in the day.

Places to Stay - bottom end

The real cheapies are either in the medina or very close to it. Most are extremely basic and often have no shower; this isn't really a problem, as there are a number of hammams dotted around.

On Rue de la Kasbah, which enters the medina near the British Embassy at Place de la Victoire, there are two hotels on the left after about 50 metres. They are both typical basic Tunisian hostelries and are not recommended for women alone. Expect to pay about TD 1.500 for a bed in a share room. The first is the *Hotel le Soleil* at No 32, and the other is the *Hotel Baghdad* a couple of doors away. The Soleil is marginally the better of the two.

Just in the new city, on the edge of the medina, is the *Hotel Royal* on Rue d'Espagne. One street to the south, the *Hotel Zarzis* (tel 248 031) is at 20 Rue d'Angleterre. The Zarzis charges TD 4 for a double room and there are (free) cold showers; the Royal is only slightly more expensive.

The *Hotel Medina* is on Place de la Victoire at the entrance to the medina. It is basic but clean enough and singles/doubles cost TD 3/6; hot showers are 500 mills. Unlike a lot of the cheapies it has a few windows and doesn't get quite as stuffy in summer.

In the new city, not far from the railway station, is the *Hotel de Bretagne* at 7 Rue de Grèce. It is quite OK: rooms have a washbasin and cost TD 4.500 for a double; showers are 500 mills.

One of the best places is the *Hotel Cirta* (tel 241 582) at 42 Rue Charles de Gaulle, five minutes' walk from the railway station and post office, 15 minutes' walk from the bus station. It has over 30 rooms, so takes a little longer to fill up in summer. Rooms cost TD 2.500 for a single, TD 5 for a double, and have a bidet and washbasin. The whole place is cleaned daily and is spotless. The only drawback is that not only do you pay 500 mills for a hot shower, but they charge the same for a cold one. The traffic noise from the street can be high at times, but this is common to virtually all the hotels. The *Hotel de l'Agriculture* right across the road is similar to the Cirta, although it's a little less friendly.

Two of the few quiet hotels are both on a small lane (Rue de Suisse) which runs between Rue de Hollande and Rue Jemal Abdelnasser, one block north of Place de Barcelone. The *Hotel de Suisse* is run by a friendly guy who speaks English (one of the few); rooms cost TD 5 for a double with washbasin, one dinar more with bath. The other place is the *Hotel Central*, which costs the same but has no singles and only cold showers.

If you really get stuck and it's too late to make the trek out to the youth hostel, you can crash out on the grass in the small park next to the railway station at the end of Rue de Russie. It's neither private nor comfortable nor highly recommended (women shouldn't even consider it), but it might do at a pinch.

Youth Hostel If you really want to stay in a youth hostel, or find that everything in the centre is full, catch a suburban (*banlieue*) train from the main station to the southern suburb of Radès. It's about a 20-minute ride from the centre. The train takes you through a disgracefully polluted area of heavy industries complete with accompanying pungent odours – a real disaster area. But I digress: the trains run every half-hour between 4.30 and 1.30 am.

From the Radès station, take the street straight up the hill and follow the road around to the left (there's a sign to the *Youth Hostel* which says 900m); after about 500 metres you come to a garden

with a white-domed building at the bottom of the hill. Turn right here, and the hostel is 100 metres along on the left. The locals all know it, so if you get lost ask for the *auberge de jeunesse*.

The hostel itself is the usual charmless barrack block and is open only from 7 to 10 pm. Charges are TD 1.500 per night, breakfast 500 mills and dinner TD 1.900; the food is just edible.

Camping The nearest site is over 20 km to the south at Hammam Plage near Hammam Lif.

Places to Stay – middle
The *Hotel Bristol* is in the small cobbled alley (Rue Lt Mohammed Aziz Tedj) one block back from Ave Bourguiba, behind the Café de Paris. It doesn't offer anything more than the cheaper places but is conveniently located. Basic rooms cost TD 7.

A bit more comfortable is the *Hotel Salammbô* at 6 Rue de Grèce. Despite its kitschy foyer decor and pink rooms, it is quite good value at TD 9 for a double with bath; breakfast is included in the price. The *Hotel Transatlantique* at 106 Rue de Yougoslavie, almost on the corner of Rue Ibn Khaldoun, is similar. Both are good value.

If you want to be right in the thick of things on Ave Bourguiba, there's the *Capitole Hotel* (tel 244 987) at No 60, right by the cinema of the same name. Room rates are TD 10.600/16 for singles/doubles, which includes a good breakfast.

Places to Stay – top end
For those people with the money and the inclination Tunis has a full quota of expensive places, some of them real architectural disasters. Take a look at the *Hotel du Lac* at the end of Ave Bourguiba behind the tourist office and you'll see what I mean.

The *Africa Hotel* on Ave Bourguiba is also a bloody great blot on the landscape, especially as it's the only high-rise building in the whole street and practically the whole city. However, even if you are not staying here, the air-con lobby with its luxurious armchairs is a welcome place to catch your breath for a few minutes on a hot and humid day. Expect to pay TD 57/70 for singles/doubles with breakfast.

Also on Ave Bourguiba, the *Hotel International Maghreb Tourisme* charges a mere TD 47.500/60 for singles/doubles.

Hilton hoppers will be happy to find their favourite here too, in Ave Salammbô in the northern suburb of Mutuelleville, 10 minutes by taxi from the centre and the airport.

Places to Eat

Tunis has plenty of cheap and moderately-priced restaurants but, although at first glance there appears to be plenty of variety, they have remarkably similar menus with about a dozen standard dishes. Service, prices and decor are the biggest variables.

For fresh fruit, the stalls around the Place de Barcelone by the railway station have a good selection of melons, peaches, grapes, figs and apples. Street vendors in and around the same area sell various things including halva, bread, nuts, cigarettes and pretzel sticks, all very cheaply.

Patisseries & Rotisseries These are at the bottom of the cheap-eats scale and are found all over the new city.

The patisseries stock all manner of sweet cakes and croissants. They usually do other things like small pizzas and savoury *pâtés*, which are generally excellent and all you need for breakfast or lunch. At the back of these places there is nearly always a café, where you can stand while eating your croissant with a coffee. Some of the best are on Rue Charles de Gaulle, between Ave Bourguiba and Rue d'Espagne.

The rotisseries cook mostly roast (or fried) chicken and chips, but also have salads and, of course, bread. They are mostly stand-up joints where you get served your food in a piece of paper; you either stand around and eat it with everyone else or take it away. You can find these places all over the *ville nouvelle*; they can usually be identified by the chicken-roasting ovens out the front.

Tunisian Restaurants There are a couple of local places, with local prices, which are popular and serve cheap and appetising food.

The best of these is the *Restaurant Carcassonne* at 8 Ave de Carthage just off Ave Bourguiba, near the Café de Paris. Although it is popular with foreigners, it is a basic place with welcome ceiling fans. The best value is the *repas*, a set menu of four courses for TD 2 which is enough to feed two people, especially when supplemented with the unlimited bread that is served here and in every other restaurant in the country. Individual dishes such as couscous and brochettes are also available for around TD 1.500 to TD 2 per plate.

Another similar place is the *Restaurant Abid* on Rue de Yougoslavie, near the corner with Rue Ibn Khaldoun. The menu is limited pretty much to chicken, haricot beans, couscous and brochettes, but the portions are more than adequate and it's a friendly place. Avoid the *Restaurant Erriadh* around the corner on Rue Ibn Khaldoun – there are so many flies in here (in summer at least) that it's a battle to get your food into your mouth before they descend.

Other Restaurants There is a fair scattering of restaurants in which, for between TD 5 and TD 10 per person, you can get a decent meal with local wine. The best of these is the *Restaurant Le Cosmos* (tel 241 610) at 7 Rue Ibn Khaldoun. Despite the awful paint job of the universe on the ceiling, this air-con restaurant serves great food at quite reasonable prices; however, the white-coated waiters are not overly friendly. The fish soup and the fresh fish (brought round on a tray for you to choose from) are both excellent. Expect to pay around TD 12 for two, and get here early (it opens at 7.30 pm) as it's popular in summer.

The *Restaurant l'Etoile* (tel 240 514) at 3 Rue Ibn Khaldoun is similar to and slightly cheaper than Le Cosmos, and is one of the best in town for the money.

Another place in the same area is the *Restaurant Savarin* (tel 244 002) in the same small street as the Hotel Bristol, Rue Lt Mohammed Aziz Tedj, at No 29. It is next to the *Restaurant Poisson d'Or* (avoid this place), which has a large illuminated yellow sign. The Savarin has a good set menu of four courses for TD 2.800 – you get an enormous amount of food. The place has a bit of a men's-club atmosphere, but is friendly and popular with locals. Also good value is the *Restaurant de la Petite Hutte* at 102 Rue Yougoslavie.

Despite the name, the *Restaurant Bella Italiana* in Rue Yougoslavie does nothing specially Italian; still, it has reasonable food for about TD 5 per head for a full meal.

At all these restaurants you need to arrive by about 8.30 pm at the latest or you miss out. Also, surprisingly, many are closed for their annual holidays for at least a couple of weeks right at the height of the season.

Cafés & Bars Café life is well established here, and there are numerous places with tables and chairs out on the footpath. The *Café de Paris* on the corner of Ave Bourguiba and Ave de Carthage is very popular; it can be a good place to pass some time, although you pay a little over the odds for coffee and the croissants are very mediocre.

The bars in Tunis are real drinking dens. They have a thick, smoky atmosphere in which many women might not feel terribly comfortable. One exception is the place next to the Restaurant Carcassonne on Ave de Carthage.

Getting There & Away

Air Tunis Air flies daily to Jerba and less frequently to Tozeur, Sfax and Monastir. It can be difficult to get a flight in the middle of summer.

Bus Tunis has two bus stations, one for departures to the north (Gare Routière Nord de Bab Saadoun) and the other for buses south and to Algeria (Gare Routière Sud de Bab el Alleoua). The north station is a brand new building 200 metres past Bab Saadoun in the north-west of the city. To get there take a No 3 bus from Tunis Marine or Ave Bourguiba opposite the Africa Hotel, and get off at the first stop after Bab Saadoun (which you can't miss, as it's a massive triple-arched gate in the middle of a roundabout); the bus station is 100 metres over to the right.

This station is for departures to Bizerte and other places on the north coast. There are SNTRI departures to: Bizerte (several daily, one hour); Tabarka (four daily, five hours); and Jendouba (eight daily, four hours). There are also SNTRI departures to Ain Draham, Mateur, Menzel Bourguiba and Beja.

From the south station, there are departures for all points in the country other than those already mentioned. As well as the SNTRI air-con buses which can be booked in advance at ticket windows No 1 and 2, some of the regional authorities also run buses to and from Tunis and have their own ticket windows at the station. It can be a bit of a battle to find out about buses and make a booking, especially as the SNTRI timetable is in Arabic. The staff in the booking office will grudgingly help you.

This station is also where you catch the international buses to Annaba (daily, 7 am, 8 hours) and Constantine (every second day, 12 hours) in Algeria; these must definitely be booked the day before departure.

SNTRI departures from Tunis south station are to:

Jerba: five daily, 11 hours
Medenine: two daily, eight hours
Tataouine: one daily, nine hours
Zarzis: one daily, 11 hours
Gabès: four daily, six hours
Matmata: one daily, seven hours
Tozeur: three daily, nine hours
Gafsa: five daily, 7½ hours
Douz: one daily, 10 hours
Nefta: one daily, 10 hours
Le Kef: six daily, four hours
Kasserine: five daily, six hours
Sfax: five daily, five hours
Sousse: seven daily, two hours
Kairouan: eight daily, 2½ hours

Train The railway station is close to the centre of town and is the most convenient place to arrive, as there are plenty of hotels within five minutes' walk. It's a modern and efficient station, with all scheduled departures and arrivals displayed on an electronic board in the terminal building. There is a small information kiosk in the foyer which is staffed irregularly.

Although the services are crowded in summer, there is no need to reserve a seat, although you can do this the day before on the air-con services to Sfax.

There are services from Tunis to: Nabeul (12 daily, two direct and the others involve a change at Bir Bou Rebka, 1½ hours); Sousse (eight daily, two hours); Mahdia (one daily, 3½ hours); El Jem (four daily, three hours); Sfax (six daily, 3½ hours); Gabès (three daily, five to six hours); Metlaoui (one daily via Sfax, 8½ hours); and Ghardimao (five daily, one continuing on to Algeria, three hours).

Taxi Louages are a good alternative to the buses. Although they are more expensive, services are also more flexible: if there are heaps of people trying to travel the louages keep running. They operate mainly in the mornings, so if you are planning on catching one you will have a shorter wait then. Things slow down considerably in the afternoon and you may have to wait a while for one to fill up.

The louage stations are often hard to find, as they are hidden away in the new city and are very informal – usually just a vacant lot. They also tend to be relocated occasionally. The main station, for departures to just about everywhere except the following places, is opposite the south bus station at the foot of the bridge over the railway line.

For louages to Sousse the station is in a yard behind a high wooden fence on Rue al Jazira.

Louages to Medenine, Tataouine and Tozeur leave from a small inconspicuous yard on Rue Sidi Bou Mendil. For Sfax the station is off Rue du Soudan, not far from the railway station.

Boat The ferries from Europe arrive at the port, which is at La Goulette at the end of the causeway across the Lake of Tunis. To get there take a TGM train to La Goulette Vieille, walk back alongside the line towards Tunis until you get to the railway crossing; then turn left and walk for 200 metres, past the kasbah, and there is a sign to the port off to the right. The whole walk takes about 20 minutes.

When arriving at Tunis, come straight out of the port, turn left at the first main intersection (by the kasbah) and walk along to the railway crossing; the station is away to the right. A taxi from the port to Ave Bourguiba shouldn't cost more than TD 1.500.

Getting a booking on a ferry out of Tunis at the height of summer can take days, as the ferries are often booked out for up to 10 days in advance. This is especially so if you are taking a vehicle. Make your reservations as early as possible.

The Tirrenia Line office (tel 242 775) is at 122 Rue de Yougoslavie; it can be a real bunfight here, with people doing battle for tickets. Turn up first thing in the morning when things are marginally less frantic.

There are regular departures to France (Marseilles) and Italy (Genoa, Trapani,

Palermo and Cagliari). See the Tunisia Getting There chapter for full details of services.

Getting Around

Airport Transport The Tunis-Carthage Airport is eight km north-east of the city. Yellow city bus No 35 runs there from the Tunis Marine terminus every 20 minutes or so between about 6 am and 9 pm. You can pick it up at the stop opposite the Africa Hotel. The trip takes about 20 minutes and costs 320 mills. A taxi to the Africa Hotel from the airport will cost around TD 2.

From the airport the bus leaves from just outside the terminal building, to the right of the exit.

Bus The yellow city buses operate to all parts of the city but, apart from getting to the airport or the Bardo Museum, you should have little cause to use them. The destination, point of origin and route number are displayed on a board by the entry door near the back. The number is also displayed in the front window. The set fare for a ride is 120 mills on most routes; 320 mills to the airport.

There are three main terminuses for the buses: Tunis Marine, which is right by the TGM station at the causeway end of Ave Bourguiba; Place de Barcelone, in front of the railway station; and Jardin Thameur, 500 metres north of Ave de France.

The No 3 bus to the Bardo and the No 35 to the airport both leave from Tunis Marine.

TGM This is the light-rail system that connects central Tunis with the beachside suburbs of La Goulette, Carthage, Sidi Bou Said and La Marsa.

It is fast, cheap and convenient, although a little crowded at times. Trains run 24 hours a day, with departures ranging from every 12 minutes during the day to every hour or so in the middle of the night. There are 1st and 2nd-class compartments. There seems to be little

point in forking out the extra for 1st class, although it is less crowded.

The 2nd-class fare from Tunis to La Goulette is 180 mills; to Carthage, Sidi Bou Said and La Marsa it's 320 mills.

Tram There is a fancy new tram service (*Métro Léger*) which runs from near the TGM station to the southern suburbs, passing right in front of the railway station. It is unlikely that you will need to use this service, as it goes nowhere of interest to the traveller.

Taxi Taxis are a fairly cheap way of getting around. They're especially good if you are visiting embassies, as the drivers always know where these are and can save you a good deal of foot slogging. They always use the meter and a trip costs about 500 mills per km.

The only problem with the taxis is that there aren't enough of them. During peak hours this is a real problem; you just have to be patient and lucky. One of the best places to pick one up is by the railway station on Ave de la Gare, while Ave Bourguiba is one of the worst places.

Around Tunis

There are quite a few places within day-trip distance of Tunis. Strictly speaking, the beach suburbs of Carthage, Sidi Bou Said and La Marsa are part of Tunis but it takes a day trip to visit any or all of them.

Further away to the south are the excellent ruins of the Roman town of Thuburbo Majus; a visit to it can be combined with the nearby town of Zaghouan to make a good day trip.

CARTHAGE
Despite its fascinating history and the position of dominance which Carthage held in the ancient world, the Romans did such a thorough demolition job on it that

Carthage map

the ruins today are a major disappointment. For a full account of the city's history, see the Facts about the Region chapter.

Most of what there is to see is of Roman origin and there's not that much of it. However, as Carthage is so accessible it's worth wandering around for a couple of hours. This can be combined with a visit to Sidi Bou Said or the beach at La Marsa.

If you have only a few hours, then the best bet is to limit yourself to the museum and the ruins of Byrsa right outside it. With half a day you could also see the Antonine Baths, the Punic ports and the theatre, and in a whole day you would be able to see the lot.

The real hassle is that the sites are quite spread out; although you can overcome this to a certain extent by making use of the TGM line which runs bang through the middle of the area, seeing everything requires a good deal of walking. In the heat

and humidity of summer this is more hassle than it's worth.

If you are intent on seeing the whole lot, the best way to tackle it is as follows: take the TGM to Carthage Salammbô and walk down to Tophet, the Punic ports and the Oceanographic Museum. From there take the TGM from Carthage Byrsa to Carthage Hannibal and head for the sea again to see the Magon Quarter. From here go back up the hill to the museum and Byrsa, and continue down the other side to the amphitheatre and cisterns; then go along the back road to the US war cemetery, from which you can cut across country to the basilica. From there, walk to the sea and the Antonine Baths via the theatre and Roman villas. Then take the street just back behind the sea to the Magon quarter, by which time you should be well and truly fucked – ha ha!! no, from where it's a short walk to the Carthage Hannibal TGM station. Covering this whole route would take the best part of a day.

Some of these sites have entry charges (usually TD 1), but you can get in free on presentation of a an ISIC student card.

Tophet

When it was first excavated in 1921 this site created a good deal of excitement, as it revealed the first evidence of child sacrifice. The area contained urns, each marked with a stele and full of burnt child remains. However, just how these children died is still open to debate. The Romans, were keen to condemn anything Carthaginian and got plenty of mileage out of the child sacrifice issue. Just how widely it was carried on is not known, although it certainly did exist and probably only died out after contacts with the Greeks and Romans. Animal sacrifice played a far bigger part in the local religion.

The word 'tophet' is in fact Hebrew and refers to a place near Jerusalem where human sacrifice was carried out. The

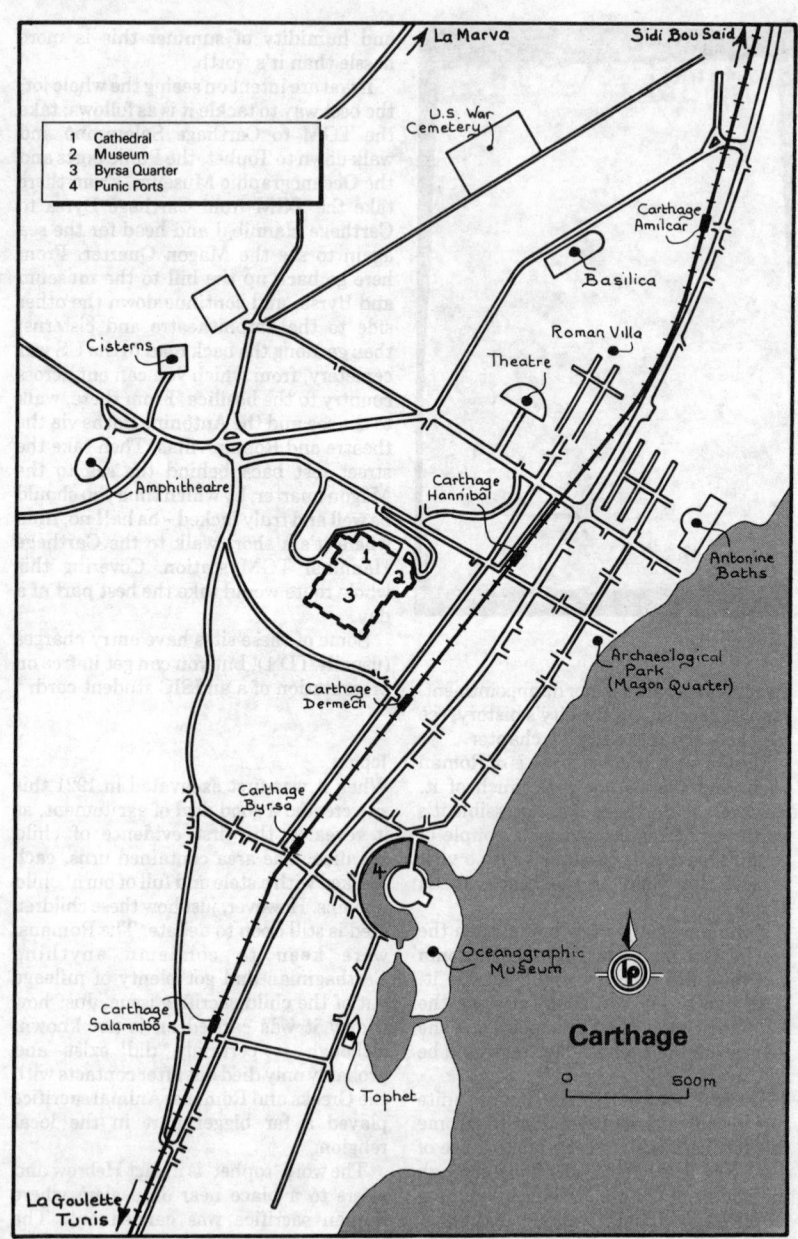

1 Cathedral
2 Museum
3 Byrsa Quarter
4 Punic Ports

La Marva

Sidi Bou Said

U.S. War Cemetery

Carthage Amilcar

Basilica

Cisterns

Roman Villa

Theatre

Amphitheatre

Carthage Hannibal

Antonine Baths

Archaeological Park (Magon Quarter)

Carthage Dermech

Carthage Byrsa

Oceanographic Museum

Carthage Salammbô

Carthage

0   500m

Tophet

La Goulette Tunis

Top: City centre, Ave Bourguiba, Tunis (HF)
Left: Cathedral, Tunis (HF)
Right: Mosque at Tataouine, Tunisia (HF)

Top: Watermelon stall in suburban Tunis (HF)
Left: Courtyard of the Great Mosque, Kairouan, Tunisia (HF)
Right: Ruined village of Chenini, Tunisia (HF)

other name for Tophet in Carthage is the Sanctuary of Tanit.

Today the small site which covers half an acre or so is basically a patch of overgrown weeds with a few excavated pits. There are also some vaults here, which are the remains of 4th-century Roman warehouses. Entry is an outrageous TD 1; you can see almost as much from over the low wall, so don't waste your money.

Punic Ports

Although they don't look too impressive today, these two basins were where the Carthaginians set sail from when they set off to challenge Rome. The northern one was the navy base and was originally circular with a diameter of about 300 metres. The island in the centre held the naval headquarters and the whole harbour was surrounded by a high wall on the landward sides. It is said that it could hold as many as 220 warships. The southern harbour was the centre of the commercial shipping.

Oceanographic Museum

This sorry display of fish and things nautical is a total waste of time. Entry is only 200 mills, however, so it won't break you if you feel like a wander around. It is open from 4.30 to 7.30 pm Tuesday to Sunday, and on Sunday mornings as well from 10 am to 12 noon; closed Monday.

Byrsa Hill

This hill dominates the area. To get to the top, head up the hill from Carthage Hannibal through this area of plush diplomats' residences and then go up the stairs to the left at the top of the hill, just near the sign for the Reine Didon (a fancy hotel). Although the museum building is on the left here, the entrance is around to the right on the other side of the cathedral.

The cathedral on top of the hill is visible for miles around. Built in 1890 and an eyesore of truly massive proportions, it was dedicated to the 13th-century French king St Louis. It has now been deconsecrated and is no longer in use.

The National Museum is the large white building at the back of the cathedral. There is surprisingly little on display, but what there is is interesting and well laid out.

The Byrsa Quarter has really the only Carthaginian ruins left. The Romans levelled off the top of the hill, burying the Carthaginian houses under the rubble. The area has been well excavated and the finds are described in full (in French) in the museum.

The Byrsa Quarter and museum are on the same site; entry is TD 1.

Amphitheatre

The amphitheatre is down the other side of the hill, about 15 minutes' walk from the cathedral. It was here that many Christians were thrown into the ring unarmed and left to defend themselves against sword-wielding gladiators or wild animals.

The limited excavations and reconstructions date from 1919. The outer circle is hard to distinguish. The caretaker here will latch on to you and babble away continuously in German or English (of sorts) if you don't speak French and then ask for TD 1.500 at the end.

Across the road from the amphitheatre are some old cisterns, which used to hold the water supply but are now ruined and not worth the scramble through the prickly pear bushes to see.

US War Cemetery & Basilica

The detour out to the war cemetery and basilica is only for the dedicated. The cemetery is extremely well kept, but the basilica across the field amounts to nothing much more than a few piles of stones.

Theatre & Villas

The theatre has been completely covered in concrete, and obscured with lighting towers and equipment for the annual Carthage Festival. It really has very little going for it.

The same applies to the Roman Villas Archaeological Park just downhill from the theatre. This is a joke: they charge you TD 1 to enter a largely decorative site which has been over-restored.

Antonine Baths

These are right down on the waterfront and are impressive more for their size and location than anything else. At the top of the steps just inland from the baths is a marble slab with a diagram of the baths, which helps to give some idea of just how big they used to be.

The entrance is about 100 metres before the sea and the charge is TD 1. From Carthage Hannibal, take the main road (Ave Bourguiba) and turn right where the enormous capital from the baths sits in the middle of the intersection.

Magon Quarter

This is another archaeological park, this time down by the water, one block south of the Antonine Baths. It has recently been excavated by a team of German archaeologists whose work has revealed a residential area. Unless you have a really keen interest in this site, you can see enough from outside the fence.

SIDI BOU SAID

This is a small, whitewashed village set high on a cliff above the Mediterranean just north of Tunis and it's on every tour-group itinerary. Despite this it is still a remarkably laid-back town, especially out of the main tourist season.

The centre of activity is the small cobbled square with its outdoor cafés and sweet stalls, which can be an agreeable place to sit for a while with a cold drink. In fact, other than this, there is very little to see in Sidi Bou Said; after a half-hour wander you will have exhausted the possibilities.

Just past the sweet stalls on the right is

a steep path and stairway which lead down to a small and relatively uncrowded beach, where there are a few fairly up-market restaurants. From here it is possible to follow the road around and back up the hill to bring you out at Carthage Amilcar TGM station. The whole walk from Sidi Bou Said takes about an hour.

Places to Stay & Eat

The *Hotel Dar Said* is about 100 metres past the main square and is a beautiful old French villa. If you can afford the TD 19 for a double with breakfast it's a great place to stay.

The *Restaurant La Bagatelle* is on the opposite corner to the Dar Said and is also worth a visit, especially at lunch time when they have specials. You need to get there around noon, as it's only a small place and the food runs out early. Expect to pay around TD 5 per person for a two-course meal.

Getting There & Away

Sidi Bou Said is on the TGM line and it takes about 25 minutes to get there from Tunis. From the station it's about a 15-minute walk up to the top of the hill and the centre of the old part of the village.

LA MARSA

This is another of the beachside suburbs and is at the end of the TGM line from Tunis. Because of that it is one of the least crowded on hot summer days, although weekends are a bad time on any beach.

Along with the area around the Byrsa Hill, La Marsa is one of the most exclusive residential suburbs of Tunis. There are a couple of good cafés and restaurants around the TGM station.

THUBURBO MAJUS

This old provincial Roman city some 55 km south-west of Tunis is easily accessible by both bus and louage from Tunis and, along with the nearby town of Zaghouan, makes an interesting day trip. If time is

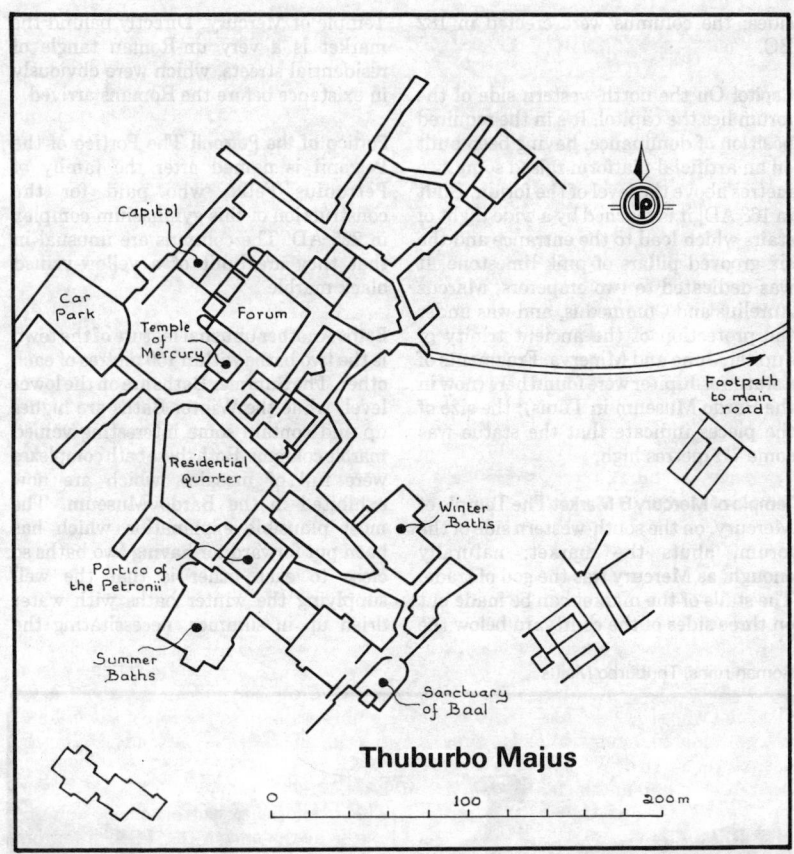

Thuburbo Majus

short, you could easily miss these places without losing any sleep.

If you are travelling from Tunis to Kairouan or vice versa it would also be possible to fit in Thuburbo Majus on the way. If you are making a day trip from Tunis to Thuburbo Majus and Zaghouan, it is easiest to go first to Thuburbo Majus and then head for Zaghouan, as the transport connections are better this way.

Thuburbo Majus thrived as a town serving an agricultural hinterland from well before Roman times, but it wasn't until the 2nd century when the emperor

Hadrian visited and declared it a municipality that the town really prospered.

The Ruins

As well as the major monuments, the ruins of various others are scattered around the edge of this site.

Forum As usual, the forum was the public focus of the city, and was where its political and economic affairs were carried out. It is colonnaded on three sides; the columns were erected in 182 BC.

Capitol On the north-western side of the forum lies the capitol. It's in the required position of dominance, having been built on an artificial platform raised some two metres above the level of the forum. Built in 168 AD, it is reached by a wide flight of stairs which lead to the entrance and the six grooved pillars of pink limestone. It was dedicated to two emperors, Marcus Aurelius and Commodus, and was under the protection of the ancient trinity of Jupiter, Juno and Minerva. Fragments of a statue of Jupiter were found here (now in the Bardo Museum in Tunis); the size of the pieces indicate that the statue was some 7½ metres high.

Temple of Mercury & Market The Temple of Mercury, on the south-western side of the forum, abuts the market; naturally enough, as Mercury was the god of trade. The stalls of the market can be made out on three sides of the courtyard below the Temple of Mercury. Directly behind the market is a very un-Roman tangle of residential streets, which were obviously in existence before the Romans arrived.

Portico of the Petronii The Portico of the Petronii is named after the family of Petronius Felix, who paid for the construction of this gymnasium complex in 225 AD. The columns are unusual in that they are built of a yellow-veined black marble.

Baths Another unusual feature of the town is the two baths within 150 metres of each other. The Summer Baths are on the lower level, while the Winter Baths are higher up and contain some interesting veined marble columns. Both these bath complexes were full of mosaics, which are now exhibited in the Bardo Museum. The most plausible explanation which has been put forward for having two baths so close to each other is that the well supplying the winter baths with water dried up in summer, necessitating the

Roman ruins, Thuburbo Majus

construction of the other baths lower down the hill.

Getting There & Away
The totally dreary rural town of El Fahs is the closest settlement to Thuburbo Majus. At over three km away it can be a stinking hot walk in summer.

Bus & Taxi Louages run from Tunis to El Fahs from the station opposite the south bus station. Tell the driver you want to go to Thuburbo Majus and get him to drop you at the *second* turn off (coming from Tunis) to it, as from here it is only a short walk. At this intersection there is a sign pointing along the side road to Thuburbo Majus but, instead of following the road, cut straight up the hill behind the sign; the ruins are just over the rise. If coming from El Fahs, you have to either walk or hitch to the turn off.

From El Fahs there are regular louages (650 mills) and buses (500 mills) to Zaghouan. Buses and louages to Tunis and Kairouan are often full, so you may have to wait a while or make a dive for a door handle when a louage arrives.

ZAGHOUAN
This sleepy town tucked in at the foot of the spectacular 1295-metre Mt Zaghouan has a couple of derisory Roman ruins, but is best known for being the place that used to supply ancient Carthage with fresh water. In those days a 70-km-long aqueduct was built to carry the water and parts of it (in remarkably good condition) can still be seen alongside the Tunis-Zaghouan road, about 20 km north of Zaghouan.

The springs are still in use today; there are a couple of gushing outlets on strategic corners in the town and the local residents still draw some of their water from these.

Places to Stay
There is a *Youth Hostel* here on the next hill over. The only hotel is the two-star *Les Nymphes* up behind the town, which charges TD 10.500/16 for singles/doubles with breakfast.

Getting There & Away
There are regular louages and buses to both El Fahs and Tunis. Louages take 40 minutes to cover the 55 km and cost TD 1.350 per person. To El Fahs a bus costs 500 mills and a louage 650 mills.

Cap Bon Peninsula

This is the tourist playground of Tunisia and consequently contains the majority of the country's resort hotels. Fortunately, the vast majority of these are centred around the Hammamet-Nabeul region on the south-east coast of the peninsula, leaving the rest of the area untouched.

Even where the resort development has taken place, the size of the hotels has been kept down to a relatively modest level and they are not too intrusive.

In summer the beaches are packed; both towns, which are gradually expanding and merging to form one, are crawling with scantily-clad package tourists and the prices hike up. Despite this it is still possible to find reasonable accommodation, and Nabeul has one of the best camp sites in the country.

Kelibia to the north offers a more relaxed atmosphere; it has a decent beach a few km away at Mansourah. The area around the small town of El Haouaria right on the northern tip is also worth exploring.

The west coast is far more rugged, so has developed little. Transport connections and accommodation are limited, but if you have your own transport there are plenty of beaches without the crowds of Hammamet or Nabeul.

NABEUL

This is where it all happens in summer. A walk down the main street will probably turn up 10 tourists to one local. The town used to be important as a service centre for the agricultural interior of the peninsula, but these days it has turned its back on the land and opened its arms to the visitors, mostly from sun-starved northern Europe, who flock here in droves. Even in the off season there are probably more tourists per square metre here than in any other part of the country.

The beaches are really nothing spec-

tacular and, unless you have a burning desire to be amongst other foreigners, you'd do well to bypass Nabeul in favour of more isolated spots such as Kelibia, 60 km to the north.

The Friday market here has become one of the major tourist events in the country. Although it is basically a tourist wank it is here that you'll find the widest range of pottery in the country, as Nabeul has long been associated with the craft. Many of the pieces on sale bear little relation to anything remotely Tunisian and owe more to the questionable tastes of the town's visitors. Because of the large number of tourists and the fact that most of them are on only a short package tour, prices in Nabeul are high and bargaining is difficult. You stand a better chance on any day other than Friday, but even then it is difficult.

Information

Tourist Office The office of the ONTT (tel 86 737), the national tourist body, is on Ave Taieb M'Hiri between the beach and the centre of town. Even when it's closed they have bus, train and accommodation information posted outside the office.

Post The main post office is on Ave Bourguiba, north of the main intersection with Ave Farhat Hached.

Money As might be expected, there are plenty of banks ready to take your money, mostly along Ave Farhat Hached and Ave Bourguiba.

Market The market is on Fridays, mainly in the morning. Things have pretty much died down by 2 pm. When it's on, Ave Farhat Hached is closed to vehicular traffic between Ave Bourguiba and Ave Habib Elkarma, and the whole stretch becomes full of tourists and traders.

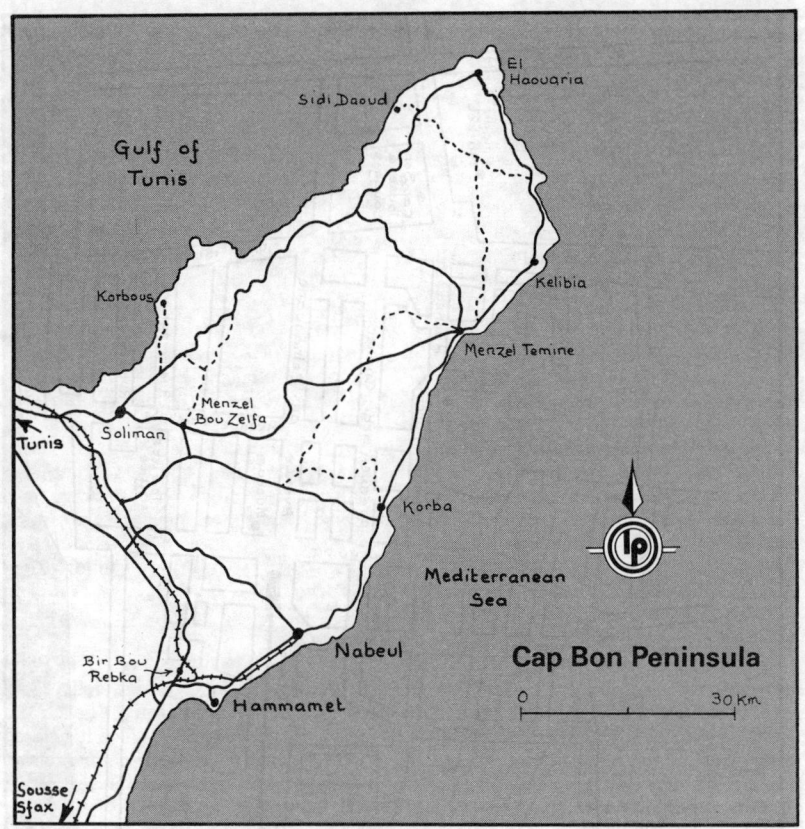

Cap Bon Peninsula

0   30 Km

Airlines The Tunis Air office (tel 85 193) is at 145 Ave Bourguiba.

Car Rental All the major agencies are represented here and/or in nearby Hammamet. The ones in Nabeul are Hertz (tel 85 027), on Ave Bourguiba, and Europcar (tel 87 085), on Ave Farhat Hached.

Museum
There is a small archaeological museum on Ave Bourguiba near the railway station but at the time of writing it was closed for renovation.

Places to Stay – bottom end
The cheapest of the few possibilities here is the *Pension les Hafsides*; it's a bit out of the way on Rue Sidi Maaouia but is easy to find, as it's signposted off Ave Habib Thameur. It is a characterless place which charges TD 4/5.000 for singles/doubles.

The *Pension el Habib*, on the noisy Ave Habib Thameur just over the Oued Souhil, is slightly better and charges the same.

Youth Hostel Although it is likely to be full in mid-summer, the *Youth Hostel* might be worth a try if you are stuck. It is down

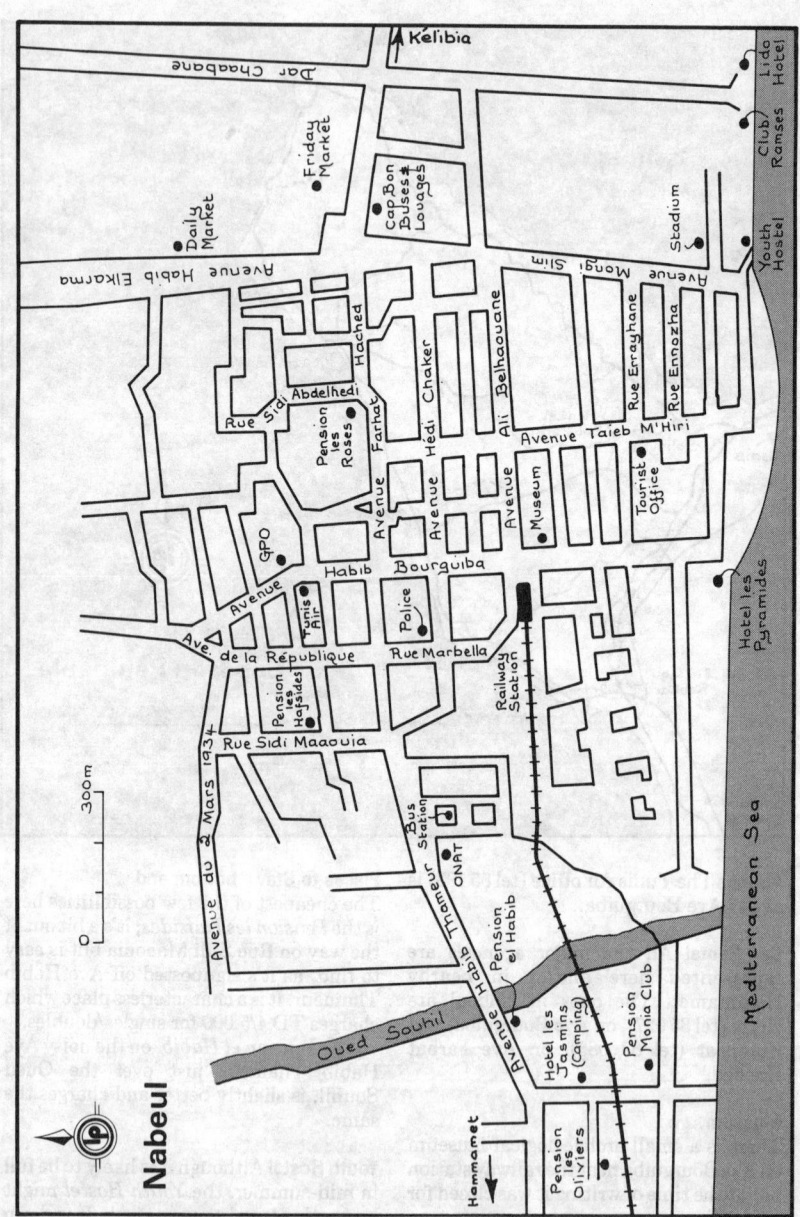

Nabeul

by the sports stadium near the beach, a solid 20-minute walk from the bus station. It follows the local tradition of making hostels as uninviting as possible.

Camping The *Hotel Les Jasmins*, signposted off to the left one km along the road towards Hammamet, has a congenial camping ground in the shady olive garden attached to the hotel. It has good privacy and security; it costs 850 mills per person and a further 500 mills for a tent.

The hotel is well situated – it's only five minutes' walk to the beach; the extra bit of distance between it and Nabeul means that the beach is relatively uncrowded. On the beach is a small café, which has some welcome shade umbrellas and serves tea, cold drinks and sandwiches.

The best way to get here is to take a bus or taxi running between Hammamet and Nabeul; get out at the Slovegnia Grill Restaurant or just ask the driver for the camping ground.

Places to Stay – middle

There are a couple of good choices here. Right in the middle of town is the *Pension les Roses* (tel 85 570), on Ave Farhat Hached. It is a friendly and comfortable place, although its proximity to one of the mosques might give light sleepers a hard time. Charges are TD 5.500/9 for singles/doubles in the high season dropping to TD 4/6 in the off season. Cold showers are free and hot showers cost 500 mills. It is right on the corner of the small open square where Ave Farhat Hached makes a dogleg in the centre of the town.

Out towards the beach is the *Pension les Oliviers* (tel 86 865). Another family-run place, it charges TD 7 per person including a filling breakfast. Close by is the *Hotel Les Jasmins* (tel 85 343), which was once a beautiful villa in an orchard. It's now a beautiful hotel in an orchard, and has a swimming pool and good restaurant. It is likely to be fully booked in summer, but if you chance on a room it

will cost TD 10.500 per person for full board.

Places to Stay – top end

The half dozen or so resorts here are almost all fully booked throughout the summer by tour and charter groups from Europe. They all have swimming pools and other sporting facilities, and it's often possible to sit on their patch of beach with the shade umbrellas, or by the pool. If you want to stay at one, expect to pay upwards of TD 15 per person; you will be lucky to find a vacancy in mid-summer. In winter prices drop and finding a room is less of a problem.

The *Hotel Les Pyramides* is typical and has about the best location if you are on foot. Its beach is ridiculously crowded and claustrophobic, and such is its isolation from the real Tunisia that topless bathing is common. It's no problem for non-residents to use the facilities here if a little discretion is exercised.

Other places close to the centre of Nabeul are the *Club Ramses* (TD 15/25 for singles/doubles with breakfast) and the *Lido Hotel* (TD 20/32); they're both on the beach, not far from the end of Ave Taieb M'Hiri.

Places to Eat

There are a few restaurants around the square in Ave Farhat Hached. The two on either side of the entrance to the Pension les Roses are both reasonable.

Things to Buy

There is an ONAT emporium on Ave Habib Thameur not far from the bus station. It has the same good-quality stuff as the other branches in the country and gives you an idea of the maximum prices you should be paying for things.

Getting There & Away

Bus & Taxi The station for buses and louages to Tunis and Hammamet is close to the centre of town on Ave Habib Thameur.

346 Cap Bon Peninsula

The regional bus service No 40 runs regularly from the Tunis south bus station. Buses to Hammamet run every half hour from 5.30 am to 7 pm. There are also small taxis which buzz back and forth, in which you pay for just a seat (150 mills). Louages to Tunis cost TD 1.650 per person.

There are bus departures for Zaghouan (three daily), Kairouan (one daily at 6 am) and Sousse (one daily, 6.45 am) as well.

For transport north, vehicles leave from a dusty lot just to the east of the intersection of Ave Farhat Hached and Ave Habib Elkarma. From here there are regular louage departures to Kelibia as well as 12 buses daily between 5 am and 6.30 pm.

There are also small white-and-red taxis which operate as shared taxis between Hammamet and Nabeul; you can pick them up opposite the bus station in Nabeul. A seat costs 150 mills.

Train The station is close to the centre of town, two blocks south of Ave Habib Thameur.

There are 12 trains daily to Tunis, but only two of these go direct. The others go to Bir Bou Rebka on the main line down to Sfax and you have to pick up another train from there. Connections are generally good, although at odd times you may have to wait for up to three hours. The direct trains leave Tunis at 2.30 and 5 pm, and Nabeul at 4.30 and 8.50 am; the journey takes 1½ hours.

Getting Around
Taxi Distances are quite big in Nabeul, and in summer it's a major effort to walk the km or so from the main street to the beach. Taxis cost only a few hundred mills and can be a life-saver; else you can take one of the many *calèches* (horse carriages), but bargain hard and agree on a price before setting off.

HAMMAMET
This is Nabeul all over again, only more so. The kasbah here has been totally over-restored, and what was once a small fishing village has now become another tourist service centre.

The reason for Hammamet's popularity is its long stretch of beach, which is one of the better ones along this coastline.

Information
Tourist Office This is in the centre of town on Ave Bourguiba.

Post The main post office is on the Nabeul road, Ave de la République, close to the centre.

Car Rental The agencies with offices here include: Avis (tel 80 303), Ave des Hôtels; Hertz (tel 80 187), Ave des Hôtels; Europcar Car (tel 80 146), Ave des Hôtels; and Topcar (tel 80 767), Ave de Koweit.

Places to Stay – bottom end
One of the cheapest places in town is the *Hotel Bennila*, which is on the Route des Hôtels. In summer the rates are TD 10/14 for singles/doubles with breakfast. The off-season rate is markedly lower at TD 4.500 per person.

Camping The *Ideal Camping* doesn't really live up to its name, but is passable. It is close to the centre on Ave de la République and charges TD 2 per person.

Places to Stay – middle
The *Pension Alya* is on the Route Touristique Hammamet Nord, the road off Ave de la République towards the beach near the camping ground. In high season it charges TD 12.500/20 for singles/doubles with breakfast; less in the off season.

Also reasonable value is the two-star *Hotel Sahbi*, on Ave de la République opposite Ideal Camping, where a double with breakfast costs TD 12/17 in summer.

Places to Stay – top end

As with Nabeul, there are stacks of resort hotels to choose from. They are all over the place but are concentrated on the Routes Touristique Hammamet Nord and Sud and the Route des Hôtels (this last is closest to the centre).

Places to Eat

The best of the cheap places is the *Café de la Poste*, which is to the left of the vast parking lot outside the kasbah.

Getting There & Away

Bus All road transport leaves from in front of the kasbah. There are regular departures for Tunis and Nabeul.

Train The railway station is one block from Ave Bourguiba. Train details are the same as for Nabeul. The direct departures for Tunis are at 4.50 and 9.10 am.

Taxi Small white-and-red taxis do the quick run to Nabeul for 150 mills per person. They leave from outside the kasbah.

KELIBIA

Suddenly you've left all the commercialism behind, and what you have is a small dusty town which survives mainly on its fishing fleet. The town itself is not of great interest, but down by the small beach, two km away, are a couple of very low-key resort hotels. The port is dominated by a picturesque fort.

Despite the backwater feeling, Kelibia has international hydrofoil connections with Trapani in Italy from June to September.

Information

All the services such as banks and post office are in the town. If you don't take your meals at the hotels or are staying at the youth hostel, you'll need to stock up with food before heading for the beach.

Fort

The Romans were the first to occupy this area but the Byzantines built the first fort here. Today the fort has been largely restored and dates from the Spanish invasions of the 16th century.

A dirt track leads up to it on the far side from opposite the youth hostel on the Mansourah road, just past the port, and it's only a short hike up to the top.

The fort is open at very irregular hours and getting in is a matter of pot luck. Once inside, it's a surprise to find a few families living here; the whole area is something of a farmyard, with chickens and cows. It's still a restricted area of some sort, so it's advisable to ask permission before taking photos and to heed the *accès interdit* signs. The views over the coastline from the ramparts are magnificent to both the north and south.

Beaches

The best beach is at Mansourah, two km to the north and 500 mills by regular shuttle taxi. The beach at Kelibia itself is very small and not that flash.

Places to Stay & Eat

There's only a limited choice of places and they are all out at the beach by the harbour. The better of the two hotels is the fading *Hotel Florida* (tel 96 248), which has a nice shaded terrace by the water's edge. Room rates are TD 8/14 for singles/doubles including breakfast and TD 12.500/23 for *pension complète*.

Next door to the Florida is the *Hotel Ennassim* (tel 96 245), which looks as though it would be more at home on the moon. The staff can be incredibly surly and unco-operative, and it's not the best value at TD 9 per person including breakfast; other meals are available at additional cost. It is invariably full in summer, but your chances of getting a room are good if you arrive before midday.

Youth Hostel The *Youth Hostel* (tel 96 105) is a third choice but is not very attractive. It is down past the harbour on the Mansourah road, and is the usual masterpiece of architectural innovation and excellence. If you have a tent or vehicle, they usually let people camp in the grounds.

Getting There & Away
Bus & Taxi The bus station is a fair three km from the harbour and beach. There are regular shared taxis doing the run between the two for 300 mills per person.

There are 10 bus departures daily along the coast to El Haouaria between 6 am and 2.45 pm. Louages leave regularly from the bus station for the 30-minute, 650-mill journey.

Hydrofoil As unlikely as it may seem, from June to September Kelibia becomes an international port, with hydrofoil departures three times a week to Trapani in Sicily, Italy. The trip takes only two hours. The agency that handles the operation is Tourafric (tel 341 481) at 52 Ave Bourguiba in Tunis.

EL HAOUARIA
This small town is tucked right in under the mountainous tip of Cap Bon. There are some interesting Roman caves just along from the tip of the cape, three km beyond the village. As there is no accommodation, you have to visit El Haouaria in a day trip. The easiest way to manage this is to visit it from either Kelibia or Nabeul, or en route between Tunis and Kelibia.

The caves are a 45-minute walk out along the road straight through town; don't be surprised if a couple of locals latch onto you to guide you (unnecessary). The road curves around to the left, and although you can take a short cut straight ahead this cuts right through the middle of the town garbage heap – bloody unsavoury smelling place it is too.

The road ends at the small Café les Grottes, and the caves are to the right of the road. In some you can see where the Romans cut out and removed building blocks for their projects in Carthage. The official guide, complete with brass nameplate, is keen to show people around.

Places to Stay
The *Hotel L'Epervier* (French for sparrowhawk; the hotel is so named because the village has been the centre of falconry in Tunisia) has been under construction for years. Maybe it will be finished by the time you get there. If not, the nearest possibilities are Kelibia or the expensive thermal resort hotel at Korbous on the west coast of the peninsula.

Getting There & Away
Bus & Taxi These leave irregularly for Tunis, the buses from the square, the louages a further 100 metres down past the Hotel L'Epervier. The bus to Tunis crawls along the north coast of Cap Bon, calling at every little village along the way, and so takes 2½ hours; the trip costs TD 2.460. Louages are a good deal faster.

There are also regular departures for Kelibia.

Since most tourists in Tunisia head for the Sahara and the beach resorts south of Tunis, the areas to the north of Tunis are far less crowded.

The beaches at Raf Raf and Sidi Ali el Mekki, between Tunis and Bizerte, are some of the best in the country and foreign tourists are relatively rare. The town of Bizerte itself is worth a quick look, and from there the road stretches west to Tabarka. The coastline along here is isolated and, if you have your own transport, there are some excellent beaches and small settlements to explore.

Tabarka is an attractive town, popular with holidaying Tunisians, and inland from here, up in the mountains and the cork forests, the town of Ain Draham is high enough to be pleasantly cool in summer while the rest of the country swelters.

The two ruined Roman cities in the north, Bulla Regia just south of Ain Draham, and Dougga, are arguably the two best sites in the country.

Bizerte

Bizerte is probably best known for being the place that the French hung on to after granting independence to Tunisia, which led to the loss of more than 1000 Tunisian lives in the attempt to oust them. The French finally withdrew on 15 October 1963 and the day has become a public holiday.

Located just a few km south of Cap Blanc (the northernmost tip of the African continent) Bizerte has some quite reasonable town beaches away to the north, and it is the best place for getting to the even better beaches of Raf Raf and Sidi Ali el Mekki to the south-east.

The French *ville nouvelle* follows the usual unimaginative grid; the medina is also true to form – a tangle of lanes and narrow streets. The two meet around the old port.

The shipping canal, first built by the Carthaginians, connects the large Lac de Bizerta (Lake Bizerte) with the Mediterranean. It has formed a natural buffer that allows the town centre to breathe without getting hemmed in by housing and development. The canal is spanned by a new bridge complete with a central span, which can be raised to allow larger ships to pass through.

Information

Tourist Offices The office of the national tourist body is on the corner of Quai Tarak ibn Ziad and Ave Taieb M'hiri. They have a reasonable hand-out map if you ask, and a useful sheet detailing the current accommodation prices for selected places in the whole northern region. It is not an exhaustive list but does give an idea of current prices.

The regional tourist office is clearly signposted on the corner of Ave Bourguiba and Blvd Hassan en Nouri, right next to the service station. The guy here speaks English and is unusually helpful – a welcome change from the monosyllabic grunts that you get from a lot of tourism staff in the country. In the window he has posted lists of bus departures and other useful bits and pieces, such as which bank is rostered to be open late. The office is open Monday to Saturday from 9 am to 1 pm and 4 to 7 pm, and on Sunday from 9 am to 12 noon, and 4 to 7 pm.

Post The main post office is on Ave d'Algérie. There is a parcel post office (*colis posteaux*) in the same building further towards Ave Bourguiba; around the back is the telecommunications office, which is open late.

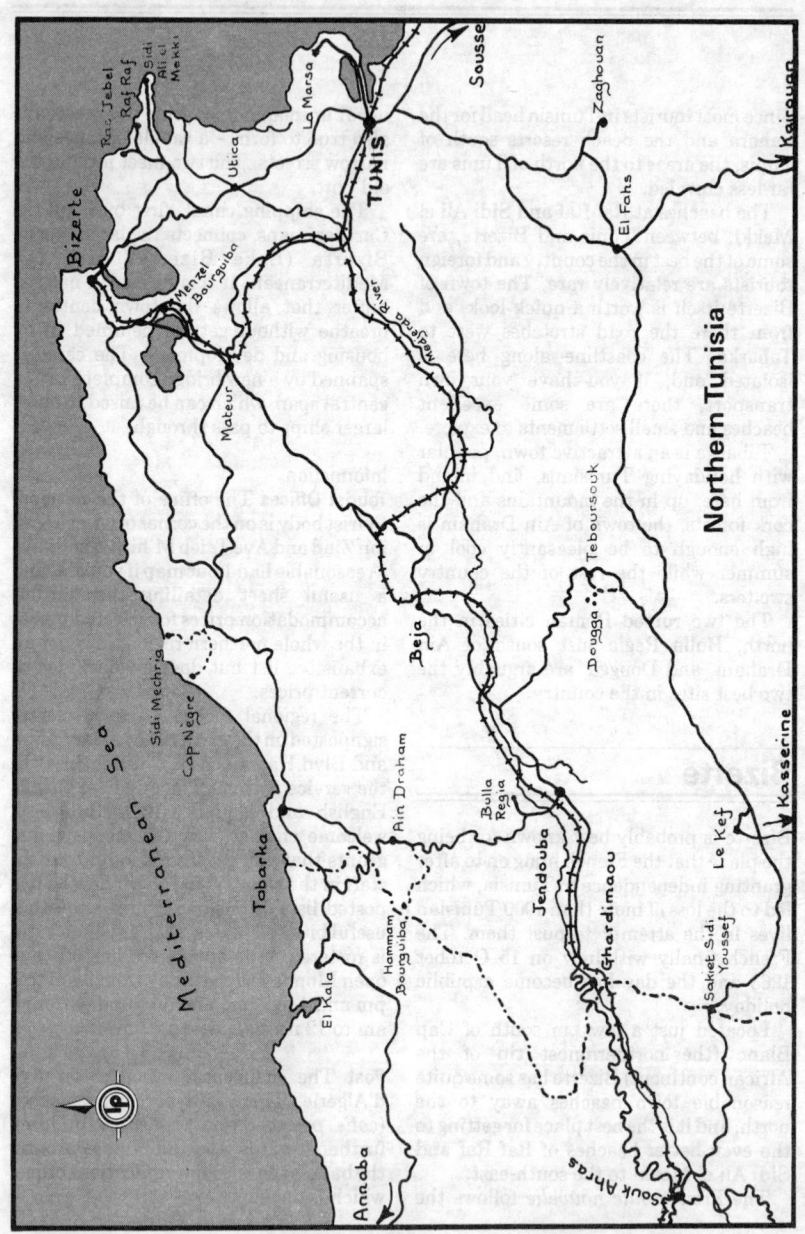

Money The banks are mostly grouped around the square with the gardens and tennis club. Normal hours are 9 am to 12 noon and 4 to 7 pm in summer, but one bank is always rostered to be open late; to find out which one check the window of the regional tourist office on Ave Bourguiba.

Airlines The Tunis Air office (tel 32 201) is at 76 Ave Bourguiba.

Car Rental The following major agencies have offices in Bizerte: Hertz (tel 33 679), Place des Martyrs; Avis (tel 33 076), 7 Rue d'Alger; Budget (tel 32 174), 7 Rue d'Alger; Europcar (tel 31 537), cnr Rue Ibn Khaldoun and Rue de Belgique.

Shipping Companies The Compagnie Tunisienne de Navigation office (tel 32 440) for ferry bookings for departures from Tunis is at 29 Rue d'Algérie.

Beaches

The beaches to the north of town towards Cap Blanc are not too bad at all. The strip of hotels has a monopoly on the first few km, but it's not too difficult to slip in and use the beach and facilities.

Further on, the beach backs directly onto the road and is very narrow – not that great. Further on still, around the first cape and along a few more km, the Les Grottes beach right at the foot of Cap Blanc is the best of the lot. Access can be a bit tedious without a car, however, as you have to rely on hitching or walking the last couple of km.

In the other direction, back towards Tunis, Remel Plage has a good strip of white sand and is a little easier to get to on your own. Buses from the main bus station heading for Raf Raf or Ras Jebel will drop you off at the turn off, from where it's a one-km walk.

Places to Stay – bottom end

The cheapest place in the city is the *Hotel Africain* on the edge of the medina. It costs TD 4 for a room with two tiny beds; the rooms at the front are noisy as hell, while the back rooms are dark and face an internal courtyard. There are no showers in the place and the entrance is through a restaurant. Not the best.

Almost next door is the *Hotel Zitouna*, which suffers from similar problems to the Africain but is marginally better; it costs TD 6 for a double.

The best of the cheapies is the *Hotel Continental* (tel 31 436) on Rue d'Espagne, but even this is not great. It is somewhere approaching clean and rooms cost TD 6 for a double. Cold showers only.

Youth Hostel & Camping There are two *Youth Hostels*. The first is up by the top end of the medina and is, as usual, more like a prison block.

The second hostel (tel 40 804) is a much better alternative. It is three km back towards Tunis. It is signposted down a dirt track at the turn off to Remel Plage. Camping is possible at this one and it is a popular place with people with their own vehicle. The hostel facilities are pretty basic but adequate, and the relaxed atmosphere and location by the beach make it a good place. The cost is TD 2 for a bed, and meals can be ordered. To get there take a bus going to Ghar el Melh, Raf Raf or Ras Jebel and get off at the Remel Plage turn off.

Places to Stay – middle & top end

The rest of the places are out along the beach strip to the north of the town. They all tend towards the top end of the scale and are usually booked out (in summer at least) with package tourists from Europe.

The cheapest of the resort-type places is the *Hotel Nador* (tel 31 846), which has a good stretch of beach, a swimming pool, tennis, poolside restaurant and all the other trappings. Charges are TD 11.300/17 for singles/doubles with breakfast in the low season and TD 16/26 in the summer.

Further out along the beach, the *Hotel*

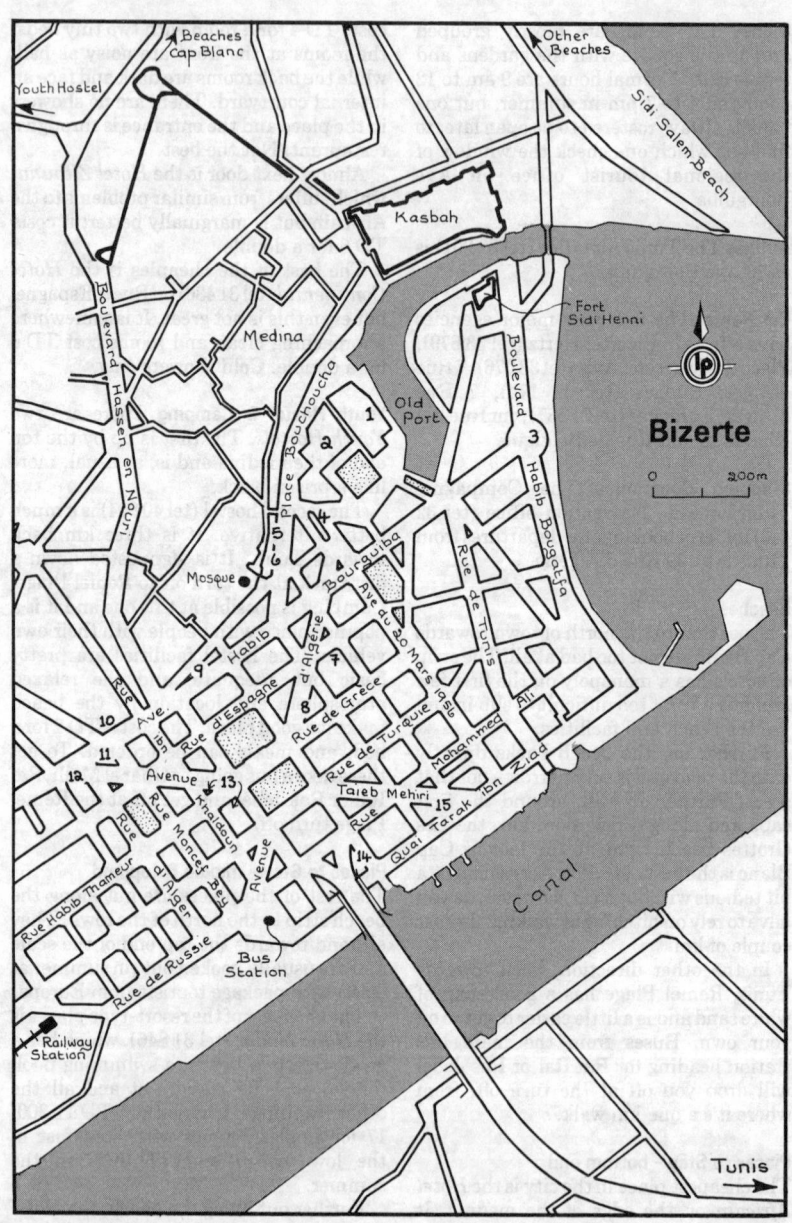

Bizerte

0   200m

1	Artisanat
2	Market
3	Buses to northern beaches
4	Louages (Regional)
5	Hotel Africain
6	Hotel Zitouna
7	Hotel Continental
8	GPO
9	Regional Tourist Office
10	Tunis Air
11	Restaurant le Coq d'Or
12	Restaurant Jeunesse
13	Banks
14	Louages (Tunis)
15	National Tourist Office

el Khayem (tel 32 120) is reasonable at TD 5.500/7 but it is a fair way out. Also, the beach here is very narrow and the road separates it from the hotel. The indescribably ugly Restaurant Zoubaida next door has to be seen to be believed.

If you can afford it, the best place for atmosphere is the *Hotel Petit Mousse* (tel 32 185), also out along the beach, although it too is separated from the beach by the road. It was built in the colonial days and good rooms cost TD 10.800/15 for singles/doubles with breakfast. Even if you don't stay here it's nice to have a drink in the bar or a meal in the garden in the evening.

Places to Eat

Bizerte is not over endowed with restaurants, but there are a few choices. The *Restaurant Bar de la Liberté* on the corner next to the Hotel Continental is clean, cool and has a courtyard. The food is cheap and quite good.

On Ave Bourguiba near the Tunis Air office, the *Restaurant le Coq d'Or* and the *Restaurant Al Quds* opposite are both typical Tunisian eateries and there's not much to choose between them – both are basic and moderately clean.

The *Restaurant Africain* is a lot better than the hotel of the same name, and does good fish and *merguez* (spicy sausages).

For just coffee, cakes and ice creams the *Patisserie de la Paix*, right opposite the

Hotel Continental, is something of a local hangout, is open long hours and has good products.

Out along the beach, past the major hotels, there are a couple more choices. The *Hotel Petit Mousse* has a very pleasant well-run outdoor restaurant where a meal, including beer, costs around TD 10 for two.

Getting There & Away

Bus The bus station is down near the canal at the end of Ave d'Algérie, less than 10 minutes' walk from the cheap hotels. There are SNTRI departures as well as more frequent regional services with SETGC.

Departures include Ain Draham (three daily), Raf Raf (five daily), Tabarka and Tunis. All the departures for Raf Raf and Ras Jebel will get you to the Remel Plage turn off for the youth hostel and camping ground.

Train The brand-new railway station is down by the port, near the end of Rue de Belgique.

There are four departures daily between 4.55 am and 6.20 pm for the 1½ hour trip to Tunis.

Taxi Louages for Tunis, Raf Raf, Ras Jebel and Ghar el Melh leave from underneath the bridge.

For Menzel Bourguiba and Tabarka they depart from a small square near the northern end of Ave d'Algérie.

Getting Around

There are local buses out to the beaches towards Cap Blanc. The No 29 runs out along Blvd Hassan en Nouri. No 2 also heads out this way, and if you want to get to the beaches right by Cap Blanc it can drop you at the T junction where the road leads off to the right to the beach. From there it's a two-km walk to Les Grottes beach, but hitching is usually possible.

AROUND BIZERTE
Ras Jebel

This is the only real town on this large promontory south of Bizerte, which ends in Raf Raf beach and Cap Farina. It is actually just a service town for the surrounding productive farming land and there's not much in the way of facilities.

The beach here is signposted from the main street but it is a three-km walk. The beaches at Raf Raf and Sidi Ali el Mekki are a better bet.

Places to Stay & Eat The only place in town is the *Hotel Okba*, signposted down towards the market from the bus stop. From there the signs peter out, but all the locals know the hotel and can direct you.

The hotel itself is very disorganised and it would appear that visitors are a rare breed here. However, it is a reasonable place to stay and charges TD 6 for a double with bath.

There are no restaurants to speak of in the town. There is a small sandwich shop with casse-croûtes and chips on the road out of town towards the Lee Cooper factory and Raf Raf.

Getting There & Away Buses leave Bizerte fairly regularly for Ras Jebel and they go on to Raf Raf. The stop in Ras Jebel is at the main intersection.

There are also louages running infrequently to both Raf Raf and Bizerte.

Raf Raf

The best of the easily accessible beaches, Raf Raf is also one of the best in the country – long stretches of white sand and relatively few people if you don't mind walking a bit.

Raf Raf beach is sheltered in a small bay, and the approach from Bizerte is spectacular: as you come over the hill from Raf Raf town (itself of no interest) the beach and bay are spread out below.

The scarred pine-clad ridge at the far end of the beach is Cap Farina, and this end of the beach is usually deserted

because it is a km or so along from the main part of the beach. You can walk along the beach or, if you have a car, you can follow the tracks around behind the town, past the mosque, to the car park (complete with parking attendant on weekends!) at the end of the track. From there a footpath leads down to the beach.

Although foreigners are rare here it is a favourite spot with holidaying Tunisians, so there are numerous up-market restaurants, grass beach huts and a hotel to cater for visitors. Raf Raf is very popular in summer, particularly on weekends. As most people come on day trips only, things really calm down in the evenings.

Places to Stay & Eat The cheapest way to stay here is to bring your own food from Bizerte and rent one of the grass huts on the beach. These are primarily built for daytime use and privacy but it's quite OK to stay the night in one. They cost TD 3 per day and have nothing in them (apart from sand), so you need to have something to sleep on. You could also sleep out in the pine forest at the far end of the beach without any problem.

The only formal place to stay is the *Hotel Dalia* at the end of the road. It's quite a good place if you can afford the TD 12 for a double with breakfast. The restaurant on the ground floor does OK food, although because it is at a tourist place the prices are a bit inflated for what you get.

The unbelievably kitsch *Café Restaurant Andalous* closer towards the water has better prices and does excellent fish.

There are quite a few other restaurants, all signposted, but these are costly and cater to the local day trippers.

Getting There & Away There is a bus stop 50 metres before the beach and from here buses operate to Ras Jebel and Bizerte. Louages also make the trip. In summer the transport gets pretty crowded, particularly around 7 pm when everyone is heading back to Tunis or Bizerte.

Hitching is possible but you need to have patience, as a lot of the cars are already full.

Sidi Ali el Mekki

On the other side of Cap Farina from Raf Raf, Sidi Ali el Mekki is the best beach in northern Tunisia. However, without your own transport it can be a six km walk from the town of Ghar el Melh. Hitching is reliable only on summer weekends, when there are quite a few day trippers in cars.

The road out to the beach skirts the lagoon of Ghar el Melh, the outlet for the Medjerda River. Although there's little reminder of it, the town has quite a history. In the 17th century it was a pirate hangout, which the famous English admiral Sir Francis Drake attacked and destroyed. In the 18th and 19th centuries the Ottoman beys fortified the town and turned it into an arsenal in the hope of making the lagoon, connected to the sea by just a small channel, into a large naval base. Their schemes were thwarted by the Medjerda River, which silted up the lagoon. Today the ruins of the forts and port are still visible, and the only boats able to sail in the lagoon are small fishing vessels.

Places to Stay & Eat The only place to stay is in one of the 30 or so grass shelters on the beach. They consist of one room and a shade area in front which is welcome in summer. Like the huts at Raf Raf they are rented for the day by day trippers, but you can stay overnight if you have something to sleep on. The custodian lives in one of them and keeps a careful eye on things so your stuff is safe. They cost TD 3 per day, or TD 4 on Sundays, the most popular day.

In summer there is a small shop here which sells very basic provisions such as bread, eggs, a few canned goods, and drinks. It also makes good casse-croûtes.

Getting There & Away Buses run infrequently from the Bizerte bus station to Ghar el Melh, and from there it's a matter of walking or hitching the six km to the beach.

Utica

At one stage after the fall of Carthage this port city was the capital of the Roman province of Africa. It was on the banks of the Medjerda River, but as the river silted up it was reduced from being a fine city into an insignificant farming village.

The ruins today are unimpressive and are a hot one-km walk signposted to the east from the small settlement of Zana on the main Bizerte-Tunis road. A visit is not really worth the effort unless you have your own vehicle.

Two km from the road on the left is the museum, which houses an extensive collection of bits and pieces found on the site. Some mosaics are displayed outside.

The site itself is a further 500 metres along the road at the bottom of the slope. The only significant ruin is the House of the Cascade, named after the fountains which used to decorate this mansion. The best mosaics, of men fishing from boats with nets and rods, are small; they're protected from the elements by wooden covers which can be lifted. For a small consideration the caretaker will splash some water on them, which really brings them to life. His real pride and joy, however, is the small garden here; he obviously devotes most of his time to this, as visitors to the site don't exactly swarm in every day.

The site is open from 8 am to 12 noon and 2 to 5 pm; entry is 800 mills and a charge of TD 2 is made if you want to take photographs.

Getting There & Away The only way to do this on public transport is to catch a bus or louage going from Tunis to Bizerte or vice versa and ask to be dropped at the turn off to the ruins. After seeing the site you will have to walk the two km or so back to the road and either hitch or wait for a bus – a lot of work for very little reward.

Menzel Bourguiba

On the southern side of Lake Bizerte, Menzel Bourguiba is a large and uninteresting provincial town, service centre for a sizeable military base and site of a major metallurgical complex.

Places to Stay There is absolutely no reason to stop here, but if you get stuck the *Hotel Younes* (tel 60 057) is a couple of km out of the town centre on the shore of the lake. The only way to get there is by taxi. Rooms cost TD 10.800 for a double, supposedly with breakfast, which somehow never seems to materialise. It is the main drinking establishment in Menzel Bourguiba and is quite pleasant in the evenings with its outdoor terrace by the water, although in summer the mosquitoes also find it very pleasant and a good hunting ground.

North Coast

Further from Bizerte towards Tabarka along the north coast there are a couple of secluded seasonal settlements. However, unless you have a vehicle these places are hard to get to and, what is more, there is really no reason to visit them.

Sidi Mechrig This has a few permanent residents as well as families who camp here for the summer. You will need to have all your own supplies if you are contemplating coming here, because although there is plenty of water, there are no provisions of any sort for sale.

The people staying here buy their things in Sejenane, 17 km inland on the Bizerte-Tabarka road. The coast here can make an interesting diversion, although you'll need your own transport; otherwise, you can ask around in Sejenane for lifts.

Cap Nègre The track to Cap Nègre branches off the Sidi Mechrig track about one km after leaving the main road. Once a small village living off the trade in coral, it is now deserted.

TABARKA

The last town along the coast before the Algerian border, Tabarka is small, scenic and friendly. It is becoming increasingly popular: people have discovered the beautiful little bay and beach which are watched over by an impressive-looking fort built by the Genoese, but the town is still a relaxed backwater.

The Carthaginians were the first to use the port. It really flourished under the Romans, who built the causeway connecting the small island with the mainland. Some of the mosaics found in the town have been displayed in the Bardo Museum in Tunis.

Tabarka was also part of the string of pirate haunts along the Barbary Coast in the 1700s. In 1741 it was annexed by the bey of Tunis.

Tabarka's most recent claim to fame, however, is the fact that Bourguiba was forced to spend a short time here in exile in 1952.

Today the town owes its existence partly to the red coral which is found just off shore; it is also a shipment point for the tonnes of cork taken from the forests of the Khroumirie Mountains, which rise sharply behind the town.

Apart from climbing up to the fort, or walking around the bay to the unusual rock formations known as Les Aiguilles ('the needles'), there's little to do except walk along the tree-lined main street (called Ave Bourguiba, just to be original), checking out the coral jewellery in the shops, or lie on the beach.

There's a tourist office on Ave Bourguiba, near the roundabout, which is open from 9 am to 12 noon and 4 to 7 pm.

Places to Stay

Accommodation is at a premium, especially in summer when you'll be lucky to find a room after midday. This is no problem if you are prepared to sleep on the beach; otherwise Ain Draham (26 km inland) offers the only other possibility.

The cheapest place is the *Hotel Corail* and even this is no bargain at TD 10 for a double. It's on Ave Bourguiba, about halfway between the roundabout and the *Hotel de France* (tel 44 577), which is the only other accommodation alternative. The latter costs TD 15 for a double and, although it's no great shakes, it does its best to cash in on the fact that Bourguiba spent time in the hotel.

Up on the hill, the three-star *Hotel Mimosas* (tel 44 376) has a commanding position and is the place to stay if you can afford the TD 27 they charge for a double with bath and breakfast.

Places to Eat

About the best place in town is the restaurant of the *Hotel de France*, although it might take a minute or two to get over the shock you get on entering the restaurant – strategically placed right in the middle of the doorway is the biggest, ugliest and most ferocious-looking stuffed wild boar you would ever want to see. Although it is a bit moth-eaten these days, it is still bloody awful. For added effect there are other assorted porcine bits around the walls. The four-course set menu for TD 3 is not bad value.

Right opposite the Hotel de France, the *Restaurant Khemis* has good calamari and passable spaghetti. The *Restaurant Triki* on Rue Farhat Hached, just off Ave Bourguiba, does good fish for TD 1.200.

Getting There & Away

Bus The SNTRI buses leave from Rue du Peuple, one block back from the Hotel Corail. Regional buses go from outside the customs house (*douane*) down at the beginning of the causeway.

There are connections with Tunis, Bizerte, Ain Draham and Jendouba.

Taxi The louages leave from the main street at the entrance to town, opposite the turn off to the Hotel Mimosas.

To/from Algeria It's possible to hitch to the border and, once across it, to the town of El Kala. Here there are hotels, a youth hostel and transport connections on to Annaba, from where you can get a direct bus to Algiers, El Oued or Constantine.

AIN DRAHAM

From Tabarka the road starts winding upwards almost immediately, and there are some spectacular views back towards the coast. All along this stretch as far as the village of Babouch there are young boys selling pine nuts, rather aggressively (and at times dangerously): they stand out in the middle of the road, almost daring the vehicles not to stop.

At Babouch there is a turn off to the Algerian border. This is 13 km away and can be reached by taxi, but there is the problem of crossing the 10 km or so of neutral territory before the Algerian post. It may be possible, if time-consuming, to hitch. The turn off leads also to Hammam Bourguiba – a three-star thermal springs resort tucked in a small valley. Charges here are TD 14/19 for singles/doubles with breakfast.

The town of Ain Draham itself clings to the side of a hill almost 1000 metres above sea level. The elevation makes it quite a bit cooler than the plains or the coast, although in winter it means that deep snow is quite common.

The town used to be popular with hunters in the days of the French administration. Today leisure activities are a lot more peaceful, and Tunisians come here to relax and escape the summer heat.

There is a bank and post office here.

Places to Stay & Eat

Accommodation is very limited, as most local tourists stay here for a week or more and rent out entire villas. The *Youth*

Hostel is at the top of the hill on the road to Jendouba.

The only other place is the scenic *Hotel Beauséjour* (tel 47 005) but it will very likely be full in summer. Rooms, if you can get them, cost TD 6/8 for singles/doubles with bath and breakfast. The building itself is covered with creepers, and its past association with game hunting is very evident thanks to all the skins and skulls hanging on the walls.

Seven km along the road to Jendouba is the *Hotel Les Chênes* (tel 47 211), which is in the middle of a cork forest. It is an old hunting lodge and, again, there are several stuffed 'trophies' around the walls. Rooms cost TD 11/16 for singles/doubles with bath and breakfast; however, you're better off paying for *pension complète*, as there is nowhere else to eat. They do allow you to camp in the grounds and use the hotel facilities for a couple of dinars per person.

In Ain Draham itself there are a couple of simple restaurants in the main street. You can get casse-croûte and plates of assorted fried food (egg, chips, chillies) – certainly no gourmet delights here. If you can't face that try the restaurant in the *Hotel Beauséjour*, but expect to pay at least TD 5 per person.

Getting There & Away
Bus Buses leave from the intersection at the bottom of town near the petrol station, 300 metres down from the hotel and youth hostel. There are infrequent buses to Tabarka and Jendouba, and one air-con SNTRI bus per day direct to Tunis.

Taxi Louages leave from the top of the hill, outside the youth hostel. They are far more frequent than the buses but only run to Tabarka and Jendouba.

BULLA REGIA
This Roman site is most famous for being the place where the Romans went underground. That is to say, they built their villas with one storey above ground

and another below ground to escape the heat.

Bulla Regia lies three km east of the Ain Draham-Jendouba road, and is six km north of Jendouba. Visiting it is easy enough and it is one of the best sites in the country. Making your way from Jendouba out to the site and back again will take you half a day.

The site was inhabited before Roman times; the Regia in the name refers to the royal Numidian kingdoms.

After the Romans moved in the residents became wealthy, living off the revenue generated by the rich grain country of the Medjerda Valley.

The Ruins
The entrance to the site is just to the left of the Memmian Baths, the most extensive of the remaining above-ground buildings.

The three main underground houses are kept locked, so make sure you ask for the keys. The caretaker seems quite happy to let you take them and return them when finished. The site is open daily from 8 am to 8 pm in summer, 8 am to 5 pm in winter, and entry is TD 1. There is a TD 2 charge for taking pictures. Most of the major points of interest are labelled with yellow signs.

The Memmian Baths on the right are impressive in size, and some of the mosaics have remained intact. The street in front of them leads to the theatre, which has loads of atmosphere; it still has a mosaic of a bear in the centre of the stage.

Following the street along to the left of the theatre brings you to the forum, which has the Temple of Apollo on the north side and the capitol to the east.

A path along an overgrown water channel takes you to a spring which is fenced off; this has a pump house which supplies Jendouba with water. From here it's a matter of scrambling over a bank to the left until you come to another excavated street. The Palace of Fishing, to the right, is one of the houses kept locked; it has a basement with fountain. Signposted just to the north-east, the House of Amphitrite (also locked) has a beautiful mosaic of Poseidon and Amphitrite surrounded by cupids.

Back next door to the Palace of Fishing is the residence known as the Palace of the Hunt. Its basement is the most impressive of the three houses, as it has a colonnade around it.

The museum outside the site across the road from the entrance doesn't have anything in it and so, logically enough, it is closed.

Getting There & Away

From Jendouba you can catch a local bus heading for Ain Draham and ask for Bulla Regia. This will drop you at a signposted intersection six km north of Jendouba, from which it's a three-km walk to the site. Hitching along this stretch is easy enough, as there is quite a bit of local traffic as well as small louages.

JENDOUBA

Jendouba is dull in the extreme. Its only redeeming feature is that it's a handy base from which to visit Bulla Regia. Perhaps the most remarkable thing about the whole place is the stork's nest on top of the police station chimney.

If you are heading for Algeria it is possible to pick up the Trans-Maghreb Express train, which runs daily to Algiers.

Life revolves around the central square, which is 100 metres north of the old main road through town. (The new road actually skirts the town to the south.) Around the square, complete with garden and fountain, you'll find the post office, bank and police station. All the hotels are nearby.

Being an important provincial town, Jendouba has branches of all the major Tunisian banks.

Places to Stay - bottom end

The *Pension Saha en Noum* is the best bet at TD 2 per person. It is on Blvd Khemais el Hajiri, not far from the square. Avoid the claustrophobic *Pension es-Saada*; it is about as attractive as a prison and has no washing facilities.

Places to Stay - middle

The town's premier establishment is the two-star *Hotel Atlas* (tel 30 566), just behind the police station. Despite the austere air, it is quite comfortable; for a room with washbasin and bidet you pay TD 7.800/10.800, which includes breakfast.

Places to Eat

There are a couple of restaurants about 100 metres east of the main square. The *Restaurant le Golfe* has a reasonable selection, and the nearby *Restaurant Carthage* is also not bad.

The nightlife is limited to the pleasant outdoor beer garden of the *Atlas Hotel* – not a bad place to be on a hot summer evening.

Getting There & Away

Bus The bus station is over the railway line on the western edge of town. There are regular connections with Ain Draham, Tunis, Ghardimao, Tebersouk and Le Kef.

Train The railway station is just off the main square, near the police station. There are five trains daily to Tunis; there are five to Ghardimao too, one of which continues on to Algiers via Annaba and Constantine.

Taxi Louages for Ghardimao leave every few minutes from the station on Blvd Sakiet Sidi Sousse, towards the main road from the square.

For Tunis they leave from Rue 1 Juin 1955, 50 metres along from the Pension es-Saada.

GHARDIMAO

If anything, Ghardimao is even more deadly boring than Jendouba. It really is the end of the line. It's certainly not worth a special trip, but you may find yourself coming through here on the way to Algeria.

Places to Stay

Just like the rest of the town the *Thubernic Hotel* is totally lacking in atmosphere, but there is no alternative. It has no sign but is the two-storey building opposite the railway station. Rooms cost TD 5 for a double.

Getting There & Away

Both the buses and the louages leave from next to the railway line, about 200 metres towards Jendouba from the station.

There are frequent louages to Jendouba, and there is one bus daily direct to Tunis.

To/from Algeria The daily Trans-Maghreb Express crawls through here at around 4 pm every day. Don't be fooled by the name: although it conjures up romantic images of a great railway journey clear across the top of the African continent, the train in fact goes only as far as Algiers (which it does in the stunning time of 21 hours); it's invariably crowded and the whole journey can be something of an endurance test.

The best bet, if you are heading for Algeria this way, is to take the train as far as Annaba, the first town of any note on the Algerian side. You could just go to Souk Ahras but, apart from the interesting countryside (which you see from the train anyway), there is stuff all to do there; if you do stop, there are buses to Constantine, Annaba and El Oued.

DOUGGA

Another of Tunisia's excellent Roman sites, Dougga has a commanding position on the edge of the Tebersouk Mountains. It is six km along a bitumen road from the small town of Tebersouk and three km up a dirt track from the even smaller town of Dougga, which now houses the residents who were moved from the ancient site to protect the ruins from further decay.

If you haven't yet had an overdose of Roman ruins, this one is well worth visiting; however, it does require a bit of effort, as there is no cheap accommodation in the immediate vicinity and public transport only takes you to within three km of the site. The best place to base yourself for a visit is the town of Le Kef, 60 km to the west.

Most of the excellent mosaics from this site are in the Bardo Museum.

History

The town of Thugga was already well established in the Punic era, and the unusual monument just below the Roman ruins (known as the Libyco-Punic Mausoleum) dates back to the 2nd century BC.

In early Roman times Thugga became one of the capitals of one of Rome's allies, a Numidian king by the name of Massinissa. Its fortunes followed the familiar pattern of Roman towns in North Africa: great prosperity in the 2nd to 4th centuries followed by a steady decline during the Byzantine and Vandal occupation. Its prosperity was aided by its ample fresh-water supplies as well as by its nearby rich agricultural land and marble quarries.

The Ruins

Theatre Having shaken off the persistent would-be guides at the entrance, the first monument you come to is the restored theatre on the right. Built in 188 by one of the city's wealthy residents, Marcus Quadrutus, it could accommodate an audience of 3500 on its 19 tiers.

Temple of Saturn A track up to the right just past the theatre leads to the Temple of Saturn, which was erected on the site of an earlier temple dedicated to the ancient Semitic god Baal.

Square of the Winds Back at the theatre, the track leads past the site administration office to an unusual winding street (the

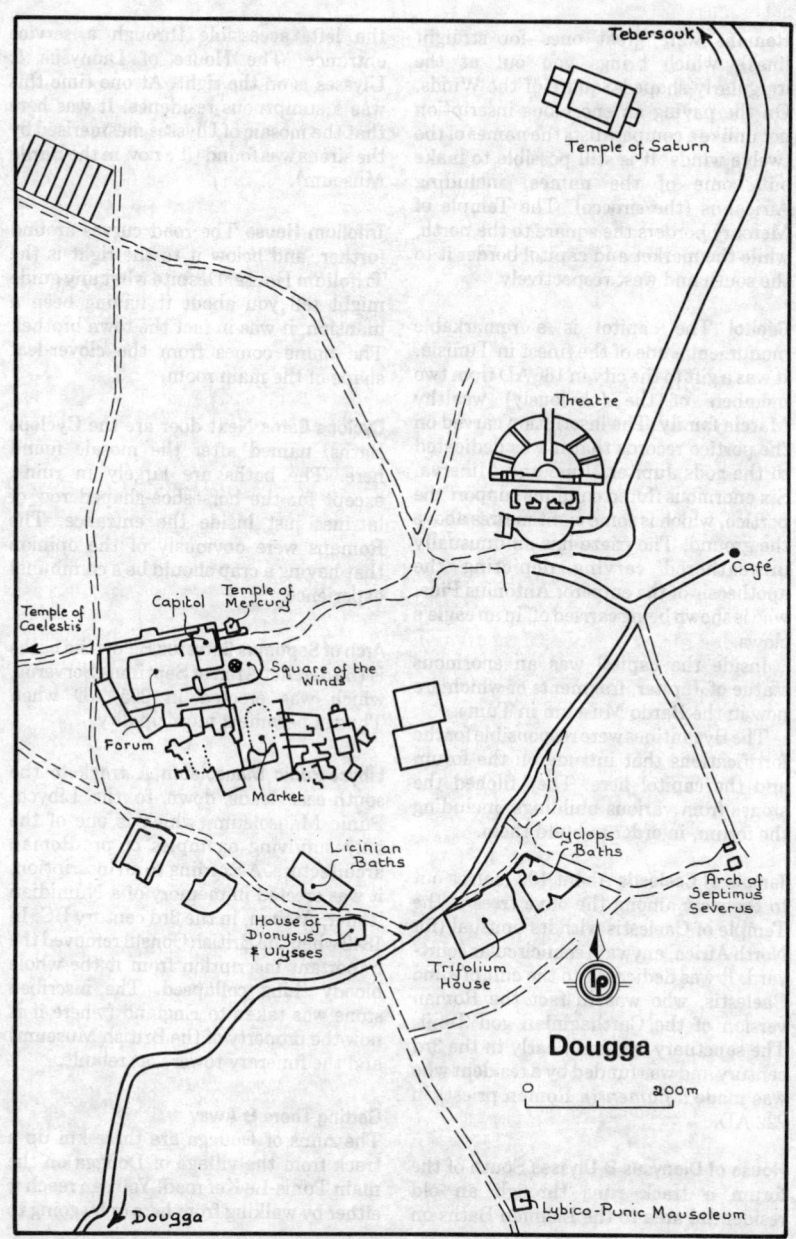

Tebersouk

Temple of Saturn

Theatre

Café

Temple of Caelestis

Capitol

Temple of Mercury

Square of the Winds

Forum

Market

Licinian Baths

House of Dionysus & Ulysses

Cyclops Baths

Arch of Septimus Severus

Trifolium House

Dougga

0   200m

Dougga

Lybico-Punic Mausoleum

Romans were great ones for straight lines), which brings you out at the irregularly-shaped Square of the Winds. On the paving an enormous inscription not unlike a compass lists the names of the twelve winds. It is still possible to make out some of the names, including Africanus (the sirocco). The Temple of Mercury borders the square to the north, while the market and capitol border it to the south and west respectively.

Capitol The capitol is a remarkable monument – one of the finest in Tunisia. It was a gift to the city in 166 AD from two members of the (obviously) wealthy Marcia family. The inscription carved on the portico records that it was dedicated to the gods Jupiter, Juno and Minerva. Six enormous fluted columns support the portico, which is some eight metres above the ground. The frieze has an unusually unweathered carving depicting the apotheosis of the emperor Antonius Pius, who is shown being carried off in an eagle's claws.

Inside the capitol was an enormous statue of Jupiter, fragments of which are now in the Bardo Museum in Tunis.

The Byzantines were responsible for the fortifications that intrude on the forum and the capitol here. They filched the stones from various buildings, including the forum, in order to build them.

Temple of Caelestis About 100 metres out to the west among the olive trees is the Temple of Caelestis with its unusual (for North Africa, anyway) semicircular courtyard. It was dedicated to the cult of Juno Caelestis, who was in fact the Roman version of the Carthaginian god Tanit. The sanctuary was built early in the 3rd century and was funded by a resident who was made a *flamen* (a Roman priest) in 222 AD.

House of Dionysus & Ulysses South of the forum a track runs through an old residential area to the Licinian Baths on the left, accessible through a service entrance. The House of Dionysus & Ulysses is on the right. At one time this was a sumptuous residence. It was here that the mosaic of Ulysses mesmerised by the sirens was found (it's now in the Bardo Museum).

Trifolium House The road curves around further, and below it to the right is the Trifolium House. Despite what any guide might tell you about it having been a mansion, it was in fact the town brothel. The name comes from the clover-leaf shape of the main room.

Cyclops Baths Next door are the Cyclops Baths, named after the mosaic found here. The baths are largely in ruins, except for the horseshoe-shaped row of latrines just inside the entrance. The Romans were obviously of the opinion that having a crap should be a communal experience.

Arch of Septimus Serverus Below the baths is the derelict Arch of Septimus Serverus, which was erected in 205 AD when Thugga became a municipality.

Libyco-Punic Mausoleum A track to the south-east leads down to the Libyco-Punic Mausoleum, which is one of the only surviving examples of pre-Roman architecture. According to an inscription, it was erected in memory of a Numidian leader, Ateban, in the 3rd century BC. In 1842 when the British Consul removed the important inscription from it the whole bloody thing collapsed. The inscribed stone was taken to England (where it is now the property of the British Museum) and the funerary tower was rebuilt.

Getting There & Away
The ruins of Dougga are three km up a track from the village of Dougga on the main Tunis-Le Kef road. You can reach it either by walking from here or by going to

Tebersouk, six km from the site, and hoping you can hitch from there.

The track up to the site is signposted by the Mobil station at the far end of the village. You can save yourself a bit of the walk by cutting through the middle of the village and asking the locals for directions. It's a solid hour's walk but, as long as the weather is not stinking hot (it invariably is in summer), it is an easy uphill grade and you will often have local people for company.

Car drivers should note that the track up from Dougga village gets very rough just below the ruins; you are better off going round via Tebersouk.

Taxi If you are coming on a louage from Le Kef, get off at Dougga. If you arrive in Tebersouk from somewhere else and can't get a lift to the site, take a local louage to Dougga township and walk from there.

TEBERSOUK

This small town sees its fair share of tourists, but no one actually seems to stop; they are all in a hurry to get to Dougga and on to the next place. Not a bad plan really, as there is stuff all here.

Places to Stay

The only reason you might want to stop here is to have a base for visiting the ruins at Dougga. The place to stay is the two-star *Hotel Thugga* (tel 65 713), down by the main road. It is quite OK at TD 12.500/20 for singles/doubles with full board, and is popular with the tour groups at lunch time.

Getting There & Away

There are louages running frequently to the village of Dougga (not the ruins), and less often to Beja, Jendouba and Tunis.

LE KEF

This is a picturesque village perched up on the side of a hill overlooking some fine agricultural land.

Although it has little in the way of

conventional attractions, its location and friendly residents make it a very pleasant place to spend a day or two. In summer its 800-metre elevation means it is significantly cooler than the plains, although it also means that it gets snow in winter.

There is at least one bank here for changing money.

Kasbah

The kasbah dominates the town from the top of the hill. Although it is in a very bad state it is still worth a wander around, and there are some excellent views over the town and surrounding countryside. Until quite recently it was inhabited by the army. There is usually someone hanging around to show you the various points of interest (Turkish mosque, prison cells, gates and walls of various vintages) if your French is up to it.

According to some of the locals there are plans afoot to turn the whole thing into a large tourist hotel but, with the slump in tourism at the moment, this hardly seems likely.

Museums

Immediately below the kasbah is a small museum housed in what was originally a basilica and then later on a mosque. The museum exhibits are not exactly riveting but entrance is free.

There is another regional museum, which is housed in a former zaouia in a small square not far from the presidential palace. The emphasis is on the nomadic Bedouin and there are some well-displayed exhibits including a tent, some crude utensils, jewellery, weaving looms showing the unusual weaving technique, and agricultural implements. The museum is open from 9 am to 12 noon and 3 to 7 pm Tuesday to Saturday, 9 am to 2.30 Sunday; closed Monday; entry is 800 mills – worth a look.

Places to Stay

The lack of both local and foreign tourists in Le Kef is reflected in the accommodation available; there are only a couple of basic but adequate places.

The brand new *Hotel Medina* (tel 20 214) at 18 Rue Farhat Hached is immaculately clean and the staff are friendly. It's in the centre of town, about 20 minutes' walk uphill from the bus station. Rooms cost TD 5 for a double including cold showers.

Just off Ave Bourguiba, the *Hotel La Source* is the next choice; it has definitely seen better days. The tiny rooms face onto a tiny glassed-in courtyard and the sickly yellow paint job doesn't help either. The front rooms are only a few metres from the minaret across the road, so be prepared for the early morning call. Rooms are overpriced at TD 6 for a double with shower.

Although it looks mildly promising from the outside, the *Hotel Auberge* close by cannot really be recommended. The dark and gloomy entrance leads to an equally dark and gloomy bar, and the hotel rooms are not much better. Avoid it if possible.

Places to Eat

As with the hotels, there's little choice. The best place is the small, popular *Restaurant el Hanaa*, 200 metres along Ave Bourguiba, opposite the new, white and ugly multi-storey Banque du Sud building. Good half chickens for TD 1.800 and couscous for 900 mills.

The *Restaurant Venus* has pretensions, is poor value and the owner certainly doesn't win any prizes for friendliness. Tunisian salad is a ridiculous TD 1 and other dishes are similarly overpriced.

Getting There & Away

Transport centres around the bus station, 20 minutes' walk downhill from the centre. Shared taxis shuttle between the town centre and the main intersection at the bottom of the hill, passing the bus station on the way.

Buses leave regularly to Tunis, Kasserine and Ain Draham. Louages are frequent, and go to Tunis, Kasserine, Jendouba and Sakiet Sidi Youssef on the Algerian border, from where there are taxis to the town of Souk Ahras.

Central Tunisia

The central coast of Tunisia has some excellent beaches and, consequently, quite a bit of tourist development. Sousse and Monastir are the major centres but, just a bit further south, the beautiful village of Mahdia is right off the tourist track.

Further south again is Sfax, an interesting regional centre. The Kerkennah Islands just off shore from here are easily accessible, and are a great place to escape the crowds and slow down a bit.

Once you leave the coast and head inland, you are among the olive trees – millions of them! The Romans were the first to plant them and the practice has revived. In fact, olive oil and olives are both important exports today.

Kairouan, the fourth holiest city in Islam, lies on the plains only a couple of hours from Sousse; tradition has it that seven visits here have as much merit as one visit to Mecca. The city was the capital of the first Arab dynasty in North Africa and today is the most fascinating city in the country.

Other attractions of the area are the massive and remarkably well-preserved Roman amphitheatre at El Jem in the olive country, and the ruins of yet another Roman city, Sufetula (Sbeitla today), out on the hot plains near Kasserine, the dull provincial capital.

Sousse

Although Sousse has a large port and is a major industrial centre, it also has an interesting medina and kasbah, and the beach, although crowded in summer, is not at all bad.

It is also a city that is extremely popular with the tour companies and they bring their clients here in droves in summer.

The strip of beach to the north of the town centre is virtually one hotel after another, but you can escape this easily if you want, as you can find quite acceptable accommodation in the medina.

One of the most unusual features of the town today is the way the main Tunis-Sfax railway line runs right along the centre of the main street; the relative calm is well and truly shattered whenever a train comes through. As there are no flashing lights, boom gates, bells or other warning devices of any kind, it's worth a precautionary look when crossing the road to make sure you don't become a decoration on the front of the 4.08 to Sfax.

History

Sousse has been a popular spot for centuries. It was an important Phoenician town before Carthage was even founded, and Hannibal, as leader of the Carthaginian forces, used it as his base against the Romans in the Second Punic War in 218 BC.

It was later occupied by the Romans, Vandals and Byzantines, each of whom gave it a different name. In the 9th century it became the main port of the Aghlabid dynasty based in Kairouan; it was taken over again in later years – first by the Normans in the 12th century, then by the Spaniards in the 16th.

Its most recent problems were in WW II, when it was being used as a German port and was bombed heavily by the Allies; however, it has all been restored since then.

Information

Tourist Offices The national tourist office (tel 25 157) is at 1 Ave Bourguiba, right on the central square, Place Farhat Hached. The only thing they have is an exhaustive list of accommodation in the Sousse

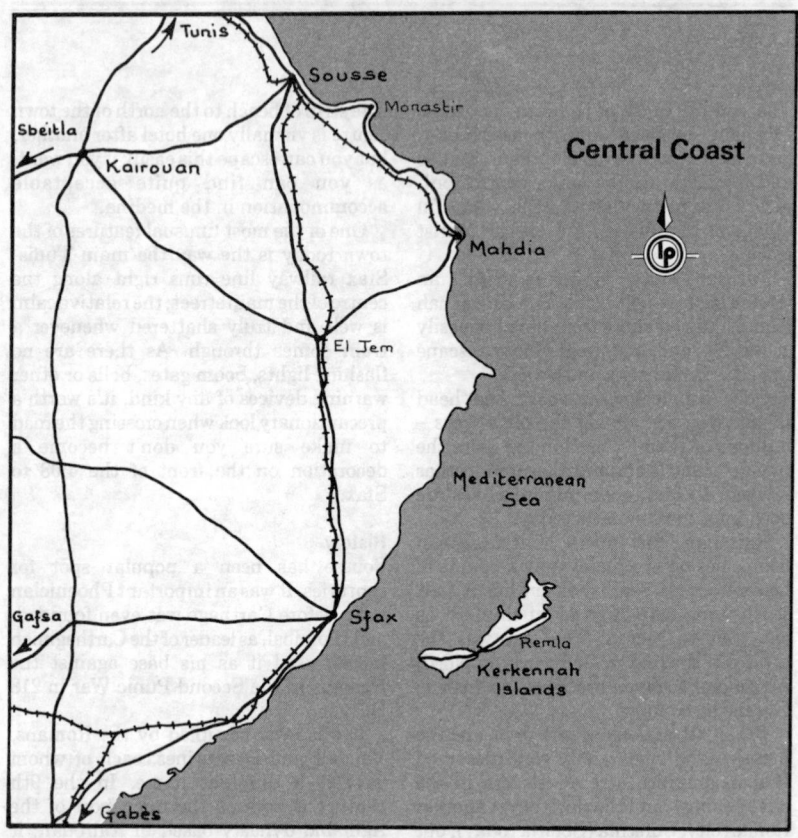

Central Coast

Tunis

Sousse

Monastir

Sbeitla

Kairouan

Mahdia

El Jem

Mediterranean Sea

Gafsa

Sfax

Remla

Kerkennah Islands

Gabès

region, although the staff are quite helpful and speak some English. In summer it is open from 7.30 am to 7.30 pm Monday to Friday and 8 am to 12 noon Sunday.

The local Syndicat d'Initiative (tel 20 431) is across on the other side of the street, in the small, white-domed building. It is here that you buy the ticket to visit the Great Mosque (300 mills).

Post The main post office is also right in the thick of things, on Ave de la République just along from Place Farhat Hached.

Money There are plenty of banks along Ave Bourguiba and up by the beach. One branch of the STB on Ave Bourguiba is open long hours in summer.

Airlines You'll find Tunis Air (tel 27 251) at 5 Ave Bourguiba.

Car Rental The companies with branches here include: Hertz (tel 25 428), Ave Bourguiba; Avis (tel 25 901), Blvd de la Corniche; Budget (tel 24 041), 63 Ave Bourguiba; and Europcar (tel 26 252), Blvd de la Corniche.

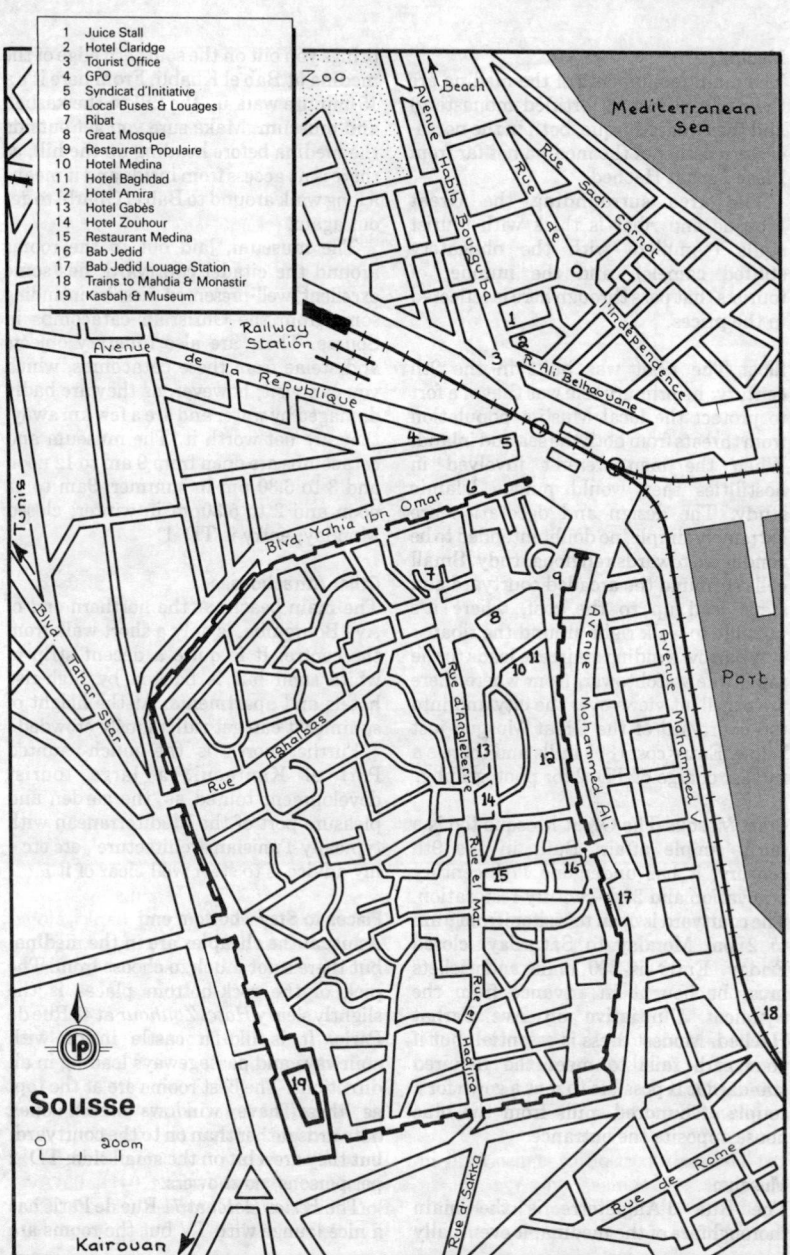

1   Juice Stall
2   Hotel Claridge
3   Tourist Office
4   GPO
5   Syndicat d'Initiative
6   Local Buses & Louages
7   Ribat
8   Great Mosque
9   Restaurant Populaire
10 Hotel Medina
11 Hotel Baghdad
12 Hotel Amira
13 Hotel Gabès
14 Hotel Zouhour
15 Restaurant Medina
16 Bab Jedid
17 Bab Jedid Louage Station
18 Trains to Mahdia & Monastir
19 Kasbah & Museum

Zoo

Beach

Mediterranean
Sea

Avenue Habib Bourguiba

Rue Sadi Carnot

Rue de l'Independence

Railway
Station

Avenue   de la   République

Tunis

Blvd Tahar Sfar

Blvd. Yahia ibn Omar

Rue Aghalbas

Rue

Rue d'Angleterre

Avenue Mohammed Ali

Avenue Mohammed V

Port

Rue el Mar

Rue el Hadira

Rue P Sakka

P Sakka

Rue de Rome

Sousse

0   200m

Kairouan

R. Ali Belhaouane

Medina

The main monuments of the medina are the ribat (a sort of fortified monastery) and the Great Mosque, both in the north-eastern corner of the medina not far from Place Farhat Hached.

The area surrounding the Great Mosque and ribat is thick with tourist stalls (complete with the obligatory stuffed camels), and the number of tourists that pass through here is reflected in the prices.

Ribat The ribat was built in the 9th century; its primary role was that of a fort to protect the local Muslim population from threats from both the sea and inland. When the men weren't involved in hostilities they would pursue Islamic study. The design and decoration are extremely simple, no doubt intended to be conducive towards religious study. Small cells surround the arcaded courtyard and steps lead up to the roof, where it's possible to walk right around the ribat.

A narrow winding staircase leads to the top of the watchtower, from where there are excellent views over the city and into the courtyard of the Great Mosque just below. Entry costs 800 mills and there's a further charge of TD 2 for photography.

Great Mosque The Great Mosque too is a fairly simple affair. Built in the 9th century, it has undergone 17th-century renovation and 20th-century restoration. The courtyard is open to visitors from 9 am to 2 pm Monday to Saturday; closed Friday. Entry is 300 mills and tickets must be bought in advance from the Syndicat d'Initiative on Ave Farhat Hached. Modest dress is essential, but if your garb fails to meet the required standard it is possible to rent a gown for a couple of hundred mills from the blue house opposite the entrance.

Museum

The Rue d'Angleterre is the main thoroughfare of the medina; it eventually brings you out on the southern edge of the medina at Bab el Khabli. From here it's a 15-minute walk up the hill to the kasbah and museum. Make sure you get outside the medina before heading up the hill, as there is no access from inside and it means a long walk around to Bab el Gharbi to get out again.

The museum, laid out in the rooms around the citadel courtyard, has some excellent, well-presented mosaics including some from the Christian catacombs in Sousse. There are also funerary objects and stelae from these catacombs, which you can visit; however, as they are badly damaged by water and are a few km away, they are not worth it. The museum and catacombs are open from 9 am to 12 noon and 3 to 6.30 pm in summer, 9am to 12 noon and 2 to 5.30pm in winter; closed Monday; entry is TD 1.

Other Attractions

The main beach, at the northern end of Ave Bourguiba, is only a short walk from the centre. It is quite a decent strip of white sand but is backed by high-rise hotels and apartments. At the height of summer it can get ridiculously crowded.

Further north is the much-vaunted Port el Kantaoui, a large tourist development touted as 'the garden and pleasure port of the Mediterranean with typically Tunisian architecture', etc etc – my advice is to steer well clear of it.

Places to Stay – bottom end

As usual the cheapies are in the medina, but there's not much to choose from. The pick of the rock-bottom places is the slightly sleazy *Hotel Zouhour* at 48 Rue de Paris. It is like a castle inside with stairways and passageways leading in all directions. The best rooms are at the top, as these have windows which open outwards rather than on to the courtyard, but they are a bit on the small side; TD 2 per persons, no showers.

The *Perles Hotel* at 71 Rue de Paris has a nice lounge with TV but the rooms are

Top: Restaurant window, Tataouine, Tunisia (HF)
Left: Underground dwelling, Matmata, Tunisia (HF)
Right: Old granary, Medenine, Tunisia (HF)

Top: Fishing boats, Jerba, Tunisia (HF)
Left: Beach backed by Genoese fort, Tabarka, Tunisia (HF)
Right: Whitewashed buildings of Sidi Bou Said, Tunisia (HF)

certainly not of the same standard; they are small and have only folding beds. They cost TD 6 for a double but this is negotiable; showers are 250 mills.

If you are desperate, the *Hotel Baghdad* by the Great Mosque has a few poky rooms around a high-walled yard and the whole place has the air of a prison. The toilets stink and the 'shower' is a well with a bucket. All these comforts and conveniences can be yours for a mere TD 2 per person.

Places to Stay – middle

Things improve rapidly here. The *Hotel Amira* (tel 26 325), inside the medina on the eastern edge near Bab Jedid, is not a bad place. It costs TD 10 for a double with bath and breakfast, which you can have served to you outside on the upstairs terrace.

The *Hotel Medina* (tel 21 722), right by the Great Mosque, has a nice airy and cool lounge room in the centre and is popular with younger tour groups; the locals are attracted to the smoky and sleazy air-conditioned bar at the back. Rooms are clean and cost TD 9.250/13.500 for singles/doubles with bath and breakfast.

On the other side of the mosque, near the ribat, the *Hotel Ahla* (tel 20 570) is conveniently located and has good rooms for TD 8.500 per person.

Just around the corner from the Amira is the *Residence Fatma* (tel 22 198), which is usually heavily booked but you may be lucky. Rooms cost TD 11 for a double with breakfast.

Lastly, outside the medina on Ave Bourguiba, the *Hotel Claridge* (tel 24 759) is a good one-star hotel in the old style. They charge TD 7.700 per person for a room with shower and breakfast.

Places to Stay – top end

The top-end resort hotels are all along the two main streets in the north of town, Blvd Hedi Chaker and Blvd de la Corniche. Most are geared to the package-tour industry and are fully booked for the season.

Some of the cheaper ones include: *Sousse Palace* (tel 25 200, on Ave Bourguiba), *Nour Justinia* (tel 26 381) and the *El Hana Beach* (tel 26 900).

Places to Eat

In the medina, the *Restaurant Medina* is in the street which leads up from Bab Jedid. The menu is in Arabic only, but they do good casse-croûtes and other Tunisian food; they also make one small concession to hygiene by keeping everything in a fly-proof cabinet. There's another good local place, the *Restaurant Populaire*, opposite the front of the Great Mosque, which doesn't have a sign in English.

As you'd expect with the number of tourists, there are plenty of restaurants catering to them. None of them offer anything out of the ordinary, and in fact most are very ordinary. Menus are often in three or four languages and the waiters can speak any or all of them. Most are along Ave Bourguiba and Place Farhat Hached. One that is quite good is the *Restaurant le Bonheur* on Place Farhat Hached, which has excellent grilled tuna steaks for TD 8 for two.

In summer, just off Ave Bourguiba in a side street next to the Hotel Claridge, there's a stall which sells a mixed fruit juice for 300 mills; it contains all sorts of mysterious things but tastes great.

Getting There & Away

Bus The bus station is to the north, some way out of the centre. It is far more convenient to arrive by train if possible.

There are at least eight departures daily for Tunis, and all the buses heading for Sfax, Gabès and Jerba pass through on the way.

For services within the Sousse region (to Monastir, Mahdia and Kairouan), buses leave from the end of Place Farhat Hached near the port entrance. To Mahdia, there are 16 buses daily from 7 am to 9.30 pm and the trip takes two hours; to Kairouan, there are seven daily from 5.30 am to 3 pm, and the trip takes 1½ hours and costs TD 1.500.

A few services (to Gabès for instance) leave from the station known as Sidi Yahia just outside the northern wall of the medina.

Train The railway station is right in the middle of town, so train is the most convenient way to arrive. The medina and hotels are only five minutes' walk from here.

For Tunis there are eight trains daily for the three-hour trip. Air-con 2nd class costs TD 2.500. For Sfax there are six departures per day (two hours); three per day for Gabès (four hours), one of which goes on to Metlaoui (for Tozeur).

There are also local trains, which run on a recently-completed line down to Monastir and Mahdia from near Bab Jedid. For Monastir they run hourly from 6 am to 9 pm and cost 600 mills. For Mahdia the services are much less frequent: about five daily, and there are none between 7 am and 1 pm.

Taxi Louages for all over the country leave from the station near Bab Jedid on Ave Mohammed Ali. Regular departures for Mahdia, Kairouan, Tunis, Kasserine and Sfax.

AROUND SOUSSE
Monastir

Situated on a headland some 15 km south of Sousse, Monastir must have at one stage been a pleasant little village. Today it has become a national showpiece, mainly because it was Bourguiba's birthplace and it is here that he has chosen to be buried.

The monuments in the centre include the Bourguiba family mausoleum with its twin cupolas, the 8th-century ribat (which overlooks the sea), and the 9th-century Great Mosque. The ribat has been used as a film set on more than a couple of occasions. Two films that have had scenes

shot here are *Life of Brian* and *Life of Christ*.

MAHDIA

Mahdia is one of the few towns on this section of coast which has managed to escape being turned into a tourist resort. It's a beautifully relaxed place, with a small medina stuck out at the end of a little promontory, 60 km or so south of Sousse.

History

The town has an important history dating back to 916, when the first Fatimid ruler, Obeid Allah, made it his capital. He was a self-declared Mahdi, 'one who is guided' (to convert the world to Islam). He belonged to the Shi'ite sect considered heretical by the Sunni majority and therefore needed a place that was easily defended. Mahdia fitted the bill neatly, as it is on a high promontory. In order to defend the town a massive wall, in places up to 10 metres thick, was built right across the neck of the spit, with just one easily guarded gate giving access.

However, in 968 the Fatimids realised their dream of becoming caliphs in Cairo and from that time on the town decreased in importance. It was still important enough for the Christians to invade in the 11th century, followed by the Normans in the 12th and the Spanish in the 16th. When the Spanish left they blew the walls down, only to have the Ottoman Turks partially reconstruct them.

Information

There is a small tourist office just inside the main gate, Skifa el Kahla, and the guy here tries to be helpful. The post office is near the Grand Hotel in the new part of town, 500 metres' walk from the Skifa el Kahla.

There are a few banks, mostly along the foreshore road on the harbour side of the promontory.

The Friday market and the daily fish market are held in the large white building opposite the fishing harbour.

Medina

The medina starts with the massive gate, Skifa el Kahla, which at one time was part of the 10-metre-thick wall that blocked off this narrow part of the promontory. The narrow vaulted passageway had various iron gates which could be lowered to block the entrance to the medina.

Once inside, the tourist office is straight ahead on the right. On the inside of the wall here are steps leading up to the top of the gate, from which you can get a good perspective of the town and see how well defended it was.

The narrow, cobbled main street first leads to a small Museum of Silk on the right, identified by a small nameplate by the door (which seems to be permanently closed). The street then leads past a hammam on the left. It eventually opens out onto an immaculate small square, complete with shady trees, vines and cafés. By day the old men sit around in the shade drinking coffee; later on the square livens up considerably, with all the men coming out for their evening coffee and game of dominoes.

The main street then continues and comes out at a larger square dominated by the Great Mosque. This is a 20th-century recreation of the original built by the Mahdi in the 10th century and it is a very simple construction. Its only major feature is the unadorned entrance, a characteristic of Fatimid design.

On the highest point of the headland is the Borj el Kebir, which was built in the 16th century and has been heavily restored. It is not worth the 800 mills entry, as there is nothing to see inside and the views from the ramparts are not that much better than from on the ground.

The road past the fort leads through an enormous cemetery to the lighthouse on the end of the headland; down to the right is what is left of the old Fatimid port, today used as a mooring for a few fishing boats.

Weaving cotton sheets and exquisite cloth for weddings on hand looms is widespread throughout the old city, and the click-clack of the shuttles is often the only sound disturbing the torpor which sets in on hot summer afternoons. Many of these small workshops have a definite air of the Dickensian workhouse about them, with poor lighting, cramped conditions and no ventilation. The guys doing the weaving are usually more than willing to break the boredom and explain the finer points of their craft. Wedding material is full of gold thread and has to be ordered at least 12 months in advance.

The water here is a clear blue and swimming is definitely possible, either from the rocks outside the Hotel El Jazira or from the beach about three km further along the coast.

Place to Stay - bottom end

The family-run *Hotel El Jazira* (tel 81 629) is not the friendliest place in the world but is one of the best bargains in the country. It is right on the water on the northern side of the headland, about 50 metres inside Skifa el Kahla. Some of the rooms look straight out over the water, although the best view is to be had from the bathroom. Beds cost TD 2 and there are hot showers. There's a table and chairs on the roof.

Places to Stay - middle

The two-star *Grand Hotel* (tel 81 256) is about 500 metres from the main gate along the Sousse road, which is the main road to the right as you come out of the gate. The hotel has a nice shaded garden, with pergolas covered in bougainvillea and even cute little cubicles to sit in privacy. Rooms cost TD 10 for a double with bath and breakfast.

The *Hotel Rand* (tel 81 448) is further again from the centre. From the Grand Hotel, take the left fork and then turn left after about 200 metres at the first major intersection; the hotel is on the right. At TD 7 for a double it's not bad value but its location makes it inconvenient.

Places to Stay - top end

Out along the beach about three km north of town is the *Hotel Sables d'Or* (tel 81 137); this is a three-star resort hotel that is nevertheless fairly low key. The beach here is clean and uncrowded; there are shade shelters on it, and small yachts and sailboards for hire. Rooms cost TD 10 or TD 15 per person for bed and breakfast depending on the season. There are blue-and-white service taxis which run out past here from the corner near the market for 200 mills per person.

Places to Eat

There's not a lot of choice here, but there's one small place which is extremely popular at lunch times and serves excellent food. This is the *Restaurant El Moez*, between Skifa el Kahla and the market. Run by a very jolly fat fellow who welcomes you with open arms, it serves the best shakshuka in the country and also has excellent fresh fish. In the evening the selection is more limited.

Getting There & Away

Bus Buses leave from the kiosk near the market up by the entrance to the fishing harbour. There are regular departures to Sousse and Monastir, and less frequent departures to Kairouan and Tunis.

Train The brand new railway station is on the other side of the Esso Station from the louages. The line from Monastir was only opened in 1987, so the station is very modern and comes complete with marble floors and potted plants.

There are five departures daily for the 75-minute journey to Sousse, but there's nothing between 7 am and 1 pm. For Tunis there is one air-con departure daily at midday which takes 3½ hours.

Taxi The louage station is right by the Esso station at the opposite end of the wide open space to the bus station. It is only about 300 metres from the centre. There are departures for Monastir, Sousse, Kairouan, El Jem and Sfax.

EL JEM

If it wasn't for the fact that El Jem has a very well-preserved Roman amphitheatre not much smaller than the Colosseum in Rome, this otherwise unremarkable town would certainly be low on the list of priorities for any visitor to Tunisia - its setting on the flat plains is dull and the summer heat is oppressive.

The amphitheatre sticks up in the middle of the town, and the tourists come flocking to see one of the most impressive Roman monuments in North Africa - it's well worth a visit.

From the 2nd century AD onwards, ancient Thysdrus prospered as the centre of an olive-growing region; it was a town with sumptuous villas adorned with some brilliant mosaics.

In 238 AD at the age of 80 Gordian was declared emperor of Rome here, and the amphitheatre is a legacy of his reign. It suffered badly in the 17th century when the guts were blown out of one side of it in order to flush out some dissidents who had taken refuge within the walls. Not only did this completely demolish a large section it also destabilised the rest of it; some fairly hasty and none-too-professional repairs were done to stop the whole thing collapsing.

The seating capacity is estimated to have been around the 30,000 mark, although none of the seats remain today. Under the arena two long passageways were uncovered, and it is believed that these held the animals, gladiators or other unfortunates who would get thrust into the ring to do battle and provide entertainment for the masses.

The amphitheatre is enclosed by a small fence and there's an entry charge of TD 1. Around the entrance are the usual hangers-on who always appear wherever there are tourists in number – camel drivers, souvenir sellers, guides, etc etc. As for the number of Land Rovers that come through here from Sousse 'on safari' fully laden with all the gear, it's really quite amazing.

About 500 metres south of the amphitheatre, along the road to Sfax, is the museum. This houses yet more mosaics, all found on the site right behind the building, which was an area of particularly rich villas. Some of the mosaics have been left *in situ* while the best have been moved into the museum. It is open from 8.30 am to 12 noon and 2.30 to 6 pm in summer, 8.30 am to 12 noon and 2 to 5.30 pm in winter; entry is TD 1, and there's a further charge of TD 2 for photography.

Across the road from the museum are the ruins of more houses and another amphitheatre, this one much smaller and barely recognisable.

Places to Stay & Eat

Although there is a hotel in town it takes only a couple of hours to see the amphitheatre and museum, so the best thing is to carry on to another destination later in the day. The railway station won't look after baggage but the guy at the entrance to the amphitheatre will keep an eye on it for a while.

The only accommodation in El Jem is the *Hotel Julius* (tel 42), right on the main road by the railway station. It's rooms are arranged around a pleasant courtyard and cost TD 7 for a double; it fills up early in summer.

There are a couple of small restaurants along the main street between the hotel and the museum, but don't expect anything more exotic than brochettes.

For coffee and tea, there are a few cafés around the square directly opposite the railway station.

Getting There & Away

Bus The SNTRI bus office is on the right just before the museum. The only departures are the buses in transit, so in summer it will be difficult to get a seat. The train is a better bet.

Train The railway station is only about five minutes' walk from the amphitheatre and is right in the centre.

For trains south, there are five daily to Sfax (one hour) between 9 am and midnight; two of these go on to Gabès (three hours), while the midnight one goes all the way to Metlaoui (six hours, change in Sfax).

For Tunis, there are only three trains which stop on the way from the south: these are at 6.15 am, 2.40 and 7 pm. The trip takes three hours.

Taxi The louages leave from the street just opposite and to the right of the train station.

Demand often exceeds supply here and it can be a bit of a scramble to get a seat. There are frequent departures to Sousse, Sfax, Kairouan and Mahdia, although things dry up a bit in the afternoon.

Kairouan

Historically, this is the most important town in the country. It ranks behind only Mecca, Medina and Jerusalem in Islam. The medina, with the Great Mosque, is compact and interesting and there are other sights around the town.

With a population of 100,000 Kairouan is the fifth-largest city in the country. It's the centre of a major fruit-growing region and is also well known for the traditional carpet-weaving which is carried out here.

Because of its importance, however, Kairouan sees more than its fair share of tourists. As a result the medina is overflowing with tourist shops, and the merchants have started resorting to a bit of good old Moroccan-style aggression to

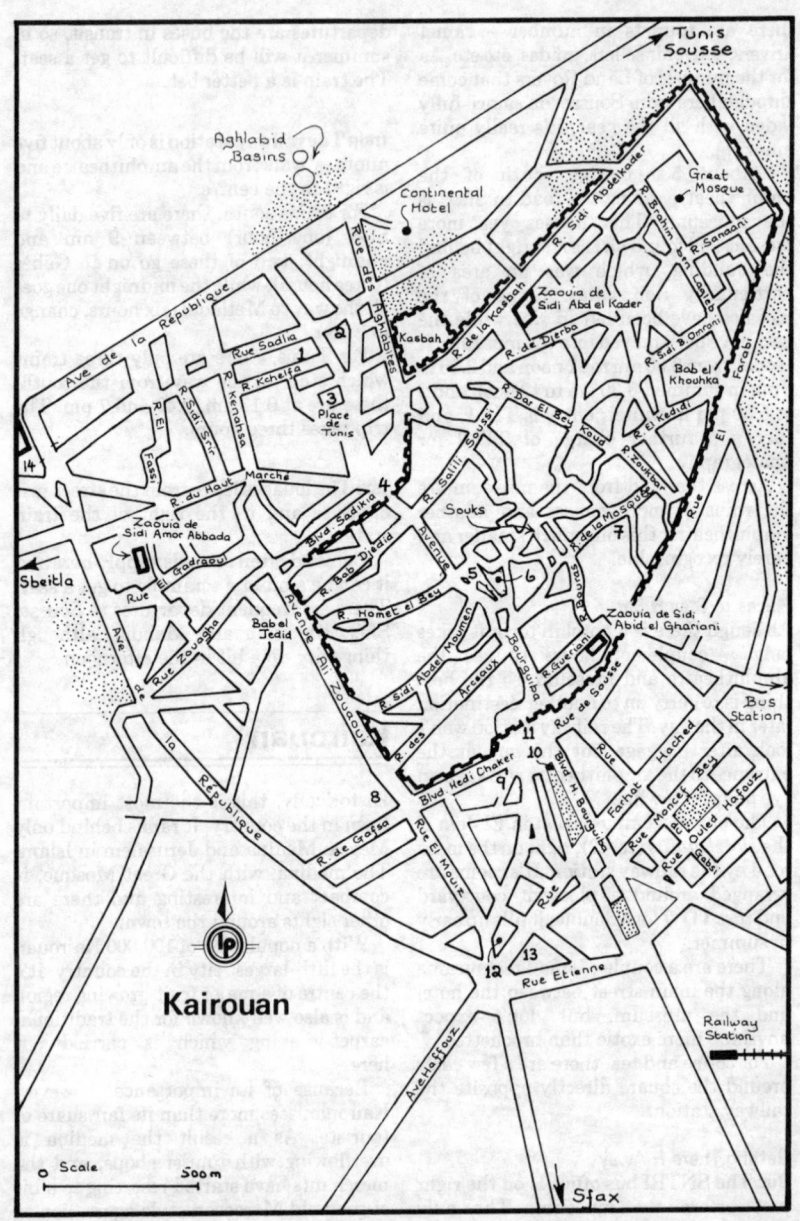

Kairouan

1	Hotel les Aghlabites
2	Hotel El Menema
3	Market
4	Bab Tunis
5	Medina Hotels
6	Bir Barouta
7	Mosque of the Three Doors
8	ONAT Emporium/Museum
9	Hotel Sabra
10	Tourist Office
11	Bab ech Chouhada
12	GPO
13	Louages
14	Zaouia of Sidi Sahab

get business; however, it's easy to cope with all this.

History
Founded in the second half of the 7th century by Aqbar ibn Nafi, Kairouan is where Islam first took hold in the Maghreb. It became the capital of the Aghlabid dynasty in 800 AD, and it was under these rulers that the Great Mosque and other buildings of religious significance were constructed.

The Fatimids conquered the city in 909. When they moved their capital to Mahdia Kairouan went through a period of decline, reaching a low point in 1057 when the Beni Hilal bedouin tribe destroyed the city at the behest of the Fatimid ruler Mustansir.

Although Kairouan was largely rebuilt in the 13th century, it was never to regain its position of political pre-eminence. However, as a religious centre it was and is still the most important place in the country.

Information
Tourist Office The tourist office (tel 20 452) of the national tourist body is right at the entrance to the old city, opposite Bab ech Chouhada (Gate of the Martyrs). Tickets for the main sites can only be bought from here. For TD 1.200 you get a combined ticket, which is valid for two days and gets you into the major monuments around the

city. The office is open from 8 am to 1.30 pm and 3 to 5.30 pm Monday to Saturday; closed Sunday, so obviously tickets for the monuments are not for sale on that day.

Post The main post office is 100 metres or so south of the of Bab ech Chouhada, at the roundabout at the corner of Ave de la République and Rue Farhat Hached.

Money There are plenty of banks for changing money. There's one just inside Bab ech Chouhada and a couple more on Blvd Bourguiba, just around the side of the tourist office.

Airlines The Tunis Air office (tel 20 422) is at 5 Blvd Bourguiba.

Car Rental The only agency in town is Budget (tel 20 528), on Ave de la République near the post office.

Medina
The walled medina is the central part of the city; the new French section spreads away to the south and follows the usual orderly plan. The wall itself is pierced by a number of entrances, the main ones being Bab ech Chouhada to the south and Bab Tunis in the north wall. A 100-metre section in the north wall near the kasbah has been removed to ease the traffic congestion and give the tour buses access to the Great Mosque.

In summer the place is crawling with tour groups, so it's best to get out and about early before they whiz in from Sousse; late afternoon is also a good time. This is also the best way to do it, as Kairouan gets bloody hot in the middle of the day.

The main street of the medina is, you guessed it, Ave Bourguiba. It is wall-to-wall souvenir shops selling every imaginable souvenir from tacky stuffed camels to really beautiful carpets. There are numerous cafés and the odd restaurant as well.

Great Mosque The Great Mosque is in the north-eastern corner of the medina and is the principal monument. The building that you see today dates from 670, although it has been restored more than once since then.

From the outside it is extremely plain, lacking in decoration of any kind, and in fact looks more like a fort. Although it has eight gates, only one of the four on Rue Brahim ben Lagleb along the west side is open today for non-Muslims.

The marble-paved courtyard is surrounded by an arched colonnade and is dominated by the square minaret on the northern side. The marble paving slopes towards the centre, where there is a decorated drain hole down which the collected rainwater falls into the 9th-century cisterns below. There are a couple of wells in the courtyard and, over the centuries, the grooves in the lips of these have been worn in by the ropes which were used to haul out the buckets of water.

It is thought that the lowest level of the 35-metre minaret dates from the 8th century, making it the oldest standing minaret in the world.

The main entrance to the prayer hall is beneath the portico with the cupola, one of five on the mosque. The large wooden doors are fairly recent, dating back to the last century; the carved panel above the doors is particularly fine. The 400 or so pillars within the prayer hall have been filched from various Roman sites throughout the country including Carthage and Sousse. At the far end of the hall it is vaguely possible to make out the precious 9th-century faïence tiles behind the mihrab, which were imported from Baghdad along with the wood for the minbar next to it.

The mosque is open daily except Friday. For people not considered suitably dressed there are robes available at the entrance.

Mosque of the Three Doors Heading back through the lanes of the medina you'll

Mosque of the Three Doors

come to the Mosque of the Three Doors, on Rue de la Mosquée not far from Ave Bourguiba. Although it has just been restored it is not open to the public, but is of interest for the rare 9th-century Arab inscriptions carved in the facade.

Zaouia of Sidi Abid el Ghariani Closer again to Ave Bourguiba is the Zaouia of Sidi Abid el Ghariani, one of the monuments on the ticket. Recently restored, the building dates from the 14th century and contains some fine wood-carving and stucco work. The custodian here is a very willing talker, and will guide you around pointing out the finer points (in French of course) such as the cedar ceiling and the new and old stucco.

Bir Barouta The biggest tourist trap in the whole city is a well, known as Bir Barouta. It is on Ave Bourguiba in the centre of the medina, at the top of a set of stairs through a high arched doorway. In quite a confined space here a poor mangy old camel trudges around and around all day, while the tourists file in and out, taking the obligatory photo and leaving the obligatory tip. Even while the well head was being restored the camel still had to stand there so that the tourists wouldn't be disappointed. The well's popularity stems from the fact that it is supposedly connected to Mecca, so to drink the water is also supposed to do wonders for you.

Other Attractions

To get to the other two monuments requires a bit of foot slogging. The Zaouia of Sidi Sahab and the Aghlabid Basins are both on the Tunis road north of the medina. It takes a couple of hours to see both of them.

The Zaouia of Sidi Sahab was built in honour of Abu Zama el Belaoui, a saint and friend of the Prophet who is renowned for always carrying three hairs from the Prophet's beard around with him. For this reason he became known as the Prophet's barber, which explains the other name of this zaouia – the Mosque of the Barber.

A very highly decorated passageway leads off the white courtyard into the main courtyard of the zaouia, which is also highly decorated with tiles and stucco work. In a room off to the left is the tomb of the designer of the Great Mosque, while the saint's tomb is in the room on the far side of the courtyard. Non-Muslims are allowed to enter as far as the courtyard only.

As at the Great Mosque, robes are available at the entrance. This is the third of the monuments on the ticket.

The Aghlabid Basins are a km to the east of the Mosque of the Barber, along the Ave de la République. These two cisterns were originally built in the 9th century and were filled by an aqueduct from a spring some 30 km away; they were some of the many which once used to supply the town with water. The larger of the two is over 130 metres in diameter and

the perimeter wall has curious buttressing. In the centre are pillars which used to hold a pavilion where the rulers could come to relax in the cool on summer evenings. They were heavily restored about 20 years ago and are all concrete, but are still worth a quick look.

Places to Stay – bottom end

The best place in town is outside the medina opposite Bab ech Chouhada. This is the big, clean *Hotel Sabra* (tel 20 260), which is popular and conveniently located; it charges TD 3.500/6 for singles/ doubles including breakfast.

There are a couple of places in the medina. The *Hotel Barouta*, on the square on Ave Bourguiba, is noisy and barely adequate; rooms cost TD 3 per person.

A better bet is the *Hotel Marhala* (tel 20 736) at 35 Souk el Belaghija, one of the covered souks off Ave Bourguiba right in the heart of the medina. The hotel is an old hostel and offers something a little different from the average medina hotel. The rooms are tiny, however, and the hard-drinking courtyard bar downstairs adds a rather sleazy atmosphere. Rooms cost TD 3.500 per person. To find the hotel, head through the big arch with crenellated top, on the right on Ave Bourguiba coming from Bab ech Chouhada. It's easy to miss during business hours, as it is obscured with all sorts of stuff from the shops selling souvenirs. The hotel is about 50 metres along on the left.

North of Bab Tunis, the new, characterless *Hotel Les Aghlabites* is a 65-room hotel with an enormous tiled courtyard, which is not unlike a mosque. All the rooms face inward and are quite good value at TD 3 per person with bath.

Places to Stay – middle

The *Hotel El Menema* (tel 20 182) is a brand new place a couple of blocks north of Bab Tunis. The rooms are all arranged around a covered courtyard but some also have windows to the outside. Charges are TD 6 per person in rooms with bath, one dinar less without bath; these prices include breakfast.

Places to Stay – top end

The *Hotel Continental* (tel 20 607) is on Ave de la République, right opposite the Aghlabid Basins. It has definitely seen better days, but is air conditioned and charges TD 19/29 for singles/doubles with breakfast. It's no real problem to just stroll in and use the pool, regardless of whether you are staying there or not.

Places to Eat

The fact that most tourists come here just for a day trip is reflected in the fact that there are very few restaurants. One that is quite good is the *Restaurant Faïzour*, well signposted but tucked away in the corner of the small square on Ave Bourguiba. You can sit outside in the evening. Be precise about what you order, or they may try to bring out all sorts of stuff and add it to the bill.

There are a couple of other Tunisian restaurants along Ave Bourguiba.

Things to Buy

Kairouan is one of the major carpet centres in the country, so if you are in the market for one this is a good place to do your shopping. The ONAT emporium/museum on Ave Ali Zouaoui not only has an excellent display of old rugs but also sells new ones; you can get a good idea of prices and what is available, although the prices here are certainly not the cheapest around.

All carpets for sale which have been inspected and classified by ONAT carry a label and seal on the back. Ones without this label may be of dubious quality, so don't buy indiscriminately.

Getting There & Away

Bus The bus station is to the south-east of Bab ech Chouhada, about 15 minutes'

walk away. Both the SNTRI and the regional buses leave from here.

There are regular departures to Sousse, Sfax, Kasserine, Gafsa and Tunis.

Taxi Louages to the north, east and south leave from opposite the post office on Rue Farhat Hached. Departures from here include Tunis and Sousse.

For departures west (Sbeitla, Kasserine and Gafsa) louages leave from a yard about 500 metres along the Sbeitla road from Ave de la République.

SBEITLA

Stuck right out in the middle of nowhere, Sbeitla is quite a good Roman site, although it is not really on the way to or from anywhere in particular. If you have your own vehicle it is worth a detour; for those without, stop off if it's on your route, otherwise don't make a special trip to see it.

The site lies only 500 metres or so from the lifeless town of Sbeitla, 40 km east of Kasserine and 120 km south-west of Kairouan.

The history of the Roman town of Sufetula is not well known, especially during the period from the 2nd to the 4th century AD, the height of Roman prosperity in North Africa.

Things to See

From the town the first monument you come across is the restored triumphal Arch of Diocletian, among the eucalypt trees to the right of the road. The site entrance, however, is a further couple of hundred metres along, between a couple of Byzantine forts.

Once inside, the ruins of interest are off to the left – there is a well-trodden path which is easy to follow. The walled forum is still easy to identify, but the dominant structures are the three temples on the north side. Although they have been largely reconstructed, they provide one of the best examples of how the centre of towns was dominated by temple buildings.

Out behind the temples are the ruins of a couple of churches. The first is a basilica with three aisles and the second a Byzantine cathedral with five aisles. Just on the forum side of the latter is a beautifully restored baptistry, complete with mosaics which include colourful floral and cross motifs.

Back towards the river, the theatre is in a bad way; at one time it must have been fantastic with its position right above the bank of the oued.

Opposite the entrance to the site is a small museum which even the custodian tells you is not worth it – sound advice.

Places to Stay

If bad luck or bad management finds you looking for a bed here, you do at least have a choice. The *Hotel Bakini* on the main street in the township would do in a pinch.

For something better there's the fancy *Hotel Sufetula*, 500 metres beyond the site on the Kasserine road. This place is designed with tourists in mind and it's reflected in the prices: TD 12.500/17.400 for rooms with bath and breakfast. One big advantage is that there is a swimming pool; also, the hotel overlooks the site itself.

Getting There & Away

Transport centres around the dusty bus station, 200 metres south of the main intersection. You can't miss it; this is only a small town.

There are connections with Tunis, Kasserine, Tozeur, Kairouan, Dahmani and Le Kef.

Sfax

With a population of over 375,000, Sfax is the second-largest city in the country. It is a major port; exports which are shipped

from here include phosphate from the Gafsa region and olive oil from the thousands of groves near the coast.

As a place to visit, Sfax is not exactly riveting. However, the walled medina is worth a wander around in, if only to see what a medina is like before it gets filled with souvenir shops. Also, the folk museum set in a typical 17th-century house is excellent.

The new city is really devoid of interest but ferries from the port give access to the nearby Kerkennah Islands. These are an ideal place to escape to and do nothing for a few days, mainly because there is nothing to do there except swim on the mediocre beaches or rent a bicycle and explore a bit.

Information

Tourist Office The local Syndicat is in the small green-roofed pavilion in a small square on Ave Bourguiba. As usual they are of very little use, and this is compounded by the fact that the office is open only in the mornings.

Post The post office is the enormous edifice on Ave Bourguiba which occupies the entire first block from the railway station. The entrance for posting letters and parcels is the small door on Ave Bourguiba under the 'Rapide Poste' sign.

Money There are plenty of banks for changing money along Ave Bourguiba and Rue de la République.

Airlines The Tunis Air office (tel 22 962) is at 4 Ave de l'Armée.

Car Rental The following agencies have offices in Sfax: Avis (tel 24 605), Rue Tahar Sfar; Hertz (tel 28 626), 47 Ave Bourguiba; and Europcar (tel 26 680), 16 Ave Bourguiba.

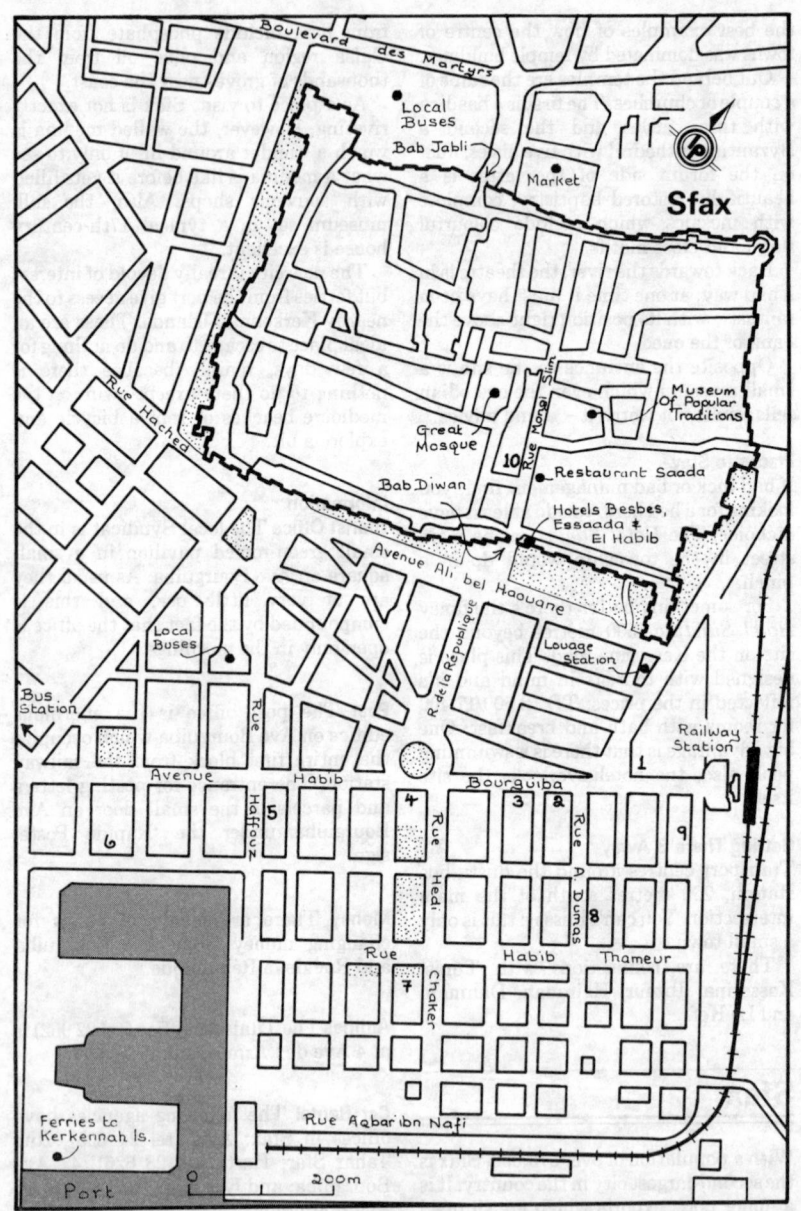

1	GPO
2	French Consulate
3	Hotel Sfax Centre
4	Town Hall & Museum
5	Pizzeria Restaurant
6	Fish Market
7	Hotel Les Oliviers
8	Hotel de la Paix
9	SNTRI Buses
10	Hotel Medina

Medina

The walls of the medina originally dated from the 9th century, but what you see today is a mixture from many periods.

The main access from the new city is through Bab Diwan in the middle of the southern wall. The main street through the medina, Rue Mongi Slim, is incredibly narrow and is little more than a footpath.

About a third of the way along is a small street to the right (next to No 54) which leads to the well set-out Museum of Popular Traditions; this is set in a 17th-century mansion, Dar Djellouli, at 5 Rue Sidi Ali Nouri. The house alone is worth a visit, with its beautiful carved wood and stucco work. The exhibits help give a better grasp of everyday life in the times of the beys – costumes, jewellery and household implements. The display of calligraphy is especially interesting. The museum is open daily in summer from 9 am to 12 noon and 3 to 6.30 pm; in winter it's open daily, except Monday, from 9 am to 12 noon and 2 to 5.30 pm; entry is 800 mills.

Just outside the north gate, Bab Djebli, is the newly constructed market, the southern wall of which is lined with the butchers' stalls – don't venture in if you can't stand the sight of butchered animals. Most stalls have the head of the animal prominently displayed, presumably so you can see what sort of a beast it was, and the stalls sell everything from tongues to testicles.

New City

The focal point of the *ville nouvelle* is the very formal main square, Place Hedi Chaker, with its statue of Bourguiba and the town hall with its clashing dome and clock tower (minus the clock).

In the town hall itself is the Museum of Antiquities, which has a few mosaics and other bits and pieces of only passing interest – you can easily pass this one up.

Places to Stay – bottom end

Once again, the medina offers a choice of cheapies. The *Hotel Besbes* (tel 27 271) is about 50 metres inside Bab Diwan to the right in amongst a group of cheap hotels. It's friendly if a little gloomy and small rooms cost TD 5 for a double. The *Hotel Essaada* next door is similar, while the *Hotel El Habib* on the other side of the road only has four-bed rooms.

There are a few more cheapies on Rue Mongi Slim. The *Hotel Medina* at No 53 charges TD 6 for a double and 500 mills for a shower. It's not a bad place but lacks privacy.

The best place in this category, however, is the friendly *Hotel de la Paix* (tel 21 436) on Rue Alexandre Dumas, outside the medina. It's very clean and a decent-sized room with bath costs TD 6 a double, one dinar less without bath. Right next door is the *Hotel Alexander*, which is a good deal more flash.

Places to Stay – top end

If you can afford it, the place to stay is the very classy *Hotel Les Oliviers* (tel 20 188) on Ave Habib Thameur, two blocks south of the town hall. It is a grand old building which still has an air of elegance. Rooms cost TD 12/18 for singles/doubles with breakfast, TD 2.500 more with air-con.

Sfax's newest monster is the four-star *Hotel Sfax Centre* on Ave Bourguiba, which is popular with the tour groups. Rooms cost TD 32/45 with air-con; there's a swimming pool and all the other frills.

Places to Eat

For cheap Tunisian food, there are a few good places just inside Bab Diwan. To the right is the clean *Restaurant Tunisien*, where a main meal costs around TD 1. There are a couple of others up to the left of Bab Diwan.

The small and cosy *Restaurant Saada* on Rue Mongi Slim also has quite reasonable food and friendly service.

Avoid the *Hamburger Diane Fast-Food* on Place Hedi Chaker – it's a blatant tourist rip-off. If you do sit down for a tea or snack check the prices first, as they will be double the usual if you don't get things straight from the outset.

The *Pizzeria Ristorante* on Rue Haffouz, not far from the port, has reasonable pizzas ranging from TD 1.200 to TD 2.200.

For just a tea or cold drink there are plenty of cafés on Place de l'Indépendence, behind the tourist office.

Getting There & Away

Bus The SNTRI office is almost opposite the railway station, at the eastern end of Ave Bourguiba. There are departures for Gabès, Jerba, Tataouine, Medenine, Matmata and Tunis, and booking in advance is advisable. However, most buses are actually only stopping in transit, so advance booking is not possible.

For regional buses to Gafsa and places south, there is a station about 15 minutes' walk west of the town hall. In summer it's a hot and dusty place, and the Gafsa buses get impossibly crowded.

Train The brand new station is right at the eastern end of Ave Bourguiba and is a grand affair. There are six departures daily to Sousse (two hours) and Tunis (four hours), two to El Jem (45 minutes) and three to Gabès (two hours).

Taxi All louages leave from one block north of the post office in a shady square. There

are departures for Tunis, Sousse, El Jem, Gabès and Kairouan.

Boat The ferries for the Kerkennah Islands leave from the port (funny about that), a 15-minute walk from the town hall. There are six departures daily (for times, see the Getting There section for the Kerkennah Islands). In summer, if you are taking a vehicle across and want to get on the first or second ferry, it is necessary to join the queue around 6 am to be assured of a place. Tickets cost 500 mills per person and TD 4.500 per car; the crossing takes about 1½ hours.

KERKENNAH ISLANDS

This group of islands lies only 25 km off the coast from Sfax but the pace of life is definitely a gear or two lower than on the mainland. If you want a place to do nothing for a couple of days, this isn't a bad choice. However, if it's a tropical island paradise you're after, this definitely isn't it: the palm trees are all very shabby, the whole place is extremely dry and the highest point is about three metres above sea level.

There are two main islands, Ile Gharbi and Ile Chergui, connected by a small causeway dating back to Roman times. Ile Gharbi has little more than the ferry port at Sidi Youssef, from which it's a 16-km drive to the causeway. Chergui has a bit more to offer – a few tourist resorts on the north coast at Sidi Fredj and the small village of Remla, the 'capital' of the islands. Despite a small amount of tourist development, the tourists are staying away in droves and the calm of the islands remains undisturbed.

Fishing is the main activity of the islanders. The water gets deep very slowly, which makes swimming pretty hopeless. However, it has enabled the locals to develop a unique fishing method whereby they make large traps out of lines of palm fronds stuck in the sea bed in a V shape. The fish are then driven into this large funnel and into a small trap at the end of the V. At least half the vehicles on the ferries from Sfax are trucks and pickups loaded with palm fronds for the traps.

El Attaya is a small village right at the far tip of Ile Chergui, 12 km from Remla. If the weather is not too scorchingly hot, it is a pleasant walk (catch a bus there or back) or bike ride.

The islands are a real backwater and it is only very recently that facilities such as a bank have been established there. It's 50 metres from the Hotel El Jazira towards the water.

Places to Stay

The only conventional hotel is the very basic *Hotel el Jazira* (tel 81 058) in Remla. It is quite clean, friendly, has showers and is right by the bus stop. Rooms cost TD 2.500 per person. The hotel is also the main social point in the islands, as it has the only bar (600 mills for a beer) and one of the few restaurants.

The resort places of the 'Zone Touristique' at Sidi Fredj are inconveniently located; you need to take them on a full-board basis, as there are no nearby restaurants. They are all quite expensive and don't offer particularly good value, especially as the beaches are only mediocre.

The *Hotel Cercina* (tel 81 562) is the most convenient if you are on foot, as it is only 200 metres from the bus stop. The only problem is that the 'rooms' are horrible little claustrophobic concrete shacks which are let out for a ridiculous TD 26 for a double with full board; however, it should be possible to bargain this down to TD 10 with breakfast only.

A much better place is the enormous *Club des Iles* (tel 81 521), a few hundred metres further along. Although it would be rare to find the place more than 25% full, the managers are not prepared to bargain and so charge the full whack of TD 14 per person with meals, or TD 12 with breakfast only. If you just want to use the beach for the day the fee is a totally ridiculous TD 5 per person! They rent

bicycles here for TD 3.200 per day (you don't need to be staying at the hotel); they also have a minibus which meets the ferries.

Further along the beach are two more places, the *Hotel Farhat* (tel 81 536) and the *Hotel Grand* (tel 81 266), both of which charge much the same as the Club des Iles.

Places to Eat

Well, sadly there's really not a lot to choose from. The best bet is the *Restaurant La Sirène* by the waterfront down the road next to the Hotel El Jazira. It has a shady terrace and reasonable food, although it's opening hours are very irregular. There is another restaurant with the same name further up the street near the El Jazira but it is not as good.

The only other place is the restaurant of the *Hotel El Jazira*, which is passable but nothing special.

For sweet snacks and drinks there is the usual assortment of patisseries and cafés.

Getting There & Away

There are six ferries daily between Sfax and Sidi Youssef in summer. Departures from Sfax are at 7.30, 9 and 11.30 am and 2, 4.30 and 6pm; from the islands the departures are at 6, 9 and 10.30 am and 1, 4 and 6 pm. The crossing takes about 1½ hours, and costs 500 mills per person and TD 4.500 for a car.

Getting Around

Bus There is a small bus network which connects the towns of the islands. There are always at least two or three to meet each ferry; one of them has the sign 'Hotel' in the window and goes via Sidi Fredj, from where it's a one-km walk to the Farhat and Grand hotels, and 500 metres to the Club des Iles. For Remla, take any of the buses. There is also a minibus which runs right to the resorts but costs TD 1 per person, as against 250 mills on the public buses.

In Remla the bus station is right next to the Hotel El Jazira. There are a couple of buses daily to El Attaya but, as there's nothing much after about 3 pm, be careful that you don't get stranded there. If you do, there is a bit of local traffic and hitching is possible.

When leaving Remla for the ferry, buses leave one hour before the ferry departures; there is a list posted in the bus station window.

Bicycle The lack of any hills higher than one metre makes bicycle the ideal way of getting around. Bikes can be hired at the Club des Iles in Sidi Fredj at the rate of TD 3.200 per day.

Southern Tunisia

The attractions in the south of the country are many – the Saharan oasis towns of Nefta and Tozeur, the shimmering chotts (saltpans), the troglodyte dwellings of Matmata, the *ksour* (fortified granaries) around Tataouine, and the resort island of Jerba, supposedly the land of the Lotus-Eaters. There's enough to keep you busy for at least a week or two, and if you are heading for Algeria and the Sahara proper you'll more than likely be coming through this way.

This area lies on the fringe of the Sahara and so, as you may well imagine, gets pretty damn hot in summer – so hot in fact that it can be a real effort to move. If you are here at this time of year it makes a lot of sense to adopt the local habit of disappearing indoors during the heat of the day. Of course the climate down here also means that while you might be shivering your butt off in Europe in winter, the temperature here will still be a very bearable 15°C or so.

Chott el Jerid

The Chott el Jerid is an immense saltpan covering almost 5000 square km, which is dry for the greater part of the year. The surface becomes incredibly blistered, and cracked and shimmers in the heat. There is a made road on a two-metre-high causeway right across the middle of it, and there are regular buses making the crossing between Kebili and Tozeur – a worthwhile trip. It is quite weird to drive across and see the water that has collected on either side of the road: because of the chemicals present it may be pink on one side and green on the other. It is even more weird to come across small cafés and souvenir stalls by the side of the road at regular intervals! Mirages are also a common occurrence, and if you have picked a sunny day to cross you're bound to see some stunning optical effects.

The oasis towns of Tozeur and Nefta are right on the edge of the Chott and are welcome patches of green in what is otherwise a totally barren area. The oases rely wholly on the fresh spring water, which gushes out and makes quite intensive agriculture possible. The main crop are the incredibly succulent *deglat nour* ('finger of light') dates, which are harvested in November – a good time to visit the area, as the weather is moderate and there is plenty of activity. Many local villagers work in other parts of the country but return home every year for the date harvest.

TOZEUR

This is the major town of the chott area and so has developed into something of a tourist centre – the number of Land Rovers and buses that come through has to be seen to be believed. This is 'accessible Sahara' and, although you really have to get into Algeria to appreciate the enormous extent of this desert, there are enough dunes and picture-postcard oases in this area to make it a compulsory stop for any package tour – a fact reflected in the number of souvenir shops which have sprung up.

These shops are colourful affairs, mainly because of all the rugs for which the area is well known. It's not a bad place to buy but quality and price vary enormously, so do a bit of comparing before buying.

Despite the pressures and prosperity which tourism brings, the town maintains a laid-back atmosphere and is indeed a pleasant place to pass a few days.

Information

There are two tourist offices in Tozeur.

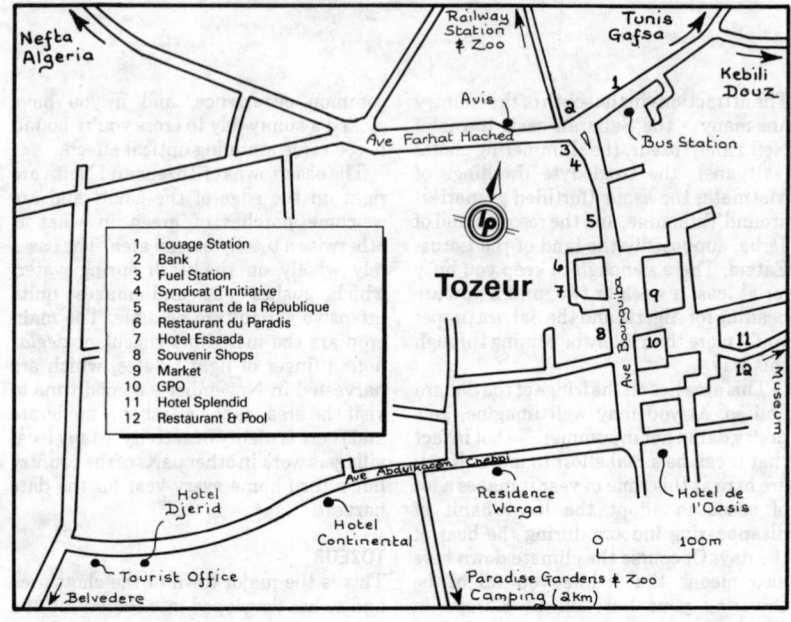

Map legend:

1. Louage Station
2. Bank
3. Fuel Station
4. Syndicat d'Initiative
5. Restaurant de la République
6. Restaurant du Paradis
7. Hotel Essaada
8. Souvenir Shops
9. Market
10. GPO
11. Hotel Splendid
12. Restaurant & Pool

Tozeur

The local Syndicat d'Initiative (tel 50 034) is on Place Ibn Châabat, right near the corner of Ave Farhat Hached. There is also a branch of the national tourist office (tel 50 088) on Ave Abdulkacem Chebbi, next door to the Hotel Djerid, about 10 minutes' walk from the post office.

Post The post office is on the main square by the market (which is busiest on Thursdays).

Money There are a couple of banks by the main intersection on the Nefta road.

Airlines The Tunis Air office (tel 50 038) is on Ave Bourguiba in the centre of town.

Car Rental There is an Avis office (tel 50 547) on Ave Farhat Hached.

Things to See

The oasis is the main attraction and,

although it is enormous, it can be explored successfully on foot. For those who don't want to walk there are camels for hire by the Hotel Continental.

The best walk is to take the track heading south off Ave Abdulkacem Chebbi signposted to 'Paradis Garden & Zoo'. It's a two-km walk to the luxuriant date garden where they sell luridly-coloured syrups of banana, rose, pomegranate and pistachio extract, all of which you can taste. The zoo is quite interesting but, as usual, the animals are kept in depressingly small cages; entry is 500 mills.

Another walk, which is quite a bit longer, is to take the track to a group of rocks known as Belvedere that are out past the main tourist office. From here you get one of the best views out over the chott, and there is a small pool which usually has enough water in it for a swim. The ground around here is littered with

sand roses, which you would have to buy elsewhere. This walk through the palmeraie takes a solid couple of hours out and back, so carry a supply of water.

In the north of town near the railway station is another zoo which is, if anything, even more depressing than the Paradis. It even has live scorpions housed in cigarette packets – 'just the thing for the mother-in-law' touts the attendant.

There is a small museum in the old part of the town, signposted past the Hotel Splendid. The 300 mills entry is hardly worth it: they have only a few bits and pieces which have been collected from the surrounding area on display. This old section of town is worth a wander around in; the architectural style is quite unusual.

Places to Stay – bottom end

The best place is the *Hotel Essaada* (tel 50 097), right in the centre just off Ave Bourguiba. It is quite basic but clean and friendly; beds cost TD 2 and hot showers are 400 mills.

Also cheap but not as convenient is the *Residence Warda* (tel 50 597), 100 metres along Ave Abdulkacem Chebbi. Beds here also cost TD 2.

Youth Hostel Tozeur also has a *Youth Hostel* (tel 50 514) but it is only for the dedicated. It is in the usual inconvenient location – at least 1½ km out of the centre on the Tunis road.

Camping There are two camp sites. The first, at Paradis Garden, has quite reasonable facilities but the big drawback is that there is absolutely no shade – a major consideration in summer. It costs TD 1.500 per person and there are free cold showers.

The second site is at Belvedere; this is a better bet, although it is quite a walk if you have no vehicle.

There is another camping ground at Degache, 16 km from Tozeur on the road to Kebili.

Places to Stay – middle

The *Hotel Splendid* (tel 50 053) right in the centre has a certain faded elegance, although it's not fantastic value. The best rooms are upstairs at the front and cost TD 7/10 for singles/doubles with washbasin. Rooms at the rear tend to be much smaller.

Places to Stay – top end

As might be expected, Tozeur has a couple of top-end hotels, both of which are on the edge of the palmeraie along Ave Abdulkacem Chebbi.

The three-star *Hotel Continental* (tel 50 411) charges TD 15/24 for singles/ doubles with breakfast, while a bit further along, the *Hotel El Jerid* (tel 50 488) is somewhat cheaper at TD 12/16. Both hotels are popular with tour groups and you may have trouble finding a vacant room.

Places to Eat

For cheap food and friendly service you can't beat the *Restaurant du Paradis*, just a couple of doors along from the Hotel Essaada. They have good soups and salad as well as all the other usual things, and the tables outside are a pleasant place to sit on a warm evening.

The only other place is the *Restaurant de la République*, which has similar stuff but is more expensive.

A local breakfast speciality is a kind of deep-fried doughnut which is very filling and guaranteed devoid of any flavour or nourishment.

There are plenty of cafés and a couple of patisseries along Ave Bourguiba. For fresh juices, try the patisserie right opposite the main mosque.

Getting There & Away

Air The Tozeur airport is four km out of town. There are flights to Tunis (Monday, 50 minutes) and Jerba (Friday, 40 minutes).

Bus The bus station for both regional and SNTRI buses is on Ave Farhat Hached near the intersection with Ave Bourguiba. There are three air-con SNTRI buses to Tunis daily, one of which comes from Nefta; buy tickets the day before.

Regional buses operate regularly but infrequently to Nefta, Gafsa, Kebili (9.30 am and 2.30 pm, TD 2.100) and Gabès. The uniformed employees who hang around the station know all the departures and are not totally unhelpful.

Train The railway station is in the north of the town but, due to lack of demand, passenger services have been discontinued and trains from Sfax only run as far as Metlaoui, 50 km to the north.

Taxi The louage station is almost opposite the bus station, in a small yard just off the street. There are regular departures to Nefta (20 minutes, 600 mills), Degache and Gafsa, and occasionally to Kebili.

NEFTA

Twenty-three km west of Tozeur is Nefta, the last town before the Algerian border. To some extent it is a smaller version of Tozeur but it does have a religious significance as well. This is the home of Sufism in Tunisia and there are a couple of important sites here.

Sufism

This mystical Islamic sect was formed by ascetics who were concerned to achieve a mystical communion with God through spiritual development rather than through the study of the Koran. This brought them into conflict with the religious orthodoxy but, because they were prepared to make concessions to local rites and superstitions, they were able to attract large numbers of people who had not embraced Islam. The Sufis also believed in the miraculous powers of saints, and saints' tombs became places of worship. A particular aspect of Berber Sufism in North Africa is maraboutism – the worship of a holy man endowed with magical powers.

Literally hundreds of different Sufi orders sprang up throughout the Islamic world. The differences between them lay largely in the rituals they performed and how far they deviated from the Koran. They were regarded with a good deal of suspicion, which was exacerbated by some of their peculiar devotional practices such as eating glass and walking on coals (which they did in order to come closer to God).

The Sufis held positions of power in Tunisia; with the breakdown of Almohad rule in the 13th century they held influential positions, particularly in rural areas.

Information

There is only one main street, Ave Bourguiba (just for a change), which is the main Tozeur-Algeria road. The bank, post office, tourist office and bus station are all on the east side of the *corbeille* (gully). There is a ring road around the north of the town and it gives access to the two flash hotels.

The tourist office is just by the ring road, on the right as you enter the town from Tozeur. The guy there is quite helpful but loses interest rapidly if you decide not to rent a camel (TD 2 per hour).

The post office is on the left, just where the road descends to cross the corbeille.

Things to See

The palmeraie here cuts right through the middle of the town, and the *corbeille* is about 30 metres deep and quite spectacular. The old part of town lies on the far (west) side, while the new French part is on the near side. At the head of this small valley water gushes out of the ground, and there are bathing pools for both men and women.

At the head of the corbeille is the Zaouia of Sidi Brahim, where this saint and some of his followers are buried.

Despite the town's attractive setting, there is really very little to do here other than wander in the palmeraie and old town. If you are not going on to Algeria, it can easily be visited in a day (or even a morning) from Tozeur.

Places to Stay & Eat

The best value is the *Hotel Marhala* (tel 57 027), one of the three excellent places run by the Touring Club de Tunisie (the others are at Matmata and Jerba). It is on the west side of town, about 20 minutes' walk from the bus station, and is actually an old brick factory - it's better than it sounds. The rooms are a bit on the small side but are spotless, comfortable and have a shower. Singles/doubles cost TD 3.400/5.600 with breakfast, or TD 5 per person for full board - good value.

Next up the scale is the *Hotel Mirage* (tel 57 041), near the northern tip of the corbeille. It's not far from the Zaouia of Sidi Brahim, around the ring road past the enormous four-star *Sahara Palace* (tel 57 046), a genuinely ugly construction.

The sum total of Nefta's eateries is a few basic restaurants on Ave Bourguiba near the bus station and the hotel restaurants. One of the better ones is the *Restaurant du Sud*.

There is a café, up on the edge of the corbeille near the Hotel Mirage, where the views are good and the drinks cold.

Getting There & Away

Bus The bus station is on the north side of Ave Bourguiba, about 100 metres past the tourist office. There is one SNTRI bus daily to Tunis (eight hours) and a few regional buses to Tozeur.

Taxi The louages leave fairly regularly

from opposite the bus station for the 20-minute ride to Tozeur (600 mills). There are also occasional departures for the Algerian border.

To/from Algeria The Algerian border is at Hazoua, 35 km to the west of Nefta. There is one bus daily from Nefta (10 am) and there are infrequent louages throughout the day. Between the two border posts is about a five-km stretch of neutral territory which you may have to walk across - be prepared with hat and water.

At the Algerian post you have to declare your money and fill in a currency form. To save hassles later, read the information on money in the Algeria section *carefully* before you reach this border.

From the Algerian border post there are shared taxis to the town of El Oued, a further 80 km along a good bitumen road. It is also possible to hitch along this stretch but traffic is very light, especially at the height of summer.

KEBILI

This small regional town at the eastern edge of the Chott el Jerid really has nothing to recommend it apart from its hot-spring baths on the road to Douz.

Facilities include a post office and bank (open for changing money from 9 am to 12 noon only.)

The baths are about a km from the centre of town. The men's pool is right by the roadside and is really pleasant, with a couple of cafés around it. The pool for women is about 150 metres upstream and is screened off by palm fronds stuck in the ground. The slightly sulphurous water gushes out of the ground at high temperature, a couple of hundred metres further up from the women's pool.

Places to Stay

The basic *Hotel l'Oasis* is about 10 minutes' walk from the centre on the Tozeur road. It is very spartan and only has cold showers but is otherwise OK. Rooms cost TD 3.500/5 for singles/

doubles, or TD 2 for a bed in a shared room.

The only other place is the somewhat up-market *Hotel des Autriches*. This is a km or so into the palmeraie; it's signposted (to 'Fort des Autriches') off to the left near the military base on the Douz road, a total of about 30 minutes' walk from the bus station. It is quite a pleasant place, with a swimming pool and terrace. Rooms are TD 9.500/15 for singles/doubles with breakfast.

Places to Eat

Considering the size of the town, there are a surprising number of restaurants. The *Restaurant Les Palmiers*, right in the centre by the bus station, does fairly good stuff.

The *Restaurant l'Oasis* is out on the Tozeur road near the hotel of the same name. There are a couple more places right by the louage station.

Getting There & Away

Bus The bus station is in fact just an office in the main street, right near the junction of the Douz, Gabès and Tozeur roads.

From here there are buses (either minibuses or regular-sized ones) to Douz at 11 am and 2, 4 and 6 pm; there are others passing through on the way from Gabès as well.

There are also regular departures for Tozeur and Gabès.

Taxi All the louages leave from a street next to the old military compound in the centre of town. Just look for the old rusty steel tower (not the post office tower).

Louages leave throughout the day for Gabès, Douz (750 mills) and occasionally Tozeur.

DOUZ

Although it tries to promote itself as 'the Gateway to the Sahara', Douz doesn't suffer from the tourist masses anywhere near as badly as Tozeur does.

It is in fact a very laid-back little oasis

village and, with the other oases to the south, it can be a pleasant place to pass a couple of days.

There is a new bank for changing money near the main intersection on the Kebili road, and opposite it is quite a good map of the town on a small signboard.

The centre of the town, for what it's worth, is the market square, 100 metres from the bus station. Around the square are a few desultory souvenir shops which have a fair range of rugs bearing local designs. Thursday is market day and so a good day to be in the area. The market square becomes a hive of activity and you need to get there early before the tour groups arrive. Down a small alley on the far side of the square is an animal market, which is interesting and doesn't have the crowds.

Douz is now the base for some of the semi-nomadic tribes of the Nefzaoua, the name given to this south-eastern region of the country.

The best way to explore the palmeraie is to walk out along the road to the Marhala and Saharien hotels, and keep going to the Place du Festival, which is set on the edge of the dunes; as the name suggests, this is the centre of activities during the Oasis Festival in December (during which time the town gets packed out). It takes about 30 minutes to walk to the palmeraie from the centre. Alternatively, you can hire camels from behind the tourist office – there are literally dozens here, but you may have a hard time dragging the owners away from the TV in the café at the tourist office.

The road to Zaafrane and El Faouar heads off to the south from next to the cemetery, almost opposite the louage station.

Places to Stay – bottom end

There are three cheapies, all in the centre near the souk and the bus station. Best of the bunch is the friendly *Hotel 20 Mars*, which has its rooms around a courtyard; there are free hot showers. The hotel used to be above the café of the same name in the corner of the market square; although there are still rooms there, you'd do best to avoid them.

The squalid *Hotel du Calme* is by the post office and should be avoided if at all possible. The other cheap place is the brand new *Hotel l'Oasis*, just opposite the entrance to the market square.

All these places charge TD 2 for a bed.

Places to Stay – middle

Signposted out along the road to the south of the town are the *Hotel Marhala* (tel 10) and the three-star *Hotel Saharien* (tel 37). Both have swimming pools and are set in the middle of the palmeraie. If you are staying out here and don't have your own transport you are more or less obliged to eat at one of the two hotels, as it is a long, dark walk into the village at night.

The Hotel Marhala is the cheaper of the two and costs TD 6/9.600 for singles/doubles with bath and breakfast. The Saharien has a more pleasant setting with a bit more shade and costs TD 7.700/11 for singles/doubles for room only.

Places to Eat

Well, for a couple of dinar you can get as full as a rat-catcher's dog in Douz. It is no gourmet's paradise but there are a couple of choices; however, because lunch is the main meal of the day, most of the restaurants don't have much left by the time dinner rolls around.

Between the Hotel 20 Mars and the bus station is the *Restaurant El Acil*, which has the usual standards. The *Restaurant de l'Oasis* at the hotel of the same name is very average.

Getting There & Away

Bus The bus station is the small kiosk just by the main intersection in the centre – you can't miss it, as there are usually one or two buses parked nearby. There is a timetable outside it, but as it's all in Arabic it's of little use.

The buses are a bit hard to pin down. There is a daily air-con SNTRI bus to Tunis at 5 am.

There are small, 20-seater minibuses which run right to El Faouar at the end of the road; departures at 6.30 am and 4 pm. There are also departures to Gabès, at 6.45 am and 2.45 pm; two hours, TD 3.

Taxi The louage station is about 50 metres around towards the telecommunications tower from the bus station. There are plenty of departures for Kebili, but they're less frequent for Gabès and Tozeur. The easiest thing is to take one to Kebili and then another from there.

AROUND DOUZ

Zaafrane & Beyond

The small oasis town of Zaafrane lies some 12 km south of Douz, right on the edge of the Grand Erg Oriental. This is where you really get to the start of the desert.

It is one of the few villages in the country where you can still see the traditional goat-hair tents of the semi-nomadic people of the Nefzaoua. Most of the inhabitants actually live in concrete-block houses and have the tents set up outside, often to give shade to the family's mules, camels or goats.

The town is busiest during the date harvest in November; for the rest of the year, many of the people migrate to the east and it slips back into the torpor that grips any desert town for much of the time.

The road continues on past other small oases as far as El Faouar, home to yet another nomadic tribe. According to the advertising signs by the side of the road near Zaafrane, there is apparently a hotel in El Faouar.

Getting There & Away The usual practice is to stand on the corner in Douz and wave down any passing vehicles. The fare to Zaafrane is 400 mills, although you may be lucky and get a free lift. The flow of traffic dries up around 4 pm and there is never anything much on Friday afternoons.

Fridays aside, it is quite a busy road and hitching out to the end to El Faouar should present no problems. The place to wait for lifts in Zaafrane is by the busy well in the middle of the village.

There are two minibuses daily which make the run from El Faouar to Douz. Departures from Douz are at 6.30 am and 4 pm. The afternoon bus stays overnight in El Faouar, before returning for Douz and Gabès at 5.45 am.

Gabès

There's very little reason to stay in this modern industrial town on the coast. It has been heavily industrialised and the pollution in both the air and water is noticeable. The town has two supposed attractions, the beach and the oasis.

The beach is raved about because it stretches so far, but it's smelly and unattractive; the oasis is nothing special either. Despite this, dozens of tour buses disgorge their daily loads on the edge of the palmeraie, the waiting *calèches* (horse carriages) take the tourists through and the buses pick them up at the other end by the depressing zoo and crocodile farm.

Information

Tourist Office The tourist office (tel 70 254) is in the small building in the middle of the intersection of Ave Habib Thameur and Ave Hedi Chaker, down towards the waterfront. The guy running it is reasonably helpful and there is a complete list of bus departures posted on the door.

Post The enormous post office is on the corner of Blvd Farhat Hached and Ave Bechir Dzir. The telephone office is through the side entrance; it is simple to make international calls from here. It is

1	Market
2	Hotel Restaurant Ben Nejima
3	Bus Station
4	Medina Hotel
5	Bus to Chenini
6	Artisanat
7	GPO
8	Louage Station
9	Youth Hostel
10	Railway Station
11	Hotels Regina & Keilani
12	Hotel de la Poste
13	Atlantic Hotel
14	Restaurant à la Bonne Table
15	Tourist Office

open Monday to Saturday from 8 am to 6 pm.

Money There are a couple of banks along Ave Bourguiba.

Airlines The Tunis Air office (tel 21 250) is in the centre of town on Ave Bourguiba.

Car Rental The major agencies here are: Hertz (tel 70 525), 30 Rue Ibn el Jazzar; Budget (tel 70 930), 57 Ave Farhat Hached; and Avis (tel 70 210), Rue 9 Avril.

Bicycle Hire The small cycle and moped shop, a couple of doors along from the Hotel de la Poste towards the souk, will usually rent out bikes for TD 2 for half a day. It's the best way to see the palmeraie, but make sure they don't give you an old broken-down clunker with minor defects such as no brakes and a swivelling seat.

Newspapers The small Tabac Nefoussi Abdallah on Ave Bourguiba, just down from the Hotel de la Poste, often has English, German and French newspapers, even if they are up to a week old.

Things to See

To get to the palmeraie, head west along Ave Bourguiba to the oued, turn left and then right across the oued. The road twists

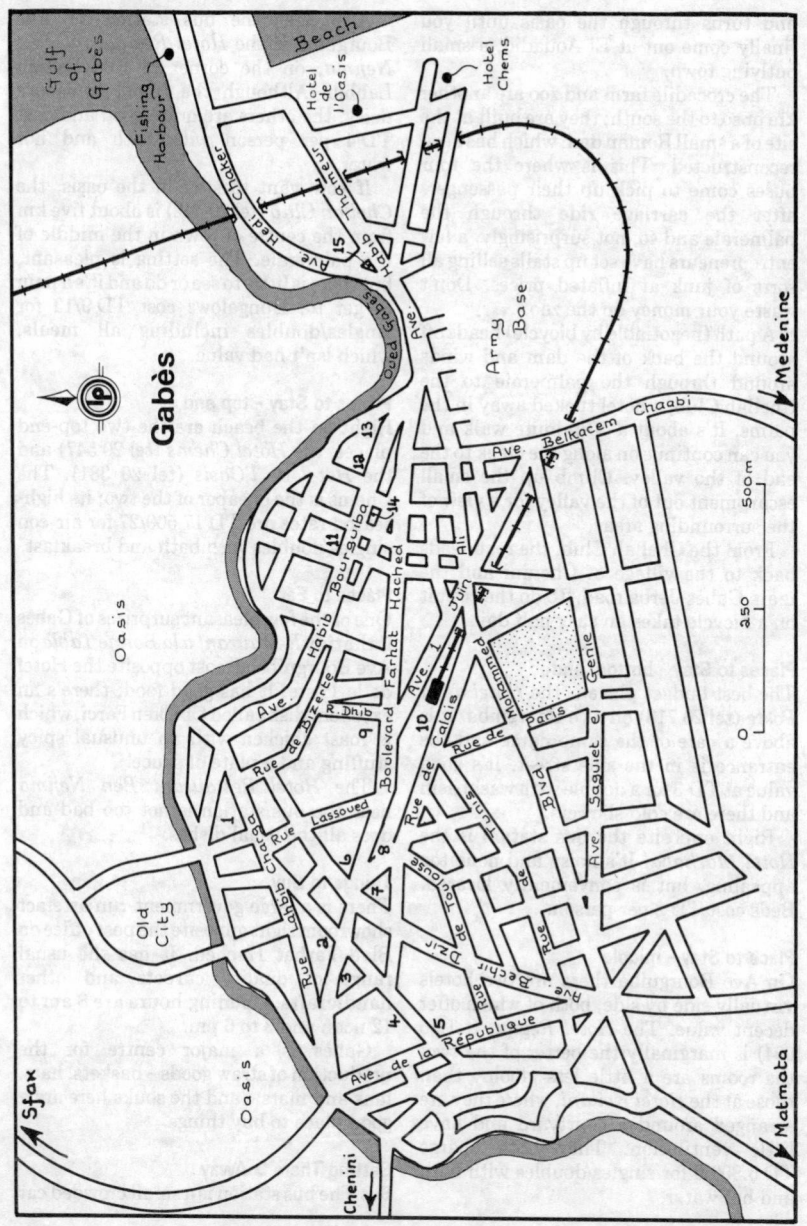

and turns through the oasis until you finally come out at El Aouadid, a small outlying town.

The crocodile farm and zoo are another km or so to the south; they are built at the site of a small Roman dam which has been reconstructed. This is where the tour buses come to pick up their passengers after the carriage ride through the palmeraie and so, not surprisingly, a few entrepreneurs have set up stalls selling all sorts of junk at inflated prices. Don't waste your money on the zoo.

A path (negotiable by bicycle) heads off around the back of the dam and winds around through the palmeraie to the Chellah Club, a hotel tucked away in the palms. It's about a 20-minute walk and you can continue on along the creek to the end of the valley. Climb up the small escarpment out of the valley for a view of the surrounding area.

From the Chellah Club, the road leads back to the village of Chenini and the main Gabès-Jerba road. To do the circuit on a bicycle takes an easy half day.

Places to Stay - bottom end

The best budget place is the *Hotel de la Poste* (tel 20 718) on Ave Bourguiba. It is above a café of the same name and the entrance is in the side street. It's good value at TD 3 for a double with washbasin and there are cold showers.

Right opposite the bus station is the *Hotel Marhaba*. It's noisy and none too appealing, but is conveniently located. Beds cost TD 2 per person.

Place to Stay - middle

On Ave Bourguiba there are two hotels virtually side by side, both of which offer decent value. The *Hotel Regina* (tel 20 094) is marginally the better of the two; the rooms are a little less gloomy than those at the *Hotel Keilani*, where they are arranged around a courtyard and have little ventilation. They both charge TD 5.800/9 for singles/doubles with bath and hot water.

Also near the bus station on Ave Bourguiba is the *Hotel Restaurant Ben Nejima*, on the corner of Rue Djilani Lahbib. Although the front rooms are noisy, the others are quite good and cost TD 4 per person with bath and hot water.

If you want to stay in the oasis, the *Chellah Club* (tel 20 442) is about five km from the centre of town in the middle of the palmeraie. The setting is pleasant, but there is little to see or do and it's a pain to get to. Bungalows cost TD 9/13 for singles/doubles including all meals, which isn't bad value.

Places to Stay - top end

Right on the beach are the two top-end places, the *Hotel Chems* (tel 20 547) and the *Hotel de l'Oasis* (tel 20 381). The Chems is the cheaper of the two; its high-season rates are TD 17.500/27 for air-con singles/doubles with bath and breakfast.

Places to Eat

One of the few pleasant surprises of Gabès is the tiny *Restaurant à la Bonne Table* on Ave Bourguiba almost opposite the Hotel de la Poste. It has good food; there's an excellent dish called Chicken Farci, which is roast chicken with an unusual spicy stuffing and a plate of sauce.

The *Hotel Restaurant Ben Nejima* near the bus station is not too bad and does all the usual dishes.

Things to Buy

There is a large government-run artefact showroom right opposite the post office on Blvd Farhat Hached. It has the usual range of quality carpets and other handicrafts. Opening hours are 8 am to 12 noon and 3 to 6 pm.

Gabès is a major centre for the production of straw goods – baskets, hats, fans and mats – and the souks here are a good place to buy things.

Getting There & Away

Bus The bus station is a small crowded car

park at the western end of Blvd Farhat Hached, about 10 minutes' walk from the hotels on Ave Bourguiba. The booking office is right in the far corner and has a listing (in Arabic only) above the door. The SNTRI office is just across the road.

There are daily departures for Matmata (eight daily, one hour, 980 mills), Kebili (two hours, TD 3), Medenine, Jerba, Gafsa, Sfax, Douz, El Faouar and Tozeur.

There are at least five SNTRI buses daily to Tunis, but most of them are coming from points further south and are often full in the summer; in winter getting a seat is not a problem.

Train The railway station is just off Ave 1 Juin, about five minutes' walk from Ave Bourguiba. There are two trains daily to Tunis (at 5.20 am and 3.50 pm) for the five-hour journey.

The line is gradually being extended to Medenine and may be open by now.

Taxi The louage station is the big dusty expanse just along from the post office. There are departures for Kebili, Medenine, Sfax and Tunis, although things quieten down considerably as the afternoon wears on.

Surprisingly, there are no louages operating between Gabès and Matmata.

Matmata

In an attempt to escape from the extreme heat the Berbers of the Matmata area went underground some centuries ago, and it was so successful that they have stayed there ever since.

Their homes are all built along the same lines: a central (usually circular) courtyard is dug down about six metres out of the very irregular terrain, and the rooms are then dug out from the sides. The main entrance is usually through a narrow

tunnel which goes out of the courtyard to ground level. Some of the larger houses had two or three courtyards, all connected, and these have now been turned into unique hotels.

Because there are only a few buildings above ground, there doesn't appear to be much to the town; however, the TV aerials and parked cars are a giveaway that there is more here than first meets the eye. A quick walk around soon reveals literally dozens of these craters. It feels very voyeuristic to be peeking over the rims at the residents going about their business; they must be utterly sick and tired of being perved at like goldfish in a bowl every day of the year. On the whole, the 5000-odd locals are not all that friendly, which is understandable.

As you might imagine with this unusual life style, Matmata is well and truly on the group-tour itineraries, and the town even has its own Hollywood-style sign on the side of the hill as you approach. Every day at least five buses roll up and the hordes troop around. Fortunately, none of them choose to stay overnight, so in the early morning and late afternoon it's possible to wander around and have the place fairly much to yourself. Because of the exposure to tourism you will no doubt be invited into the houses – which you may think is a nice gesture until you get pressured to buy handicrafts.

The best villages are in the surrounding area and Matmata makes a good base for visiting them.

There is no bank or post office in Matmata; these facilities are all at New Matmata, five km or so back along the road to Gabès.

Places to Stay

The three hotels in town are all traditional holes in the ground. They're well signposted and are within 10 minutes' walk of the bus stop.

The best for value is the *Hotel Marhala* (tel 30 015), which is run by the Touring Club de Tunisie. The unfortunate thing about this hotel is that the staff are without exception a miserably grumpy lot who tend to view guests as an unavoidable nuisance. Still, it's the best place and is good value at TD 3.500/5.900 for spotlessly clean rooms, all of which open off two courtyards. As there is not much restaurant choice, the best bet is to take a room *demie-pension* for TD 5 per person. The hotel restaurant is used by the tour groups at lunch time but is better in the evenings. It may or may not interest you to know that it was also where the disco scene out of *Star Wars* was filmed. The hotel is only a few minutes' walk beyond the bus stop along the Toujane road.

The other two hotels, the *Hotel Les Berbiers* (tel 30 024) and the *Hotel Sidi Driss* (tel 30 005) are not as good as the Marhala and charge TD 2.500 and TD 2.600 per person respectively.

Youth Hostel There is also a *Youth Hostel* in the town but, as it's a modern above-ground construction, it does not have the appeal of the other places. It is cheap, however, and may be a good fall-back if the other places are full. It costs TD 1.500 for a bed and is right up towards the entrance to the town.

Places to Eat
Apart from the hotels, there is very little choice; just a couple of places by the marketplace on the main drag, neither of which are terribly inspiring.

Getting There & Away
The buses terminate at the marketplace in the centre of town. There are departures to Gabès (seven daily between 7.30 am and 5 pm) and one to Tamezret at 1.30 pm, leaving for the return trip at 4 pm.

There is one SNTRI bus daily for Tunis at 9 pm.

AROUND MATMATA
Haddej
This is a smaller village three km off to the

east of the Matmata-Gabès road. It is much less developed than Matmata (no electricity or restaurants) and the most substantial building in town is the school.

The people here are much more friendly than in Matmata, and an invitation into a family home is liable to be genuine rather than motivated by the chance to make a bit of money.

You can get someone to show you the underground olive press, where big mill stones are turned by a camel in an impossibly small space. There is also a press operated by weights and levers which is used to extract the oil from the olives once they have been crushed. The guy who runs the small shop and post office can arrange for someone to take you there.

Getting There & Away The easiest way is to catch a Gabès bus from Matmata for the four km to the village of Tijma, which is nothing more than the turn off to Haddej. From there it's a three-km walk to Haddej; there is the occasional vehicle.

If the weather is favourable, it is an excellent walk back to Matmata along the mule track which cuts direct through the hills. It'll take you about 1¼ hours at a steady pace. Just ask the locals to point it out to you, as it's not obvious where it starts. Once you are on it, it's well trodden and easy to follow.

Tamezret
This is an above-ground village which sees very few tourists. It's an interesting place, but the bus schedule makes it difficult to spend more than a couple of hours there unless you can get a lift or are invited to stay.

Getting There & Away The bus leaves Matmata at 1 pm and returns around 4 pm. The trip takes about one hour for the 10 km.

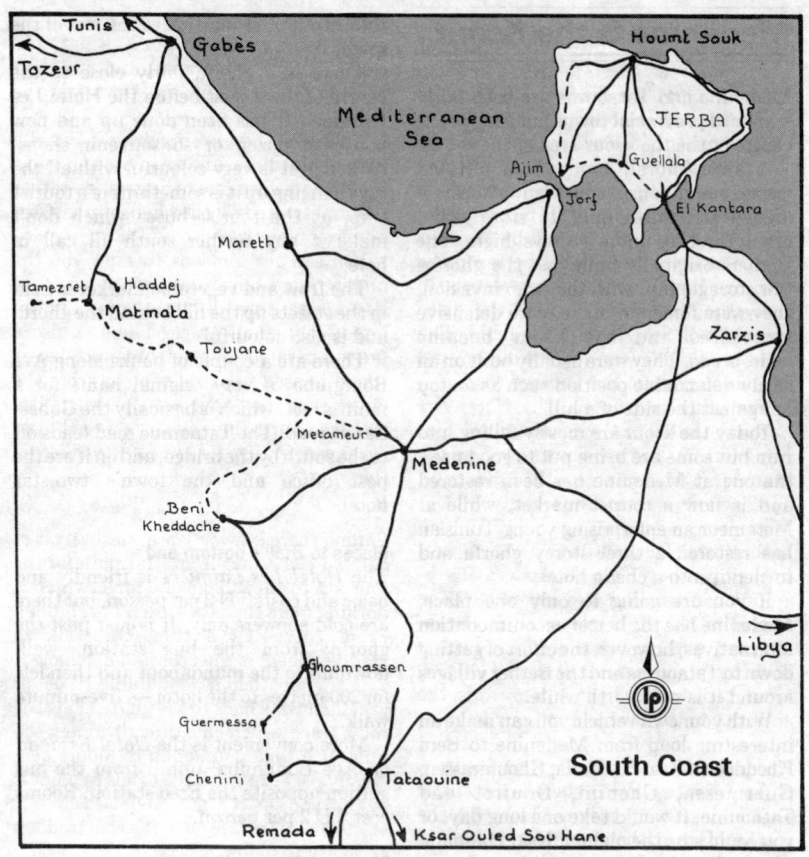

Toujane

Toujane is built right on the edge of the range of hills, on the rough track which runs from Matmata to Medenine. It is an isolated place but sees its fair share of tourists, as the Land Rovers rumble through here on their way to Matmata.

The road is of more interest than the village itself, as it runs through some pretty wild country, much of it covered by esparto grass which the locals gather and use for making all sorts of things, from mats to mule harnesses.

Getting There & Away There is no scheduled transport along this route but you may be able to organise a lift from the Hotel Marhala, as this is where most people stay.

Despite what you may be told, the Matmata-Medenine road *is* negotiable *with care* by even the smallest of the rented cars, although the rental companies would no doubt have a fit if you told them that was where you intended to going.

Medenine & the Ksour

Medenine and Tataouine are both fairly standard provincial towns but they're the centre of the the ksour area of the south.

A ksar (plural: ksour) is a fortified granary and consists of many *ghorfas* – arched structures built to store grain, often three or more storeys high. The Berbers originally built just the ghorfas (for storage) but, with the Arab invasion, they were forced to make more defensive structures and the ksour became widespread. They were usually built on an easily defendable position such as on top or against the side of a hill.

Today the ksour are mostly falling into ruin but some are being put to good use – the one at Medenine has been restored and is now a tourist market, while at Metameur an enterprising young Tunisian has restored a three-storey ghorfa and turned it into a cheap hotel.

If you are going to only one place, Medenine has the better accommodation alternatives; however, the effort of getting down to Tataouine and the Berber villages around it is well worth while.

With your own vehicle you can make an interesting loop from Medenine to Beni Kheddache, Ksar Haddada, Ghoumrassen, Guermessa, Chenini, Douiret and Tataouine. It would take one long day, or you could stop the night at Ksar Haddada where a ksar has been turned into a hotel. The roads around here are usually not in fantastic condition and are poorly signposted – getting lost is not that difficult, but there are small villages and houses dotted around where you can ask directions. It doesn't rain very often, but when it does many of the roads become impassable.

MEDENINE
Medenine is unexciting in the extreme but not a bad place to stop if the need arises. The skyline is dominated by the gigantic regional hospital, which seems totally out of proportion to the rest of the town.

There is a ghorfa fairly close to the centre of town, just before the Hotel Les Palmiers. It has been done up and now houses a dozen or so souvenir shops. Although it is very colourful with all the rugs hanging up it is something of a tourist trap, as the tourist buses which don't make it any further south all call in here.

The fruit and vegetable market is held in the streets up the hill behind the ghorfa and is also colourful.

There are a couple of banks along Ave Bourguiba, a very original name for a main street, which is basically the Gabès-Zarzis road. The Tataouine road leads off to the south by the bridge, and on it are the post office and the town's two-star hotel.

Places to Stay – bottom end
The *Hotel Les Palmiers* is friendly and basic and costs TD 2 per person, but there are cold showers only. It is just past the ghorfa; from the bus station, walk downhill to the roundabout and then left for 200 metres to the hotel – a five-minute walk.

More convenient is the *Hotel Essaada* on Ave Bourguiba, uphill from the bus station opposite the Esso station. Rooms cost TD 2 per person.

Places to Stay – middle
The *Hotel Sahara* (tel 40 007) is over the bridge and around to the right, next to the post office. Expect to pay around TD 4 per person.

Places to Eat
The *Restaurant Carthage* is opposite the bus station. The food is quite adequate, but the place gets no prizes for friendliness.

There are a couple of shops selling casse-croûtes, and there's another restaurant in the same street.

The restaurant in the *Hotel Sahara* is

the best in town and you get wine with a meal.

Getting There & Away

Bus The bus station is in the centre of the town on Rue 18 Janvier.

There are four buses daily to Tataouine between 9.30 am and 5 pm.

To Jorf, for the ferry to Jerba, buses leave at 5.30 and 8 am and 3 and 5 pm.

There are buses which take you all the way to Houmt Souk but, as they go via Zarzis, they take a good deal longer.

Taxi Louages leave from the small side street directly opposite the bus station. There are departures for Tataouine, Jorf, Zarzis and Ben Guerdane.

AROUND MEDENINE
Metameur

The attraction of this small village, six km from Medenine and one km off the main Medenine-Gabès road, is the old ghorfa on the high point of the village.

The town itself dates back to the 15th century but the ghorfas are obviously later constructions. In one of the courtyards near the mosque, a ghorfa in one corner has been restored and turned into a unique low-key hotel. It's easy to recognise by the bright whitewash and the yellow doors. It is quite isolated, perfect if you just want a spot to escape to and do nothing in for a few days. The charge for a room is TD 3 per person with breakfast. They will cook other meals for you as well; else it's a matter of bringing food from Medenine, as there is nothing much in the village.

Getting There & Away The cheapest way to get to Metameur is to hitch out along the Gabès road. The turn off to Metameur is well signposted off to the left and you can see the village not far off.

There are local shared taxis which run to the neighbourhood villages; these are Peugeot 404 pick-ups with a painted red licence plate on the tailgate. A lift in one of

these from the Metameur turn off into Medenine costs 150 mills.

The back road to Matmata through Toujane runs through here, so it may be possible to hitch; however, practically the only people using this road are other tourists in rental cars.

Joumaa

This is a magnificent hill-top site, 36 km south-west of Medenine. The village, visible from the road where the bus stops, is built on a spur and appears to be just a blank wall.

Inside, however, are a couple of streets, a mosque, a courtyard and water tanks.

Getting There & Away There are buses from Medenine at 8.15 and 10 am; they return from Joumaa at 10 am and 2 pm; the trip costs 600 mills.

Beni Kheddache

From Joumaa you can continue on to Beni Kheddache, a market and administrative village in the hills with a low-lying ksar. It has been largely demolished but what remains is still in use.

There is no accommodation here but there are a couple of restaurants. There are regular minibuses back to Medenine.

TATAOUINE

The other major centre of the ksour region is Tataouine, which is largely an administrative town with little of interest. It is, however, a friendly place and the best time to be here is Monday or Thursday because that's when the market is on.

It would be much improved as a base for exploring the nearby ksour if it had some decent budget accommodation.

The post office is at the end of the main street, tucked in beneath the jebel – just look for the radio tower. There are a couple of banks in the streets nearby.

Things to See

The Ksar Megabla is within walking distance; it's a couple of km from the centre, signposted to the right off the Remada road. It takes about an hour to walk up to it, and there are good views of the town and surrounding area. The ksar itself is not in the best condition – in fact you need to be a bit careful when poking about in the courtyard. The villagers still keep their livestock in the cells.

Places to Stay & Eat

The budget hotel situation here is a bit grim. The better of the two places available is the *Hotel Ennour*, about 500 metres from the centre on the main Medenine road. It is certainly nothing special and charges TD 1.500 per person.

The other cheapie is the *Hotel Elksour*, right in the centre, but it is dirty and uninviting.

If you can afford it, by far the best place is the two-star *Hotel La Gazelle* (tel 10) up near the post office. Rooms with bath, hot water and breakfast cost TD 9/13 in summer; in winter the price drops to TD 6.500 for a single.

There are a couple of restaurants worth a mention. The small one on the left just down the street directly in front of the post office is quite friendly, and they do a good couscous for 800 mills. The place has no name in English but has a chef painted on the window, giving the thumbs-up sign.

Further along the same street, near the statue, is the *Restaurant B Moussa*. This is the best place in town, with good food and prices.

Getting There & Away

Bus The bus station is on Rue 1 Juin 1955, pretty much in the centre of things.

There are buses to Medenine at 6.30, 8 and 9.30 am, and at 2.30 pm. The 9.30 am bus continues on to Zarzis and Houmt Souk.

For Ghoumrassen, there are departures at 10.30 am and 4.30 pm. The afternoon bus leaves Ghoumrassen at 7.30 am the next day for the return trip.

There is one SNTRI air-con bus to Tunis daily at 9 pm.

Taxi The louages leave from the same street as the buses. Things are much busier in the mornings.

There are daily departures for Ghoumrassen, Remada, Medenine, Zarzis and Tunis.

AROUND TATAOUINE
Chenini

Don't miss this place. It is a Berber village perched on a narrow escarpment on the edge of the mountains, 18 km west of Tataouine.

The houses themselves consist of a cave room, which has a fenced courtyard out the front with maybe a couple more rooms. On the peak of the ridge is an old ksar which is largely in ruins. It was originally a fort built to defend the local inhabitants from the invading Arabs but it later became a granary.

On a saddle between the ksar and the other more substantial ridge is a beautiful white mosque. The whole setting is superb, and the village has a commanding position over the plains to the north.

Chenini is very much on the Land Rover trail, but if you can get out here in the early morning the light is excellent and you should have the place to yourself.

Just around from the mosque and below the ksar, one of the enterprising locals has turned his house into an informal museum and will show you around for a small consideration.

Places to Stay & Eat The *Relais Restaurant* is at the bottom of the hill by the car park. It specialises in lunch-time banquets for the tour groups. It is possible to stay here if you don't mind roughing it, which in this case means sleeping on the floor or the roof.

Getting There & Away This is the real snag. There is no public transport to Chenini, so it's a matter of hitching or chartering a louage.

Hitching is OK but can be slow, as most

of the vehicles coming out this way are tour-group Land Rovers which usually have up to 11 people crammed in anyway!

To charter a louage, ask around with the drivers in Tataouine. It shouldn't cost more than TD 10 for the round trip and it's quite possible that the driver will act as guide when you get there. An hour is the minimum time necessary for a leisurely scramble around, so make sure the driver knows that you want to stay at least that long.

Douiret

This is really something, perched as it is on a hill with its dazzling whitewashed mosque. The village is inhabited in parts and is a fascinating place to wander around.

The site is very well preserved, and from above you can get a good view of the layout of the houses. The main buildings for animals front onto the road, then there's a walled courtyard, and then the living quarters built 10 metres or so into the rock.

There are several camel-powered olive presses – just look for the tell-tale black streaks down the hill sides.

Getting There & Away As usual in this neck of the woods, transport is a bit of a hit-and-miss affair. There is a village *camionette* (Peugeot 404 pick-up) which makes the run from Tataouine but it can be hard to track it down – ask around the louages at Tataouine.

Failing that you can catch a louage to Dabbab and hitch from there; you may be in for a long wait, as there is very little traffic along this road. You will get there in the end, however.

Ksar Ouled Soultane

This is the best preserved of the ksour, and also the most difficult to get to. Buses and camionettes from Tataouine run as far as Maztouria, passing the ksour of Beni Barka and Kedim on the way.

From Maztouria the road to Remada turns to dirt; after eight km there's a signpost for Ksar Ouled Soultane and from here it's a further three km.

Although not built on a particularly big rise, the ksar is visible for miles around and was obviously easily defendable. The ghorfas rise to four levels in two courtyards and the climb to the top of the stairs can be dizzying.

This is the best place to visualise the ksar as a storage place and not just as a ruin. There are a couple of small shops and a café in this town, which sees only a handful of tourists.

Ghoumrassen

This is the largest of the southern Berber villages and is the only one regularly accessible by public transport. It is surrounded by rocky cliffs on all sides and there are cave dwellings dotted all over the place.

The most interesting aspect of the place is that many of the dwellings have only recently been deserted; wandering through some of them, in which utensils and tools are still lying around, it's easy to get the feeling that the owners are going to return any minute and catch you snooping. Bring a torch if you have one; even matches would be a help in exploring some of the deeper dwellings.

There is a bank and a couple of restaurants but no place to stay, so it is necessary to return to Tataouine.

Getting There & Away There are infrequent buses and louages to and from Tataouine.

Jerba

Well, if the locals are to be believed, this is the mythical land of the Lotus-Eaters where Ulysses was delayed on the way back from the scrap at Troy. If that's the case, then the island today is populated by the descendants of these people, who

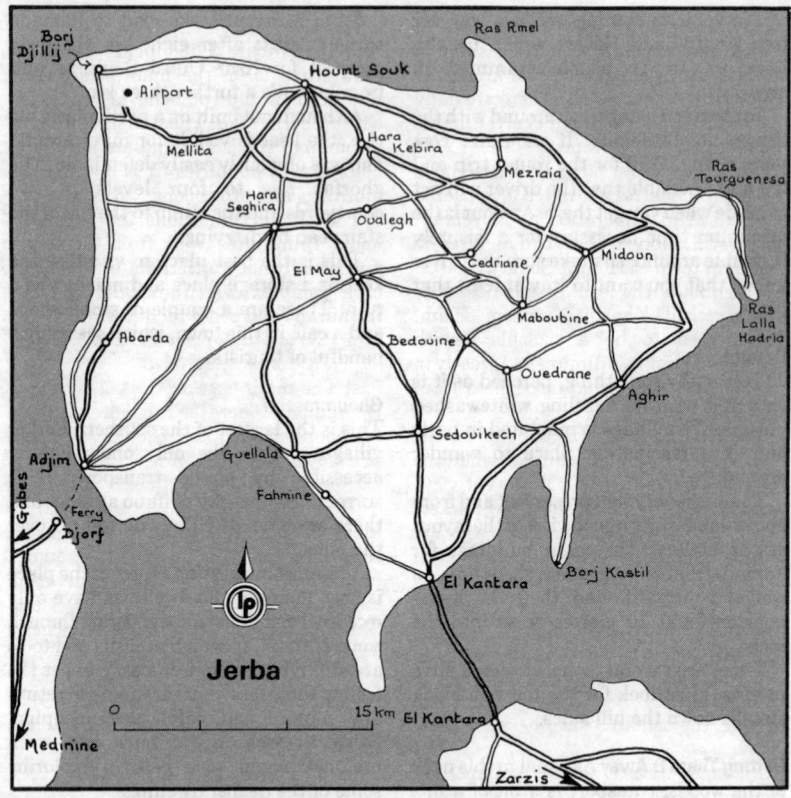

Jerba

15 km

lived 'in indolent forgetfulness, drugged by the fruit of the legendary honeyed-fruit'. The fruit is variously thought to have been hashish, jujuba or the lotus. Fantasy or not, it makes a good exotic story to draw the tourists with.

The low-lying island is in the Gulf of Gabès. Its southerly location gives it a climate much envied by the people of Europe – so envied in fact that it has become a major tourist destination complete with international airport and resort hotels. In the summer months, the place is crawling with tourists – you're better off visiting out of season, when it's cheaper and facilities are less in demand.

The architecture of Jerba is very distinctive. The island is dotted with square whitewashed houses (known as *menzels*) which, from the outside, look more like small fortresses. It is unlikely you will be invited inside at any stage unless you are lucky enough to befriend a local resident – there have been too many foreigners here for the locals to get any thrill out of inviting someone in for a tea. This is not to say they are unfriendly – just reserved.

With an area of about 500 square km, Jerba is connected to the mainland by a ferry from the south-western tip; there's also a causeway in the south-eastern corner which links it with the town of Zarzis, another place which is cashing in on the tourist dollar (or yen, or kroner, or whatever). As well as this there are daily flights to Tunis and direct charter flights to points all over Europe.

Since the highest point on the island is less than 30 metres above sea level, Jerba lends itself to exploration by bicycle or, better still, moped. Both can be hired in the main town of Houmt Souk.

The bulk of the local people belong to the heretical Kharijite sect of Islam. There used to be a sizeable Jewish community but this diminished greatly in number with the formation of the state of Israel.

The Kharijite sect was popular among the Berbers in the 7th century; when the Fatimids wiped them out in the early 8th century, Jerba was one of the few pockets to survive. It is the Kharijites who are largely responsible for the huge number of mosques on the island – 213 in all.

History

The Phoenicians were the first to realise the potential of a virtually land-locked gulf and were the first of many invaders to occupy the island over the next 2500 years.

In Roman times it became an important commercial centre and the causeway connecting it to the mainland was built. Since the Romans left the island has been occupied by Spaniards, Barbarossa pirates, Italians and then, in the 1500s, by the Turks.

HOUMT SOUK

The main town of the island, Houmt Souk, is on the north coast. The 6500 residents depend fairly heavily on tourism for their livelihood; the other, more traditional source of income is the fishing industry.

Out of season it's an easy-going place; the few hotels and restaurants are virtually deserted and the shopkeepers don't even bother hassling for a sale.

Information

Tourist Offices The local Syndicat d'Initiative is on the main street (Ave Bourguiba would you believe?) and is set back from the road. The staff have a handout map of the island and are also quite helpful with enquiries. It is open in the mornings and afternoons.

The office of the national tourist body is about 15 minutes' walk from the centre and is really not worth the effort. It is part of a complex which includes a fancy restaurant and other facilities. It is open from 8.30 am to 12 noon and 3 to 5.45 pm.

Post The main post office is also on Ave Bourguiba. There is an international telephone office around the side, although you may have to fight your way in as it gets extremely crowded at times.

Money There are a number of banks on Ave Bourguiba and around the squares just off it. There is always one bank rostered to be open on Saturdays and Sundays. The Syndicat d'Initiative has a current list.

Airlines The Tunis Air office (tel 50 586) is at the southern end of Ave Bourguiba, a block in front of the bus station.

Car Rental Jerba is a popular place to hire cars for trips around the island and to sights around the south of the country. All the major companies have offices both in town and out at the airport, where the phone number for them all is 50 233.

The offices in town are: Avis (tel 50 151), Ave Mohammed Badra; Budget (tel 50 185), Rue 20 Mars 1934; Hertz (tel 50 196), Ave Abdelhamid el Cadhi; Europcar (tel 50 357), Ave Abdelhamid el Cadhi; and Topcar (tel 50 536), Rue 20 Mars 1934.

Bicycle & Moped Rental Bikes are available for rent from any of the hotels in Houmt Souk. In fact they just act as agent and take a small cut. Some of the bikes are in

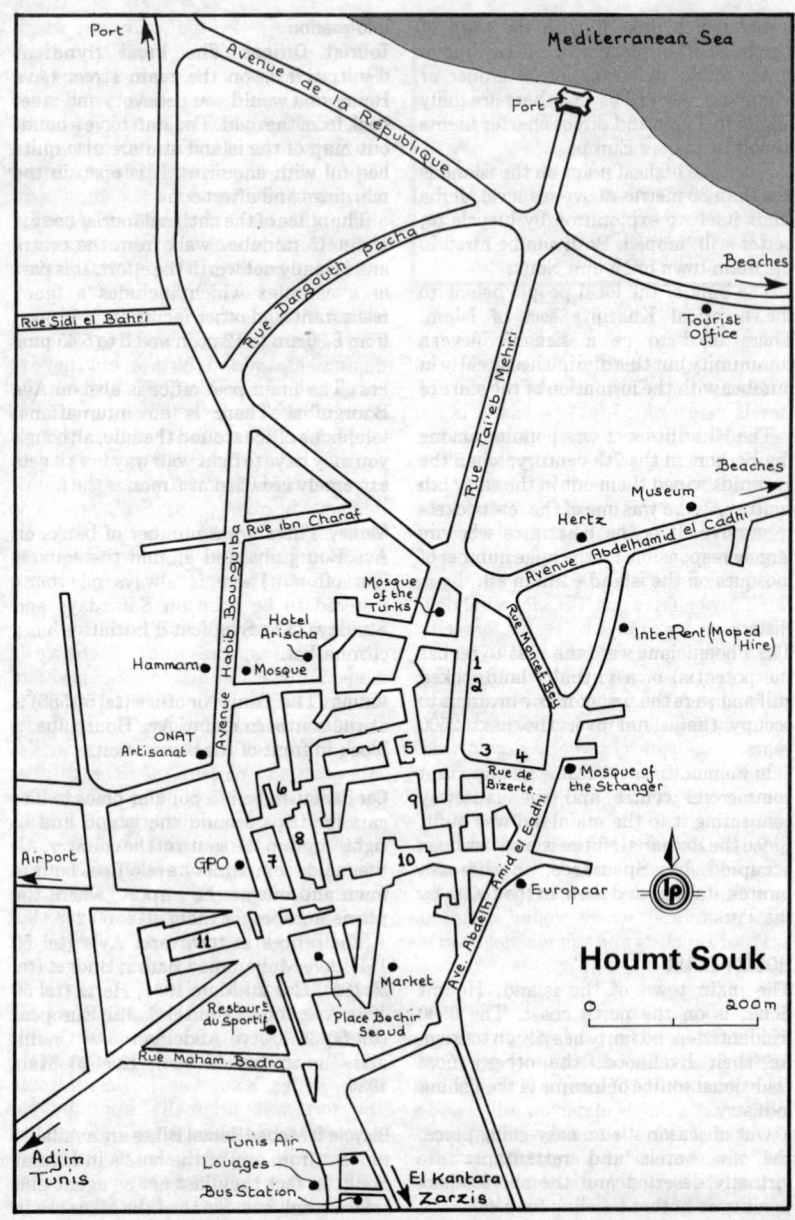

Houmt Souk

0   200m

1	Hotel Marhala
2	Youth Hostel
3	Hammam
4	Zaouia of Sidi Brahim
5	Hotel Sable d'Or
6	Place Sidi Abdelkader
7	Place Mongi Bali
8	Hotel Sindbad
9	New Hotel
10	Place Hedi Chaker
11	Syndicat d'Initiative

pretty poor shape, so make sure you get a decent one.

The amount you can see by bicycle in a day is very limited, as the island is too large to see the lot. If there were places to stay in the other towns you could make a great three or four-day circuit, but unfortunately this is not possible at the moment unless you just sleep out somewhere.

Rental costs are 700 mills per hour, TD 2 per half day and TD 3 for a full day.

Mopeds are a much better bet for seeing the whole island; in half a day you can cover pretty well the whole thing, although a full day makes for a much more leisurely trip. Again, the hotels act as agents, or you get them direct from InterRent. They cost TD 2 per hour, TD 8 for half a day (six hours) and TD 12 for a full day.

When riding a moped you are not covered by any insurance. Be extremely careful, especially out in the smaller villages inland where young children, wayward cyclists and suicidal dogs can be a real hazard.

Souk
Houmt Souk is compact enough to make seeing everything on foot quite practical. The old souk is the centre of things and consists of a tangle of narrow alleys and a few open squares with cafés. The place is full of souvenir shops and, although the prices are high, there is some excellent-quality stuff for sale.

There are a few old *fondouks*, which used to provide lodging for pilgrims and the merchants of the camel caravans; some of these have been turned into excellent cheap hotels. The rooms are on two floors around a central courtyard, in the middle of which is a large cistern which provided water for the guests and animals. One of the hotels, the El Arischa, has converted the cistern into a very small swimming pool.

Islamic Monuments
There are a few interesting Islamic monuments around the town but they are all closed to non-Muslims. Just on the edge of the souk, the Zaouia of Sidi Brahim has the tomb of the 17th-century saint. Today it is used as a place of prayer. On the other side of the road is the multi-domed Mosque of the Strangers. The 18th-century Mosque of the Turks is north of the souk; it has a distinctly Turkish minaret.

Museum of Popular Arts & Traditions
About 200 metres out along Ave Abdelhamid el Cadhi is the Zaouia of Sidi Zitouni, which now houses the Museum of Popular Arts & Traditions. This has quite a good range of local costumes as well as other bits and pieces. One room still has the original terracotta-tile ceiling. The museum is open daily, except Friday, from 9 am to 12 noon and 2 to 5.30 pm in winter, 9 am to 12 noon and 3 to 6.30 pm in summer; entry is 800 mills. The ticket office is the small traditional weaver's hut near the main entrance.

Borj el Kebir & Around
From the Mosque of the Turks, the main street is lined with beautiful shady eucalypt trees and leads to the fort on the water's edge. Known as the Borj el Kebir, the fort was originally built by the Aragonese (members of an independent kingdom in north-eastern Spain) in the 13th century, and was extended in the 16th century under the Spaniards. Later

the same century the Turks captured the fort and massacred the Spanish garrison. The skulls of the victims were stacked in a pile a couple of hundred metres along from the fort, and this macabre tower of skulls stood for over two hundred years until the soldiers were given a formal burial. The site is still marked by a monument.

The fort itself is good for a quick wander around, if only for the views along the coast. It is open the same hours as the museum.

The fishing harbour is only a little further along. It is a hive of activity during the day, with the fishermen mending nets and preparing for the evening's outing.

Places to Stay – bottom end

The cheapest hotels (including the youth hostel, which for once is not a bad place to stay) are old converted caravanserais, which provide good accommodation.

Pick of the bunch is the *Hotel Marhala* (tel 50 146), another one in the chain of three run by the Touring Club de Tunisie. As usual the standard is excellent, and it is not bad value at TD 4.700/8 per person with breakfast. In winter it is a bargain at TD 2.600 per person. Cold showers are free but for a hot one you pay a steep 700 mills. The rooms are all arranged around the traditional colonnaded courtyard.

The *Hotel Arischa* (tel 50 384) is just north of the souk and is another caravanserai. It costs much the same as the Marhala at TD 4.500/7 for a single/double with breakfast, slightly less in winter. In this place the central cistern has been turned into a tiny swimming pool.

The *New Hotel* (tel 50 756) is the cheapest at TD 2 per person; it's not that bad, it's just that the other places are better. Close by is the *Hotel Sable d'Or* (tel 50 423), which is also not bad for TD 3.500 per person.

On Place Mongi Bali in the centre, the *Hotel Sindbad* (tel 50 047) is a bit run down and overpriced at TD 5 per person, although this is definitely negotiable in winter.

Youth Hostel The *Youth Hostel* has only recently moved to its present location in the fondouk next to the Hotel Marhala. The staff are friendly, and the hostel is open throughout the day until at least 10 pm. In summer this may be the only place with a vacancy. Beds cost TD 1.500.

Camping The only camping ground is attached to the *Hotel Sidi Slim* (tel 57 023), one of the resort hotels on the eastern corner of the island. It is on a decent beach, so if you just want to spend a few

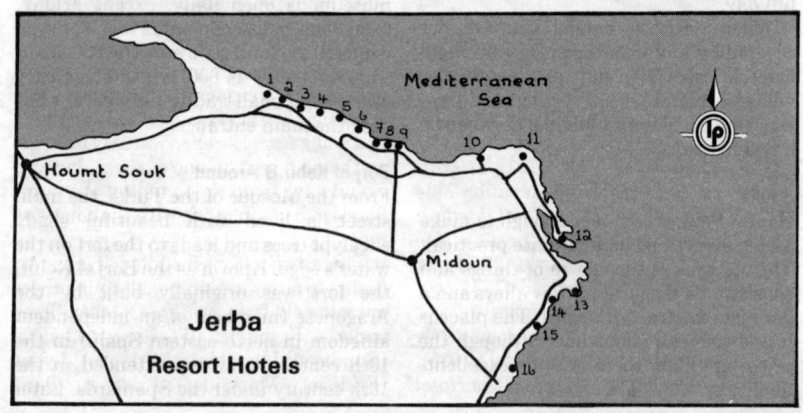

1	Ulysses
2	Mimosas
3	Al Jazira
4	Strand
5	Medina
6	Les Sirènes
7	Abou Nawas
8	Palm Beach
9	El Bousten
10	Dar Jerba
11	Yati
12	Tanit
13	Jerba Menzel
14	La Douce
15	Calypso
16	Sidi Slim

days doing nothing it's not a bad place to be; otherwise, it can be a bit isolated. The Sidi Slim is on the coast, south-east of Midoun.

Places to Stay – middle & top end

All the resort hotels are scattered along the north-eastern coast of the island, along the Sidi Mahares beach. Prices in summer are generally high across the board, but there are a few places which really drop their prices out of season.

Top of the range is the *Dar Jerba* (tel 57 191), which is a totally over-the-top construction complete with cinemas, conference halls, and beds for over 2000 people – just the thing for a quiet getaway? There are even tricycles that you can hire to explore the complex! The place is in fact four hotels rolled into one and prices range from TD 14 to TD 41 for a single. Much more sensible is the *Hotel Tanit* (tel 57 132), further around the coast, where rooms cost TD 19/27 with breakfast (dropping to an affordable TD 9/12 in winter). The *Hotel Medina* (tel 57 171) with its excellent beach is also good. Charges here are TD 26/41 for singles/doubles, which drop to TD 12.500/19 in winter.

Other beach hotels which are moderately priced are the *Hotel Al Jazira* (tel 57 015), the *Hotel Yati* (tel 57 106) and the *Hotel*

Sidi Slim (tel 57 023), which also has the camping ground.

Places to Eat

Around Place Hedi Chaker are three of four tourist-oriented restaurants. The menus are posted outside, usually in four languages, and there is not a great deal to choose between them – they are all good and have much the same prices. The prices are also aimed at the tourists – expect to pay about TD 5 (or more) per person. Beware of the owners who try and get you to have a 'special meal', as the price will be pretty bloody special as well unless you clarify beforehand just how much you are prepared to pay.

One place with a similar menu but cheaper prices because of its location is the *Restaurant Central* on Ave Bourguiba near the bus station.

The main Tunisian restaurant, where a meal costs about half as much as the other places, is the *Restaurant du Sportif* on Ave Bourguiba.

If you are staying out at the hotel strip you will have to eat out there as well because the area is not well served by the buses and taxis are not cheap.

Getting There & Away

Air Tunis Air has daily flights to Tunis at 6 am in winter. In summer there are up to three flights daily and you need to book in advance to get a seat. Tickets for the 40-minute flight cost TD 21 one way.

Jerba is also an international airport and in the summer months there is a constant stream of charter flights coming and going from Europe. You may be lucky and score a seat on one of these, but you would have to do the rounds of the resort hotels and get in touch with the company reps.

There are also scheduled Tunis Air flights to cities in Europe, although these operate only from April to October. They include: Frankfurt (Tuesdays); Geneva (Sundays); Luxemburg (Fridays); Lyons (Fridays); Marseilles (Fridays); Paris

(Saturdays, Sundays); and Zürich (Sundays).

Bus The uncharacteristically well-organised bus station is at the southern end of Ave Bourguiba. All the scheduled departures are listed on a board above the ticket windows.

There is a nightly SNTRI bus to Tunis, and local departures to Zarzis, Medenine, Tataouine and Gabès.

Taxi The louages leave from just outside the bus station. There are departures for Zarzis, Gabès and Tunis.

Many of the mainland louage services go only as far as Jorf. From there you need to catch the ferry across, and then a bus or louage to Houmt Souk. Some services do go all the way but they usually do so via Zarzis, which makes the trip a good deal longer.

Getting Around the Island

Airport Transport The airport is eight km from the centre of Houmt Souk, signposted out past the village of Mellita. There is one bus daily at 6.30 am, which is obviously useless if you are catching the 6 am flight to Tunis.

The taxis congregate in the middle of Ave Bourguiba, near the Tunis Air office. They have meters, and the run out to the airport shouldn't cost more than TD 1.500.

Bus There are local services which connect the larger towns of the island, but the coverage is erratic and trying to use the buses successfully can be a frustrating experience.

There is a timetable and a colour-coded route map of the services around the island above the ticket windows in the bus station.

Taxi The blue-and-white Peugeot taxis can be hired for the day for trips around the island or just to specific places on the island. A daily charter shouldn't cost more than TD 25.

The taxis are forever cruising the hotel strip for fares into Houmt Souk. In summer demand far exceeds supply and it can be difficult to get hold of one in Houmt Souk, especially in the early afternoon when things close up for a couple of hours and everyone is returning to Sidi Mahares.

Moped & Bicycle Moped is an excellent way to see the island, bicycle less so because the winds are often strong and the distances are quite large – it is 22 km from Houmt Souk to Ajim, for instance, and a similar distance from Houmt Souk to the lighthouse at Ras Tourgueness in the middle of the resort strip.

Both mopeds and bicycles can be rented by the hour, half day or day in Houmt Souk.

AROUND THE ISLAND
Midoun

This is the second major town of the island and is best known for its busy Friday market. Most of the items on sale are really only tacky tourist rubbish but a few local stalls set up to sell fruit and vegetables.

Foreigners far outnumber locals here on Fridays. It's not unusual for a tour group on horseback to make a total bloody nuisance of themselves and come pushing their way through the crowds.

The women of this area dress distinctively in white *sifsaris* which have a border of bright embroidery. They also wear small straw hats with a coloured ribbon tied to the back.

Hara Seghira

Once an exclusively Jewish settlement, Hara Seghira lies just off the main Houmt Souk-Zarzis road. With the mass migration of Jews to Israel the population is now predominantly Muslim, but there are still a number of synagogues.

The most important Jewish synagogue is El Griba, signposted a km south of the town. It is a major place of pilgrimage during the Passover festival. The site is believed to date back to pre-Christian times, although the present building dates back only as far as early this century. The inner sanctuary is said to contain one of the oldest *torahs* in the world.

The site was apparently chosen after a stone fell from heaven; it is also said that an unknown woman turned up and performed a miracle or two in helping the builders.

It is open to the public but you need to be modestly dressed, and men have to don *yarmulkes* (skullcaps) on entering. Donations are compulsory but you don't have to leave much.

Guellala

This is a tiny village on the south coast which is known for its pottery. In the past the pottery was sold on the mainland but these days almost all of it is sold on site.

The dozen or so workshops and galleries line the main road. They all sell much the same stuff, which unfortunately falls into the 'tacky souvenir' category with ease.

From Guellala there is a dirt track

which skirts around a bay, where fishermen paddle around in waist-deep water, to the village of Ajim, where the ferries connect with the mainland.

Ajim

No attractions here, but if your transport goes only as far as Jorf on the mainland you'll have to catch a louage from here to Houmt Souk.

The ferry dock is about 500 metres from the centre and the ferries run 24 hours a day, although the frequency drops in the middle of the night to about once an hour.

West Coast

There is very little along the whole western coastline. There's just one dirt track, which hugs the swampy coast all the way.

The ruins of the 18th-century Turkish fort Borj Djillij are out past the airport, but you needn't waste your time trying to get out here unless you have a moped and an overpowering passion for ruined Turkish forts.

Glossary

This glossary is a list of Arabic (a), Berber (b) and French (f) words commonly used in the three Maghreb countries.

Words followed by a capital letter in brackets are those which are used principally in one country – Algeria (A), Tunisia (T) and Morocco (M).

Adrar (A) – mountain.
Agadhir – escarpment.
Aid – see Eid.
Ain – see In.
Aghlabids – 9th-century Arab rulers of Tunisia.
Akhbar (a) – great.
Al – see El.
Allah (a) – God.
Andalous – Muslim Spain and Portugal.

Bab (a) – gate.
Babouche (M) – traditional leather slippers.
Bali (a) – new.
Baraka (a) – divine blessing or favour.
Barbary – European term used to describe the North African coast from the 16th to 19th centuries.
Basilica – type of Roman administrative building; later used to describe churches.
Beni (a) – tribal name.
Berbers – indigenous inhabitants of North Africa.
Bey – provincial governor in Ottoman Empire.
Borj (a) – fort.
Burnous (a) – traditional full-length cape with a hood, worn by men throughout the Maghreb.

Capitol – main temple of Roman town, usually situated in the forum.
Chechia (T) – term for the traditional red felt hats, only worn by the older generation these days.
Chott (a) – salt lake.
Couscous – semolina, staple food of North Africa.

Daira (A) – Algerian equivalent of a local government.
Dar (a) – house.
Dey – title given to commanders of Turkish janissaries.

Eid (a) – feast.
El (a) – the article 'the'; can change according to the first letter of the following word, eg **Ech, Es, En, Et**.
Erg (a) – sand 'sea' or region.

Forum – open space at centre of Roman towns.
Fouggara (a) – system of underground water channels used to supply an oasis; found mainly near Adrar in Algeria.
Foum (a) – gorge, defile.
Foundouk (a) – caravanserai.

Gare routière (f) – bus station
Ghar (a) – cave
Ghorfa (a) – room; used in Tunisia to describe grain storage rooms in a ksar.
Guerba – waterbag made from the skin of a goat or sheep, seen hanging on the side of many Saharan vehicles; they look the part, but certainly add a bit of flavour to the water and are not very efficient, as they rely on evaporation (water loss) to keep the contents cool.

Hajj (a) – pilgrimage to Mecca; hence **Hajji**, one who has made the pilgrimage.
Hammada – stony desert.
Hammam – Turkish-style bathhouse with sauna and massage; there's at least one in virtually every town in the Maghreb.
Harira (M) – bean soup.

Ibn (a) – son of.
Imam – Islamic prayer leader.
In (a) – water-source, spring.

Janissaries – the elite of the Turkish army.
Jebel (a) – hill, mountain.
Jedid (a) – new.
Jezir (a) – island.
Jemaa (a) – mosque.
Jemil (a) – camel.

Kasbah – fort, citadel; often also the administrative centre.
Kef – cliff.
Kissaria – commercial centre of medina.
Koubba – sanctuary, marabout.
Ksar (a) – (pl: **ksour**) fortified stronghold in the south of Tunisia.

Maghreb (a) – west (lit: where the sun sets); used these days to describe the area covered by Morocco, Algeria and Tunisia.

Marabout – holy man or saint; often used to describe the mausolea of these men, which are places of worship in themselves.

Mechouar – royal assembly place.

Medina (a) – city; used these days to describe the Arab part of modern towns and cities.

Medressa (a) – college for teaching theology, law, Arabic literature and grammar; widespread throughout the Maghreb from the 13th century.

Mellah – Jewish section of medina.

Mihrab (a) – prayer niche in wall of mosque indicating direction of Mecca.

Minbar (a) – pulpit in mosque; the imam delivers the sermon from one of the lower steps because the Prophet preached from the top step.

Moulay (M) – ruler.

Mozabite – a Berber inhabitant of the M'Zab, the name given to the area around Ghardaia in Algeria.

Muezzin (a) – mosque official who sings the call to prayer from the top of the minaret.

Oued (a) – river.

Pasha – high official in Ottoman empire.

Piste (f) – a track, often a couple of km wide, in the Sahara.

Ras (a) – headland.

Reg – stony desert.

Ribat – monastery and fort in one.

Sebkha (a) – saltpan.

Sidi (a) – honorific reserved for saints and holy men.

Sifsari (T) – off-white robe worn by Tunisian women.

Souk (a) – market.

Sufism – mystical strand of Islam; adherents concentrate on their inner attitude in order to attain communion with God.

Tajine (M) – stew, usually with meat as the main ingredient.

Tassili – the word for plateau in the Touareg language Tamashek.

Tizi – mountain pass.

Touareg – nomadic Berbers of the Sahara, sometimes known by romantics as the Blue Men, because of their indigo-dyed robes which gives their skin a bluish tinge; however, these days the cloth comes ready-dyed from Europe.

Vizier – another term for a provincial governor, usually in the Ottoman Empire.

Wilaya (A) – province; there are 43 of them Algeria.

Zaouia – religious fraternity based around a marabout.

Zeriba (A) – house built of reeds and grass; found in southern Algeria.

Zitouna (a) – olive tree or grove.

Index

MAPS

Temperature

To convert °C to °F multiply by 1.8 and add 32

To convert °F to °C subtract 32 and multiply by ·55

Length, Distance & Area

	multiply by
inches to centimetres	2.54
centimetres to inches	0.39
feet to metres	0.30
metres to feet	3.28
yards to metres	0.91
metres to yards	1.09
miles to kilometres	1.61
kilometres to miles	0.62
acres to hectares	0.40
hectares to acres	2.47

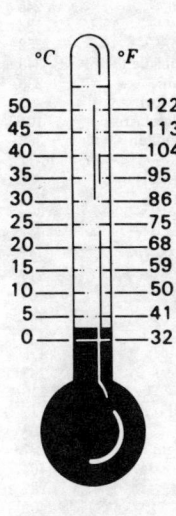

Weight

	multiply by
ounces to grams	28.35
grams to ounces	0.035
pounds to kilograms	0.45
kilograms to pounds	2.21
British tons to kilograms	1016
US tons to kilograms	907

A British ton is 2240 lbs, a US ton is 2000 lbs

Volume

	multiply by
Imperial gallons to litres	4.55
litres to imperial gallons	0.22
US gallons to litres	3.79
litres to US gallons	0.26

5 imperial gallons equals 6 US gallons
a litre is slightly more than a US quart, slightly less
than a British one

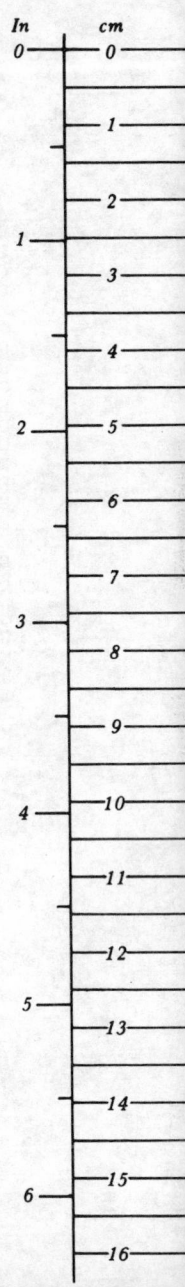

Guides to Africa

Africa on a shoestring
From Marrakesh to Kampala, Mozambique to Mauritania, Johannesburg to Cairo – this guidebook gives you all the facts on travelling in Africa. It provides comprehensive information on more than 50 African countries – how to get to them, how to get around, where to stay, where to eat, what to see and what to avoid.

East Africa – a travel survival kit
Whether you want to climb Kilimanjaro, visit wildlife reserves, or sail an Arab dhow, East Africa offers a fascinating pastiche of cultures and landscapes. This guide has detailed information on Kenya, Uganda, Rwanda, Burundi, eastern Zaire, Tanzania and the Comoros Islands.

West Africa – a travel survival kit
This book has all the necessary information for independent travel in 16 countries – Benin, Burkino Faso, Cape Verde, Gambia, Ghana, Guinea, Guinea Bissau, Ivory Coast, Liberia, Mali, Mauritania, Niger, Nigeria, Senegal, Sierra Leone and Togo.

Swahili phrasebook
Swahili is widely spoken throughout East Africa – from the coast of Kenya and Tanzania through to Zaire.

Central Africa – a travel survival kit
Central Africa offers the visitor incomparable wildlife and scenery, and the essence of African culture. Countries covered include Cameroon, Central African Republic, Chad, The Congo, Equatorial Guinea, Gabon and Zaïre.

Guides to the Middle East

Egypt & the Sudan – a travel survival kit
The sights of Egypt and the Sudan have impressed
visitors for more than 50 centuries. This guide takes you
beyond the spectacular pyramids to discover the villages
of the Nile, diving in the Red Sea and many other other
attractions.

Israel – a travel survival kit
This is a comprehensive guidebook to a small, fascinating
country that is packed with things to see and do. This
guide will help you unravel its political and religious
significance – and enjoy your stay.

Jordan & Syria – a travel survival kit
Roman cities, ancient Petra, Crusader castles – these
sights, amongst many others, combine with Arab
hospitality to make this undiscovered region a fascinating
and enjoyable destination.

Turkey – a travel survival kit
Unspoilt by tourism, Turkey is a travellers' paradise,
whether you want to lie on a beach or explore the ancient
cities that are the legacy of a rich and varied past. This
acclaimed guide will help you to make the most of your
stay.

West Asia on a shoestring
A complete guide to the overland trip from Bangladesh to
Turkey. Information for budget travellers to Afghanistan,
Bangladesh, Bhutan, India, Iran, Maldives, Nepal,
Pakistan, Sri Lanka, Turkey and the Middle East.

Yemen – a travel survival kit
One of the oldest inhabited regions in the world, the
Yemen is a beautiful mountainous region with a unique
architecture. This book covers both North and South
Yemen in detail.

Lonely Planet Guidebooks

Lonely Planet guidebooks cover virtually every accessible part of Asia as well as Australia, the Pacific, Central and South America, Africa, the Middle East and parts of North America. There are four main series: 'travel survival kits', covering a single country for a range of budgets; 'shoestring' guides with compact information for low-budget travel in a major region; trekking guides; and 'phrasebooks'.

Australia & the Pacific
Australia
Bushwalking in Australia
Papua New Guinea
Papua New Guinea phrasebook
New Zealand
Tramping in New Zealand
Rarotonga & the Cook Islands
Solomon Islands
Tahiti & French Polynesia
Fiji
Micronesia

South-East Asia
South-East Asia on a shoestring
Malaysia, Singapore & Brunei
Indonesia
Bali & Lombok
Indonesia phrasebook
Burma
Burmese phrasebook
Thailand
Thai phrasebook
Philippines
Pilipino phrasebook

North-East Asia
North-East Asia on a shoestring
China
China phrasebook
Tibet
Tibet phrasebook
Japan
Korea
Korean phrasebook
Hong Kong, Macau & Canton
Taiwan

West Asia
West Asia on a shoestring
Trekking in Turkey
Turkey

Mail Order

Lonely Planet guidebooks are distributed worldwide and are sold by good bookshops everywhere. They are also available by mail order from Lonely Planet, so if you have difficulty finding a title please write to us. US and Canadian residents should write to Embarcadero West, 112 Linden St, Oakland CA 94607, USA and residents of other countries to PO Box 617, Hawthorn, Victoria 3122, Australia.

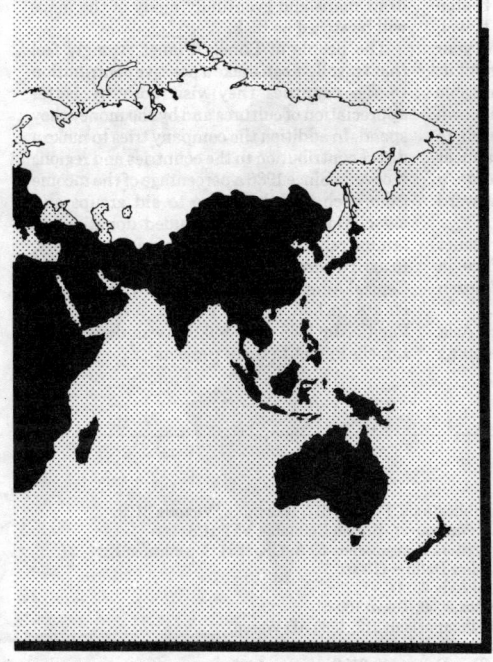

Lonely Planet

Lonely Planet published its first book in 1973. Tony and Maureen Wheeler had made a lengthy overland trip from England to Australia and, in response to numerous 'how do you do it?' questions, Tony wrote and they published *Across Asia on the Cheap*. It became an instant local best-seller and inspired thoughts of a second travel guide. A year and a half in South-East Asia resulted in their second book, *South-East Asia on a Shoestring*, which they put together in a backstreet Chinese hotel in Singapore in 1975. The 'yellow book', as it quickly became known, soon became *the* guide to the region and has gone through five editions, always with its familiar yellow cover.

Soon other writers came to them with ideas for similar books – books that went off the beaten track with an adventurous approach to travel, books that 'assumed you knew how to get your luggage off the carousel,' as one reviewer put it. Lonely Planet grew from a kitchen table operation to a spare room and then to its own office. It's international reputation began to grow as the Lonely Planet logo began to appear in more and more countries. In 1982 *India – a travel survival kit* won the Thomas Cook award for the best guidebook of the year.

These days there are over 70 Lonely Planet titles. Over 40 people work at our office in Melbourne, Australia and another half dozen at our US office in Oakland, California.

At first Lonely Planet specialised in the Asia region but these days we are also developing major ranges of guidebooks to the Pacific region, to South America and to Africa. The list of walking guides is growing and Lonely Planet now has a unique series of phrasebooks to 'unusual' languages. The emphasis continues to be on travel for travellers and Tony and Maureen still manage to fit in a number of trips each year and play a very active part in the writing and updating of Lonely Planet's guides.

Keeping guidebooks up to date is a constant battle which requires an ear to the ground and lots of walking, but technology also plays its part. All Lonely Planet guidebooks are now stored and updated on computer, and some authors even take lap-top computers into the field. Lonely Planet is also using computers to draw maps and eventually many of the maps will be stored on disk.

The people at Lonely Planet strongly feel that travellers can make a positive contribution to the countries they visit both by better appreciation of cultures and by the money they spend. In addition the company tries to make a direct contribution to the countries and regions it covers. Since 1986 a percentage of the income from each book has gone to aid groups and associations. This has included donations to famine relief in Africa, to aid projects in India, to agricultural projects in Nicaragua and other Central American countries and to Greenpeace's efforts to halt French nuclear testing in the Pacific. In 1988 over $40,000 was donated by Lonely Planet to these projects.

Lonely Planet Distributors

Australia & Papua New Guinea Lonely Planet Publications, PO Box 617, Hawthorn, Victoria 3122.
Canada Raincoast Books, 112 East 3rd Avenue, Vancouver, British Columbia V5T 1C8.
Denmark, Finland & Norway Scanvik Books aps, Store Kongensgade 59 A, DK-1264 Copenhagen K.
India & Nepal UBS Distributors, 5 Ansari Rd, New Delhi – 110002
Israel Geographical Tours Ltd, 8 Tverya St, Tel Aviv 63144.
Japan Intercontinental Marketing Corp, IPO Box 5056, Tokyo 100-31.
Netherlands Nilsson & Lamm bv, Postbus 195, Pampuslaan 212, 1380 AD Weesp.
New Zealand Transworld Publishers, PO Box 83-094, Edmonton PO, Auckland.
Singapore & Malaysia MPH Distributors, 601 Sims Drive, #03-21, Singapore 1438.
Spain Altair, Balmes 69, 08007 Barcelona.
Sweden Esselte Kartcentrum AB, Vasagatan 16, S-111 20 Stockholm.
Thailand Chalermnit, 108 Sukhumvit 53, Bangkok 10110.
Turkey Yab-Yay Dagitim, Alay Koshu Caddesi 12/A, Kat 4 no. 11-12, Cagaloglu, Istanbul.
UK Roger Lascelles, 47 York Rd, Brentford, Middlesex, TW8 0QP
USA Lonely Planet Publications, PO Box 2001A, Berkeley, CA 94702.
West Germany Buchvertrieb Gerda Schettler, Postfach 64, D3415 Hattorf a H.
All Other Countries refer to Australia address.